A New German Idealism

A NEW GERMAN IDEALISM

Hegel, Žižek, and Dialectical Materialism

ADRIAN JOHNSTON

COLUMBIA UNIVERSITY PRESS *NEW YORK*

Columbia University Press
Publishers Since 1893
New York   Chichester, West Sussex
cup.columbia.edu
Copyright © 2018 Columbia University Press
Paperback edition, 2019
All rights reserved
Library of Congress Cataloging-in-Publication Data
Names: Johnston, Adrian, 1974- author.
Title: A new German idealism: Hegel, Zizek, and dialectical materialism / Adrian Johnston.
Description: New York: Columbia University Press, 2018. | Includes bibliographical references and index.
Identifiers: LCCN 2017052046 | ISBN 9780231183949 (cloth) | ISBN 9780231183956 (pbk.) | ISBN 9780231545242 (e-book)
Subjects: LCSH: Dialectical materialism. | Hegel, Georg Wilhelm Friedrich, 1770–1831. | Zizek, Slavoj.
Classification: LCC B809.82.G3 J64 2018 | DDC 199/.4973—dc22
LC record available at https://lccn.loc.gov/2017052046

Cover image: Chronicle / Alamy Stock Photo

To S.—for pushing me

Nature should not be rated too high nor too low ... awakening consciousness takes its rise surrounded by natural influences alone (*nur in der Natur*), and every development of it is the reflection of Spirit back upon itself in opposition to the immediate, unreflected character of mere nature. Nature is therefore one element in this antithetic abstracting process; Nature is the first standpoint from which man can gain freedom within himself, and this liberation must not be rendered difficult by natural obstructions. Nature, as contrasted with Spirit, is a quantitative mass, whose power must not be so great as to make its single force omnipotent (*allmächtig*).

—G. W. F. Hegel

When will all these shadows of God cease to darken our minds? When will we complete our de-deification of nature? When may we begin to "*naturalize*" humanity in terms of a pure, newly discovered, newly redeemed nature?

—Friedrich Nietzsche

Contents

Preface: Drawing Lines—Žižek's Speculative Dialectics xi

Acknowledgments xxxv

Introduction: Sublating Absolute Idealism—Žižekian Materialist Reversals 1

ONE   "Freedom or System? Yes, Please!": Spinozisms of Freedom and the Post-Kantian Aftermath Then and Now 11

TWO   Where to Start?: Deflating Hegel's Deflators 38

THREE   Contingency, Pure Contingency—Without Any Further Determination: Hegelian Modalities 74

FOUR   Materialism Sans Materialism: Žižekian Substance Deprived of Its Substance 129

FIVE   Bartleby by Nature: German Idealism, Biology, and Žižek's Compatibilism 151

Conclusion: Driven On—the (Meta)Dialectics of Drive and Desire 187

CONTENTS

Notes 249

Bibliography 299

Index 321

Preface
Drawing Lines—Žižek's Speculative Dialectics

A New German Idealism: Hegel, Žižek, and Dialectical Materialism, an extended critical engagement with Slavoj Žižek's most recent theoretical labors, rests upon certain fundamental agreements with him about G. W. F. Hegel's philosophy. I wholeheartedly concur with Žižek that a contemporary "return to Hegel" is urgent in the intellectual and sociopolitical contexts of the early twenty-first century. Moreover, like him, I too construe Hegel's System as the primary forerunner of dialectical materialism. Žižek and I also recast Hegelianism as an ontologically ambitious philosophical framework within which the dimensions of the natural and the contingent play central roles—contrary to widespread, still-prevailing views of Hegelian "absolute idealism" (including "deflationary" qua antimetaphysical renditions of Hegel).

However, this consensus between Žižek and me also makes possible a real debate. As Hegel indicated many times in many ways, the only critiques worth conducting are immanent ones as opposed to external ones, because the latter tend to be unproductive exercises in comparing apples and oranges. In Žižek's Marxist-Leninist terms, the most promising and productive exchanges are "inner-party disputes." My endeavors here operate in the spirit of this Hegelian-Žižekian precept.

Perhaps the most basic contention between us is about the beginnings of ontology and metaphysics: Which comes first, the positivity of contingent material facticity or the negativity of a primordial Void? Schematically speaking, I defend the former option while Žižek advocates the latter. In

A New German Idealism, I argue that fidelity to both Hegel and dialectical materialism requires eschewing appeals to any version of an underived initial Nothing(ness).

A series of other disagreements arise from how Žižek and I interpret Hegel's philosophy and, on the basis of these interpretations, combine Hegelianism with politics, science, and psychoanalysis. Regarding the internal architectonics of the Hegelian System itself, I maintain that Žižek's reading of Hegel, in line with many other readings past and present, continues to inordinately privilege Hegel's *Logik* at the expense of the more-than-logical *Realphilosophie* (Hegel's Philosophy of the Real contains both his Philosophy of Nature and Philosophy of Mind or Spirit, with social and political dimensions falling under the heading of *Geist*). In contrast with Žižek, I treat the *Realphilosophie* as at least as important as the Logic, arguing that this treatment is essential for a proper appreciation of Hegel as a philosopher who anticipates the theories of Marxian historical and dialectical materialism and its corresponding political practices.

Questions proliferate about the relations between Hegelian speculative dialectics (exemplified in the Logic) and extraphilosophical fields and disciplines (embodied as the real of the Philosophy of the Real). How do Hegelianism generally and a Hegelian materialism specifically answer to the knowledge-claims and epistemological-methodological constraints of the empirical, experimental sciences of nature? When and how should Hegelianism, psychoanalysis, and the natural sciences be triangulated? Which aspects of analysis and the sciences should be prioritized for a Hegelian materialism?

Žižek and I, starting from a set of shared convictions, offer different answers to these questions. Žižek's universe privileges the structures and dynamics of quantum physics, denies all sociopolitical foresight to historical materialism, and depicts libidinal economies as revolving around the enigmatic "x" of a primal emptiness. My ontological perspective focuses on how biology and its branches provide indispensable bridges between natural substances and denaturalized subjects, grants limited predictive powers to Marxism, and recasts the negativities of drives and desires as secondarily emergent vis-à-vis evolutionary natural history. These are distinct visions, although they are equally rooted in an ensemble of axioms, decisions, intuitions, and references that Žižek and I hold in common. A belief animating this book is that exploring the tensions between Žižek's version and

PREFACE

my version of a contemporary Hegelianism with political, scientific, and psychoanalytic ramifications will help renew leftist materialism in our times.

* * *

Karl Marx, in a letter to Friedrich Engels dated January 16, 1858, mentions fortuitously rereading Hegel's mature Logic—at a moment when Marx is immersed in the economic research for *Capital*.[1] He then remarks, "If ever the time comes when such work is again possible, I should very much like to write 2 or 3 sheets making accessible to the common reader the *rational* aspect of the method which Hegel not only discovered but also mystified."[2] Two letters to Ludwig Kugelmann (of March 6, 1868, and June 27, 1870) similarly allude to Marx having a methodology deriving but also deviating from that of Hegel.[3]

Alas, as is well known, Marx never found the time to compose a separate treatise on this method. Sometimes, this determinate absence (or Rumsfeldian "known unknown") in Marx's corpus is covered over by the projections from his audience that this absence solicits (much like how the ellipsis where the manuscript of the third volume of *Capital* abruptly breaks off prompts readers to fill it in with guesses about what Marx was about to say there about classes). When those handling the Marxian oeuvre refrain from indulging themselves in such projecting, the mature Marx's comments about Hegel in three places in particular (the introduction to the *Grundrisse* from 1857, the preface to *A Contribution to the Critique of Political Economy* from 1859, and the postface to the second edition of the first volume of *Capital* from 1873) are made to serve, understandably and not without justification, as substitutes for the missing book on this methodology (sometimes in conjunction with the young Marx's more detailed and extended critical engagements with Hegel circa 1843 and 1844). This absent volume on dialectical method is the nonexistent book whose nonexistence is perhaps most painfully felt and deeply regretted by generation after generation of readers of Marx.[4]

Fortunately, the same cannot be said for readers of Žižek, an author for whom both Hegel and Marx, along with the twentieth-century French psychoanalyst Jacques Lacan, are avowedly sources of inspiration. Already before 2012, Žižek's many works contain frequent, sustained treatments of Hegel's philosophy, though these treatments, admittedly, are scattered across numerous texts and placed within discussions of various figures and topics unrelated to Hegel or philosophy. However, *Less Than Nothing: Hegel and the*

Shadow of Dialectical Materialism (2012), supplemented by *Absolute Recoil: Towards a New Foundation of Dialectical Materialism* (2014), amounts to, among other things, Žižek's definitive and exhaustive settling of accounts with his Hegelian conscience. In addition to enriching the Marxian tradition of dialectical materialism through a contemporary materialist resurrection of Hegelian absolute idealism, the Žižek of *Less Than Nothing* and *Absolute Recoil* provides thorough expositions of what could be called, with reference to Marx, his Hegel-indebted dialectical method. An initiation into this mature Žižekian dialectics requires a preliminary acquaintance with Hegel himself. Only thereafter can Žižek's Hegelianism be properly appreciated and assessed.

When considering speculative dialectics as the fundamental nucleus of Hegel's philosophical apparatus, one of several possible associations is an oft-quoted line from Johann Wolfgang von Goethe's *Faust*: "gray are all theories, and green alone Life's golden tree."[5] Hegel himself, at the start of a section of the *Phenomenology of Spirit* (published in 1807, the first of his magnum opera) that describes a Faustian figure (*Gestalt*) of consciousness (that is, the figure of "Pleasure and Necessity"), gestures at this line by Goethe.[6] The idea here relies on Hegel's fundamental distinction, departing (in both senses of the word) from Immanuel Kant's philosophy, between the understanding (*Verstand*) and reason (*Vernunft*).[7] Specifically, many readers of Hegel equate theoretical grayness with the understanding and living greenness with reason. On such a reading, Hegel's speculative dialectics, as rational (*als Vernunft*), sweeps aside the colorless husks of *Verstand* so as to seize directly without further ado the flourishing branches of a scintillatingly vibrant, many-hued reality that is otherwise buried within the drab nets of the understanding's abstractions.

However, this manner of distinguishing the understanding and reason amounts to a *Verstand*-style binary opposition at odds with both the letter and the spirit of Hegelian *Vernunft*—hence a betrayal of Hegelian rationality committed in its name. Moreover, Hegel himself, even before the *Phenomenology*, warns against one-sidedly favoring kinetic reason over static understanding because the latter is nothing more than a set of deficiencies to be overcome and left behind by the former.[8] To begin with, an entry from his "Aphorisms from the Wastebook," written in Jena before 1807, bluntly declares that "Reason without understanding is nothing, but the understanding is still something without reason" ("*Die Vernunft ohne Verstand ist nichts, der*

Verstand doch etwas ohne Vernunft").⁹ Likewise, the older Hegel, in the third volume of the *Encyclopedia of the Philosophical Sciences* (specifically, the "Psychology" section of the *Philosophy of Mind*), insists that the understanding is "a necessary moment of rational thinking" (*"ein notwendiges Moment des vernünftigen Denkens"*).¹⁰

Whether in the guise of pre- or post-Kantian mystical trances, spiritualist visions, or intellectual intuitions, a supposedly pure reason attempting "like a shot from a pistol" to bypass, rather than pass through, the logic and concepts of the understanding does not thereby get its hands on "Life's golden tree" (or anything else determinate) in all its vivid, undiluted greenness.¹¹ Instead, such reason-without-understanding simply ends up blindly wandering through a "night in which all cows are black" empty-handed.¹² In a twist on the color language of Goethe's Mephistopheles, reality's subtle shades of gray become visible, for Hegel, only starting from and moving within the understanding's black-and-white divisions and dichotomies (and their blurring). In Hegel's view, speculative *Vernunft* (as a *Vernunft mit Verstand* rather than a *Vernunft ohne Verstand*) is an Owl of Minerva that spreads its wings exclusively after the establishment of *Verstand*, solely following the onset of the understanding's self-induced dialectical twilight.

The *Phenomenology*, despite the potentially misleading reference it later makes to *Faust*, cautions against playing the theoretical grayness of the understanding against the living greenness of reason. Specifically, a well-known paragraph of the *Phenomenology*'s deservedly celebrated preface (a paragraph Žižek extols at one point in *Less Than Nothing*)¹³ identifies *Verstand* as "the most astonishing and mightiest of powers, or rather the absolute power" (*"der verwundersamsten und größten oder vielmehr der absoluten Macht"*).¹⁴ This same paragraph then proceeds to portray the abstracting, analyzing understanding as "the tremendous power of the negative" (*"die ungeheurer Macht des Negativen"*), as "the energy of thought, of the pure 'I'" (*"die Energie des Denkens, des reinen Ichs"*)—in short, as that with which Hegelian rational *Geist* must "tarry" (*verweilen*).¹⁵ In this specific context, Hegel associates the understanding thus characterized both with subjectivity proper (*das Subjekt*) and with "death" (*der Tod*), "devastation" (*der Verwüstung*), and "dismemberment" (*der Zerissenheit*).¹⁶ (Žižek's fundamental theoretical thesis equating the subject as negativity of German idealism with the death drive [*Todestrieb, pulsion de mort*] of Freudian-Lacanian psychoanalysis is not without its clear and direct Hegelian precedents.)¹⁷ As if to rebuke Goethe's Mephistopheles in

PREFACE

advance, Hegel rejects an aesthetic path supposedly leading to "Life's golden tree" as the dead end of *"kraftlose Schönheit"* (impotent/powerless beauty)[18] in favor of the analytic path of a subjective "tarrying with the negative" in all its stark, awkward ugliness. (It is anything but accidental that, of Žižek's own philosophical works, the title of one of his favorites is *Tarrying with the Negative*.)

The later Hegel of both the *Science of Logic* and *Encyclopedia* further underscores the unequal priority of *Verstand* over *Vernunft*. In the *Science of Logic*, a cautionary clarification about the relationship between the understanding and reason, one signaled already in the preface to the first edition of this work, published in 1812,[19] occurs in the first chapter ("The Notion" [*Der Begriff*]) of this treatise's third and final major division ("The Doctrine of the Notion" [*Die Lehre vom Begriff*]), namely, at the start of the "Subjective Logic" (*Die subjektive Logik*). The passages I have in mind begin with Hegel noting the recurrent post-Kantian idealist and Romantic complaints about the austere and inflexible traits, the "fixity" (Festigkeit), of *Verstand*.[20] Immediately after this acknowledgment, he cautions that

> we must recognize the infinite force of the understanding (*die unendliche Kraft des Verstandes*) in splitting the concrete into abstract determinatenesses and plumbing the depth of the difference (*das Konkrete in die abstrakten Bestimmtheiten zu trennen und die Tiefe des Unterschieds zu fassen*), the force that at the same time is alone the power that effects their transition (*welche allein zugleich die Macht ist, die ihren Übergang bewirkt*). The concrete of *intuition* is a *totality*, but a sensuous one (*Das Konkrete der* Anschauung ist Totalität, *aber die* sinnliche)—a real material which has an indifferent, *sundered* (auseinander) existence in space and time; but surely this absence of unity in the manifold (*diese Einheitslosigkeit des Mannigfaltigen*), where it is the content of intuition, ought not to be counted to it for merit and superiority over intellectual existence.[21]

These remarks about the understanding's "infinite force" (*unendliche Kraft*) audibly echo the *Phenomenology*'s identification of it as "the absolute power" (*der absoluten Macht*). Moreover, this passage subtly but firmly signals why and how Hegel's unique brand of speculative dialectics is an embodiment of philosophical-scientific rationality significantly different in kind from *Vernunft* as conceived by late-eighteenth- and early-nineteenth-century Schellingian and Romantic intellectual intuitings. The latter amount, for Hegel, to post-Kantian instances of (regressions to) pre-Kantian, Spinozistic-style pure reason qua *Vernunft ohne Verstand*. From Hegel's perspective, such cases of *reinen Vernunft* precipitously plunge themselves headlong into a monochromatic, moonless midnight in which everything is black (including all cows); they do so by dissolving every difference under the sun into the undifferentiated, ever-self-same Identity of an Absolute reduced to the impoverished, featureless uniformity of a mere indeterminate Being (whether called "All," "One," "the Infinite," "Substance," "Identity," "God," "*hen kai pan*," "*natura naturans*," "the Point of Indifference," or whatever else along these lines) transcendently standing beyond, behind, or beneath each determinate being and becoming.

Hegel associates *Verstand* with the determinate and the differentiated ("splitting the concrete into abstract determinatenesses and plumbing the depth of the difference"). Hence, a reason-without-understanding, in preferring to circumvent (rather than tarry with) the negativities of the understanding and its immanently self-wrought dialectics, is inherently and inevitably unable to hold on to and preserve the kaleidoscopic multitude of distinctions and individuations, of particularities and singularities, displayed by reality and captured in the categories and concepts of *Verstand*. Additionally, Hegel, in the passage just quoted, insists that uniquely in and through nothing other than the understanding do dialectical-speculative reason and its splitting and syntheses of the understanding's categories and concepts arise ("alone the power that effects their transition").

Finally, this passage implies a contrast between a sensibly intuited totality or unity qua initially given beginning and a rationally ideated totality or unity qua subsequently produced outcome. The latter, on Hegel's assessment, is obviously of immeasurably greater worth than the former. Moreover, and as should be quite evident by now, Hegel prizes "the infinite force of the understanding" specifically because "the tremendous power of the negative" peculiar to *Verstand* breaks up the passively present whole of perceptual intuition while assembling the actively synthesized new whole of conceptual (as dialectical-speculative) reason (*Vernunft*). If the colors of "Life's golden tree" are those of sensuous concreteness, then Hegel is anything but Goethe's Mephistopheles.

Shortly after the passage from the *Science of Logic* just quoted, Hegel further buttresses his spirited defense of the rights and value of the understanding against proponents of the purported higher powers of *Vernunft ohne Verstand*. He adds:

> Since ... understanding exhibits the infinite force (*die unendliche Kraft*) which determines the universal, or conversely, imparts through the form of universality a fixity and subsistence to the determinateness that is in and for itself transitory, then it is not the fault of the understanding if no progress is made beyond this point. It is a subjective *impotence of reason* (*eine subjektive* Ohnmacht der Vernunft) which adopts these determinatenesses in their fixity, and which is unable to bring them back to their unity through the dialectical force (*dialektische Kraft*) opposed to this abstract universality, in other words, through their own peculiar nature or through their Notion. The understanding does indeed give them, so to speak, a rigidity of *being* (Härte *des Seins*) such as they do not possess in the qualitative sphere and in the sphere of reflection; but at the same time it *spiritually impregnates* them and so sharpens them (*aber durch diese Vereinfachung begeistet er sie zugleich und schärft sie so zu*), that just at this extreme point (*dieser Spitze die Fähigkeit*) alone they acquire the capability to dissolve themselves and to pass over into their opposite (*in ihr Entgegengesetztes überzugehen*). The highest maturity, the highest stage, which anything can attain is that in which its downfall begins (*Die höchste Reife und Stufe, die irgend etwas erreichen kann, ist diejenige, in welcher sein Untergang beginnt*). The fixity of the determinateness into which the understanding seems to run, the form of the imperishable, is that of self-relating universality. But this belongs properly to the Notion (*Begriffe*); and consequently in this universality is to be found expressed, and infinitely close at hand, the *dissolution* of the finite (*die* Auflösung *des Endlichen*).[22]

In the first half of this passage, Hegel's exculpation of the understanding begins with shifting responsibility for any lack of dialectical-speculative progress beyond *Verstand* from the understanding itself to dialectical-speculative reason. The "*Ohnmacht der Vernunft*,"[23] and not stubbornness on the part of *Verstand*, is to blame for all ossifications of the categories and concepts forming the understanding's ideational determinations.

Moreover, in the second half of this passage, Hegel goes even further in his defense of *Verstand*. He argues that it is exclusively in and through an unreserved intensification of the understanding's analytic, divisive, and dichotomizing tendencies that the genesis of dialectical-speculative *Vernunft* becomes possible. Counterintuitively, the determinations of the

PREFACE

understanding sublationally (*als Aufhebung*) pass over or are transubstantiated into the fluidity of the moments of reason precisely at the (tipping) point of their maximum degree of "fixity" or "rigidity" (that is, nonfluidity). In a coincidence of opposites, fixed/rigid *Verstand* transitions into fluid or supple *Vernunft* specifically at the very height of its fixity/rigidity; the understanding comes closest to reason exactly when the former appears to be at the greatest distance from the latter, when *Verstand* contracts into the most extreme, exaggerated versions of its (seemingly) subrational (qua neither dialectical nor speculative) defining characteristics (such as the understanding's insistence on the absoluteness of classical bivalent logic). The third volume of Marx's *Capital* provides a concretizing sociohistorical case of this counterintuitive proximity between opposites precisely at the most intense point of their distancing opposition to each other. In a chapter titled "The Role of Credit in Capitalist Production," Marx asserts that monopoly capitalism, in which capitalism's inherent contradictory tension between the private property of the wealthy few and the public productivity of the impoverished many reaches its very peak, is, despite appearances to the contrary, the threshold of socialism.[24]

Therefore, in this light, an essential aspect of the art of dialectical-speculative reasoning is the "sharpening," rather than smudging and dissolving, of *Verstand*-style binary distinctions, mutually exclusive either-ors, black-and-white polar oppositions, and the like—contrary to commonplace impressions regarding what a Hegelian manner of proceeding entails. Reason is reached only by pushing the understanding (or, more accurately, by the understanding pushing itself) to the breaking point. As will soon be seen, this underappreciated dimension of Hegelian speculative dialectics is crucial for both Žižek's general modus operandi and his specific form of materialism. For Žižek, the first task of dialectical thinking is to draw firm, clear lines.

Before I touch upon Hegel's further stipulations concerning the relation between *Verstand* and *Vernunft* at the start of the *Encyclopedia Logic*, one last paragraph from the *Science of Logic* deserves quoting and commentary. (Indeed, this paragraph sets up a quick and direct segue to what I will address in the *Encyclopedia Logic*.) Soon after the previous passage quoted, Hegel maintains that

> the usual practice of separating understanding and reason is, from every point of view, to be rejected. When the Notion (*der Begriff*) is regarded as irrational

(*vernunftlos*), this should be interpreted rather as an incapacity of reason (*eine Unfähigkeit der Vernunft*) to recognize itself in the Notion. The determinate and abstract Notion is the *condition* (*die* Bedingung), or rather an *essential moment of reason* (wesentliche Moment der Vernunft); it is form spiritually impregnated (*begeistete Form*), in which the finite, through the universality in which it relates itself to itself, spontaneously catches fire (*sich in sich entzündet*), posits itself as dialectical and thereby is the *beginning* of the manifestation of reason.[25]

Obviously, these remarks contain some synoptic repetition of points already covered (the categorical refusal to partition *Verstand* from *Vernunft*, a blameworthy rational powerlessness, the understanding as already pregnant with reason, and dialectical-speculative thinking as having to pass through and not bypass the understanding). But the crucial nuance this passage introduces, one subsequently stressed by Hegel in the *Encyclopedia Logic* (as will be seen), is that *Verstand* is not only not separate from *Vernunft*, but "an *essential moment*" of *Vernunft*. Specifically, the understanding is the pivotal "*beginning*" of reason. Similarly, Hegelian *Verstand* could be said, in the words of the *Phenomenology*, to freely "do violence to itself at its own hands";[26] the understanding independently dialecticizes and sublates itself through self-criticism, since it is its own best immanent critic ("it . . . spontaneously catches fire"), as well as its only one. Reason proper, as dialectical-speculative (and not *reinen Vernunft ohne Verstand*), cannot and should not try to operate as an external critic swooping down upon the understanding from an unspecified (and unspecifiable) transcendent Beyond or Elsewhere.

One of the upshots of this is that, for Hegel, the distinction between the understanding and reason is always already sublated *als Aufhebung* (that is, simultaneously canceled, destroyed, negated, or surpassed and elevated, preserved, [re]affirmed, or retained). Put differently, both identity and difference are operative at the same time in the rapport between *Verstand* and *Vernunft*. In yet other words, the understanding is different from reason, but this difference is not absolute as a hard-and-fast, impermeable barrier between the two.

At the actual beginning of the *Encyclopedia Logic*, before the start of "The Doctrine of Being," the *Logic*'s first major subdivision, Hegel frames the text in a section titled "More Precise Conception and Division of the *Logic*." The first two subsections of this concise overview, sections 79 and 80 of the *Encyclopedia*, further clarify and reinforce his rendition of the relationship between the understanding and reason. Section 79, in reference specifically to dialectical-speculative logic, refashions and refines the dyad of *Verstand* and *Vernunft* into a triad: "With regard to its form, the *logical* has three sides: (α) *the side of abstraction* or *of the understanding*, (β) *the dialectical* or *negatively rational side*, [and] (γ) *the speculative* or *positively rational* one."[27] Hegel adds: "These three sides do not constitute three *parts* of the Logic, but are *moments of everything logically real* (Momente jedes Logisch-Reellen); i.e., of every concept or of everything true in general (*jedes Begriffes oder jedes Wahren überhaupt*). All of them together can be put under the first moment, that *of the understanding*; and in this way they can be kept separate from each other, but then they are not considered in their truth (*Wahrheit*)."[28] As is evident from the first of these two quotations, the two of the understanding and reason becomes three through the latter being divided into the dialectics and the speculation of negative and positive reason.[29] (Žižek, early on in *Absolute Recoil*, underscores the importance of this distinction between the dialectical and the speculative sides of Hegelian reason.)[30] The second quotation then promptly stipulates that these "three sides" of dialectical-speculative Logic are equiprimordial "moments."[31] That is to say, both *Verstand* and the two faces of *Vernunft* are "in their truth" (*Wahrheit*) inseparable, namely, always already inextricably intertwined in actuality—and this truth is that of the organic-relational holism gestured at in the preface to the *Phenomenology* (that is, "The True is the whole" ["*Das Wahre ist das Ganze*"]).[32]

The *Zusätz* to section 80 contains, among other things, unmistakable echoes of Hegel's praise for and prioritization of *Verstand* in the awe-inspiring potency of its abstracting and negating activities, which he articulated in the period before 1817, and which I have already mentioned.[33] Reiterating an old insistence, Hegel maintains that "the thinking of the understanding must unquestionably be conceded its right and merit."[34] Likewise, he once again proposes that "philosophy cannot do without the understanding."[35]

In connection with the superficially counterintuitive thesis in section 79 positing the subsumption of the triad of the understanding and the two dimensions of reason under the understanding itself ("All of them together can be put under the first moment, that *of the understanding*"), the addition to section 80 also contains a further supplementary clarification of this thesis. Hegel specifies that "the understanding . . . is the first form of logical thinking."[36] In other words, negative and positive *Vernunft* are to be subsumed under *Verstand* precisely insofar as the latter is the beginning out of which both dialectics and speculation immanently arise.[37] (As Hegel scholar H. S. Harris observes, Hegelian speculation is conditioned by nonspeculative contents.)[38]

Yet, at the same time, the understanding is just a beginning. Beginnings in general are enormously important for Hegel. However, they are not all important. A true and proper start is crucial, but it is only a start. The closing paragraph of the *Zusätz* to section 80 emphasizes exactly this: "The understanding must not go too far.... The understanding cannot have the last word (*das Verständige allerdings nicht ein Letztes*). On the contrary, it is finite, and, more precisely, it is such that when it is pushed to an extreme it overturns into its opposite (*auf die Spitze getrieben in sein Entgegengesetztes umschlägt*)."[39] In Hegelian speculative dialectics, every initiation or origin is sublated in the precise sense of Hegel's *Aufhebung*. The understanding has the first word, but only the first word, in the encyclopedic System formed by both *Logik* and *Realphilosophie*. Moreover, Hegel stresses in these lines from the addition to section 80, as already underscored in the earlier *Science of Logic*, that subrational *Verstand* sublationally transubstantiates itself into true *Vernunft* uniquely in and through an intensification and sharpening of its (seemingly) antirational characteristics (such as its distinctive inclinations toward analysis, division, and dichotomization). That is to say, the understanding tips into (dialectical-negative) reason precisely when it appears to be at a maximum distance from the latter, namely, when it is most invested in its categorial and conceptual binaries and oppositions that are neither dialectical nor speculative ("when it is pushed to an extreme it overturns into its opposite").

The prior condensed survey of the rapport between the understanding and reason in Hegel's speculative dialectics makes it possible to properly appreciate Žižek's Hegelian modus operandi both generally and in *Less Than Nothing* and *Absolute Recoil*. For those clinging to images of Hegel as the thinker whose gaze unwaveringly is focused upon the supposed greenery of "Life's golden tree" à la the Mephistopheles of Goethe's *Faust*, as the philosopher of fluid dynamics blurring and liquidating all established and definite categorial and conceptual distinctions, Žižek often might seem to be quite un-Hegelian, despite his recurrent and insistent avowals of an adamant, uncompromising Hegelianism. In particular, Žižek's penchant (one he shares with his fellow-traveler Alain Badiou) for distilling clear-cut contrasts and divisions from the murky waters of confusingly complex situations and intermingling ideational currents risks striking some as subrational and antispeculative, namely, as fundamentally at odds with the sensibility, procedure, and outlook of Hegel himself. When Žižek brusquely brushes aside tangled thickets of ambiguous intricacy and disorienting subtlety to confront his audiences with either-or choices between nakedly opposed binary alternatives ("yes or no?," "for or against?," "advance or retreat?," "persist or desist," and so on), is this not regressively to sink to the lowest levels of the understanding that Hegel denigrated? As my overview of Hegel's own articulations of the relationship between *Verstand* and *Vernunft* (including the intrarational difference between the negative-dialectical and the positive-speculative) already shows, impressions of Žižek as unwittingly or covertly non- or anti-Hegelian are themselves generated by a thoroughly un-Hegelian understanding (as misunderstanding) of Hegel himself.

In both *Less Than Nothing* and *Absolute Recoil*, Žižek speaks to these same Hegelian issues at multiple times and in varied fashions. The first of several relevant passages in his magnum opus from 2012 declares:

> Everything turns on how we are to understand this identity-and-difference between Understanding and Reason: it is not that Reason adds something to the separating power of Understanding, reestablishing (at some "higher level") the organic unity of what Understanding has sundered, supplementing analysis with synthesis; Reason is, in a way, not more but *less* than Understanding, it is—to put it in the well-known terms of Hegel's opposition between what one wants to say and what one actually says—what Understanding, in its activity, *really does*, in contrast to what it wants or means to do. Reason is therefore not another faculty supplementing Understanding's "one-sidedness": the very idea that there is something (the core of the substantial content of the analyzed thing) which eludes Understanding, a trans-rational Beyond out of its reach, is the fundamental illusion of Understanding. In other words, all we have to do to get from Understanding to Reason is to *subtract* from Understanding its constitutive illusion.[40]

Žižek continues:

> Understanding is not too abstract or violent, it is, on the contrary, as Hegel remarked of Kant, *too soft towards things*, too afraid to locate its violent movement of tearing things apart in the things themselves. In a way, it is epistemology versus ontology: the illusion of Understanding is that its own analytical

power—the power to make "an accident as such ... obtain an existence all its own, gain freedom and independence on its own account"—is only an "abstraction," something external to "true reality" which persists out there intact in its inaccessible fullness. In other words, it is the standard critical view of Understanding and its power of abstraction (that it is just an impotent intellectual exercise which misses the wealth of reality) which contains the core illusion of Understanding. To put it in yet another way, the mistake of Understanding is to perceive its own negative activity (of separating, tearing things apart) only in its negative aspect, ignoring its "positive" (productive) aspect—Reason is Understanding itself in its productive aspect.[41]

Žižek's emphasis in these paragraphs on the "subtractive" (in Badiouian parlance) nature of Hegelian *Vernunft* vis-à-vis *Verstand* is, as my earlier exegetical efforts indicate, justified on the basis of Hegel's texts. Following Hegel, and appropriately making the apparent opposites of the understanding and reason converge, Žižek identifies the seemingly most anti-*Vernunft* traits of *Verstand*—the understanding's maximally nonrational features are its tendencies toward the reductive, the abstract, the one-sided, the analytic, the formal, the bivalent, the dualistic, the dichotomous, and the like—as precisely the loci at which understanding always already tips over into reason, into itself becoming properly rational ("Reason is Understanding itself in its productive aspect").

Hence, as in Žižek's own style and method of philosophical (and political) practice, properly dialectical-speculative thinking necessarily involves moving directly in and through, rather than evasively around, black-and-white mutual exclusivities. A fidelity to Hegel's genuine legacy demands theoretical and practical confrontations with hard choices in relation to challenging conflicts between sharply antagonistic constituents, instead of avoiding difficult decisions through precipitous flights into the pseudodialectics or pseudospeculation of indeterminacy and undecidability, the multi- and the poly-. As Žižek puts this in *Absolute Recoil* in regard to an active forgetfulness of reality's apparent wealth of kaleidoscopic details, "Hegelian forgetting is ... not a weakness to be feigned, but the expression of Spirit's highest, 'absolute,' power—the absence of this power of forgetting (which is effectively a specific aspect of negativity) causes a debilitating indecision" (debilitating for both theory and practice).[42] Or, as the concluding line of his rewritten version of Sophocles's *Antigone* states, "wise men know how to suspend the chaos and decide."[43]

Additionally, the two preceding block quotations from *Less Than Nothing* outline how one is to effectuate authentically Hegelian transitions from *Verstand* to *Vernunft*. Žižek proposes a single maneuver that itself can be viewed as consisting of two interrelated, inseparable steps. First, the understanding, always enjoying a precedence vis-à-vis a reason whose dialectics and speculation are parasitic upon it, must shift its perspective on itself. To be more precise, *Verstand* has to "look awry" at itself such that it comes to invert its previous prioritization of what it subjectively intends over what it objectively accomplishes (according to Žižek, "what one wants to say" or "what it wants or means to do" over "what one actually says" or "what" it "in its activity, *really does*"), instead prioritizing the latter over the former. This Hegelian distinction first and most famously surfaces in the momentous opening chapter of the *Phenomenology*, "Sense-Certainty: Or the 'This' and 'Meaning' [*Meinen*]," where the ball of Hegel's mature dialectics gets rolling (and which is the moment Žižek is alluding to).[44]

Specifically, Hegelian-Žižekian understanding needs sooner or later to come to the realization that it never actually arrives at the supposed transcendent Beyond of ultimate harmonies, identities, totalities, and unities (understanding's pre- or nondialectical image of "pure reason," of what being rational would bring about) toward which, in its Sisyphean stubbornness, it means to move according to the teloi of its pre- or nonrational subjective intentionality (an intentionality transfixed by an "illusion," as Žižek has it). Moreover, the understanding's very efforts to pursue this Elsewhere of wholly synthetic rationality succeed only at driving this Beyond ever further away, namely, at effectively generating additional dialectical consequences (qua antinomies, conflicts, and so on). *Verstand*, rather than misperceive its (self-)subversion of the mirage of *reinen Vernunft* that it tends to chase after in vain, can and should come to perceive this seeming failure as, in fact, real success.

In the second Hegelian-Žižekian step in the transition from the understanding to reason, after *Verstand* takes the first step of losing its illusions about what *Vernunft* or being rational truly would be—in fitting Lacanian locution, this could be described as "traversing the fantasy" of an imagined pure reason—it becomes free to embrace dialectical negativity, which the understanding cannot help but ceaselessly reintroduce, as a virtue rather than a vice, as an asset rather than a liability. In thus becoming self-affirming, the understanding becomes reason. The fundamentally subtractive aspect of Žižek's rendition of this movement is that, for him, *Vernunft* is nothing more than *Verstand* minus the latter's fantasies about the former.

Žižek also aligns the transition from the understanding to reason as parallel with a shift from epistemology to ontology ("it is epistemology versus ontology"—I will address this shift at length in chapter 1). Succinctly stated for the time being, *Verstand* passes over into *Vernunft* when it comes to see what it previously took to be its ignorance (qua epistemological impotence, the inaccessibility of being to thinking) as, instead, insight (qua ontological potency, the accessing of being by this same thinking). Žižek frequently translates these features of his "return to Hegel" into Lacanese. On Žižek's reconstruction, Hegel's "absolute knowing" (*das absolute Wissen*) amounts to insight into the general nature of the rapport between the understanding and reason (as I have outlined this rapport). Given this, Žižek insistently equates what this notorious Hegelian phrase designates with Lacan's thesis that "the big Other does not exist" (*le grand Autre n'existe pas*), that this Other is "barred," that is, ridden with and saturated by antagonisms, contradictions, inconsistencies, and the like.[45]

Kant limits the understanding-generated dialectics of reason (that is, Hegel's negative moment of *Vernunft*) to the purely epistemological dimension of a thinking separate from being. He thereby keeps the ontological dimension of things in themselves (that is, beings beyond thinking) unscathed by the dialectical negativities he discovers within the cognizing subject's categories and concepts (as spelled out in the *Critique of Pure Reason* under the heading "Transcendental Dialectic," the second half of the first *Critique*). In Žižek's Lacanian terms, Kant believes in the existence of a big Other as a self-consistent, conflict-free noumenal Beyond. By contrast, Hegel, on the basis of a multipronged critique of Kant's subjectivist transcendental idealism, renders this Kantian Other nonexistent by revealing the dialectical (including the dialectics of the first *Critique*'s "Transcendental Dialectic") to be ontological as well as epistemological, an aspect of being in addition to one of thinking. According to Žižek, Hegel's absolute knowing amounts to insight into this absence of an ultimately harmonious and unified Being transcending the cacophonous fray of the dialectical negativities that show up within subjective cognition. (Chapters 1 and 2 delineate in detail these features, among others, of the Kant-Hegel connection and Žižek's perspectives on this pivotal philosophical relationship.)[46]

In addition to Lacan's refrains about the big Other as barred and nonexistent, Žižek also employs, in the same vein, a Lacanian distinction between "alienation" and "separation."[47] The transition from alienation to separation, with the former as a subject's sensed lack of wholeness (that is, a sense of discord, incompleteness, and the like), occurs if and when the alienated subject comes to two interrelated realizations (with a clinical analysis, for Lacan, facilitating the arrival at these twin epiphanies): (1) its alienation is structurally necessary rather than gratuitously contingent; (2) all subjects, as subjects, are likewise thus alienated. In separating from fantasies of a nonalienated Other (or others as other subjects), the subject achieving this separation can thereby reframe and reposition him- or herself in relation to his or her alienation.[48] (A further therapeutic gain is that, through separation, alienation is transformed from the overwhelming intensity of neurotic pathos into the bearable dullness of ordinary suffering, to paraphrase Sigmund Freud himself.)[49] In Žižek's eyes, Hegel separates from the alienation of Kant's critical epistemology, in which the dialectical is taken to mark the estrangement of thinking from being, by jettisoning the very idea of a dialectics-transcending being free of the negativities plaguing thinking (that is, the notion of a nonalienated Other qua cohesive and at one with itself). With Hegel's ontologization of the understanding and the negative-rational dialectics it immanently generates, the lesson of Hegelian separation is once again that "*le grand Autre n'existe pas*," a lesson barring any heavenly Elsewhere of final synthesis and highest totality.[50] More generally, in Žižek's combination of Lacan's alienation-separation couplet with Hegel's philosophy, Hegelian separation-as-reconciliation is nothing other than, in a way, reconciliation with alienation.[51]

Similarly, Žižek's celebration of the powers of *Verstand* involves a less-is-more perspective. (Such praise of the understanding is indeed profoundly Hegelian despite certain expectable impressions to the contrary.) In *Less Than Nothing*, Žižek observes: "How does a notion emerge out of the confused network of impressions we have of an object? Through the power of 'abstraction,' of blinding oneself to most of the features of the object, reducing it to its constitutive key aspects. The greatest power of our mind is not to see more, but to see *less* in a correct way, to reduce reality to its notional determinations—only such 'blindness' generates the insight into what things really are."⁵² A page later, he adds: "Hegel does not overcome the abstract character of Understanding by substantially changing it (replacing abstraction with synthesis etc.), but by perceiving in a new light this same power of abstraction: what at first appears as the weakness of Understanding (its inability to grasp reality in all its complexity, its tearing apart of reality's living texture) is in fact its greatest power."⁵³

These remarks are echoed subsequently in *Absolute Recoil*, where Hegelian abstraction also gets associated with the Freudian-Lacanian notion of the nodal "unary trait" (*ein einziger Zug, le trait unaire*).⁵⁴ Now, of course, "to see *less* in a correct way," rather than in an "incorrect way" (whether due to carelessness, ignorance, obliviousness, stupidity, or whatever else along these lines), one previously and initially needs to "see more" (that is, "the confused network of impressions we have of an object," "most of the features of the object," "reality in all its complexity," "reality's living texture"). Only through beginning with a prior acknowledgment and appreciation of this "more" can the selections and subtractions of the understanding's abstracting labor resulting in a certain "less" be "correct" qua considered, deliberate, informed, and principled. As Hegel himself would put it, one has to start by surveying the entirety of whatever is given before identifying the differences therein between what possesses mere being-there or existence (*Dasein/Existenz*) as peripheral and inessential and what possesses authentic actuality or reality (*Wirklichkeit*) as central and essential (for more on this Hegelian distinction, see chapter 3). Exclusively after flying over the "more" of the full sweep of a specific terrain can the philosophical Owl of Minerva accurately discern within this landscape the "less" of what is properly actual/real.

Later in *Less Than Nothing*, Žižek adds a supplementary twist to his Hegelian vindication of the importance and indispensability of *Verstand*. He argues that

> what makes Hegel's "concrete universality" infinite is that *it includes "abstractions" in concrete reality itself, as their immanent constituents*. To put it another way: what, for Hegel, is the elementary move of philosophy with regard to abstraction? It is to abandon the common-sense empiricist notion of abstraction as a step away from the wealth of concrete empirical reality with its irreducible multiplicity of features: life is green, concepts are gray, they dissect, mortify, concrete reality. (This common-sense notion even has its pseudo-dialectical version, according to which such "abstraction" is a feature of mere Understanding, while "dialectics" recuperates the rich tapestry of reality.) Philosophical thought proper

begins when we become aware of how *such a process of "abstraction" is inherent to reality itself*: the tension between empirical reality and its "abstract" notional determinations is immanent to reality, it is a feature of "Things themselves." Therein lies the anti-nominalist accent of philosophical thinking—for example, the basic insight of Marx's "critique of political economy" is that the abstraction of the value of a commodity is its "objective" constituent. It is life without theory which is gray, a flat stupid reality—it is only theory which makes it "green," truly alive, bringing out the complex underlying network of mediations and tensions which makes it move.[55]

First of all, my opening warning about the risk of being misled by Hegel's references to Goethe's *Faust* into believing that Hegel plays a purely speculative reason against a nonspeculative (and unequivocally disparaged) understanding resonates with this passage. What is more, at the end of this quotation, Žižek, in the very name of genuine Hegelianism itself, goes so far as to invert Mephistopheles's famous pronouncement regarding the respective colorings of the theoretical (in its purported abstract grayness) and the living (in its purported concrete greenness).

Obviously, the preceding passage also explicitly refers to and unpacks one of Žižek's favorite concepts in Hegel's philosophy, namely, that of "concrete universality" (specifically as the precursor of "real abstraction" à la Marx and legged structures "marching in the street" à la Lacan—see also chapter 1).[56] In the background of this Žižekian gloss on this concept lurks the Hegelian view according to which the notion of the concrete apart from the abstract is itself the height of abstraction. This view encapsulates Hegel's opposition to the nominalism of every common-sensical, antiphilosophical empiricism.

It might seem, at first glance, that Žižek's parsing of Hegelian concrete universality entails an unqualified rejection of the nominalist common sense of *Verstand*-type empiricism. However, Žižek, consistent with his stress on Hegel's (underappreciated) positive assessments of the understanding, by no means categorically dismisses such empiricist nominalism. Rather than speculatively liquidating the understanding's dichotomy between the abstractions of subjective thinking and the concretenesses of objective being—in this dichotomy, the understanding, by contrast with Hegelian-Žižekian speculative dialectics, avoids conceiving of the subject's symbolic-linguistic-cognitive representations as beings endowed with ontological standing—Žižek ontologizes this very distinction, inscribing it into the Real itself ("*such a process of 'abstraction' is inherent to reality itself*: the tension between empirical reality and its 'abstract' notional determinations is immanent to reality, it is a feature of 'Things themselves'"). This Žižekian gesture implies that dialectics, at least sometimes, involves not negating as utterly illusory but, quite the contrary, affirming as fully existent nondialectical distinctions and incompatibilities (such as, in this context, the nominalist's antagonistic binary opposition between the abstract and the concrete, an opposition explicitly ontologized by Žižek).[57] Put differently, Hegel's and Žižek's dialectical approaches take the understanding's sub- or antidialectical categories and concepts more (not less) seriously than the understanding itself does.

In line with this, both *Less Than Nothing* and *Absolute Recoil* emphatically underscore the centrality of the nondialectical to the dialectical. As Žižek himself indicates,[58] the entire seventh chapter of *Less Than Nothing* (titled "The Limits of Hegel") is devoted to it.[59] *Absolute Recoil* concisely states in this same vein that

> yes, one should look for a non-dialecticizable moment of the dialectical process, but this moment is not to be sought in an external starting point which triggers it: the aspect of the process which cannot be dialecticized is its very motor, the repetitive "death drive" as the basic form of what Hegel calls "negativity." The relationship between Hegel's negativity and Freud's death drive (or compulsion to repeat) is thus a very specific one, well beyond their (hidden) outright identity: what Freud was aiming at with his notion of the death drive—more precisely, the key dimension of this notion to which Freud himself was blind, unaware of what he discovered—is the "non-dialectical" core of Hegelian negativity, the pure drive to repeat without any movement of sublation (idealization). In Kierkegaard-Freudian pure repetition, the dialectical movement of sublimation thus encounters itself outside itself, in the guise of a "blind" compulsion-to-repeat. And it is here that we should apply the great Hegelian motto about the internalizing of the external obstacle: in fighting its external opposite, the blind non-sublatable repetition, the dialectical movement is fighting its own abyssal ground, its own core; in other words, the ultimate gesture of reconciliation is to recognize in this threatening excess of negativity the core of the subject itself.[60]

I already have treated in detail elsewhere (in my 2008 book *Žižek's Ontology: A Transcendental Materialist Theory of Subjectivity*) Žižek's fundamental thesis positing an equivalence between the negativities of German idealist subjectivities and Freudian and Lacanian versions of the death drive.[61] Moreover, I take up Žižek's accounts of drive (including the *Todestrieb*) and desire as he discusses them in his books from 2012 and 2014 in my conclusion. (Incidentally, the Žižekian version of the Lacanian distinction between drive and desire can and should be aligned with Hegel's and Žižek's duo of non- or antidialectical understanding and dialectical-speculative reason respectively.) So, setting aside these aspects of this quotation, I want here to highlight the Žižekian thesis according to which the root-source powering the dynamics of dialectics is itself something nondialectical that is immanent to and inherent in all dialectical processes.

In relation to this postulate regarding the nondialectical nucleus of dialectics, Žižek mobilizes the paired categories of "condition of possibility" and "condition of impossibility." For instance, in *Less Than Nothing*, he proposes as a basic, essential principle of dialectics *überhaupt* that "The shift to be made in a proper dialectical analysis . . . goes from the condition of impossibility to the condition of possibility: what appears as the 'condition of impossibility,' or the obstacle, is in fact the condition that enables what it appears to threaten to exist."[62] Later in this same book, a number of examples and illustrations of this "shift" are deployed, ones drawn from Hegelian and Marxian reflections on sociopolitical history as well as psychoanalytic considerations about sexuality and sexual difference.[63]

Absolute Recoil also contains a general formulation of the dialectical tout court as generated on the basis of an interplay between conditions of possibility and impossibility. Žižek writes:

> Is not the notion of a "bone-in-the-throat" remainder, which is simultaneously the condition of possibility and the condition of impossibility of the dialectical process, at the very core of the Hegelian dialectic? What happens in the concluding reversal of that process is not the magical dissolution/reintegration of the "bone" into the circle of dialectical movement, but merely a shift of perspective which makes us see how the "bone" is not merely an obstacle which cannot be sublated but, precisely as such, a positive condition of the movement of sublation—the obstacle retroactively engenders what it is an obstacle to.[64]

Rejoining the discussion at the beginning of this preface, I would suggest now that, at the most fundamental of methodological/systematic levels, it is nothing other than the understanding according to Hegel (that is, the structures and dynamics of Hegelian *Verstand*) that functions as Žižek's "bone-in-the-throat" of speculative dialectics, the nondialectical condition of impossibility as also condition of possibility for every dialectical motion. The understanding's dualistic, black-and-white categorial and conceptual distinctions are conditions of possibility for Hegelian reason equally in its negative (that is, dialectical) and positive (that is, speculative) dimensions; for both Hegel and Žižek, as seen earlier, there is an asymmetry in the relation between the understanding and reason such that, while there indeed can be *Verstand ohne Vernunft*, there definitely cannot be *Vernunft ohne Verstand*, namely, "pure reason" (whether in its pre- or post-Kantian permutations).[65]

Nevertheless, these same *Verstand*-level binaries, dichotomies, and oppositions are conditions of impossibility for dialectical-speculative *Vernunft* insofar as they generate the very frictions resisting the kinetics of Hegelian reason. The antidialectical, subspeculative understanding, as the ultimate barrier (or, more accurately, Fichtean-style *Anstoß* as both check/hindrance and spur/catalyst)[66] to dialectical-speculative reason, is nonetheless productive of this same reason, with the latter thereafter remaining dependent and parasitical upon this very understanding. As Žižek puts it in the preceding block quotation, "the obstacle retroactively engenders what it is an obstacle to." And he already expresses this in his book from 2012 in reference to the paradigmatic operator of Hegel's speculative dialectics, namely, sublation *als Aufhebung*, the emblematic, signature gesture of Hegelian *Vernunft*: "Therein resides the properly utopian misunderstanding of *Aufhebung*: to distinguish in the phenomenon both its healthy core and the unfortunate particular conditions which prevent the full actualization of this core, and then to get rid of those conditions in order to enable the core to fully actualize its potential."[67]

Against this *méconnaissance* of genuine sublation à la Hegel, Žižek, in this observation just quoted, implicitly but clearly opposes a counterassertion to the effect that all efforts (enacted under the malign influence of a "utopian" pseudoversion of *Aufhebung*) to extract the "core" of reason from its embeddedness in and entanglements with the "conditions" of the understanding results in the destruction of this very core itself. That is to say, in a mixture of language from both *Less Than Nothing* and *Absolute Recoil*, the repetitive "stuckness" of *Verstand*-type rigidity and stasis precedes and enables (while nevertheless continuing to resist and disrupt) the differential motility of

Vernunft-type fluidity and kinesis.[68] As in the biblical lapsarian narratives referenced by Hegel and Žižek, "the Fall" (whether as original sin or the constitutive, founding errors and falsehoods of the understanding) comes first, and even, moreover, makes possible eventual redemption (whether as the reconciliation between God and humanity or the sublations of dialectical-speculative reason).[69] Or, to risk resorting to the terms of a (spontaneously dialectical) cliché, Hegelian-Žižekian reason cannot live with yet cannot live without the understanding.

Whenever one approaches Žižek the Hegelian, regardless of whether the Žižek in question is explicitly referring to Hegel by name in a given context, this prioritization of the understanding's violent cuts, abrupt polarizations, and mortifying analyses as ontologically real or concrete (and not just epistemologically formal or abstract) must always be kept in mind. Hence, any genuinely immanent-critical confrontation with Žižek must place a premium, as he does himself, on first drawing sharp, unambiguous lines in the creation and delineation of a *Kampfplatz* as the site for a specifically Žižekian encounter with Žižek's thinking. Similarly, one should continually remember that it is precisely when Hegel and Žižek look to be at their least Hegelian, as thinkers of antinomic oppositions and parallax splits, that they are, in fact, at their most Hegelian (rather than pre-Hegelian-*cum*-Kantian).[70] Despite potential appearances to the contrary, this overlapping of the nondialectical and the dialectical (in which the latter relies upon the former) is a coincidence of seeming opposites absolutely central and essential to both Hegel's and Žižek's modi operandi. One of the many lessons of the ongoing Žižekian "return to Hegel" is that true fidelity to the Hegelian legacy demands its apparent betrayal. Perhaps the same could be said in turn about what is in the process of becoming the Žižekian legacy.

Albuquerque, December 2016

Acknowledgments

To begin with, I delivered several lectures on the basis of material in this manuscript: an abbreviated version of chapter 2 as "Where to Start?: Robert Pippin, Slavoj Žižek, and the True Beginning(s) of Hegel's System" at the Department of Philosophy of the University of New Mexico in the fall of 2014; an abbreviated version of chapter 3 as "Absolutely Contingent: Slavoj Žižek and the Hegelian Contingency of Necessity" at the University of Western Ontario in the fall of 2015; and an abbreviated version of chapter 5 as "Bartleby by Nature: German Idealism, Biology, and the Žižekian Compatibilism of *Less Than Nothing: Hegel and the Shadow of Dialectical Materialism*" at the Townsend Humanities Center of the University of California, Berkeley, in the spring of 2014. I am very grateful to the organizers of and participants at these events. Their questions, comments, and critical feedback enabled me to refine these portions of this book.

Earlier drafts of this book's contents have appeared as chapters in edited collections: chapter 1 as " 'Freedom or System? Yes, Please!': How to Read Slavoj Žižek's *Less Than Nothing: Hegel and the Shadow of Dialectical Materialism*," in *Repeating Žižek*, ed. Agon Hamza (Durham: Duke University Press, 2015), 7–42; part of chapter 3 as "Absolutely Contingent: Slavoj Žižek and the Hegelian Contingency of Necessity," in *Rethinking German Idealism*, ed. Joseph Carew and Sean McGrath (Basingstoke: Palgrave Macmillan, 2016), 215–245; part of chapter 4 as "Materialism Without Materialism: Slavoj Žižek and the Disappearance of Matter," in *Slavoj Žižek and Dialectical Materialism*, ed. Agon Hamza and Frank Ruda (Basingstoke: Palgrave Macmillan, 2015), 3–22; chapter 5 as "Bartleby by Nature: German Idealism, Biology, and the Žižekian Compatibilism of *Less Than Nothing: Hegel and the Shadow of Dialectical Materialism*," in *Žižek and the Law*, ed. Laurent de Sutter (New York: Routledge, 2015), 121–152; and part of the conclusion as "Repetition and Difference: Žižek, Deleuze, and Lacanian Drives," in *Lacan and Deleuze: A Disjunctive Synthesis*, ed. Bostjan Nedoh and Andreja Zevnik (Edinburgh: Edinburgh University Press, 2016), 180–202. I thank these publishers for permission to include revised versions of these essays in the present book. Moreover, I also thank the editors and reviewers of these pieces for their very thoughtful insights and advice.

Furthermore, earlier drafts of other portions of this book's contents have appeared as journal articles: chapter 2 as "Where to Start?: Robert Pippin, Slavoj Žižek, and the True Beginning(s) of Hegel's System," special issue, "Critique Today," ed. Agon Hamza and Frank Ruda, *Crisis and Critique* 1, no. 3 (2014): 371–418; and part of chapter 3 as "Contingency, Pure Contingency—Without Any Further Determination: Modal Categories in Hegelian Logic," special issue, "German Idealism After Finitude," *Logos: Russian Journal of Philosophy and Humanities* 1, no. 2 (2017): 23–48. I likewise thank these journals and editors for their permission and extremely helpful suggestions.

Additionally, I am grateful to the students and auditors in my spring 2013 seminar on Žižek's *Less Than Nothing* in the Department of Philosophy at the University of New Mexico. Their lively engagements with Žižek inspired further enthusiasm in me for writing the present book. The conversations in that seminar significantly aided me in organizing and exploring my ideas about the Žižekian "return to Hegel."

Finally, Todd McGowan and Tom Brockelman have my deepest gratitude for their generously given and incredibly perspicacious recommendations and criticisms.

A New German Idealism

Introduction

Sublating Absolute Idealism—Žižekian Materialist Reversals

MY BOOK *ŽIŽEK'S Ontology*, published in 2008, was originally written between 2002 and 2005. In revising it for publication, I managed to have it address Žižek's texts up through his philosophical treatise *The Parallax View*, published in 2006. My book *Badiou, Žižek, and Political Transformations: The Cadence of Change*, published in 2009, treats his oeuvre up through *In Defense of Lost Causes*, published in 2008.

With the appearances of *Less Than Nothing* and *Absolute Recoil*, I since have come slightly to regret that *Žižek's Ontology* in particular was composed and published before the releases of these books by Žižek from 2012 and 2014, both of them major, substantial components of his philosophical corpus in process. Of course, such is the obvious danger, then and now, of writing on a very much alive and thinking figure. Nonetheless, here I am, once again running the same risk in writing this critical assessment of and response to *Less Than Nothing* and *Absolute Recoil* as itself a sequel to *Žižek's Ontology*.

For the sake of progress rather than perseveration, I refrain here from extensive rehashing of topics Žižek addresses in his works from before 2012 that I covered in previous publications. Therefore, my focus will be on *Less Than Nothing* and *Absolute Recoil* (with references in the notes to *Disparities*, published in 2016), and I will devote the bulk of my attention to the innovative and novel aspects of these recent sizable statements by Žižek of his philosophical commitments. That is to say, I intend, in the book, to dwell primarily upon the distinctive features of Žižek's efforts from 2012 and

2014 to revivify Hegelianism in connection with the tradition of dialectical materialism partly inspired by Hegel.

There is a natural question at this point: What exactly is new or creative in *Less Than Nothing* and *Absolute Recoil* in relation to Žižek's body of work from before 2012? Specifically in light of my concerns in *Žižek's Ontology*, what additional contributions do Žižek's books from 2012 and 2014 make in terms of both his renditions of German idealism and psychoanalytic theory and his interlinked account of subjectivity and materialist ontology? To begin with, *Less Than Nothing* in particular, weighing in at just over one thousand pages, is by far his most sustained reckoning with Hegel to date (before 2012, his lengthiest single engagement in English with Hegel's philosophy is to be found in *For They Know Not What They Do: Enjoyment as a Political Factor*, published in 1991). As anyone even minimally familiar with Žižek knows, Hegel is at least as important to him as Lacan. Žižek's unprecedentedly detailed and thorough consideration of every facet of Hegel's sprawling, encyclopedic philosophical edifice in *Less Than Nothing* and *Absolute Recoil* deserves and promises to repay careful scrutiny. Such scrutiny is further warranted and demanded by the fact that this Žižek also precisely delineates what he sees as the shortcomings and flaws of Hegel's System.

Hence, chapters 1 through 3 involve, among other things, examinations of Žižek's relations with German idealism generally and Hegel especially. Much of chapter 1 (" 'Freedom or System? Yes, Please!': Spinozisms of Freedom and the Post-Kantian Aftermath Then and Now") is devoted to retelling the history both of the emergence of German idealism from Kantianism and the latter's surrounding contemporaneous context and of the emergence of Hegelianism from post-Kantian idealism, doing so with an eye to Žižek's own retelling of this historical sequence. This narrative exercise is important not only for illuminating the history of ideas forming the main background framing *Less Than Nothing* and *Absolute Recoil*; the Žižekian theoretical agenda is in no small part motivated by its pursuit of a contemporary reactivation of the questions and problems at the very heart of Kantian and post-Kantian German idealism. Thus, my revisitation of the German-speaking intellectual universe of the late eighteenth and early nineteenth centuries is at least as much about the (or, at a minimum, Žižek's) philosophical present as it is about the historical past. Chapter 1 concludes by distilling from the history of philosophy from Kant to Hegel the criteria that make possible properly immanent-critical judgments on the successes or failures, virtues or vices, of the (post-)Hegelian dialectical materialism articulated in *Less Than Nothing* and *Absolute Recoil*.

Chapter 2 ("Where to Start?: Deflating Hegel's Deflators") shifts to reflecting upon recent and current non-Žižekian reckonings with Hegelianism. The proper name *Hegel* lies at the origins of the century-old split between "continental" and "analytic" philosophical traditions, with the latter arising in part on the basis of a sharp repudiation of the excesses of nineteenth-century British Hegelianism by Bertrand Russell, G. E. Moore, and company. But, starting in the 1970s, particularly thanks to Charles Taylor's engagements with Hegel's thought, Hegel became acceptable and interesting within certain circles in the world of Anglo-American philosophy. However, this analytic uptake of Hegel has been dominated by various "deflationary" approaches, namely, interpretations and reconstructions sharing in common the downplaying, excising, or rubbishing of the more metaphysically ambitious dimensions of the Hegelian System. The "deflated" Hegel is a non- or postmetaphysical thinker, whether as an epistemologically conservative Kantian, a philosopher of the "linguistic turn" avant la lettre, or a historically minded ethicist and sociopolitical theorist.

In both *Less Than Nothing* and *Absolute Recoil*, Žižek frontally assaults the deflationary, antimetaphysical versions of Hegel still so popular in today's philosophical milieus. These assaults are additional distinctive features specific to Žižek's books from 2012 and 2014 (that is, content not to be found in his work from before 2012). Žižek and I concur that Hegel's metaphysics, including his ontology and *Naturphilosophie*, is both unavoidable for any historically accurate rendition of Hegelian philosophy and quite defensible and justified, a "live option," in the philosophical *hic et nunc*. Nonetheless, as chapter 2 spells out, I take issue with what strikes me as two crucial missteps made by Žižek in his attacks focused especially upon Robert B. Pippin, today's leading representative of the Kantian-style deflation of Hegel's philosophy: first, Žižek's acceptance of a widespread consensus according to which the Hegelian System in its entirety is grounded in and begins with the Logic alone; second, his neglect of the task of directly challenging Pippin's basic thesis about the pivotal role of Kantian subjectivity (à la Kant's "transcendental unity of apperception") in Hegelian Logic, a thesis underpinning Pippin's Kantianized (pseudo-)Hegelianism as a whole. In making up for this neglect by critiquing Pippin along these very lines, I also sketch a map of the architectonic of Hegel's System in which his philosophies of nature and spirit or mind (*Geist*) are equiprimordial vis-à-vis his Logic. The bigger picture of Hegel that comes to light differs in a number of ways from both deflationary and antideflationary versions of systematic Hegelianism put forward by Pippin, Žižek, and many others.

Although Žižek's heterodox presentation of Hegel as a thinker of contingency rather than necessity long predates *Less Than Nothing* and *Absolute Recoil*, his emphasis on the modal category of the contingent intensifies in these two recent books. Hence, after my situating of Žižek's Hegel in relation to other Hegels past and present (in chapters 1 and 2), chapter 3 ("Contingency, Pure Contingency—Without Any Further Determination: Hegelian Modalities") turns to Hegel's logical doctrine of modal categories. (Although, in chapter 2, I problematize the impression that the Logic by itself is the unique *Ur*-nucleus of the Hegelian System, I nevertheless readily acknowledge its utterly central importance to his philosophy.) Doing so leads me to an ambivalent assessment of Žižek on Hegelian contingency. On the positive side, my scrutinizing of contingency and its relations with other modalities in the *Science of Logic* and *Encyclopedia Logic* largely vindicates Žižek's stress on the primacy of the contingent for Hegel. On the negative side, I find that Žižek, perhaps under certain anachronous influences (stemming from Alexandre Kojève and Lacan, among others), errs in two ways here: first, he places himself at odds with Hegel by reversing the relations between the logical and the real (specifically, the historical as real qua extralogical), thereby inadvertently going too far in the direction of historicizing Hegel's doctrine of modal categories; second, he utilizes his historicized rendition of Hegelian modalities to draw what is, by my lights, an excessively stark, exaggerated contrast between the impossibility and actuality of foresight into the historical future in Hegelianism and classical Marxist historical materialism. In chapter 3, I seek to correct these two Žižekian errors.

Chapter 3 also sets up chapter 4 ("Materialism Sans Materialism: Žižekian Substance Deprived of Its Substance"). The third chapter's defense of historical materialism à la Marx and Engels contains a reconsideration of the understandings and misunderstandings operative in Engels's materialist affirmation of what he takes to be Hegel's compatibilism (as the mutual compatibility between the worlds of autonomous mind and heteronomous matter), which is bound up with Hegel's doctrine of modalities. (The topic of compatibilism in connection with German idealism and dialectical materialism according to Žižek is the primary preoccupation of chapter

5.) Žižek's repudiation of Engels in particular, along with so-called scientific socialism, addressed in chapter 3 brings up the matter of Žižek's relations with post-Hegelian Marxist materialism.

The subtitles of both *Less Than Nothing* and *Absolute Recoil* refer to "dialectical materialism." Another novel feature of these two books is their firm and sustained embrace of a twenty-first-century permutation of this materialist orientation informed by Hegel. Although Joseph Dietzgen and Karl Kautsky separately coined the phrase *dialectical materialism* in the same year (1887), the Engels of such texts as *Anti-Dühring*, *Dialectics of Nature*, and *Ludwig Feuerbach and the Outcome of Classical German Philosophy* is the key inspiration for this phrase and the notion it designates of a generalization into a philosophical worldview of Marx's historical materialism as a framework for critically examining social structures. Furthermore, whereas Western Marxists, starting with the young Georg Lukács, decisively break with Engelsian dialectical materialism (particularly with its "dialectics of nature"), Eastern (that is, Soviet) Marxists, starting with such figures as V. I. Lenin, affirm and advance this specific materialist current originating with Engels, including its controversial *Naturdialektik*.

Despite Žižek's Leninist political leanings, he theoretically veers sharply away from the Engelsian-Soviet line of materialism as a philosophical position. As already underscored in chapter 3, Žižek follows in the footsteps of such Western Marxists as Walter Benjamin, the mature Jean-Paul Sartre, and the later Louis Althusser in purging Marxism of any teleological necessitarianism in response to the twentieth century's multiple defiances of Marx's nineteenth-century predictions. (His replacement of necessity with contingency in historical materialism is not without precedent in the prior Marxist tradition.) Moreover, Žižek also opposes the Lenin of *Materialism and Empirio-Criticism*, as highlighted in chapter 4. In particular, he faults Lenin's damning in 1908 of philosophical forays into the then-new field of post-Newtonian physics as sadly self-defeating and a missed opportunity for the science-shaped materialism Lenin perceives himself as upholding. Yet another distinguishing aspect of Žižek's books from 2012 and 2014 is their rich elaborations of his theoretical appropriations of quantum physics (appropriations only outlined in such texts from before 2012 as *The Indivisible Remainder: An Essay on Schelling and Related Matters*, published in 1996).

There is much that I agree with in Žižek's insightful and provocative criticisms of Engelsian and Leninist variants of dialectical materialism.

Chapter 4, in detailing these criticisms in its first half, nonetheless voices certain reservations about and disagreements with them. Specifically, I confront these criticisms with two lines of counterargumentation: first, Žižek's distance-taking from Engelsian-Leninist dialectical materialism pushes him too far in the direction of forms of antimaterialist idealism; second, his Hegelian-Lacanian brand of dialectical materialism harbors risky ambiguities that threaten to dissolve the distinction he wishes to maintain between his position and those of other contemporary currents of materialism that he loudly and rightly condemns as materialist only speciously.

Yet, as the second half of chapter 4 concedes, there is, at the same time, another Žižek who makes up for these idealist deviations. A novel facet of Žižek's latest sizable philosophical tomes is their nuanced reflections upon German idealist *Naturphilosophie* (especially that of Hegel). His extractions and reassembly of materialist moments in the works of the German idealists are of great interest for intellectual history on their own. They are also philosophically significant by virtue both of problematizing standard, received impressions about the rapport between German idealism and historical or dialectical materialisms and of indicating what a nonreductive materialism viable in the present would have to involve. What is more, Žižek's reconceptualization of the very idea of nature via the German idealists elicits my deepest sympathies. This is one of several Žižeks with whom I feel the utmost solidarity.

A common denominator uniting Kant, J. G. Fichte, F. W. J. Schelling, and Hegel into a single orientation (that is, "German idealism") is their shared enthusiastic commitment to making an idea of human freedom inspired by the French Revolution absolutely foundational for any systematic philosophy after 1789. With the advent of the post-Fichtean objective and absolute idealisms of Schelling and Hegel respectively, this commitment to subjective-spiritual spontaneity is presented as simultaneously having to be squared with a Spinozistic vision of pre- or nonsubjective Being *an sich*, with this Being going by various names in both Schellingian and Hegelian philosophies, including the Absolute, the Idea, Identity, the Infinite, and Nature. In short, Schelling's and Hegel's efforts to systematically combine a Kantian- and Fichtean-style conception of self-determining subjectivity with a Spinozistic-style, quasi-naturalist ontology are endeavors to develop a certain sort of compatibilism. (In chapter 1, I narrate at length the history sketched in this paragraph.)

INTRODUCTION

Žižek, fully aware of his indebtedness to this dimension of German idealism (among others), likewise can be fairly depicted as a specific type of compatibilist (as could Badiou too, with his Lacan-inspired syntheses of Althusserian structural determination and Sartrean existential freedom). Having explored, with a mixture of sympathy and criticism, the contours of Žižek's dialectical materialist ontology in chapter 4, I shift, in chapter 5, to considering his theory of the autonomous subject as compatible with his ontology of the a- or transsubjective. (Incidentally, regarding this theory of subjectivity, the third chapter of *Less Than Nothing* furnishes readers with what is by far Žižek's most sustained consideration to date of Fichte, the German idealist who, before 2012, receives the least attention of the big four he constitutes together with Kant, Schelling, and Hegel.) I carefully examine how Žižek assembles his unique variant of compatibilism through distinctive combinations of references to German idealism, Freudian-Lacanian psychoanalysis, quantum physics, neurobiology, and cognitive science. This compatibilism productively lays the invaluable foundations (specifically, the necessary conditions) for a satisfying reconciliation that is materialist yet nonreductive of, to put it in Hegelian parlance, subject with substance. But the verdict I arrive at in this chapter is that Žižekian compatibilism, at least as elaborated by Žižek thus far, leaves unspecified what the sufficient conditions (over and above the necessary ones) would be for the immanent emergence of the subjective (qua denaturalized and more than-material) out of the substantial (qua natural-material). Hence, Žižek's dialectical materialist depiction of subjects crucially sets the correct agenda for further future research in this same vein while nonetheless not yet having fulfilled this agenda itself.

Finally, the conclusion brings sustained scrutiny to bear on the Žižekian redeployment of Lacan's distinction between drive (*Trieb, pulsion*) and desire (*Begierde, désir*). This distinction features throughout Žižek's oeuvre. However, as I have already suggested toward the end of the preface, the dialectical materialist return to Hegel of *Less Than Nothing* and *Absolute Recoil* not only forcefully reiterates the thesis according to which German idealist subjective negativities and the psychoanalytic *Todestrieb* conceptually capture identical phenomena; it also identifies drive (especially the death drive) with the nondialectical animating heart of dialectics itself, the unsublatable repetitiveness sustaining successive different sublations. Moreover, I would add here that, especially given Žižek's fondness for the middle-period

INTRODUCTION

Schelling's unfinished *Ages of the World* project, the transition from substance to subject sometimes appears coded as a shift from presubjective *Trieb* (as in the Schellingian "vortex of drives" à la the *Weltalter* mythology of the "eternal past") to subjective *Begierde* (or, expressed in Lacanian mathemes, the transition from S to $).

Žižek, in his philosophical statements of 2012 and 2014, speculates that the very tension between drive (and, associated with it, both nondialectical *Verstand* and presubjective substance [S]) and desire (and, associated with it, both dialectical-speculative *Vernunft* and desubstantialized subject [$]) arises out of the irreducible, "unprethinkable" (*unhintergehbar, unvordenkbar*, to borrow the language of the later Schelling) *Ur*-origin of a primordial Void. The book concludes by drawing to a close with the contention that Žižek's recent (un)grounding of his fundamental ontology on such a (less than) Nothing is tantamount to a relapse back into a pre-Hegelian idealism, against his express intention to advance a Hegelian materialism. As in the Fichte critique of Friedrich Hölderlin from 1795 (see chapter 1), Žižek inadvertently flirts here with basically Neo-Platonic and Spinozistic motifs. He thereby is in jeopardy of a de facto, objective regression to what would amount to a negative-theological, obscurantist-mystical absolutization of the lone Void or Nothing(ness) as the mother of all beginnings. Both Hegel and Hegel's Marxist materialist successors leave behind these types of ontological models. So too, I would argue, should Žižek himself.

From a larger perspective, Žižek and I clearly are invested in constructing materialisms that would be both post-Hegelian and post-Marxian—and, hence, neither vulgarly reductive nor crudely naturalistic. Furthermore, I completely concur with Žižek's current assessment that any such materialism must be arrived at by passing through (rather than passing by) idealism (an assessment echoing the first of Marx's "Theses on Feuerbach"). But such a passage is risky (as discussed in chapter 4). The danger is that one gets stranded in or remains entangled with idealism. Ostensible sublations (as in Hegel's *Aufhebung* in its double-sidedness) of idealism can go awry by entailing too much conservation and not enough cancelation. As a cliché warns, the road to (idealist) hell is paved with good (materialist) intentions.

Žižek and I indeed agree on the need to run the risk of this materialist passage through idealism. However, we disagree about how to do it so as not to get mired before finally reaching a (re)consolidated postidealist materialism. The disagreements cluster around such factors as our differing

INTRODUCTION

interpretations of Hegel's System, Marxist materialisms, Freudian-Lacanian psychoanalysis, and the natural sciences—as well as the relations between these shared points of inspiration and reference.

Any Hegelian, Žižek and me included, ought to welcome the "inside jobs" of immanent critiques (such as my Žižekian critiques of Žižek himself) as the most fruitful catalysts for pushing forward shared intellectual pursuits. I continue to find the emerging differences between Žižek's own dialectical materialism and my Žižek-inspired transcendental materialism to be indispensable stimulants for my ongoing labors. Let a hundred flowers bloom!

ONE

"Freedom or System? Yes, Please!"

Spinozisms of Freedom and the Post-Kantian Aftermath Then and Now

AN EXTREMELY BRIEF period between the end of the eighteenth and beginning of the nineteenth centuries sees an incredible explosion of intense philosophical activity in the German-speaking world, perhaps rivaled solely by the birth of Western philosophy itself in ancient Greece (although Badiou passionately maintains that postwar France is philosophically comparable to these other two momentous times and places).[1] Inaugurated by Kant and accompanied by the Romantics as cultural fellow-travelers, the set of orientations that has come to be known by the label "German idealism"—this movement spans just a few decades—partly originates in the 1780s with the debates generated by F. H. Jacobi's challenges to modern secular rationality generally as well as Kant's critical transcendental idealism specifically.[2] One of the most provocative moves Jacobi makes is to confront his contemporaries with a stark forced choice between either "system" or "freedom" (to use language Schelling, a German idealist giant, employs to designate this Jacobian dilemma and its many permutations and variants).[3] In Jacobi's Pietist Protestant view, the systematization of the allegedly contradiction-ridden Kantian philosophy—the post-Kantian idealists at least agree with Jacobi that Kant indeed falls short of achieving thoroughly rigorous, self-consistent systematicity—inevitably must result, as with any rationally systematic philosophy on Jacobi's assessment, in the very loss of what arguably is most dear to this philosophy itself in its contemporaneity with both the Enlightenment and the French Revolution: in a word, autonomy (in Kant's specific case, the transcendental subject's powers of spontaneous judgment and self-determination).[4] Suffice it to say, Jacobi is far from satisfied with the attempted resolution of the third of the "antinomies of pure reason" in the *Critique of Pure Reason*.[5] This dissatisfaction is supported by Jacobi's undermining of the Kantian distinction between the noumenal and the phenomenal through his criticisms of the thing in itself (*das Ding an sich*),[6] criticisms subsequently broadened and deepened by the "big three" of post-Kantian German idealism: Fichte, Schelling, and Hegel.

With the unintended effect of igniting a fascination with Baruch Spinoza among a younger generation of intellectuals, Jacobi, as part of his anti-Enlightenment agenda, contentiously claims that Spinoza's monistic substance metaphysics is the one and only system inevitably arrived at by all unflinchingly consistent and consequent philosophical reasoning. Construing this metaphysics as materialistic and naturalistic, Jacobi equates Spinozist ontology with freedom-denying, subject-squelching determinism (that is, "fatalism") and therefore also with atheistic "nihilism."[7] The "pantheism controversy" (*Pantheismusstreit*) triggered by Jacobi's polemicizing saddles Kant's idealist successors, insofar as they wish to systematize Kantian philosophy, with the task of formulating a totally coherent metaphysics (qua a seamlessly integrated epistemology and ontology) that nonetheless preserves space within itself for the spontaneity of self-determining subjectivity.[8]

Inspired by the failed efforts of K. L. Reinhold, the first (but far from foremost) post-Kantian German idealist, to ground Kant's critical transcendental edifice in the firmer foundation of an apodictic first principle (that is, an indubitable *Grundsatz* methodologically akin to René Descartes's Archimedean proposition *Cogito, ergo sum*),[9] Fichte opts for a radical "primacy of the practical" as the key to a systematized (post-)Kantianism. It is necessary to skip over numerous details here, but generally Fichte's position, in his *Wissenschaftslehre* from 1794, which is rooted in nothing more than the free activity of spontaneous subjectivity, is itself quickly found to be wanting in turn by certain of his contemporaries and soon-to-be immediate successors. Hölderlin's fragment "Über Urtheil und Seyn" ("On Judgment and Being"), penned in 1795 by someone fresh from hearing Fichte lecture on this "scientific teaching," lays down the initial sketches for his Tübingen seminary classmates Schelling's and Hegel's myriad subsequent arguments against the allegedly excessive subjectivism of Fichte's (and Kant's) brand of idealism.¹⁰ Hölderlin suggests the ultimate unavoidability of presupposing or positing a non- or presubjective ground of being in relation to which the transcendental subject of Kant and Fichte is a secondary outgrowth. His fragment heralds the final, post-Fichtean phase of classical German idealism (starting with Schelling's very public break with Fichte in 1801)¹¹ insofar as this phase is animated by, among other things, the pursuit of a "Spinozism of freedom," namely, a dialectical-speculative synthesis of Spinoza (qua a proper name for the system of substance) with Kant and Fichte (qua proper names for the freedom of the subject).¹² Hegel's insistence, in the deservedly celebrated preface to his *Phenomenology of Spirit*, on "grasping and expressing the True, not only as *Substance*, but equally as *Subject*" ("*das Wahre nicht als* Substanz, *sondern ebensosehr als* Subjekt *aufzufassen und auszudrücken*")¹³ is only the most famous articulation of this far-reaching ambition, which was kindled in him and Schelling by their dear old school friend, the philosophically minded great poet.¹⁴

Dated a year later than "Über Urtheil und Seyn," the short "Earliest System-Program of German Idealism" can be read as resonating with Hölderlin's text. Although written in Hegel's handwriting, the authorship of this fragment from 1796 remains a matter of dispute among specialists in German idealism, with Hölderlin, Schelling, and Hegel all being put forward as possibly responsible for its contents. Regardless of who originally composed it—I happen to favor those scholars, such as Otto Pöggeler and H. S. Harris, who make the case for Hegel being its original author (against, for instance, Dieter Henrich)¹⁵—the "program" announced and outlined in it undeniably sets lasting priorities for the subsequent philosophical agendas of both Schelling and Hegel.¹⁶

As the beginning of the project of a post-Fichtean, Hölderlin-inspired Spinozism of freedom in particular, "The Earliest System-Program of German Idealism" gestures specifically at the project of reverse engineering a (quasi-)naturalistic fundamental ontology (dealing with substance as featuring in a *Naturphilosophie*) out of an axiomatically postulated affirmation of the actual and factual existence of spontaneous, autonomous selves (that is, the subjects of transcendental idealist reflections).¹⁷ This fragment's author declares:

> Since the whole of metaphysics falls for the future within moral theory ... this ethics will be nothing less than a complete system of all ideas or of all practical

postulates (which is the same thing). The first idea is, of course, the presentation of myself as an absolutely free entity. Along with the free, self-conscious essence, there stands forth—out of nothing—an entire world, the one true and thinkable creation out of nothing.—Here I shall descend into the realms of physics; the question is this: how must a world be constituted for a moral entity? I would like to give wings once more to our backward physics, that advances laboriously by experiments.[18]

The text continues: "Thus, if philosophy supplies the ideas, and experience the data, we may at last come to have in essentials the physics that I look forward to for later times. It does not appear that our present-day physics can satisfy a creative spirit such as ours is or ought to be."[19] Hegel and Schelling, regardless of who originally composed these lines, both go on to carry out the endeavor called for in these passages.[20] So, appropriately combining the two pairs of terms *substance* and *subject* (à la Hegel) and *system* and *freedom* (à la Schelling)—these terms refer in part to Hegel's and Schelling's subsequent fulfillments of this "program" from 1796—the "physics" (*Physik*)[21] demanded here would amount to nothing less than an ontological system of natural substance as itself autodialectically self-denaturalizing ("a world . . . constituted for a moral entity"), because it has internally generated the freedom of autonomous subjectivity ("myself as an absolutely free entity") as a transcendence in immanence relative to it. (Both Jean Hyppolite and Adrien Peperzak speak of a horizontal, rather than vertical, transcendence, and Ettore Barbagallo invokes "the immanence of immanence and non-immanence.")[22] In this context, the names *Spinoza*, on the one hand, and *Kant* and *Fichte*, on the other hand, stand for the monist-naturalist system of substance and the transcendental idealist freedom of the subject, respectively.[23]

Žižek's *Less Than Nothing* and *Absolute Recoil* require for their proper evaluation being interpreted in relation to the historical background I have just summarized rather quickly. (Incidentally, Badiou's sustained Lacan-inspired efforts to synthesize the existentialism of Sartre and the structuralism of Althusser likewise should be viewed as reengaging in the pursuit of a Spinozism of freedom—thanks to their avowed inheritance of Spinozism [in the case of Althusser] and transcendental idealism [in the case of Sartre];[24] in *Absolute Recoil*, Žižek similarly depicts Lacan's "inconsistent, non-All, symbolic structure" as breaking through the antinomic deadlock between Sartre

"FREEDOM OR SYSTEM? YES, PLEASE!"

and Claude Lévi-Strauss.)[25] In the introduction to his magnum opus from 2012, Žižek explicitly situates this book with respect to the hypercompressed history of German idealism in its full sweep. To begin with, he insists that the history of philosophy as philosophy proper only truly gets underway with Kant (an insistence he has voiced elsewhere too),[26] with this history rapidly gaining momentum through Kant's immediate successors.[27] Žižek speaks of "the unbearable density of thought … provided by the mother of all Gangs of Four: Kant, Fichte, Schelling, Hegel."[28]

Žižek's preliminary retelling of the story of German idealism as an introductory framing of *Less Than Nothing* focuses primarily on Kant's critical transcendental turn as epitomized by the second half of the *Critique of Pure Reason*, namely, the "Transcendental Dialectic," where Kant purports to reveal the ultimate vanity of pure reason's pretensions to enjoy direct epistemological access to the independent ontological reality of such things in themselves as the soul, the cosmos, and God (that is, the three "ideas of reason" generated by the "interest of reason" in achieving ultimate, unconditioned points of englobing synthesis: the "psychological," "cosmological," and "theological" ideas). Žižek, in his introduction, contrasts Kant's epistemological dialectics with the ontological dialectics of Schelling and Hegel, all the while acknowledging the profound indebtedness of the latter two to the former. As he spells out here, Kant's reactivation and redeployment of the ancient art of dialectics (paradigmatically on display in Plato's *Parmenides*, with which Žižek proceeds to engage)[29] begin by irreparably shattering pre-Kantian metaphysical worldviews, introducing corrosive antinomies, contradictions, and the like into them. In the hands of the post-Kantians Schelling and Hegel, this Kantian revival of dialectics ends up, as it were, destroying the world itself qua image of being a monolithic, unified One, a harmonious, coherent All. In other words, the ontologization of Kantian critical epistemology as found in the first *Critique*'s "Transcendental Dialectic" means not only that the thinking of being is inconsistent, but that being *an sich* is itself inconsistent too.[30] Hegel achieves this breakthrough during his pre-*Phenomenology* period in Jena when he finally drops the distinction between logic (as the thinking of epistemology) and metaphysics (as the being of ontology), with the consequence that the speculative dialectics of logic come to infect metaphysics and ontology.[31] As for Schelling, Žižek restricts his praise along these lines to Schelling's middle period, running from 1809 (with the *Freiheitschrift*) to 1815 (with the third draft of the

Weltalter manuscripts).[32] Furthermore, in the cases of both the mature Hegel and the middle-period Schelling, Žižek perspicuously discerns a decisive advance over Hölderlin's pioneering vision in "Über Urtheil und Seyn" from 1795: whereas the Spinozism of freedom à la Hölderlin posits the ultimate substance of being as a seamless, undifferentiated Absolute (in the style of a Neo-Platonic One), the versions of Hegel and Schelling beloved by Žižek radicalize this post-Fichtean project by injecting antagonisms, conflicts, gaps, splits, and so on into this Absolute itself.[33] (However, I think Žižek overlooks select moments in the young Schelling's *Naturphilosophie* that foreshadow, as early as 1798, the theosophical framings of primordial negativity in his subsequent middle period [1809–1815],[34] even though a study that Žižek praises,[35] Wolfram Hogrebe's *Prädikation und Genesis*, published in 1989, delineates along these lines the threads of continuity between the early Schelling and the later one of the *Weltalter* project.)[36]

In *Žižek's Ontology*, I stress the importance for Žižek of construing the transition from Kant to Hegel as one from epistemological to ontological dialectics, with Hegel (and a specific Schelling) "ontologizing" the critical Kant.[37] At multiple junctures in *Less Than Nothing*, Žižek continues to characterize the rapport between Kant and Hegel in these same terms, as he also appears to do more recently in both *Absolute Recoil* and *Disparities*.[38] However, at other moments in the book, he goes out of his way to correct this (mis)characterization (a new gesture of his surfacing for the first time in *Less Than Nothing*).[39] I suspect that, without him explicitly saying as much, this is both a self-critique of his earlier depictions of Kant *avec* Hegel and a critique of my exegesis in this vein in *Žižek's Ontology*. Žižek's critical qualifications begin thus:

> Kant ... goes only half-way in his destruction of metaphysics, still maintaining the reference to the Thing-in-itself as an external inaccessible entity, and Hegel is merely a radicalized Kant, who moves from our negative access to the Absolute to the Absolute itself as negativity. Or, to put it in terms of the Hegelian shift from epistemological obstacle to positive ontological condition (our incomplete knowledge of the thing becomes a positive feature of the thing which is in itself incomplete, inconsistent): it is not that Hegel "ontologizes" Kant; on the contrary, it is Kant who, insofar as he conceives the gap as merely epistemological, continues to presuppose a fully constituted noumenal realm existing out there, and it is Hegel who "deontologizes" Kant, introducing a gap into the very texture of

"FREEDOM OR SYSTEM? YES, PLEASE!"

reality. In other words, Hegel's move is not to "overcome" the Kantian division, but, rather, to assert it "as such," to *remove the need for its "overcoming,"* for the additional "reconciliation" of the opposites, that is, to gain the insight—through a purely formal parallax shift—into how positing the distinction "as such" already *is* the looked-for "reconciliation." Kant's limitation lies not in his remaining within the confines of finite oppositions, in his inability to reach the Infinite, but, on the contrary, in his very search for a transcendent domain beyond the realm of finite oppositions: Kant is not unable to reach the Infinite—what he is unable to see is how he *already has what he is looking for*.[40]

Kant might retort that it is not he who is invested in a "search for a transcendent domain," but the faculty of reason (*Vernunft*) itself, whose operations he merely describes, including its interest-driven, illusion-generating "constitutive" abuses (rather than legitimate "regulative" uses) of its ideas (that is, the ideas of the soul, the cosmos, and God).[41] He also perhaps would underscore that, on a couple of occasions in the second edition (B version) of the first *Critique* (and possibly in response to certain reactions to the first edition [A version]),[42] he deems his "Transcendental Analytic" of the understanding (*Verstand*) as well as his transcendental philosophy *überhaupt* to be replacements for traditional ontologies erroneously and vainly aiming at transcendent things in themselves.[43] (However, one readily could counterargue that the subjective idealism of Kantian critique offers an "ontology" only on the basis of a glaringly equivocal employment of this word.) Anyhow, Žižek proceeds to reiterate that "At its most elementary, Hegel's move is a reduction, not an enrichment, of Kant: a *subtractive* move, a gesture of taking away the metaphysical ballast and of analyzing notional determinations in their immanent nature."[44] Or, as he puts it again a little later:

> With his philosophical revolution, Kant made a breakthrough the radicality of which he was himself unaware; so, in a second move, he withdraws from this radicality and desperately tries to navigate into the safe waters of a more traditional ontology. Consequently, in order to pass "from Kant to Hegel," we have to move not "forward" but backward: back from the deceptive envelope to identify the true radicality of Kant's breakthrough—in this sense, Hegel was literally "more Kantian than Kant himself." One of the points where we see this clearly is in the distinction between phenomena and noumena: Kant's explicit justification of why we need to introduce noumena remains well within the confines

of traditional ontology with its distinction between appearance and true reality.[45]

As I indicated, not only in his earlier writings but even at other points in *Less Than Nothing* Žižek sometimes still has recourse to the depiction of Hegel ontologizing Kant despite the (seeming) inversions of this depiction just quoted. For now, I wish to show that the apparent contradiction between ontologizing and deontologizing in Žižek's 180-degree reversal is just an appearance. That is to say, my contention (perhaps with Žižek, perhaps against him) is that these are two sides of the same coin; rather than contradicting each other, they are of a piece, namely, the recto and verso of a single rendition of the transition from Kant to Hegel. How so?

The key to dispelling the semblance of incompatibility in talk of Hegel "ontologizing" and "deontologizing" Kant resides in appreciating the relation (or lack thereof) between epistemology and ontology in Kant's critical framework (particularly that of the *Critique of Pure Reason*). As Žižek observes in *Less Than Nothing*, "one cannot avoid ontology."[46] This observation is directly relevant here because, on a certain reading, Kant indeed attempts to "avoid ontology" in his transcendental turn. To be more exact, the first *Critique* prohibits traditional ontological investigations insofar as it rules out as epistemologically invalid any robustly realist metaphysics purporting to directly address mind-independent objective (as asubjective) beings (that is, the being qua being of things in themselves). Epistemology-obsessed critique bans and itself replaces every ontology ostensibly getting its hands on being over and above thinking. But as with the John Locke of the inconsistency-riddled *An Essay Concerning Human Understanding*, published in 1690 (this tome intends to sidestep ontological issues in focusing exclusively on [empiricist] epistemological inquiries),[47] so too with Kant:

> No philosophy can avoid entirely certain foundational ontological commitments. . . . Even Kant's critical philosophy, which defensibly can be construed as an extremely careful and rigorous attempt to turn philosophizing away from speculations into the bedrock substantial reality of what is and toward primarily epistemological concerns, fails to refrain from dogmatically endorsing select presuppositions about the fundamental nature of being apart from subjectively mediated knowledge of it. Prior to Kant, the much more obvious and striking inconsistencies of an important empiricist textual precursor of key aspects of

"FREEDOM OR SYSTEM? YES, PLEASE!"

Kant's first *Critique*, John Locke's *An Essay Concerning Human Understanding*, arguably are symptomatic points of torsion and conflict within Kantian transcendental idealism too. Therein, Locke basically seems to say such self-contradictory things as "We can't intelligibly talk about substance in itself, but only our mental ideas of it. . . . Now, let's talk about substance in itself." However, given Kant's significantly greater philosophical sophistication and finesse as compared with Locke (at least at the level of theoretical, if not practical, philosophy), the inconsistencies glaringly manifest in the latter's 1690 text, inconsistencies resulting from the ontology repressed in favor of epistemology intrusively and insistently returning in a variety of ways, are less visible in the *Critique of Pure Reason*. Thanks to his highly skillful and refined systematicity, Kant, whether purposefully or not, is better at smoothly concealing what Locke, in his relative clumsiness, stumbles into openly revealing—namely, that an epistemology of the subjective mind cannot succeed at completely avoiding the violation of its own self-imposed limits (such as the [in]famous Kantian "limits of possible experience") by hypothesizing things about the ontology of the objective world *an sich*.[48]

On such a construal of Kantian transcendental idealism, the critical apparatus, inadvertently but inevitably contradicting itself, of necessity inconsistently presupposes or posits a spontaneous ontology in tandem with its epistemology and vainly attempted ontological agnosticism.[49] This ontology manifests itself primarily in the guise of the notorious distinction between, on one side, subjective and intersubjective phenomenal objects as appearances and, on another side, asubjective noumenal things in themselves. As is common knowledge, one of the unifying features of post-Kantian German idealism is its pointed rejection of this very distinction, taking to heart Jacobi's quip about *das Ding an sich* (as a "presupposition" in relation to the *Critique of Pure Reason*) that "*without* that presupposition I could not enter into the system, but *with* it I could not stay within it."[50]

Fichte, Schelling, and Hegel, in often overlapping manners, all launch multiple assaults against the defensibility and coherence of *das Ding an sich*, itself the crystallization of what they take to be a systematically untenable two-worlds metaphysics implicit in Kant's mature philosophy.[51] (The fact that legions of subsequent Kant scholars have strained mightily to exculpate Kant of any commitment whatsoever to a two-worlds metaphysics tacitly testifies to the devastating strength of the German idealists' criticisms of those aspects of Kant's texts flirting with, if not outright embracing, such

"FREEDOM OR SYSTEM? YES, PLEASE!"

a metaphysics.) Hence, post-Kantian German idealism generally and Hegel specifically "deontologize" this Kant, namely, the one who, despite the breathtakingly inventive ingeniousness of his "Copernican" critical transcendental revolution,[52] nonetheless continues to remain attached to a traditional mind-world image of the order of being(s) that is ultimately no more sophisticated than, for instance, that of Locke's vulgar, quotidian "common sense."[53] In particular, Hegel's repeated demonstrations of the self-induced dialectics subversively sublating from within such load-bearing pillars of Kant's Weltanschauung as the thing in itself and the *Verstand*-level dichotomies between subject and object as well as phenomena and noumena are immanent critiques of the spontaneous ontology of Kantian transcendentalism as "subjective idealism." Hegel's recurrent stress (echoed by Žižek)[54] on the self-undermining (il)logical nature of the figure of the "limit" relied upon by Kant (with his central "limits of possible experience") attacks both just-mentioned dichotomies at their root,[55] in addition to the numerous separate criticisms of each dichotomy on its own.

But one of the main aims of post-Fichtean idealism is precisely to (re)"ontologize" where critique tried (but failed) to deontologize. Schelling's "objective idealism," in his youthful philosophies of nature and identity circa the late 1790s and early 1800s, and Hegel's "absolute idealism" are both efforts to overcome the alleged one-sided subjectivism of Kant's and Fichte's transcendental idealism. (In line with Žižek's Hegelian partisanship—as Žižek remarks in *Less Than Nothing*, "For Hegel, the true ['concrete'] universality is accessible only from an engaged 'partial' standpoint"[56]—I here obviously employ and endorse Hegel's tripartite distinction between subjective, objective, and absolute idealisms.)[57] Schelling's and Hegel's talk of "the Absolute," "the Infinite," "Nature," "Substance," and so on, whatever differences there admittedly are both between these terms themselves and between Schellingian and Hegelian senses of them, essentially involves reference to ontological dimensions repressed by Kantian and Fichtean transcendental idealisms. Schelling and Hegel adamantly contend that these dimensions must return within a fully systematized postcritical philosophy, one violating the letter in the name of the spirit of Kant's philosophy.

Schelling aside for now, Hegel's critiques of Kant result in a sublation *als Aufhebung* of transcendental idealism (as is to be entirely expected with Hegel). That is to say, these critiques are not mere indeterminate negations as one-sided cancelations or razings of Kant's philosophy from outside it, namely, simple annihilations or obliterations of this philosophy leading to nothing else specific in its place beyond this voiding destruction. Rather, exemplifying the two-sidedness characteristic of Hegel's dialectical-speculative *Aufhebung*,[58] his critiques of Kant are "determinate negations"[59] qua movements arguably immanent to the structures and dynamics of Kant's own position. As Lacan would put it, Hegel seeks to trace trajectories that are "extimate" (that is, intimately and internally external, endogenously exogenous) with respect to Kant insofar as they are consequent extensions of Kantianism "in Kantianism more than Kantianism itself."[60] Right before his death, in his Berlin course on the *Encyclopedia Logic* from 1831, Hegel himself observes that "What is most interesting are the points where Kant reaches beyond himself."[61] Put differently, Hegel, in both senses of the prefix "post-" (as the continuity of coming after and as the discontinuity of moving beyond), is, with an ambivalence appropriate to dialectical speculation, a post-Kantian (rather than seeking to be a regressive pre-Kantian reacting against the critical Copernican revolution).[62]

More specifically, Hegel embraces and extends Kant's modern critical revivification of ancient dialectics[63] (as found in the latter half of the first *Critique*) while nonetheless still jettisoning anything in Kantian transcendental idealism even so much as hinting at a two-worlds metaphysics (such as *das Ding an sich*, the distinction between noumena and phenomena, and the figure of the limit à la the ostensible limits of possible experience). The implications of this composite gesture that both affirms and negates vis-à-vis Kant bring me back to Žižek and the question of whether Hegel ontologizes or deontologizes Kant's critical transcendental framework. As I underlined earlier, Žižek, in *Less Than Nothing*, both alternates between invoking ontologization and invoking deontologization with respect to the transition from Kant to Hegel and insists on the inevitability and necessity of ontological commitments even for philosophers (such as Locke and Kant) who wish to remain ontologically noncommittal. With these features of Žižek's reflections in his book from 2012 in conjunction with my discussion of Kantian and Hegelian philosophies in mind, it now can be readily comprehended why I asserted that Hegel's cancelation of the spontaneous ontology implicit in Kant's critical apparatus (that is, the latter's subjective idealist two-worlds metaphysics) is an elevation to a new ontology, as it is a dialectical gesture in which destruction is at the same time creation. Hegel's liquidation of Kantian two-worlds metaphysics is combined with his simultaneous retention of Kant's transcendental dialectics (with the latter being, for Kant himself, purely epistemological, ideational, and subjective, namely, de- or non-ontological). If, as asserted by both the post-Fichtean idealists and Žižek, ontology ultimately is unavoidable,[64] then, after Hegel's negation of any noumenal Beyond as the transcendent subsistence of contradiction-free, self-consistent things in themselves, the contradiction-ridden, inconsistent realm of experience is all there is. With the unavoidability of the ontological, the antinomy-plagued not-All of multiple teeming phenomena must itself be treated as the very Real of being qua being. For Hegel, epistemology without ontology is impossible. This impossibility, were it possible, would be a nonmetaphysical theory of knowing and thinking subjectivity sans presuppositions or posits about asubjective being *an sich* (which would include Kant's subjectively idealist critical approach as non- or postmetaphysical).[65] With Hegel's post-Kantianism, this leaves the field of phenomena already dialecticized by the *Critique of Pure Reason* as the sole reality for the ontology of a one-world metaphysics devoid of any transcendent Elsewhere (that is, as the Absolute in a certain Hegelian sense).[66] As Žižek expresses in the third chapter of *Less Than Nothing* ("Fichte's Choice"), *"the 'Absolute' beyond appearances coincides with an 'absolute appearance,' an appearance beneath which there is no substantial Being."*[67] (I will refer to this quoted line again.)

A passage in a longish letter dated October 23, 1812, from Hegel to his friend and professional protector, the Bavarian minister of education, Friedrich Immanuel Niethammer, on whom he pins his hopes for a desperately desired university post, is especially revealing along these lines. Writing while he is in the midst of working on the *Science of Logic*, Hegel explains (in connection with his pedagogy as a *Gymnasium* teacher in Nuremberg):

> According to my view, metaphysics . . . falls entirely within logic. Here I can cite Kant as my predecessor and authority. His critique reduces metaphysics as it has existed until now to a consideration of the understanding and reason. Logic can thus in the Kantian sense be understood so that, beyond the usual content of so-called general logic, what he calls transcendental logic is bound up with it and set out prior to it. In point of content I mean the doctrine of the categories, or reflective concepts, and then of the concepts of reason: analytic and dialectic. These objective thought forms constitute an independent content [corresponding to] the role of the Aristotelian *Categories* [*organon de categoriis*] or the former ontology. Further, they are independent of one's metaphysical system. They occur

in transcendental idealism as much as in dogmatism. The latter calls them determinations of being [*Entium*], while the former calls them determinations of the understanding. My objective logic will, I hope, purify this science once again, expositing it in its true worth, but until it is better known those Kantian distinctions already contain a makeshift or rough version of it.[68]

As I noted, Hegel, during his pre-*Phenomenology* period in Jena, had already taken the crucial step of dissolving the distinction between ideational logic (as subjectivist and epistemological) and ontological metaphysics (as philosophically practiced by pre-Kantians ranging from Aristotle to the early-modern rationalist substance metaphysicians [Descartes, Nicolas Malebranche, Spinoza, Gottfried Wilhelm Leibniz, and their ilk] and, even closer in time and place to the German idealists, Christian Wolff and his Leibnizian school). For the mature Hegel, logic properly conceived is the one and only possible metaphysics ("metaphysics ... falls entirely within logic").[69] Furthermore, this quotation reveals that Kant's "transcendental logic" furnishes the rudiments for the first two-thirds of Hegel's post-Jena System of speculative philosophical *Wissenschaft* (that is, the "Objective Logic" of "The Doctrine of Being" and "The Doctrine of Essence" in both the *Science of Logic* and *Encyclopedia Logic*).[70] (Hegel here stipulates that, with the phrase "transcendental logic," he means to encompass dimensions from both the "Transcendental Analytic" of the understanding and the "Transcendental Dialectic" of reason in the first *Critique*.) As he says, "those Kantian distinctions already contain a makeshift or rough version of it" ("it" being Hegel's "Objective Logic").

The beginning of the "Objective Logic," as the beginning of Hegel's Logic *überhaupt*, starts with mere "Being" (*Sein*). The *Phenomenology* (1807), as itself an "introduction" of a peculiar kind to the Hegelian System proper, leads to this starting point. This peculiarity is due to the *Phenomenology* being always already immanently within the post-Spinozistic genuine (instead of bad or spurious) infinity of a System necessarily brooking no independent externalities as non- or extrasystemic transcendences.[71] That is to say, if an introduction to something is external to (as preceding) that which it introduces (as something else separate from and coming after it), then the *Phenomenology* is not an introduction since it is, from its inception and in its entirety, situated completely within what it nevertheless introduces in its own strange way(s).[72] Additionally, the *Phenomenology* is defensibly describable as the (pre) history of self-sublating presuppositions (that is, the *Gestalten* of consciousness [*Bewußtsein*] and/as Spirit [*Geist*]) leading up to what is presented as the "presuppositionless" initiation of the structured dynamics of more-than-phenomenological (or, perhaps, less-than-phenomenological) Logic strictly speaking.[73]

In his preface to the *Encyclopedia Logic* (specifically, sections 26 to 78 of the *Encyclopedia of the Philosophical Sciences*, under the heading "Preliminary Conception"), Hegel employs a process-of-elimination argumentative strategy against alternative, non-Hegelian positions. One might feel licensed to reread the *Phenomenology*, with the benefit of the *Encyclopedia*, as a single, massive process-of-elimination argument executed by the figures and shapes of consciousness or Spirit bringing about their self-wrought ruin through "doing violence to themselves at their own hands."[74] More precisely, this "elimination" is sublation *als Aufhebung*, rather than plain old negation as simple, straightforward elimination-without-remainder. These eliminations are, in truth, self-eliminations.

The post-*Phenomenology* logical beginning of both the *Science of Logic* and the *Encyclopedia* therefore nondogmatically presupposes, among other things, the (self-)sublation of Kant's two-worlds metaphysics and its accompanying supports. Dogmatism is avoided thanks to the positing of the immanent critical arguments thoroughly delineated by the *Phenomenology*; the arguments particularly relevant to Hegel's critiques of Kant's theoretical philosophy occur in, among other places in the *Phenomenology*, the second and third chapters, "Perception: Or the Thing and Deception" and "Force and the Understanding: Appearance and the Supersensible World."[75] Thus, the Being begun with at the logical start of the System as a whole, with this beginning being preserved (insofar as it is sublated [*als aufgehobene*]) throughout everything that follows,[76] is, contra the critical strictures of Kant's post-Lockean epistemological "limits of possible experience," something ontologically grounding a post-Kantian metaphysics (that is, the "future metaphysics" that Hegel maintains Kant did not realize he essentially already possessed in outline in the form of his transcendental logic).[77]

So, referring back to Žižek again, Hegel deontologizes Kant precisely through immanently critiquing his two-worlds metaphysics (a spontaneous metaphysics or ontology entailed by the limits of possible experience, themselves inextricably intertwined with the rigid dualism partitioning a subjective realm of phenomenal objects as appearances and an objective realm of noumenal things in themselves). However, Hegel affirms, extends, and intensifies Kant's analytics and, especially, dialectics of *Verstand* and *Vernunft* (particularly the dialectical antinomies of pure reason).[78] He is thus compelled, by his own systematic rationality, to ontologize the explicit epistemology that these components of Kant's critical edifice constitute, since these are the only components left after the exorcism of any unknowable transcendent Beyond.

However, the Hegelianism of *Less Than Nothing* should not be misunderstood as categorically canceling out the notion of "appearance" à la Kantian transcendental idealism. In fact, a certain precise conception of appearances forms one of the unifying motifs (if not the unifying motif) of the whole thousand-page course of Žižek's tour de force. Of course, with regard to Hegel in this context, the first association likely to come to anyone's mind is a well-known passage from the third chapter of the *Phenomenology* ("Force and the Understanding"):

> The inner world (*Das Innere*), or supersensible beyond (*übersinnliche Jenseits*), has, however, *come into being*: it *comes from* the world of appearance, which has mediated it; in other words, appearance is its essence (*die Erscheinung ist sein Wesen*) and, in fact, its filling. The supersensible is the sensuous and the perceived (*das Sinnliche und Wahrgenommenen*) posited as it is *in truth*; but the *truth* of the sensuous and the perceived is to be *appearance*. The supersensible is therefore *appearance qua appearance* (Erscheinung *als* Erscheinung). We completely misunderstand (*verkehrtes Verstehen*) this if we think that the supersensible world is *therefore* the sensuous world, or the world as it exists for immediate sense-certainty and perception; for the world of appearance is, on the contrary, *not* the world of sense-knowledge and perception as a world that positively *is*, but this world posited as superseded (*als aufgehobene*), or as in truth an *inner world*. It is often said that the supersensible world is *not* appearance; but what is here understood by appearance is not appearance, but rather the *sensuous* world as itself the really actual (*reelle Wirklichkeit*).[79]

Just before these observations, Hegel vehemently insists upon the null-and-void philosophical vacuity of Kantian-style subjective idealist versions of this "supersensible beyond" as an inaccessible realm of hidden, withdrawn noumenal presences.[80] (This reiterates some of Hegel's criticisms of Kant's thing in itself already advanced by him before the *Phenomenology* itself in *Glauben und Wissen*, published in 1802.)[81] Now, the phenomenological genesis of the category of appearance in the *Phenomenology*'s third chapter is preceded and made possible by its first two chapters, namely, the sensuous immediacies and perceptual things (*das Sinnliche und Wahrgenommenen*) of "Sense-Certainty" (*sinnliche Gewißheit*) and "Perception" (*Wahrnehmung*), respectively. These prior two types of phenomenal objects of conscious experiences become appearances as such, in Hegel's precise sense of "appearance" here, if and when consciousness responds to the dialectics afflicting Sense-Certainty and Perception by morphing into "the Understanding" (*Verstand*) per se (that is, the third figure or shape of consciousness after these first two). In other words, this metamorphosis occurs if and when the contradictions plaguing sensuous immediacies and perceptual things succeed at prompting an apperceptive shift in consciousness such that it proceeds to hypothesize the being of a nonphenomenal essence, ground, or substratum subsisting behind, beneath, or beyond the manifest façade of fragmentary, unstable phenomena.[82]

In transforming from Perception into the Understanding, phenomenological consciousness apperceptively transubstantiates phenomena into appearances strictly speaking. But what, for Hegel, is the difference between, on the one hand, a sensuous immediacy (à la Sense-Certainty) or perceptual thing (à la Perception) and, on the other hand, an appearance (à la the Understanding)? The former two categories of phenomena both treat their manifestations as direct disclosures of the objective being of the real world manifesting itself in and through such phenomena. The latter (that is, appearance), by contrast, entails a doubling of reality whereby phenomena become, at best and at most, indirect manifestations of nonmanifest entities or events. The very notion of appearance always already brings with it by way of automatic implication the image of a veil of appearances, an image dear to the tradition of two-worlds metaphysics. That is to say, conceiving of a phenomenon as an appearance necessarily involves presupposing or positing a distinction between the appearing of the appearance itself and the underlying "what" of the nonappearing "x" presumably responsible for the appearance. Put differently, the Understanding divides the real world of Sense-Certainty and Perception into an "outer world" (that is, the visible surface of the manifest phenomenon) and an "inner world" (that is, the invisible depth of the nonmanifest noumenon or similar non-Kantian equivalent). Given the Hegelian phenomenological account, this inner world (*das Innere als übersinnliche Jenseits*) is a secondary effect rather than a primary cause. It "has ... come into being" instead of, as according to traditional two-worlds metaphysics (Kantian transcendental idealism as subjectivism included), the supersensible preexisting and producing the sensible.

What is more, *das Innere* is generated specifically through the deployment by intentional consciousness of the category of appearance ("it *comes from* the world of appearance"). Hence, Hegel proclaims that "The supersensible is therefore *appearance qua appearance* (Erscheinung *als* Erscheinung)." That is to say, thinking of phenomena precisely as appearances in accordance with the strict meaning of "appearance" (that is, as *"appearance qua appearance"* rather than as either appearance qua sensuous immediacy or appearance qua perceptual thing) is, at one and the same time, also to think of them as the sensible (mis)representatives of supersensible beings. As the *Differenzschrift* (1801) already puts it, "appearing and dichotomy [of subject and object] are the same thing" (*"Erscheinen und Sich-Entzweien ist eins"*).[83] Subsequently, in various versions of his Logic, Hegel furnishes the logical scaffoldings of the dialectical-phenomenological dynamics of appearing in the earlier Jena-period *Phenomenology*.[84]

Hegel retains the category of appearance despite his critical reflections regarding it (as is fitting in the process of sublation). In the block quotation from the *Phenomenology* just given, he alerts readers to the fact that he is not collapsing appearances back into phenomena as either sensuous immediacies or perceived things ("We completely misunderstand [*verkehrtes Verstehen*] this if we think that the supersensible world is *therefore* the sensuous world, or the world as it exists for immediate sense-certainty and perception"). Only for a wrongheaded, upside-down understanding (as "*verkehrtes Verstehen*") is the denial of a supersensible Beyond automatically tantamount to the (re)affirmation of a flat sensible here and now. This topsy-turvy *Verstand*, still as a figure or shape of Consciousness as discussed in the first section of the *Phenomenology* (and, thus, still wedded, like Sense-Certainty and Perception before it, to asubjective objectivity as its self-imposed standard of the Whole Truth), lapses into this false dilemma between a supersensible Beyond or a flat sensible here and now because, for it, *das Innere als übersinnliche Jenseits* can be only an external, objective inner world, namely, an outer inner, so to speak. In Hegel's eyes, the transition from sensed and perceived phenomena to apperceived appearances indeed counts as genuine dialectical progress.

In fact, at this stage in the *Phenomenology*, Hegel hails the emergence of the supersensible Beyond in and through appearance as providing the first phenomenological glimpse of "Reason" (*Vernunft*) proper,[85] with the latter (as discussed in the third section of the *Phenomenology*, titled "Reason") already being the initial incarnation of Hegel's own absolute idealism.[86] For Hegel, insofar as the Understanding's misunderstanding of its inner world as an objective interiority is a 180-degree inversion of the truth, it needs merely to be stood upright back on its own feet as, instead, a subjective interiority. In other words, phenomena are actually appearances insofar as there indeed is an inner world beyond them ("the world of appearance is, on the contrary, *not* the world of sense-knowledge and perception as a world that positively *is*, but this world posited as superseded [*als aufgehobene*], or as in truth an *inner world*"). However, this inner world is nothing other than apperceiving subjectivity itself. Hence, as Hegel proposes at the end of the *Phenomenology*'s chapter on "Force and the Understanding" (the conclusion of the entire first section on "Consciousness"), what Consciousness uncovers when it finally manages to tear aside the veil of appearances is just its own activity; behind this veil is, as it were, a mirror.[87] Consciousness becomes conscious of itself (that is, Self-Consciousness, the subject of the next section of the *Phenomenology*) as a supersensible inner world to the extent that it now experiences itself as a Beyond superseding the objective outer world of the sensible, the phenomenal, and the apparent.

All of the preceding discussion on the topic of Hegel on appearances is immensely important to Žižek himself throughout various texts constituting his still-unfolding oeuvre.[88] The theme of appearance is especially central to *Less Than Nothing*. Already on its fourth page, Žižek asserts that "beyond the fiction of reality, there is the reality of the fiction."[89] This "reality of the fiction" is incarnated in a number of guises in the Žižekian theoretical universe, including "concrete universality" (taken from Hegel), "real abstraction" (taken from Marx), and "structures that march in the streets" (taken from Lacan).[90] Žižek and Alenka Zupančič also sometimes refer to this set of closely interrelated notions with the phrase "the Real of an illusion."[91]

With respect to German idealism generally and Hegel particularly, Žižek signals early in the introduction to *Less Than Nothing* that a major preoccupation throughout this gargantuan piece of work will be the topic of appearances. He addresses this topic along three precise lines of inquiry: (1) There is the line of inquiry responding to connected questions of how and why being appears to itself, that is, how and why *Sein an sich* doubles itself in becoming self-reflective/reflexive by giving rise to appearances out of its own substantial, monistic flatness.[92] (Neither Schelling nor Hegel consider their dear Spinoza as having asked and answered these ultimately unavoidable, mandatory queries,[93] and Žižek likewise indicts Badiou's materialism as guilty of the same failure.)[94] (2) There is the line of inquiry dealing with the connected questions of how and why the internal genesis of appearance in and through being also generates subjectivity as a transcendence-in-immanence vis-à-vis its ontological ground *als Ur-* or *Un-Grund*. (Žižek considers the Hegel of the *Phenomenology*'s third chapter as largely having resolved this issue; however, Žižek's ambitions arguably go beyond Hegelian phenomenology to the extent that he aims to broaden and deepen Hegel's account of the emergence of self-conscious subjectivity in "Force and the Understanding" to the levels of Hegel's post-phenomenological Logic and corresponding *Realphilosophie* of *Natur und Geist*.) (3) There is the line of inquiry about the fundamental question of what sort of ontology results from reinscribing the interlinked phenomena of appearances and subjects within the ontological fields from which these far-from-epiphenomenal phenomena originally arose, as found in the contemporary reactivation of objective and absolute idealisms à la Schelling and Hegel. (Žižek, both in *Less Than Nothing* and throughout his corpus, relentlessly pursues investigations regarding how being qua being must be thoroughly reconceptualized in light of the facts both that it sunders itself into the parallax split between subjectivity and objectivity and that subjective reflectivity or reflexivity continues to remain immanent, although nonetheless irreducible, to it.) For Schelling's and Hegel's post-Fichtean idealisms alike (and in line with both Hölderlin's "On Judgment and Being" and the "Earliest System-Program of German Idealism," as I discussed earlier), substance must be thought also as subject and vice versa (to phrase this in Hegel's language from the preface to the *Phenomenology*). Particularly in *Less Than Nothing*, Žižek can be fairly portrayed as focused primarily on this "vice versa," namely, on thinking subject also as substance (along with the requisite parallel rethinking of substance to the extent that it is now thought of as harboring transcendent[al]-while-immanent subjectivity within itself).[95] As he puts it later in this book, "The real difficulty is to think the subjective perspective as inscribed in 'reality' itself."[96] This difficulty is nothing less than that of thinking the Hegelian Absolute:[97] "the 'absolute' does not add some deeper, more substantial, dimension—all it does is include (subjective) illusion in (objective) truth itself."[98] As Herbert Marcuse succinctly states, "Seeming-being, qua non-essential, is not nothing."[99] Stanley Rosen likewise observes, "Illusion is something, not nothing in the sense of the void or complete vacuity,"[100] and "Life may be an illusion, but illusions exist."[101] Furthermore, Klaus Düsing renders this point even more precise along realist qua absolute idealist lines: "Everything believed in is; but not all that is is believed in."[102] Therefore, any systematic philosophy *als Wissenschaft*, with its complete, non-one-sided ontology, must include within itself an account of illusions and related phenomena as more than nothing.

Tellingly, the first chapter ("'Vacillating the Semblances'") of *Less Than Nothing*, as the word *semblance* in its title hints at the get-go, already contains an extended ensemble of reflections on the matter of appearances. Žižek herein utilizes the Hegelian thesis according to which "the supersensible is *appearance qua appearance*" (supplemented with Lacan's variations on this theme)[103] so as to narrate a specific sequence running from Plato (more precisely, a heterodox Platonism inspired by Badiou)[104] through Hegel and up to Lacan and Gilles Deleuze.[105] At one point, he proposes that "essence is 'appearance as appearance.' . . . Essence appears in contrast to appearance within appearance. . . . *The distinction between appearance and essence has to be inscribed into appearance itself.*"[106] Žižek's proposition gestures at the complexity of Hegel's ontology as neither nominalism nor metaphysical realism.[107] On the one hand, Hegel is definitely not a nominalist, for many reasons, including his immanent dialectical critiques both of Sense-Certainty and Perception in the *Phenomenology* and of finite figurations of Being in "The Doctrine of Being" of his mature Logic.[108] On the other hand, Hegel is also not a metaphysical realist since, within his triad of Universality (*Allgemeinheit*), Particularity (*Besonderheit*), and Individuality or Singularity (*Einzelheit*), there are actually not only no brute, raw particulars as imagined by nominalism, but also no pure, transcendent universals as envisioned by metaphysical realism.[109] For Hegel, everything enjoying actuality (*Wirklichkeit*) is individual or singular qua a synthesizing sublation of universal and particular dimensions.[110] Žižek's remarks about appearance and essence emphasize, among other facets of Hegel on appearances, Hegel's immanentist conception of the more-than-apparent and more-than-particular (that is, essences as supersensible universals).[111] Later in *Less Than Nothing*, Žižek underscores the absolutely immanent status of the transcendent(al) in Hegelian metaphysics, with the latter mainly as "negativity" (such as the negativity involved, in the *Phenomenology*'s third chapter, in the inner world that becomes self-conscious subjectivity opening up simultaneously along with the surfacing of the category of appearance, with such subjects also superseding the appearances with which they are coemergent).[112]

While endorsing the Hegelian speculative handling of the dialectics of appearance and essence as a partial account of the genesis of transcendent(al)-while-immanent subjective negativity, Žižek nevertheless wants to push this line of speculation through to a more foundational ontological level. In a footnote to the second chapter of *Less Than Nothing*, he articulates, echoing some of his earlier work,[113] a revealing characterization of "Hegel's reversal of the classic metaphysical question" as a "shift" from querying "how can we see through false appearances to their underlying essential reality?" to "how has appearance emerged out of reality?"[114] Subsequently, he likewise asks, "how we pass from being to appearing, how and why does being start to appear to itself?"[115]

Other moments in *Less Than Nothing* testify to Žižek's insistence on orthodox Hegelian answers to these Hegelian (and Schellingian) questions. Very much faithful to the agenda set for German idealism during its rapidly shifting development in the mid-1790s,[116] Žižek maintains that, "in appearing to the subject, the Absolute also appears *to itself*. . . . The subjective reflection of the Absolute is the Absolute's self-reflection."[117] Two pages later (in a passage I have already quoted), he asserts that *"the 'Absolute' beyond appearances coincides with an 'absolute appearance,' an appearance beneath which there is no substantial Being."* This second assertion, in order to be interpreted correctly, requires recalling another aspect of the *Phenomenology*'s third chapter, "Force and the Understanding," related to the discussion of "appearance qua appearance." In particular, Hegel indicates that the positing of a supersensible Beyond through the shift to treating phenomena as appearances (that is, as outer [mis]representations of an underlying, veiled inner world) is motivated, at least in part, by a powerful impulse to calm and unify the fluctuating, fragmented field of phenomenal experience (an impulse perhaps akin to Kant's "interest of reason").[118] Whether as the Kantian domain of noumenal things in themselves or the Newtonian universe of mechanical laws of efficient causality (not to mention the Platonic realm of purely intelligible forms or ideas), the nonapparent Beyond coemergent with and corresponding to the apparent *hic et nunc* provides minded subjectivity with "the *stable* image of unstable appearance."[119] Therefore, Žižek's "*'absolute appearance' . . . beneath which there is no substantial Being*" is not a subjective idealist reduction of everything to the phenomenal experience of consciousness. Rather, he is drawing attention to the Hegelian dialectical gesture of negating the picture of being as a serene invisible Elsewhere (that is, the inner world of the supersensible Beyond as the stable image of unstable appearance),[120] while simultaneously retaining its evident discord, incoherence, and volatility at the surface level of appearances themselves. With the combination of this cancelation of being's transcendence with the sublation of subjective idealisms, this means that the remaining monistic ontology of lone immanence contains both being and appearing—and, hence, that appearing's conflicts, contradictions, and chaos are part of being itself, with the latter thereby undergoing desubstantialization through being permeated by antagonisms, inconsistencies, tensions, and the like (that is, being deprived of its substantiality qua solid, indivisible oneness).[121]

On the basis of this line of thought, Žižek distinguishes between three different philosophical approaches (with *Absolute Recoil* further nuancing this typology).[122] He states:

> We can . . . identify three positions: metaphysical, transcendental, and "speculative." In the first, reality is simply perceived as existing out there, and the task of philosophy is to analyze its basic structure. In the second, the philosopher investigates the subjective conditions of the possibility of objective reality, its transcendental genesis. In the third, subjectivity is re-inscribed into reality, but not simply reduced to a part of objective reality. While the subjective constitution of reality—the split that separates the subject from the In-itself—is fully admitted, this very split is transposed back into reality as its kenotic self-emptying (to use the Christian theological term). Appearance is not reduced to reality; rather the very process of appearance is conceived from the standpoint of reality, so that the question is not "How, if at all, can we pass from appearance to reality?" but "How can something like appearance arise in the midst of reality? What are the conditions for reality appearing to itself?"[123]

This trinity can be translated into the triad of transcendental realism (that is, metaphysics), transcendental idealism (that is, transcendentalism), and objective or absolute idealism (that is, speculation). In this context, metaphysics as transcendental realism is perhaps best epitomized by the different substance ontologies of the early-modern rationalists (such as Descartes, Spinoza, and Leibniz), all of whom seek to investigate the supposed mind-independent objective realities of such metaphysical objects as the soul, the cosmos, and God (that is, Kant's three ideas of reason as the principal targets of precritical philosophical inquiry). Transcendentalism as transcendental idealism is obviously represented exclusively by the subjectivisms of Kant and Fichte. Finally, speculation as objective or absolute idealism is, of course, embodied by Schelling and Hegel. Throughout *Less Than Nothing*, Žižek is a fierce partisan on behalf of the speculative orientation as itself a sublation of the metaphysical and transcendental orientations.

Speculation, as Žižek defines it, involves several distinctive features. First of all, its reinscription of the appearance-subject couplet into the one and only plane of real being by no means entails a reduction or elimination of this couplet itself. Subjectivity and the appearances it participates in (transcendentally) coconstituting in interaction with objectivity do not lose their effective independence so as to become sterile, illusory epiphenomena. Second, the divide between subject (as the for-itself) and substance (as the in-itself) is preserved despite the asserted becoming-immanent of the former to the latter. That is to say, a gap persists between the substantial *an sich* and the subjective *für sich* (as itself substance *an und für sich*) entirely within the confines of the substantial *an sich*. Schelling and Hegel, in self-conscious adherence to Spinoza, rightly insist that the distinction between the infinite and the finite is a distinction internal to the infinite itself (contra a *Verstand*-type opposition between the finite and the infinite, which results in the limitation and, hence, deinfinitization of infinity itself).[124] Likewise, as indicated in the dialectical-speculative slogan "the identity of identity and difference," which Schelling and Hegel shared (and which Spinoza's insight into the true nature of the infinite as per authentic *Vernunft* inspired),[125] the discrepancy between substance and subject is a discrepancy internal to substance itself. For Žižek, the orienting concern of speculation is therefore the enigma of how the negativity of this rift opens up out of being in the first place (as he says in the previous block quotation, "the question is not 'How, if at all, can we pass from appearance to reality?' but 'How can something like appearance arise in the midst of reality? What are the conditions for reality appearing to itself?'"). Because of this concern, when all is said and done, Žižek must also explain how this split itself and its subjective side achieve and sustain self-determining autonomy or spontaneity vis-à-vis their ontological ground(s), thus being more than mere delusions, fantasies, fictions, hallucinations, unrealities, and the like (that is, causally inefficacious epiphenomena).

Much later in *Less Than Nothing*, what earlier is called "speculation" is relabeled "transcendental materialism."[126] In the context of critiquing Quentin Meillassoux's "speculative materialism," Žižek puts forward a preliminarily rendition of transcendental materialism:

> One can make out the contours of what can perhaps only be designated by the oxymoron "transcendental materialism." . . . All reality is transcendentally constituted, "correlative" to a subjective position, and, to push this through to the end, the way out of this "correlationist" circle is not to try to directly reach the In-itself, but to inscribe this transcendental correlation *into the Thing itself*. The path to the In-itself leads through the subjective gap, since the gap between For-us and In-itself is immanent to the In-itself: appearance is itself "objective," therein resides the truth of the realist problem of "How can we pass from appearance For-us to reality In-itself?"[127]

It can now readily be appreciated that transcendental materialism involves, among other things, modifying and updating the dialectical-speculative objective or absolute idealisms of Schelling and Hegel within the circumstances of present-day conjunctures. In other words, as the latest system-program of German idealism (tracing its roots back to the earliest one of 1795–1796), Žižekian transcendental materialism strives to be what amounts to a new Spinozism of freedom. More precisely, and as expressed in *Less Than Nothing*, it seeks to accomplish a systematic combining of, on the one hand, a materialist, quasi-naturalist ontology of substance and, on the other hand, a theory of more-than-material, denaturalized transcendent(al) subjectivity in its nonepiphenomenal autonomous spontaneity and self-determining. Put differently, Žižek intends to "repeat Hegel and Schelling," creatively reactivating in the context of the early twenty-first century their struggles of two centuries ago to combine the apparent opposites of the naturalistic monism of Johann Gottfried von Herder's Spinoza and Kant's antinaturalist dualism.[128] All the German idealists after Kant are animated by the controversy about pantheism and Spinozism triggered by Jacobi's attempt, partly with respect to the Kantian critical edifice, to force an either-or choice between system (as allegedly always in the end deterministic or fatalistic and, thus, nihilistic) and freedom. (Apart from Jacobi, Salomon Maimon's and G. E. Schulze's neo-Humean skeptical challenges to Kantianism also further motivate the post-Kantian idealists to systematize Kant's thinking and thereby immunize it from such doubts.)[129] Starting with Reinhold, each post-Kantian idealist seeks to refute Jacobi through achieving the construction of a rigorously rational philosophical system that, in its very systematicity, does full justice to freedom as instantiated by human agency. (As I noted, Reinhold, Fichte, Schelling, and Hegel at least agree with Jacobi that Kant himself fails to be thoroughly systematic within and between his three *Critiques*.) Žižek (along with Badiou) is a direct heir of this legacy, albeit with the Spinozism appropriated by Schelling and Hegel replaced with the postidealist developments of the (seemingly) more deterministic dimensions presented by Marxist historical or dialectical materialism, Freudian-Lacanian psychoanalysis, and the natural sciences of the past century (in Žižek's case, both quantum physics and biology).[130]

Just before introducing the phrase "transcendental materialism" in *Less Than Nothing*, Žižek poses a series of queries. He asks:

> How can one explain the rise of subjectivity out of the "incomplete" ontology, how are these two dimensions (the abyss/void of subjectivity, the incompleteness of reality) to be thought together? We should apply here something like a weak anthropic principle: how should the Real be structured so that it allows for the emergence of subjectivity (in its autonomous efficacy, not as a mere "user's illusion")?[131]

The topic of ontological incompleteness aside for now, a version of this last question is similarly formulated by Ilya Prigogine and Isabelle Stengers: "we need an account of the material world in which it is not absurd to claim that it produced us."[132] (Terrence Deacon quoted this specific formulation quite recently.)[133] That said, what arguably amounts to Žižek's decision to begin with or from this "weak anthropic principle"—this principle is requisite in order, as *Absolute Recoil* phrases it, "to approach head-on the question of how the pre-human real has to be structured so as to allow for the emergence of the symbolic/normative dimension"[134]—resonates with Fichte's starting point as part of his primacy of the practical. (I consider it to be no coincidence that *Less Than Nothing* contains an important chapter devoted to Fichte.)[135] Moreover, it also audibly reverberates with "The Earliest System-Program of

German Idealism," whose author (whether Hegel, Schelling, or Hölderlin) evidently pushes off from Fichte's chosen beginning and proceeds to the same basic question raised in slightly different terms by Prigogine, Stengers, Deacon, and Žižek himself: "The first idea is, of course, the presentation of myself as an absolutely free entity. . . . Here I shall descend into the realms of physics; the question is this: how must a world be constituted for a moral entity?" With the "I" as a "moral entity" qua "absolutely free entity" (that is, transcendental subjectivity à la Kant and Fichte) and *Physik* (physics) as the empirical, experimental natural sciences of modernity, it appears that this two-hundred-year-old mystery setting the agenda for post-Fichtean German idealism (as objective or absolute) remains a pressing theoretical motivator to this very day. In this vein, both dialectical and transcendental materialism can be construed as materialist inheritors of this venerable program, one whose fulfillment, if ever attained by Hegel or Schelling over the course of their intellectual itineraries, seems to have been undone by developments intervening between then and now. To be faithful to this project, its contemporary defenders must alter it in heterodox fashions.

I wholeheartedly agree with Žižek's Hegelian insistence that only immanent critiques are worthwhile, with merely external ones being unproductive and ineffective.[136] The whole of my preceding commentary is intended primarily for the initial establishment of the historical and philosophical background against which a thorough, immanent, and critical assessment of *Less Than Nothing* and *Absolute Recoil* should be conducted. In light of this stage-setting, a verdict on the cogency of Žižek's transcendental materialist endeavors in his magnum opus from 2012 and its sequel from 2014 must be reached on the basis of whether he satisfactorily speaks to the following six interrelated, overlapping issues: (1) a strictly materialist establishment and explanation, at least compatible with, if not based upon, the sciences of nature, of the purported incompleteness of being in and of itself; (2) a detailed account of the exact nature of the relationship between an incomplete ontology (as the being of substance) and a theory of self-relating spontaneity (as the thinking and appearances of the subject); (3) a narrative of the emergence of appearing out of being that does not surreptitiously presuppose apperceiving subjectivity as always already there and phenomenologically operative beforehand; (4) the sufficient conditions for the immanent genesis of transcendent(al) actors out of the sole baseless base of natural, material objects and processes over and above the necessary conditions for this;

"FREEDOM OR SYSTEM? YES, PLEASE!"

(5) the possibility and actuality of strongly emergent subjects reciprocally coming to exert so-called downward causation on the substances from which they originally arose; (6) the priceless bridges, if any there are, between matter and mind as well as mere indeterminism and robust freedom (that is, solutions to everything ranging from Kant's third antinomy to David Chalmers's "hard problem").[137] The degree to which Žižek succeeds at synthesizing German idealism with postidealist materialisms and naturalisms depends upon the extent to which he resolves these difficulties. What is more, whether transcendental materialism enjoys a viable, enduring future hinges on its coming to grips with such demanding philosophical challenges.

TWO

Where to Start?

Deflating Hegel's Deflators

ONE OF THE significant stakes of the Žižekian return to Hegel is the issue of the very possibility of a robustly realist post-Kantian ontology. In other words, the big question here is whether, in the aftermath of Kant's transcendental idealist critique of pre-Kantian ontologies, a theory of asubjective being(s) remains an epistemologically defensible option. Is there a way, in the wake of the first *Critique*'s decisive problematizations of "pure reason," to reengage in metaphysics (as involving ontology and not just epistemology, the *an sich* and not merely the *für sich*) that would not regressively rely upon permutations of pre-Kantian intellectual intuition?

Both Žižek and I, along with a number of others, consider one of Hegel's major accomplishments to be the forging of a metaphysics meeting (rather than indefensibly ignoring) the epistemological challenges to traditional ontology posed by Kant. In particular, one of the key innovative features of the Hegelian dialectic, first systematically deployed in the *Phenomenology of Spirit*, is its role as a replacement for intellectual intuition in light of Kantian critique's devastating objections to the latter. Moreover, Hegel's dialectics not only enable him to regain epistemologically justified access to "the Absolute" in the teeth of the epistemology of critical transcendental idealism; his approach, applied to Kant, generates an immanent critique of Kantian critique itself, undoing from within Kant's antirealist subjectivism on its own terms and by its own standards.

WHERE TO START?

Yet, over the course of approximately the past four decades, one of the most popular styles of rendering Hegel's philosophy, still dominant nowadays especially among English-speaking Hegel scholars, is a "deflationary" approach in which his metaphysics, if he is even admitted to have one, is done away with as an embarrassing anachronism. Deflationist Hegelians treat the metaphysical Hegel as an antiquated irrelevance in relation to what is alleged to be a postmetaphysical contemporary philosophical Zeitgeist. Hegel's purportedly nonmetaphysical features (whether these are identified as his lingering Kantianism, historical consciousness, political perspectives, or linguistic sensitivities) are held up by deflationists as the true Hegelian legacy for today's thinkers. According to these deflationists, a Hegelian critique of metaphysics, rather than a Hegelian metaphysics, is the only remaining live option.

Hence, for Hegelian philosophers such as Žižek and me, efforts to construct a solid Hegel-inspired ontology or metaphysics require, among other things, rebutting the interpretations and arguments of deflationist (pseudo-)Hegelians. The present chapter sets out to accomplish this. It focuses on what I take to be the strongest version of deflationary Hegelianism, namely, Pippin's Kantianizing reading, according to which Kant's "transcendental unity of apperception" persists as the ultimate grounding core of Hegel's System. Defeating this reading of Hegel goes a long way toward relegitimizing an ontology or metaphysics that is Hegelian qua post-Kantian.

So as to initiate a more detailed engagement with Žižek's return to Hegel under the shadow of deflationary Hegelianisms, I want to start, suitably enough, by addressing the nature of beginning(s) in Hegel's thinking. In an earlier book, *The Indivisible Remainder*, published in 1996, Žižek identifies "the *problem of Beginning itself*" as "the crucial problem of German Idealism."[1] (More recently, Gilles Marmasse has done so with regard to Hegel specifically.)[2] *Less Than Nothing* contains a reference to this problem with respect to the opening of Hegel's Logic:

> When he writes about the passage from Being to Nothingness, Hegel resorts to the past tense: Being does not pass into Nothingness, it has *always already passed* into Nothingness, and so on. The first triad of the Logic is not a dialectical triad, but a retroactive evocation of a kind of shadowy virtual past, of something which never passes since it has always already passed: the actual beginning, the first

entity which is "really here," is the contingent multiplicity of beings-there (existents). To put it another way, there is no tension between Being and Nothingness which would generate the incessant passage of one into the other: in themselves, prior to dialectics proper, Being and Nothingness are directly and immediately the same, they are indiscernible; their tension (the tension between form and content) appears only retroactively, if one looks at them from the standpoint of dialectics proper.[3]

Žižek in the next paragraph claims that the beginning of Hegelian Logic thus interpreted already in and of itself furnishes readers with the groundless ground of a materialist ontology of radical, ultimate contingency.[4] (I discuss Hegel's and Žižek's treatments of contingency in chapter 3.) Before evaluating whether Žižek is entitled to this claim on the basis he provides in this instance, this quotation needs to be exegetically unpacked.

In it, Žižek (like, for instance, Robert Wallace and Stanley Rosen)[5] chooses to pinpoint "Determinate Being"/"Being-there" (*das Dasein*) as the true starting point of Hegel's ontological/metaphysical Logic (that is, book 1, section 1, chapter 2 of the *Science of Logic* and what is inaugurated with section 89 in the *Encyclopedia Logic*). Of course, since the mid-twentieth century, the German word *Dasein* has come to be most closely associated with Martin Heidegger and his existential phenomenology. This is quite ironic in that Hegel's logical dialectics of Being, Nothing, and Becoming (including implicitly in Žižek's interpretation) can be understood as entailing a pointed critique avant la lettre of Heidegger's pivotal conception of "ontological difference."[6] Hegel likely would accuse Heidegger of being logically inconsequent in his distinguishing between Being and beings, thereby remaining unproductively confined to the initial moments of (onto)logical thinking in his fascination with a Being that is indistinguishable from Nothing (which is on display in, for instance, Heidegger's well-known essay "What Is Metaphysics?" from 1929).[7] Moreover, for Hegel, the opening moments of his Logic also capture what is essential to the chronological origins in ancient Greece of the history of Western philosophy,[8] with Heidegger's fetishization of these Greeks and their language, a fetishism inherited from the German Romantics, thus further testifying to a dialectical-speculative inhibition or limitation marking Heideggerian phenomenological ontology. Hegel emphasizes repeatedly that pure Being on its own before any further determination (such as the Heideggerian ontological apart from the ontic) is the most meager and abstract of (onto)logical moments.⁹ (Some were and still are tempted to mistake the undeveloped poverty of its vacuous superficiality for the accumulated wealth of profound depths of mysterious, ineffable meanings.)

Heidegger aside, Žižek's pinpointing of the "real beginning" of Hegelian Logic is an instance of a long-running, ongoing activity among scholars of Hegel and German idealism: debating about from where the Hegelian System actually starts. Some of the biggest questions (if not the biggest question) concerning how to appreciate the relationship (or lack thereof) between the *Phenomenology of Spirit* and the various versions of the mature Logic hinge on the topic of when and how Hegelian philosophy proper gets well and truly underway. (I will disregard those significant questions related to the *Phenomenology* in the present context of considering what Žižek asserts about the beginning of the Logic alone and will return to them later.) One could say about the three major divisions of both the *Science of Logic* and the *Encyclopedia Logic* (that is, the three books of the "doctrines" of "Being" [*Sein*], "Essence" [*Wesen*], and "Concept" [*Begriff*]) that each division has been claimed by specific Hegel scholars as the genuine primordial nucleus of the Hegelian logical network. Recent examples arguably would include Stephen Houlgate for "The Doctrine of Being" (with the thesis that Hegel begins precisely where he appears to begin, namely, without presuppositions and with indeterminate Being),¹⁰ Dieter Henrich for "The Doctrine of Essence" (with the thesis that "The Doctrine of Being" implicitly presupposes from its very outset, in order to get the dialectical-speculative ball rolling even just from Being to Nothing, the categorial and conceptual distinctions explicitly posited only subsequently with "The Doctrine of Essence"),¹¹ and Robert Pippin for "The Doctrine of the Concept" (with the thesis that Hegel's praise in "The Doctrine of the Concept" for Kant's "transcendental unity of apperception" of the *Critique of Pure Reason*'s "Transcendental Deduction" signals that the Logic arises from and is anchored by Kantian-style cognizing subjectivity as indicated by the "Subjective Logic" coming after the first two doctrines together constituting the "Objective Logic").¹² At least in *Less Than Nothing*, Žižek seems to be a partisan of "The Doctrine of Being" as the true launching platform for Hegelian Logic, albeit (by contrast with, for instance, the example of Houlgate) with the caveat that the launch gets delayed until determinate Being-there congeals out of Becoming.

WHERE TO START?

For the questions and controversies about beginning(s) in Hegel's philosophy, I elect to zero in on Pippin as a privileged foil for Žižek for two reasons: first, in *Less Than Nothing*, *Absolute Recoil*, and *Disparities*, Žižek himself does this; second, Pippin, by my estimation, has good reasons for challenging the kinds of exegetical positions regarding the true start of Hegelian Logic put forward by, among many others, Houlgate and Henrich. In reference to the second reason, Pippin's position draws support from the fact that Hegel both characterizes Logic from start to finish as a "thinking about thinking"[13] and treats it as a circle whose end ("The Doctrine of the Concept") rejoins its beginning ("The Doctrine of Being"), with the former retroactively making explicit what the latter always already implicitly was (in the manner of T. S. Eliot's "to arrive where we started and know the place for the first time").[14] In reference to the first reason, one of Žižek's main objections to Pippin has to do with the latter's renowned "deflationary" (that is, post- or antimetaphysical) rendition of Hegel.

Of course, Pippin is not the first or only advocate of a nonmetaphysical version of Hegelianism. A far from exhaustive alphabetical list of the names of champions of this (diverse) family of reconstructions would include Robert Brandom, Klaus Hartmann, Jean-François Kervégan, Terry Pinkard, Paul Redding, and Allen Wood (with Karl Ameriks providing a helpful overview of some of the main representatives and orientations within this constellation of Hegel interpretations as well as criticizing Pippin in particular).[15] Especially in the Anglophone world, this cluster of overlapping reconstructions of Hegelian thought has profoundly influenced the past four decades of Hegel scholarship, starting with Hartmann's and Charles Taylor's[16] interventions in the 1970s. Although Taylor proposes a metaphysical reading of Hegel, he knowingly depicts this purportedly "cosmic" metaphysics to be too ridiculously puffed up to be a palatable, plausible option for philosophers of the present age, thus furnishing a sort of reductio ad absurdum (one accepted by Wood, among others) in favor of deflationary discardings of the metaphysical aspects of Hegel's System. Žižek rightly rejects Taylor-style depictions of Hegelian metaphysics.[17]

However, even more recently, a number of scholars of German idealism have begun to push back against the still rather fashionable non-/antimetaphysical renditions of Hegel. Among the growing ranks of deflationism's discontents are Frederick Beiser, Brady Bowman, Markus Gabriel, Rolf-Peter Horstmann, Houlgate, James Kreines, Sally Sedgwick, Robert Stern, Kenneth

Westphal, myself,[18] and Žižek. Despite differences between the multiple advocates of various flavors of deflated Hegelianism—there have been direct, detailed debates between some of them[19]—they share in common, as Beiser lucidly explains in language borrowed from none other than Marx, the conviction that the "rational kernel" of Hegel's investments in Kantian transcendentalism or sociohistorical angles of philosophical approach should be salvaged from the "mystical shell" of his more ambitious global ontology, especially as embodied by his *Realphilosophie* of nature (that is, those aspects of Hegel's musings that appear to veer into [Neo-]Platonic or Romantic visions of a metaphysically real Godlike Notion as a kind of cosmic superorganism or Mega-Mind).[20] Pippin, over the course of his own intellectual career, has shifted his attention and focus between the two basic poles of the deflationist spectrum, from an early emphasis on Hegel's fidelity to Kant's transcendental idealism (in his groundbreaking, now-classic study *Hegel's Idealism: The Satisfactions of Self-Consciousness*, published in 1989) to a later highlighting of the social and historical dimensions of the Hegelian edifice (in such texts as *Hegel's Practical Philosophy: Rational Agency as Ethical Life*, published in 2008, and *Hegel on Self-Consciousness: Desire and Death in the Phenomenology of Spirit*, published in 2011, texts in which Hegel seems to be presented as a social-rationality pragmatist of a Brandomian inferentialist kind avant la lettre, with this presentation being made possible by Pippin's underlying [over]emphasis on the theme of apperception in Hegel).

Quite appropriately in the fourth chapter of *Less Than Nothing*, titled "Is It Still Possible to Be a Hegelian Today?," Žižek targets deflated Hegelianism à la Pippin (along with mention of the post-Sellarsian Pittsburgh neo-Hegelianism of Brandom and John McDowell).[21] His remarks in this vein, ones echoed in *Absolute Recoil*,[22] are worth quoting:

> If . . . in ontological terms, spirit naturally evolves as a capacity of natural beings, why not simply endorse materialist evolutionism? That is to say, if—to quote Pippin—"at a certain level of complexity and organization, natural organisms come to be occupied with themselves and eventually to understand themselves," does this not mean that, precisely in a certain sense, nature itself *does* "develop into spirit?" What one should render problematic is precisely Pippin's fragile balance between ontological materialism and epistemological transcendental idealism: he rejects the direct idealist ontologization of the transcendental account of intelligibility, but he also rejects the epistemological consequences of the

ontological evolutionary materialism. (In other words, he does not accept that the self-reflection of knowledge should construct a kind of bridge to materialist ontology, accounting for how the normative attitude of "accounting for" itself could have emerged out of nature.)[23]

On the next page, Žižek proceeds to argue that

the point is not that one should take sides and opt for one consistent stance, either evolutionary materialism or speculative idealism. The point is rather that one should fully and explicitly accept the gap which manifests itself in the incompatibility of the two stances: the transcendental standpoint is in a sense irreducible, for one cannot look "objectively" at oneself and locate oneself in reality; and the task is to *think this impossibility itself as an ontological fact*, not only as an epistemological limitation. In other words, the task is to think this impossibility not as a limit, but as a positive fact—and this, perhaps, is what at his most radical Hegel does.[24]

This Hegel, "at his most radical," is the Žižekian one in whose "parallax view" apparent gaps in knowledge (maintained as merely epistemological by Kantianism, including by Pippin's Kantianized Hegel as transcendental idealist) reappear as real gaps in being qua being *an und für sich*.[25] Once again (as I discuss in chapter 1), this involves the transition from Kant to Hegel being portrayed as a matter of a shift from the positing of breaks exclusively at the level of epistemology (Kant) to the assertion of these very same breaks (also) at the level of ontology (Hegel).[26] For Žižek, the proper Hegelian gesture to be performed vis-à-vis Pippin's allegedly inconsistent position with respect to the split between the seemingly incommensurable ontological options of "either evolutionary materialism or speculative idealism" is not to force a decision one way or the other according to the parameters of this binary opposition, which are taken for granted. Instead, the Žižekian Hegel eschews the Kantian inclination to shield the noumenal Real of *Sein an sich* from the rifts and ruptures phenomenally manifesting themselves within the cognizing subject's experience or knowing, and he treats the apparent choice between the first-person perspective of idealism and the third-person perspective of materialism as a false dilemma. The consequence of this is that the appearance of discrepancy between these perspectives is not just the mere appearance of an epistemological epiphenomenon deprived of any ontological status and weight.

Elsewhere in *Less Than Nothing*, Žižek makes this same set of moves with respect to the division within the Marxist tradition between its two fundamental approaches to theorizing human beings. The gap between the "social" à la historical materialism and the "natural" à la dialectical materialism is not to be closed in favor of one approach over the other. Rather, it is to be affirmed as directly reflecting a real gap actually perturbing from within the substance of humanity's very being itself.[27] *Absolute Recoil*, in the context of elaborating upon *Less Than Nothing*'s criticisms of Pippin, similarly remarks that "the gap separating the normative from the factual should be simultaneously conceived as a gap immanent to the factual itself."[28] Moreover, as a close reading of the early moments of *Less Than Nothing* readily makes evident, the topic of appearance, featuring centrally in Žižek's critical handling of Pippin, is one of the most important red threads tying together the entirety of his hulking philosophical masterpiece from 2012 (as I discuss in chapter 1). But, before employing this thread to circumnavigate back to my main concern here (that is, establishing how to read *Less Than Nothing* in an immanently critical fashion based on its initial framing by Žižek himself), I want to push the critique of Pippin's deflationary Hegelianism further and, in so doing, address both Pippin's and Žižek's conceptions of where, when, and how Hegel's Logic actually begins.

Pippin hangs an enormous amount of interpretive weight on one single passage in particular from "The Doctrine of the Concept" in the *Science of Logic*.[29] (Brandom likewise highlights the same passage.)[30] Arguably, Pippin's overarching Kantianization of Hegel's philosophy as a whole, in addition to his reading of the Logic specifically, hinges on this particular stretch of text. Preliminarily addressing "the concept in general" at the start of the "Subjective Logic" formed by the third book of the *Science of Logic*, Hegel declares at great length:

> It is one of the profoundest and truest insights to be found in the *Critique of Pure Reason* that the *unity* (Einheit) which constitutes the nature of the *Notion* (das Wesen des Begriffs) is recognized as the *original synthetic* unity of *apperception* (die ursprünglich-synthetische *Einheit der* Apperzeption), as unity of the *I think*, or of self-consciousness. This proposition constitutes the so-called *transcendental*

deduction of the categories; but this has always been regarded as one of the most difficult parts of the Kantian philosophy, doubtless for no other reason than that it demands that we should go beyond the mere *representation* (*die bloße* Vorstellung) of the relation in which the *I* stands to the *understanding*, or notions (Begriffe) stand to a thing and its properties and accidents, and advance to the *thought* (Gedanken) of that relation. *An object*, says Kant, is that in the *notion* of which the *manifold* of a given intuition is *unified*. But all unifying of representations demands a *unity of consciousness* in the synthesis of them. Consequently it is this *unity of consciousness* which alone constitutes the connection of the representations with the object and therewith their *objective validity* and on which rests even the *possibility of the understanding*. Kant distinguishes this unity from the *subjective unity* of consciousness (*die* subjektive Einheit *des Bewußtseins*), the unity of representation whereby I am conscious of a manifold as either *simultaneous* or *successive*, this being dependent on empirical conditions. On the other hand, the principles of the *objective* determination of notions (objectiven Bestimmung der Vorstellungen) are, he says, to be derived solely from the principle of the *transcendental unity of apperception* (*der* transzendentalen Einheit der Apperzeption). Through the categories which are these objective determinations, the manifold of given representations is so determined as to be brought into the *unity of consciousness*. According to this exposition, the unity of the notion is that whereby something is not a mere *mode of feeling*, an *intuition*, or even a mere *representation* (*bloße* Gefühlsbestimmung, Anschauung *oder auch bloße* Vorstellung), but is an *object* (Objekt), and this objective unity is the unity of the ego with itself (*welche objektive Einheit die Einheit des Ich mit sich selbst ist*). In point of fact, the *comprehension* of an object (*Das Begreifen eines Gegenstandes*) consists in nothing else than that the ego makes it *its own*, pervades (*durchdringt*) it and brings it into *its own form* (seine eigene Form), that is, into the *universality* that is immediately a *determinateness*, or a determinateness that is immediately universality. As intuited or even in ordinary conception, the object is still something *external* and *alien* (Äußerliches, Fremdes). When it is comprehended, the being-in-and-for-self (Anundfürsichsein) which it possesses in intuition and pictorial thought (Vorstellen) is transformed into a *positedness* (Gesetztsein); the *I* in *thinking* it pervades it. But it is *only* as it is in thought that the object is truly *in and for itself*; in intuition or ordinary conception it is only an *Appearance*. Thought sublates the *immediacy* with which the object at first confronts us and thus converts the object into a positedness; but this its *positedness* is *its-being-in-and-for-self*, or its *objectivity* (Objektivität). The object (*Gegenstand*) therefore has its objectivity in the Notion

(Begriffe) and this is the *unity of self-consciousness* into which it has been received; consequently its objectivity, or the Notion, is itself none other than the nature of self-consciousness, has no other moments or determinations than the *I* itself.[31]

The first sentence of the next paragraph states, "Thus we are justified by a cardinal principle of the Kantian philosophy in referring to the nature of the *I* in order to learn what the *Notion* is."[32] Hegel explicitly refers to B137 in the "Transcendental Deduction" (section 17, titled "The Principle of the Synthetic Unity of Apperception Is the Supreme Principle of All Use of the Understanding") of the *Critique of Pure Reason*.[33] On Pippin's construal, the Kantian transcendental unity of apperception is likewise "the supreme principle" of Hegel's philosophy as itself ultimately grounded in and by the Logic—insofar as such a unity is taken to be the underlying agency of cognition responsible for driving the entire activity of logical, dialectical-speculative thinking (as a "thinking about thinking") from its very inception with pure Being alone. Both the *Science of Logic* and the *Encyclopedia Logic* thereby look to be rectifications of what Hegel sees (along with many other of Kant's contemporaries and immediate successors) as the unacceptable absence of a systematic, scientific (*als Wissenschaft*) derivation of the categories and concepts of the understanding from the transcendental unity of apperception in the "Transcendental Analytic" of the first *Critique* (with Reinhold and Fichte kicking off post-Kantian German idealism through their anti-Jacobian efforts to remedy this lack of sufficient systematicity/scientificity in the Kantian critical transcendental apparatus).[34]

In addition to Žižek's criticisms of the deflationary depiction of Hegelianism à la Pippin, what else might be objectionable about Pippin's anchoring of his reconstruction of Hegel in the passage from the *Science of Logic* praising Kant's unity of apperception as found in the B-version of the "Transcendental Deduction"? To thoroughly answer this question would be to destabilize Pippin's deflationary Hegelianism at its very root, to undermine the fundamental load-bearing pillar of this exegetical edifice. Žižek does not go for the jugular in either *Less Than Nothing* or *Absolute Recoil*, although doing so would serve him well. Moreover, other dissenters from Pippin's Kantianized Hegel such as Harris, Sedgwick, and Stern, despite their different objections to Pippin, all concede that his construal of Hegel's relationship to Kant's transcendental deduction is one of the great strengths of his approach (if not the greatest strength), granting that this construal illuminates places in the Hegelian corpus such as the preceding quotation from the *Science of Logic*.[35]

Rather than seek to rebut Pippin through explicitly contesting his stress on Hegel's references to apperception while implicitly conceding the accuracy of Pippin's interpretation of these same references (as some of his other critics have done), I will, in what follows, attempt to demonstrate why and how the very moment to which Pippin appeals actually does not bring Hegel back into the proximity of the specifically subjective idealism of Kantian transcendentalism. As is appropriate in a Hegelian discussion about Hegel, my critique of Pippin is immanent rather than external, working from the inside and developing itself out of Pippin's own chosen starting point. That said, a first manner of objecting to Pippin would be to note that Hegel's praise for Kant's transcendental unity of apperception is preceded by moments in both the *Phenomenology of Spirit* and the *Science of Logic* itself (as well as other articulations of the Logic) in which the alleged two-worlds metaphysics of the subjectivism of Kantian (and Fichtean) transcendental idealism is dialectically sublated.[36] This means that, as one might describe it, Hegel pays Kant a backhanded compliment, with the principle of unity extolled already being, at this late stage in Hegelian Logic, so heavily qualified by Hegel's critique of Kant as to no longer really be Kantian per se.

Pippin appears not to appreciate in the lengthy passage from the *Science of Logic* just what a huge difference Hegel's own distinction between subjective idealism and objective or absolute idealism makes to the significance of his reference to Kant's transcendental unity of apperception (although such Hegelians as Westphal and Thomas Wartenberg do appreciate this).[37] This Hegelian distinction surfaces both in the *Phenomenology* and in the stages of the various versions of the Logic coming well before the "Subjective Logic" consisting in "The Doctrine of the Concept" inordinately privileged by Pippin.[38] For Kant, this principle of unity at the heart of the first *Critique*'s "Transcendental Deduction" is the core of all genuine knowledge both actual and possible. But this very nucleus of the theoretical part of critical philosophy is, of course, ensconced within the framework of the subjectivism of transcendental idealism. Consequently, for Hegel, Kantian subjective idealism results in the ridiculous thesis that, as he puts it in the introduction to the *Science of Logic*, cognizing subjects are limited to having true knowledge solely of false appearances.[39] (This makes a mockery of the very notions of truth and knowledge; as Marcuse remarks and clarifies in some detail,[40] "that truth is an aspect of Being and not of knowledge is a fundamental premise of Hegel's thought that is repeatedly emphasized.")[41] Hegel observes: "This is like attributing to someone a correct perception (*richtige Einsicht*), with the rider (*Zusatz*) that nevertheless he is incapable of perceiving (*einzusehen*) what is true (*Wahres*) but only what is false (*Unwahres*). Absurd as this would be, it would not be more so than a true knowledge (*wahre Erkenntnis*) which did not know the object (*Gegenstand*) as it is in itself (*wie er an sich ist*)."[42] Hegel uses the word *Gegenstand* in both this quotation and the long passage from the *Science of Logic* that Pippin relies on (in the latter, he alternates between *Gegenstand* and *Objekt* when referring to the "object" forming the correlate of the subject qua transcendental unity of apperception). By contrast with subjective idealism as Kantian transcendentalism (here specifically its antirealism regarding objects treated as mere phenomenal appearances [that is, as "false"] deprived of the actuality of ontological heft [that is, as "true"]), Hegelian absolute idealism is robustly realist regarding the objectivities related to by subjectivities.[43] (In the *Differenzschrift*, published in 1801, Hegel is willing, *pace* Kant, Fichte, and a certain Reinhold, to acknowledge that even a materialism such as that of Baron d'Holbach is not without its relevance to his and Schelling's absolute idealism.)[44] However, Hegel arrives at this absolute idealist position in a nondogmatic and properly post-Kantian fashion by virtue of achieving a reaffirmed ontological realism precisely via an immanent critique passing through (and not simply bypassing altogether) Kant's critical problematizations of pre-Kantian realist ontologies.[45]

In light of Henry Allison's quite plausible interpretation of the "Transcendental Deduction," according to which Kant posits a "reciprocity thesis" holding that the transcendental unity of apperception entails a mutual, two-way interdependency of knowing subject and known object upon each other (with the claim that the subject can know itself as a unifying producer only in and through the produced unity reflected back to it by the objects it itself is responsible for unifying), Hegel's absolute idealist appropriation of Kant's subjective idealist transcendental unity of apperception cannot but involve a fundamental transformation of the sense and implications of the latter.[46] A famous one-liner from the *Critique of Pure Reason*, one directly related to what Allison has in view about the alleged reciprocity between apperceiving subjectivity and apperceived objectivity, has it that "The *a priori* conditions of a possible experience in general are at the same time conditions of the possibility of the objects of experience."[47] With his absolute idealism as, in part, a sublation of subjective idealism in its antirealist, deontologized one-sidedness, Hegel arguably radicalizes the reciprocity at the base of Kant's "Transcendental Deduction" such that the (epistemological) truthfulness of this one-liner from the first *Critique* must be counterbalanced by also positing the equal (ontological) truthfulness of its inversion: "Conditions of the possibility of the objects of experience (i.e., the 'in itself' [*an sich*] delineated in the 'Objective Logic' prior to the 'Subjective Logic' of 'The Doctrine of the Concept') are at the same time the *a priori* conditions of a possible experience in general (i.e., the 'in and for itself' [*an und für sich*] delineated in the 'Subjective Logic' only after the 'Objective Logic')."[48]

Additional clarity and concreteness can be lent to this by another return to Hegel's *Phenomenology of Spirit*: specifically, the opening of its third section on "Reason" (*Vernunft*). (Ameriks and Harris both correctly note that Pippin, although preserving a crucial role for the *Phenomenology* in the mature Hegelian System [after 1807], ignores this section in his focus on the preceding first two sections dealing with "Consciousness" [*Bewußtsein*] and "Self-Consciousness" [*Selbstbewußtsein*].)[49] In the wake of the dialectics running from Consciousness through Self-Consciousness, the Reason arising at the start of this third section is characterized by Hegel as being "certain" of the existence of fundamental structural isomorphisms between its minded subjectivity and worldly objectivity; however, at this juncture, it still has yet to prove the "truth" (*Wahrheit*) of its certainty (*Gewißheit*) through the tests of its experiences.[50] Reason balances out the lopsided preponderances of object and subject posited by the earlier figures of Consciousness and Self-Consciousness, respectively. Having been driven by the preceding dialectical moments sublating the shapes in the *Phenomenology* coming before it, Reason does so by adopting the view that

> self-consciousness (*Selbstbewußtsein*) and being (*Sein*) are the same essence (*Wesen*), the same, not through comparison, but in and for themselves (*an und für sich*). It is only the one-sided, spurious idealism (*einseitige schlechte Idealismus*) that lets this unity (*Einheit*) again come on the scene as consciousness (*Bewußtsein*), on one side, confronted by an *in-itself* (Ansich), on the other. But now this category or *simple* (einfache) unity of self-consciousness and being possesses difference *in itself*; for its essence is just this, to be immediately one and selfsame in *otherness* (Anderssein), or in absolute difference (*absolute Unterschiede*). The difference

therefore *is*, but is perfectly transparent, and a difference that is at the same time none. It appears as a *plurality* of categories.[51]

To begin with, the objection to Kantian transcendental idealism as subjectivism in this passage is so obvious as to not require deciphering and explanation. Moreover, Hegel's wording here in the Phenomenology is echoed in Pippin's preferred later moment in the Science of Logic, thus indicating that the latter text's kind words for the transcendental unity of apperception of the B-Deduction are significantly tempered by a rejection of the type of idealism to which Kant shackles this transcendentally deduced unity. In the Science of Logic, Hegel recasts Kant's transcendental unity of apperception as (to paraphrase the Phenomenology) the becoming-subject of substance, namely, a preexistent objectivity in itself ("something *external* and *alien*") being "comprehended," "pervaded," and thereby "idealized" so as to achieve the status of (also) being in and for itself via subjectivity (with subjectivity in this instance being nothing other than the self-reflectivity or -reflexivity of substantial objectivity itself).[52] As the quotation manifestly shows (along with adjacent material in the same text),[53] this recasting transpires in the Phenomenology even before it occurs in the Science of Logic.

Additionally, Hegel's recourse in this passage to the language of post-Kantian dialectical-speculative logic (in particular, nonbivalent ideas about the identity of identity and difference) marks a break with Kant (in particular, the classical logic of Kant's faculty of the non- or prespeculative understanding [*Verstand*]) that allows Hegel to be both an idealist and a realist. As he maintains in the Science of Logic's first book, on the heels of stringently criticizing Kant and Fichte, "the opposition of idealistic and realistic philosophy has no significance."[54] Already in his Differenzschrift, Hegel indicates that true idealism also involves realism (*pace* Kant's and Fichte's subjectivism qua antirealism).[55] In the article "How the Ordinary Human Understanding Takes Philosophy (as Displayed in the Works of Mr. Krug)," published in 1802, he gestures at a form of (post-)Kantian idealism that overcomes the false dilemma between realism and idealism: "Transcendental idealism does not just concede . . . but asserts the reality of the external world, just as much as its ideality."[56] His "First Philosophy of Spirit," written in Jena and dated 1803/1804, is scathing about the antirealism of subjective idealism.[57] And he repeats these stipulations when discussing idealism in the Encyclopedia.[58] Since Hegel maintained this stance on the distinction between realism and idealism in various texts from 1801 until his death, Pippin's dismissal of the *Science of Logic*'s "Remark on Idealism" in "The Doctrine of Being" as unrepresentative of Hegel's own convictions is quite dubious.[59]

Immediately after the quotation from the *Phenomenology* just given, Hegel voices the complaint he often repeats, along with his fellow post-Kantian idealists, about Kant's allegedly dogmatic, unsystematic cutting and pasting from antiquated logic textbooks in the composition of his "Transcendental Analytic" of the categories and concepts of the understanding (that is, the lack of a properly scientific deduction of these categories and concepts).[60] In the same context, he also addresses the matter of the Kantian transcendental unity of apperception in a manner undeniably foreshadowing his later comments upon it in the *Science of Logic*:

> Only in the unity of apperception lies the truth of knowing (*nur die Einheit der Apperzeption ist die Wahrheit des Wissens*). The pure Reason (*Die reine Vernunft*) of this idealism, in order to reach this "other" (Anderen) which is *essential* to it, and thus is the *in-itself* (Ansich), but which it does not have within it, is therefore thrown back by its own self on to that knowing which is *not* a knowing of what is true (*Wahren*); in this way, it condemns itself of its own knowledge and volition to being an untrue kind of knowing, and cannot get away from "meaning" (*Meinen*) and "perceiving" (*Wahrnehmen*), which for it have no truth (*Wahrheit*). It is involved in a direct contradiction (*schlechthin Entgegengesetztes*); it asserts essence (*Wesen*) to be a duality of opposed factors, the *unity of apperception* and equally a *Thing* (*das Ding*); whether the Thing is called an extraneous impulse (fremder Anstoß), or an empirical or sensuous entity (empirisches *Wesen oder* Sinnlichkeit), or the Thing-in-itself (das Ding an sich), it still remains in principle the same, i.e. extraneous (*Fremde*) to that unity.[61]

These assertions audibly resonate with Hegel's reduction, in a portion of the *Science of Logic* I referenced earlier, of the epistemology of Kantian transcendental idealism to the absurdity of treating "true" knowledge as a knowing of admittedly false appearances (that is, ideal phenomenal objects unrelated to and different in kind from real noumenal things, the latter including, on this reading, supposed pure intuitions [*als Sinnlichkeit*] as passively received hypothetically before their transubstantiation into actual objects of experience by the categories and concepts of the understanding).[62] Kant's antirealist subjectivism, with its non- or prespeculative, *Verstand*-style oppositional dualism between subject (as the transcendental unity of apperception) and object (as *das Ding an sich*), backs him into this indefensible corner. (Via the phrase *fremder Anstoß* in the quotation, Hegel signals that Fichte, as likewise a subjectivist transcendental idealist, is in the crosshairs too.) But what qualifies as an alternative version of the transcendental unity of apperception that manages to be both realist and idealist in ways that reflect Kant's valuable epistemological insights?

This question can be answered with a single proper name: Francis Bacon, the founding figure of British empiricism, who, in his *New Organon* (1620), erects the basic scaffolding of modern scientific method (at the same time that Galileo contributes another key component to the foundations of scientific modernity, namely, the identification of mathematics as the language of nature).[63] Bacon not only provides the lone epigraph for the *Critique of Pure Reason*;[64] Kant, in the preface to the second edition of the first *Critique* from 1787, also compares the Copernican revolution of his critical transcendental turn at the level of first philosophy (as metaphysics qua integrated epistemology and ontology) with "the suggestion of the ingenious Francis Bacon" at the level of natural science.[65] In particular, Kant credits Bacon with a spontaneous, protoidealist realization to the effect that the order, pattern, and regularity of the apparently lawful world of nature must be produced through the practices of minded and like-minded subjects. (In Bacon's case, nature reveals its laws only in and through the process of scientific investigators actively submitting it to empirical, experimental interrogation and probing directed in advance by theoretical and methodological guidelines.)[66] In Kant's prefatory narrative here, the first *Critique*'s transcendental idealism raises Baconian empiricism to the dignity of its notion (as Hegel might put it) by insisting that subjectivity makes possible every knowable and known objectivity, whether in the natural sciences or any other branch of whatever could count as genuine knowledge per se.[67]

In the opening pages of the section of the *Phenomenology of Spirit* devoted to "Reason," particularly the start of this section's first major division on "Observing Reason" (*Beobachtende Vernunft*), Hegel is referring implicitly to this Bacon in addition to (as seen in the quotations I discussed earlier from the *Phenomenology*) the Kant of the "Transcendental Deduction." The figure of Observing Reason, which culminates in the self-subverting dead end of phrenology's infinite judgment that "Spirit is a bone,"[68] represents the Weltanschauung of modern science circa the seventeenth and eighteenth centuries, especially this worldview's naturalism, with its obsessive (and ultimately self-destructive qua autodialecticizing) pursuit of natural laws.[69] The very first paragraph of the subsection "Observing Reason" can be understood solely through appreciating Bacon's tacit presence in its background:

> It is true that we now see this consciousness (*Bewußtsein*), for which Being [*Sein*] means what is its own [*Seinen*], revert to the standpoint of "meaning" (*Meinen*) and "perceiving" (*Wahrnehmen*); but not in the sense that it is certain of what is merely an "other" (*Anderen*). Previously, its perception and *experience* (*erfahren*) of various aspects of the Thing (*Dinge*) were something that only *happened to* consciousness; but here, consciousness *makes its own* observations and experiments. "Meaning" and "perceiving," which previously were superseded *for us* (*für uns früher sich aufgehoben*), are now superseded by and for consciousness itself. Reason sets to work to *know* the truth (*die Wahrheit zu wissen*), to find in the form of a Notion (*Begriff*) that which, for "meaning" and "perceiving," is a Thing; i.e. it seeks to possess in thinghood (*Dingheit*) the consciousness only of itself. Reason now has, therefore, a universal *interest* in the world (*allgemeines* Interesse *an der Welt*), because it is certain of its presence in the world, or that the world present to it is rational. It seeks its "other," knowing that therein it possesses nothing else but itself: it seeks only its own infinitude (*Unendlichkeit*).[70]

Hegel's primary concern in this paragraph is to distinguish the Reason (*Vernunft*) of the third section of the *Phenomenology* from the Consciousness (*Bewußtsein*) of the first section. Despite potential misunderstandings to the contrary, the Reason whose initial incarnation is in the rational observation of nature (as in the empirical, experimental, mathematized sciences of modernity cofounded by Bacon and Galileo early in the seventeenth century) is not tantamount to a simple regressive return, in the aftermath of the dialectical self-sublation of the Self-Consciousness (*Selbstbewußtsein*) of the *Phenomenology*'s intervening second section, to the phenomenologically previous standpoint specifically of the first two figures of Consciousness, namely, Sense-Certainty (*sinnliche Gewißheit*) and Perception (*Wahrnehmung*). For Hegel, the primary significant difference between Sense-Certainty and Perception, on the one hand, and Observing Reason, on the other hand, has to do with, as he emphasizes in the block quotation, the contrast between passivity and activity—with Bacon's stress on the active role of the scientific investigator being pivotal both historically and (phenomeno)logically in this context.[71]

Consciousness overall, including Sense-Certainty and Perception, sets as its own standard of the ultimately True a notion of objectivity as utterly independent of subjectivity and passively received or registered by subjectivity. (The Self-Consciousness of the subsequent section reverses Consciousness's prioritization of objectivity over subjectivity.) Reason, by contrast, sublates both Consciousness and Self-Consciousness such that its orienting standard of the Whole Truth is a rationally articulable ensemble of structures and dynamics common to both subjectivity and objectivity. These structures and dynamics are described by Hegel in language that risks being misconstrued as subjectively idealist in that he speaks of "concepts," "ideas," "logic," "judgments," "syllogisms," and the like,[72] terms that have strong associations with images of mindedness in which subjective mind is set apart from objective world à la pre-Hegelian (that is, nondialectical or nonspeculative) versions of the subject-object distinction (with Hegel warning of this risk and the need to avoid it, a caution underscored by, among others, Ermanno Bencivenga, Düsing, Marcuse, Sedgwick, Ludwig Siep, and Westphal).[73] However, by this point in the *Phenomenology* with Reason, subjective idealism (including the Kantian transcendental variety) has been sublated (both in the final subsection on "Consciousness" [in the chapter titled "Force and the Understanding"] and in the section "Self-Consciousness" in its entirety). That is to say, starting with Reason, the *Phenomenology* presents a non- or postsubjective idealism (that is, an objective or absolute idealism) in which apparently subjectivist language actually designates a rational reality comprising configurations that cut across the subject-object divide, being both objective (as substantially "in themselves" apart from all knowing subjects) and subjective (if and when they also become "for themselves" through human mindedness and like-mindedness) and reflected in isomorphisms between conceptual logics operative in subjects and objects alike.[74] After the advent of Reason in the *Phenomenology*, any endorsements by Hegel of idealism, including Kant's variety with its transcendental unity of apperception, both in the rest of this book from 1807 and in his post-*Phenomenology* System in its entirety must be appreciated as invariably qualified by his immanent critical sublation of subjectivism, especially the subjectivism coloring Kantian and Fichtean transcendental idealisms on Hegel's readings of them.[75]

Reason generally and Observing Reason particularly rise out of the ashes of the preceding section of the *Phenomenology* on Self-Consciousness (culminating in the "Unhappy Consciousness" of primarily medieval Christianity). Through his specific staging of the transition between Self-Consciousness and Reason, Hegel intends to convey the claim that the Christianity of the Unhappy Consciousness historically and (phenomeno)logically paves the way and serves as a possibility condition for the modern secular sciences of nature born early in the seventeenth century—even though the rational scientific Weltanschauung that takes shape thanks to the contemporaries Bacon, Galileo, and Descartes promptly comes to generate a tension between itself and the religion of its historical background. This is definitely an instance of, as the *Phenomenology*'s introduction puts it, a transition between figures of phenomenal consciousness (as Self-Consciousness and Reason, in this case) transpiring "behind the back of consciousness."[76] Simply stated, science fails to recognize or remember its indebtedness to the religion out of which it emerges and with which it quickly enters into lasting conflict after its emergence.[77] Moreover, Hegel indicates that Reason, first and foremost as Observing Reason, is especially prone to ahistorical amnesia (the proof of this being that working scientists need not and often do not pay much attention to the history of their disciplines).[78]

To be more precise, Hegel has in mind in the context presently under consideration the role that God fulfills in Descartes's philosophy as expressed in the latter's *Meditations on First Philosophy*, from 1640/1641. There, the singular Supreme Being is reduced to serving as not much more than an ultimate guarantor of the veracity of both perceptually based empirical (a posteriori) knowledge and conceptually based nonempirical (a priori) knowledge. As with, approximately three centuries later, Albert Einstein's God, who does not play games with dice, Descartes's divinity is not an unreliable deceiver or trickster. In addition to Bacon's contribution of an epistemologically formalized and generalized methodology and Galileo's contribution of the identification of mathematics as the language of nature, Descartes, at least tacitly, contributes to the foundations of modern science its supporting assumption that being is a rule-bound, stable field of existence knowable by thinking, with the signifier *God* naming this presupposition.[79] Without such an assumption, scientific investigators never could launch into their inquiries in the first place with the requisite inaugural confidence and conviction that, at least in principle, reality is law-like and, hence, comprehensible in the form of posited laws with predictive power. This nonempirical article of faith provides an indispensable metaphysical ground for the empirical disciplines themselves, including modernity's experimental, mathematized sciences of nature. The God of the Unhappy Consciousness (that is, what Hegel designates in this subsection of the *Phenomenology* "the Unchangeable,"[80] thus already foreshadowing this depiction of Descartes's) in which Self-Consciousness culminates continues to live on in and through the apparently secular (or even atheistic) rationality sublating (as both preserving and negating) Him.[81] Likewise, the "Holy Spirit" of the universal fellowship of believers united by faith and recognition in God morphs into the community of scientists, a community whose presence is entailed already in Baconian scientific method itself and whose powers of recognition are responsible for determining what counts as authentic, true knowledge. An earlier moment of Self-Consciousness also persists into and contributes to the new scientific rationality: the technological apparatuses, devices, implements, instruments, and tools, as well as the technical skills to employ them, jointly constituting a savoir faire crucial to Bacon's *Novum Organum Scientiarum*, which essentially involves experimentation (and which is, hence, crucial to scientific savoir tout court),[82] are inherited by Reason from the history of labor beginning with the slavery famously figuring in the subsection of Self-Consciousness titled "Lordship and Bondage" (with serfs, artisans, craftspeople, and so on conserving and enriching this historically accumulated know-how extending across anonymous generations of unsung laborers).[83]

The opening paragraph of the section on Reason in the *Phenomenology* portrays this new shape of consciousness as taking over and translating into its own terms a number of elements initially characteristic of the Unhappy Consciousness of Self-Consciousness. Utilizing his nonsubjectivist logical language, Hegel here employs the structure of the syllogism so as to establish the parallels and continuities between Self-Consciousness and Reason: *Vernunft*, first incarnated as the rational scientific observer of nature, becomes aware of itself as a syllogistic middle term (that is, the mediator assuming the position previously occupied for Unhappy Consciousness by the priest as clerical conduit mediating relations with the divine) between a universal term (that is, God qua the Unchangeable that becomes the God's-eye "view from nowhere" of modern science's methodologically secured objective viewpoint on the world) and a particular term (that is, the individual persons qua members of the congregation that become the specific empirical entities and events of concern to the scientist).[84] This syllogistic formulation helps further sharpen the distinction between Consciousness (particularly as Sense-Certainty and Perception) and Reason. Not only, as I already noted, is Consciousness passive and Reason active (with this emphasis on activity reflecting Reason's successor position as an inheritor of the intervening legacies of Self-Consciousness); while the objects of Consciousness are conceived by it nominalistically as sensory-perceptual individualities qua utterly unique thises, thats, and others, the "same" objects are, for *Vernunft* in its modern scientific shape, particular embodiments or manifestations of universal patterns and rules (that is, laws amenable to formalized generalizations, such as causal laws of nature). In other words, Reason's primary concern is with what is intelligibly universal in sensuous particulars, whereas Consciousness is fixated on and in thrall to the latter alone,[85] a point Hegel later underscores in his Berlin-era history-of-philosophy lecture on Bacon.[86]

Now, having clarified the historical and (phenomeno)logical backdrop to Reason as the preliminary appearance of what becomes Hegelian absolute idealism proper (or, one could say, of *Vernunft* as the *an sich* of absolute idealism *an und für sich*), I still have to respond to two questions raised by my preceding remarks: First, how does Hegel's implicit reference to Bacon in 1807 inform his appropriation of Kant's transcendental unity of apperception (both in the *Phenomenology* itself and in the passage of the *Science of Logic* repeatedly brandished by Pippin)? Second, how does the answer to the previous question affect Pippin's interpretation of apperception in Hegel's idealism? In response to the first of these queries, Hegel reverses Kant's narrative, in the preface to the B-version of the first *Critique*, about the relationship between Bacon and critical transcendental idealism. Kant sees the Copernican revolution of his idealism as the consequent advancement and coming to fruition of the germinal seed of Bacon's insight into the contribution of the inquirer's subjective activities necessary to what is revealed as the objective content of true knowledge in and through these same inquiries. By contrast, for Hegel, Kant's (subjective) idealism is retrograde in comparison with Bacon's protoidealism, lagging behind what it claims to be merely one of its historical precursors.[87] Not (yet) burdened by the baggage of an antirealist subjectivism freighted with fatal, (self-)dialecticizing inconsistencies, Bacon, with his combination of an empiricist, naturalist realism and a protoidealist appreciation of active subjectivity as a coconstituter of known reality, is philosophically closer to Hegel's absolute idealist metaphysics than Kant's transcendental idealist epistemology is to Hegel—and this despite the chronological (and geographical and cultural) proximity between Kant and Hegel. Even in the *Phenomenology*, the logical arguably has priority over the chronological, one consequence of this being that speculative solutions to dialectical problems sometimes occur historically out of sequence, with answers to questions surfacing in linear historical time before the questions themselves have been (explicitly) posed.[88] By Hegel's lights, the relationship between Bacon and Kant is an illustration of precisely this. Baconian *Vernunft* already overcomes the self-subverting one-sidedness of the subjectivism of Kantian critical transcendental idealism in a manner foreshadowing Hegel's own absolute idealist sublation of Kantianism. In line with the *Vernunft* of Hegelian absolute idealism, Bacon already sketches the rudimentary contours of an immanent unity of apperception—more precisely, such a unity as a subjectivity sharing a dialectical-speculative identity-in-difference with objectivity within an overarching one-world metaphysics (as opposed to Kant's two-worlds metaphysics).[89]

In response to the question of how this affects Pippin's reconstruction of the relationship between Kant and Hegel, my highlighting of Hegel's interweaving of simultaneous references to both Bacon and Kant in the "Reason" section of the *Phenomenology* (an interweaving with respect to which Pippin remains silent) I hope drives home the point that the Pippinian brand of deflationary Hegelianism is a highly selective revision of Hegel's actual philosophy, one replacing absolute with subjective idealism wholesale. (Here, my verdict on Pippin agrees with that pronounced by Houlgate,[90] although Houlgate and I reach this shared judgment by different exegetical and argumentative routes.) Taking the "absolute" out of absolute idealism and ignoring the absolute idealist dialectical-speculative sublation of subjectivist one-sidedness (that is, sidelining and neglecting both Hegel's critique of Kantian transcendentalism as subjective idealism and his elevation in 1807 of Bacon over Kant in regard to the metaphysics of active subjective agency) certainly allow for a creative reconstruction of Hegel as, for the most part, a good Kantian. But, simply put, this is not Hegel.[91] Especially considering the weight of the evidence I have provided thus far for this critical contention directed against Pippin—this evidence is drawn mainly from textual moments before Pippin's favorite passage on the transcendental unity of apperception from "The Doctrine of the Concept" in the *Science of Logic*—additional testimony drawn from textual moments following Pippin's key piece of evidence for his Kantianizing interpretation further substantiates my counterclaims against this interpretation. As I will show, Hegel himself would reject the post-Kantian antirealism that Pippin tries to attribute to him. Hegel's somewhat pro-Bacon, anti-Kant account of Reason breaks with Kant's subjectivism, resting as this subjectivism does on untenable dualisms of a *Verstand* type, namely, subrational dualisms supporting antimaterialist, antinaturalist perspectives alien to both Bacon's and Hegel's idealisms.[92]

As in the *Science of Logic*, Hegel, in the prefatory treatment of Kantian critical philosophy in the *Encyclopedia Logic*, also pronounces a few approving words with respect to the transcendental unity of apperception.[93] But, once again, as soon as he voices this sympathy, he significantly qualifies it, immediately adding these remarks with respect to Kant's pure apperceiving "I":

> Now this certainly expresses correctly the nature of all consciousness (*die Natur alles Bewußtseins*). What human beings strive (*Streben*) for in general is cognition of the world; we strive to appropriate it and to conquer it (*sie sich anzueignen und zu unterwerfen*). To this end the reality of the world (*die Realität der Welt*) must be crushed (*zerquetscht*) as it were; i.e., it must be made ideal (*idealisiert*). At the same time, however, it must be remarked that it is not the subjective activity of self-consciousness that introduces absolute unity into the multiplicity in question; rather, this identity is the Absolute, genuineness itself (*Zugleich ist dann aber zu bemerken, daß es nicht die subjektive Tätigkeit des Selbstbewußtseins ist, welche die absolute Einheit in die Mannigfaltigkeit hineinbringt. Dieses Identität ist vielmehr das Absolute, das Wahrhafte selbst*). Thus it is the goodness of the Absolute (*die Güte des Absoluten*), so to speak, that lets singular [beings] (*Einzelheiten*) enjoy their own selves (*Selbstgenuß*), and it is just this that drives them back into absolute unity (*treibt sie in die absolute Einheit zurück*).[94]

To begin with, both here and in his other invocations of the transcendental unity of apperception (which I quoted earlier), Hegel, contra Pippin's subjectivist antirealism, implies that the absolute idealist sublated version of this Kantian principle involves positing that "the reality of the world," as already unified and formed in itself ("it is not the subjective activity of self-consciousness that introduces absolute unity into the multiplicity in question"), objectively preexists the synthesizing and unifying activities of subjectivity.[95] That is to say, if this real world is "appropriated," "conquered," "crushed," and "idealized," it must already be there, as a pre- or nonsubjective presence, to be submitted to these "strivings" of the apperceiving, (self-)conscious subject.[96] When Pippin himself quotes this passage from the *Encyclopedia* in support of his Kantian antirealist version of Hegel, he ignores this directly implied preexistence of an asubjective real as unified and formed in and of itself.[97]

Furthermore, in this quotation from the *Encyclopedia Logic*, the "drunk on God" (à la Novalis) talk of "the Absolute" so anathema to all permutations of deflationary Hegelianism (Pippin's included) promptly follows and directly qualifies the ambivalent characterization of Kant's transcendental unity of apperception. This serves as a reminder of a fundamental feature of post-Fichtean German idealism beginning with Hölderlin's "Über Urtheil und Seyn" of 1795 and "The Earliest System-Program of German Idealism" of 1796, a feature coming to form a red thread running across the entire length of Hegel's intellectual journey. The infinite Absolute as substance also becomes self-reflective/reflexive in and through finite, minded subjectivity, with the latter and its cognizing (self-)conscious activities remaining fully immanent to the substantial, absolute infinity as the ontological ground out of which it arose. (If finite subjective reflection were to fall outside of this infinity, the infinite would be rendered finite, the Absolute less than absolute.)[98] As the deservedly celebrated preface to the *Phenomenology* already maintains, the Absolute, in its proper absoluteness, includes within itself reflection on the Absolute (something maintained on the heels of the famous "*Substance . . . equally as Subject*" line).[99] Hegel warns there that "reason is . . . misunderstood when reflection is excluded from the True, and is not grasped as a positive moment of the Absolute" ("*Es ist . . . ein Verkennen der Vernunft, wenn die Reflexion aus dem Wahren ausgeschlossen und nicht als positives Moment des Absoluten erfaßt wird*")[100]—with "the True" here being "the Whole" ("*Das Wahre ist das Ganze*"),[101] namely, the dialectically self-sundering absolute substance dividing into itself and its (self-)reflection in and through subjectivity.[102] Hence, *pace* Pippin's repeated maneuver of drawing Hegel close to Kant's epistemological finitism via the former's mentions of the latter's transcendental unity of apperception, Hegelian absolute idealism, in

WHERE TO START?

contrast with Kantian transcendental idealism, recasts this unity as a transcendent-while-immanent transcendental function (re)unified with an infinite ontological base.[103] Pippin's deflationary finitization qua epistemological deontologization and deabsolutization of Hegel de-Hegelianizes Hegel himself.

Additional moments in Hegel's corpus bearing witness against Pippin's Kantianization of him via the topic of apperception are to be found in "The Doctrine of the Concept" as the "Subjective Logic" of the *Science of Logic* (that is, in the place from where Pippin extracts Hegel's admiring remarks about the first *Critique*'s "Transcendental Deduction"). In fact, just a couple of pages later, the fourth paragraph after the paragraph extolling the importance of Kant's transcendental unity of apperception (albeit, as seen, with significant caveats and reservations) states:

> The Notion (*der Begriff*) is to be regarded not as the act of the self-conscious understanding (*selbstbewußten Verstandes*), not as the *subjective understanding* (*subjektive Verstand*), but as the Notion in its own absolute character (*der Begriff an und für sich*) which constitutes a *stage of nature* (Stufe *der* Natur) as well as of *spirit* (Geistes). Life, or organic nature, is the stage of nature at which the Notion emerges, but as blind, as unaware of itself and unthinking (*nicht denkender Begriff*); the Notion that is self-conscious and thinks pertains solely to spirit. But the logical form of the Notion is independent of its non-spiritual (*ungeistigen*), as also of its spiritual (*geistigen*), shapes (*Gestalten des Begriffs*).[104]

Later in the *Science of Logic*, Hegel devotes the entirety of the introduction to the third and final section of "The Doctrine of the Concept," "the Idea" (*die Idee*), to dismissing subjective idealist understandings of the ideational. He emphasizes, by contrast, that his Idea is an absolute idealist one essentially involving the identity-in-difference of the subjective and the objective.[105] All of this qualifies Hegel's appropriations of Kantian critical philosophy both in the *Science of Logic* itself and elsewhere.

With its proximity to the invocation of Kant's "Transcendental Deduction," the preceding block quotation is crucial to appreciate at this juncture. The transcendental unity of apperception is situated at (and as) the very heart of the first *Critique*'s analysis of *Verstand*. Hence, it is firmly circumscribed within the field of phenomenal experience and its limits as coconstituted by the two faculties of intuition and the understanding.

WHERE TO START?

Therefore, Hegel's disqualification of *"subjective understanding"* qua "the act of the self-conscious understanding" strikes at nothing other than the apperceiving activity of synthesizing self-consciousness according to the "Transcendental Deduction" ambivalently referenced four paragraphs earlier in the *Science of Logic*. Unlike in transcendental idealism, with its subjectivism (and corresponding aversions to realism, naturalism, and materialism), *"der Begriff an und für sich"* is as much "non-spiritual" (that is, asubjectively objective qua natural, substantial, and the like) as it is "spiritual" (that is, subjective, whether as individual [self-]consciousness or the sociohistorical collectivities of "objective spirit").[106] Moreover, the Notion or Concept (*der Begriff*) as self-aware thinking subjectivity (that is, the side of this closer to Pippin's Kant) is explicitly rendered by Hegel here, already anticipating the philosophical anthropology and psychology of the third volume of the *Encyclopedia* (*Philosophy of Mind*), as emergent vis-à-vis nature generally and organic, living beings specifically.[107] This posit or anything like it would be inadmissible within the epistemological confines of the Kantian critical transcendental idealism leaned upon by Pippin.

As I have shown, Žižek, both implicitly and explicitly throughout *Less Than Nothing*, challenges in various ways Pippin's tendency to situate Hegelian subjectivity within the antimaterialist, antinaturalist, and antirealist framework of the subjectivism of Kantian transcendental idealism as grounded in the apperceptive unity of (self-)consciousness. The second paragraph of the preface to Hegel's *Differenzschrift* provides yet more ample support for opposition (whether Žižekian or not) to Pippin's deflationary rapprochement between the Kant of the "Transcendental Deduction" and Hegel (and, with Pippin himself citing this very same paragraph in support of his Kantianizing interpretation,[108] I am opting once again, as with the passage in the *Science of Logic*'s "Doctrine of the Concept" on the transcendental deduction, for an immanent-critical line of contestation):

> The Kantian philosophy needed to have its spirit (*Geist*) distinguished from its letter (*Buchstaben*), and to have its purely speculative principle lifted out of the remainder that belonged to, or could be used for, the arguments of reflection (*der räsonierenden Reflexion*). In the principle of the deduction of the categories Kant's philosophy is authentic idealism (*echter Idealismus*); and it is this principle that Fichte extracted in a purer, stricter form and called the spirit of Kantian philosophy. The things in themselves—which are nothing but an objective

expression of the empty form of opposition—had been hypostasized anew by Kant, and posited as absolute objectivity like the things of the dogmatic philosophers. On the one hand, he made the categories into static, dead pigeonholes of the intellect (*Intelligenz*); and on the other hand he made them into the supreme principles capable of nullifying the language that expresses the Absolute itself—e.g., "substance" in Spinoza. Thus he allowed argumentation (*negative Räsonieren*) to go on replacing philosophy, as before, only more pretentiously than ever under the name of critical philosophy. But all this springs at best from the form of the Kantian deduction of the categories, not from its principle or spirit (*Prinzip oder Geist*). Indeed, if we had no part of Kant's philosophy but the deduction, the transformation (*Verwandlung*) of his philosophy [from speculation into reflection] would be almost incomprehensible. The principle of speculation is the identity of subject and object (*die Identität des Subjekts und Objekts*), and this principle is most definitely articulated in the deduction of the forms of the intellect (*Verstand*). It was Reason (*Vernunft*) itself that baptized this theory of the intellect.[109]

Hegel unambiguously distinguishes between the nonspeculative qua subjective idealist "letter" and the speculative qua absolute idealist "spirit" of Kant's "Transcendental Deduction." Already in 1801, he heavily qualifies his praise of the Kantian transcendental unity of apperception in the same manner he does later in such texts as the *Science of Logic*. (I cited and unpacked these instances earlier.) Moreover, he signals that his post-Kantianism is a sublation *als Aufhebung*, being at least as much "post-" in the sense of surpassing as "post-" in the different sense of preserving. In regard to both the transcendental unity of apperception and transcendental idealism *überhaupt*, Hegelian "speculation" (that is, absolute idealism) is a "transformation" (*Verwandlung*), instead of a continuation, of Kantian "reflection" (that is, subjective idealism).

As the passage from the *Differenzschrift* indicates, Hegel's interpretation of the "Transcendental Deduction" is very much along the lines of the Allisonian "reciprocity thesis" reading (albeit avant la lettre). Indeed, an equivalence can be maintained between Hegel's "identity of subject and object (*die Identität des Subjekts und Objekts*)" and Allison's "reciprocity" between apperceiving subjectivity and apperceived objectivity. This reciprocity thesis, as subject-object identity, is the *Critique of Pure Reason*'s "purely speculative principle," namely, that by virtue of which "Kant's philosophy is authentic idealism (*echter Idealismus*)" (that is, absolute, rather than subjective, idealism). In the preceding block quotation, Hegel treats everything other than this moment of identity in the first *Critique* as "the remainder that belonged to, or could be used for, the arguments of reflection (*der räsonierenden Reflexion*)" (that is, a subjective idealist worldview with a *Verstand*-style opposition between subjectivity qua ideal thinking and objectivity qua real being, with the former as entirely external to, but reflecting, the latter). Hegel suggests an exegetical thought experiment in which one faces the "Transcendental Deduction" on its own, freed from its position as sandwiched between "the remainder" formed by the "Transcendental Aesthetic" (as insisting upon the strict ideality of space and time)[110] and the "Transcendental Dialectic" (as buttressing this antirealist insistence of the Aesthetic through supposedly demonstrating the contradictory, illogical consequences of any robustly realist option).[111] He justifiably sees the Kantian Aesthetic and Dialectic, which surround the Deduction in the first *Critique*, as working together to cement in place the two-worlds metaphysics of the reflective intellect or understanding, a *Weltanschauung* in which the subject-object reciprocity of the Deduction is confined to one world (that is, the subjective or ideal one of phenomenal experience with its objects as appearances) separate from another world (that is, the objective or real one of noumenal things in themselves). Worded in Hegelian fashion, the Kantian unity of subject and object is a unity internal to the subject itself (that is, a one-sided unity).[112]

Additionally, even though Fichte, for the Hegel of the *Differenzschrift*, makes progress beyond Kant by jettisoning *das Ding an sich*, Fichtean transcendental idealism is as subjectivist as the Kantian variety or even more so. As Hegel insists in 1801, Fichte's subject-object identity remains a lopsided, wrongly absolutized identity confined exclusively to the subject alone.[113] Tellingly, Pippin stresses the importance of Fichte for Hegel and depicts the Hegelian identity of subject and object in the shadow of the dissolution of Kant's thing in itself as a Fichtean subjective idealist identity that is internal solely to subjectivity itself.[114] This not only downplays Hegel's sustained critique of Fichte in the *Differenzschrift*; it neglects Schelling's importance, with Schelling's philosophies of nature and identity representing a Hölderlin-heralded, post-Fichtean objective or absolute idealism to which Hegel remains steadfastly committed throughout his mature intellectual itinerary (even long after his break with Schelling). Of course, as is well known, Hegel's first philosophical publication of 1801 largely sides with Schelling's identity-philosophical counterbalancing of the subjective subject-object of Fichtean transcendental idealism with the objective subject-object of the Schellingian Philosophy of Nature.[115] (Pippin symptomatically mentions as an influence on Hegel's development the young Schelling's *System of Transcendental Idealism*, published in 1800, which represents the more Fichtean side of his early endeavors, before his rupture with Fichte, which was publicly announced through the publication of "Presentation of My System of Philosophy" in 1801.)[116]

At various points throughout his oeuvre, Hegel sublates the dualist metaphysics of Kantian transcendental idealism as a self-subverting (attempted) absolutization of the subject-object dichotomy upheld by the external, formal understanding in the guise of an inflexible, brittle dualism between mental thinking and worldly being.[117] In particular, his vision in 1801 of the Deduction minus both the Aesthetic and the Dialectic is one in which the "object" of subject-object identity is no longer merely the phenomenal object as appearance but, instead, a genuinely objective (as extra- or nonsubjective) object *an sich* (that is, not the "formless lump" of *das Ding an sich*,[118] but, instead, an asubjective yet formed and unified objectivity). That is to say, Hegel's immanent critiques of the two-worlds metaphysics of transcendental idealism, with its antirealist subjectivism as embodied in the related theses about the strict ideality of space and time and about the existence of things in themselves, allow for interpretively appropriating the transcendental unity of apperception of the "Transcendental Deduction" such that this unity is no longer enclosed within the limits of the purely conscious, mental, and subjective as deontologized, epistemological, and exclusively ideal. This immanent-critical possibility for sublating Kant's Deduction testifies to the fact that, although Kant himself debatably restricts his subject-object identity (or, as in Allison, reciprocity) to the one side of the subject only, this identity is open to an absolute idealist speculative rereading once the antirealist arguments of the first *Critique*'s Aesthetic and Dialectic are justifiably left by the wayside (with this openness helping to explain what Hegel means when he says in 1801 that "It was Reason [*Vernunft*] itself that baptized this theory of the intellect"). Thus, the *Differenzschrift* adds yet more weight to my prior claim that Pippin misconstrues Hegel's references to Kant's transcendental unity of apperception as drawing the former closer to the subjective idealism of the latter.[119]

WHERE TO START?

Given that I began this chapter with the question of beginnings in Hegel's philosophy and in Žižek's perspectives on German idealism, how is my problematization of Pippin's use of the transcendental unity of apperception to establish a certain continuity between Kant and Hegel linked to this point of departure? As earlier remarks already indicate, the link is simple and direct: insofar as Pippin identifies his Kantianized version of "The Doctrine of the Concept" as the genuine logical start of the Hegelian System (by contrast with those, such as Houlgate, Henrich, and Žižek, who advocate for "The Doctrine of Being" or "The Doctrine of Essence" as the locus of proper beginning in Hegel's Logic), my critique of Pippin's portrayal of Hegel's relationship to the "Transcendental Deduction" of the first *Critique* inhibits the gesture of elevating Kant's transcendental unity of apperception to the status of grounding primordial moment of Hegel's philosophical edifice as a whole. In fact, I wish to move toward a conclusion to this chapter with the proposal that the entire debate among readers of Hegel about where the Hegelian System well and truly gets underway in the Logic rests on two questionable assumptions shared by participants in this debate (despite their otherwise fierce disagreements among themselves): first, there is a stable beginning, a fixed starting point, to be found somewhere within the Logic; second, the Logic itself (or, at least, some moment[s] within it) is the foundational, one and only proper beginning of Hegel's systematic philosophical apparatus in its entirety (as also recently asserted by, for instance, Rosen).[120]

Contra these two assumptions, I have two assertions: First, the Logic in its full expanse comprises a series of (spectacular) failed attempts to begin with thinking alone (with thinking, at the end of this series, driving itself out of and beyond itself into the Real of the *Realphilosophie*, initially as objectively real spatiotemporal nature in its externality).[121] Second, there is no single *Ur*-beginning in Hegel's philosophy, but, instead, at least three different beginnings incommensurable yet equiprimordial with respect to one another. (These two proposals are more specific versions of suggestions also gestured at by Hans Friedrich Fulda and Sedgwick.)[122] In connection with my first assertion, a snippet from the collection *Žižek's Jokes* is fitting:

> There is the ultimate good news/bad news doctor joke that reaches the dark limit of a joke; it starts with the good news, which, however, is so ominous that no further bad news is needed: "Doctor: First the good news: we definitely established

that you are not a hypochondriac." No need for a counterpoint here. (Another version: "Doctor: I have some good news and some bad news. Patient: What's the good news? Doctor: The good news is that your name will be soon a household name all around the world—they are naming a disease after you!") Is this a nondialectical short circuit? Or is it rather the proper dialectical beginning that immediately negates itself? Something like this joke happens at the beginning of Hegel's logic, not a passage to the opposite, but the beginning's immediate self-sabotage.[123]

The back cover of the collection containing this passage cites Ludwig Wittgenstein's statement that "a serious and good philosophical work could be written consisting entirely of jokes." My suggestion for how to read Hegel's Logic could be construed as involving a reversal of this Wittgensteinian assertion: the *Science of Logic* (or other versions of the Logic, such as the first volume of the *Encyclopedia*) amounts to a long sequence of jokes delivered in the form of a serious and good philosophical work (further support for this can be found in Ernst Bloch's reflections on "Hegel and Humor").[124] In *Less Than Nothing*, *Žižek's Jokes*, and *Absolute Recoil*,[125] Žižek denies that the very beginning of the Logic (that is, the initial triad of Being, Nothing, and Becoming) is really a beginning. However, as I highlighted at the opening of this chapter, the Žižek specifically of *Less Than Nothing* claims that "Determinate Being" or "Being-there" (*das Dasein*), the immediate successor moment to Becoming in "The Doctrine of Being," is indeed to be understood as the actual start of Hegelian Logic after the false starts of its opening trinity. (Similarly, both Hans-Georg Gadamer and Bernard Bourgeois identify Becoming as the true beginning of Logic after the false starts of Being and Nothing.)[126] That is to say, Žižek limits "the beginning's immediate self-sabotage" in Hegel's *Science of Logic* and *Encyclopedia Logic* to these texts' literal beginnings with the triad of Being, Nothing, and Becoming. This not only leaves him exposed to the objections that the likes of a Henrich or a Pippin would raise to treating any moment whatsoever of "The Doctrine of Being" as the proper starting point of the Logic; it is less than optimally consistent with the specifically dialectical materialist version of Hegelian philosophy aimed at by *Less Than Nothing* and *Absolute Recoil*.

This leads to my second assertion regarding the three distinct varieties of beginnings in Hegel's framework, with each one enjoying its own mode of precedence or priority vis-à-vis the other two. As with Lacan's Borromean knot, the Hegelian System is a configuration whose existence and integrity depend upon all three of its dimensions as equally indispensable constituents, this arguably being part of what is at stake in some of Hegel's (often opaque) remarks about syllogistic structures.[127] Of course, the *Encyclopedia*, as articulating the core of Hegelian *Wissenschaft*, is structured by two basic organizing divisions, a two-part and a three-part division: first, a two-part division between *Logik* and *Realphilosophie*; and second, a three-part division between *Logik* and *Realphilosophie* as divided into *Naturphilosophie* and *Geistesphilosophie* (that is, the three divisions familiar in the form of the three volumes of the *Encyclopedia*, namely, *Logic*, *Philosophy of Nature*, and *Philosophy of Mind*).[128] Stated roughly and quickly, my idea is that Hegel's three beginnings correspond approximately to the divisions of the Hegelian System as follows: metaphysical (Logic), material (Philosophy of Nature), and historical (Philosophy of Mind, including Phenomenology, with both ontogenetic and phylogenetic histories being involved in mindedness and like-mindedness).

The *Phenomenology of Spirit* provides the prehistory leading up to the presuppositionless initiation of the Logic.[129] (Indeed, this first systematic work of the mature Hegel can defensibly be read as a massive dialectical process-of-elimination argument in which all non-Hegelian presuppositions, embodied in the *Phenomenology*'s myriad figures and shapes of consciousness, dialectically eliminate themselves through sublation.) Given both that Hegel is no metaphysical realist and that he distinguishes between the logical and the real (as in the division between *Logik* and *Realphilosophie*), the Logic can then be construed as spelling out the dialectical-speculative network of categories and concepts making possible all *Realphilosophie* precisely as knowledge of the Real. (Any knowing of Nature or Mind [*als Geist*] necessarily relies directly upon at least some of the constellations delineated in the Logic.) However, this making possible is done not in the epistemological manner of Kant's subjectively idealist transcendental, but, instead, in the ontological fashion of Hegel's absolute idealist Idea (*Idee*) qua the identity-in-difference between the objectively real and the subjectively ideal dimensions of categories and concepts (with, as I have shown at some length, categories and concepts indeed being both objectively real and subjectively ideal for Hegel).[130] Hence, the intelligibility of all things real, be they natural or mental (again, *als geistige*), is made possible by them always already being formed in and of themselves along lines traced by the Logic.

Nonetheless, the structures and dynamics of the Logic do not magically float in the rarified air of a mysterious, eternal time-before-time (despite a famous Hegelian passage misleadingly suggesting this).[131] They exist only in and through the natural and spiritual realities that are themselves immanent realizations of logical categories and concepts. For Hegel, and *pace* metaphysical realism, the metaphysical by itself is not the real. Therefore, the Logic is a beginning strictly in the circumscribed sense of laying down the skeletal metaphysical abstractions serving as necessary conditions or ingredients for an ontology of intelligible being(s)[132]—with this "-logy" formulated at a determinate point of spiritual history from the contextually situated standpoint of philosophy's backward glance (à la the Owl of Minerva) as itself invariably embodied in individual human creatures of nature as well as culture. (Along these lines, Althusser approvingly underscores Hegel's refusal of any nonfactical Origin-with-a-capital-O, and Harris emphasizes that, with Hegel, one must accept beginning in medias res.)[133] These qualifications I just now attached to the logical beginning of Hegel's absolute idealism already hint at the different priorities belonging to the two fundamental dimensions of *Realphilosophie*, those of *Natur und Geist*.

One of the accomplishments of the *Phenomenology of Spirit*, *Science of Logic*, and *Encyclopedia Logic* taken together is that they permit Hegel to posit real beginnings both material/natural (as in *Realphilosophie als Naturphilosophie*) and historical or mental (as in *Realphilosophie als Geistesphilosophie*) in thoroughly nondogmatic, postcritical ways.[134] In particular, Hegelian Logic not only makes possible knowledge of the Real à la the *Realphilosophie* (as real knowledge);[135] it also argumentatively supports Hegel's realism generally (by immanently critiquing such antirealist options as Kantian transcendental idealism) as well as his beginning, at the start of the *Philosophy of Nature*, with space and time as objectively real specifically.[136] The course of Hegel's mature Logic begins with Being and ends with the transition to Nature, the latter being external to thinking (including the thinking of and about thinking that is the Logic itself). This is significant, especially considering that Hegel, as I noted, proclaims the structure of his Logic to be circular, with the end reconnecting (somehow or other) with the beginning. Of course, the Logic initially gets underway with the attempt to start with Being from within pure thinking. Hence, its conclusion, as a move that is neither temporal nor causal from the Logical to the Real of Nature as an externality in excess of pure thinking, entails that the "onto-" in ontology is really to be found over and above a "-logy" alone, namely, to be located in *Natur an sich*.[137]

WHERE TO START?

If I am right in reading the entire Logic as a series of false starts, then it becomes a failed ontology. However, surprisingly, its failure is epistemologically productive. Initiated without presuppositions and set in motion with the self-induced dialectics of the attempt to begin with mere Being per se, the Logic keeps failing to properly begin. The sequence of failures to begin inexorably drives thought up to the point of thinking Nature's externality, ready to do so equipped with the categorial and conceptual resources generated precisely by the sublimely, stunningly productive failures, as "determinate negations,"[138] constituting the full sweep of the Logic. With the Logic's circularity, this means that Being, its false start, is truly recovered first as spatiotemporal objective reality (that is, the start of *Realphilosophie* with *Natur*), an intelligible reality whose intelligibility is made possible by the Logic itself (as a metaphysical, but not yet real, beginning). Therefore, the *Philosophy of Nature* can be construed as furnishing a second beginning for Hegel's System, that is, its material preconditions and presuppositions.

Finally, and as the deservedly renowned preface to Hegel's *Elements of the Philosophy of Right* (1821) powerfully proposes, philosophy generally (including Hegelian systematic, scientific philosophy) is invariably and inevitably a "child of its time," namely, constructed from the perspective of the backward glance of the Owl of Minerva.[139] In this sense, what I am here identifying as the third, historical beginning of Hegelian *Wissenschaft*, in addition to the other two beginnings, the metaphysical one (with *Logik*) and the material one (with *Naturphilosophie*), enjoys the priority of embodying the spiritual-contextual starting points conditioning Hegel's philosophy *überhaupt*. As the introductory "First Part" of a "System of Science," the *Phenomenology of Spirit*, particularly with its prominent sociohistorical components, already hints, well before 1821, that both *Logik* and *Realphilosophie* (that is, the entirety of the encyclopedic nucleus of the System) are actual and possible only insofar as the history of human mindedness and like-mindedness has eventuated in Hegel the philosopher's particular early-nineteenth-century European time and place.[140] However, although Hegel posits such conjunctural and situational presuppositions as (pre)conditions of his philosophy as well as philosophy tout court, he nonetheless avoids crudely and unreservedly reducing the philosophical to the historical. For instance, his own Logic, his own Philosophy of Nature, and large portions of the Phenomenology and Philosophy of Mind are put forward as possessing at least a relative autonomy vis-à-vis their sociohistorical catalysts and influences, with these components' validity not simply rising and falling with the waxing and waning of given contextual circumstances.

Two fundamental questions are at stake in Žižek's recent disagreements with Pippin (and other deflationists) over the non- or antimetaphysical Hegel: First, what is the true nature of beginning(s) for Hegel's philosophical framework? Second, how and why, in the current aftermath of deflationary variants of Hegelianism (especially Pippin's Kantianizing one), is anybody entitled to put forward a historical and dialectical materialist Hegel? As I have discussed, I answer the first question differently than Žižek does. Whereas he locates a single *Ur*-beginning in the Logic's "Doctrine of Being" (more precisely, in "Determinate Being" or "Being-There" as preceded by the triad of Being, Nothing, and Becoming) and Pippin does so within "The Doctrine of the Concept," I treat the Logic in toto as only one of three different yet equiprimordial beginnings, that is, as a metaphysical beginning distinct from equally indispensable material ones (as in *Naturphilosophie*) and historical ones (as in *Geistesphilosophie*). Furthermore, this move of mine, particularly by virtue of its restoring to Hegel's *Realphilosophie* equal standing with respect to *Logik* within his System as a whole, answers the second question by inverting it: How and why, in taking seriously Hegel's thoughts and texts, is anybody entitled to put forward an antimaterialist, antinaturalist, or antirealist (in a word, deflated) Hegel? In *Less Than Nothing* as well as throughout his still-unfolding oeuvre, Žižek indeed reads Hegel in this same spirit, clearly considering the Philosophy of the Real to be as essential to Hegel's philosophy as the Logic. However, this exegetical approach not only requires the sort of additional argumentative and textual support I have tried to provide in the preceding; some of Žižek's interpretive maneuvers with respect to Hegel (such as the beginning he claims to find in "The Doctrine of Being") are at odds with a globally consistent overall reading of Hegel's System as a historical and dialectical materialism avant la lettre. As seen at the start of this chapter, Žižek, immediately after claiming in *Less Than Nothing* that Hegel's System initially gets underway quite early in the Logic with the Being-there of Determinate Being, claims that there is a properly Hegelian materialist ontology. One thing I think I have managed to show here is that these two claims are in tension with each other and that Žižek would be well advised to drop the former claim if he wants to hold on to the latter.

Deflationists might respond to all of this by appealing to a distinction between historically accurate readings and philosophically interesting reconstructions, identifying themselves as pursuing projects of the latter type. With this line of response, it is either assumed or asserted that much of the actual and factual Hegel of yore (for instance, the grand system-builder, the ambitious metaphysician, and the philosopher of nature) long ago ceased to be alive, relevant, or valid for later generations of readers and thinkers. (I believe Rosen is right to construe such assumptions and assertions as symptomatic of a currently reigning hegemony of subjective idealism.)[141] Such deflationists take it for granted that the various and sundry postmetaphysical turns in the continental and analytic philosophical traditions are (or, at least, should be) historical points of no return marking a trajectory of presumed intellectual progress. In this, they are neither sufficiently (self-)critical nor philosophically interesting. For them, there are two key questions: Where does Hegel stand with respect to the present? What remains interesting or palatable in Hegel's philosophy judged by today's philosophical criteria and tastes?

But, for anyone risking the encounter of a true engagement with a giant of the philosophical past such as Hegel (a past that, echoing William Faulkner, is never even past) with as few (usually anachronistic) presuppositions as possible, there are also always two additional key questions: Where does the present stand with respect to Hegel (or any member of the pantheon of the "mighty dead")? How would Hegel (or any other philosopher of the never-even-past past) judge today's philosophical criteria and tastes? That is to say, recognizing Hegel (or anyone else) as truly worthy of sustained attention in the present, as an interlocutor irreplaceable by other recent or current thinkers, ought to entail those conferring this recognition being willing and able to have their present itself called into question and challenged by the object of this recognition. This amounts to a reversal of Žižek's question "Is it still possible to be a Hegelian today?": Is it still possible to be contemporary (that is, to presume as well founded today's established standards for judging Hegel's enduring value or lack thereof) in the face of an honest, thorough reckoning with Hegel himself in all his glorious untimeliness? Anything short of this reckoning signals a disrespectful underestimation throwing the doors wide open to the surreptitious replacement of Hegel with a dummy made for exploitation by post-Hegelian ventriloquists.

THREE

Contingency, Pure Contingency—Without Any Further Determination
Hegelian Modalities

OVER THE LENGTHY arc of his still-unfurling intellectual itinerary, Žižek has consistently combatted various textbook caricatures of Hegel.[1] This struggle, one with deep roots in certain venerable strains of the Marxist tradition,[2] to recover and redeploy a "real Hegel" (a dialectical materialist one avant la lettre) who appears strikingly unfamiliar and heterodox by the standards of established understandings of Hegelianism is indeed the central red thread in both *Less Than Nothing* and *Absolute Recoil*. Žižek currently remains predominantly occupied with a return to Hegel profoundly akin to, and, in fact, partly modeled on, Lacan's return to Freud.[3]

One of several stock stories about Hegel's philosophy is that it privileges the modality of necessity to such an excessive extent as to engage in what would be tantamount to a lamentable or laughable post-Kantian regression, within the traditions of German philosophy, to pre-Kantian Leibnizianism.[4] That is to say, from this kind of all-too-common perspective, Hegel, like Leibniz before him,[5] elaborates a theodicy (however much secularly disguised or not) according to which reality, in its categorial and conceptual determinations via the metaphysically real Godlike mega-Mind of "the Absolute Idea," necessarily is exactly as it is and cannot be otherwise. Purportedly like Leibniz's divinity, the Hegelian Absolute's sufficient reason(s) make it such that there is no space whatsoever left open for anomaly, arbitrariness, caprice, contingency, difference, facticity, indeterminism, irrationality, meaninglessness, randomness, and the like.

CONTINGENCY, PURE CONTINGENCY

Of course, near the start of his philosophical career in the early 1800s, Hegel (in his Jena period, leading up to the *Phenomenology of Spirit*) already encountered objections to German idealism overall along these lines from the pen of W. T. Krug, an otherwise trifling writing instrument made (in)famous thanks exclusively to Hegel's stinging responses to Krug's critical challenges.[6] And, before Hegel's corpse was even cold, the later Schelling, faithfully executing his state-ordained duty given by his Prussian summoners to "stamp out the dragon seed of Hegelianism" while occupying the philosophical chair at the University of Berlin vacated by the death of his former friend, initiates what have become repetitive refrains among subsequent critics of Hegelian philosophy: Hegel's System is centered on the Logic alone; the machinery of this absolute idealist apparatus dissolves the real into the logical; Hegelian "negative philosophy" (to be opposed by a Christian "positive philosophy") entirely excludes and is powerless to account for the extralogical real, especially in terms of an undeducible factual "thatness" evading the grasp of any deducible categorial "whatness," a contingent givenness unassimilable by mediated necessity.[7]

I will show, among other things, that this Schellingian dance on Hegel's grave, the first of many such performances, does not have a leg or even terra firma upon which to stand (let alone move gracefully). Hegel's modal doctrine in the Logic, combined with his more-than-logical Philosophy of the Real, is a rebuttal in advance (a refutation from the crypt, as it were) of Schelling's opportunistic attacks upon him. Schelling and all those who reduce Hegel's philosophy to the Logic on its own fail to recognize that the System is the *Encyclopedia of the Philosophical Sciences* in its entirety, within which *Logik* is only one part, along with *Naturphilosophie* and *Geistesphilosophie* (as discussed in chapter 2). Additionally, as Klaus Düsing perspicaciously observes, the late Schelling presupposes, without supporting arguments, a modal doctrine in his positive-philosophical critique (with its notion of factical thatness) of Hegel's allegedly Logic-centric negative philosophy. Hegelian *Logik*, by contrast, posits, with supporting arguments, precisely such a doctrine.[8]

Opposed to the widespread misreading of Hegel as the philosopher of absolute necessity par excellence, Žižek prioritizes contingency as the alpha and omega of true, undistorted Hegelianism.[9] In *Less Than Nothing*, he repeatedly and forcefully reaffirms the primacy of this modality in Hegel's thinking, adamantly underscoring the contention that necessity itself is

[75]

contingent for Hegel.[10] Although at odds with the superficial impressions of Hegelian speculative dialectics prevailing among nonspecialists of various types within and beyond the world of professional academic philosophy, this Žižekian premium placed on contingency is echoed by certain other scholars with expertise regarding German idealism generally and Hegel especially. Such diverse interpreters of Hegel's texts as (in a nonexhaustive alphabetical list) Louis Althusser, Ermanno Bencivenga, John Burbidge, André Doz, Dieter Henrich, Jean Hyppolite, Jean-Marie Lardic, Gérard Lebrun, Georg Lukács, Bernard Mabille, Catherine Malabou, Herbert Marcuse, Gilles Marmasse, Terry Pinkard, Emmanuel Renault, and Stanley Rosen[11] converge on a consensus (one in which Žižek too participates) that the Hegelian Absolute intrinsically entails an irreparable lack of greater metalevel grounding grounds, an ineliminable, factical "without why" (*ohne Warum*)—in short, an ultimate, unsurpassable contingency. Within the admittedly broad spectrum of readings of Hegel on contingency represented by this group of authors, Žižek is to be situated on one far end of it, within which the contingent not only is said to be acknowledged in Hegel's corpus, but is argued to enjoy an unrivaled ultimacy in this oeuvre.

Having dealt elsewhere both with Žižek on Hegelian contingency before 2012 (in the third part of my book *Žižek's Ontology*, published in 2008) as well as with the contingent in Hegel's *Naturphilosophie* specifically,[12] I will scrutinize only Žižek's more recent glosses in *Less Than Nothing* and *Absolute Recoil* on the contingent in Hegelianism. Following this Žižek, I will accompany this scrutiny of him with a focus on how Hegel conceptualizes contingency within the apparatus of the versions of his Logic from 1812 and after. The contingent indeed features in myriad guises throughout both *Phänomenologie* and *Realphilosophie* as branches of the Hegelian System distinct from *Logik* per se. Like Žižek, I too will touch upon some of these phenomenological and real-philosophical (in addition to logical) instances. But the final third ("Actuality" [*Wirklichkeit*]) of the second book ("The Doctrine of Essence" [*Die Lehre vom Wesen*]) of both the *Science of Logic* and the three successive editions (1817, 1827, and 1830) of the *Encyclopedia Logic* (as well as the Berlin *Lectures on Logic* from 1831) contains in logically and categorially distilled purity Hegel's decisive treatments of the modalities of actuality, possibility (*Möglichkeit*), necessity (*Notwendigkeit*), and contingency (*Zufälligkeit*). Hence, my interpretations of Hegel, as articulated in this chapter with an eye to

Žižek's Hegelianism of the contingent, will dwell primarily on this stretch of Hegel's mature Logic.

But, before shifting attention directly to Hegel himself, the intimate link in Žižek's current thinking between Hegelian contingency and post-Hegelian dialectical materialism should be examined in some detail. Of course, the phrase *dialectical materialism* appears in the subtitles of both *Less Than Nothing* and *Absolute Recoil* (as I noted in the introduction). Revealingly, the former tome goes so far as to contend that "the true foundation of dialectical materialism is not the necessity of contingency, but the contingency of necessity. In other words, while the second position opts for a secret invisible necessity beneath the surface of contingency ... the first position asserts contingency as the abyssal ground of necessity itself."[13]

First and foremost, given my purposes in the present context, it should be noted that Žižek himself openly asserts a direct connection between the contingent à la Hegel and the dialectical materialism that his ongoing philosophical labors aim to revivify for the twenty-first century. The baseless base of an absolute, ultimate *Ur*-contingency (that is, "the contingency of necessity" qua "the abyssal ground of necessity itself") is said by him to be "the true foundation of dialectical materialism."[14] Of a piece with this, *Less Than Nothing* also calls for playing off Hegel against Marx by bringing to light a dialectical materialist version of the former.[15] In Žižek's eyes, reinventing dialectical materialism for today requires extracting it out of nothing other than Hegelian philosophy properly construed,[16] a philosophy at least as concealed and misrecognized as revealed and recognized by the Marxist tradition within which "dialectical materialism" explicitly arises by name approximately four years after Marx's death.[17] (In 1887, Dietzgen and Kautsky[18] each coin the very phrase under the inspiration of Engels, especially the Engels of the trilogy formed by *Anti-Dühring*, *Dialectics of Nature*, and *Ludwig Feuerbach and the Outcome of Classical German Philosophy*, as much as Marx himself.)

As if to emphasize this asserted superiority of Hegelian dialectical materialism avant la lettre to Marxian dialectical materialism après la lettre, Žižek, at another moment in *Less Than Nothing*, criticizes the later Althusser for allegedly excluding Hegel from the eclectic, motley ranks of the "underground current" in the philosophical history of "the materialism of the encounter" (that is, an "aleatory materialism" in which contingencies qua unpredictable chance events disrupt and displace the necessities posited as causal laws by the mechanical materialisms and teleological processes of certain permutations of Marxian historical and dialectical materialism). Žižek remarks that

> the point of Hegelian dialectical analysis is not to reduce the chaotic flow of events to a deeper necessity, but to unearth the contingency of the rise of necessity itself—this is what it means to grasp things "in their becoming." So when, in his late text "The Subterranean Current of the Materialism of the Encounter," Althusser endeavors to discern, beneath the hegemonic idealist orientation of Origins/Sense, etc., the subterranean tradition of "aleatory materialism"—Epicurus (and the Stoics?) versus Plato, Machiavelli versus Descartes, Spinoza versus Kant and Hegel, Marx, Heidegger—the least one can say is that he is wrong to locate Hegel in the hegemonic "idealist" line.[19]

Admittedly, this particular Althusser does not highlight Hegel's name as prominently included in the pantheon of the "mighty dead" of the hidden history (that is, the "underground current") of the aleatory materialism of the encounter (with the word *encounter* signifying the primacy of contingency over necessity).[20] And Althusser indeed suggests that (a certain) Hegel(ianism) is partly responsible for the nonaleatory materialisms within the Marxist tradition that he seeks to combat in the final phases of his theorizing (such as Stalinism's notorious *diamat* of deservedly ill repute).[21]

Nonetheless, at various junctures throughout Althusser's theoretical career (including ones roughly contemporaneous both chronologically and conceptually with "The Underground Current of the Materialism of the Encounter" from the early 1980s), he approvingly credits Hegel with replacing every necessary, meaningful "in the Beginning" (with the capital B, signaling a nonfactical Origin) with a contingent, meaningless in medias res (as factical givenness or thrownness).[22] Moreover, "The Underground Current of the Materialism of the Encounter" and closely related texts explicitly identify this very replacement that Althusser elsewhere acknowledges Hegel executes to be one of the hallmark defining characteristics of aleatory materialism.[23] In fact, on multiple occasions, he underscores a number of Hegel's virtues. One virtue is his insistence on the depth and breadth of historical mediation.[24] A second virtue is the stress on modern bourgeois capitalism's creation of a steadily swelling rabble (*Pöbel*) through relentlessly increasing the disparity between market-generated wealth and poverty[25] (a topic so intensely dear to the recent Žižek, along with Frank Ruda in *Hegel's Rabble* [2011], that he even invokes Hegel's *Pöbel*, also invoked by Georgi Plekhanov,[26] as key evidence of the greater contemporary relevance of Hegel in comparison with Marx, the argument being that the oppressed masses of today's capitalism are better represented as a Hegelian rabble economically excluded than a Marxian proletariat economically exploited).[27] A third virtue is the denial of predictive power to the philosopher or theorist.[28] (For Hegel in the preface to *Elements of the Philosophy of Right* in 1821, the Benjamin of 1940 in "Theses on the Philosophy of History," the later Althusser, and Žižek alike,[29] traditional, "orthodox" Marxism can and should give up its dubious claim to the effect that historical materialism enjoys science-like predictive power as regards sociohistorical futures, with *Less Than Nothing* praising the modesty of Hegel's "absolute idealism" for its acceptance that its Absolute is the result of the Owl of Minerva's backward glance from the present over the past, a position always liable to being unforeseeably deabsolutized thanks to undoing by the impossible-to-anticipate *à venir*.)[30]

What is more, Althusser's short, fragment-like late piece "Portrait of the Materialist Philosopher" contains a list of historical and contemporary heralds of aleatory materialism that includes Hegel by name. Referring to the philosopher of the encounter, Althusser writes: "He reads the Hindus and Chinese (Zen), as well as Machiavelli, Spinoza, Kant, Hegel, Kierkegaard, Cavaillès, Canguilhem, Vuillemin, Heidegger, Derrida, Deleuze, and so on. Thus, without having intended to, he becomes a quasi-professional materialist philosopher—not that horror, a *dialectical* materialist, but an aleatory materialist."[31] The "dialectical materialist horror" decried in this quotation is nothing other than the official philosophical dogma of Soviet Really Existing Socialism, namely, J. V. Stalin's *diamat*.[32] As I have argued elsewhere, Althusser, despite his rejection of the Stalinist version of dialectical materialism, can defensibly be construed as far from wholly and consistently opposed to possible non-Stalinist reappropriations of this label.[33] Combined with the positive side of Althusserian ambivalence vis-à-vis Hegel, at least certain sides of Althusser would not be opposed (despite what Žižek seems to believe) to Žižek's heterodox reinvention of "dialectical materialism" via Hegel. (Incidentally, the later Althusser even evinces hesitation and uncertainty about the correctness of his grasp of Hegelian philosophy when he confesses in a letter to Fernanda Navarro that "Hegel . . . remains, after all, the fundamental reference for everyone, since he is himself such a 'continent' that it takes practically a whole lifetime to come to know him well.")[34] Additionally, in "The Underground Current of the Materialism of the Encounter," aleatory materialism is directly associated with the Hegelian dialectical dynamic of the becoming-necessary of the originally contingent:

> No determination of the being which issues from the "taking-hold" of the encounter is prefigured, even in outline, in the being of the elements that converge in the encounter. Quite the contrary: no determination of these elements can be assigned except by *working backwards* from the result to its becoming, in its retroaction. If we must therefore say that there can be no result without its becoming (Hegel), we must also affirm that there is nothing which has become except as determined by the result of this becoming—this retroaction itself (Canguilhem). That is, instead of thinking contingency as a modality of necessity, or an exception to it, we must think necessity as the becoming-necessary of the encounter of contingencies.[35]

Like Althusser here ("there can be no result without its becoming"), Žižek repeatedly draws attention to the significant fact that such paradigmatically Hegelian terms as the Absolute, the Concept, the Idea, and the like designate, for Hegel, results, namely, outcomes rather than origins, bottom-up and immanent One-effects rather than top-down and transcendent One-causes.[36] As I will indicate (and have already indicated on another occasion),[37] this result status of Hegel's core notions is closely related to nonteleological contingencies and the Žižekian interpretation of the contingent in Hegelian philosophy (especially as epitomized toward the conclusion of "The Doctrine of Essence" in the various versions of the mature Logic).

The Althusser of the block quotation sees the addition of a Canguilhemian supplement to Hegel as requisite to arrive at the conception of "necessity as the becoming-necessary of the encounter of contingencies." By contrast, the credit this Althusser withholds from Hegel and extends to Georges Canguilhem is generously granted to Hegel by Žižek. Žižek's psychoanalytically inflected reading of Hegel's philosophy insists on the crucial role of retroaction (along the lines of Freud's *Nachträglichkeit* and Lacan's *après-coup*) within this philosophy.[38] (This thread too is integrally woven into the Žižekian narrative about Hegelian contingency.)[39] Nonetheless, both the late Althusser (through a combination of Hegel and Canguilhem) and Žižek (through Hegel alone) arrive at an aleatory or dialectical materialism resting upon the thesis according to which (and appropriately worded in Hegelian fashion) the distinction between the categories of contingency and necessity is a distinction internal to the category of contingency itself. That is to say, for Althusserian aleatory materialism (as partly Hegelian) and Žižekian dialectical materialism (as fully Hegelian) alike, the contingent is the ultimate, abyssal *Ur*-modality.[40]

I will put Althusser aside for the rest of this chapter and Žižek aside until later in the chapter. I want now to elaborate an extended, detailed exegesis of Hegel's handling of the contingent, especially in the variants of his mature *Logik*. I will deviate from chronology in what follows, focusing first on the *Encyclopedia Logic* and then turning to the more intricate and difficult *Science of Logic*. This protracted exegetical exercise is an unavoidable prerequisite for properly appreciating and evaluating Žižek's reconstruction of Hegelian philosophy as a dialectical materialism of contingency.

As I noted, the modalities of actuality, possibility, necessity, and contingency are addressed by Hegel at the close of "The Doctrine of Essence," itself bringing the entirety of the "Objective Logic" (that is, "The Doctrine of Being" [*Die Lehre vom Sein*] plus "The Doctrine of Essence") to an end in transitioning into the "Subjective Logic" formed by the third book of the Logic, namely, "The Doctrine of the Concept" (*Die Lehre vom Begriff*). To understand Hegel's modal doctrine (and, in so doing, to arrive at a proper perspective from which to adequately survey and assess Žižek's claims and arguments regarding contingency according to Hegel) demands beginning where Hegel himself begins in this doctrine, namely, with the logical-categorial determination or moment of *Wirklichkeit*. Of course, *Wirklichkeit* (actuality) is a particularly (in)famous Hegelian term of art specifically because of the appearance it makes in the renowned (or notorious) preface to *Elements of the Philosophy of Right*. There, as is all too well known, Hegel declares, in the form of what has come to be known as the *Doppelsatz*, that "what is rational is actual; and what is actual is rational" ("*Was vernüftig ist, das ist wirlich; und was wirklich ist, das ist vernünftig*").[41] Countless critics past and present (starting with Rudolf Haym)[42] indicting this Hegel for being an apologetic mouthpiece for the conservative Prussia of Friedrich Wilhelm III latch on to this one-liner as exhibit A for their indictment. But, in so doing, they ignore the precise technical sense of *wirklich* and thereby carelessly trample over Hegel's strict distinction between *Wirklichkeit* and *Dasein/Existenz* (being-there, existence).⁴³ In section 6 of the *Encyclopedia Logic*, Hegel directly refutes those accusing him of pronouncing a Leibnizian-Panglossian benediction over everything that happens to be the case in his given status quo as necessitated and justified by a theodicy of an omniscient and omnipotent *Weltgeist*. For this Hegel, much of what happens to be the case in his given status quo is merely there or exists, but is not fully real qua actual *als wirklich*. Such mere beings-there or existences would include, for the Berlin-era Hegel, what he construes as the futile, doomed Germanic reaction against the ultimately irresistible progressive currents represented by the French Revolution and Napoleon, the emperor embodying and epitomizing Hegel's notion of history *überhaupt* as inexorably surging toward ever-greater realizations of human freedom. In this instance, actuality *als Wirklichkeit* and, hence, rationality (*Vernünftigkeit*) reside on the side of revolution rather than reaction—revolutionary rationality is "the rose in the cross of the present"⁴⁴ of a reactionary *Dasein/Existenz*—with reaction straining in vain against "the inner pulse" (*inneren Puls*) incarnated in and by revolution.⁴⁵ Hegel's dictum from the 1820s "What is rational is actual; and what is actual is rational" is anything but an older, comfortably established man's cynical or craven repudiation of the progressive or revolutionary passions of his restless, volatile younger years.⁴⁶ This one-liner's author remains the same person who faithfully toasted Bastille Day year after year, including publicly, and with audacity, in mixed company during the height of Prussian conservative repression.⁴⁷

But, as Hegel's own defense of himself in the *Encyclopedia Logic* against the criticisms triggered by his proclamation regarding the rational and the actual in the preface to *Elements of the Philosophy of Right* indicates, his definitive determinations of the category of *Wirklichkeit* are to be found within the framework of the *Logik* (rather than within branches of *Realphilosophie*, such as *Rechtsphilosophie* or *Geschichtsphilosophie*). In the *Encyclopedia Logic*, Hegel opens the section "Actuality" by stating, with its very first sentence, that "actuality is the unity (*Einheit*), become immediate (*unmittelbar*), of essence (*Wesens*) and existence (*Existenz*), or of what is inner and what is outer."⁴⁸ The entire prior two thirds of "The Doctrine of Essence" is structured around what fundamentally amounts to a two-worlds metaphysics. This Doctrine's first two sections, "Essence as Reflection Within Itself" ("*Das Wesen als Reflexion in ihm selbst*," *Science of Logic*) or "Essence as Ground of Existence" ("*Das Wesen als Grund der Existenz*," *Encyclopedia Logic*) and "Appearance" (*Die*

Erscheinung) both unfold variations on the basic theme of the distinction between supersensible essential ground and sensible apparent existence. To cut the long story of the entirety of "The Doctrine of Essence" very short, this second of the three divisions of the Logic culminates with *Wirklichkeit* as the sublation of the closely interrelated families of dichotomies structuring the prior moments of the *Wesenslehre*.[49] That is to say, the "unity" (*Einheit*) that Hegel speaks of in the opening sentence of section 142 of the *Encyclopedia Logic*, which I just quoted, is specifically a dialectical-speculative *Aufhebung* of the "two worlds" (as ground versus existence, essence versus appearance, inner versus outer, and similar variations on this theme) at stake in the first two-thirds of "The Doctrine of Essence."[50]

One of many consequences of actuality's sublation of the oppositions making possible any two-worlds metaphysics is the dialectical going-under of what Hegel sees as perhaps the most sophisticated and formidable version of such a metaphysics, namely, Kant's critical transcendental framework as subjectively idealist in Hegel's precise sense of "subjective idealism" (as distinct from "objective" and "absolute" idealisms, as discussed in chapter 2). The addition (*Zusatz*) to section 142 of the *Encyclopedia Logic* emphatically links *Wirklichkeit* to absolute idealism in terms of this idealism's antisubjectivist realism, namely, its non- or post-Kantian insistence that objective (qua extra- or more-than-subjective) reality *an sich* is, before and independently of knowing subjectivity, always already formed, structured, and the like in and of itself.[51] Given Kant's omnipresent shadow looming over an ambivalently post-Kantian Hegel, this point is crucial. Kant, in the *Critique of Pure Reason*, treats the topic of modalities (that is, according to Kant's Table of Categories, the pairs possibility/impossibility, existence/nonexistence, and necessity/contingency) under the heading of his subjectively idealist "Transcendental Analytic."[52] By contrast, Hegel, in his mature *Logik*, narrates the modalities as emerging out of an actuality that itself involves, among other things, an absolute idealist sublation of antirealist transcendental idealism (and all other two-worlds metaphysics along with it). This means that, for Hegel, modalities are not just subjectively ideal categories, as they are for Kant, but also objectively real ones. In other words, contra Kant and in an inversion of a famous line from the preface to the *Phenomenology of Spirit*, subject (the categories of modality as subjectively ideal) must be thought, through a thinking responding to the compelling force of the movement of Hegelian Logic up through the culmination of the *Wesenslehre* in *Wirklichkeit*, also as substance (the categories of modality as objectively real in addition to subjectively ideal).⁵³

In the addition to section 143 of the *Encyclopedia Logic*, Hegel stipulates that, "of course, it is not just what is immediately there (*unmittelbar Daseiende*) that should be understood as actual (*das Wirkliche*)."⁵⁴ (Incidentally, this clarification regarding a strict distinction between *Dasein* and *Wirklichkeit* buttresses the non- or anticonservative interpretation of "what is rational is actual; and what is actual is rational.") Earlier, in Hegel's Nuremberg lectures on the "Philosophical Encyclopedia" for advanced *Gymnasium* students, the category of determinate being-there (that is, *Dasein* as immediate existence [*Existenz*]) is already deployed in connection with actuality: "The Actual itself is the unity of its possibility and its existence (*Daseins*)."⁵⁵ In this quotation from Hegel's Nuremberg texts, the pairing of the category of being-there/existence (*Dasein/Existenz*) with the category of possibility arguably suggests that the former, like the latter, is also a modal category (or, at least, has a modal valence) in this precise context. Put differently, *Dasein*, in being an ingredient in *Wirklichkeit* distinct from that of possibility, is or represents a modality distinct from that of possibility itself. In yet other words, if being-there or existence is distinguished from possibility as a modality, then this seems to suggest that being-there or existence is or instantiates a modal category.

Before proceeding further, a radically anti-Leibnizian upshot to Hegel's Logic at this specific stage of its development must be highlighted. Only after the logical genesis of actuality toward the end of "The Doctrine of Essence" does the particular category of the modality of possibility explicitly arise— and, with it, the general (meta)category of modality overall (that is, any modality). Hence, for Hegel, actuality precedes every possibility. By sharp contrast, in Leibniz's theosophical metaphysics with its Christian theodicy possibility precedes actuality (with a benevolent, omniscient, omnipotent, and perfect God selecting among an infinitude of possible worlds before actualizing, through the act of creation, the only and only, optimally good "best of all possible worlds"). (This aspect of Leibnizianism resurfaces in multiple secular (dis)guises within the twentieth-century Anglo-American analytic philosophical tradition.) Thus, Hegel, already from within the pure conceptual abstractness of his logical apparatus, announces a principled, categorical opposition to the spiritualist idealism of Leibniz's ontologically prioritized metaphysical reality of possibilities purportedly existing before anything actual.

Now that I have noted Hegel's anti-Leibnizian prioritizing of actuality over possibility, the identifications of *Wirklichkeit* as a dialectical-speculative, sublational (*als Aufhebung*) synthesis ("unity" [*Einheit*]) of "immediate thereness" or "existence" and possibility still require further exegetical unpacking here. Something being actual automatically entails it also already being possible too. In this sense, were this something impossible, it simply would not be. However, the peculiarity of this sort of possibility as invoked by Hegel at this stage of the Logic is that it is not a possibility preceding and existing before the being-there or existence of the actuality for which it is the very possibility. Instead, the given actuality generates simultaneously both its own possibility and its being-there or existence. In other words, *Möglichkeit* and *Dasein/Existenz* are contemporaneously coemergent from *Wirklichkeit* as their shared ground. The first paragraph of section 147 of the *Encyclopedia Logic* corroborates this reading.[56]

At this point, two things are to be appreciated. First, as I just explained, actuality logically (that is, dialectically and speculatively) gives rise out of itself to the jointly arising pair of possibility and being-there or existence. In so doing, actuality initially introduces modality tout court into the movement of Hegelian *Logik*. Put differently, modality as such begins with the being-there of an actuality that, as really existing, is at the same time really possible. Second, if the determination or moment that introduces modality into the Logic is being-there or existence qua possible, then the modality of contingency surfaces before that of necessity. Therefore, the contingent definitely appears to enjoy a certain priority over the necessary in Hegelian thinking (with the *Science of Logic* furnishing confirmation of my interpretive reasoning here).[57]

Indeed, Hegel discusses contingency before necessity, emphasizing the former in section 145 and the latter in section 147 of the *Encyclopedia Logic*. The *Zusatz* to section 145 states that

> contingency... does deserve its due in the world of ob-jects (*gegenständlichen Welt*). This holds first for nature, on the surface of which contingency has free rein, so to speak. This free play should be recognised as such, without the pretension (sometimes erroneously ascribed to philosophy) of finding

[85]

something in it that could only be so and not otherwise (*nicht anders sein Können*). Similarly . . . the contingent also asserts itself in the world of spirit, since will contains the contingent within itself in the shape of freedom of choice, though only as a sublated moment. In regard to the spirit and its activity, we also have to be careful that we are not misled by the well-meant striving of rational cognition into trying to show that phenomena that have the character of contingency are necessary, or, as people tend to say, into "constructing them a priori." For example, although language is the body of thinking, as it were, still chance indisputably plays a decisive role in it, and the same is true with regard to the configurations of law, art, etc. It is quite correct to say that the task of science and, more precisely, of philosophy, consists generally in coming to know the necessity that is hidden under the semblance of contingency; but this must not be understood to mean that contingency pertains only to our subjective views and that it must therefore be set aside totally if we wish to attain the truth. Scientific endeavors which one-sidedly push in this direction will not escape the justified reproach of being an empty game and a strained pedantry.[58]

Throughout this quotation, starting with its very first sentence, Hegel thrusts to the fore the objectively real status of the modality of contingency in his logical framework—in sharp contrast, at least implicitly, with its subjectively ideal status in Kantian critical transcendentalism. One of Hegel's central assertions here, at least as much against Spinoza and Leibniz (and perhaps the early Schelling too) as against Kant, is that the contingent is far from always symptomatic merely of epistemological ignorance (that is, the knowing subject's failure to grasp a concealed underlying necessity in objective being *an sich*). Sometimes, this seeming ignorance is, in fact, direct ontological insight (that is, the knowing subject's success, whether appreciated by this subject or not, at grasping the actual absence of necessity within objective being *an sich*). Hegel warns that the far-from-unproductive, not-always-unjustified rationalist tendency or drive to search for real necessity hidden behind or beneath apparent contingency, if left lopsidedly unchecked by not giving to the contingent its countervailing metaphysical due, inevitably results in "an empty game and a strained pedantry."

To begin with, I again would suggest that Leibniz exemplifies such a teller of these risible rationalist just-so stories (famously lampooned by Voltaire). Within Leibniz's theodicy of the purported "best of all possible worlds," each seeming contingency is nothing more than an index of finite human knowers' lack of full understanding of God-the-creator's sufficient reasons for things being exactly so and not otherwise. In Leibnizian Christian-theosophical philosophy, the combination of the laws of classical, bivalent logic with the principle of sufficient reason guarantees that everything in creation necessarily and with certainty is precisely as it is, with no "illogical" or "irrational" breathing room for any really existent contingencies whatsoever.

Additionally, and still in the context of the passage from section 145 just quoted, I also would maintain that there is a secular, as well as theistic (i.e., Leibnizian), epitomization of the contingency-denying rationalism derided by Hegel as predictably eventuating in absurd rationalizations: a modern, natural scientific Weltanschauung in which nature and all things natural or naturalizable (including living beings generally and even human beings specifically) can and should be reduced to structures and dynamics governed by laws qua deterministic causal rules imposing an iron-clad, inviolable necessity on all entities and events. Hegel, in this quotation, sees fit to mention nature first when insisting upon certain contingencies as in fact being objectively real, with his motif of "the weakness of nature" (*die Ohnmacht der Natur*) palpably in the background. The necessitarian worldview of the natural sciences and scientists of the seventeenth and eighteenth centuries (a worldview that lingers on in the early twenty-first century) is parodied as bringing about its own ridiculous self-wrought ruin in the section "Observing Reason" in the *Phenomenology of Spirit*, culminating with the preposterous, comical pseudoexplanations of Franz Josef Gall's phrenology (with its attempts to eliminate such phenomena as "will" qua "freedom of choice" [section 145] in favor of dumb bumps on inert bones). These phrenological pseudoexplanations are this naturalistic worldview's immanently generated *reductio ad absurdum*. According to Hegel's narrative from 1807, the scientific Weltanschauung taking form in the seventeenth and eighteenth centuries begins to run into troubles with contingency particularly when it shifts its attention to the organic and human realms over and above physics and chemistry.[59] (I have addressed both Hegel's *Ohnmacht der Natur* and phenomenological figure or shape [*Gestalt*] of "Observing Reason" at length in other contexts.)[60]

Furthermore, Hegel, particularly in the preface to the second edition of the *Science of Logic*, published in 1831,[61] insists that thinking, including that of the most purely logical sort, is inextricably intertwined with natural language(s) (as he also elaborates in the accounts of the linguistically mediated and facilitated emergence of distinctively human intelligence in various versions of his *Philosophie des Geistes*, itself a part of *Realphilosophie* rather than *Logik* alone).[62] As seen from the previous block quotation, Hegel, in section 145 of the *Encyclopedia Logic*, makes reference to this language-bound character of cognition. His point in this passage is that thinking, in thinking either itself (as in Logic) or anything else (as in the Philosophy of the Real), cannot avoid the contingent insofar as all natural languages without exception are shot through with myriad contingencies (as the more-than-linguistic histories impacting etymologies, as what Saussurian structural linguistics designates under the heading "the arbitrariness of the signifier," and so on).[63] A simple syllogism is enough to encapsulate Hegel's argument here: first, human sapience is made possible by and always operates within natural language(s); second, all natural languages are riddled with contingencies; therefore, cognitive intelligence cannot avoid entanglement with and working through incarnations of the modality of contingency.

Before turning attention to section 147 of the *Encyclopedia Logic*, I want to highlight that, in the quotation from section 145, Hegel renders the modality of necessity as "could only be so and not otherwise (*nicht anders sein Können*)." Although this is a quite conventional way of defining the necessary, Hegel's recourse to it soon will prove to be important with the benefit of hindsight. For now, suffice it to note that Hegelian necessity, as introduced at this moment in the Logic, is determined as no more and no less than the impossibility of any additional "otherwise" (*anders sein*).

The time has come to parse a portion of section 147 of the *Encyclopedia Logic*. While the main body of section 147 portrays actuality as simultaneously realizing in and through itself the coemergent pair of possibility and being-there or existence—as I have already explained in regard to *Wirklichkeit*—its "Addition" goes into more detail about necessity. Hegel declares:

> The process of necessity (*Der Prozeß der Notwendigkeit*) begins with the existence of dispersed circumstances (*der Existenz zerstreuter Umstände*) that seem to have no concern with one another and no inward coherence. These circumstances are an immediate actuality (*eine unmittelbare Wirklichkeit*) that collapses inwardly; and from this negation a new actuality (*eine neue Wirklichkeit*) emerges. We have here a content that has a dual character within it in respect to its form: first, as the content of the matter (*Inhalt der Sache*) that is at issue, and secondly, as the

content of the dispersed circumstances (*Inhalt der zerstreuter Umstände*) that appear to be something positive, and initially assert themselves as such. Because of its inward nullity (*Nichtiges in sich*), this content is inverted into its negative, and so becomes the content of the matter. As conditions, the immediate circumstances go under, but at the same time they are also preserved as the content of the matter (*Die unmittelbaren Umstände gehen als Bedingungen zugrunde, werden aber auch zugleich als Inhalt der Sache erhalten*).[64]

The upshot of this passage is the thesis that necessity itself (that is, the "process of necessity" [*Prozeß der Notwendigkeit*]) originally arises out of contingency.[65] In other words, there is an *Ur*-contingency preceding and at the root of the necessary[66] (a Hegelian claim central to Žižek's concerns). Conversely but correlatively (and contrary to so many ridiculous, flagrant bastardizations of Hegel), there is no transcendent, metaphysically real *Ur*-necessity, a divinely supernatural cosmic Idea or world Spirit, imposing in a top-down fashion the Platonic-style *teloi* of a preordained theodicy upon the being-there of really existing actuality.[67] Instead, every necessity or teleology is a delayed effect and belated outcome of a primordially neither necessary nor teleological *Wirklichkeit* qua possibility just happening to exist.[68] Alternatively, the only *Ur*-necessity recognized by Hegelian Logic is the necessity of *Ur*-contingency as a modal category with logical priority vis-à-vis the modal category of necessity.[69] As Rosen expresses this sense of the necessity of contingency, "contingency itself, namely, as a category, is not itself contingent."[70] To this should be added Lukács's observation that "in Hegel the annulment of contingency takes place on the assumption that it cannot be annulled."[71]

What logically comes first and, hence, has a certain categorial precedence in Hegel's philosophy is the being-there (*Dasein*) of (an) actuality (*Wirklichkeit*) that, as existing, is also at the same time possible (*möglich*).[72] And a merely possible existence would amount to a contingency. Thus, a given actuality qua contingent is the factical ground, the baseless base, of a necessity that is always after the fact. The *Science of Logic* directly ties existence (*Existenz*) to facticity as itself groundless (*Grundlose*),[73] to an anti-Leibnizian, post-Kantian *ohne Warum*.[74] That is to say, for Hegel, necessity is, in its very logical essence as a metaphysical category, invariably the result of a movement of becoming, with this kinetic trajectory (that is, "the content of the matter" [*Inhalt der Sache*]) within which necessity takes shape pushing off from an initially contingent set of conditions,[75] namely, "the existence of dispersed circumstances (*der Existenz zerstreuter Umstände*) that seem to have no concern with one another and no inward coherence," "circumstances" that "are an immediate actuality (*eine unmittelbare Wirklichkeit*) that collapses inwardly."

Some of the wording in the quotation from section 147 should be highlighted. Arguably, the word *Existenz* in "the existence of dispersed circumstances (*der Existenz zerstreuter Umstände*)" is used here by Hegel in its technical sense (that is, as equivalent to determinate being-there [*Dasein*]). Likewise, when he depicts these same circumstances as "an immediate actuality (*eine unmittelbare Wirklichkeit*)," this resonates with the phrase "immediately there (*unmittelbar Daseiende*)" as employed in section 143 to designate one of the two coemergent modal dimensions of actuality (along with the modality of possibility). Both of these terminological details further reinforce the interpretive thesis (advanced by Žižek, among others) regarding the primacy of contingency over necessity within Hegelian Logic itself. Finally, at the end of the passage from section 147, Hegel indicates that (*Ur-*)contingency gets sublated, but never negated altogether, by the resultant necessity to which it gives rise. (Such contingencies "go under, but at the same time they are also preserved [*gehen . . . zugrunde, werden aber auch zugleich . . . erhalten*].")[76] Put differently, everything necessary bears upon itself a navel-like mark of its contingent origin, of its origin as contingent (that is, as a prior actuality [*Wirklichkeit*] qua both existent and possible). Consistent with the immediately preceding, Žižek, in *Absolute Recoil*, remarks, "The key problem is . . . that of the umbilical cord connecting a formal-transcendental structure to its contingent historical content: how is the Real of history inscribed into a structure?"[77]

In connection with Žižek's mention of the topic of history, perhaps the best corroborative instantiation of the just-summarized Hegelian logic of modality in the more-than-logical *Realphilosophie* is to be found in the *Philosophy of History*. Specifically, the last stretch of this text's introduction, a section titled "Geographical Basis of History,"[78] indicates that, for Hegel, the grand arc of human history in its complex, extended entirety arises out of the grounds of factual contingencies, such as the geographical dispersal of different populations and the variations of climate, resources, and the like available to these scattered groups. Before everyone from Marx to Jared Diamond—Plekhanov, among others, holds up the "Geographical Basis of

History" as evidence of Hegel's historical materialist leanings avant la lettre[79]—Hegel already argues that, whatever necessities eventually come to hold sway and be retroactively discernible across sequences of human history, these necessities ultimately, when all is said and done, are secondary results, products of a becoming-necessary, emerging out of primary contingencies qua "the existence of dispersed circumstances (*der Existenz zerstreuter Umstände*)" as "immediate actuality (*unmittelbare Wirklichkeit*)" (section 147)—in this case, dispersed geographical circumstances and the variables these circumstances bring with them. Moreover, to anachronously invoke the Ernst Haeckel of "ontogeny recapitulates phylogeny," the becoming-necessary of the contingent in phylogenetic collective history is mirrored, in Hegel's philosophy, by the same dynamic in ontogenetic individual history, as illustrated by the Faust-inspired figure of "Pleasure and Necessity" in the *Phenomenology of Spirit* (a *Gestalt* springing phoenix-like from the phrenological skull of "Observing Reason").[80]

At this juncture, I want to put forward an argument gathering together what I have traced thus far in terms of the intertwined threads from the *Encyclopedia Logic* (an argument I will further substantiate in connection with the *Science of Logic*). This line of thought might best be introduced through reference to another set of moments in the addition to section 143. This *Zusatz* opens with Hegel forcefully inverting the common misperception according to which possibility is greater than actuality and enjoys priority over it:

> The notion of possibility appears initially to be the richer and more comprehensive determination, and actuality, in contrast, as the poorer and more restricted one. So we say, "Everything is possible, but not everything that is possible is on that account actual too." But, in fact, i.e., in thought, actuality is what is more comprehensive, because, being the concrete thought (*konkrete Gedanke*), it contains possibility within itself as an abstract moment (*abstraktes Moment*). We find this accepted in our ordinary consciousness, too: for when we speak of the possible, as distinct from the actual, we call it "merely" possible (nur *Mögliches*).[81]

He continues with the following paragraph:

> It is usually said that possibility consists generally in thinkability (*Denkbarkeit*). But thinking is here understood to mean just the apprehending of a content in the form of abstract identity (*abstrakten Identität*). Now, since any content can be

brought into this form, providing only that it is separated from the relations in which it stands, even the most absurd and nonsensical suppositions can be considered possible. It is possible that the moon will fall on the earth this evening, for the moon is a body separate from the earth and therefore can fall downward just as easily as a stone that has been flung into the air; it is possible that the Sultan may become Pope, for he is a human being, and as such he can become a convert to Christianity, and then a priest, and so on. Now in all this talk of possibilities it is especially the principle of a "grounding" (*das Denkgesetz vom Grunde*) that is applied.... according to this principle, anything for which a ground (or reason) (*Grund*) can be specified is possible. The more uneducated (*ungebildeter*) a person is, the less he knows about the determinate relations in which the objects that he is considering stand and the more inclined he tends to be to indulge in all manner of empty possibilities (*leeren Möglichkeiten*); we see this, for example, with so-called pub politicians (*Kannengißern*) in the political domain.[82]

There is much to be illuminated in these two paragraphs. To begin with, Hegel deploys a distinction between the "concrete thought (*konkrete Gedanke*)" of actuality and "empty possibilities (*leeren Möglichkeiten*)." *Wirklichkeit* and the concrete thinking of it contain within themselves nonempty possibilities, namely, those possibilities that are made concretely possible by an already-there (as *Dasein*) actuality endowed with the ontological weight of *Existenz*. Such *Wirklichkeit* internally harbors these nonempty possibilities as its own possibilities, as the multiple potential future actualities with real chances (that is, nonnull probabilities) to be actualized in the *à venir* out of the previously actualized. This actuality therefore is a presence embodying not only the or its past and present, but also the or its future specifically in the form of this actual present's own immanently self-generated possibilities as its corresponding not-yets. Actuality's presence shelters within itself its own future as its autoproduced "abstract moment (*abstraktes Moment*)." To go even further, what makes a given actuality the very actuality that it indeed is in the present is, in no small part, what it has the potential to become in the future. All of this is buttressed with a characteristically Hegelian appeal to the (contingent) conventions of "ordinary language."[83] ("We find this accepted in our ordinary consciousness, too: for when we speak of the possible, as distinct from the actual, we call it 'merely' possible [*nur Mögliches*].")

However, with Hegel's mention of "abstract identity (*abstrakten Identität*)"—he here means nothing other than the law of identity (A = A), the recto whose verso is the law of noncontradiction (A ≠ ¬A), the load-bearing pillar of classical, bivalent logic—it is clear that he associates the emptily possible with mere logical possibility alone. Once again, through his references both to the law of identity and to the principle of sufficient reason ("the principle of a 'grounding' [*das Denkgesetz vom Grunde*]"), Hegel evidently is taking yet more swipes at Leibniz.[84] But, as was seen in connection with the *Zusatz* to section 145 of the *Encyclopedia Logic*, Hegel's handling of modalities has critical consequences for certain secular scientific targets in addition to monotheistic religious ones. To be precise, I suspect, because of Hegel's chosen examples, that some of his mockery of the bare thinkability of logical-but-empty possibilities is scorn heaped upon the empiricist David Hume and his confronting of the sciences with the problem of induction.[85] Hegel, for a number of reasons, has a somewhat low estimation of Hume's philosophy,[86] a philosophy inspiring such developments in the late-eighteenth- and early-nineteenth-century German-speaking intellectual milieu that Hegel disliked as Kantian critical-epistemological antirealism and the neo-Humean skepticism of such contemporaries as Maimon and Schulze.

Whether as the immeasurable vastness of the metaphysical reality of countless possible worlds à la the Leibnizian theodicy, the indefinite number of unpredictable future patterns of observed entities and events à la the Humean problem of induction, the wild, free-wheeling sociopolitical hypotheses and predictions of drunk and uninformed barflies (that is, "so-called pub politicians [*Kannengißern*]"), or whatever other imaginative playing upon the basic skeletal structure of logical possibility in its untempered purity (that is, unconstrained by any considerations regarding probability), all instantiations of the simply logically possible count, from Hegel's perspective, as just so many empty possibilities. Their emptiness is due to an emptying from the possible, whether through inadvertent ignorance or intentional neglect, of the possible's determinate contents endowed to it exclusively by virtue of it arising from the concreteness of established actuality. This *Wirklichkeit*, as the extant ground of its corresponding nonempty possibilities, renders a certain number of possibilities, a quantity far short of the incalculably large number of logical possibilities, actually possible (with the actually possible being those "abstract moments" "contained within" [section 143] the concreteness of the actual as the latter's "ownmost" possibilities, to resort to Heideggerian jargon). In other words, the limited number of possibilities projected from and tethered to a given actuality are nonempty thanks to their anchoring in and expression of the actual potentials and probabilities of a really existent, already-there Wirklichkeit. The excessive surplus of the greater number of formal-logical possibilities over and above the significantly lesser number of these concretely real possibilities amounts to the arid, boring expanse of empty, fantastical possibilities never to pass. Like the undisciplined, untrained mind of the inebriated "pub politician"—this is the pathetic, pitiable figure to which all intoxicated speculators foolishly betting upon the unreal prospects of formal-logical possibility alone reduce (whether they be Leibnizians, Humeans, Meillassouxians, or whoever else)—the boundless, sprawling space of the logically possible beyond the confines of the really possible is vacuous and unformed (*ungebildeter*). Both are equally worthy of disregard and dismissal in Hegel's eyes.

Earlier, and in connection specifically with the addition to section 145 of the *Encyclopedia Logic*, I placed a spotlight on Hegel's rendition of necessity as "could only be so and not otherwise (*nicht anders sein Können*)." Now, with the link between actuality and possibility as elaborated in the *Zusatz* to section 143 discussed, the significance of the modality of necessity according to section 145 can be properly explained and appreciated. Given the ground I have already covered here regarding the Hegelian logical doctrine of the modalities, it can be said that *Wirklichkeit* embodies the modality of contingency.[87] It also can be said that such logically primary contingency is the concrete being-there (*Dasein*) out of which grow all real, actual possibilities (as opposed to the superfluous, frivolous limitlessness of empty formal-logical possibilities by themselves). On this basis, Hegelian necessity, as a modality qua logical category, can and should be comprehended as nothing other than the internally differentiated unity formed by the modal ensemble of the actual-qua-contingent and this actuality's correlative actual possibilities. Beyond this pairing of existent (*als Existenz*) contingency and the concretely possible corresponding to and sheltering within it, nothing else or more is possible. That is to say, although there is the wiggle room of the "otherwise" (*anders sein*) within concrete actuality for its multiple accompanying possibilities as nonempty or real—and, for Hegel, every present actuality is itself the actualization of possibilities generated by past actualities—the proliferation of mere logical possibilities in excess of actuality's own possibilities cannot really (come to) be. Put differently, outside the modal pair of contingent actuality and its correlative actual possibilities, "it cannot be otherwise," namely, no other, additional possibilities are really possible. Therefore, if the necessary is the modality of "cannot be otherwise," then, as is done in Hegel's Logic, necessity can be equated with the set constituted by the combination of *Wirklichkeit* and its own possibilities. In terms of modal categories, *Notwendigkeit* is the produced logical outcome resulting from the prior dialectical-speculative synthesis of *Zufälligkeit* (as incarnated by *Wirklichkeit*) and an accompanying *Möglichkeit*.

This specification of Hegelian necessity can be clarified further and certain of its implications indicated through recourse to what arguably amounts to a partial misreading of Hegel's modal doctrine made popular by Engels in particular. (However, unlike Wallace, I do not believe that Engels is guilty of a complete misreading.)[88] In Engels's *Anti-Dühring*, he famously attributes to Hegel the thesis that freedom is simply known necessity (an attribution repeated by others in the Marxist tradition, such as Plekhanov, Nicolai Bukharin, and a somewhat Spinozist Althusser):[89]

> Hegel was the first to state correctly the relation between freedom and necessity. To him, freedom is the appreciation of necessity. "Necessity is *blind* only *in so far as it is not understood*." Freedom does not consist in the dream of independence from natural laws, but in the knowledge of these laws, and in the possibility this gives of systematically making them work towards definite ends. This holds good in relation both to the laws of external nature and to those which govern the bodily and mental existence of men themselves—two classes of laws which we can separate from each other at most only in thought but not in reality. Freedom of the will therefore means nothing but the capacity to make decisions with knowledge of the subject. Therefore the *freer* a man's judgment is in relation to a definite question, the greater is the *necessity* with which the content of this judgment will be determined; while the uncertainty, founded on ignorance, which seems to make an arbitrary choice among many different and conflicting possible decisions, shows precisely by this that it is not free, that it is controlled by the very object it should itself control. Freedom therefore consists in the control over ourselves and over external nature, a control founded on knowledge of natural necessity; it is therefore a product of historical

development. The first men who separated themselves from the animal kingdom were in all essentials as unfree as the animals themselves, but each step forward in the field of culture was a step towards freedom.[90]

With respect to Engels, I will start with the "bad news" first, namely, with the errors in his interpretation of Hegel on freedom and determinism. Although, along with many other readers of Hegel, I agree with Engels that Hegel is indeed some sort of compatibilist on this issue canonically crystallized in the third of Kant's "Antinomies of Pure Reason,"[91] I nevertheless disagree with Engels about what exact sort of compatibilism Hegel's philosophy advances (I discuss compatibilism more in chapter 5).

To begin with, one should notice Engels's unqualified rejection of the very existence of freedom as "arbitrary choice." As he declares in the passage just quoted, "Freedom of the will therefore means nothing but the capacity to make decisions with knowledge of the subject." This "knowledge" is precisely that of natural or historical necessity in terms of the ostensibly inviolable causal laws of nature or history, with dialectical materialism (which combines the natural sciences with a *Naturdialektik* partly inspired by Hegelian *Naturphilosophie*)[92] handling nature's laws (that is, "the laws of external nature") and historical materialism (epitomized by Marx's mature "critique of political economy") handling history's laws (that is, "the laws . . . which govern the bodily and mental existence of men themselves," although these would also involve, at least for Engels, natural laws).[93] A later discussion of "scientific socialism" (itself modeled along the lines of the causal explanatory schemas of the natural sciences) in *Anti-Dühring* testifies to the political importance for Engels of this characterization of Hegelian compatibilism.[94]

Nonetheless, as already seen, particularly with reference to the addition to section 145 of the *Encyclopedia Logic*, Hegel would definitely indict this Engels for failing to "give contingency its due." In that *Zusatz* that I have quoted, Hegel insists upon the objective reality of nonnecessary contingencies within the realms of both *Natur* (with its impotence or weakness [*Ohnmacht*]) and *Geist* (with the arbitrary caprice of "freedom of choice" being explicitly mentioned as an example of spiritual or mental contingency). (Countless other textual instances of Hegel invoking the human will's autonomy qua the subject's spontaneity could be cited against Engels's categorical denial of any relation whatsoever between freedom and contingency in Hegel's thought.)

This Engels is closer to Spinoza than Hegel in that, as does Spinoza's *Ethics*,[95] so too does Engels's *Anti-Dühring* propose that apparent freedom of choice is merely apparent. For both Spinoza and Engels, the strength of the sense of subjective self-determination via reflective deliberation and decision is precisely proportional to the degree of the subject's ignorance of the sum total of causes that converge upon him or her, making him or her think what he or she thinks and do what he or she does. Removal of this ignorance eliminates the purportedly illusory sense of freedom as autonomous, spontaneous willing ("uncertainty, founded on ignorance . . . seems to make an arbitrary choice among many different and conflicting possible decisions").

But, unfortunately for this Engels, Hegel is not Spinoza.[96] By contrast with both Spinozism and the not-unrelated Enlightenment-era natural scientific *Weltanschauung* monopolizing Engels's field of vision, Hegel is not only a compatibilist, but a vehemently antireductive one. (I foreground Hegel's resistances to reductivism, mechanism, and epiphenomenalism on other occasions.)[97] In the quotation from *Anti-Dühring*, Engels, alluding to ideas from his essay "The Part Played by Labour in the Transition from Ape to Man," composed circa 1876 and contained in *Dialectics of Nature*, published in 1883,[98] appears crudely to reduce historical to dialectical materialism (as found in his *Naturdialektik*), and, even worse, to reduce dialectical materialism itself in turn to a flat, deterministic monism scientistically modeled on the image of natural laws as necessary, unbreakable efficient causal connections. ("Two classes of laws which we can separate from each other at most only in thought but not in reality," "the control over ourselves and over external nature, a control founded on knowledge of natural necessity"—I provide a partly sympathetic, partly critical examination of Engels's "dialectics of nature" elsewhere.)[99] Of course, Hegel himself has a dialectical-speculative *Naturphilosophie*, one not without its influences upon Engelsian *Naturdialektik*. Nevertheless, Hegel's Philosophy of Nature does not depict even nature *überhaupt* as determined by the sort of efficient causal necessity envisioned by Engels. Such deterministic necessitation by efficient causes holds for the mechanical and physical regions of natural beings perhaps up to inorganic chemistry, but loses exclusive dominance already within the organic realms of nature that are not yet properly spiritual. Moreover, and still within the *Realphilosophie*, the emergence of *Geist* from *Natur* is precisely a further break, in addition to the objective reality of the final causes of nature-immanent organic structures and dynamics, with the sort of naturalist, scientific determinism or necessitarianism that Engels flirted with.[100]

Additionally, if my preceding interpretations of Hegel's logical framing of modal categories is correct, then Engels's rendition of Hegelian compatibilism bases itself upon a confusion of what Hegel means by "necessity" in the Logic with necessity as efficient causal determinism à la the empirical, experimental sciences of nature. For Hegel, the latter would be, at most, merely one real-philosophical species of the logical genus of necessity per se qua the bonds between an actuality and its nonempty possibilities. Furthermore, with Hegelian necessity, although there is no possibility for an "otherwise" beyond this necessity (that is, no other possibilities, such other possibilities being empty qua purely formal-logical), there is, within this necessity, nevertheless a spectrum of actual possibilities "otherwise" in comparison both with each other and with the existent actuality from which they spring. Within Hegel's Logic, Organics, and Philosophy of Mind/Spirit (that is, every portion of his encyclopedic System save for the Mechanics and Physics of the Philosophy of Nature), necessity cannot be, as Engels appears to do, squeezed and collapsed into rigid, narrow channels of one-to-one necessary connections between single causes and correlated single effects. (Hegel says precisely this near the conclusion of "The Doctrine of Essence" in the *Science of Logic*.)[101] Instead, all that is necessary is a connection between a given actuality and its plurality of corresponding real possibilities. Especially for minded and like-minded human agents, there is plenty of elbow room, space for free decisions and deeds however contingently arbitrary or noncontingently principled, both between the actual and its possibilities and among these multiple actual possibilities. Therefore, contra the Engelsian interpretation, to know Hegelian necessity is not to know scientific determinism. Rather, it is to know (1) how to distinguish in the past and present between actuality (*Wirklichkeit*) and mere being-there/existence (*Dasein/Existenz*) and (2) what future possibilities this thus-discerned actuality really does and does not make possible (that is, the difference between nonempty and empty possibilities respectively, with the former as more than just logical possibilities alone). If, in Hegel's doctrine of the modalities, *Notwendigkeit* equals *Wirklichkeit als Zufälligkeit* plus corresponding *Möglichkeit*, then this necessity is far from deterministically necessitarian.

Select examples from Hegel's corpus, ones Engels undoubtedly has in mind as supporting his (mis)interpretation of Hegel, can and should be reread in light of my preceding exegetical proposals. In particular, I am thinking of Hegel's several references to "world-historical individuals" (that is, major history-forming actors, such as Napoleon) in connection with his interrelated conceptions of freedom and the modalities.[102] Hegel and Engels concur that such individuals achieve their undying greatness on the stage of humanity's history only insofar as they act according to, and not in defiance of, "necessity." Those who defy such "necessity" are swiftly overwhelmed and swept aside by it into the dustbin of historical anonymity, achieving little or nothing (and certainly not everlasting fame).

However, Hegel and Engels, despite the latter's confusion to the contrary, do not agree on the very meaning of the word *necessity* here. In Engelsian "scientific socialism," the historically necessary amounts to a single causal pathway running from the past to the future through the present and deterministically brooking no deviations from its one and only trajectory. Here, the "freedom" of world-historical individuals is that, by virtue of scientific socialism (that is, historical materialism as a "science of history" modeled on the natural sciences, with both right-wing [for example, Second International economism] and left-wing [for example, Stalinist *diamat*] deviant versions), they know the laws of history and its unique fated teleology. Thus, they are "free" to attain legendary immortality by, thanks to their knowledge, being able to participate in the invincible march forward of History-with-a-capital-H.

By contrast, in Hegelian absolute idealism properly conceived, the historically necessary amounts to multiple pathways running from, on one side, a contingent, factical actuality (*Wirklichkeit*) given by the past and present to, on another side, a plurality (limited but plural) of real, nonempty possibilities potentially actualizable on the basis of the already-there, status quo actuality. Hence, in however consciously or unconsciously knowing the necessary as the combination of the actual and the possible, Hegel's world-historical individual, unlike Engels's, does not know inviolable, unbreakable causal fatalism, but, instead, the actually realistic scope for successfully acting in various freely chosen ways such as to bring about a desired outcome in a subsequent actuality *à venir*. This Hegelian individual explicitly or implicitly comprehends, first, what elements of the present are actual and what elements are merely existent and, second (and based on this first comprehension), what really is and is not possible on the basis of the current actuality. Unlike in Engelsian deterministic compatibilism (as pseudo-Hegelian), different individuals, in Hegelian nondeterministic compatibilism, have varying, albeit far from limitless, degrees of room for subjectively spontaneous maneuvering within and between past, present, and future.

Yet there still remains some "good news" for Engels and those that follow him. As I already indicated, I do not believe Engels is 100 percent wrong in his interpretation of freedom and necessity in Hegel's philosophy. To begin with, although Hegel would not accept Engels's reduction of necessity solely to the kind of necessitation paradigmatically operative in the efficient causal laws of inorganic nature, he nonetheless grants that this kind of necessitation is indeed one of the species (within *Realphilosophie*) of the genus necessity (as itself a modal category of *Logik*). Especially when Hegel describes human labor in relation to its natural environment (with labor and nature being topics dear to Engels as both a historical and a dialectical materialist), he indicates that part of the cunning of human reason involves making nonhuman natural forces and factors work on behalf of human interests.[103] In particular, the modern empirical, experimental sciences of nature standing under Bacon's shadow assemble a knowledge—the "knowledge of natural necessity" qua "product of historical development" of which Engels speaks in *Anti-Dühring*—translating into a technological know-how through which, as Bacon has it, knowledge is power.[104] For Hegel and Engels, this power is humanity's freedom specifically as the ability of human beings to actively bend nature to their wills, to have their purposes realized in and through it, rather than passively be overpowered and broken by their indifferent material surroundings. At least as regards modernity's scientific savoir and technological savoir faire, Hegel likely would endorse, albeit with caveats and qualifications, Engels's notion of freedom as known necessity.

At the start of the block quotation from *Anti-Dühring*, Engels himself quotes a line from the *Zusatz* to section 147 of the *Encyclopedia Logic*— "Necessity is *blind* only *in so far as it is not understood*" ("*Blind ist die Notwendigkeit nur, insofern dieselbe nicht begriffen wird*").[105] Ironically, in the remarks coming immediately after this line, Hegel proceeds to pointedly rebuke those who would accuse his Philosophy of History of being in any way fatalistic,[106] something for which Engels incorrectly praises him. That said, Engels is correct in claiming that, within Hegel's philosophy, the necessary, in transitioning from the metaphysical status of the nonconscious *an sich* (that is, in itself qua implicit and blind) to that of the (self-)conscious *an und für sich* (that is, in and for itself qua explicit and sighted), is *aufgehoben* into the free. In this same vein, Hegel, in the addition to section 158 of the *Encyclopedia Logic*, stipulates that, "to be sure, necessity as such is not yet freedom; but freedom presupposes necessity and contains it sublated within itself" ("*Allerdings ist die Notwendigkeit als solche noch nicht die Freiheit; aber die Freiheit hat die Notwendigkeit zu ihrer Voraussetzung und enthält dieselbe als aufgehoben in sich*").[107] Likewise, the *Science of Logic* speaks of "*free necessity*" ("*freie Notwendigkeit*").[108]

Again, the difference between Hegel and Engels here is that, for the former, the various necessities that can and do come to be known (and, thereby, shift from impeding to facilitating the exercise of freedom) are far from reducible to the necessity embodied by the efficient causal laws of nonliving mechanical or physical nature. By contrast with the deterministic narrowness of Engelsian necessity, Hegelian necessity's broadness encompasses multiple species of organic and spiritual relations between actualities and their correlative possibilities in addition to the one-to-one cause-and-effect couplings epitomized by the laws of mechanics and physics. However, this difference aside, Hegel agrees with Engels (and Bacon too) that scientific knowledge and technological know-how in relation to the mechanical and physical objects and processes of the inorganic world governed by efficient causality indeed allow for individual and collective human agencies to realize their self-determined aims, ends, and goals in and through these very objects and processes. Furthermore, for both Engels-the-materialist and Hegel-the-protomaterialist, there would simply not be such human agencies in the first place without mechanical and physical nature (that is, no organics without inorganics and no mindedness or spiritedness without organics).[109]

I have one last comment to make regarding Engels before proceeding further. With reference again to the quotation from *Anti-Dühring*, Engels there acknowledges that scientific *savoir* (that is, Engels's "knowledge of natural necessity") "is ... a product of historical development." His fashion of recognizing this suggests an associative resonance with Marx's famous one-liner from the *Grundrisse*: "human anatomy contains a key to the anatomy of the ape."[110] For this Marx and this Engels alike, advents of new knowledges (whether in the natural or social sciences) sometimes give rise to certain benefits of hindsight. In the case of the Marx of the *Grundrisse*, the eighteenth-century emergence of the discipline of political economy enables not only a grasp of contemporaneous industrial capitalism itself (that is, "human anatomy"), but also, belatedly, an after-the-fact comprehension of the precapitalist sequences of human history (that is, "the anatomy of the ape").

Similarly, in the case of the Engels of *Anti-Dühring*, the natural sciences of modernity come to make known not only nature's necessities (that is, its efficient causal laws) in the modern era, but also, retroactively, these necessities as having been in force throughout all of premodern history too. For Marx, the capitalism-induced birth of the knowledge that is historical materialism permits the prior, blindly lived "necessity" of socioeconomic "history hitherto," as a nonconscious, alienated *an sich*, to be transubstantiated into the unprecedented "freedom" of a history *à venir*, as a self-conscious, nonalienated *an und für sich*. This transpires via the genesis of proletarian class consciousness and its actualization in and through the socialist revolution leading eventually to communism as a classless society of socially cooperative producers collaboratively shaping their own historical development. For Engels, the historical-materialist-induced birth of the knowledge that is dialectical materialism (itself conditioned by both capitalism and the modern sciences of nature) permits the prior, blindly lived "necessity" of both natural forces and the sociohistorical evolution of the natural sciences to be transubstantiated likewise into a historically unprecedented socialist or communist "freedom."

On this point too, Engels again achieves a proximity to Hegel. In Hegel's terms, the historical advances of modernity's empirical, experimental sciences of nature, with their technological offspring, represent at the level of "objective spirit" (that is, institutionally and instrumentally actualized human like-mindedness) the progress through history of *Geist* in its greater and greater realization of its own freedom, including as increasingly free from *Natur* and with increasing power over it. As Engels puts this at the end of the quotation from *Anti-Dühring*, "each step forward in the field of culture was a step towards freedom" (with "culture" here designating scientific and technological culture as the products of socioeconomic objective spirit).

Finally, before turning to Hegel's treatment of modalities in the *Science of Logic*, an additional extra-Hegelian reference (besides the one to the Engels of *Anti-Dühring*) promises to make even more tangible my preceding interpretation of the triad of actuality, possibility, and necessity as it appears primarily in the *Encyclopedia Logic*. I have in mind Freud's notorious one-liner declaring, in a paraphrase of Napoleon, that "Anatomy is destiny" (*Die*

Anatomie ist das Schicksal).[111] Žižek himself, in both *Less Than Nothing* and *Absolute Recoil*, proposes a Hegelian reading of this declaration as a "speculative judgment" in which the "truth" of the subject-term is to be found in (that is, entirely "passes over" into) the predicate-term. According to Žižek, the truth of biological, organic anatomy, what it truly amounts to, is extra-biological, more-than-organic destiny.[112] Without in the least contesting this Žižekian gloss, I want to offer a different Hegelian take on Freud's "*Die Anatomie ist das Schicksal*," one that distinctly clarifies this Freud as well as further illuminates Hegel's modal doctrine.

Hegelian actuality and possibility can be associated with Freudian anatomy and destiny, respectively. In this association, Hegel and Freud share in common, contrary to widespread, prevailing misunderstandings and caricatures of these two figures, rejections of mechanistic materialisms, reductive naturalisms, scientistic determinisms, and the like. In Hegel's logic of modal categories, as already witnessed, a given actuality tends to generate a bandwidth of multiple corresponding real possibilities; Hegelian necessity is nothing other than the whole formed by an actuality and its accompanying possibilities. Likewise, in Freud's metapsychology of libidinal life, a given anatomy (as the contingency of a bodily *Wirklichkeit*) tends to generate a bandwidth of multiple corresponding real destinies. However, by contrast with the English *destiny*, the German *Schicksal* does not automatically connote the deterministic necessitarianism of fate, instead allowing for a plurality, albeit constrained, of possible courses of subsequent vicissitudes. Hence, Freudian *Schicksal* is indeed an instantiation of Hegelian *Möglichkeit*. Therefore, the "necessity" of Freud's "destiny" is no more fatalistic, in an allegedly vulgar biologistic fashion, than Hegel's *Notwendigkeit* accurately construed.

The moment has finally arrived for examining the modal categories as they feature in Hegel's *Science of Logic*. My focus in what follows will be on "The Doctrine of Essence," "Section Three: Actuality," "Chapter 2: Actuality." This specific chapter is divided into three main subsections: "A. Contingency, or Formal Actuality, Possibility, and Necessity" (*Zufälligkeit oder formelle Wirklichkeit, Möglichkeit und Notwendigkeit*); "B. Relative Necessity, or Real Actuality, Possibility, and Necessity" (*Relative Notwendigkeit oder reale Wirklichkeit, Möglichkeit und Notwendigkeit*); and, "C. Absolute Necessity" (*Absolute Notwendigkeit*). On the basis of the table of contents alone, one can readily see that, for Hegel, contingency precedes necessity, with the "absolute" version of the latter being a late outcome or result (rather than an eternally preexistent alpha, beginning, or origin) of the dialectical-speculative dynamics of *reale Wirklichkeit*, itself arising out of *Zufälligkeit*. In this vein, Žižek remarks that, "necessity is ... nothing but the 'truth' of contingency, contingency brought to its truth by way of its (self-)negation."[113]

In "A. Contingency, or Formal Actuality, Possibility, and Necessity," Hegel directly links the dialectical-speculative relations between actuality and possibility with those between contingency and necessity. Referring specifically to the "two determinations" of actuality and possibility (in which the latter is coemergent with the being-there/existence [*Dasein/Existenz*] of the former in its contingent, immediate givenness), Hegel states: "This *absolute unrest* of the *becoming* (*Diese* absolute Unruhe *des* Werdens) of these two determinations is *contingency* (Zufälligkeit). But just because each immediately turns into its opposite (*jede unmittelbar in die entgegengesetzte umschlägt*), equally in this other it simply *unites with itself* (mit sich *selbst* zusammen), and this identity (Identität) of both, of one in the other, is *necessity* (Notwendigkeit)."[114] One could say that the determinations of *Wirklichkeit* and *Möglichkeit* are doubly contingent. First, as I already observed in connection with the *Encyclopedia Logic*, the actual itself is fundamentally a contingency as a merely possible being-there that also happens to exist. Second, no single one of the multiple real possibilities generated and contained within a given actuality is itself necessary qua destined or fated to be the one and only next actuality produced out of the current actuality as the latter's successor moment. Any one of the plurality of nonempty possibilities, as possible future actualities bound up with a present actuality, could contingently become the subsequently realized actuality.

As Hegel has it, *Wirklichkeit* and *Möglichkeit* are "opposites" qua complimentary pair of mutually entangled dialectical determinations. Additionally, they are enrichments of the logical category of Becoming (*Werden*). Of course, Becoming famously surfaces near the very beginning of the main body of the Logic, doing so precisely as the *Aufhebung* of the first two moments of "The Doctrine of Being," namely, Being (*Sein*) and Nothing (*Nichts*).[115] The much later logical moment of "Actuality" near the conclusion of "The Doctrine of Essence" retroactively adds to Becoming modal determinations. In the quotation, *Werden* acquires as characteristics the modalities of possibility, contingency, and necessity. What is more, this modally enriched Becoming (that is, the "*absolute unrest* of the *becoming* [*Diese* absolute Unruhe *des* Werdens]" in the passage just quoted) is one involving the two determinations or moments of actuality and possibility. There, "each immediately turns into its opposite (*jede unmittelbar in die entgegengesetzte umschlägt*)" insofar as (1) a current actuality becomes a subsequent actuality by transitioning into one of the actual possibilities it already harbors within itself and (2) possibilities ceaselessly transition into being actualities in and through the perpetual movement (that is, "absolute unrest") where posterior actualities continually take shape out of prior ones. In short, actuality passes over into possibility (with this possibility thereby becoming the new, next actuality) and possibility passes over into actuality (with this actuality producing in and through itself further possibilities). More succinctly stated still, the actual becomes the possible and vice versa. Even if I put aside temporal connotations that always risk being problematic in relation to Hegel's Logic in its strict logical abstractness, the categorial determinations of actuality and possibility structurally imply each other within the Hegelian framework. Every actuality is itself an actualization of a possibility. And every possibility in Hegel's precise sense (that is, as real or non-empty qua more than simply a formal issue of mere logical possibility alone) is tied to an extant actuality making this possibility an actual possibility. With Hegelian actuality and possibility thus conceptualized, the one essentially and necessarily entails the other.

Last, as Hegel stipulates at the close of the preceding quotation from the *Science of Logic*, necessity is the "identity (Identität)" (specifically as a dialectical-speculative unity via sublation) of actuality and possibility. That is to say, the necessary is the *Aufhebung*-attained identity-of-identity-and-difference between the actual and the possible. In yet other words, necessity preserves the distinction between actuality and possibility while being nothing other than what results from the interminable restlessness of the passage of *Wirklichkeit* and *Möglichkeit* into each other (this passage being the immanent dialectics of the actual and the possible, their self-subversion as autosublation). But, as I already stressed regarding the *Encyclopedia Logic*, Hegelian *Notwendigkeit* is nothing more or other than this, namely, the contingency-ridden relations between actualities and their accompanying limited-but-open plethoras of possibilities. Along these precise lines, it bears repeating that necessity à la Hegel is, contrary to countless caricatures, anything but a metaphysically real predestination flawlessly manifesting itself as a unique, contingency-free fate, teleology, or theodicy.

The title of the second subsection of "Chapter 2: Actuality" of "Section Three: Actuality" of "The Doctrine of Essence" in the *Science of Logic* clearly contrasts with that of the preceding subsection of this same chapter. Whereas subsection "A" deals with "Contingency, or Formal Actuality, Possibility, and Necessity," subsection "B" deals instead with "Relative Necessity, or Real Actuality, Possibility, and Necessity." Obviously, the "formally actual" as contingent now has become the "really actual" as "relatively necessary," with the three logical categories of actuality, possibility, and necessity shifting from being "formal" to being "real." As formal, the three dimensions of contingent actuality, possibility, and necessity are not really distinguished from one another. Subsection "A," as I explained earlier, makes clear that contingent actuality and possibility are ultimately identical, with this identity being necessity itself. Minus the reality of any content, there is nothing to realize the formal differences between these modalities in subsection "A." But now in subsection "B," the addition of the reality of content enables the implicit formal differences between modalities to become explicit real differences. With a really existent content, the actuality of this content as present can be seen to be distinct from any of its not-(yet-)present possibilities.[116]

With an eye already to the third and final subsection ("C. Absolute Necessity") of "Chapter 2: Actuality," a focus on necessity in subsection "B" is an appropriate reflection of the dialectical-speculative transition, the very movement of *Wirklichkeit* itself, from contingency to absolute necessity. Discussing real necessity, Hegel specifies that "this necessity is . . . *relative*. For it has a *presupposition* from which it begins, it has its *starting point* in the *contingent*" ("*Diese Notwendigkeit . . . ist . . .* relative. *—Sie hat nämlich eine* Voraussetzung, *von der sie anfängt, sie hat an dem* Zufälligen *ihren* Ausgangspunkt").[117] Insofar as necessity is the result of the relationship between contingent actuality and the latter's accompanying possibilities—the necessary presupposes the combination of the contingently actual and the actually possible—it is "relative" to *Wirklichkeit* as itself, at least initially, contingent.

Hegel proceeds to posit that "in point of fact real necessity is *in itself* also contingency. . . . Real necessity . . . contains contingency" ("*In der Tat ist . . . die* reale Notwendigkeit an sich *auch* Zufälligkeit. . . . *Die reale Notwendigkeit enthält . . . die Zufälligkeit*").[118] He soon adds that "Here, therefore, the unity of necessity and contingency is present *in itself* or *in principle*; this unity is to be called *absolute actuality*" ("*An sich ist also hier die Einheit der Notwendigkeit und Zufälligkeit vorhanden; diese Einheit ist die* absolute Wirklichkeit *zu*

CONTINGENCY, PURE CONTINGENCY

nennen").[119] As I elucidated much earlier here when discussing both section 147 of the *Encyclopedia Logic* and the "Geographical Basis of History" in the introduction to the *Philosophy of History*, contingency, as the *Ur*-modality-of-modalities, sets in motion the *"absolute unrest* of the *becoming"* in which actuality and possibility constantly pass over into each other. The contingent thereby self-sublates by immanently generating out of itself *"absolute actuality"* as necessary insofar as nothing other than this *absolute Wirklichkeit* is possible. Put differently, no possibilities for things being "otherwise" than this actuality beyond the nonempty, more-than-formal or more-than-logical possibilities already contained within *Wirklichkeit* are truly possible. This particular "cannot be otherwise" is Hegelian real necessity, which, as an outcome or product of the interrelations between actuality and possibility primordially activated and launched by contingency, "contains contingency" as this necessity's basis that is sublated but impossible to expunge altogether, the groundless ground of its originary factical givenness ineliminably preserved in whatever *Aufhebung* it undergoes.[120]

Hegel succinctly reiterates the immediately preceding at the very start of "C. Absolute Necessity,"[121] the sub-section bringing "Chapter 2: Actuality" to a close. He goes on to characterize absolute necessity thusly—"It is, *because it is*. . . . It has only itself for ground and condition. It is the in-itself, but its in-itself is its immediacy, its possibility is its actuality. *It is, therefore, because it is*" ("*es ist*, weil *es ist*. . . . *es hat nur sich zum Grunde und Bedingung. Es ist Ansichsein, aber sein Ansichsein ist seine Unmittelbarkeit, seine Möglichkeit ist seine Wirklichkeit.—Es ist also, weil es ist*").[122] Hegel's depiction of *absolute Notwendigkeit* here already suggests what is emphatically emphasized two paragraphs later, in the penultimate paragraph of subsection "C": With the absolute of necessity (or also the necessity of the Absolute), a dialectical-speculative "convergence of opposites" transpires in which *Ur*-contingency is *Ur*-necessity and *vice versa*. As that penultimate paragraph states:

> this *contingency* is . . . absolute necessity; it is the *essence* (Wesen) of those free, inherently necessary actualities *(freien, an sich notwendigen Wirklichkeiten)*. This essence is *light-shy* (Lichtscheue), because there is in these actualities no *reflective movement* (Scheinen), no reflex, because they are grounded purely in themselves alone (*nur rein in sich gegründet*), are shaped for themselves (*für sich gestaltet sind*), and manifest themselves only to *themselves*, because they are only *being* (Sein). . . . Contingency is absolute necessity, it is itself the presupposing of that

first, absolute actuality (*sie selbst ist das Voraussetzen jener ersten absoluten Wirklichkeiten*).[123]

So, contingency is not only the first of the modalities to be introduced in Hegel's Logic; it returns as (part of) the last of the modalities (that is, absolute necessity) too. Thus, contingency is, in a certain sense, genuinely both the alpha and the omega of the modal categories of Hegelian *Logik*.

Any necessity (whether formal, real, or absolute) is a subsequent result arising from or supervening on a prior contingency—specifically, a merely possible actuality just so happening to also enjoy being-there/existence. As Žižek maintains along these lines, "Hegel is ... the ultimate thinker of autopoeisis, of the process of the emergence of necessary features out of chaotic contingency, the thinker of contingency's gradual self-organization, of the gradual rise of order out of chaos."[124] Such necessity sublates but, as is the well-known nature of Hegel's *Aufhebung*, does not negate entirely and without remainder this always-already-there contingency to which necessity remains tethered.[125] (As Hegel puts it in the previous quotation, "absolute necessity ... is itself the presupposing of that first, absolute actuality," with this always-prior *absolute Wirklichkeit* incarnating ineliminable Urcontingency.) Furthermore, every necessity, even when "absolute" (this absoluteness can be construed as referring to primordial origins, unsurpassable horizons, absence of an otherwise, or lack of any Beyond/Outside), confronts thinking, when all is said and done, with a spade-turning "it is, because it is." In *Less Than Nothing*, Žižek employs the necessity embodied by scientific laws of nature, the efficient causal necessitation of predictable concatenations of natural entities and events, as examples of the contingency of necessity qua "it is, because it is,"[126] and he also equates Hegelian nature with the "*contingency of necessity*" (by contrast with Hegelian freedom as the "*necessity of contingency*," namely, the becoming-necessary through consequent ontogenetic and phylogenetic vicissitudes of initially nonnecessary, notfated decisions and deeds).[127] This tautology expresses the convergence of opposites in which this convergence, rather than being an equal, balanced synthesis between the opposed modalities of contingency and necessity, lopsidedly favors contingency. "It is, because it is" articulates the ultimate contingency of necessity. As Žižek's *Less Than Nothing* words it, "it is contingency itself which encompasses both itself and necessity."[128] Likewise, the Hegelian Absolute *überhaupt* (obviously invoked as part of the phrase *absolute necessity*), whatever else it might be, is also just such a coincidence of the apparently contradictory modal determinations of contingency and necessity.

Finally, Hegel cautions that this dialectical-speculative identification of the absolutely necessary with the contingent is *"light-shy* (Lichtscheue)." He indicates that this has to do with the fact that absolute necessity, as absolute, is self-grounding ("necessary actualities . . . are grounded purely in themselves alone [*nur rein in sich gegründet*], are shaped for themselves [*für sich gestaltet sind*], and manifest themselves only to *themselves*"). The notion of self-grounding is shrouded in obscurity precisely because of its dialectical ambiguity. On the one hand, the self-grounded is grounded insofar as it supplies itself with a ground. On the other hand, the self-grounded is groundless insofar as it rests on nothing beyond, behind, or beneath itself. In the Hegelian System, absolute necessity specifically and the Absolute generally, in their shared lack, given their absoluteness, of any Other or Externality, involve this ambiguous combination of being simultaneously with and without ground qua reason: "with why" (*mit Warum*) as autojustifying and self-supporting (that is, with a base of grounded necessity), but, at the same time, also "without why" (*ohne Warum*) as unjustified and unsupported (that is, with a baselessness of groundless contingency).[129]

For the black-and-white vision of the understanding (*Verstand*), with its congenital blindness to the colors of reason (*Vernunft*), the ambiguities of absoluteness are difficult, if not impossible, to discern (that is, these ambiguities are "light-shy").[130] They are really there nonetheless. Here, the Hegelian circle closes, with the Absolute rejoining the *"Being, pure Being, without any further determination"* ("*Sein, reines Sein,—ohne alle weiterer Bestimmung*")[131] of the very start of the System at the (apparent) beginning of the Logic (an opening line highlighted and appropriated by the recent Žižek).[132] As Düsing states, "the third, the synthesis, is in truth the first, the original unity; or: the beginning is the result."[133] Or, as Marcuse rightly maintains, "contingency is the final and deepest character of all being."[134] Hence, the Absolute of Being or the Being of the Absolute resultantly have turned out to be, in truth, *Contingency, pure Contingency*—without any further determination.

At long last, the time has come to circumnavigate back to Žižek's rendition of Hegelianism as a dialectical materialism of *Ur*-contingency (that is, a sort of proto-Althusserian aleatory materialism of the encounter avant la lettre). I hope that my preceding reconstruction of Hegel's logical doctrine of the modal categories has succeeded at making the privileging of contingency in Hegelian philosophy by Žižek and certain other Hegel interpreters highly plausible and readily defensible. If nothing else, this reconstruction shifts the burden of proof squarely onto the shoulders of all those who would cling stubbornly to doubts about the centrality of the contingent in Hegel's System, namely, those who would persist in portraying Hegel as a pre-Kantian wolf (or "Wolff" à la the Leibnizianism of Wolff) in post-Kantian clothing (that is, a theosopher of divine necessitation, a metaphysical realist about a transcendent destiny, and so on). I believe myself to have shown that Žižek stands on solidly Hegelian terra firma when asserting that "necessity is itself grounded in a contingency."[135]

Equipped with the Hegelian resources that I have assembled, I want to now examine Žižek's handling of, in relation to Hegel, the immensely important topic of teleology. Žižek addresses things (allegedly) teleological in Hegelianism mainly at the real-philosophical (that is, more-than-logical) level of history. *Less Than Nothing*, in the context of contrasting Hegel's philosophy as self-avowedly blind to the future (à la the Owl of Minerva) with Marx's historical materialism as a "science of history" purportedly possessing predictive powers,[136] observes that "historical Necessity does not pre-exist the contingent process of its actualization, that is . . . the historical process is also in itself 'open,' undecided."[137] Žižek continues: "This is how one should read Hegel's thesis that, in the course of the dialectical development, things 'become what they are': it is not that a temporal deployment merely actualizes some pre-existing atemporal conceptual structure—this atemporal conceptual structure is itself the result of contingent temporal decisions."[138]

These remarks, consistent with Hegel himself, amount to insisting that historical structures and dynamics as in *Geschichtsphilosophie* as a branch of *Realphilosophie* indeed instantiate the structures and dynamics of the modal categories as in *Logik* (as least according to my readings of the *Science of Logic* and *Encyclopedia Logic*). In line with Hegel's depiction of the necessary as a subsequent result qua outcome or product immanently generated out of the contingent, Žižek stresses, "*if*, due to contingency, a story emerges at the end, *then* this story will appear as necessary. Yes, the story is necessary, but its necessity is itself contingent."[139] This echoes Hegel's "it is, because it is" of "absolute necessity" in the *Science of Logic*. This also suggests that there is an unavoidable and inescapable "necessary illusion" (to risk using a Kantian phrase) for the backward glance of the philosopher of history, making it such that the sequence of historical actualities leading from the past up through the present always must appear to this glance as necessary. The *hic et nunc* would not be what it is had history been otherwise; for any given historical present to be the present that it is, its historical past is necessary qua "cannot be otherwise."[140] A couple of pages later, Žižek adds, "The Hegelian dialectical process is not this 'saturated,' self-contained, necessary Whole, but the *open and contingent process through which such a Whole forms itself.*"[141] Again, this "Whole," whether as the Absolute, necessity, or whatever else along these Hegelian lines, is an omega rather than an alpha, an effect rather than a cause.

At the same moment in *Less Than Nothing*, Žižek inserts the stipulation that the kinetic interactions between contingency and necessity in Hegelian history also involve retroactions of the present and future upon the past.[142] He then connects this historical *Nachträglichkeit/après-coup* with a critique of the pretensions of certain Marxist materialists to enjoy powers of foresight into the *à venir*:

> Does Hegel's thought harbor such an openness towards the future, or does the closure of his System a priori preclude it? In spite of misleading appearances, we should answer yes, Hegel's thought is open towards the future, but precisely on account of its closure. That is to say, Hegel's opening towards the future is a *negative*: it is articulated in his negative/limiting statements like the famous "one cannot jump ahead of one's time" from his *Philosophy of Right*. The impossibility of directly borrowing from the future is grounded in the very fact of retroactivity which makes the future a priori unpredictable: we cannot climb onto our own shoulders and see ourselves "objectively," in terms of the way we fit into the texture of history, because this texture is again and again retroactively rearranged.[143]

With this reference to Hegel's "*Hic* Rhodus, *hic* saltus" from the preface to *Elements of the Philosophy of Right*,[144] Žižek makes two interesting moves. First, he maintains that retroactive temporality is the specific factor to blame for the Hegelian philosopher's avowed congenital blindness to the yet-to-come. In Žižek's account, the after-the-fact, deferred action of the present and future on the past is precisely what dictates the impossibility of leaping forward through foresight into a God's-eye, view-from-nowhere, end-of-time perspective on "objective history," whatever that would be.

Second, Žižek rebuts a woefully commonplace story—according to which Hegel hubristically promotes a delusional "theory of everything" enclosing all of reality under the sun in a fixed and frozen necessitarian framework—by turning the particular feature prompting the narration of this story (that is, the [apparent] closure of the Hegelian System) into the very means of refuting it. To be more exact, Žižek's tactic appropriately mobilizes a dialectical-speculative convergence of opposites in which the closed and the open coincide with each other. In this case regarding Hegel's philosophy of history, the totalizing closure of the past enacted by the present (that is, by the flight of the Owl of Minerva on a given evening) necessarily cannot but leave unseen and untouched the openness of the future (that is, the dawn of the next day). The closed character of systematic *Geschichtsphilosophie* simultaneously signals the insurmountably, indissolubly open character of the *à venir*. Another favorite Žižekian reference hovers in the wings here: the Lacanian analyst Octave Mannoni's famous encapsulation of the logic of fetishistic disavowal (that is, Freudian *Verleugnung*)[145] with the line *"je sais bien, mais quand même . . ."* ("I know full well, but nonetheless . . .").[146] In this instance, Hegel is not so much "the most sublime of hysterics" (as Žižek has put it on multiple other occasions), but rather the most sublime of fetishists. That is to say, Žižek's version of the Hegelian philosopher of history knows full well (that the yet-to-come is unpredictably open, that this invisible future will retroactively alter the visible past and present, that the current closure of the systematized historical whole will be shattered and reconfigured by the *à venir*, that seeming historical necessities are both created and destroyed by contingencies, and so on) but nonetheless . . . (remembers the past in a present totalizing recollection, recounts the progressive march forward of rational world history, discerns with hindsight prior teleological trajectories necessitating in advance the contemporary conjuncture . . .).

At this point, I wish to voice some Hegelian reservations (stemming from my earlier exegeses of Hegel's texts) about these two admittedly innovative and insightful maneuvers by Žižek. To begin with, I think that Hegel might object to Žižek's insistence that temporal retroactivity is the particular cause responsible for rendering "the future a priori unpredictable." Why? Ultimately, this has to do with the fundamental architectonic of Hegel's System. This System, whose nucleus is formed by the entirety of the *Encyclopedia of the Philosophical Sciences*, is divided into *Logik* and *Realphilosophie*, the latter being subdivided into *Naturphilosophie* and *Geistesphilosophie*. For Hegel, *Geschichtsphilosophie* is a branch of *Geistesphilosophie*. The constellations and motions of historical temporality in which retroactivity features centrally—again, they are what Žižek appeals to as resulting in the future's constitutive unpredictability—are ingredients of *Geschichtsphilosophie*.

Thus, in Hegelian eyes, Žižek is in danger of riding roughshod over Hegel's distinction between Logic and the Philosophy of the Real. The more-than-categorial concept of time per se (initially as objectively real time in pre- or nonspiritual nature) does not come on the systematic scene for Hegel until the beginning of *Realphilosophie*, specifically as the second moment of *Naturphilosophie*.[147] Properly human historical time, as yet another, even richer more-than-categorial concept, does not arise in the System until the penultimate subdivision of the entire *Encyclopedia*, namely, "Section II: Mind Objective" (*Der objektive Geist*) of the *Philosophy of Mind*.[148]

The crucial upshot in this context is that, in light of these architectonic considerations, Hegel would likely contend, *pace* Žižek, that the non-/pretemporal and a-/transhistorical interrelations between the logical categories of the modalities are the ultimate *Ur*-cause of the a priori unpredictability of the future.[149] In particular, the pivotal place of contingency both at the (baseless) base of actuality and between actuality and actuality's own possibilities—and, as both Hegel and Žižek maintain, any necessity is only ever a secondary consequence of these other, more foundational modalities—means that no one possibility or set of possibilities, as not-yet-but-potentially-actual, can be deemed necessary along predictable, deterministic lines. Insofar as the historical temporalities of objective spirit (*objektive Geist*) are, as are all things in Hegelian *Realphilosophie*, essentially and immanently formed by absolute idealism's categories, the unforeseeable nature of the future vis-à-vis the past and the present is an effect or manifestation of the logical modalities.

Exclusively thereby, at the level of *Logik*, is one entitled to uphold, as Žižek does, a specifically a priori (qua transhistorical) status for the future's antifatalistic defiance of predictions. Yet Žižek, as seen, implicitly inverts the Hegelian order of priority between Logic and the Philosophy of the Real (an inversion in line with Lenin and the Soviets,[150] despite Žižek's explicit taking of distance from this non-Western branch of dialectical materialism, as I discuss in chapter 4). He identifies the temporal retroaction of future history as the cause and basis of the nonnecessity arguably central to Hegel's

System precisely as (according to Žižek himself, among others) a philosophy of contingency par excellence. Incidentally, Hegel's treatment of the categories of cause and effect—in "The Doctrine of Essence," this treatment, in which an effect causes its cause to be a cause,[151] follows on the heels of the discussion of the modalities—constitutes a logical condition for the real-philosophical retroaction of human historical time (doing so along with the dialectical-speculative logic of contingency and necessity).

Even if I set aside the question of whether and when one should remain faithful to whatever counts as the best reconstruction of Hegel's thinking at present, an authentic debate could indeed be had about the pros and cons of Žižek's tacit reversal of relations between *Logik* and *Realphilosophie* (a reversal in which, as just witnessed, logical categories are the by-products, rather than essential forms, of historical processes). That said, I strongly suspect that this inversion reflects two aspects of Žižek's twentieth-century French intellectual background. First, the post-Kojèvian reception of Hegel in France, due to Kojève's own privileging of the more anthropological and historical dimensions of Hegelian phenomenology, exhibits a tendency toward elevating *Geistesphilosophie* over *Logik* (even sometimes flirting with the gesture of treating the latter as an overdetermined outgrowth of the former).[152] As I noted, Žižek indeed appears to make the logical modal categories determined results (instead of determining forms or essences) of human historical temporalities.

Second, Lacan, a figure arguably at least as important for Žižek as Hegel, places special emphasis on temporal retroaction (as the *après-coup*, the future anterior, and so on) through his radicalizations of Freud's *Nachträglichkeit* (deferred action). Žižek's stress upon this motif in his spirited defense of Hegel against certain hackneyed critical refrains is perhaps a symptom of the influence of this Lacanian emphasis. Additionally, in discussing temporality, Žižek goes so far in his recent Hegelian meditations as to equate negativity à la Hegel directly with time.[153] But, within Hegel's System proper, time is only one of many species of the genus negativity. Since time per se does not arise until the start of *Realphilosophie* with *Naturphilosophie* (time being the second determination or moment of the latter), Hegel would resist conflating strictly logical negativity with anything temporal.

If Hegel were alive today, I am confident he would not be an orthodox Hegelian adhering to the letter of the text. To be more exact, I believe that a contemporary, resurrected Hegel would see fit to significantly revise substantial swathes of his *Realphilosophie* in particular. Confronted with the past two centuries of scientific and historical developments, Hegel's early-nineteenth-century *Naturphilosophie* and *Geistesphilosophie* clearly require updates, modifications, and even, in certain instances, profound overhauls. Žižek acknowledges this too, especially with respect to post-Hegelian science and psychoanalysis.[154] I have little doubt that Hegel himself would be ready, willing, and able to undertake such broad and deep revisions of his Philosophy of the Real.

But, when it comes to his *Logik*, I am equally confident that Hegel would stick to his guns. *Realphilosophie* is conditioned by and sensitive to the more-than-logical Real qua the a posteriori, empirical, experiential, historical, and the like. It is the Philosophy of the Real specifically that Hegel famously describes, in the preface to *Elements of the Philosophy of Right* (with *Rechtsphilosophie* as a branch of *Geistesphilosophie*, itself a branch of *Realphilosophie*), as "its own time comprehended in thoughts" ("ihre Zeit in Gedanken erfaßt").[155] In this same preface, he implicitly contrasts this depiction of philosophy with the fully completed execution (*ausführen*) of "science," namely, *Wissenschaft als Wissenschaft der Logik*.[156] Now, *Logik*, although its explicit emergence is enabled by historical factors (the introductory role of the entire *Phenomenology of Spirit* in relation to the Logic and System as a whole is one among many pieces of evidence for this enabling),[157] allegedly achieves independence from these catalytic factors. In this vein, Hegel makes several connected claims for his Logic: it forms a seamlessly integrated network or web of categories that are simultaneously ontological and epistemological; this network or web amounts to an exhaustive totality; no further new logical categories remain to be discovered or invented; any future revisions to this Logic would (and should) be minor refinements at the level of presentation, rather than major revisions at the level of substance.[158] These claims establish a sharp, glaring contrast between the open incompleteness of *Realphilosophie* and the closed completeness of *Logik*.

Furthermore, the Logic both epistemologically and ontologically makes possible knowledge of the Real. *Logik* appears before *Realphilosophie* in the *Encyclopedia of the Philosophical Sciences* precisely because the former, as metaphysics (that is, as a systematically integrated ontology and epistemology), plays this transcendental role with respect to the latter (that is, *Realphilosophie*). Additionally, although, for Hegel, the historical future of human *Geist* is a priori unpredictable, it is definitely not, once it arrives as actually here and now, a priori unknowable. Hegel's critique of Kant—Hegel rejects the finitism of Kant's subjectivist transcendental idealism, with its interlinked "limits of possible experience" and thing in itself (as I discuss in chapters 1 and 2)—entails the (notorious) "infinitude" of the *Begriff/Idee*.[159] Properly comprehended, the Concept or Idea is infinite not as having attained "Absolute Knowledge" by digesting all of reality without any leftovers. Hegel is careful to speak of "Absolute Knowing" (*das absolute Wissen* as a kinetic verb), not "Absolute Knowledge" (as a static noun). Instead, the Concept or Idea is not finite in the sense of being limited in advance by any alterity or transcendence (that is, a Kantian *Ding an sich*) forever insurmountably refractory by its essential nature to the incursions of categorially determined, conceptually mediated knowing. Real-philosophical knowing is always in (metaphysical) principle infinitely expandable vis-à-vis the Real itself, although never in (historical) fact infinitely expanded.[160] Rosen, in his sizable recent study of the *Science of Logic*, remarks that, for Hegel, "to be is to be thinkable."[161] However, this observation about the ontology of Hegel's Logic-informed metaphysics requires the crucial accompanying caveat that being thinkable is not tantamount to actually being automatically, necessarily, or inevitably thought.[162]

In tandem with Hegel's assertions about the status of his Logic as history generated but history transcending, future history, as the spiritual yet-to-come, is logically guaranteed ahead of time to be both cognizable and cognized, to be a conceptually intelligible reality conforming to the systematically, scientifically established configurations of the logical categories. In the Hegelian encyclopedic framework, this future, including its retroaction upon the past and present, can invariably be recognized and registered again and again solely because of the Logic's priority over the Philosophy of the Real. Žižek's inversion of this priority inadvertently risks turning futurity into a quite anti-Hegelian noumenal "x." His reversal at least allows for the possibility, which Hegel does not, of the invisible, inaudible arrivals, however sooner or later and frequently or infrequently, of an unrecognizable and unregisterable future.

Žižek, as already observed, rightly opposes the Hegel of the preface to *Elements of the Philosophy of Right*, with the Owl of Minerva as "*a child of its time*,"[163] to all those Marxists who claim for historical materialism predictive powers regarding the socioeconomic *à venir*. However, on the basis of my preceding Hegelian criticisms of Žižek's interpretation of Hegel, I feel justified in maintaining that he is in danger of rendering this contrast between Hegelianism and Marxism excessively stark. One way to put this reservation is to say that (with reference back to the block quotation from *Less Than Nothing*) Hegel's negative propositions about the future in the preface to *Elements of the Philosophy of Right* are not (just) "negative/limiting statements," as Žižek has it. Instead (or also), these propositions are positive statements about futurity as the potent power of negativity, especially in relation to the being-there/existence of the status quo.

This point can be driven home compellingly with reference to a detail from Hegel's *Rechtsphilosophie* featuring centrally in the Žižekian playing off of Hegel against Marx, namely, the *Pöbel*. As I explain in a review of Ruda's book *Hegel's Rabble*:

> Hegel suggests that the economic and political dynamics resulting in poverty, itself functioning as a breeding ground for the rabble mentality, are inherent to the then-new political economies of modernity (of course, he also highlights how the steadily widening gap between poverty and wealth under capitalism creates a corresponding rabble mentality in the rich, who come to believe that their gains contingently gotten through gambling on civil society's free markets absolve them of duties and obligations *vis-à-vis* the public spheres of the *polis*). Moreover, on Hegel's assessment, no modern society (yet) appears to be willing and able adequately to address this internally generated self-undermining factor of rabble-rousing impoverishment. Without doing so, these historically youthful collective systems are at risk of destroying themselves sooner or later. Hence, rather than marking a pseudo-Hegelian "end of history," such societies, Hegel insinuates, have a very uncertain future ahead of them.[164]

I continue:

> As is common knowledge, the preface to the 1821 *Philosophy of Right* characterizes philosophy as "the Owl of Minerva" which spreads its wings solely at dusk, when the deeds and happenings of the day are done. In the same context, Hegel emphasizes that the philosopher is limited to gathering up materials furnished to him/her by the past and the present, constrained to conceptually synthesize his/her *Zeitgeist* and nothing more beyond this. Like the "angel of history" in Walter Benjamin's "Theses on the Philosophy of History," the philosopher—Hegel doubtlessly includes himself here—always has his/her back turned towards an

unpredictable future (and this by contrast with the Marxist historical materialism soon to follow in Hegel's wake).[165]

Finally, I add:

> Given that the problem of the rabble is underscored in the text prefaced by these very remarks, the radical leftist Hegelian conclusion that, even for the author of the *Philosophy of Right*, capitalism faces the prospect of eventually doing fatal violence to itself at its own hands is hardly unreasonable as a defensible exegesis of Hegel's socio-political thinking. The defensibility of this is further reinforced substantially by the fact that Hegel, also in the preface to the *Philosophy of Right*, explicitly stipulates that the ability of philosophy to sublate the material of its times in thoughts signals the entering into decay and dissolution of the realities thus sublated; the sun must be setting when the wise owl takes flight. Consequently and by his own lights, Hegel's capacity to distill the essence of capitalist modernity heralds that the bourgeois social order of his age already is on its way off the stage of history. Taking into account the multiple connections between Hegel and Marx, the Hegelian *Pöbel* might very well represent, within the confines of the *Philosophy of Right*, those who will unchain themselves one fine day in order to expedite capitalism's twilight labor of digging its own grave.[166]

The rabble is symptomatic of an internally self-generated negativity of capitalist modernity, of a real, true actuality (*als Wirklichkeit*) at work within this conjuncture, corroding it and, in so doing, signaling its imminent implosion. Hence, this *Pöbel* might very well be a (if not the) "rose in the cross of the present" ("*die Rose im Kreutze der Gegenwart*"), the very spot for reveling so as to welcome the immanently arising future on its eve ("*Here* is the rose, dance *here*" ["Hier *ist die Rose,* hier *tanze*"]).[167] Curiously, in the preface to the *Phenomenology of Spirit*, Hegel associates *Wirklichkeit* with "the Bacchanalian revel in which no member is not drunk."[168]

With a surreptitiousness and circumspection understandable on the part of a prominent public intellectual with an official post under the repressive pressure of a reactionary government authority suffused with suspicion, Hegel, circa 1821, is forecasting, in coded, censor-evading fashion, the coming negation of this conservative state of affairs. Such conservatism, built on German nationalist resistance (aroused in the "Wars of Liberation" or

"Napoleonic Wars") to the progressivism of the French Revolution as incarnated by Napoleon, is a nonactual *Dasein/Existenz* resisting in futility the prevailing currents of the undertow, "the inner pulse," of historical *Wirklichkeit*. In his contemporaneous Berlin lectures on the *Philosophy of History*, Hegel is unambiguous in his lyrical celebration of the French Revolution as "a glorious mental dawn" (*"ein herrlicher Sonnenaufgang"*).[169] This should be read in tandem with that moment in Hegel's correspondence when he avows that "I am daily ever more convinced that theoretical work accomplishes more in the world than practical work. Once the realm of representation [*Vorstellung*] is revolutionized, actuality [*Wirklichkeit*] will not hold out."[170]

All of this is to say that Žižek perhaps exaggerates the width of the divide between Hegelian *Geschichtsphilosophie/Rechtsphilosophie* and Marxian historical materialism. As the preface to *Elements of the Philosophy of Right* also shows, Hegel is certainly against unphilosophically and vainly micromanaging ahead of time the empirical details of sociohistorical arrangements. (The examples of this he gives are Plato's advice to nurses on physically handling children and Fichte's rationalizations regarding the design of passports.)[171] In Žižek's favor, this indeed suggests a principled refraining on Hegel's part from uttering empirically contentful and detailed predictions about specific aspects of yet-to-transpire social history (unlike, for instance, vulgar Marxist partisans of supposedly "scientific" socialism).

But, not in Žižek's favor, Hegel, however subtly and covertly, appears to invest himself, like Marx after him, in the prediction that the sociohistorical *Sittlichkeit* of modern capitalism will, at the hands of the rabble, commit suicide in the not-too-distant future (just as the ethical order of ancient Greece did "violence to itself at its own hands" along the specific fault lines of collective tensions reflected in Sophocles's *Antigone* and Plato's *Trial and Death of Socrates*).[172] Both the *Pöbel* and, in the preface to *Elements of the Philosophy of Right*, the indication that Hegel's ability to capture capitalist modernity in philosophical thoughts signifies that this socioeconomic order is already dying amount to Hegel discerning a limit to his present. As Žižek himself underscores, two types of limit are operative in Hegelian philosophy: *Grenze* ("a simple external limit . . . I don't even perceive . . . as a limitation since I have no access to any external point with which to compare it") and *Schranke* ("When *Grenze* changes into *Schranke*, it becomes a limitation proper, an obstacle I am aware of and try to overcome").[173] Precisely in the mode of a *Schranke*, Hegel's Logic posits a limitation to any existent actuality by its immanent possibilities and, what is more, his Philosophies of Sprit, History, and Right posit an imminent limitation to his present sociohistorical situation (that is, modern capitalism). Especially in regard to the latter, Hegel clearly sees himself as one step ahead (but one step only) of his *Zeitgeist*. For him, the immediate, impending sociohistorical future is at least minimally a *Schranke* rather than a *Grenze*.

Admittedly, Hegel, unlike Marx and company, does not treat this imminent and immanent dialectical negation of capitalist modernity as a "determinate negation"[174] whose destruction is simultaneously the creation of a subsequent socialist and communist historical future. Again, he neither forecasts far off into later, yet-to-arrive stages of social history nor fabricates fleshed-out visions of the nitty-gritty concreteness of *die sittliche Zukunft*. Nonetheless, and contra Žižek, Hegel slyly anticipates the negation of his particular sociohistorical status quo in the near-term future. Although whether a phoenix will rise and, if so, what kind of bird this will be—this phoenix of the future would be the close avian relative of the Owl of Minerva—are issues about which Hegel is deliberately silent, he definitely anticipates, subtly but firmly, that at the very least there soon will be ashes.

What is more, Hegel's Logic, starting with its third categorial moment of Becoming in "The Doctrine of Being" (a moment subsequently enriched in "The Doctrine of Essence" by its acquisition of actuality with the modalities of contingency, possibility, and necessity), indicates that the categorial structuring of the Real by dialectical-speculative Logic qua metaphysics essentially inclines this Real, especially the historical temporalities of *Geist*, in the direction of ceaselessly restless transformations. Given that this inclination is logical (that is, transhistorical), this entails the expectation of such recurrent alterations being perpetual off into the future (although the determination of the exact cadences of such recurrences is left open). There might be something worth salvaging in Engels's much-derided, Marx-inspired identification of Hegelian philosophy's "rational kernel" with the theories of change(s) put forward in the guise of speculative dialectics.[175] But, given my complete agreement with Žižek that the main thing to be combatted is the propagandistic cartoon of Hegel as an absurd, antiquated, Leibnizian hyperrationalist, I am sympathetic to Žižek's recommendation that it would be better and more accurate to speak of recovering the "irrational core" (that is, contingency, facticity, groundlessness, and the like) dwelling at the center of Hegel's System.[176]

CONTINGENCY, PURE CONTINGENCY

Before concluding the chapter, I want to do justice to some additional, illuminating reflections on matters teleological by Žižek. In *Less Than Nothing*, he states:

> Hegel's dialectic itself is not yet another grand teleological narrative, but precisely an effort to avoid the narrative illusion of a continuous process of organic growth of the New out of the Old; the historical forms which follow one another are not successive figures within the same teleological frame, but successive re-totalizations, each of them creating ("positing") its own past (as well as projecting its own future). In other words, Hegel's dialectic is the science of the gap between the Old and the New, of accounting for this gap; more precisely, its true topic is not directly the gap between the Old and the New, but its self-reflective redoubling—when it describes the cut between the Old and the New, it simultaneously describes the gap, within the Old itself, between the Old "in-itself" (as it was before the New) and the Old retroactively posited by the New. It is because of this redoubled gap that every new form arises as a *creation ex nihilo*: the Nothingness out of which the New arises is the very gap between the Old-in-itself and the Old-for-the-New, the gap which makes impossible any account of the rise of the New in terms of a continuous narrative.[177]

A few pages later, Žižek, in a passage that also makes a modified reappearance in *Absolute Recoil*,[178] links this to Hegel's doctrine of the modalities:

> Hegel has . . . a lot to teach us about the topic of possibility versus actuality. What is involved in a dialectical analysis of, say, a past event, such as a revolutionary break? Does it really amount to identifying the underlying necessity that governed the course of events in all their apparent confusion? What if the opposite is true, and dialectical analysis *reinserts possibility into the necessity of the past*? There is something of an unpredictable miraculous emergence in every passage from "negation" to "negation of negation," in every rise of a new Order out of the chaos of disintegration—which is why for Hegel dialectical analysis is always the analysis of *past* events. No deduction will bring us from chaos to order; and to locate this moment of the magical turn, this unpredictable reversal of chaos into Order, is the true aim of dialectical analysis.[179]

Subsequently in *Less Than Nothing*, this passage is once again tightly tied to the theme of (temporal) retroaction.[180] In regard to teleology, the key thesis of these just-quoted passages is that teleological trajectories (seem to) exist exclusively with the benefit of hindsight, from the perspective of the Owl of Minerva's backward glance. As Žižek puts it here, "for Hegel dialectical analysis is always the analysis of *past* events." And, as I put it elsewhere (at some length):

> Hegel, . . . *contra* prevailing interpretive orthodoxy, is not the crude teleological thinker he's all too frequently made out to be. . . . To take the example of the *Phenomenology*, which, as Hegel's first *magnum opus*, sets the stage for much of the rest of his later philosophizing, it appears therein that a deep, irresistible current of progress functions as an undertow carrying the figures of non-philosophical consciousness along a preordained pathway leading to the telos of philosophical "Absolute Knowing." Moreover, this odyssey seems to be laid out in a particular order of stages and phases forming a fixed, necessary sequence through which consciousness is condemned to journey under the pre-arranged schedule of an always already established logical/metaphysical itinerary. But, the case can be made that, for Hegel, nothing guarantees in advance that progress will occur. Any progress is an after the fact effect to be discerned only retroactively (and whose temporally antecedent causes are contingencies); any necessity, as the preface to the *Philosophy of Right* spells out with pointed frankness, can be seen solely by the Owl of Minerva. Stated with greater precision, in the *Phenomenology*, a dialectically self-generated deadlock or impasse afflicting a shape of consciousness does not contain within itself the promise of the fated actual arrival of a progressive step Beyond *qua* a resolution or exit. The immanent critiques of themselves these shapes produce, as determinate negations in the technical Hegelian sense, merely outline what a resolution/exit could be if—this "if" arguably is a matter of conditional contingency rather than teleological necessity—a new figure of consciousness, one fulfilling what is demanded in terms of a resolution/exit, happens to come along in the future course of time. The dialectical self-subversions of consciousness, through their immanent determinate negations of themselves, just sketch the rough contours of what a possible solution to the problems they create for themselves would have to look like if such a solution arrives unpredictably one fine day. In other words, the thus-generated foreshadowings of subsequent progress, in the guise of approximate criteria for what would count as moving forward past specific cul-de-sacs, do not have the authoritative power to assure, as a matter of a simplistic teleology, the popping up in factual reality of realized escapes from these quagmires. Whether

or not consciousness remains stuck is, ultimately, a matter of chance, left up to the caprice of the contingent.[181]

Žižek and I concur that a cardinal feature of Hegelian thinking is the appreciation of the lack of links of necessitation from *Wirklichkeit* to *Wirklichkeit*. Between any two (or more) consecutive actualities (with their accompanying beings-there/existences), there are multiple actually possible possibilities, no one of which is noncontingently necessary in the standard sense. Even in the limit case of the efficient causality of inorganic mechanics or physics, in which an antecedent actuality (that is, a cause) necessitates one and only one consequent actuality (that is, an effect), this necessity itself (that is, the causal law of nature qua necessary connection) is contingent à la the contingency of necessity. No metanecessity, such as the sufficient reason(s) of a Leibnizian God, supplements the necessity of natural laws with the purposive final cause(s) of a teleology.

When Žižek, as quoted earlier, proposes that "dialectical analysis *reinserts possibility into the necessity of the past*," this is tantamount to a two-fold insistence. On the one hand, the past as it really was is necessary for the present as it is, with the historical then becoming, through the *Nachträglichkeit/après-coup* of the future anterior, the necessary teleological presequence eventuating in the contemporary now (this being the very real *"necessity of the past"*). On the other hand, this same *"necessity of the past"* is itself contingent, for two reasons: first, the concatenation of prior actualities is a chain assembled on the basis of the successive actualizations of nonnecessary, one-among-many possibilities between actualities; second, each after-the-fact teleology that is visible exclusively in hindsight is relative to the present of a situated backward glance—with unpredictable, contingent future presents promising to retroactively alter or overturn altogether such teleologies through positing their own new teleologies. As Žižek puts this, "There is something of an unpredictable miraculous emergence in every passage from 'negation' to 'negation of negation,' in every rise of a new Order out of the chaos of disintegration."

However, the second half of the block quotation from my "The Voiding of Weak Nature" marks a divergence between Žižek and me. Combining this quoted content with much of the preceding analysis in this chapter, Hegel looks, on my interpretation of him, to navigate subtly between the Scylla of the complete blindness to the future that Žižek's reconstruction ascribes to him and the Charybdis of the delusional clairvoyance feigned by scientific-socialist vulgarizations of Marx's historical materialism. To paraphrase the Benjamin of "Theses on the Philosophy of History" (with his "*weak* messianic power"),[182] Hegel's Philosophy of History, undergirded, like the entirety of *Realphilosophie*, by the Logic, modestly claims for itself a weak predictive power—something in between the polar extremes of the false humility of no predictive power and the equally false hallucination of strong predictive power.[183] On my reading, Hegel, at least with respect to the historical actuality of his specific context in the 1820s (if not more generally), lays claim to very limited foresight (but foresight nevertheless) about two things: first, an imminent demise of the status quo to be brought about by negativities internal to and already operative within this same situation (such as the increasing frictions between modern societies and their growing rabbles); and, second, an apprehension, based on the aforementioned conjuncture-immanent negativities, of what would count as subsequent rational progress. To be more precise, this rational progress would be a "speculative" resolution of these dialectical negativities, if—this "if" is a contingent conditional not guaranteed or necessitated by any preordained teleology—such a resolution is achieved eventually, if such an advance beyond the impasses of the present just so happens to occur in the future.

To stay with the example of Hegel's *Pöbel*, one could say that, even though the rabble is the unique instance in the entire Hegelian corpus of a problem mentioned by Hegel for which he offers no solution or even hint of one, this instance establishes one of the criteria for what would count as sociohistorically progressive by rational-qua-dialectical-speculative standards. The rabble embodies a problem that can become a determinate negation (rather than simple negation as destruction) of the present only if a future arrives in which this symptom and its underlying causes are more adequately addressed. Hence, with Hegel, deadlocks of a current actuality already foreshadow and outline the parameters of what an immediately succeeding future actuality would have to be were it (conditionally, contingently) to count as a genuine step beyond the blockages and limits of the *hic et nunc*. Admittedly, Hegel deliberately avoids preaching prophecies about necessary developments to come or concrete occurrences in the distant future. Yet, he still, for multiple systematic reasons logical and real-philosophical, indicates, first, that his present is ailing and soon will die (modern capitalism ultimately will destroy itself thanks to the exponentially widening gap between rich and poor) and, second, what would count as an actually new form of life overcoming this old ailment if and when this new form of life surfaces in the future (a *Sittlichkeit* with an economy in which, in a way that seems to elude being envisioned in advance, capitalism's self-destructive socioeconomic dynamics are tamed, domesticated, and surpassed). However near-sighted and uncertain of itself, this Hegelian weak predictive power is predictive power all the same.

I am convinced there is something to Zizek's assertion that Hegel has greater contemporary relevance in the early twenty-first century than Marx.[184] In line with this Žižekian contention, I would maintain that Hegel's weak predictive power circa the 1820s resonates with current circumstances much more than Marx's dictum from the (in)famous preface to *A Contribution to the Critique of Political Economy* from 1859 that "mankind ... inevitably sets itself only such tasks as it is able to solve."[185] This dictum (as well as the text in which it features) is emblematic of those moments in Marx when he, as a child of the Enlightenment, inadvertently paves the way for the not-so-secular theodicies of both Second International economism and Stalinist *diamat*. On this score, Hegel is closer to such twentieth-century Marxists as the Benjamin of "Theses on the Philosophy of History," the mature Sartre of the *Critique of Dialectical Reason*, and the later Althusser of "the aleatory materialism of the encounter"—these three, each in his own fashion, plead for a historical or dialectical materialism of contingency (as Žižek does) in tandem with their repudiations of the teleological necessitarianisms of both economism and Stalinism—than to Marx himself.

In fact, Hegel's philosophy in particular, if we take into account both Žižek's and my differing interpretations of Hegel, can be seen as especially and uncannily appropriate for capturing today's social, economic, and political conjunctural combinations of actualities and beings-there/existences. Žižek, in connection with his insistence that Hegelianism denies itself prophetic foresight, wisely cautions that "especially as communists, we should abstain from any positive imagination of the future communist society. We are, of course, borrowing from the future, but how we are doing so will only become readable once the future is here, so we should not put too much hope in the desperate search for the 'germs of communism' in today's society."[186] Žižek and I agree that Hegel and all true Hegelians abstain as a matter of principle from making foolishly detailed long-term forecasts (such as "any positive imagination of the future communist society"). Moreover, there are not only systematic Hegelian justifications at the levels of both *Logik* and *Realphilosophie* for this abstention; a long string of losses, failures, and missed opportunities have made any kind of scientific-socialist, messianic-prophetic power into a sad, antiquated fiction. A far from exhaustive list of these historical catastrophes includes, in addition to two Worlds Wars, 1848 (Europe's crushed workers' uprisings), 1871 (the bloodily defeated Paris Commune), 1918–1919 (the German Revolution, Spartacist Uprising, and consequent murders of Rosa Luxemburg and Karl Liebknecht), 1922 (Benito Mussolini becoming Italy's head of state), 1924 (Lenin's death as paving the way for Stalin's betrayal of the Bolshevik Revolution, for the Stalinist Thermidor), 1929 (the nonmaterialization of leftist revolts in capitalist countries hit hard by the Great Depression), 1933 (Adolf Hitler's solidification of control over Germany), 1938–1939 (both the publication of Stalin's *Dialectical and Historical Materialism* as well as his relationship with Hitler in the guise of the Molotov-Ribbentrop Pact), 1965–1967 (Suharto's overthrow of Sukharno in Indonesia and the mass slaughter of Indonesian communists and leftists), 1973 (Augusto Pinochet's coup against the government of Salvador Allende and the latter's ensuing death), 1978 (Deng Xiaoping's post-Mao reforms ushering in "socialism with Chinese characteristics" partly inspired by Singapore's Lee Kuan Yew), 1979–1980 (Margret Thatcher's and Ronald Reagan's electoral mandates for their neoliberal counterrevolutions), 1983 (François Mitterrand's *tournant de la rigueur*), 1989 (the wheezing collapse of Really Existing Socialism), 1992/1997 (the victories of Bill Clinton's New Democrats and Tony Blair's New Labour as further consolidations, via the pseudoleftist "Third Way," of neoliberalism's triumph). Today looks just as bad, if not worse: skyrocketing wealth inequality not seen since before World War I; endless amounts of tax cuts and corporate welfare for the ultrarich; equally endless amounts of disempowerment and dispossession for both the employed and the unemployed masses alike; postmodern returns of late-nineteenth- and early-twentieth-century-style big power imperialist rivalries and resultant violent conflicts; and, the fetid, toxic tide of far-right populisms, nationalisms, fundamentalisms, and racisms sloshing around the entire globe (Donald Trump, Brexit, Vladimir Putin, Marine Le Pen, and on and on). Only the coldest of comfort is provided by Benjamin's observation that "every rise of Fascism bears witness to a failed revolution."[187] Perhaps the sole hope in such circumstances is that at least a few fascisms potentially bear witness to future successful revolutions that have not yet happened in addition to bearing witness to failed revolutions whose failure is nothing other than to have not materialized in the past.

Contrary to Marx's hypothesis from 1859 that "mankind always sets itself only such tasks as it can solve," these discouraging lessons of the past two centuries seem to unanimously teach instead that the humanity represented by the Marxist tradition repeatedly sets itself tasks that it is anything but ready, willing, or able to solve. Consequently, like Hegel in 1821 (on my reading of him), radical leftists nowadays find themselves uncomfortably stuck with a strange sort of antinomic parallax view (to employ a Žižekian turn of phrase). On the one hand, a viciously reactionary state of affairs looks to be in the process of unwittingly driving itself to internally generated destruction partly by virtue of phenomena common to the nineteenth and late twentieth and early twenty-first centuries (such as excessively grotesque and obscene wealth inequalities as well as the building tensions of great-power rivalries). On the other hand, nobody appears to be capable of articulating an actually possible and potentially feasible alternative order as a successor *Sittlichkeit* to the currently imploding socioeconomic reality. In short, a Hegelian leftist today neither can imagine the status quo continuing on into the future nor can imagine it not continuing. It seems as though capitalism cannot go on and yet, simultaneously, cannot not go on (echoing the last line of Samuel Beckett's *The Unnamable*—"You must go on, I can't go on, I'll go on").

Hegel's resolution, if it can be called such, of this parallactic antinomy at the level of his *Realphilosophie* (as *Geschichtsphilosophie* and *Rechtsphilosophie*) is to gesture at the flickering shadow of the imminent self-wrought ruin cast by a specific feature of his times (in this instance, the *Pöbel*) while not gesturing at any concrete constellations of actualities and beings-there/existences *à venir*. And, at the level of Hegel's *Logik*, the interlinked negativities of becoming (*Werden*), contingent actualities (*Wirklichkeiten*), and possibilities (*Möglichkeiten*) repeatedly cast the penumbra of an imminent actuality-to-come onto a given actuality-that-is, a difficult-to-see penumbra nonetheless visible to certain discerning gazes.

Although I concur with Zizek's warning that "we should not put too much hope in the desperate search for the 'germs of communism' in today's society," I also still believe that a properly Hegelian leftist can and should hold on to the germs of negativity within the present as sustaining sources of hope (however vague and tenuous), namely, the currently actual symptoms within the here and now of the imminent future actuality (that is, the germs of anticapitalism, although not of communism or even socialism). Perhaps Hegel's advice to today's leftists would be more or less the same as in the 1820s: Here is the shadow of tomorrow, revel here. But be prepared for the likelihood of a long, brutal hangover the morning after these enthusiastic Bacchanalian festivities and, as Mao Tse-Tung would say, the probability (but not certainty) of near-to-medium-term defeat.[188]

FOUR

Materialism Sans Materialism
Žižekian Substance Deprived of Its Substance

LESS THAN NOTHING and Absolute Recoil both strive, as their subtitles indicate, to reinvent for the twenty-first century the Marxist tradition of "dialectical materialism." Although this philosophical label is closely associated with such names as, first and foremost, Engels and Lenin, Žižek seeks to develop a permutation of it deviating markedly in a number of ways from the classical Engelsian and Soviet versions of it. As is to be expected, he pursues this via his characteristic blend of German idealism and psychoanalysis, employing especially Hegel and Lacan in order to creatively update dialectical materialism.

In particular, Žižek openly adopts two manifestly anti-Leninist approaches to the reinvention of dialectical materialism. First, in opposition to the Lenin of *Materialism and Empirio-Criticism*, published in 1908, he enthusiastically celebrates "the disappearance of matter" purportedly to be observed in quantum physics[1] (as well as, more recently and dramatically, in string theory). Second, inverting the emphasis on finding materialism within idealism in Lenin's remarks on Hegel's *Science of Logic* in the former's *Philosophical Notebooks*,[2] Žižek insists (implicitly echoing the first of Marx's eleven "Theses on Feuerbach")[3] upon the urgent need to infuse materialism with idealism, especially transcendental and post-Kantian varieties of the latter.[4] Of course, Žižek's anti-Leninism at the level of theoretical philosophy is striking in light of his politics as Leninist (to a certain extent) at the corresponding level of practical philosophy. That said, I intend to argue in the first half of this chapter along two related lines. First, Žižek deviates too far in an idealist qua nonmaterialist direction in his anti-Leninist revisions of dialectical materialism. Second, Žižek's own Hegelian-Lacanian dialectical materialist negotiations of such relations as those between *Natur und Geist* (as in Hegel) and the Real and reality (as in Lacan) not only raise crucial questions yet to be answered; they contain dangerous ambiguities sometimes bringing Žižek's materialism into disturbing proximity with certain of those contemporaneous "materialisms" he explicitly and correctly denounces as pseudomaterialist.

This chapter is organized chronologically, with its first half focusing on Žižek's ambivalent relations with the earlier Soviet and Leninist tradition of dialectical materialism. Then, in its second half, I turn to Žižek's contemporary variant of dialectical materialism. In so doing, I will play off Žižek against himself in his favor, showing how, in both *Less Than Nothing* and *Absolute Recoil*, there are other moments when he makes up for what I present as idealist deviations in his criticisms of traditional dialectical materialism. These moments involve him incisively addressing Hegel's *Naturphilosophie*, especially in its relations to both *Logik* and *Geistesphilosophie*. (And, although some of Žižek's treatments of the pair Nature and Spirit risk calling into question his dialectical materialist credentials, other treatments of this pair by him burnish these very credentials.) In so doing, Žižek reinforces the same materialism his flirtations with idealist revisions weaken. This reinforcement is brought about through him recovering and remobilizing the kind of carefully qualified naturalism essential to both Hegel and the post-Hegelian tradition of Marxist dialectical materialism.

Žižek opens *Absolute Recoil* by calling for an immanent critique of *Materialism and Empirio-Criticism*. As is well known, Lenin's overriding concern, in this text from 1908, is with combatting idealist exploitations by multiple philosophers and scientists of the revolutionary upheavals in physics overturning Newtonianism, which were new then. For the author of *Materialism and Empirio-Criticism*, such scientistic, ideological exploiters opportunistically seek to take advantage of a crisis in the natural sciences so as to attack, whether directly or indirectly, precisely the sort of materialist positions he sees as integral to Marxism *überhaupt*.[5]

Žižek's concisely damning verdict, conveyed in the opening lines of *Absolute Recoil*, is that Lenin, in striving so vehemently to defend the uncompromisingly robust realism of materialism, falls far short of a criterion for materialism that both he and Engels uphold[6]—"In Chapter 5 of his *Materialism and Empirio-Criticism*, invoking Engels' claim that materialism has to change its form with each new scientific discovery, Lenin applies the point to Engels himself."[7] Žižek continues: "Today, in turn, we should apply this motto to Lenin himself: if his *Materialism and Empirio-Criticism* clearly failed the task of raising philosophical materialism to the level of relativity theory and quantum physics, neither can it help us grasp other breakthroughs such as Freudian psychoanalysis, not to mention the failures of twentieth-century communism."[8] Certainly, *Materialism and Empirio-Criticism*, given its conjuncturally prompted preoccupation with abruptly striking down moves to provide (pseudo)scientific support for antimaterialist and antirealist stances, ignores the dialectical materialist potentials arguably latent within post-Newtonian physics from its very inception. (Of course, in *Less Than Nothing*, *Absolute Recoil*, and earlier works, Žižek engages in efforts to combine quantum physics in particular with his hybrid German-idealist, Marxist, and Lacanian philosophical framework.)[9] Lenin addresses such physics only insofar as it functions as a misappropriated weapon in the hands of his theoretical and ideological adversaries. This treatise from 1908 appears not to put forward, in its frontal assaults upon its opponents, a genuinely dialectical materialist alternative to the worldviews it hotly contests. Given this, Žižek is indeed justified in stressing the need to "repeat Lenin" (philosophically as well as politically), to move beyond him specifically by performing in the early twenty-first century, just over a hundred years after *Materialism and Empirio-Criticism*, the same gesture with respect to him that he recommends enacting vis-à-vis Engels. However, the relations between *Materialism and Empirio-Criticism* and properly dialectical materialism are much more complicated than the preceding brief remarks indicate. (I have addressed these complexities in detail elsewhere.)[10]

Materialism and Empirio-Criticism undeniably involves a missed encounter between philosophical materialism and quantum physics. What is more, as Žižek persuasively charges on a number of occasions, the materialism of this work from 1908 is even guilty of being "contemplative" (qua insufficiently historical and dialectical) in the precise sense critiqued in Marx's first thesis.[11] Nonetheless, some devil's advocacy on Lenin's behalf might be appropriate here.

Lenin arguably does not intend for *Materialism and Empirio-Criticism*, as a contextually conditioned intervention occasioned by certain antimaterialists' scientistic maneuvers, to stand alone as a complete, self-sufficient statement of his theoretical materialism in its entirety (let alone to address such topics as communism per se or Freudian psychoanalysis). A standard (Soviet) line going back to Bukharin, among others, is that Leninist dialectical materialism is (or should be) constructed on the basis of a combination of the dialectics of Lenin's *Philosophical Notebooks* and the *Materialism and Empirio-Criticism*.[12] One would have to concede to Žižek that the *Philosophical Notebooks* certainly do not return to the topic of the new physics. But it just so happens to be a historical fact (one meticulously and soberly documented by Loren R. Graham especially) that many philosophers and scientists in the Soviet Union, pushing off from a dialectical materialism fundamentally informed by a combination of *Materialism and Empirio-Criticism* and the *Philosophical Notebooks*, seriously practiced and interpreted the sciences of quantum mechanics, relativity theory, and cosmology and cosmogony (not to mention chemistry and the life sciences over and above physics).

I would contend that, whereas numerous radical leftists rightly protest against noisy ditchings of "the idea of communism" (to employ Badiou's phrase) in the aftermath of the fall of the Berlin Wall and related occurrences in the late twentieth century, they have tended to overlook and remain silent about the quiet rubbishing of the products of the labors of Soviet natural scientists and dialectical materialist philosophers of science. That is to say, while contemporary Marxists have mightily resisted the crude anti-Marxist gesture of indefensibly equating Marxist politics tout court with the figure of Joseph Stalin, they appear, for the most part, to have fought less fiercely (if at all) against equally crude reductions of Marxist theory qua the Engelsian-Leninist dialectics of nature, with its unique Soviet legacy, to the lone figure of Trofim Denisovich Lysenko.[13] In my view, there are lamentable scientific and philosophical casualties, as well as disastrous, catastrophic political-ideological ones, from the collapse of Really Existing Socialism in the Soviet Union and its satellites. (This is yet another sad instance of what Benjamin is getting at when, in "Theses on the Philosophy of History," he warns that *"even the dead* will not be safe from the enemy if he wins. And this enemy has not ceased to be victorious.")[14] I fear that Žižek's swift dismissals of *Materialism and Empirio-Criticism* risk inadvertently heaping even more obscuring dirt on the burial sites of these unjustly unmourned losses. What is more, I believe that both his materialism specifically and a newly resurrected dialectical materialism generally would benefit in intellectual-historical as well as philosophical and political depth from revisiting the multidisciplinary ideas and debates centered upon *Naturdialektik* in the Soviet Union from Lenin's time onward.

Admittedly, Žižek, at one point in *Less Than Nothing*, refers approvingly in passing to Soviet dialectical materialism and creatively recasts the distinction between historical and dialectical materialisms. He ontologizes this distinction as reflecting a "parallax gap," a real antagonistic split, internal to human beings themselves in their natural (as in dialectical materialism) and social (as in historical materialism) incarnate existences.[15] This innovative gesture implicitly contests the young Lukács's mobilization of a historical materialism of mediating and mediated human practices contra a dialectical materialism of immediate natural processes. *History and Class Consciousness*, published in 1923, and related texts argue that, for a proper Marxist as a historical materialist, "nature" and the natural sciences always must be treated as nothing more than ideologically compromised and socially structured artificial configurations[16] (in opposition to the confidently unqualified naturalism and realism of the Engelsian dialectics of nature and its offshoots).[17] Žižek's implicit contestation of the early Lukács is explicitly confirmed later in *Less Than Nothing* when Žižek pleads against this Lukács (and his many Western Marxist descendants) for the urgency of resuscitating Hegelian *Naturphilosophie* and Marxian *Naturdialektik*.[18] And to cut a well-known story short (a story to which Žižek alludes in *Absolute Recoil*),[19] the Lukács of *History and Class Consciousness*, with his playing off of historical against dialectical materialism, establishes the difference between Western-European and Eastern/Soviet Marxisms, which thereafter becomes definitive.[20]

Alfred Schmidt's *The Concept of Nature in Marx*, published in 1962, although originally a dissertation supervised by Theodor Adorno and Max Horkheimer (themselves generally followers of the young Lukács in regard to the empirical, experimental sciences of nature),[21] represents a voice of partial internal dissent within the Frankfurt School, at least regarding naturalist materialism. Much like Schmidt, Žižek attempts to strike a delicate balance between the historicist social constructivism of historical materialism and the realist (quasi-)naturalism of dialectical materialism.[22] As Žižek puts it in an interview from 1996, "not everything is cultural.... Although you cannot pinpoint a moment which is pure nature, which is not yet mediated by culture, in spite of this you must not draw the conclusion that everything is culture. Otherwise you fall into 'discursive idealism.' "[23] (This stipulation is echoed in *Absolute Recoil*.)[24] Two premises can be extracted from Žižek's remarks: first, the distinction between nature (as Real) and culture (as Imaginary-Symbolic realities) is internal to the latter;[25] second, an anti-idealist materialism is to be affirmed nevertheless (against such examples as the early Lukács's version of historical materialism, "discursive idealism," and the like). From these two premises, it might be concluded that what Žižek requires is a metadialectical materialism delineating the dialectics between the domains covered by dialectical materialism (that is, the Real as nature) and historical materialism (that is, Imaginary-Symbolic realities as culture).[26] Put differently, if, as *Absolute Recoil* has it, "the limit that separates the Real from the symbolic is simultaneously external and internal to the symbolic,"[27] then a certain amount of (meta)dialectical finesse will be demanded of a materialism striving to walk a fine line between the Scylla of every pre-/nondialectical materialism and the Charybdis of all idealisms (including pseudo-Marxist ones).

As I already have hinted, Žižek insinuates that the materialism of the Lenin of 1908 amounts to a regression behind Marx circa 1845 and back to the contemplative stance of Ludwig Feuerbach and his eighteenth-century French materialist predecessors. However, Marx himself is not left unscathed in the context of Žižek's push for a contemporary reworking of dialectical materialism. Lenin is not only criticized via Marx; Marx is criticized in turn via Hegel. In *Less Than Nothing*, Žižek asserts, in addition to some Althusserian indictments of the young (pre-1845) Marx both for being too Aristotelian and for assuming the potential effective existence of a thoroughly nonalienated human nature,[28] that "today, one should return from Marx to Hegel and enact a 'materialist reversal' of Marx himself."[29] I would suggest reading this assertion alongside Žižek's thesis, central to *Absolute Recoil*, that "the only way to be a true materialist today is to push idealism to its limit."[30] In this instance, the only way to be a true Marxist historical and dialectical materialist today is to push Hegelian absolute idealism to its limit. Žižek hints that Marx himself, in his mature work, already starts doing something along these lines specifically in relation to the structures and phenomena involving "real abstractions."[31] He later expands upon this thesis, using concepts and language borrowed from the Badiou of *Logics of Worlds*:[32]

MATERIALISM SANS MATERIALISM

The predominant philosophical struggle occurs today *within* materialism, between democratic and dialectical materialism—and what characterizes dialectical materialism is precisely that it incorporates the idealist legacy, against vulgar democratic materialism in all its guises, from scientist naturalism to the post-Deleuzian assertion of spiritualized "vibrant" matter. Dialectical materialism is, first, a *materialism without matter*, without the metaphysical notion of matter as a full substantial entity—in dialectical materialism, matter "disappears" in a set of purely formal relations. Second, despite being materialism without matter, it is not idealism without an idea—it is a *materialism with an Idea*, an assertion of the eternal Idea outside the space of idealism. In contrast to idealism, whose problem is how to explain temporal finite reality if our starting point is the eternal order of Ideas, materialism's problem is how to explain the rise of an eternal Idea out of the activity of people caught in a finite historical situation.[33]

At the beginning of *Absolute Recoil*, Žižek provides a succinct yet incisive inventory of current strands of nondialectical materialisms (all of which he subsumes under the Badiouian heading of "democratic materialism" in this quotation). He points out that none of them incorporates within materialism the philosophical resources of Kantian and post-Kantian German idealisms in particular (with these, and especially the absolute idealism of Hegel, embodying the ultimate apex of "the idealist legacy").[34] Moreover, despite the problematizations of Badiou's own version of materialism articulated in multiple manners throughout *Less Than Nothing* and *Absolute Recoil*,[35] Žižek fundamentally endorses *Logics of Worlds*'s characterization of the "materialist dialectic" (in contrast with democratic materialism)[36] as the genuine dialectical materialism to be advanced in the twenty-first century. Like Badiou, Žižek, in the conclusion to *Less Than Nothing*, calls for a materialism going beyond the limits set by a Foucauldian-Agambenian biopolitics of animalistic "bare life."[37]

Staying with the details of the passage from *Absolute Recoil* just quoted, I want to begin raising some concerns and reservations from a (dialectical) materialist perspective about Žižek's characterizations of dialectical materialism qua properly dialectical. Before doing so, though, it should be noted that I share Žižek's (and Badiou's) antipathies and objections to, in Badiouian terms, all those brands and flavors of biopolitical democratic materialism to be combatted ferociously by a new (or renewed) materialist dialectic or dialectical materialism. I also am in profound solidarity both with Žižek's occasional pleas for reviving Hegelian *Naturphilosophie* and Engelsian *Naturdialektik* and with his doubts about the authentically materialist credentials of Badiou's ontological framework.[38]

That said, Žižek appears to me hastily to conflate two different possible senses of "a *materialism without matter*." The first possible sense refers to a materialism in which physical nature itself is deprived of its traditionally imagined positivity qua consistency, density, solidity, and unity. Instead, nature in this case is envisioned as shot through and permeated with the immanent negativities of antagonisms, conflicts, discrepancies, and tensions. Godlike Nature-with-a-capital-N as an omnipotent and omniscient big Other or Whole/Totality as One-All is replaced with, in hybrid Hegelian-Lacanian-Žižekian parlance, weak (*ohnmächtig*), rotten (*pourri*) nature(s) as a nonwhole/not-all (*pas tout*) barred Real.[39]

By contrast, the second possible sense of "a *materialism without matter*" refers to a "materialism" in which everything material is dissolved into the "purity" of logical (whether symbolic or dialectical-speculative) or mathematical "forms." This ontology is difficult to distinguish from Pythagorianism and Platonic metaphysical realism. Moreover, such a realism by no means entails necessarily either dialectics or anything material in a way distinguishable from the ideational.

For the sake of abbreviated clarity and convenience, I will designate the first possible sense of "a *materialism without matter*," a sort of conflict ontology in which "matter disappears" only as nonconflicted, as a dialectical materialism of weak nature (with *Less Than Nothing* identifying Democritean atomism as historically inaugurating this option in the guise of a materialism of the Nothing or Void qua desubstantialized substantiality).[40] I will designate the second possible sense, a kind of hyperstructuralist ontology in which matter disappears tout court, as a "dialectical materialism" (being really neither essentially dialectical nor materialist) of strong form (one closer to Pythagoras and Plato than to Democritus and the atomists). This second "dialectical materialism" is arguably akin to what is captured by Žižek's consumer-culture examples of the diet version of a substance (*materialism*) deprived (*without*) of its substance (*matter*), free of alcohol, caffeine, and fat (thereby being unappetizing and unsatisfying). This matter-free "materialism" of strong form calls for doubts about Žižek's materialist credentials identical to those Žižek casts upon Badiou's formalist, pure-mathematical, set-theoretic ontology.

These two distinct alternatives of what "a *materialism without matter*" could be are run together by Žižek in a single sentence, separated only by a dash: "Dialectical materialism is, first, a *materialism without matter*, without the metaphysical notion of matter as a full substantial entity—in dialectical materialism, matter 'disappears' in a set of purely formal relations." Before the dash, one has a dialectical materialism of weak nature. But, after the dash, one has a "dialectical materialism" of strong form instead. Therefore, there are two parallel, separate fashions in which Žižek tries to "push idealism to its limit": one in which a "limit" qua tipping point at which a twisting transition is made to materialism proper is traversed (weak nature) and another in which a "limit" qua maximum or peak of idealism is reached (strong form). There is no difficulty in guessing what the Lenin of *Materialism and Empirio-Criticism* would have to say, with some justification, about the second of these two Žižekian reinventions of dialectical materialism.

But the problems with Žižek's elaborations of his updated dialectical materialism do not end with this risky ambiguity about "a *materialism without matter*." Even when advocating a materialist ontology of weak nature (rather than a pseudomaterialist ontology of strong form), Žižek, in violation of his own weak-naturalist stipulations regarding "the disappearance of matter" (qua "the metaphysical notion of matter as a full substantial entity"), seems to surreptitiously slide back into a belief in a strong Nature as a holistically self-cohesive field of being. This probably inadvertent and unconscious slippage usually happens, within the pages of *Less Than Nothing* and *Absolute Recoil*, in close proximity to employments of the Hegelian dialectical-speculative distinction between "substance" and "subject" (translated by Žižek into the Lacanian mathemes of S and $, respectively).[41] In good materialist fashion, Žižek insists upon the ontological and temporal or genetic priority of substance over subject, with the latter emerging out of the former.[42] But, when he does so, he also tends to flirt with the notion that substantiality before the emergence of subjectivity (that is, prehuman nature *an sich*) is not weak (as in Hegel's *Ohnmacht der Natur*) but, rather, strong qua a Whole organically at one with itself and its parts. In *Less Than Nothing*, he stresses that "the subject always, constitutively, comes second, it refers to an already given Substance, introducing into it abstract distinctions and fictions, tearing apart its organic unity,"[43] and goes on to claim that "man *is* . . . an anamorphic distortion of nature, a perturbance of the 'natural' rhythm of generation and corruption."[44] Although the quotation marks around "natural" in the second of these two lines allude to nuancing caveats, the basic gist of these lines involves presupposing or positing the smooth "rhythm" of an "organic unity," something glaringly at odds both with other formulations by Žižek and, arguably, with Žižek's ontology in its most fundamental, systematic dimensions.

Žižek's glosses on Hegel's substance *als Natur* and subject *als Geist* in *Absolute Recoil* likewise problematically imply that there actually is (or was), in fact, a substantial harmony subsequently disrupted with the genesis of subjectivity. He states that "the Spirit is itself the wound it tries to heal, that is, the wound is self-inflicted. 'Spirit' at its most elementary is the 'wound' of nature. The subject is the immense—absolute—power of negativity, the power of introducing a gap or cut into the given-immediate substantial unity, the power of differentiating, of 'abstracting,' of tearing apart and treating as self-standing what in reality is part of an organic unity."[45] These lines recur almost verbatim in *Disparities*.[46] In addition to this talk of "substantial," "organic unity," Žižek also, in the same context, speaks of "broken symmetry," the "ruining" of "the preceding peace," and "the full and sane Body into which the wound was cut."[47] In short, substance (S), before the emergence of subject ($), enjoys, as Žižek's mathemes themselves suggest, an unbarred (that is, harmonious, smooth, unified) status, namely, strong positive plenitude rather than weak negative deficiencies.

However, some of Žižek's other formulations in this vein that clearly avoid the stealthy reintroduction of Nature-with-a-capital-N as a substantial big Other and self-consistent One-All bring with them their own difficulties in turn. In *Less Than Nothing*, he recommends a "properly dialectical-materialist" move involving "not, of course, the direct spiritualization of nature in the mode of Romantic *Naturphilosophie*, but an immanent de-naturalization of nature"[48] (a line he repeats in *Absolute Recoil*).[49] I must avow my very deepest sympathies with this idea of "an immanent de-naturalization of nature." But these sympathies are nonetheless partly conditional upon precisely how one understands what, exactly, Žižek has in mind here.

Throughout Žižek's current work related to a resurrected dialectical materialism, he tends to speak of nature in and of itself as desubstantialized qua conflicted, disharmonious, inconsistent, and so on, especially when addressing such topics as humanity's distinctiveness (or lack thereof) in terms of animality, freedom, and sexuality (as well as when he touches upon ecology and "green thinking").[50] This type of talk importantly differs from his other elaborations along the lines of "a *materialism without matter*" as a hyperstructuralist ontology of strong form(alism) (what I have rejected as a betrayal, rather than reinvention, of dialectical materialism). Yet Žižek sometimes, when articulating the tenets of a dialectical materialism of weak nature, seems too quickly to identify subject with insubstantial substance, *Geist* with *die Ohnmacht der Natur*, the barred subject of culture with the barred Real of nature (as does Zupančič too from time to time in some of her recent reflections).[51] At this juncture, it must be recalled that Žižek's earlier-mentioned attacks upon contemporary pseudomaterialist orientations subsumable under the heading of "democratic materialism" include dismissals of Deleuze-inspired "new materialisms" as indefensibly panpsychist, as implausibly spiritualizing nature (qua *natura naturans* and even *natura naturata*) in a regressive, mystical fashion.[52] But, if the move is made of directly equating the two negativities of natural (in)substantiality and denaturalized or more-than-natural subjectivity, then how is this not tantamount to yet another panpsychism, albeit one with the historical distinctiveness of replacing an emphasis upon cosmic organic unity with one upon ubiquitous antagonisms and strife (Empedocles rather than Parmenides)?

At this point, it might seem as though the Žižek of *Less Than Nothing* and *Absolute Recoil* is inconsistent such that readers are pushed into choosing between two incompatible options, both intensely unpalatable for any materialist agreeing with much of what Žižek expresses so marvelously across the arc of his corpus. About "pushing idealism to its limit," the choice would be between either making "matter disappear" tout court (that is, the Pythagorean-Platonic idealist metaphysical realism of strong form) or lapsing into a disavowed panpsychism of the barred psyche (that is, a spiritualization of nature in which the main difference from most other panpsychisms is that the spirit at work is split, rather than undivided, subjectivity [$]). Now, I am convinced that Žižek possesses and frequently utilizes claims and arguments delineating a compelling, novel variant of dialectical materialism avoiding and surpassing both of these distasteful options. As on previous occasions,[53] I see myself in this context as yet again conducting an immanent critique of Žižek himself, challenging some of his utterances on the basis of what I take to be the most charitable and powerful reconstruction of a systematic Žižekian metaphysics. All the same, this reconstruction requires carefully sifting through the black-letter contents of Žižek's texts, selectively amending or disputing certain of their details.

Playing Žižek contra Žižek, what sketch am I able to offer of a dialectical materialism remaining faithful to the spirit, while criticizing the letter, of *Less Than Nothing* and *Absolute Recoil*? From my perspective, there are five lines of thought contained in these two monumental recent statements of Žižek's philosophical position that fit together tightly. They constitute a theoretical core both supporting neither an idealism of metaphysically real forms nor a panpsychism of the split psyche and able to be held up as a legitimate extension of the Marxian-Engelsian dialectical materialist tradition (as well as an inheritor of the enduringly valid aspects of the Hegelian Philosophy of Nature).[54] In what follows, I will pinpoint and briefly characterize these five facets of (partially) Žižekian dialectical materialism.

First, Hegel's Logic, in all its mature versions, is not to be misconstrued as the Hegelian System in its entirety or even as the unique *Ur*-core of this System. In contrast with Platonic metaphysical realism, Hegel puts forward his *Logik* as, on its own in abstraction from *Realphilosophie als Naturphilosophie und Geistesphilosophie* (that is, Logic as merely the first part of the three-part *Encyclopedia of the Philosophical Sciences*), "pre-ontological" (Žižek) instead of properly ontological.[55] The Logic unfolds the dialectical-speculative network of categories as themselves both epistemological conditions of possibility for the subjective thinking of the natural and spiritual realities of the Philosophy of the Real and (pre)ontological conditions of possibility for the materialized, more-than-logical being of these same realities.[56] But these categories, confined strictly within the pure abstraction of the Logic's "thinking about thinking," are not metaphysically real, acquiring such full ontological status (that is, real being) only in and through the immanence of the actual (*als Wirklichkeit*) existences of *Natur und Geist*.[57] (Chapter 2 already provides the evidence and justifications for the assertions in this paragraph.)

Second, Žižek's militant fidelity specifically to this non-Platonist Hegel categorically rules out his deviations in the direction of a matter-less hyper-structuralism of unsullied, strong forms (that is, a formalist-idealist *"materialism without matter"*). Žižek reinforces this properly materialist repudiation of metaphysical realism when, in the context of demarcating the limits of Hegel's philosophy, he indicates that the combination, definitively characteristic of the modern natural sciences, of *Verstand*-level mathematics and empirical experimentation could not be done justice to by Hegel himself but still must be affirmatively incorporated by Hegelian materialists today.[58] Moreover, Žižek's entirely correct dismissals of the Koyréian French neo-Cartesian rationalism of Badiou and Meillassoux as indefensibly reducing scientificity to pure mathematical(-style) formalization alone similarly signal a reassuring (for a materialist) commitment, however qualified, to empiricist and naturalist epistemological and ontological elements.[59] Likewise, he is careful to note that quantum physics itself cannot be treated as a matter of nonapplied, armchair mathematics alone.[60]

Third, and following on the heels of the second, Žižek, despite his pronounced taste for speculations regarding theoretical physics as his favored empirical, experimental natural-scientific partner for a rejuvenated contemporary dialectical materialism, sometimes recognizes how and why the life sciences are of such overriding importance for Marxian materialist traditions past and present[61] (not to mention for Hegelian *Naturphilosophie* too).[62] He recurrently evinces an appropriate awareness and appreciation of a lineage running from the Kant of the *Critique of the Power of Judgment* (specifically the "Critique of the Teleological Power of Judgment") through Schelling's and Hegel's Philosophies of Nature and onward into Engels's *Naturdialektik* and its primarily Soviet furtherance. Within this orientation, biological organics occupies a special position for "a *materialism with an Idea*" (*Absolute Recoil*) qua a nonreductive materialist ontology of desubstantialized substantiality (that is, weak or rotten nature) inextricably intertwined precisely with nothing other than a theory of full-fledged, nonepiphenomenal subjectivity (that is, $s endowed with powers of downward causation). Specifically, biology is simultaneously (1) a natural science and region of nature emergent from but irreducible to physics and chemistry as well as (2) the threshold realm out of which arise sentient and sapient subjects.

Fourth, Žižek's periodic affirmations of emergentism (as I just appealed to in the previous paragraph) helpfully mitigate against a pansubjectivism of $ in which barred substance and barred subject are conflated with each other completely (an unfortunate equivocation or short circuit to which, as I showed earlier, Žižek occasionally has recourse despite himself). However, this mitigation is conditional upon the emergence of $ specifically from living matter (itself emergent in turn vis-à-vis nonliving matter) and not, as potentially insinuated by much of the engaging with quantum physics in *Less*

Than Nothing and *Absolute Recoil*, from subatomic particles and processes (at least not directly and immediately). Along the lines of my critical stipulations with respect to quantum physics à la Žižek elsewhere,[63] I would say here that an emergentism of subjectivity proper straight from quantum-physical, rather than organic, substance(s) violates the fundaments of dialectical materialism and Žižekian ontology by being extremely reductive and holistic, abruptly collapsing real distinctions between multiple intermediate emergent levels and layers (atomic, molecular, chemical, genetic, cellular, and so on), as I also discuss in chapter 5.

Fifth and finally, Žižek, when, for instance, wisely cautioning that quantum indeterminacy is not tantamount to subjective freedom qua self-determinacy[64] (that is, that contingency and randomness do not equal autonomy and agency), reveals himself to be cognizant of the simple but pivotal distinction between necessary and sufficient conditions. For a current, genuine dialectical materialism, by contrast with the pseudomaterialist ontology of a panpsychism of the divided psyche, the incompleteness of being as the weakness or rottenness of nature makes possible, without automatically or inevitably making actual, $. Put differently, the barred Real is necessary but not sufficient for the barred subject. And, methodologically following in the wake of certain aspects of Kantian and post-Kantian German idealism, such transcendental yet natural or material catalysts for subjectivity (as themselves pre- or nonsubjective) can and should be reverse-engineered *après-coup* out of this same subjectivity. Maintaining the distinction between necessary and sufficient conditions indispensably assists with guarding against falls straight back into the fetters of a "great chain of Being." There is nothing to lose here but the cheap and empty disposable packaging of materialism-free materialisms.

But what about Žižek's self-redemptions as a proper Hegelian-Marxian dialectical materialist I promised at the start of this chapter that I would underscore in its second half? As I said then, these are to be found primarily in connection with his lucid, demystifying interpretations of Hegel's *Naturphilosophie*, itself sometimes obscure and vulnerable to a multitude of misunderstandings. One of the many important services performed by the Žižekian return to Hegel is its demonstration, sometimes contrary to the belief of Marx and his descendants, that the gaps between Hegelianism and Marxism are not as numerous or wide as Marxists take them to be (and sometimes they are not even located where Marxists believe they are). Žižek's handling of Hegel's Philosophy of Nature as a dialectical materialist naturalism avant la lettre is a case in point. Moreover, Žižek, however intentionally or not, brings himself back into the good company of Marxist materialists in and through his materialist rendition of Hegelian *Naturphilosophie*.

The conclusion of Hegel's mature Logic—the *Science of Logic* and successive editions of the *Encyclopedia Logic* all share very similar closing paragraphs—explicitly marks the transition from *Logik* to *Realphilosophie*, with the initial form of the latter being *Naturphilosophie*.[65] (Admittedly, exactly how, for Hegel, this dialectical-speculative segue from the logical to the natural works [or does not work] is a matter of some confusion and dissensus among his readers.) *Less Than Nothing*, with reference to this pivotal but enigmatic moment in the Hegelian encyclopedic System, exegetically emphasizes the textual fact that the logical Idea, upon completing itself, suddenly allows Nature to come into actual being as an independent, extralogical existence unto itself.[66] Žižek then utilizes as an illustration of this allowance content from Hegelian Aesthetics:

> Hegel accounts for the rise of "dead nature" paintings (not only of landscapes, flowers, etc., but of food and dead animals) in the following way: precisely because, in the development of art, subjectivity no longer needs the visual as the principle medium of its expression—the accent having shifted to poetry as a more direct means of expressing the subject's inner life—the natural is "released" from the burden of expressing subjectivity and can thus now be approached, and visually depicted, on its own terms.[67]

On the next page, he asserts that "the release of Nature into its own ... lays the foundation for Spirit proper, which can develop itself only out of Nature, as its inherent self-sublation."[68] Regarding Hegel and Žižek's Hegelianism, these observations by Žižek signal several points. First of all, they underscore that, even with the "Absolute Idea" of the Logic, Hegel's "absolute idealism," contra numerous falsifications of it as an antirealist macrosolipsism, is both realist generally (as discussed in chapters 1 and 2) and realist specifically regarding Nature qua the pre-/nonsubjective Real *an sich*.

Second, logical subjectivity's releasing (*als Entlassung*) of natural objectivity sets *Natur* as well as *Geist* free as sovereign, self-standing realities unto themselves precisely by making neither heteronomously depend upon the other. Nonetheless, Žižek, in a true Hegelian manner, is careful to qualify the emergent, achieved freedom of Mind or Spirit vis-à-vis Nature. The spiritual, precisely as the "inherent self-sublation" of the natural, is a nature-generated negation of nature, namely, an overcoming of the natural arising from the natural itself, an antinature immanent to what it transcends and opposes.[69] The very prepositional phrase *out of* (as in "develop itself only out of Nature") employed by Žižek in the previous quotation conveys the essential ambiguity of this sublation (as well as of *Aufhebung überhaupt*). On the one hand, "out of" signifies "escape from"—in this context, Spirit becoming autonomous by escaping from Nature (that is, sublation as negation). On the other hand, "out of" (also) signifies internal, bottom-up genesis—in this context, Spirit welling up from within, and thereafter permanently owing its creation and continued being to, Nature (that is, sublation as preservation).

These themes receive further elaboration both elsewhere in *Less Than Nothing* and in *Absolute Recoil*. Later in his tome from 2012, Žižek posits that "we not only work upon and thus transform nature—in a gesture of retroactive reversal, nature itself radically changes its 'nature.'"[70] (His sequel in 2014 returns to this same retroactivity.)[71] This statement is somewhat perilously ambiguous. As discussed in the first half of this chapter, a number of Žižek's assertions in 2012 and 2014 about material nature problematically come close to expressing vitalist or panpsychist perspectives, to unreservedly "spiritualizing" *Natur an sich*. Likewise, this line from *Less Than Nothing* could potentially be (mis)interpreted as announcing a transubstantiation without remainder of Nature by Spirit via a *nachträglich* digestion by spiritual subjectivity of natural objectivity sans leftovers (a danger all the greater given the idealist-qua-vitalist/panpsychist notes sounded at other moments in Žižek's recent work, which I criticized earlier in this chapter). Subsequently in *Less Than Nothing*, Žižek even seems both to take Hegel himself to task for not pushing through the *après-coup* denaturalization of nature to the exceptionless end (thereby leaving at least some of Nature unmediated by Spirit) and to insist that the denaturalizing mediations of spiritual subjectivity indeed exhaustively transform natural objectivity.[72] Is this not an instance of Žižek strangely chastising Hegel for, of all things, failing to live up to the parodies of him as a cosmic idealist-spiritualist vehemently hostile to realism, naturalism, and materialism? How can Žižek, specifically as a self-declared Hegelian dialectical materialist, be making such suggestions?

Obviously, on any remotely charitable interpretation crediting Žižek with even a minimal capacity for being consistent with himself, he cannot seriously be suggesting this line of thought. Indeed, other moments in *Less Than Nothing* and *Absolute Recoil* call for such charity. Elsewhere in his book from 2012, Žižek, in the context of challenging certain aspects of the (false, guilty, and pseudosecular) consciousness of ecological green thinking, maintains that "there is no nature."[73] By this, he definitely does not mean that the physical universe does not exist, that the material world is a veil of illusions behind which lurks only a supernatural metaphysical reality of mind, spirit, ideas, and the like. Instead, what is unreal for this Žižek is merely a particular image of nature as a peaceful balanced harmony (which, in the eyes of those of the ecologically minded he is attacking, is accidentally and gratuitously thrown into lamentable disorder and crisis by the tragic technoscientific sins of hubristic humanity as externally meddling with nature's beings and rhythms). Žižek's *il n'y a pas de nature* conveys the Hegelian thesis according to which nature does not exist as a placid orchestrated unity precisely because nature itself internally generates the human agencies that are nature-immanent but nature-disruptive and that are responsible for (some of what appears to be) the imbalance and disharmony associated with the human qua emblematic of antinature and denaturalization. The humans seeming to shatter the fantasized organic consistency of nature are themselves the products of nature. Hence, nature itself is self-shattering. Or, as Žižek puts it in *Absolute Recoil*, Spirit-*als-Geist* is the "wound" of a self-wounding *Natur*, the desubstantializing sundering of a self-sundering substance.[74] With the distinction between "the factual" and "the normative" as aligning with that between Nature and Spirit respectively, "the gap separating the normative from the factual should be simultaneously conceived as a gap immanent to the factual itself."[75]

Furthermore, when Žižek criticizes Hegel's own handling of the distinction between Nature and Spirit as insufficiently dialectical-speculative due to its leaving intact natural dimensions in an immediacy externally confronting spiritual mediation (a criticism I just noted), this is not, despite possible appearances to the contrary, an unreserved liquidation of the independent reality of the natural. How so? Here, invoking the Hegelian distinction between the "in itself" and the "in and for itself" is once again crucial. Žižek's Hegelian objection to Hegel, properly construed, is that *Natur*, although *an sich* a free-standing, self-subsistent existence apart from *Geist*, nevertheless, after the emergence of the latter, cannot manifest itself to Spirit(s) as something utterly alien. What Nature is *an und für sich* is equivalent to what it is "for us" insofar as the consciousness and self-consciousness of human beings are immanent to Nature, are Nature appearing to itself through itself. What I take Žižek to be saying is that while there really are and continue to be natural dimensions enjoying the ontological independence of a pre- and nonhuman "in itself," these dimensions cannot be experienced as such by human mindedness and like-mindedness. In manifesting itself to itself via Spirit, Nature introduces a split into itself between, on the one hand, what it is and remains "in itself" and, on the other hand, what it is (or seems to be) "for itself" (with this "for itself" being "for us").

Also in *Less Than Nothing*, Žižek further buttresses his Hegelian contention that humanity embodies the autointerrupting, self-fragmenting character of *Natur* through recourse to Hegel's "Anthropology," the opening section of the third and final volume of the *Encyclopedia*, the *Philosophy of Mind*. Of course, this section builds indispensable bridges between *Naturphilosophie* and *Geistesphilosophie*, constructing the pivotal transition from pre-/nonhuman Nature to properly human Spirit. The subject of Hegelian philosophical anthropology is the human "soul" (*Seele*), itself the animal-organic foundation of human nature as still very much natural (as protospiritual but not yet fully, properly *geistige*). Žižek turns specifically to Hegel's famous discussion of "habit" (*die Gewohnheit*) there.[76]

Having dealt with Žižek's reflections on the habitual à la Hegel on prior occasions[77]—I also address this topic again in the conclusion—I will move to the relevant upshot here of Hegelian habit in *Less Than Nothing*. Hegelian-Žižekian habits are, on the one hand, natural developments insofar as they crystalize in and through the nature-immanent human soul. But, on the other hand, they incarnate in singular human beings idiosyncratic forms of bodily and behavioral asymmetry, imbalance, lopsidedness, and the like—namely, "unnatural" developments qua interruptions and subversions of nature envisioned as symmetrical, balanced, harmonized, well-proportioned, and so on. Furthermore, as acquired rather than innate, habits constitute a second nature, albeit one made possible by the human organism's first-natural potential and inclination for acquiring them. The conclusion Žižek draws from the preceding is that, with the habit-prone human *Seele* as internal to organic nature, this nature is self-disruptive and autosublating. Hence, "there is no Nature" as a presupposed harmonious unity free from the negativities of humanity.[78] Human organisms represent the real dialectics of the organic immanently producing out of itself what I call the "anorganic" (specifically as a negation of the organic that itself is not simply a return to the inorganic as the merely mechanical, physical, or chemical).[79]

Select moments in *Absolute Recoil*, from my perspective, go even further in strengthening Žižek-the-Hegelian-dialectical-materialist against other Žižeks who seem to stray from the line of the former Žižek. Early on in his book from 2014, he declares that it is crucial "to approach head-on the question of how the pre-human real has to be structured so as to allow for the emergence of the symbolic/normative dimension."[80] In response to this declaration, I suggest that Žižek is an authentic, die-hard Hegelian dialectical materialist at those points when he identifies this "pre-human real" as nature understood in specific senses. Conversely, I likewise suggest that when he instead slides into portraying this Real as a mysterious primal Nothingness/Void or omnipresent protosubjectivity, he drifts toward a certain negative theology or vitalist panpsychism respectively (as I discussed in the first half of this chapter, and as I will discuss again in the conclusion).

Later moments in *Absolute Recoil* indeed involve Žižek aligning his "pre-human real" with the natural. For instance, he proposes an "inverted perspective" according to which the direction of questioning should be "not 'What is nature for language? Can we grasp nature adequately in/through language?' but 'What is language for nature? How does its emergence affect nature?'"[81] The word *language* here should be read as equivalent to what Žižek, in the quotation before this one, refers to as "the emergence of the symbolic/normative dimension," namely, in Hegelian parlance, objective spirit and, in Lacanian parlance, the sociolinguistic big Other. Hence, the fundamental query being formulated is, essentially, "What is *Geist* for *Natur*?" And, as I clarified a short while ago, Žižek can be construed as answering questions about Spirit's "emergence" from Nature and the former's impact on the latter in two ways simultaneously: first, positing the natural as a self-sundering, autodisruptive Real splintering off from itself the spiritual that thereafter immanently transcends this pre- or nonspiritual nature; and, second, stipulating that *Natur*, without thereby losing its self-standing objectivity, nonetheless cannot appear to *Geist* as a pure *an sich* Real. The first explanatory line receives additional elaboration in *Absolute Recoil*.

Žižek subsequently returns to the distinction between the linguistic and the natural in *Absolute Recoil*. He proposes:

> Should we not take a step further beyond the ontological break between language and the living body and ask: how must the real be structured so that that break can emerge within it? In other words, language colonizing the living body from without cannot be the last word since, in some sense, language itself has to be part of the real. How to think this belonging outside the naturalization of language? There is only one consistent answer: by de-naturalizing nature itself.[82]

Žižek continues:

> Lacan himself oscillates here between the (predominant) transcendental approach and timid gestures in the direction of its beyond. Lacan's standard topos is the radical discontinuity between (biological) life and the symbolic: the symbolic derails life, subordinating it to a foreign compulsion, depriving it forever of its homeostasis—the move from instinct to drive, from need to desire. Within this perspective, the symbolic order is "always already there" as our unsurpassable horizon, and every account of its genesis amounts to a fantasmatic obfuscation of its constitutive gap. In this Lacanian-structuralist version of the "hermeneutic circle," all we can do is circumscribe the void or impossibility which makes the symbolic non-All and inconsistent, the void in which the external limit coincides with the internal one (the void delimits the symbolic from the Real, but this limitation cuts into the symbolic itself). However, from time to time, and more often in the later Lacan, we find echoes of the Schellingian-Benjaminian-Heideggerian topic of a suffering in nature itself, a pain which comes to be expressed/resolved in human speech—the Freudian *Unbehagen in Der Kultur* is thereby supplemented by an uncanny *Unbehagen in Der Natur* itself.[83]

When, in the first of these quotations, Žižek speaks of "de-naturalizing nature itself," this indicates that familiar, established (one might say, "natural" qua second-natural) pictures of nature must be abandoned and replaced once one accepts that Nature (as "the pre-human real," "the living body," and the like) generates "the ontological break" between itself and Spirit (as "the symbolic/normative dimension," "language," and so on). With the benefit of metaphysical hindsight compelled by the nature-internal genetic emergence of denaturalized, socio-historico-linguistic humanity, the natural can no longer seem so natural. Non/pre-human *Natur* must be thought of quite differently once *Geist* is non-reductively rendered immanent to it.[84]

In particular, Žižek, in both the second of these quotations and passages immediately after it, takes a stance according to which specific kinds of negativity must be attributed retroactively to "the pre-human real" of *Natur an sich* in order to account for the very fact of the historical rise of the human out of the natural. He associates such negativity with certain negative affects under the heading of *"das Unbehagen in der Natur."* Just after doing so, he ties this to a phrase recurrently employed by Hegel himself: *"die Ohnmacht der Natur."*[85] (I have written at length about this elsewhere, including in connection with Lacan.)[86] For Žižek, Hegel's "weakness of nature" is tantamount to the fact that "pre-human reality is itself 'exceptional,' incomplete, unbalanced, and this ontological gap or incompleteness emerges 'as such' with humanity."[87]

This Žižek adamantly insists that, "in humanity, the exception constitutive of nature appears as such."[88] I consider it unsurprising that, in this very context, a pair of Žižek's favorite references surface: Schelling and quantum physics,[89] along with Heidegger and Benjamin, as seen in the previous block quotation. At this juncture, I must qualify my extension of charity to Žižek and say that, while I consider the questions he asks regarding permutations of the *Natur-Geist* relationship in *Absolute Recoil* to be both Hegelian and materialist, I have doubts about whether his answers to these questions are always in step with Hegel's philosophy or the legacy of dialectical materialism. Specifically, Žižek's solutions to materialist problems deployed under the banner of "quantum physics with Schelling" are arguably in tension with both Hegelianism and materialism (an incompatibility I further underscore in the conclusion).

The Schellingian model to which Žižek avowedly has recourse in such remarks as "in humanity, the exception constitutive of nature appears as such" repeatedly manifests itself throughout the full arc of Schelling's corpus, despite this thinker's partly deserved reputation as mercurial and protean. Starting with his philosophies of identity and nature in the late 1790s, Schelling again and again opts to explain (or, less sympathetically, explain away) anthropogenesis in particular—which is also what is at stake for the Žižek under discussion—via a sort of Spinoza-inspired vitalist panpsychism. (At this point, one should recall why and how I expressed reservations with respect to certain potentially panpsychist or pansubjectivist moments in Žižek's thinking earlier in this chapter.) About this Schelling, one could say that the rabbit he pulls out of his hat is the one he put there beforehand. The human organism and its forms of subjectivity "emerge" from Schellingian nature because the latter is always already an eternally preexistent macro-/mega-Subject, namely, the spontaneous agency of *natura naturans*, a divine productive power as the ground (*Grund*) or *Ur*-potency of all beings. The final phases of Schelling's intellectual itinerary during the decades of the 1830s and 1840s—a period characterized by vehement anti-Hegelianism coupled with outright Christian religiosity—can defensibly be interpreted as a consequent extension of the nondialectical spiritualism haunting Schelling's oeuvre from its inception onward. In approvingly drawing upon this strain of Schellingianism, Žižek pulls himself away from both the Hegelianism and dialectical materialism to which he so ardently swears unwavering fidelity.[90]

In *Absolute Recoil*, Žižek quite justifiably attacks theoretical prohibitions on inquiries into the origins of minded and like-minded human subjectivity and everything associated with these subjects (language, culture, normativity, and so on)—for instance, these prohibitions as linked to a structuralist privileging of synchrony over diachrony, including (pseudo-)Lacanian versions of this privileging.[91] Against such dubious bans forbidding investigations into the immanent geneses of more-than-material *Geist* out of material *Natur*, he rightly maintains that "the Hegelian wager is that one *can* account for such emergences."[92] I could not agree more with this. Nonetheless (and as I will reinforce in the conclusion), it remains for me questionable whether Žižek makes good on this wager in a consistently proper Hegelian-materialist manner.

FIVE

Bartleby by Nature
German Idealism, Biology, and Žižek's Compatibilism

ŽIŽEK, AS IS entirely appropriate and, indeed, requisite for a self-identifying materialist, wrestles again and again with versions of the perennial mind-body problem, one of the biggest questions in the history of Western philosophy. Likewise, he also repeatedly confronts the equally daunting and persistent divide between freedom and determinism from various angles. As a single, massive summation of Žižek's current theoretical framework, *Less Than Nothing* extends and develops his dialectical materialist ways of treating these two fundamental philosophical topics. He does so primarily through staging encounters between, on one side, classical German philosophy (à la Kant, Fichte, Schelling, and Hegel) and, on another side, today's empirical, experimental sciences of nature (especially quantum physics and biology).

To those unfamiliar with Žižek, this combining of German idealism and natural science would likely sound like a recipe for yet another death match between partisans of freedom (represented by German idealism) and advocates of determinism (represented by natural science) on an old *Kampfplatz* devoid of hope. But, as anyone familiar with Žižek's ideas already knows, such is never the case for him. Žižek is well aware of how the original forms of the idealisms of the late-eighteenth- and early-nineteenth-century German-speaking world (especially the idealists' philosophies of nature and the natural sciences) have been rendered partially problematic and limited in connection with an intervening two hundred years of significant scientific advances.¹ Nonetheless, he not only seeks to salvage for the present what from German idealism has continued to remain enduringly valid and valuable for the past two centuries; he also arguably shows why and how contemporary understandings of various matters, including nature according to those sciences concerned with it, can and must be altered in response to redeployments of Kantian and post-Kantian philosophical systems.

The present chapter critically examines the compatibility, for Žižek, between autonomous denaturalized subjectivity and heteronomous natural substantiality. I scrutinize how Žižek constructs his distinctive version of compatibilism via creative syntheses of German idealism, psychoanalysis, and the sciences of nature. Žižekian compatibilism, on my reconstruction of it, identifies certain necessary conditions for subjective spontaneity within the constrains of a strictly materialist, albeit antireductive, ontology. But the conclusion I reach at the end of this chapter is that this compatibilism, at least as articulated by Žižek so far, has yet to stipulate what the sufficient conditions, in addition to the necessary ones, are for the genesis of subjectivity out of substantiality. Therefore, Žižek's dialectical materialist account of subjects importantly helps to lay solid foundations for future intellectual labors along these same lines while nevertheless not yet having finished the tasks required for this account's theoretical completeness.

In *Less Than Nothing*, Žižek begins approaching the issue of autonomy via the now-familiar pairing of Kant *avec* Lacan. On the basis of Lacan's psychoanalytic appropriations of Kant's deontological ethics of pure practical reason in such texts as the seventh seminar of 1959–1960 on *The Ethics of Psychoanalysis* and the contemporaneous *écrit* "Kant *avec* Sade," numerous interpreters of Lacan, including Žižek, Zupančič, myself, and many others, have previously discussed this pairing at detailed length. Hence, I will try to avoid in what follows excessively or needlessly recapitulating these earlier discussions.

As in much of Žižek's prior corpus, *Less Than Nothing* has recourse to Lacan's concept of the "act." (I critically examine Lacan's and Žižek's variations on this concept elsewhere.)² Žižek states that, "for Lacan, properly ethical acts are rare: they occur like 'miracles' which interrupt the ordinary run of things; they do not 'express' the entire 'personality' of the subject, but function as a break in the continuity of 'personal identity.'"³ On the next page, he adds: "An ethical act is one that does not comprise or express the entire person, but is a moment of grace, a 'miracle' which can occur also in a non-virtuous individual. This is why such acts are difficult to imagine, and why, when they do occur, one tends to invent a narrative which normalizes them."[4]

This line of thought recurs in *Absolute Recoil* too.[5] With such phrases as "the ordinary run of things," "entire 'personality' of the subject," " 'personal identity,' " "entire person," and "individual," Žižek is designating a dimension featuring centrally in both Kant's and Lacan's conceptions of ethics: in Kant, the all-too-human phenomenal "I," the empirical "me" with its self-seeking pathological inclinations aimed at private gratification, pleasure, satisfaction, and the like; in Lacan, the ego entwined through the related pleasure and reality principles with Imaginary-Symbolic realities. A basic stance held in common between Kant and Lacan is their shared insistence that the domain of this type of personal identity is not all there is to subjectivity. One even could say that, for these two thinkers, the subject proper is something different in kind from such selfhood.[6]

Amply supported by earlier investigative efforts into Lacan's heterodox Kantianism by both himself and others, Žižek therefore feels licensed to draw a straight line closely connecting the categorically imperative moral law of pure rational duty à la Kant with the circuits of *désir* and *jouissance* operating "beyond the pleasure principle" à la Lacan. He explains:

> The first thing to state categorically is that Lacanian ethics is not an ethics of hedonism: whatever "do not compromise on your desire" means, it does *not* mean the unrestrained rule of what Freud called "the pleasure principle," the functioning of the psychic apparatus that aims at achieving pleasure. For Lacan, hedonism is in fact *the* model of postponing desire on behalf of "realistic compromises": it is not only that, in order to attain the greatest amount of pleasure, I have to calculate and economize, sacrificing short-term pleasures for more intense long-term ones; what is even more important is that *jouissance hurts*. So, first, there is no break between the pleasure principle and its counterpart, the "reality principle": the latter (compelling us to take into account the limitations that thwart our direct access to pleasure) is an inherent prolongation of the former. Second, even (Western) Buddhism is not immune to the lures of the pleasure principle; the Dalai Lama himself wrote: "The purpose of life is to be happy"—*not true for psychoanalysis*, one should add. It was Nietzsche who observed that "human beings do not desire happiness, only the Englishmen desire happiness"—today's globalized

hedonism is thus merely the obverse of the fact that, in the conditions of global capitalism, we are ideologically "all Englishmen" (or, rather, Anglo-Saxon Americans ...). So what is wrong with the rule of the pleasure principle? In Kant's description, ethical duty functions like a foreign intruder that disturbs the subject's homeostatic balance, its unbearable pressure forcing the subject to act "beyond the pleasure principle," ignoring the pursuit of pleasures. For Lacan, exactly the same description holds for desire, which is why enjoyment is not something that comes naturally to the subject, as a realization of his or her inner potential, but is the content of a traumatic superegoic injunction.[7]

The content of this passage is also echoed subsequently in the same book.[8] Of course, *Beyond the Pleasure Principle*, published in 1920, is the text in which the later Freud introduces his hypothesis of the *Todestrieb*. Hence, Žižek's identification of this particular "beyond" as a direct link of commonality between Kant and Lacan is of a piece with his larger endeavor to establish an equivalence between the autonomous subject as in Kantian and post-Kantian German idealism and the death drive as in Freudian-Lacanian psychoanalysis. (He recurrently insists that this synthesis of freedom as in idealism and *Todestrieb* as in analysis is the core concern of his entire oeuvre.)[9] Žižek further reinforces the bond between Kant and Lacan through stressing that both Kantian and Lacanian ethics equally eschew reliance upon, in Lacan's terms, a hypothesized "big Other" as an ethical "subject supposed to know," namely, a transcendent, omniscient authority eternally guaranteeing the ultimate rightness (or wrongness) of one's decisions and deeds.[10] Thus, the decontextualized formal emptiness of Kant's categorical imperative, as itself the cornerstone of his metaphysics of morals, is depicted as a virtue rather than a vice insofar as its formal emptiness condemns the ethical subject to being responsible for freely determining every specific instantiation of this imperative. Incidentally, Žižek's defense of this formal emptiness implicitly goes against Hegel's recurrent criticisms of the empty formalism of Kantian philosophy generally and Kant's practical philosophy especially.[11]

Žižek proceeds, in *Less Than Nothing*, to lend additional precision to the notion of the act he appropriates from Lacan. Specifically, he situates it as part of a tripartite distinction:

> A radical revolution does (what previously appeared as) the impossible and thereby creates its own precursors—this, perhaps, is the most succinct definition

of what an authentic *act* is. Such an act proper should be located in the trilogy (which strangely reflects the "European trinity" of English, French, and German): *acting out, passage à l'acte, Tat-Handlung* (Fichte's neologism for the founding gesture of the subject's self-positing in which the activity and its result fully overlap). *Acting out* is a hysterical outburst within the same big Other; *passage à l'acte* destructively suspends the big Other; *Tat-Handlung* retroactively rearranges it. As Jacques-Alain Miller put it, "the status of the act is retroactive": a gesture "will have been" an act; it becomes an act if, in its consequences, it succeeds in disturbing and rearranging the "big Other." The properly dialectical solution of the dilemma "Is it really there, in the source, or did we just read it into the source?" is thus: it is there, but we can only perceive and state this retroactively, from the perspective of the present.[12]

In line with Žižek's fundamental theoretical agenda, this quotation further reinforces the tie between German idealism and psychoanalysis. As seen earlier, there are not only threads of continuity conjoining Kant and Lacan, especially at the level of ethics; Fichte, with his (post-)Kantian refounding of transcendental idealism on the basis of the spontaneous subject of practical philosophy, foreshadows Lacan's concept of the act with his pivotal idea of the *Tat-Handlung*. The Fichtean *Tat-Handlung* ("fact/act") can be understood here as a structural dynamic in which subjectivity, as acting agency, and objectivity, as produced action, are moments of one and the same unity. In the case of the theory of self-consciousness central to Fichte's philosophy, the "I," in being conscious of itself, is simultaneously and irreducibly both the transcendental subject intellectually intuiting itself as well as the object thereby intuited.[13]

However, Žižek's Lacanian retrieval of Fichte already tacitly entails certain nonnegligible modifications of the Kantian and Fichtean conceptions of transcendental subjectivity. In particular, Kant's and Fichte's presuppositions and posits about the relation (or lack thereof) between the transcendental and the empirical are implicitly challenged by the Žižekian Lacanianization of Kant and Fichte themselves:

What about the retroactivity of a gesture which (re)constitutes this past itself? This, perhaps, is the most succinct definition of what an authentic *act* is: in our ordinary activity, we effectively just follow the (virtual-fantasmatic) coordinates of our identity, while an act proper involves the paradox of an actual move which (retroactively) changes the very virtual "transcendental" coordinates of its agent's being—or, in Freudian terms, which not only changes the actuality of our world but also "moves its underground." . . . While the pure past is the transcendental condition for our acts, our acts not only create new actual reality, they also retroactively change this very condition.[14]

Or, as Žižek rearticulates this much later, "every authentic act creates its own conditions of possibility."[15] Now, neither Kant nor Fichte temporalizes the transcendental of their transcendental idealisms. Their idealistic subject qua set of possibility conditions for empirical, experiential structures and phenomena itself remains beyond, behind, or beneath everything situated in time. Arguably, transcendental subjectivity as in Kant's and Fichte's idealisms is unchanging, a constant relative to the variables of temporally volatile empirical beings and happenings. One must bear in mind that Žižek here stretches Fichte's concept of the *Tat-Handlung* to cover (Lacanian) acts other than just the (f)act of the "I"'s self-positing (something Fichte would not do). He also assumes a more Hegelian (than Fichtean) dialectical-speculative, reciprocal interpenetration of self qua form (that is, acting subject) and nonself qua content (that is, objects as what are acted upon as well as performed acts themselves). Given this, Žižek's subjectivity of the act (in both senses of the genitive), if it still can be described as "transcendental," is doubly temporal: (1) chronological, genetic, and historical as well as (2) after-the-(f)act à la Freudian-Lacanian *Nachträglichkeit/après-coup* (that is, deferred action as signaled in the verb tense of the future anterior). That is to say, the Žižekian acting subject, as the nonempirical locus of ineliminable autonomy, freedom, and spontaneity, changes in its very transcendental contours and configurations as it moves forward in linear time precisely thanks to this subject being (auto)affected by the effects and influences of its own acts flowing backward in retroactive time. This whole circuit in its entirety amounts to a temporally elongated dynamic of self-reflexivity stretching out over past, present, and future.[16]

Although Žižek already moves beyond Fichte while still explaining the latter's often misunderstood idealist philosophy, he also carefully highlights Fichte's extrapolations from and progress beyond Kant's transcendentalism. In particular, Žižek employs Fichte so as to render Kant more exact and true to himself. On Žižek's construal of the Fichtean version of Kantian transcendental idealism, transcendental subjectivity, as free qua autonomous and spontaneous, is neither merely a phenomenal object as appearance (nonetheless, as seen in chapter 1, the Žižekian German idealist subject is indeed enmeshed with appearances) nor immediately a noumenal thing in itself.[17] (However, as Žižek rightly observes, Kant sometimes conflates transcendental subjectivity with *das Ding an sich* as "this I, or He, or It (the thing), which thinks.")[18] As Žižek points out, Fichte's rejection of Kant's thing in itself—a rejection he shares in common with Jacobi, Schelling, and Hegel, among others (as discussed in chapter 1)—is motivated, at least in part, by a desire to foreclose a specific possibility (one entertained by Kant himself):[19] Subjectivity rests on an underlying noumenal seat and, at this supersensible level, everything really is determined, namely, no autonomy or spontaneity is to be found there. In other words, by jettisoning *das Ding an sich* and, along with it, the (occasional) Kantian equation of the transcendental "I" immanent to the realm of phenomenal appearances with a noumenal "x" transcendent vis-à-vis this same realm, Fichte moves to safeguard the freedom esteemed as of unsurpassably great importance by him, Kant, and the German idealist movement in its entirety. With Žižek's reconstruction of Fichte's theory of the subject (as itself absolutely central to the latter's entire philosophical edifice as a subjectivist transcendental idealism [explained in chapter 1]), there remains, in the post-Kantian aftermath of the dissolution of anything noumenal, only the lone plane of multiple different phenomena and the kinetic negativity of (self-)positing subjectivity internal to this same plane.[20]

In relation to the immediately preceding, Žižek, as is to be expected from the author of *Less Than Nothing*, proceeds to highlight Hegel's crucial step beyond Kant and Fichte. Regarding what is alleged to be "Kant's and Fichte's inability to conceive positively of the ontological status of this neither-phenomenal-nor-noumenal autonomous-spontaneous subject," he proposes that "Hegel's solution here involves the transposition of the epistemological limitation into ontological fact: the void of our knowledge corresponds to a void in being itself, to the ontological incompleteness of reality."[21] Despite Žižek's implicitly self-critical insistence, at other points in *Less Than Nothing*, on reconceptualizing the shift from Kant to Hegel as a matter of the latter "deontologizing" (rather than "ontologizing") the former, this is an instance of him sticking to his older narrative according to which Kantian epistemological ignorances can and should be transformed into Hegelian ontological insights (as discussed in chapter 1). Incidentally but interestingly, in the context of critiquing Meillassoux's speculative materialism much later in

Less Than Nothing, Žižek cautions that not all minuses at the level of epistemology are to be automatically and immediately transubstantiated into pluses at the level of ontology (given that Meillassoux performs with respect to Hume and his problem of induction an ontologization of this empiricist's epistemology akin to what Žižek's Hegel does with Kant).[22] Žižek warns that "not every epistemological limitation is an indication of ontological incompleteness."[23] The main question this raises is, What are the criteria, whether philosophical or empirical, for determining if and when an apparent absence of knowledge is actually the real presence of a true direct rapport between thinking and being?

However, Žižek seems to faithfully follow Hegel's criticisms of the subjectivist essence of Kant's and Fichte's idealisms (as first formulated by Hegel in his *Differenzschrift*, published in 1801, and repeated regularly by him thereafter [as highlighted in chapter 1]). Both Kant and Fichte, in Žižek's Hegelian eyes, spoil many of their best insights into transcendental subjectivity by self-interpreting their own theories of the subject in subjectivist qua transcendent (as distinct from transcendental) terms. The two giants of transcendental idealism (representing the first main phase of German idealism, the one preceding the rise of objective and absolute idealisms with Schelling and Hegel) succeed at disclosing an incomplete, disunited phenomenal field of dialectically unstable organizations and operations, including a more-than-phenomenal subjectivity nonetheless inextricably intertwined with this same field. But Kant and Fichte, each in his own manner, shrink back from the ultimate ontological consequences potentially to be unfurled out of their philosophical efforts. Kant tends to treat his own critical transcendental analyses as strictly epistemological and sometimes succumbs to the temptation to hypothesize (or, one might say, hypostatize) a noumenal self as a transcendent "I"-Thing. Both Kant and Fichte, as subjectivists in Hegel's sense, are extreme and stubborn antirealists, treating their own discourses as exclusively about (self-)conscious thinking *für sich* and not also nonconscious being *an sich*. For Žižek, if a Fichtean in particular wants to defend the reality of freedom as amounting to the authentic, radical causal efficacy of nonappearing subjectivity (that is, the self-positing transcendental subject) and its corresponding appearances, then he or she should become a Hegelian by, as Hegel might phrase it, thinking subject also as substance (yet again, as discussed in chapter 1). That is to say, for the autonomous or spontaneous subject of Fichte's philosophy to be robustly and unambiguously nonepiphenomenal, it and the surface of phenomena to which it remains immanent must, in the absence of a Kantian noumenal Elsewhere (as an other world of things in themselves transcending this world here), be ontologized—even if only by default insofar as the phenomenal here and now is the sole existence that enjoys being in the wake of the dissolution of any absolute Outside of noumena. Despite his repudiation of Kant's *Ding an sich*, Fichte still fails to abandon the antirealist subjectivism closely associated with this very Thing.

Regarding a properly Hegelian sublation of the idealist accounts of freedom within the Kantian and Fichtean edifices, Žižek expresses this with the help of Lacanian language. Near the end of the third chapter of *Less Than Nothing* (the chapter titled "Fichte's Choice"), he suggests: "What kind of structure do we have to think so that it effectively involves the subject, not only as its epiphenomenal 'effect,' but as its immanent constituent? Lacan's answer, of course, is that the condition of freedom (of a free subject) is the 'barred' big Other, a structure which is inconsistent, with gaps."[24] This line of thought subsequently is reiterated: "We are free because there is a lack in the Other, because the substance out of which we grew and on which we rely is inconsistent, barred, failed, marked by an impossibility"[25] and "I am free if the substance of my being is not a full causal network, but an ontologically incomplete field."[26] Žižek has in mind, across the span of these quoted remarks, both sociosymbolic and natural-real versions of the Lacanian barred big Other.[27] Put differently, the "structures" that must be "inconsistent," "incomplete," and the like for the effective existence of nonepiphenomenal autonomous, spontaneous subjectivity are those of the substance(s) both of nonhuman nature and of the "objective spirit" of cultural-linguistic symbolic orders (that is, barred Reals as well as barred Symbolics).[28] Put in Hegelian terms, Hegel and Lacan, for Žižek, sublationally raise Kant and Fichte to the dignity of their Notions by ontologizing Kantian and Fichtean epistemological and subjectivist negativities as necessary nonsubjective conditions for Kant's and Fichte's transcendental subjects.[29]

Less Than Nothing goes on to spend sustained energy in explaining the details of nature as, in Lacanese, the lacking Other of a barred Real of material substances at odds with one another. Of course, Schelling's and Hegel's post-Fichtean Philosophies of Nature already prepare the ground for much of what Žižek does here, as he well knows.[30] Žižek's aim in so doing is, as I indicated, to establish the ultimate ontological-material bases qua necessary conditions of possibility for free subjects immanently transcending these same bases. In addition to working through core components of the problem of freedom and determinism via an enchaining together of Kant, Fichte, Hegel, and Lacan, he also brings into the conversation references to biology and cognitivism:

> Compatibilists such as Daniel Dennett have an elegant solution to the incompatibilists' complaints about determinism: when incompatibilists complain that our freedom cannot be combined with the fact that all our acts are part of the great chain of natural determinism, they secretly make an unwarranted ontological assumption: first, they assume that we (the Self, the free agent) somehow stand *outside* reality, then they go on to complain about how they feel oppressed by the notion that reality in its determinism controls them totally. This is what is wrong with the notion of us being "imprisoned" by the chains of natural determinism: we thereby obfuscate the fact that we are *part of* reality, that the (possible, local) conflict between our "free" striving and the external reality that resists it is a conflict inherent in reality itself. That is to say, there is nothing "oppressive" or "constraining" about the fact that our innermost strivings are (pre)determined: when we feel thwarted in our freedom by the pressure of external reality, there must be something in us, some desire or striving, which is thus thwarted, but where do such strivings come from if not this same reality? Our "free will" does not in some mysterious way "disturb the natural course of things," it is part and parcel of this course. For us to be "truly" and "radically" free would entail that there be no positive content involved in our free act—if we want nothing "external" and particular or given to determine our behavior, then "this would involve being free of every part of ourselves." When a determinist claims that our free choice is "determined," this does not mean that our free will is somehow constrained, that we are forced to act *against* our will—what is "determined" is the very thing that we want to do "freely," that is, without being thwarted by external obstacles.[31]

Žižek, at the beginning of this passage, is referring specifically to arguments in Daniel Dennett's book *Freedom Evolves*, published in 2003.[32] One straightforward way to rearticulate Žižek's compatibilism is to observe that, for both him and Dennett, incompatibilists, as antinaturalistic dualists, rely upon a useless standard of freedom whose uselessness is due to an empty abstraction ("an unwarranted ontological assumption"). This empty abstraction is the vacuous pseudoidea of a wholly pure "I" completely devoid of content by virtue of this self's transcendence of anything determinate. One way to make this point is to assert that the image of "imprisonment" entails a false distinction between prisoner (that is, the incompatibilist's self) and prison (that is, what the incompatibilist misperceives in the guise of deterministic nature as this self's Other). Arguably, Kant and Fichte (unlike Schelling and Hegel) both flirt with, if not outright embrace, such incompatibilism, at least sometimes and to certain degrees.

In the quotation, a position in Anglo-American analytic philosophy of mind—Dennett's specific brand of compatibilism bearing upon the issue of freedom and determinism, which is itself entangled with the divide between monist naturalism and dualist antinaturalism—is justifiably situated as, unbeknown to itself, a permutation of the "system-program" of post-Fichtean German idealism to think subject also as substance (as delineated in chapter 1).[33] In other words, if there really is such a thing as free subjectivity (qua autonomous, spontaneous, and self-determining), then, for a thoroughly materialist theory of such a subject, this freedom must be rendered as an outgrowth of natural substances. ("Our 'free will' does not in some mysterious way 'disturb the natural course of things,' it is part and parcel of this course.") To again resort to a Hegelian style of phrasing, to the extent that there is a true and irreducible distinction between determination (via natural substance) and self-determination (via more-than-natural or denaturalized subjectivity), this must be a distinction internal to determination itself. Furthermore, at the level of a theoretical-philosophical ontology, there are not only reasons to insist upon the immanence of the subjective to the substantial contra any dualistic transcendence in which subjects stand entirely over and above all material actualities; Žižek, fully in line with Hegel, also suggests that the unreal, impossible purity of the voided "I" of incompatibilisms is objectionable at the level of a practical-philosophical ethics or politics insofar as its purity comes at the price of not being able to be either motivated by or committed to doing anything specific. ("For us to be 'truly' and 'radically' free would entail that there be no positive content involved in our free act.") Such a contentless, indeterminate "I" is reminiscent of versions of the "beautiful soul" (and similar figures or shapes of consciousness) harshly derided throughout Hegel's writings.[34]

Dennett, with his thesis in *Freedom Evolves* that there is no inconsistency in claiming that human beings are naturally determined to be free, himself indicates much of what I just explained. But Žižek consistently exhibits a comparatively stronger, clearer, and more unambiguous fidelity to staunch antireductionism and a related greater wariness of a biologizing naturalism that would risk compromising or mitigating the freedom of concern to both himself and Dennett. In the block quotation just given, as elsewhere, the distinguishing feature of Žižek's own version of compatibilism is his emphasis on antagonism, inconsistency, and so on. ("We are *part of* reality ... the (possible, local) conflict between our 'free' striving and the external reality that resists it is a conflict inherent in reality itself.") In *Less Than Nothing*, he quickly moves to develop this feature through interrelated invocations of retroaction and incompleteness:

> We are ... simultaneously less free and more free than we think: we are thoroughly passive, determined by and dependent on the past, but we have the freedom to define the scope of this determination, to (over)determine the past which will determine us.... I am determined by causes, but I (can) retroactively determine which causes will determine me: we, subjects, are passively affected by pathological objects and motivations; but, in a reflexive way, we have the minimal power to accept (or reject) being affected in this way, that is, we retroactively determine the causes allowed to determine us, or, at least, the *mode* of this linear determination. "Freedom" is thus inherently retroactive: at its most elementary, it is not simply a free act which, out of nowhere, starts a new causal link, but a retroactive act of determining which link or sequence of necessities will determine us. Here, one should add a Hegelian twist to Spinoza: freedom is not simply "recognized/known necessity," but recognized/assumed necessity, the necessity constituted/actualized through this recognition.[35]

In the immediately following paragraph, Žižek proceeds to link this retroaction to a certain sort of incompleteness: "The key philosophical implication of Hegelian retroactivity is that it undermines the reign of the Principle of Sufficient Reason: this principle only holds in the condition of linear causality where the sum of past causes determines a future event—retroactivity means that the set of (past, given) reasons is never complete and 'sufficient,' since the past reasons are retroactively activated by what is, within the linear order, their effect."[36] Subsequently in *Less Than Nothing*, these points are recapitulated thus:

The common-sense "dialectics" of freedom and necessity conceives of their articulation in the sense of the famous lines from the beginning of Marx's *Eighteenth Brumaire of Louis Bonaparte*: "Men make their own history, but they do not make it as they please; they do not make it under self-selected circumstances, but under circumstances existing already, given and transmitted from the past." We are partially, but not totally, determined: we have a space of freedom, but within the coordinates imposed by our objective situation. What this view fails to take into account is the way our freedom (free activity) retroactively creates ("posits") its objective conditions: these conditions are not simply given, they emerge as the presuppositions of our activity. (And vice versa: the space of our freedom itself is sustained by the situation in which we find ourselves.) The excess is thus double: we are not only less free than we think (the contours of our freedom are predetermined), we are simultaneously more free than we think (we freely "posit" the very necessity that determines us). This is why, to arrive at our "absolute" freedom (the free positing of our presuppositions), we have to pass through absolute determinism.[37]

There is an enormous amount in need of unpacking in these quotations. (This requisite labor will occupy me for some while in what follows.) In the first of these three quoted passages, Žižek alludes to a paraphrase transposing Freud's statement "the normal man is not only far more immoral than he believes but also far more moral than he knows"[38] into "the normal man is not only far more determined than he believes but also far freer than he knows." (Zupančič and I deploy this exact paraphrase.)[39] Although Žižek does not do so in this instance, he elsewhere explores a more psychoanalytic angle of the matters at stake in this context by speculating about agency, choice, freedom, and the like (also on the basis of German idealism) specifically in relation to the Freudian-Lacanian unconscious.[40] In *Absolute Recoil*, he nicely captures the dialectics of freedom and determinism in psychoanalysis,[41] noting that the human predicament along these lines as revealed by analysis is that, "while we are never fully free, at the same time we cannot ever escape being free."[42]

However, in *Less Than Nothing*, Žižek indeed rightly rebukes those, such as Pippin (and Manfred Frank), who erroneously conflate the analytic unconscious with the id qua roiling primitive ocean of animalistic organic instincts and thereby oppose such crude mindedness to the subjective self-reflexivity so powerfully thematized within the tradition of German idealism. As Žižek quite correctly observes, Lacan's return to Freud brings out how the unconscious (as unthought thinking or unknown knowing) is intimately folded within the very reflexivity of self-relating or reflecting subjectivity à la Kant, Fichte, Schelling, and Hegel.[43] Indeed, a key Lacanian lesson regarding Freudian psychoanalysis is that the unconscious properly speaking is not to be confused with the id.[44] However, Žižek's depiction of subjects as simultaneously more and less free than they think can be taken in both psychoanalytic and nonpsychoanalytic senses, depending on whether one is considering freedom and determinism as unconscious qua defensively occluded from thought (that is, as in the analytic unconscious bound up with intrapsychical defense mechanisms) or as unconscious qua simply nonconscious (that is, as in nonanalytic notions about what remains unthought).

Furthermore, Žižek's ensuing specifications regarding what he means by individuals being simultaneously "less free and more free than we think" hint at an intricate tapestry of references in the background of his claims and arguments. I will identify in chronological order the different constituents involved in this complex contextual framing of his remarks. Kant is the first major presence, casting a long shadow over these considerations. To be more precise, Žižek here appropriates Allison's interpretation of Kantian practical philosophy via what Allison calls the "incorporation thesis"[45] (distinct from Allison's "reciprocity thesis" as an element of his reading of Kantian theoretical philosophy, which I consider in chapter 2). According to this Žižekian appropriation of Kant and Allison together, the Kantian subject's free self-determination amounts to its ability to spontaneously decide which potential determinants of its actions will have been these actions' actual determinants: "I am determined by causes, but I (can) retroactively determine which causes will determine me: we, subjects, are passively affected by pathological objects and motivations; but, in a reflexive way, we have the minimal power to accept (or reject) being affected in this way."

One should notice that, perhaps under Allison's influence, Žižek here offers a more sympathetic depiction of Kant's ethical subjectivity by comparison with his Hegel-inspired indications, mentioned earlier, which suggest that Kant, given the incompatibilism of his antimaterialist and antinaturalist dualisms, renders the properly ethical subject empty, ineffective, and impotent through "purifying" it of all relations to any real or possible determinate content. Allison's Kant sidesteps the dead-end of sterile, vacuous indeterminism insofar as he insists that the actor's autonomy consists precisely in a second-order power to "incorporate" (that is, freely identify with and opt to be determined by) omnipresent and ultimately unavoidable first-order determinants, with the latter including an ever-varying array of empirical entities and events along with the self's responses to them. Also, much of this resonates with Lacan's description from 1959 of desire per se as always "in the second degree" qua "desire of desire,"[46] as well as, in the analytic philosophical canon, Harry Frankfurt's seminal paper "Freedom of the Will and the Concept of a Person," published in 1971.[47]

In fact, the Allisonian incorporation thesis provides Žižek with a means of discerning a Hegelian dimension within the structures of the Kantian metaphysics of morals. Specifically, he mobilizes Hegel's distinction between "presupposing" (associated by Hegel with the "in itself" [*an sich*]) and "positing" (associated by Hegel with the "for itself" [*für sich*]) in characterizing freedom à la Kant as enacted in "the free positing of our presuppositions." (This Hegelian distinction is important for Žižek throughout his corpus.)[48] On Žižek's construal of Kant's practical philosophy in this context, the subject's capacity to be spontaneously self-determining consists in nothing more than its ability to freely determine (that is, posit) which potential determinants (that is, presuppositions as the palpable background of various pressing circumstances, inclinations, situations, urges, and so on) will be actually determining of its effectively realized conduct. Through the present moment of such an autonomous decision, the subject chooses which past influences bearing upon this *hic et nunc* will become, in the immediate future, what will have been the decisive, sufficient motivators of its consequent eventual deed.[49] What is more, this Žižekian Hegelianization of Kant (via Allison) also tacitly relies on the Hegelian logic of cause and effect, according to which the effect is the cause of its cause (as discussed in chapter 3). That is to say, a potential cause becomes an actual cause only after-the-(f) act of generating an ensuing actual effect. The logical status of "cause" is conferred upon something *après-coup* through the retroaction of something else subsequently being conceptualizable as an "effect" in connection with this prior something.[50] Or, one could say, the effect posits its cause as its preceding presupposition.

Before I highlight an additional Hegelian facet of Žižek's compatibilist reinterpretation of the problem of freedom and determinism in Kantian and post-Kantian German idealism, I wish to bring to the fore another contemporary reference silently lurking within the passages currently under consideration. Although not in *Less Than Nothing*, Žižek elsewhere directly cites Benjamin Libet's neurobiological research.[51] Libet is the experimental investigator credited with discovering the late quality of conscious awareness of an impulse to action in relation to the nonconscious initiation of the synaptic firing sequences that, left to run their course, will eventuate in the performance of this very action (the temporal discrepancy between these being an approximately five-hundred-millisecond delay of onset of conscious awareness).[52] I will come back to Žižek's glosses on Libet's findings in due course, since both Libet and Žižek address the difficulty of freedom and determinism from combined philosophical, psychoanalytic, and scientific perspectives. For now, suffice it to note Libet's hypothesis according to which "free will," although not responsible for the originally neuronal triggering of intentions to act (hence the threatening character of Libet's discoveries for advocates of traditional versions of free will), is nonetheless an effective reality as a power to veto these synaptic sequences once consciousness becomes aware of them after an approximately five-hundred-millisecond time lag (but before these sequences fully run their course and terminate in an action).[53]

Implicitly endorsing Libet's hypothesis, Žižek takes it to dovetail with his interpretation of Kantian ethical subjectivity (in light of Allison's incorporation thesis). For him, Libet's vetoing consciousness is the neurobiological epitomization of Kant's autonomous agent "positing its presuppositions." On this Žižekian reading, the presuppositions are the neuronal firing patterns initially arising nonconsciously and automatically within the central nervous system. And the subsequent, lagging first-person introspective awareness of these patterns correspondingly posits, through how it denies (by vetoing) or permits (by not vetoing) them to pass on to eventual actualizations (as behaviors, performances, and so on), what will and will not have been the causally efficacious presuppositions behind the conscious subject's manifested conduct. According to Žižek, this amounts to a materialist-qua-neuroscientific substantialization of a Kantian model of subjectivity. Again, I will return to these issues soon.

Another aspect of the previous set of three quotations from *Less Than Nothing* is that Žižek's invocations of the modality of necessity according to Hegelian philosophy cannot but prompt associations to Hegel's treatments of necessity in relation to contingency as its modal complement. Throughout his career-long engagement with Hegel, Žižek unwaveringly insists that, contrary to certain popular misrepresentations of this giant of German idealism, Hegel does not privilege necessity over contingency (as, for example, metaphysically real logical or world-historical Ideas or Spirits qua timeless teleological dictators reigning from on high over the empirical-material realities of finite spatiotemporal creatures and creations). On the contrary, the Žižekian Hegel prioritizes contingency over necessity, making the latter a secondary outgrowth of the former.[54] As I demonstrated at detailed length in chapter 3, there is indeed significant support in Hegel's own texts for this Žižekian interpretive line.[55] Hence, Žižek's invocations of a Hegelian dialectic between necessity and freedom in the passages from *Less Than Nothing*, when both Hegel's speculative-dialectical logic of necessity and contingency and Žižek's frequent emphasis on contingency's centrality in Hegelian philosophy are considered, leads straight to the following question: How are the concepts of freedom and contingency compared and contrasted by Žižek? As with the Libet material, I will circumnavigate back to this critical query shortly.

The role of retroaction in the preceding brings up Žižek's reliance on Freud, Lacan, and Badiou. *Pace* the vulgar misunderstanding according to which time in psychoanalysis is no exception to the commonplace assumption that it flows in only a single linear-chronological direction (with analysis presumably just stressing the past's determination of the present), Freudian-Lacanian *Nachträglichkeit/après-coup* underscores the pivotal and pervasive workings of "deferred action" as the backward-flowing influence of the present and future on the past.[56] Of particular relevance and importance in the current context, retroactive temporality is integral to the later Lacan's conception of the "act," a concept that has come over the years to occupy a place at the very heart of Žižek's theoretical apparatus. Succinctly stated, for Lacan, whether or not a given action (as a piece of comportment, a deed, or a doing) will have been an act (as a true disruption of established Imaginary-Symbolic reality)[57] gets determined after-the-(f)act.[58] For Žižek, as he emphasizes repeatedly, whether or not a given instance of behavior is to count as free, as a manifestation of freedom, is also a matter of retroactivity's future anterior.[59] Likewise, in *Absolute Recoil*, he closely associates *Nachträglichkeit*, the unconscious, and freedom.[60]

However, there nonetheless appears to be a nonnegligible difference between the act à la Lacanian psychoanalysis and autonomy à la Žižekian

German idealism (with the latter as the activity of spontaneously positing one's presuppositions). Although both involve retroactivity, the distinct facets of subjectivity illuminated here by Lacan and Žižek seem to contrast markedly. The account of the subject entailed by Lacan's theory of the act stresses the subject's nonexistence before the act that brings it into being.[61] Lacan emphasizes that his subject of the act is definitely not an already-there locus of (self-)awareness whose deliberations and reflections precede and produce the act in question. Due both to the act's relationship to the analytic unconscious and to the act's dependence for its deferred, belated act-level status on its ensuing resonances or dissonances with transsubjective sociosymbolic matrices, the Lacanian act is more the prior cause than the subsequent effect of its subject. Moreover, whatever freedom is involved with the *après-coup* subject of the act, it looks to be distinct from Kantian freedom as consisting in a capacity for willful, conscious self-determination[62] (if only, as in Žižek's appropriations of Allison and Libet, as a power to selectively incorporate, through blocking vetoes, which presently palpable inclinations and influences will be allowed to determine realized courses of acting).

Furthermore, Žižek's quasi-Lacanian German idealist depiction of freedom similarly sometimes gives the impression of cross-resonating also with Badiou's (partially Lacan-inspired) theory of "evental" subjectivity. But such echoes, while not entirely misleading (Badiou too sketches a dynamic of retroactive positing of presuppositions in his portrayal of subjects of events),[63] arguably distort as much as they disclose. In certain respects, Badiou's account of the rapport between event and subject is closer to Lacan's account of the rapport between act and subject than it is to Žižek's more Kantian characterization of free agency.[64] (This is apart from the various discrepancies between Lacan's and Badiou's concepts of act and event, respectively.)[65] Other potentially relevant details aside, the Badiouian subject of the event, like the Lacanian subject of the act, in no way whatsoever preexists the given event to which it owes its very (coming into) being.[66] Moreover, in addition to the Kantian and post-Kantian characteristics of Žižekian autonomous agency (with its reflective and reflexive vetoing powers of self-determination), Žižek's specific synthesis here of German idealism and neurobiology (via Libet) would likely be unappealing to Badiou, considering the latter's aversions to both the German idealists and the life sciences.

BARTLEBY BY NATURE

Finally, and once again with reference to the three interrelated passages from *Less Than Nothing* (in particular, the second of these three), Žižek interestingly draws a radical conclusion about the principle of sufficient reason from his compatibilist considerations of subjective freedom. The free subject's ability in the present to determine what past forces and factors will become the causes determining this same subject's activities renders the past by itself "insufficient." In other words, the past alone, as the ensemble of presuppositions qua influences pressing upon the present, lacks the capacity to directly posit (qua cause, command, determine, dictate, and the like) realized effects at the level of subjects' cognition and comportment. Or, put differently once more, preceding chains of entities and events, with respect to free actors, transition from insufficiency to sufficiency only *après-coup* through the subsequent supplements of choices to block (or not to block) their translations into materialized decisions and deeds.

In his reflections on the principle of sufficient reason, Žižek's opening up of the past by decompleting it through its reciprocal relations with ever-unfurling presents and futures cannot but call to mind a theme recurrent throughout his works, including *Less Than Nothing*: an ontology of incompleteness (as discussed in chapter 4). Often with reference to Lacan's notion of the "not-all" (*pas tout*) and the related dictum according to which "the big Other does not exist" (*il n'y a pas de grand Autre*), Žižek regularly stresses that both Imaginary-Symbolic realities and the Real of being in itself are "barred," namely, detotalized and permeated with antagonisms, conflicts, gaps, ruptures, tensions, and the like.[67] In remarks from *Less Than Nothing* I already cited some time ago, he identifies a Hegelian-Lacanian ontology of nonwholeness as providing the ultimate metatranscendental basis of transcendental subjectivity itself qua spontaneous and self-determining. For Žižek, genuine freedom, as nonepiphenomenal subjective autonomy, is possible only if the Real of being *an sich* is not "complete" as a causally closed One enjoying seamless self-consistency. The insufficiency of the realized past alone, according to Žižek's take on the principle of sufficient reason, looks to be of a piece with his recurrent emphasis on ontological incompleteness.

However, at this juncture, two possibly major problems for Žižekian compatibilism should be made explicit. First, a danger of vicious circularity seems to threaten Žižek's explanation of the rapport between present subjective freedom and past objective (in)sufficiency. On the one hand, the positing activity of the subject's spontaneous self-determination through its veto power (as in the combination of Kant, Allison, and Libet) retroactively renders the presuppositions of already-there potential determinants insufficient on their own apart from this positing. On the other hand, the very same insufficiency of these past presuppositions appears to be itself an ontological-temporal and metatranscendental condition of possibility for this very same subject's autonomy qua free (self-)positing. Succinctly stated, with no free present, there is no insufficient or incomplete past; with no insufficient or incomplete past, there is no free present. How, if at all, does Žižek avoid falling into this trap?

Second, there arguably are, as I noted earlier, cross-resonances between Žižek's Hegelian recasting of Allison's Kantian incorporation thesis and his repeated insistence that Hegel ultimately prioritizes contingency over necessity. However, if such reverberations are indeed audible (even if not entirely intended), then it sounds as though Žižek is in peril of indefensibly equivocating between contingency and freedom by associating autonomous spontaneity with a modality involving arbitrariness, capriciousness, chanciness, randomness, and so on. Bluntly stated, contingency as mere indetermination is far from being freedom as full-blown self-determination. This certainly is the view of the vast majority of Western philosophers past and present, holding with special strength for Kant and his German idealist successors. As will be seen shortly, Žižek's references to quantum physics, particularly in *Less Than Nothing*, often only intensify the sense that he illegitimately conflates the indeterminate with the self-determinate. So, does Žižek actually operate with a subtle, refined distinction between contingency and freedom despite the worrying impression that he fails to recognize or respect this distinction?

At one moment during his extended speculations regarding theoretical physics in *Less Than Nothing*, Žižek invokes the now-familiar compatibilist use of quantum indeterminacy as a means to debunk materialist and naturalist determinisms of the type epitomized by Laplace's demon.[68] To believe that simply exorcizing this demon is tantamount to establishing the causally efficacious reality of robust human freedom would obviously be to rely on the invalid equation of the indeterminate with the self-determinate. Subsequent quantum-physical moments in *Less Than Nothing* only partly indicate Žižek's innocence of this equivocation. On the one hand, he clearly identifies and rejects this very equivalence (with reference back to Lenin's *Materialism and Empirio-Criticism*):[69]

> Lenin's gesture should be repeated in the context of denouncing spiritualist appropriations of quantum physics. For example, there is no direct link or even a sign of equation between (human) freedom and quantum indeterminacy: simple intuition tells us that if an occurrence depends on pure chance, if there is no causality in which to ground it, this in no way makes it an act of freedom. Freedom is not the absence of causality, it occurs not when there is no causality, but when my free will is the cause of an event or decision—when something happens not without cause, but because I wanted it to happen. On the opposite side, Dennett proceeds all too quickly in naturalizing freedom, that is, in equating it with inner necessity, with the deployment of an inner potential: an organism is "free" when no external obstacles prevent it from realizing its inner inclinations—again, simple intuition tells us that this is not what we mean by freedom.[70]

Before continuing to track the matter of the distinction between contingency and freedom in relation to quantum physics à la Žižek, I feel it worthwhile to draw attention to the fact that the latter half of this quotation importantly qualifies Žižek's endorsement of Dennett's compatibilism earlier in *Less Than Nothing* (an endorsement I quoted previously). The Dennett criticized in the present context is the one who, however wittingly or unwittingly, basically redeploys a Humean rendition of human freedom (itself of primarily Lockean inspiration)[71] couched in the more up-to-date naturalist language of today's life sciences.

However, Žižek's criticism here does not signal on his part a knee-jerk swing over to the opposite extreme of science-phobic antinaturalism, despite the understandable and likely expectation that a thinker situated in the lineage of post-Kantian continental philosophy, such as Žižek, would readily embrace such a position of opposition to the naturalism of an analytic philosopher of mind and biology, such as Dennett. Motivated by his underlying materialist commitments, Žižek, as seen, is sympathetic to compatibilism generally and even Dennett's version of it specifically (as found in *Freedom Evolves*). What is more, Žižek's already-noted recourse to the work of Libet, a neuroscientist, in articulating a compatibilism also reliant upon Kant, Hegel, and Allison (among others) further invalidates any reading according to which his objection to Dennett-style naturalism is a categorical rejection of naturalism tout court. *Less Than Nothing* spends ample time philosophically scrutinizing and absorbing material from the natural sciences with the utmost seriousness and care.

Contra most naturalisms (Dennett's included), a Žižekian compatibilism in which a Kantian-Hegelian incorporating subject positing its own presuppositions is materialized through being embodied in Libet's neurobiological findings entails a naturalism of nature (especially nature as manifested in and through the human natures immanent to it) as itself "barred" and "not-all" (that is, internally inconsistent, at odds with itself, and so on). Žižek's use of the word *organism* in his criticism of Dennett is telling, and the former's counterclaim against the latter could be formulated as "there is no human organism." That is to say, although human beings are "organisms" in the sense of living creatures, they do not conform to organicist pictures (as, arguably, fantasy images) of unified wholes successfully subordinating and synthesizing their constituent parts and organs.[72]

For instance, a compatibilist naturalization of Kant via Libet preserves (rather than reduces or eliminates) the strife-ridden split between conflicting dimensions of subjectivity. In Kantian ethics, these dimensions are incarnated in the division between the noumenal universality of the legislating will of pure practical reason and the phenomenal particularity of the animalistic individual's pathological inclinations. Furthermore, such a naturalization renders this split fully immanent to the central nervous system, with the veto power of Libet's prefrontal cortex being the bodily instantiation of Kant's moral legislator or, at least, of this legislator's effective enforcer. In short, from a Žižekian perspective, Dennett-style organicist naturalism leaves no room for taking into account the peculiar negativities brought to light so forcefully in German idealist theories of the subject. However, it is abundantly evident that Žižek, as a materialist, calls here for an alternative, nonorganicist naturalism, rather than for an outright antinaturalism.

To pick up again the braided threads of contingency, necessity, and "quantum physics with Žižek," the first half of the block quotation several paragraphs ago unambiguously identifies the illegitimacy of equating indetermination with self-determination. But a few pages later in *Less Than Nothing*, Žižek arguably muddies the waters again regarding this distinction between the mere absence of determination and the full presence of freedom. Redeploying lines of reflection going back to earlier works such as *The Indivisible Remainder* (1996),[73] he remarks: "A fact rarely noticed is that the propositions of quantum physics which defy our common-sense view of material reality strangely echo another domain, that of language, of the symbolic order—it is as if quantum processes are closer to the universe of language than anything one finds in 'nature,' as if, in the quantum universe, the human spirit encounters itself outside itself, in the guise of its uncanny 'natural' double."[74] Žižek continues: "The 'spookiness' of quantum physics is not its radical heterogeneity with regard to our common sense, but, rather, its uncanny resemblance to what we consider specifically human—here, indeed, one is tempted to say that quantum physics 'deconstructs' the standard binary opposition of nature and culture."[75] Finally, on the next page, he adds:

> Should we risk a step further and claim that there is something which strangely recalls (or points towards) symbolic structures already present in "physical" reality itself? If we do draw that conclusion, then the entire "spontaneous philosophical ideology" of the gap that separates nature from culture (a form of ideology often clearly discernible in Lacan himself) has to be abandoned. According to this "spontaneous ideology," nature stands for the primacy of actuality over potentiality, its domain is the domain of the pure positivity of being where there are no lacks (gaps) in the strict symbolic sense; if, however, we take the ontological consequences of quantum physics seriously, then we have to suppose that the symbolic order pre-exists in a "wild" natural form, albeit in what Schelling would have called a lower potency. We thus have to posit a kind of ontological triad of quantum proto-reality (the pre-ontological quantum oscillations), ordinary physical reality, and the "immaterial" virtual level of Sense-Events.[76]

Having already critically considered much of the content of these passages elsewhere,[77] I will be highly selective in my responses in the current setting. To begin with, autonomous spontaneity is an integral feature of the human subject qua *parlêtre* according to Žižek's combination of German idealism and Lacanianism. Hence, the parallels he draws between symbolic-linguistic human *Geist* and quantum objects and processes risk falling afoul of his own Leninist "denouncing" of "spiritualist appropriations of quantum physics."

Yet the recourse to Schellingian *Naturphilosophie* at the end of the third of these three quotations holds out the promise of an absolute idealist defusing of this danger. (I address the topic of post-Fichtean absolute idealism in chapters 1 and 2.) Schelling's "potencies" (*Potenzen*) can be interpreted as integrally of a piece with a nonreductive realist naturalism involving a strong emergentism in which emergent powers exhibit a speculative-dialectical continuity-in-discontinuity (à la Schellingian-Hegelian identity-in-difference, discussed in chapter 1) vis-à-vis the ontological grounds out of which they emerge.[78] Žižek here identifies three such potencies or powers, namely, his "ontological triad of quantum proto-reality (the pre-ontological quantum oscillations), ordinary physical reality, and the 'immaterial' virtual level of Sense-Events." Therefore, following this Schelling, Žižek could consistently deny that material or natural indetermination is equivalent to more-than-material or more-than-natural self-determination (that is, that contingency does not equal freedom) while treating human autonomy as internally arising out of natural heteronomy.

Moreover, absolute idealism (whether Schelling's or Hegel's) permits a nonpanpsychist (that is, an antispiritualist) panlogicism in which the recognition of structural and dynamical isomorphisms between human and nonhuman dimensions (as in, for example, "to suppose that the symbolic order pre-exists in a 'wild' natural form") is hardly tantamount to a one-sided anthropomorphizing of nature.[79] Instead, as Žižek's handling of the distinction between nature and culture suggests, rendering cultural subjectivity immanent to natural substantiality (in line with the absolute idealist agendas of Schelling and Hegel [as characterized in chapter 1]) does not reduce one pole of the distinction to the other. Rather, it thoroughly sublates (*als Aufhebung*) the traditional, *Verstand*-style dichotomy between nonhuman nature and nonnatural culture by transforming both sides of this distinction simultaneously and in tandem with each other.

As I have argued on prior occasions, there are multiple empirical-scientific as well as theoretical-philosophical reasons for hesitating to endorse unreservedly Žižek's mobilizations of quantum physics.[80] Without recapitulating those arguments here, I simply will reiterate my claim that, at least for now, the life sciences, much more than the physical sciences, are the real proving grounds for a materialist theory of subjectivity (or, more exactly, a materialist ontology that is distinctive precisely in containing within itself, as a core feature, such a theory—the dialectical or transcendental materialisms that both Žižek and I forward contain this theoretical feature). Hence, from this perspective, it is better to consider Žižek's compatibilism within the register of (to use the Schellingian language he favors) the "potency" of biology (especially the neurosciences). It is unclear in *Less Than Nothing* whether he intends to extend his compatibilist position to cover the "lower potency" of quantum physics. Žižek refrains from directly basing human freedom on quantum indeterminacy, although he seems still to edge toward this gesture. Indeed, some of Schelling's philosophy pushes strongly in this direction with the idea of subjective spontaneity as the resurgence, at a higher power (that of *Existenz*), of the groundlessness of the Ur/Un-Grund.[81] This middle-period (1809–1815) Schellingian discourse is already foreshadowed by Schelling's early appropriations of Spinoza in the Philosophies of Nature and Identity, with the autonomous "I" being the resurfacing, among the determinate products of *natura naturata*, of the primordial productive force of freely active *natura naturans*.[82] (This is discussed in chapter 4.) Recourse to Schelling might exacerbate the temptation to dubiously short-circuit the level distinction between, on the one hand, natural quantum objects and processes as neither sentient nor sapient and, on the other hand, significantly larger spiritual (*als* Hegelian *Geist*) constellations and operations as bound up with uniquely human sentience and sapience.[83] In, for instance, *The Indivisible Remainder*, Žižek appears to openly flirt with this very temptation.[84]

Nonetheless, through the recourse to Libet's research (strongly implicit in *Less Than Nothing* and explicit elsewhere), Žižek offers the beginnings of an anchoring of his compatibilism in the life sciences. Two of his direct references to Libet, one in *Organs Without Bodies* (2004) and the other in *The Parallax View* (2006), are particularly revealing of Žižek's specific compatibilist position, showing how it combines German idealism, psychoanalysis, and neurobiology. Addressing "Benjamin Libet's (deservedly) famous experiments" in *Organs Without Bodies*, he states:

> What makes them so interesting is that, although the results are clear, it is not clear what they are arguments *for*. It can be argued that they demonstrate how there is no free will: even before we consciously decide (say, to move a finger), the appropriate neuronal processes are already underway, which means that our conscious decision just takes note of what is already going on (adding its superfluous authorization to a fait accompli). On the other hand, consciousness does seem to have the veto power to stop this process already underway, so there seems to be at least the freedom to *block* our spontaneous decisions. And yet, what if our very ability to veto the automatic decision is again conditioned by some

"blind" neuronal processes? There is, however, a third, more radical option. What if, prior to our conscious decision, there already was an *unconscious* decision that triggered the "automatic" neuronal process itself? Prior to Freud, Schelling developed the notion that the basic free decisions made by us are unconscious. So, with regard to Libet's experiment, from the Freudian standpoint, the basic underlying problem is that of the status of the Unconscious: are there only conscious thoughts (my belated conscious decision to move a finger) and "blind" neuronal processes (the neuronal activity to move the finger), or is there also an unconscious "mental" process? And, what is the ontological status of this unconscious, if there indeed is one? Is it not that of a purely virtual symbolic order, of a pure logical *presupposition* (the decision *had to be made*, although it was never effectively made in real time)?[85]

The next paragraph proceeds thus:

> It is with regard to such questions that the cognitivist project seems unable to provide a materialist answer. It either denies them or takes refuge in a "dualist" idealist position. When Daniel Dennett almost compulsively varies the theme of how dangerous "Darwin's idea" is, one is tempted to raise the suspicion that his insistence conceals/reveals the opposite fear: what if Darwin's idea (the radical contingency of evolution, the emergence of intentionality and mind itself out of a blind process of genetic variations and selection) is the one whose message is pacifying (take it easy, there is no meaning or obligation in our lives . . .)? What if, in a Kierkegaardian way, the true "danger," the truly unbearable trauma, would be to accept that we *cannot* be reduced to an outcome of evolutionary adaptation, that there is a dimension eluding cognitivism? No wonder, then, that the most succinct definition of cognitivism is internalized behaviorism: a behaviorism of the interior (in the same way that, in contrast to a Jew, a Christian has to be "inwardly circumcised"). That is to say, does it not (re)apply the behaviorist reduction (a reduction to observable positive processes) to internal processes: mind is no longer a black box, but a computational machine?[86]

The invocations both of the Schellingian cutting deed of the primordial, unconscious decision (*Ent-Scheidung*) founding one's character in the always-already past prehistory of one's actual life history and of the Freudian "choice of neurosis" (*Neuronenwahl*) as the eclipsed origin of one's symptom-ridden selfhood are Žižekian staples.[87] In *Absolute Recoil*, he likewise discusses

Schelling, Freud, and Libet together along these same lines.[88] Having treated Žižek's appropriations of these two related notions at length before,[89] I here will restrict myself to playing devil's advocate on behalf of the cognitivism Žižek seeks to undermine in these passages.

Although I am convinced that the more expansive systematic framework of Žižek's ontology can and does justify his interpretation of Libet and his corresponding critique of Dennett et al., I nevertheless view the critical formulations in the preceding two quotations as inadequate on their own by virtue of being vulnerable to a quick retort from proponents of more deterministic flavors of cognitivism. Žižek momentarily entertains the hypothesis that the veto power uncovered by Libet's experiments is not an incarnation of the subject's free spontaneity, but itself merely another heteronomous effect of underlying neurological and evolutionary causal determinants ("And yet, what if our very ability to veto the automatic decision is again conditioned by some 'blind' neuronal processes?"). As seen, he immediately proceeds to counterpropose "a third, more radical option," namely, a hybrid Schellingian-Kierkegaardian-Freudian idea according to which an unconscious-but-subjective choice or act irreducible to anything bodily precedes and provokes the neuronal firing sequences involved in the very capacity of consciousness to block other such sequences. But, without additional supporting argumentation, what prevents the opening up of an interminable, irresolvable tit-for-tat regress? Such a regress would consist in the cognitive determinist replying to this Žižekian philosophical and psychoanalytic move by grounding Žižek's (unconscious) autonomy in a yet deeper neurobiological or evolutionary-genetic asubjective, unfree basis—with Žižek in turn positing behind the cognitivist's deeper basis an even more primordial "abyss of freedom" and on and on ad infinitum (and ad nauseum).

This essentially would be to fall back into the confines of Kant's third antinomy, thereby lending it further plausibility (an undesirable outcome for Žižek's post-Kantian compatibilism). Moreover, this situation resonates with a bit of humor, one nicely capturing the peculiarity of the Schellingian temporality of the de-cision or deed, utilized by Bruno Bosteels in a Badiouian critique of Žižek: "A joke ... puts two fools together in an insane asylum as they get caught up in a heated shouting match. The first yells: 'You're a fool!' And the second: 'No, *you're* a fool!' 'No, *you!*' and so on, back and forth, until the first person finally shouts out with a certain pride: 'Tomorrow, I will wake up at five a.m. and I will write on your door that you're a fool!' to which the second person answers smilingly: 'And I will wake up at four a.m. and wipe it off!' "[90] In order to block this regress, to avoid such a degenerative slide into a Kantian antinomic impasse, the Žižekian compatibilist should not rely so heavily upon a not-unambiguously-materialist conception of human freedom (that is, Schelling's *Ent-Scheidung* and Freud's *Neuronenwahl* as appropriated by Žižek) as a foil against the reductive naturalist materialism of certain brands of cognitivism. Instead, what is needed so that this compatibilism can overcome these determinist cognitivisms while itself remaining firmly materialist and (quasi-)naturalist (and yet simultaneously staunchly antireductive) is nothing less than a metaphysics of nature in which anything resembling Laplace's demon and the absolutizing of the Newtonian mechanics of efficient physical causes (assumed as valid in Kant's *Critique of Pure Reason* generally and third antinomy specifically) is decisively refuted. A *Naturphilosophie* achieving this would establish at least the preliminary necessary (albeit not necessarily sufficient) metatranscendental conditions of possibility for the autonomous subjectivity that Žižek's compatibilism wishes to save and defend (as I discuss in the conclusion). This would be a twenty-first-century philosophy of nature embodying the "Spinozism of freedom" sketched in "The Earliest System-Program of German Idealism," the program which was pursued by Hölderlin as well as by both Hegel and Schelling, the latter two each developing post-Kantian *Naturphilosophien* (as outlined in chapter 1).

Before turning to Libet's reflections and speculations regarding his own research, Žižek's glosses on him in *The Parallax View* are worth quoting and examining. Žižek elaborates:

> There is another lesson to be learned from Libet: the function of *blocking* as the elementary function of consciousness. This negative function is discernible at two main levels: first, at the level of "theoretical reason," the very strength of consciousness resides in what may appear to be its weakness: in its limitation, in its power of abstraction, of *leaving out* the wealth of (subliminal) sensory data. In this sense, what we perceive as the most immediate sensual reality is already the result of complex elaboration and judgment, a hypothesis which results from the combination of sensual signals and the matrix of expectations. Secondly, at the level of "practical reason," consciousness, while in no way able to instigate a spontaneous act, can "freely" impede its actualization: it can veto it, say "No!" to a spontaneously emerging tendency. This is where Hegel comes in, with his

praise of the infinite negative power of abstraction that pertains to understanding: consciousness is possible only through this loss, this delay with regard to the fullness of immediate experience—a "direct consciousness" would be a kind of claustrophobic horror, like being buried alive with no breathing space. Only through this delay/limitation does the "world" open itself to us: without it, we would be totally suffocated by billions of data with, in a way, no empty breathing space around us, directly part of the world.[91]

This recourse to the distinction between theoretical and practical philosophy brings Kant's shadow into view. In particular, the aspects of Hegel's philosophy mobilized by Žižek here—the abstracting negativity associated with Hegelian subjectivity, so crucial in both the *Phenomenology of Spirit* and elsewhere (as explained in the preface),[92] cuts across the divide between the theoretical and the practical in this block quotation from *The Parallax View*—are partially foreshadowed, as is often the case with Hegel, by Kant. More precisely, the first *Critique* powerfully presents the case that what is experienced by human beings as their reality is not some brute, raw, primitive givenness, namely, direct disclosures of mind-independent objective things and occurrences manifest and registered as presumably simple, immediate sensory-perceptual data. (The first *Critique*'s case for this is made particularly in its "Transcendental Deduction," with its transcendental unity of apperception [treated in chapter 2], as well as in its "Axioms of Intuition," "Anticipations of Perception," and "Analogies of Experience"[93]—all of this under the heading of the "Transcendental Analytic" with its "Analytic of Principles.") Rather, in the Kantian picture inspiring subsequent assaults on "the myth of the given" from Hegel to Wilfrid Sellars,[94] McDowell, and Pippin, "what we perceive as the most immediate sensual reality is already the result of complex elaboration and judgment, a hypothesis which results from the combination of sensual signals and the matrix of expectations" (as Žižek puts it in the quotation).

Furthermore, when Žižek says, "the very strength of consciousness resides in what may appear to be its weakness: in its limitation, in its power of abstraction, of *leaving out* the wealth of (subliminal) sensory data," he alludes to psychoanalysis in addition to German idealism. Freud's metapsychological conception of what he labels the "perception-consciousness system" indicates that one of the principle functions of awareness (if not the principal function) is not to receptively open up to influxes from the wider world, but, by contrast, to cancel, dampen, diminish, reduce, or screen out these very influxes. That is to say, on an analytic account, consciousness functions more to block out than to let in sensory-perceptual impressions. Freud explicitly speaks of a "shield against stimuli." And, of course, such restrictive and restricted awareness operates not only against external natural and sociocultural realities; it also functions intrapsychically so as to repel and exclude from (self-)awareness unbearably extimate aspects of psychical reality (that is, as Žižek would label them, "things from inner space").[95]

In terms of the practical-philosophical upshots of Libet's work on Žižek's reading, a connection can be established to another neurobiological investigator: Antonio Damasio. In particular, Damasio's early "somatic marker hypothesis" (in his book *Descartes' Error*, published in 1994) is relevant here.[96] In the preceding block quotation, Žižek speaks of how "a 'direct consciousness' would be a kind of claustrophobic horror. . . . We would be totally suffocated by billions of data with, in a way, no empty breathing space around us, directly part of the world." At the level of praxis, the Libetian delaying and blocking functions of consciousness, especially when parsed in conjunction with a Žižekian combination of German idealism and psychoanalysis, are biomaterial conditions of possibility for decision-making. Without these filters, the human mind would be paralyzed into inactivity through being thoroughly overwhelmed by an indigestible poverty of riches such that neither in its cognitions nor comportments would it be able to act as a free agent.

Likewise, Damasio demonstrates that affectively charged somato-psychical centers of intraneuronal/mental gravity, ones situated below the threshold of explicit self-awareness, are crucial to the reliability and effectiveness of conscious operations of reasoning and deliberating about choices. *Pace* common-sensical folk wisdom past and present, neuropathological cases in which the emotional dimensions of individuals' brains or minds are diminished or destroyed do not result in people who, by virtue of the minimization or elimination of feelings and passions, are better, more rational decision-makers. These patients, who indeed can and do reason "in cold blood," turn out to make either poor decisions or no decisions at all; they are worse than average at choosing or even too impaired to be able to choose in the first place. Damasio's observational and experimental findings appear to lend further support to Žižek's hypotheses about the practical implications of Libet's neurobiologically grounded buffers or screens.

But what about Libet himself? What does he have to say about the multiple issues raised by Žižek's analyses? Libet's presentations of his specific empirical discoveries (that is, those concerning the approximately five-hundred-millisecond time lag for the onset of conscious awareness regarding neural firing sequences) not only reinforce much of what Žižek does with these same discoveries; Libet's broader theoretical speculations are startlingly in line with some of the philosophical and psychoanalytic angles of Žižek's musings. To start at the broadest of philosophical levels, Libet espouses what fairly could be described as an emergent dual-aspect monism. In other words, Libet's preferred ontology and corresponding theory of subjectivity are surprisingly proximate to Žižekian dialectical or transcendental materialism. For Libet, more-than-material mind emerges from material brain, with the former thereafter becoming irreducible to the latter.[97]

Libet even proposes that this asserted strongly emergent irreducibility of the mental to the physical or organic could, at least in principle, be experimentally tested. If and when sufficiently sophisticated surgical instruments and techniques allow for isolating areas of the brain while still keeping them alive (that is, surgically severing all of these areas' synaptic connections to the rest of the brain's neural networks while leaving the blood vessels sustaining these areas of living tissue fully intact), it will be seen whether the cognitive, emotional, or motivational capacities correlated with these isolated areas remain integrated within the synthetic mental sphere of consciousness. If so, this would suggest that conscious mindedness possesses a functional unity independent (at least in certain respects) of its material basis in the anatomy and physiology of the central nervous system.[98] Despite Žižek's ambivalence about emergentism—in *Less Than Nothing*, he voices reservations about it despite also conceding, at least tacitly, that he nevertheless relies upon a robust version of it admitting of "downward causation"—his materialist compatibilism, like Libet's emergent dual-aspect monism, posits the immanent genesis of thereafter-irreducible mind/subject from matter/substance.[99]

The cross-resonances between Žižek and Libet reverberate more profoundly still. Even though Freud had to fight fiercely against a long-standing, deeply entrenched assumption according to which the mental and the conscious are coextensive and equivalent, one of Freud's historical triumphs (despite the somewhat spurious appearance of his contemporary defeat) is that nobody in the "psy-" disciplines nowadays seriously questions the notion that a great deal of mental life transpires under the radar of explicit cognizance. Libet echoes this post-Freudian consensus with his repeated assertions that a sizable amount of neuronal and mental processes integral to cognitive, emotional, and motivational functioning remains implicit qua nonconscious.[100] But if this were all that he echoed, the connection with psychoanalysis would be tenuous indeed. The Freudian unconscious proper is not merely the absence of consciousness.

However, Libet goes further here in two ways. First, he suggests that, in the roughly five-hundred-millisecond interval between an initiated neural firing sequence and a belated awareness of this sequence as an intention to act, unconscious defense mechanisms might be able to take advantage of this interval so as to distort, inflect, modify, or nudge how late-to-arrive consciousness takes note of and responds to the underlying intention in question.[101] Hence, Libet avowedly sees his research as uncovering a fundamental feature of neurobiologically based mental life whose existence lends support to core Freudian views. Second, he maintains that the time lag his investigations reveal shows that any region of the brain capable of affecting consciousness can also work unconsciously (because every such region works in and through the temporal gaps of delays).[102] Additionally, like Freud and Žižek, Libet emphasizes that the delayed temporal quality of consciousness acts as a filter protecting minded awareness against the potential incapacitating flood of sensory-perceptual overloading.[103]

At one point, Libet comments that "perhaps all conscious mental events actually *begin unconsciously* before any awareness appears."[104] In light of Žižek's mobilization of Schelling et al. against cognitivism in *Organs Without Bodies*—as seen, Žižek there argues that the *Ent-Scheidungen* of unconscious decision-making are the nonneurobiological possibility conditions for the neurobiological processes highlighted by Libet's investigations—everything hinges on the ontological standing of Libet's unconscious beginning. Whether with Libetian emergent dual-aspect monism or Žižekian dialectical materialism—both positions share in common a compatibilist orientation, among other things—there are, to put this in Hegelian parlance, a number of presuppositions in need of positing.

As seen earlier, Žižek, in *Organs Without Bodies*, asks, in relation to his anticognitivist unconscious, "what is the ontological status of this unconscious, if there indeed is one? Is it not that of a purely virtual symbolic order, of a pure logical *presupposition* (the decision *had to be made*, although it was never effectively made in real time)?" Žižek's invocation of "a purely virtual symbolic order" arguably refers to his combination of the concepts of Hegelian "objective spirit" and the Lacanian big Other (that is, the cultural-linguistic symbolic order). The "virtual reality" in question here is that of the transindividual networks of collective beliefs, customs, habits, institutions, laws, mores, practices, rituals, traditions, and so on. These matrices of material and more-than-material shared configurations structure individuals who become and remain proper subjects through how these individuals internalize and instantiate such configurations. At the same time, because Hegel, Lacan, and Žižek are not classical metaphysical realists, objective spirits, symbolic orders, and the like are not transcendent realities unto themselves. These realities exist only in and through their specific instantiations at the level of particular individuals.[105]

Thus, regarding the hybrid Schellingian-Kierkegaardian-Freudian unconscious that Žižek mobilizes against certain cognitivisms, he appears to be making the Hegelian-Lacanian suggestion that the virtual-yet-objective reality of a *geistige grand Autre* condemns particular persons to the abyssal freedom of groundlessly, spontaneously deciding how to subjectify themselves in response to the coordinates of this preexistent, partially deterministic order. Put differently, a web of real abstractions composing a given sociohistorical context into which specific individuals are factually hurled always already compels these individuals to choose their subjectivities on the basis of this web's parameters and permutations.[106] The very "barring" of this big Other as inconsistent, conflicted, and the like is a crucial part of what allows and pulls for acts of underdetermined decisions as necessary moments of processes of subjectification.[107] Yet, what would prevent Žižek's cognitivist adversary from promptly responding with the claim that this primordial subjectifying *Ur*-choice (that is, Schelling's *Ent-Scheidung* or Freud's *Neuronenwahl*) vis-à-vis "a purely virtual symbolic order" is itself just another heteronomous effect determined by such causes as electro-chemical reactions in the brain or genetically encoded evolutionary dictates?

Assuming that the Žižekian anticognitivist unconscious is indeed to be understood along the lines sketched in the preceding paragraphs, it could plausibly be maintained that Žižek and Libet both need a theory of subjectivity drawing on models of "extended mind" (as these models are dubbed in analytic philosophy of mind). Especially for Žižek's compatibilism, part of what makes his philosophical-psychoanalytic subject irreducible to the biomateriality of its corresponding central nervous system alone is its being bound up with and distributed over the "virtual" extension constituted by everything associated with Hegel's objective spirit or Lacan's symbolic order, an expanse vastly exceeding single, isolated organisms. Žižekian subjectivity is brought into effective existence by virtue of the mediating influences of transindividual, sociolinguistic forces and factors.[108] (However, Žižek also nonetheless justifiably insists in turn upon the irreducibility of this subjectivity to the spiritual or social mediators helping to generate and sustain it.)[109]

Because of the implicit extended-mind dimensions of Žižek's compatibilist picture of autonomous, full-fledged subjectivity, this picture requires explicit posits (with the support of accompanying argumentation) at two levels. What are called for are interlinked, coordinated phylogenetic and ontogenetic renditions of the emergence of the cultural out of the natural. At the ontogenetic level, fundamental questions of the following kind would have to be asked and answered:[110] How is the anatomy and physiology of the human animal receptive to being permeated and modulated by external milieus, especially of a sociolinguistic sort? Why are these overriding (or, as Lacan would prefer, overwriting) impositions from without not rejected like failed organ transplants by the libidinally charged bodies onto which they are impressed, but supported and perpetuated by these very bodies? What accounts of the constituents and operations of both the individual's central nervous system and the mediating matrices of transindividual symbolic orders (and the interactions between these two dimensions, neuronal and symbolico-linguistic) explain the asserted autonomy of signifier-entangled subjectivity, itself a transcendence-in-immanence with respect to its corporeal grounds as themselves necessary conditions for every subject's existence? How do the reflexivity and recursivity of the subject of the signifier enable it to become nonepiphenomenally self-determining (à la Kantian and post-Kantian German idealist depictions of subjective spontaneity) despite it remaining ontologically dependent upon the physical basis of its underlying bodily being (particularly its brain)? How and why does "natural" substance become (also) "cultural" subject? How and why is the latter free in and through the former?

At the phylogenetic level, a related series of queries likewise proliferates for Žižekian compatibilist materialism:[111] What larger-scale philosophy of nature and the natural sciences is required to substantiate the move of barring Laplace's demon (as a figure representing reductive, totalizing scientistic determinisms in general)? What is involved in the genesis of human history out of natural history? Assuming human history in fact does so, how does it achieve (at least partially) a separateness from natural history? How and why does nature enable and participate in this, namely, a break with it permitted and catalyzed from nowhere other than within itself? What exactly would a *Naturphilosophie* with an ontology of self-sundering, autodenaturalizing nature look like that is both uncompromisingly materialist and (quasi-)naturalist qua responsible with respect to the empirical, experimental sciences of nature? And how are these phylogenetic topics to be systematically combined with the ontogenetic ones outlined earlier?

I would be the first to admiringly acknowledge that Žižek should be credited both with articulating many of the key insights establishing the theoretical foundations for a possible dialectical or transcendental materialist compatibilism and with richly elaborating these insights in relation to German idealism and Lacanian metapsychology (not to mention Badiou's philosophy). What is more, he has done much to reactivate, within the context of European philosophical traditions and their offshoots, serious engagements with the natural sciences of a sort foreshadowed by Schellingian and Hegelian Philosophies of Nature as well as certain Marxian dialectical materialisms (precursors largely overshadowed and overlooked during roughly the past one hundred years of "continental philosophy" as dominated by antirealist idealisms, constructivisms, and relativisms). However, as the plethora of questions raised in the preceding two paragraphs already indicates, I also would contend that much still remains to be done in consolidating and solidifying a materialism nonreductively yet (quasi-)naturalistically resolving the antinomies between the autonomous/free and the heteronomous/determined. Further expansions and elaborations of philosophically and psychoanalytically informed inquires concerning, in particular, evolutionary theory, epigenetics, neuroplasticity, emergentism, recursion, downward causation, extended mind, and analytic philosophy of mind in general are requisite if Žižekian materialism is to continue to develop and advance further. Žižek deserves recognition not only for his trailblazing labors of paving lengthy portions of the path of this novel materialism; his work thus far also outlines with precision what still must be accomplished in the years ahead by him, sympathetic-yet-critical others, and an interdisciplinary "general intellect" conditioning whatever future philosophical breakthroughs along these materialist lines might be possible.

Conclusion

Driven On—the (Meta)Dialectics of Drive and Desire

Hegel's Extimacy: The Nondialectical Ground of Dialectics

Over the course of many years now, Žižek has repeatedly emphasized that the fundamental underlying concern and overriding ambition of his intellectual efforts is to argue for a counterintuitive identity between the *Cogito*-like subject of German idealism and the death drive (*Todestrieb, pulsion de mort*) of Freudian and Lacanian psychoanalysis.[1] Consistent with this emphasis, the short circuit of this coincidence of apparent antagonists (that is, subject and death drive) also features centrally in the pages of *Less Than Nothing* and *Absolute Recoil*.[2] In these two philosophical works, Žižek, as could readily be guessed at this point, is concerned in part with confronting Hegel in particular (of the "big four" of German idealism) with Freud's and Lacan's theories of libidinal economics (as involving the death drive). Both the *Todestrieb* and a Lacanian distinction between drive (*Trieb, pulsion*) and desire (*Begierde/Wunsch, désir*) are presented by Žižek as requiring of Hegel's philosophy certain revisions and changes while simultaneously being foreshadowed by this same philosophy.

In *Less Than Nothing*, Žižek goes so far as to put forward the death drive as the extimate nucleus of Hegelianism, as that which this philosophy, as it were, neither can live with nor can live without. He explains:

CONCLUSION

> Is not absolute negativity, this central notion of Hegelian thought, precisely a philosophical figure of what Freud called the "death drive?" Insofar as—following Lacan—the core of Kant's thought can be defined as the "critique of pure desire," is not the passage from Kant to Hegel then precisely the passage from desire to drive? The very concluding lines of Hegel's *Encyclopedia* (on the Idea which enjoys repeatedly traversing its circle) point in this direction, suggesting that the answer to the standard critical question—"Why does the dialectical process always go on? Why does dialectical mediation always continue its work?"—is precisely the *eppur si muove* of the pure drive. This structure of negativity also accounts for the quasi-"automatic" character of the dialectical process, for the common reproach concerning its "mechanical" character: belying all the assurances that dialectics is open to the true life of reality, the Hegelian dialectic is like a processing machine which indifferently swallows up and processes all possible contents, from nature to history, from politics to art, delivering them packaged in the same triadic form.[3]

Žižek continues:

> Heidegger was thus right with his thesis that Hegel does not render thematic his basic operation of negativity, but he is, as it were, right for the wrong reason: the core of Hegelian dialectics, inaccessible to Hegel himself, is the repetitive (death) drive which becomes visible after the post-Hegelian break. But why should there not be at the base of dialectics a tension between dialectics and its non-dialecticizable core? In this sense, the death drive or the compulsion to repeat is the heart of negativity, Hegel's non-thematized presupposition—inaccessible not only to him, but, perhaps, to philosophy as such: its outlines were first deployed by a theologian (Kierkegaard) and a (meta-)psychologist (Freud), and a century later a philosopher (Deleuze) incorporated Kierkegaard's and Freud's lesson. With regard to the precise status of negativity, the situation is thus in a way reversed: it is Hegel who offers a series of *Vers*, of displaced variations of negativity, and it is only in psychoanalysis, through Freud and Lacan, that we can formulate the elementary form of negativity.[4]

In line with a stress on groundless contingency as the *Ur*-modality of Hegelianism's absoluteness (as laid out in chapter 3), Žižek identifies as "the core of Hegelian dialectics" (that is, the main engine of Hegel's System) nothing other than "the death drive or the compulsion to repeat" in its brute, dumb

CONCLUSION

facticity. This motor is a recurrent circling movement exhibiting an acephalous, idiotic character resembling a mechanical automaton rather than a human subject. Žižek's move here displays a convergence of (seeming) opposites in which the heights of meaning or sense (Hegel's dialectically systematic absolute Idea as the entire integrated network of categories and concepts both logical and real) coincide with the depths of meaninglessness or nonsense (a nondialectical repetitiveness making possible the Hegelian System and yet, at the same time, perpetually evading this System's comprehension).

Of the four post-Hegelians Žižek mentions by name in the block quotation just given, it is, unsurprisingly, Lacan who is most important for his purposes in this context (as in many others). A Lacanian psychoanalytic Owl of Minerva permits an *après-coup* making explicit of (as a raising to the dignity of its Notion) a Hegelian philosophical presupposition (as *an sich*) waiting to be delivered by its belated positing (as *an und für sich*). Lacan's psychoanalytic conceptions of drive and repetition are put forward by Žižek as the keys to "positing the presuppositions" that are, precisely, Hegel's implicit conceptions of the contingent Absolute and its dialectical developments propelled along by a nondialecticizable negativity interminably reiterating itself.

Properly appreciating and assessing Žižek's identification of psychoanalytic drive theory as, to paraphrase Lacan appropriately in this context, "in Hegel more than Hegel himself" obviously require examining how Žižek conceptualizes *Trieb* generally and the *Todestrieb* specifically. Throughout this conclusion, I will be tacitly but heavily relying upon (without explicitly rehearsing) my reconstruction of Freud's, Lacan's, and Žižek's accounts of drives and libidinal economies in my book *Time Driven: Metapsychology and the Splitting of the Drive*, published in 2005. I also explore Žižek's parsings of metapsychological drive theory from before 2012 at various moments in my book *Žižek's Ontology*, explorations likewise in the background of what ensues.

The remaining four sections of this conclusion carry out an interlinked series of related tasks: delineating Žižek's German-idealist-inspired reconstruction of the libidinal economy à la Lacanian psychoanalytic metapsychology (in the second section); revisiting Freud's and Lacan's own theorizations of matters libidinal in light of the divergences between how Žižek and I each conceive of a post-Hegelian materialism for the twenty-first century (in the third and fourth sections); and, on the basis of the preceding Hegel-inflected renditions of drive theory, pinpointing the fundamental philosophical bones of contention between Žižek's dialectical materialism and my transcendental materialism (in the fifth section). Now, the best place to start this examination is with Žižek's distinction, based on a certain interpretation of Lacan, between drive and desire. Indeed, the Žižekian conception of drive is utterly dependent upon this distinction. Moreover, drive is, for Žižek, perhaps the ultimate extimate (that is, intimately external, internally foreign) factor, the key unposited presupposition, of the entire Hegelian System. Hence, this topic is an ideal lightening rod for capturing and condensing the issues of concern both to Žižek and to me throughout this book.

From Kantian Aim to Hegelian Goal: Žižek Between Desire and Drive

The contrast between drive and desire is invoked by Žižek multiple times in *Less Than Nothing*. There, the first and most substantial articulation of this difference, an initial articulation upon which subsequent returns to this topic in both *Less Than Nothing* and *Absolute Recoil* draw, begins thus:

> What does drive mean from a *philosophical* standpoint? In a vague general sense, there is a homology between the shift from Kant to Hegel and the shift from desire to drive: the Kantian universe is that of desire (structured around the lack, the inaccessible Thing-in-itself), of endlessly approaching the goal, which is why, in order to guarantee the meaningfulness of our ethical activity, Kant has to postulate the immortality of the soul (since we cannot reach the goal in our terrestrial life, we must be allowed to go on *ad infinitum*). For Hegel, on the contrary, the Thing-in-itself is not inaccessible, the impossible does happen here and now—not, of course, in the naïve pre-critical sense of gaining access to the transcendent order of things, but in the properly dialectical sense of shifting the perspective and conceiving the gap (that separates us from the Thing) as the Real. With regard to satisfaction, this does not mean that, in contrast to desire which is constitutively non-satisfied, the drive achieves satisfaction by way of reaching the object which eludes desire. True, in contrast to desire, the drive is by definition satisfied, but this is because, in it, satisfaction is

achieved in the repeated failure to reach the object, in repeatedly circling around the object.⁵

Žižek's opening question is motivated by his thesis, examined earlier, that drive theory à la Lacanian psychoanalysis is the best means for retroactively positing a pivotal presupposition in speculative dialectics à la Hegelian philosophy (that is, the ceaseless restlessness of dialectical negativity). Additionally, Žižek self-consciously mobilizes two tightly intertwined strands of Hegel's critique of Kant, namely, objections both to Kant's "postulates of pure practical reason" and to the "bad/spurious infinite" allegedly operative in Kantian practical philosophy (as well as in the Fichtean *Wissenschaftslehre*, with its primacy of the practical, as mentioned in chapter 1).

Hegel, from some of his earliest writings onward, consistently treats Kant's postulates as symptomatic of a failure to move from bad or spurious to good or genuine infinity.⁶ Of special focus in this regard is, as Žižek indicates, the postulate of the soul's immortality as permitting the possibility of infinite progress toward a perfect goodness impossible to realize within the this-worldly existence of mortal, flesh-and-blood persons.⁷ In Hegel's critical view—which lends further credence to Žižek's overall picture of Hegel as a materialist of a certain sort—the Kantian elevation of an empirically unattainable moral perfection to the status of a normatively authoritative regulative ideal results in an ethics that, in being too good for this world, is, in actuality, not good enough. This one and only world here has no need (and, indeed, should not have a need) for the otherworldly, even if only as the "noble lies" of fictitious, hypothetical postulates.

Moreover, as Hegel observes, Kant's deontological ethics of pure practical reason, by identifying the goodness of the noumenal, rational will with its disregard for and defiance of the phenomenal, subrational inclinations, self-defeatingly makes it such that moral perfection is impossible to achieve. Even worse, if such perfection were to be attained, it would immediately cancel itself out, ceasing to be moral by virtue of nullifying itself in closing the gap between the will and the inclinations. If the will can be good only in and through its resistance to the inclinations, then eliminating the tension between these two is tantamount to eliminating morality tout court.⁸

Of course, much of Hegel's critique of Kantian ethics is foreshadowed by Friedrich Schiller in his *Letters on the Aesthetic Education of Man*, published in 1795. These letters made a powerful and lasting impression on the early

Hegel,[9] among many others (including, for instance, Schelling). Additionally, both the Kant of the *Critique of Practical Reason*, with his "drives of pure practical reason" (*Triebfedern der reinen praktischen Vernunft*),[10] and this Schiller, with his "play drive" (*Spieltrieb*),[11] provide Žižek with motivating prompts for connecting psychoanalytic drive (*Trieb*) theory with German philosophical sources.

However, and still in reference to the block quotation from *Less Than Nothing*, Žižek there proceeds to make what should strike the eye as a surprising move. In drawing the parallel between Kant and Hegel and desire and drive respectively—which he draws again later in *Less Than Nothing* and in *Absolute Recoil*[12]—Žižek associates Hegel with *pulsion* specifically as *désir* "looked at awry" (to paraphrase the title of one of Žižek's early books) by "shifting the perspective and conceiving the gap (that separates us from the Thing) as the Real." That is to say, one among several of Žižek's (tacit) suggestions seems to be that Hegel's dialectical-speculative solution to Kant's contradiction-plagued, dualistic "metaphysics of morals" is to jettison the latter's postulates and affirm what remains (that is, a finite individual agent internally and irreconcilably divided between rationality and animality) as the good itself, goodness incarnate. Defending this portrayal of Hegel's positioning vis-à-vis Kant's practical philosophy would require the assistance both of a great deal of interpretive massaging of the relevant texts and of multiple lines of complex argumentation. Even with such substantial historical and philosophical supplementation, it would still be highly debatable.

But, beyond the questionable, contentious depiction of the Hegelian sublation of Kantian ethics implied (however intentionally or not) by Žižek in the passage from *Less Than Nothing*, his manner of aligning Kant and Hegel with desire and drive respectively reinforces the heterodoxy of his Hegelianism. In other words, and in a gesture familiar to connoisseurs of the Žižekian oeuvre, Žižek's Hegel abruptly transubstantiates Kantian epistemological defeat (as equated with the "That's not it!" of the "hysteria" of Lacanian *désir*) directly into ontological victory (as equated with the "That's it!" of the "perversion" of Lacanian *pulsion*).[13] Put differently, Žižekian Hegelianism involves a kind of interminably and compulsively repeated enjoyment of negativity, an automatic, inhuman, and senseless orbiting around certain centers of gravity akin to black holes in physics or attractors in mathematics (that is, Žižek's "*eppur si muove* of the pure drive").[14]

CONCLUSION

Less Than Nothing then continues elaborating upon the distinction between drive and desire and this distinction's theoretical significance. Žižek promptly proceeds to introduce the topic of Lacan's *objet petit a* into this discussion, asking, "does the *objet a* function as the object of desire or of the drive?"[15] His answer here (an answer recurring subsequently in *Less Than Nothing*)[16] runs as follows:

> The true object-cause of desire is the void filled in by its fantasmatic incarnations. While, as Lacan emphasizes, the *objet a* is also the object of the drive, the relationship is here thoroughly different: although in both cases the link between object and loss is crucial, in the case of the *objet a* as the object-cause of *desire*, we have an object which is originally lost, which coincides with its own loss, which emerges as lost, while, in the case of the *objet a* as the object of the drive, the "object" *is directly the loss itself*—in the shift from desire to drive, we pass from the *lost object* to *loss itself as an object*. That is to say, the weird movement called "drive" is not driven by the "impossible" quest for the lost object; it is *a drive to directly enact the "loss"—the gap, cut, distance—itself*. There is thus a *double* distinction to be drawn here: not only between the *objet a* in its fantasmatic and post-fantasmatic status, but also, within this post-fantasmatic domain itself, between the lost object-cause of desire and the object-loss of the drive.[17]

Žižek proceeds:

> This is what Lacan means by the "satisfaction of the drives": a drive does not bring satisfaction because its object is a stand-in for the Thing, but because a drive, as it were, turns failure into triumph—in it, the very failure to reach its goal, the repetition of this failure, the endless circulation around the object, generates a satisfaction of its own. To put it even more pointedly, the object of the drive is not related to the Thing as a filler of its void: the drive is literally a counter-movement to desire, it does not strive towards impossible fullness and then, being forced to renounce it, get stuck onto a partial object as its remainder—the drive is quite literally the very "drive" to *break* the All of continuity in which we are embedded, to introduce a radical imbalance into it, and the difference between drive and desire is precisely that, in desire, this cut, this fixation onto a partial object, is as it were "transcendentalized," transposed into a stand-in for the void of the Thing.[18]

Tightly tethered to Žižek's rereading of German idealism generally and Hegelianism especially, these passages, as well as others in which Žižek likewise insists upon a strict split of mutual exclusivity and insurmountable incompatibility between *désir* and *pulsion*,[19] indicate that, for him, the central motor mechanism powering the kinetics of Hegelian dialectical negativity is a metadialectical "parallax" between drive and desire.[20] Put differently, Žižek's psychoanalytic, drive-theoretic revisitation of Hegel's philosophy quite deliberately suggests that something nondialectical (that is, a *Verstand*-type binary opposition) generates and underlies the dialectical (that is, *Vernunft* as speculative dialectics), as demonstrated in the preface.

Similarly, when, in the second of the two block quotations just given, Žižek speaks of "the very 'drive' to *break* the All of continuity in which we are embedded, to introduce a radical imbalance into it," this sympathetically can be heard as accurately capturing Hegel's post-Spinoza, anti-Schelling insistence on "grasping and expressing the True, not only as *Substance*, but equally as *Subject*" (as discussed in chapter 1). Here, subjectivity, identified by Žižek as equivalent to (the death) drive, is an excrescence of substantiality (that is, "the All of continuity in which we are embedded") disrupting this very substantiality from within and out of itself. This substantiality therefore is, in proper Hegelian fashion, self-sundering and autodialecticizing.[21] Hence, in Žižek's discourse, "subject" and "drive" are two names, in German idealism and psychoanalysis respectively, for the same thing, namely, an existent negativity both produced by and simultaneously interfering with the ground of *Substanz* qua a chain of (rough) equivalences including the Absolute, the One, the All, the Infinite, the Totality, the Whole, and so on.

A page after the two quotations in *Less Than Nothing*, Žižek further enriches the concept of drive by contrasting it with instinct (in addition to the contrasts already drawn with desire). He states:

> The specifically human dimension—drive as opposed to instinct—emerges precisely when what was originally a mere by-product is elevated into an autonomous aim: man is not more "reflexive"; on the contrary, man perceives as a direct goal what, for an animal, has no intrinsic value. In short, the zero-degree of "humanization" is not a further "mediation" of animal activity, its reinscription as a subordinated moment of a higher totality (for example, we eat and procreate in order to develop our higher spiritual potentials), but a radical narrowing

of focus, the elevation of a minor activity into an end-in-itself. We become "humans" when we get caught up in a closed, self-propelling loop of repeating the same gesture and finding satisfaction in it.... This rotary movement, in which the linear progress of time is suspended in a repetitive loop, is the *drive* at its most elementary. This, again, is "humanization" at its zero-level: this self-propelling loop which suspends or disrupts the linear temporal enchainment. This shift from desire to drive is crucial if one is to grasp the true nature of the "minimal difference": at its most fundamental, the minimal difference is not the unfathomable X which elevates an ordinary object into an object of desire, but, rather, the inner torsion which curves libidinal space and thus transforms instinct into drive.[22]

Although Hegel is not mentioned directly by name here, this entire passage fundamentally expresses an ambivalence with respect to him. On the positive side of this ambivalence, Žižek is once again characteristically correcting certain standard, commonplace misinterpretations of Hegelianism. In regard to Hegel's conception of the distinctiveness of humans vis-à-vis nonhuman animals, Žižek's remarks here warn against construing this specific philosophical anthropology as the straightforward progress narrative of a teleological development in which simple animality is superseded by comparatively more complex humanity ("the zero-degree of 'humanization' is not a further 'mediation' of animal activity, its reinscription as a subordinated moment of a higher totality [for example, we eat and procreate in order to develop our higher spiritual potentials]"). With such instances as the famous discussion of habit in the *Encyclopedia*'s treatment of the human soul clearly in mind (as invoked in chapter 4), Žižek contends that human animals become properly human (qua [partially] deanimalized) by passing through a concentration into the more, rather than less, rudimentary (that is, the repetitive, the narrow, the habitual, the fixed, the driven, and so on).

Additionally, when Žižek asserts that "man perceives as a direct goal what, for an animal, has no intrinsic value," this alludes to aspects of Freud's and Lacan's accounts of distinctive features of specifically human libidinal economies (in addition to its allusions to Hegel's philosophical anthropology). In regard to Freud, one could take as an example here the Freudian oral drive. The hunger of an instinct (*als Instinkt*) to obtain nourishment would, in the case of a human infant, invest in milk as the nourishing substance *an sich*. But, the oral drive (*als Trieb*) parasitically accompanying this instinct instead cathects (*als Besetzung*) such not-directly-nourishing objects and activities as the sensory-perceptual representatives of the breast and the repetitive motor movements of the mouth and tongue involved in sucking (that is, in Žižek's terms, "mere by-products" of sating instinctive hunger).

In regard to Lacan, I cannot help but recall a humorous moment during his elaborations in the early 1950s of the mirror stage in "Some Reflections on the Ego." (Many other Lacanian texts and topics could be mentioned in this context fittingly.) There, he contrasts human and nonhuman primate responses to reflective surfaces. The nonhuman primate quickly realizes that the mirror image is nothing but a semblance, the flat, superficial illusion of a conspecific who is not really there, and then quite reasonably loses interest in it as unreal. However, the human being becomes permanently enthralled by this image, getting lured into the spectral vortex of a virtual reality in which appearances, fictions, semblances, and the like become more valued and important than anything "real." On this occasion, Lacan is not only engaging in a bit of tongue-in-cheek human self-deprecation (with human idiots stupidly falling again and again for mirages and deceptions readily and wisely turned away from by humanity's closest animal relatives); he is also taking a swipe at his archenemies, the pseudo-Freudian ego psychologists, for whom "adaptation to reality" is the gold standard of human mental health. Lacan's counterpoint is that a hallmark feature of humanity is an original dis- or maladaptation to reality, a preference for the unreality of illusory images and fictitious phantasms instead of the reality adaptationally favored by nonhuman animals, including the other primates. One implication is that ego psychology's insistence on patients "adapting to reality" is literally dehumanizing, stunningly blind and deaf to essential facets of the so-called human condition.[23]

But, back to Hegel, and on the negative side of Žižek's ambivalence toward him in the prior block quotation, Žižek views Hegel's philosophy as sometimes lapsing into precisely the pseudo-Hegelianism Žižek's positive, pro-Hegel remarks in the same passage seek to rectify. This should not, despite the likelihood of the contrary, come as a shock, since Žižek, in both *Less Than Nothing* and *Absolute Recoil*, explicitly makes clear that his general interpretive modus operandi with respect to his chosen cardinal points of reference (such as Hegel, Marx, Freud, and Lacan) is, at least when suitable, to play them off against themselves, thereby bringing to light that which is extimately in "x" (Hegel, Marx, Freud, Lacan) more than "x" him-/herself. ("What characterizes a really great thinker is that they misrecognize the basic dimension of their own breakthrough.")[24] Žižek describes this critical-exegetical procedure as "thinking with Freud against Freud, or with Hegel against Hegel,"[25] and similarly maintains that "the only way beyond Lacan is through Lacan."[26] *Less Than Nothing* pinpoints a number of topics, such as rabble-rousing poverty, mathematized experimental science, the psychoanalytic unconscious, and Freudian-Lacanian drives (especially the *Todestrieb*), arguably addressable and assimilable by Hegelianism only if the latter undergoes significant metamorphoses involving immanent self-critiques (that is, Hegelian critiques of Hegel[ianism]).[27]

To refer once more to the previous quotation: For Žižek, Hegel mishandles human sexuality as something quasi-animalistic to be subordinated to the sociosymbolic mediations of the family as itself an element of *Sittlichkeit*. But the analytic Owl of Minerva, with the benefit of hindsight afforded specifically by its conceptualization of the largely unconscious, drive-centered, sexual-libidinal economy of human psychical subjects, accurately sees that this sexuality, with its everyday and not-so-everyday obsessions and fixations (including fetishes and other perversions), fits elsewhere in Hegel's System than Hegel realizes.[28] To be exact, it fits in the "Anthropology" of the "Philosophy of Subjective Spirit," with the soul and its habits so near to and yet so far from animality, rather than much later in the subsequent "Philosophy of Objective Spirit." From Žižek's perspective, it is not that Hegel's System cannot accommodate at all such post-Hegelian developments as the psychoanalytic theory of human sexuality and is rendered obsolete by them. Instead, this System allegedly can accommodate them, but in ways other than those that Hegel himself might favor. Fidelity requires a certain amount of betrayal. This dialectical truth applies as much to relations with dialectical thinkers (such as Hegel and Žižek) as to those with nondialectical ones.

The last sentence of the preceding block quotation is somewhat enigmatic. It triangulates desire, drive, and instinct in a not-entirely-transparent fashion. To quote it again: "This shift from desire to drive is crucial if one is to grasp the true nature of the 'minimal difference': at its most fundamental, the minimal difference is not the unfathomable X which elevates an ordinary object into an object of desire, but, rather, the inner torsion which curves libidinal space and thus transforms instinct into drive."[29]

Subsequently in *Less Than Nothing*, Žižek similarly triangulates drive, instinct, and *objet petit a* (the latter implicitly referring to desire, given its Lacanian definition as the "object-cause of desire"):

> While drive and instinct have the same "object," the same goal, what differentiates them is that the drive finds satisfaction not in reaching its goal, but in circling around it, repeating its failure to reach it. One can say, of course, that what prevents the drive from reaching its goal is the *objet a* which is decentered with regard to it, so that, even if we reach the goal, the object eludes us and we are condemned to repeat the procedure; however, this *objet a* is purely formal, it is the curvature of the space of the drive, hence the "shortest way" to reach the object is not to aim directly at it but to encircle it, to circle around it.[30]

In these two sets of stipulations, it almost seems as though Žižek either completely cuts desire out of the picture of the relationship between drive and instinct or renders desire a parasitic, secondary by-product arising only after the transition from instinct to drive. I strongly suspect that the first alternative cannot be the case, because of Žižek's frequent recourse to Lacanian *désir* throughout his corpus, including in *Less Than Nothing* and *Absolute Recoil*.

The second alternative strikes me as more plausible, for two reasons: first, Žižek denies that the structures and dynamics of desire are to be positioned as the ontogenetic vanishing mediator between instinct and drive ("the minimal difference is not the unfathomable X which elevates an ordinary object into an object of desire"); second, when Žižek's insistence on drive having its own distinctive rapport with *objet petit a* (that is, the latter is not exclusive to *désir* alone) is taken into account, this "object" appears to be cast by Žižek as originally an "inner torsion" or "curvature" in and through which natural animal instincts are transubstantiated into denaturalized human drives. Hence, *objet petit a*, preceding desire as its "cause," is, before the very genesis of *désir* proper, initially a sort of perverse twisting or warping of instinct producing *pulsion* first. However, even with these specifications, there is much that still remains mysterious and opaque at this point.

Additional clues are to be found both elsewhere in *Less Than Nothing* and in *Absolute Recoil*. The former text contains a pertinent consideration of *Trieb* in relation to the distinction between "nature" and "culture": "The drive ... is a Force thwarted in its goal, finding its aim in repeating the very failure to reach its goal. The drive does not express itself, it stumbles upon an external element or obstacle; it does not pass from one to another of its manifestations or expressions, it gets stuck on one of them. It is not driven back to itself through overcoming or annihilating its expressions, but through *not being able to do so*."[31] Žižek continues:

> The drive has nothing whatsoever to do with psychology: the death drive (and the drive as such is the death drive) is not a psychic (or biological) striving for death and destruction—as Lacan emphasizes repeatedly, the death drive is an ontological concept, and it is this properly ontological dimension of the death drive which is so difficult to think. Freud defined *Trieb* (drive) as a limit-concept situated between biology and psychology, or nature and culture—a natural force known only through its psychic representatives. But we should take a step further here and read Freud more radically: the drive is natural, but the natural thrown out of joint, distorted or deformed by culture; it is culture in its natural state. This is why the drive is a kind of imaginary focus, or meeting place, between psychoanalysis and cognitive brain sciences: the paradox of the self-propelling loop on which the entire Freudian edifice is based and which the brain sciences approach in metaphoric formulations, without being able to define it precisely. Due to this in-between status, the insistence of the drive is "immortal," an "undead" striving that insists beyond life and death.[32]

I want to start elucidating Žižek's quite accurate and precise references to Freud and Lacan by interjecting here, via what will be an extended detour through Freud's work in particular, a few of my own friendly amendments to his remarks (partly based and profoundly reliant on some of my prior work, such as, for instance, *Time Driven* and *Žižek's Ontology*). This extended detour is not only centered upon the theoretical content of *Beyond the Pleasure Principle*; however wisely and justifiably or not, I also, in the spirit of this same Freudian text from 1920, take the liberty in what follows of indulging in a number of lines of metapsychological speculation, of highly tentative conjecturing and hypothesizing. What ensues should be taken in this manner.

CONCLUSION

Unprincipled Instincts: Returning to Freud After Žižek

Now, to begin with, the word *stuck* in the first of the two quotations just given designates the notion of "stuckness" Žižek attributes to Eric Santner (a notion I will return to again as it functions in Žižek's updating of Hegelianism).[33] This stuckness is the stupid stubbornness of compulsive repetitiveness.[34] But such (seemingly) senseless (or, one might say, loopy) looping is not self-evidently a feature exclusive to *Trieb* and does not necessarily distinguish it from *Instinkt*. That is to say, instincts too, insofar as they are conceived of as evolutionarily and genetically preprogrammed behavioral repertoires oriented toward specific sorts of stimuli and entities, compel repetition, dictating perpetually recurring actions of certain types. Arguably, *Wiederholungszwang*, in a broader sense than perhaps originally intended by Freud, is a prominent aspect of instinct qua instinct, with instinct's difficult-to-resist imperatives to obey its hard-wired programs.

With reference to the Freudian death drive initially surfacing in *Beyond the Pleasure Principle*, what really perplexes Freud and prompts him to create the notion of the *Todestrieb* is not repetition compulsion in and of itself, on its own. Rather, it is the compulsive repeating of failed efforts to (re)install the intrapsychical hegemony of the pleasure principle. The mature Freud's radical revision of his drive theory initiated at the start of the 1920s is prompted by observations of subjects' persistently, insistently recurrent attempts in vain to tame and domesticate things that are too painful, intense, or excessive, namely, overwhelming excitations that flood and short-circuit the psyche. It is the repetition specifically of that which is futile that rightly catches Freud's discerning analytic attention. In *Less Than Nothing*, Žižek, in step with Lacan, vehemently maintains that, despite Freud mentioning a "Nirvana principle," the *Todestrieb* cannot and should not be confused with this principle.[35] Yet, consistent with certain other aspects of Žižek's construal of the death drive (aspects I will address), the *Todestrieb*, I suggest, is indeed associated with a failed Nirvana principle, namely, with the psychical subject's failure to return to a placid libidinal-affective homeostasis (whether that of "Nirvana" or "pleasure") resembling the presumed quiescence of the absolute zero of no sentience or sapience whatsoever.

Furthermore, it also should be remarked here that the Freudian pleasure principle, as with *Wiederholungszwang*, does not by itself establish a sharp and strict difference in kind between the instinctual and the driven, the animal and the human, the somatic and the psychical. Insofar as this principle orders the simultaneous pursuit of pleasure and corresponding avoidance of unpleasure, it is hardly unique to the sentient and sapient mindedness distinctive of humans. Is there a form of feeling life that does not follow a fundamental tendency along the lines of such a principle? In this vein, there is nothing accidental, careless, or haphazard about the later Freud, with his recasting of the pleasure principle in tandem with the new duality of Eros and the *Todestrieb*, permitting himself indulgence in speculations roaming far and wide across the expanses of the animate (and even inanimate) world. Similarly, one can readily understand why this Freud, who deliberately hearkens back to such forerunners as Empedocles, is justifiably construed by Lacan and Žižek not as an empirical psychologist with a garden-variety naturalism, but as a philosophical metapsychologist with a strange, special ontology (one that brings with it subversive, transformative implications for the very idea of "nature," as indicated in chapter 4). Of course, in Žižek's theoretical universe, the Freudian-Lacanian death drive is bound up with the Hegelian ontological constellations and operations of both substance and subject.

At one point in *Absolute Recoil*, Žižek endorses Jonathan Lear's critical recasting of Freud's death drive.[36] I have discussed Žižek's previous endorsements of this Lear elsewhere, and will be relying on those discussions here.[37] Lear accuses *Beyond the Pleasure Principle* especially of hypostatizing misfirings of the pleasure principle in the form of the *Todestrieb*. That is to say, the later Freud, by Lear's lights, mistakenly reacts theoretically to revelations of the pleasure principle's frailty and malfunctioning—as is well known, prior to 1920, Freud upholds the pleasure principle as the ultimate sovereign law governing psychical life—by positing a second principle, an even more profound law producing these manifest disruptions and glitches: the death drive interfering with Eros. As Lear elegantly encapsulates his objection, "what lies 'beyond the pleasure principle' isn't another principle, but a lack of principle."[38] Or, as I put it on another occasion when discussing Lear's critique, "There is just the dysfunctional pleasure principle and nothing more."[39]

For both Žižek and me, there are significant ramifications to be extracted from the Learian take on the death drive. I maintain elsewhere that

CONCLUSION

In line with Lear's perspective, one reasonably could conclude that the pleasure principle is not sufficiently clever or strong enough to do better. As a mental legislator, it possesses relatively limited powers. And it has no more powerful Other standing behind it as a secret, profound metalaw steering things when its feeble regime is in default and disarray. These implications of the 1920 dethroning of the pleasure principle as the invariantly operative fundamental inclination of mental life are often overlooked by those seduced by Freud's musings about a mysterious, enigmatic drive-toward-death.[40]

I soon continue:

Combining the neglected aspect of *Beyond the Pleasure Principle* (i.e., the shift from a strong to a weak pleasure principle, as arguably distinct from the shift to another dual-drive model involving the death drive) with its rejected aspect (i.e., Freud's anchoring of his hypotheses and speculations in bio-material nature itself) has the startling consequence of pointing to a somewhat counterintuitive notion: Nature itself is weak, vulnerable to breakdowns and failures in its functions. This challenges the intuitive notion of it as being an almighty monistic nexus of seamlessly connected elements controlled by inviolable laws of efficient causality. In such a vision of the material universe, human nature can be imagined only as an overdetermined subcomponent of a macrocosmic web of entities exhaustively integrated through causal relations. By contrast, a nature permitting and giving rise to, for example, beings guided by dysfunctional operating programs not up to the task of providing constant, steady guidance doesn't correspond to the fantasy of a quasidivine cosmic substance as a puppet master from whose determinative grasp nothing whatsoever, including forms of psychical subjectivity reduced to the status of residual epiphenomena, escapes.[41]

Back to Freud himself, it now could be claimed that his puzzlement in the face of the failings of the pleasure principle, a perplexity he speciously resolves with precipitous flight toward the pseudosolution of the *Todestrieb* qua second principle *Jenseits des Lustprinzips*, arises, in no small part, from his having not thoroughly traversed the fantasy of there being a *grand Autre* (to put it in Lacanian parlance). Freud's (unconsciously) fantasized big Other would be an ultimate executive Legislator-with-a-capital-L responsible for what thereby is not glaring, blatant anomie (that is, the lawlessness of the suspension of the pleasure principle) but the rule of a deeper, shadowy *nomos* (that is, the metalevel lawfulness of the death drive as the secret method behind the apparent madness of what only seems to be mere, sheer anomie).

In yet more Lacanese, if the pleasure principle is the lone *grand Autre* of the psyche for Freud before 1920 (that is, the psyche's one and only final authoritative law), this principle's evident falterings and lapses prompt Freud, starting in 1920, to posit an "Other of the Other" (that is, an invisible second authority, the *Todestrieb*, both causing and compensating for the shortcomings of the visible first authority). In non-Lacanian language, Freud's surprise at there being a "beyond" to the pleasure principle is perhaps unjustifiably overblown. It is generated, at least in part, by two questionable presuppositions. First, animalistic-instinctual nature and what is arguably one of its human versions in the guise of the pleasure principle are "strong" qua robustly, reliably adaptational and functional (rather than "weak" qua easily and readily prone to maladaptation and dysfunction). Second, both nature generally and human nature specifically are consistently lawful, with their organizations and functions always obeying if not one law (that of Eros), then another (that of the *Todestrieb*).

If, as in Lacan, neither the big Other nor its redoubling (that is, an Other of the Other) exists, then a Lacanian reconsideration of the Freudian death drive (one carried out somewhat differently by Lear, Žižek, and myself) must involve recasting *Todestrieb* as a name for something negative rather than positive, for lawlessness (qua a failing principle) instead of lawfulness (qua a succeeding metaprinciple). The Freud of *Beyond the Pleasure Principle* and related texts is brought into the proximity of garden-variety scientific naturalism not only in and through his references to things biological; he shares with this Weltanschauung a rationalistic belief in, so to speak, the established, effective rule of law, namely, in an always-principled ordering of the entities and events, structures and dynamics of concern to him. Echoing Hegel (as he features in chapter 3), one could say that this article of faith, although admittedly serving Freud well much of the time and indeed making possible essential features of analytic thinking, can nonetheless be taken too far (as Freud arguably does in the case of the death drive) and result in miscalculating contingency's due, short-changing it. A Hegelian view would likewise see Freud's dystopian, pessimistic narratives of the *Todestrieb* as an inverted permutation of Leibniz's utopian, optimistic tales of "the best of all possible worlds"; both are, from this view, mirror-image, recto-and-verso rationalist just-so stories presuming much more lawful necessitation in the world than is really in force.

Yet Freud's inconsistent, contradiction-ridden musings about the death drive contain within and between themselves the means for moving beyond these very same inconsistencies and contradictions. This is consonant with Žižek's assertion that some of the brilliance of Freud and others of comparable intellectual stature resides in their conceptual networks generating breakthroughs to these same networks' own impasses precisely via the execution of recursive immanent critiques. My own specific immanent-critical, dialectical-speculative reconstruction of this Freud in particular should begin with reference to certain notions of the instinctual arguably permeating the later Freud's thinking, especially about the *Todestrieb*. As I claimed earlier, neither *Wiederholungszwang* nor the *Lustprinzip* by themselves embodies a clear-cut, hard-and-fast divide between human drives and animal instincts. Instinctive animals, like driven humans, compulsively repeat behavioral strategies and tactics for seeking pleasure and avoiding pain.

Of course, Freud early on grasps and illuminates the peculiarities of distinctively human libidinal economies. As is common knowledge, the groundbreaking first edition of his *Three Essays on the Theory of Sexuality* lays the foundations, in 1905, of the distinction between *Instinkt* and *Trieb*. It does this by amassing and persuasively parsing an overwhelming amount of evidence showing just how far and wide humans' myriad forms of libidinal gratification deviate from what would be prescribed or proscribed by any supposed sexual instinct of a natural kind (that is, an assumed irresistible urge to procreate through heterosexual genital copulation with any available member of the opposite sex).

When this deservedly celebrated fundamental dimension of Freudian psychoanalysis is taken into consideration, one can say, with respect to the differences between human and nonhuman organisms entwined with the distinction between drive and instinct, that humans exhibit singular idiosyncrasies so different in degree from other animals as to be tantamount to a difference in kind. In other words, the drives of human animals distinguish themselves in displaying far less transindividual regularity and uniformity than, by glaring contrast, the instincts of nonhuman animals dictating species-typic patterns of comportment across individuals. That is to say, although both animal instincts and human drives compulsively repeat pleasure-seeking and pain-avoidance—these aspects do not on their own demarcate a

CONCLUSION

real boundary between them, being instead lowest common denominators—*Triebe* manifest much more diversity and variability in how and what they compulsively repeat than *Instinkte*. This is one of several truly (rather than speciously) distinguishing features between drive and instinct.

As I mentioned earlier, Freud's penetrating gaze fixates in *Beyond the Pleasure Principle* upon the compulsive repetition specifically of floundering efforts to reinstate the lapsing authority of the pleasure principle. One of the catalysts for the crystallization of the death drive in 1920 is this puzzlement in the face of failure (to be precise, the failure of a *Lustprinzip*, which was maintained, before 1920, to be the final, inviolable law of laws of mental life, always triumphant in enforcing its ultimate, inescapable rule). Freud's explicitly expressed perplexity vis-à-vis dysfunctional perseverations necessarily presupposes a standard of functionality. According to this implicit measure, when a given form of acting proves to be maladaptive in the sense of not conducive (or even in the sense of detrimental) to the happiness and well-being of the acting creature, the creature in question, if functional qua adaptive, will presumably adjust its comportment accordingly, adopting new actions to replace the old, unsuccessful ones.

As I already observed, Freud's astonishment at phenomena "beyond the pleasure principle" is made possible by the background assumption of an instinctual adaptiveness automatically abandoning (rather than idiotically repeating) courses of conduct failing to result in happiness and well-being (that is, "pleasure," whether as discharge, equilibrium, homeostasis, quiescence, satiety, or something similar). This assumption is enshrined in the Freudian corpus before 1920 in the guise of nothing other than the *Lustprinzip* itself. And this principle from before 1920, independent of any additional caveats, nuances, or supplements, does not, on its own, support bold contrasts and differentiations between human and animal, drive and instinct, or related distinctions along these same lines. Driven humans and instinctual animals alike could be said to strive to maximize pleasure and minimize pain. In and of itself, the pleasure principle alone, as an ideal model in the bare isolation of being an unqualified metapsychological conceptual construct, is an aspect of life in general shared among all sentient beings qua sentient (that is, able to feel, with every feeling being [able to be] situated on a spectrum between the pleasurable and the painful).

Although it takes Freud until 1920 to call into question and problematize the absolute intrapsychical sovereignty of his *Lustprinzip* at the level of theoretical positing *an und für sich*, this radical shift occurring in *Beyond the Pleasure Principle* makes explicit things long in evidence (however unthematized) throughout Freud's lengthy prior analytic career. First and foremost, there are the self-sabotaging dynamics of countless sufferers of various neuroses, with their talents for invariably snatching defeat from the jaws of victory, for pissing off themselves and others, for transubstantiating gifts of gold into shit, for recurrently fucking (over) themselves and their dissatisfied and dissatisfying partners, and so on. Well before *Jenseits des Lustprinzips*, Freud is all too familiar with such neurotic misfirings and breakdowns of the pleasure principle from clinical and personal experience. After the advent of the *Todestrieb* in 1920, self-punitive tendencies translating into an unexpected worsening, rather than an expected improvement, in certain neurotics' symptoms with progressive gains of insight over the courses of their analyses are subsumed under the heading of "negative therapeutic reaction."

Closer to the time of *Beyond the Pleasure Principle*, further deviations from this principle thrust themselves to the fore, whether, for instance, as "conscience" à la "On Narcissism: An Introduction" in 1914 or as "melancholia" à la "Mourning and Melancholia" in 1917. (In both of these instances, the psyche spontaneously and gratuitously inflicts discomfort or even anguish on itself.) What is more, World War I furnishes Freud's couch with traumatized veterans brutalized and ravaged by the excruciating symptoms of "shell shock," namely, what has come to be labeled "post-traumatic stress disorder" (PTSD). In recent times, this DSM term has sadly gone from the realms of the technical to popular discourse for a number of lamentable socioeconomic and political reasons. In addition to conscience, melancholia, and PTSD, there is also the famous scene, described by Freud in *Beyond the Pleasure Principle*, of his eighteen-month-old grandson Ernst Halberstadt playing the *Fort-Da* game in the wake of Ernst's mother's departure.

The hegemony before 1920 of the pleasure principle is epitomized by the central thesis of *The Interpretation of Dreams*, the landmark turn-of-the-century work founding psychoanalysis strictly speaking, that all dreams without exception obey the pleasure principle by representing, in however distorted and deceptive a guise, the fulfillment of wishes. By the lights of this thesis from 1900, foregrounded content of a displeasurable nature in the "manifest dream text" (triggering in the dreamer or dream-recounter such negative affective states as anxiety, confusion, discomfort, dread, embarrassment, fear, foreboding, panic, shame, terror, unease, and the like) is really due to the "dream work" having to disguise certain "latent dream-thoughts" (that is, [infantile] wishes aroused by particular "day residues") so as to get around the censorship imposed by specific repressions. Hence, even nightmares are not actual exceptions to or refutations of the pleasure principle, being interpretively reducible, through proper analysis, to repression-evading encryptions of gratifying wish fulfillments, to censor-skirting encodings of the satisfactions of impulses that cannot consciously be avowed as such.

Moreover, this Freud takes the example of the dream of an analysand that defies being analytically interpreted along the immediately preceding lines as the unacknowledged expression of an unconscious, transferential desire on this analysand's part that he (Freud the analyst, with his thesis that all dreams represent wish fulfillments) be wrong—hence a dream whose manifest content is the antithesis of wish fulfillment. Thus, even this negation of wish fulfillment in a dream fulfills a wish (namely, the wish that Freud be mistaken and fallible). The primacy of the pleasure principle in Freud's early dream theory often leads to accurate and insightful interpretations (such as, perhaps, in the just-mentioned example of the analysand wishing this very theory to be erroneous, dreaming a dream that seems to refute it). But the relentlessly recurring night terrors of Freud's PTSD victims eventually convince him that not all dreams show obedience to the *Lustprinzip*, that the thesis regarding wish fulfillment is stretched too far when rendered universal without exceptions.

In confronting such phenomena, the later Freud indeed comes to concede that the pleasure principle is intrapsychically neither omnipresent nor omnipotent. This principle's reign is limited and prone to (intermittent) suspension. Nonetheless, Freud still tries to smooth over what would otherwise be the very rough edges of an abrupt break violently punctuating his intellectual itinerary in 1920. His compromise is to temper this concession regarding the pleasure principle's weakness with the accompanying assertion to the effect that the displeasurable repetitions of concern in *Beyond the Pleasure Principle* are nonetheless attempts to reinstall the wobbly regime of the *Lustprinzip*. Despite being powerfully struck by the compulsion to repeat the painful instead of the pleasurable, Freud allays this struckness with the supplemental hypothesis that such stuckness (Žižek) is, as Lacan might put it, not without (*pas sans*) its rapport with the pleasure principle. According to Freud's supplemental hypothesis, this stuckness, however inadequately or counterproductively, still works for the *Lustprinzip*, the former intending (but failing) to reenthrone the latter.

But, with this, what remains for Freud and everyone after him is what still should be a source of analytic wonder: the fact that the fruitlessness and futility of this *Wiederholungszwang* in its purported pleasure-preparatory function, a function whose aim these sorts of repetition compulsions thwart even while they attempt to carry it out, do not eventually lead, sooner or later, to an adaptive change in favor of different approaches. As the second coming, the return to power, the restoration of the pleasure principle interminably keep not arriving, why is there obstinately continued observance of the well-worn rites and rituals themselves serving in actuality only to postpone and forestall indefinitely such redemption and salvation? Why does the Sisyphean labor of endlessly trying but failing to "bind" (à la Freudian binding [*Bindung*]) traumatic breaches of the pleasure principle's fortifications indefinitely continue despite its indefinitely continued failing and self-defeating counterproductivity?

Performing a Hegelian-style pirouette in step with both Žižek and Lear, I would suggest that the difficulty of these questions is itself already an indication of the real answer. That is to say, the proper answer to this "why" query is *ohne Warum* (without why [as discussed in chapter 3]). To go into more detail, Žižek, Lear, and I concur that, starting in 1920, Freud takes the misstep of hypostatizing malfunctions of the pleasure principle, turning them into functions of a metaprinciple, namely, the death drive. He transforms the failures of one intentionality, with its final causes (that is, the reasons as "whys" of the *Lustprinzip*), into the successes of another intentionality (that is, the *Todestrieb*), with its own, different final causes. However knowingly or not, the later Freud appears to remain faithful to Franz Brentano, with whom he studied as a younger man at the University of Vienna. Even at the stage of *Beyond the Pleasure Principle*, the Freudian psyche remains always and invariably governed by intentional logics, even if these are now those of a death drive opposing the pleasure principle.

Therefore, by attributing an intentionality with its final-causal reasons to instances "beyond the pleasure principle," Freud foists upon himself the obligation to ask and answer questions along the lines of the ones just posed. But Žižek, Lear, and I agree that such a line of inquiry is itself badly framed in the first place, that the questions themselves are wrongly posed to begin

CONCLUSION

with insofar as they pull for the "why" of final causality. In accepting the interlinked, cross-resonating Lacanian propositions according to which "the big Other does not exist," "there is no Other of the Other," and "there is no truth about the truth"[42] (not to mention Hegel's logical doctrine of the modalities as centered on contingency [again, as treated in chapter 3]), one should reject those versions of the Freudian *Todestrieb* in which it operates as a meta-Other or metatruth, namely, as a positive principle unto itself intentionally pursuing the final ends of death and destruction.

Nevertheless, leaving these things at a sudden full stop simply with a curt *ohne Warum* would be too quick and easy as well as misleadingly inaccurate. At this stage, the main matter that remains to be illuminated is how exactly the pleasure principle goes awry, the factors responsible for its (self-)disruptions. Devils reside in the details of its malfunctioning. As I demonstrate at length in *Time Driven* and elsewhere,[43] "death drive" names not a consistent, integrated concept in Freud's writings from 1920 onward, but a jumbled, tangled cluster of observations and hypotheses that are associated with one another to varying degrees of tightness—or even, sometimes, that are entirely incompatible with one another. As I have suggested on other occasions, the inconsistencies and contradictions plaguing Freud's formulations of the *Todestrieb* may very well be intellectual symptoms of unresolved issues from his (inevitably incomplete) self-analysis having to do with his mortality and pronounced *Todesangst*. Thus, although certain of Freud's characterizations of the death drive are to be set aside, others represent invaluable insights that ought to be retained and put to work. As with his psychoanalytic edifice in general, so too with the notion of the *Todestrieb* in particular: an immanent-critical gesture of recursively applying certain aspects of the edifice or notion in question to the edifice or notion itself is precisely what facilitates overcoming and sublating its own deadlocks and impasses.

My reconstruction of Freudian and Lacanian drive theory in *Time Driven* relies heavily upon and takes very seriously Freud's speculation according to which the *Todestrieb* is not a drive unto itself, but a designation of dimensions essential to any drive qua drive, to *Trieb als Trieb* (a speculation also endorsed by Žižek).[44] The objections to the death drive common to Žižek, Lear, and myself have to do with versions of it in which Freud speaks of it as though it really were one drive among others, a positive force coming into conflict with other positive forces (as in the clashes between it and Eros). However, treating the *Todestrieb* as a reflection of facets inhering in all drives as drives per se does not necessarily involve the type of hypostatization eliciting such objections (although it still could). That said—the evidence and justifications for what I am about to claim are to be found in *Time Driven*—Freud's death drive should be recast as a metapsychological conceptualization capturing a maladaptation and dysfunctionality inherent in the very nature of *Trieb*, intrinsic to every drive as a drive.

Freud, both before and after 1920, tends to assume there being an instinct-like, unfailingly lawful governance of the psychical apparatus, whether as the monopoly of the pleasure principle (before 1920) or the duopoly of Eros and the *Todestrieb* (after 1920). The necessitating reasons of the final causes of intentionality reign supreme, whether as the plans and purposes of the *Lustprinzip* alone or its thwarting by an opposed (meta)principle with its own distinctive (and diabolical) plans and purposes. The possibility to which Freud does not give due consideration, as entertained by Žižek, Lear, and me, is that there might be utterly unintentional failures, namely, malfunctions and misfirings without rhyme or reason, why or wherefore. To be more specific, maybe the intrapsychical influence of the pleasure principle is sometimes interrupted not by another law or rule, but by its own limitations, its own feebleness and finitude—with its "beyond" being nothing other than an absence of principle rather than a supplementary second principle.

As I contended earlier, Freud's *Lustprinzip* by itself does not distinguish driven humans from instinctive animals, with sentient organic life in its countless forms exhibiting inclinations to seek pleasure and avoid pain. If anything, this principle in abstraction is of a piece with the naturalistic scientific (or scientist) Weltanschauung, with its emphases on the lawful regularity of material nature, that Freud inherits from the likes of Gustav Fechner and Hermann von Helmholtz via one of his teachers in particular, Ernst Brücke. Throughout Freud's career, including contemporaneously and in connection with his later musings about the death drive, this sort of naturalism lingers on as a background influence coloring and inflecting his reflections (a naturalism epitomized by, in turn-of-the-century Europe, Fechnerian psychophysicalism, but perennially recurring throughout the history of ideas up through today). Lacanian, French, and continental engagements with Freud—Žižek is a notable and admirable exception here (as indicated in chapters 4 and 5)—generally favor an external-critical dismissal and jettisoning of Freud's naturalistic leanings as retrograde self-misunderstandings on his part. However, these same leanings, taken in tandem with a particular construal of the *Todestrieb*, facilitate a judo-like immanent-critical maneuver in which a naturalism inclusive of drive generally and the death drive specifically entails revolutionary transformations of the very notion of nature bequeathed to Freud by certain of his nineteenth-century predecessors.

My handling of a Freudian naturalism of drives as a Trojan horse for revolutionarily transforming naturalism overall from within its own confines hinges on four pivotal, enchained claims. First, drives arise from, are sustained by, and remain (partly) composed of "natural" qua biomaterial elements (that is, drives are immanent, even if not reducible, to nature). Second, drives are complex, heterogeneous, collage-like assemblages of multiple constituents (with Freud's "source" [*Quelle*], "pressure" [*Zwang*], "aim" [*Ziel*], and "object" [*Objekt*] as the four basic ingredients of *Trieb als Trieb*, of drive qua drive) and drives are split from within, internally divided against themselves (which is the central contention of *Time Driven*, according to which every drive is riven along the lines of two discrepant temporal dimensions, namely, a cyclical, repetitive "axis of iteration" [source and pressure] and a projective-retrojective, differing "axis of alteration" [aim and object]). Third, "death drive," taken as a phrase referring to falterings and crashes of drives or the pleasure principle, is an essential, intrinsic feature of human libidinal economies and the subjectivities bound up with them. Therefore, fourth, insofar as nature and evolution happened to have eventuated in beings (that is, driven subjects) configured in and through the sorts of conflicts that psychoanalysis places at the very center of human psychical life, nature itself permits and produces negativity, at least in the case of the *Todestrieb* on my specific construal of it.

Contrary to countless varieties of naturalism imagining nature to be Godlike, to be All, One, Total, and Whole as well as harmonious, lawful, omnipotent, and regular, a nature generating and containing the kinds of beings of concern to psychoanalysis cannot be something along these lines (despite what Freud himself says periodically). In Lacanese, nature is not an organically unified big Other, but a not-all (*pas tout*) barred Other.[45] What is more, this conclusion can be reached precisely by moving with, rather than against, Freud's naturalist tendencies, by naturalizing his psychical subjects in all their suboptimal bizarreness. Put differently,

Freudian naturalism is self-dialecticizing to the extent that naturalizations of the metapsychological and clinical contents of psychoanalysis bring about an undermining and subversion of load-bearing tenets of this same naturalism's worldview.

In addition to *Time Driven*, my subsequent explorations and elaborations of the idea of a "weak nature"—efforts foreshadowed by *Time Driven*, although not explicit there—are likewise operative in the background of the present discussion. Without the time, space, or inclination to rehearse those on this occasion, it is nonetheless important for me to situate in this context the (self-subverting) Freudian naturalism of drives stipulated in the four points just given in relation to the conceptual thematic of the weakness of nature (a naturalism tracing back, as with so many other theoretical things of the past two centuries, to Hegel, with his *Ohnmacht der Natur*.)[46] In particular, I wish to head off what I anticipate to be certain readers' reservations or protests about situating psychoanalysis with respect (rather than disrespect) to evolutionary nature, because I treat human beings with their drives, like nonhuman animals with their instincts, as products of natural history, not just of their own history.

These preemptive replies to such worries or complaints can be sorted, in good Žižekian fashion, into broadly Hegelian and Lacanian lines of response. To begin with, although Hegel infamously articulates objections to contemporaneous foreshadowings of Charles Darwin's theses (I address this controversial topic elsewhere),[47] I would maintain that Hegel's account of the modalities (as reconstructed in chapter 3) provides, in his terms, the most adequate "logical" (that is, categorial, metaphysical, and dialectical-speculative) scaffolding for post-Hegelian, Darwinian evolutionary theory as itself "real-philosophical." (Specifically, evolutionary theory, in the architectonic of the Hegelian System, would be part of both the "organics" of *Naturphilosophie* and the "anthropology" of *Geistesphilosophie*.) From the perspectives of both Hegelian philosophy and Darwinian theory, the realities they consider are ultimately, at their baseless bases, nonteleological, contingency-propelled concatenations of factual givens. Similarly, for Hegelians and Darwinians alike, "necessity" is a name for the spectrum of multiple (although not limitless) real, more-than-logical possibilities generated in and out of a given actuality (*Wirklichkeit*). This thus entails underdetermination relative to *Verstand*-type understandings of necessity as an overpowering determination in which one, and only one, effect is dictated by a preceding cause. Such deterministic necessitation is the Hegel-admitted exception to a Hegelian rule where one actuality, as a cause, gives rise to a plurality of really possible successor actualities (as this prior actuality's potential effects).

In Darwinian and post-Darwinian frameworks, this Hegelian looseness of "necessity" is in evidence in two ways. First, the rather minimal evolutionary constraint of, as it were, "good enough to survive long enough to reproduce"—as a German speaker might observe, *Dumm fickt gut*—sets outer boundaries for what is actually possible (beyond which there are only not-actually-possible logical possibilities as empty, unreal, and the like) in evolution at any specific moment in natural history without, for all that, determining a single, unique pathway of development ahead. Running with Marxist critical depictions of Darwinism as an unconscious, ideologically compromised projection onto nature of the human socioeconomic relations peculiar to industrial capitalism, one could say in a noncritical manner that evolutionary pressures regulate with a light touch, maintaining a laissez-faire arrangement in which what is not directly prohibited by requirements to survive and reproduce is permitted. Even if nature is "red in tooth and claw," it does not, as an American republican or British liberal would put it, impose excessive amounts of red tape. This might be yet another instance of, following the Marx of the *Grundrisse*, "human anatomy" furnishing "a key to the anatomy of the ape," a dictum that can be read as allowing for possible vindications and validations of some of Darwin's inadvertent retrojections of the capitalistic onto the natural.[48] As evidenced by everything from the overwhelming biomass of bacteria and insects to the symptoms and pathologies of the human sufferers of concern to psychoanalysis, evolution has nothing to do with inexorably bringing about ever-greater "perfection" as more and more smoothly integrated, highly functioning complex organic systems. The simple and the suboptimal flourish evolutionarily, even if not, in the case of human beings, psychically.

The second way in which a Hegelian looseness of "necessity" is in evidence in Darwinian and post-Darwinian frameworks has to do with a manner in which evolutionary theory deviates from a fundamental standard of scientificity. For modernity's empirical, experimental sciences of nature, "science" generally involves predictive power. Among other of their characteristics, properly scientific hypotheses are propositions making experimentally testable predictions about future states of affairs, very specifically forecasting exact, replicable relations among determinate kinds of entities and events. With physics as the presumed disciplinary exemplar of the various branches and subbranches of the natural sciences, this conception of scientificity as involving predictive power implicitly presupposes or explicitly posits a metaphysics of nature—for better or worse, no science is able to avoid the philosophical accompaniments of a nonempirical *Naturphilosophie*—in which natural realities are assumed or argued to be governed by "necessity" as deterministic necessitation by efficient causal laws, with their one-to-one connections between single causes and corresponding single effects. Evolutionary theory does not meet this standard of scientificity. Precisely because of its unwitting, tacit Hegelianism in the form of its fashion of prioritizing the modality of contingency and correlatively relaxing the very sense of "necessity," Darwinism finds itself occupying a role akin to that of Hegel's Owl of Minerva. Like the Hegelian philosopher enjoying hindsight but not foresight, the Darwinian biologist hews to a principled avoidance of overly specific predictions about the evolutionary future, deliberately limiting him- or herself to surveying natural history from the then up through the now (and no further). As with its famous philosophical conspecific (and, perhaps, unrecognized parent), Darwin's owl of biological wisdom, with its retrospective but not prospective vision, discerns necessities exclusively in the guise of chains of past contingencies that cannot be otherwise if the present (contingent) evolutionary landscape is to be what it itself actually happens to be and not otherwise.

Before delineating my Lacanian responses to likely apprehensions about invocations of biology and evolution in relation to psychoanalysis, I ought to note one more Hegelian point that should assuage such antinaturalist misgivings and science-phobic qualms. For many, putting Freud into proximity with Darwin conjures up the alarming specter of heavy-handed evolutionary psychology, with its reductive, oversimplifying just-so stories. However, nothing provides a better means of detecting and debunking the genetic fallacies forming the stock in trade of this pseudodiscipline than Hegel's speculative thinking, with such features as its dialectics of quantity and quality, continuity and discontinuity, evolution and revolution. With Hegelianism, the generally prevailing emphasis, countering that of evolutionary psychology's fallacious basic assumption that initial origins always determine final ends, is on effects exceeding their causes, existences outgrowing their grounds, subjects turning back upon (and against) their substances, and so on. In short, there is no risk, in a specifically Hegel-arranged marriage between Darwinian evolutionary theory and Freudian (as well as Lacanian) psychoanalysis, of dissolving the latter into the miserable, monochromatic muck of the intellectual crudeness and vulgarity of reductive evolutionary psychology. For my approach at least, this is not a danger about which to fret.[49]

In reference to Lacan, and consistent with Žižek's Otherless ontology, evolution need not and, indeed, should not be idolized as yet another *grand Autre*. Hegel's "weakening" of nature already signals as much. Instead of there being a big Evolution-with-a-capital-E as a single developmental trajectory of orchestrated and synthesized objects and processes, there are only multiple evolutionary concatenations of disparate beings and kinetics ultimately lacking any centralized or centralizing agency, force, law, organization, principle, rule, telos, or the like (above and beyond the minimal parameters maintained by selections-for and selections-against at the levels of survival and reproduction). The paradigmatic embodiment of this, one absolutely crucial for my psychoanalysis-related purposes, is nothing other than the central nervous system. As I have stressed repeatedly elsewhere,[50] the "kludginess" of this system of systems—the human brain is one of the most intricate, complex, multifaceted objects in the known universe—both contributes to the psychical conflicts prioritized by (materialist) psychoanalysis and incarnates the fact that this brain is the product of a plurality of diverse, uncoordinated natural-historical periods and influences. The brain is a hodgepodge contraption slapped together by a plethora of blind, noncooperating evolutionary eras and pressures, resulting in, within the human organism, an intraorganic crystallization of the "uneven development" (to borrow a Marxist phrase) of natural history. From its evolutionarily older brain stem to its evolutionarily newer neocortex—these distinct, discrepant strata of neuroanatomy and neurophysiology are plopped carelessly onto each other by evolution and are (incompletely) synchronized only well enough for human organisms to survive long enough to reproduce—the central nervous system, if indeed the crown jewel of evolution, refracts within itself evolution's real status as anything but that of a Godlike sovereign power.

Back to the thread of psychoanalytic drive theory. Drives themselves, in both their Freudian and their Lacanian metapsychological conceptualizations, partly mirror (among myriad other things) the brain that is their material-ontological necessary (but not, by itself, anywhere close to sufficient) condition of effective existence. To be more precise, *Triebe* are, as Freud and Lacan each emphasize in his own fashion (and as I show in *Time Driven*), kludgy, namely, collage-like juxtapositions of components somatic and psychical, affective and cognitive, energetic and representational. As compound contraptions consisting (however inconsistently) of sources, pressures, aims, and objects, Freudian-Lacanian drives are highly distributed far and wide across the variegated, folded regions of the human central nervous system. Hence, they reflect at least some intraneural tensions and clashes. In particular, what I identify as the split within every *Trieb* between an axis of iteration and an axis of alteration arguably is partially rooted in discordances and disharmonies between evolutionarily older and newer strata of the brain, with their different (and sometimes discrepant) anatomies and physiologies produced out of the uneven development of evolution's various natural histories in the plural.[51]

As I have argued here and elsewhere, the Freudian death drive "beyond the pleasure principle" is best employed as a concept capturing the dysfunction-inducing negativity of a rift antagonistically dividing all drives from within themselves. Moreover, in line with the later Freud's tightly interwoven speculations about the *Todestrieb* and nature, I have maintained that the life sciences powerfully and strikingly corroborate the hypothesis of there being, within humans especially, an intraorganic "anorganicity" (that is, a breakdown or interruption of organic organization generated in and by this same organization) resulting in a proneness to misfirings and short-circuitings of pleasure-principled drives.[52] In fact, one could therefore argue, as I do, that nature itself, at least as human nature if drives with their "deathly" dimension are immanent to (human) nature, is impotent or weak qua not able to reliably uphold its own basic laws (such as the animalistic-instinctual *Lustprinzip*). As Lear and Žižek contend, there is only a feeble, fragile pleasure principle alone, with at least some of its failures being just that, namely, failures rather than successes of another, opposed (meta)principle (that is, Freud's hypostatized version of the *Todestrieb*). If I am correct that the *Lustprinzip* is in and of itself "natural" as shared in common between human and nonhuman animals, then nature, at least within its biological levels and contrary to certain notions and images of it, allows for some of its mechanisms to be suboptimal and to succumb to periodic (self-)disruptions.

CONCLUSION

However, I by no means seek to minimize or deny what psychoanalysis in particular brings with special force to the fore as the idiosyncrasies and peculiarities of humans (both as individuals and as a species) that distinguish them from all other animals. Of course, evolutionary nature is completely indifferent to success or failure, adaptation or maladaptation, functionality or dysfunctionality in regard to human and nonhuman forms of life alike. As Deleuze puts this, "nature . . . is not hostile and does not hate us, even when she deals death, but always turns to us a threefold face: cold, maternal, severe."[53] But I would venture to hypothesize that maladaptation or dysfunction is more exogenous than endogenous in nonhuman animals and, in human beings, it is at least as much endogenous as it is exogenous.

A tendency to seek pleasure and avoid pain on its own is not only hardly specific to human beings alone; the compulsive repetition of certain actions or activities is also not unique to humanity. That is to say, like Freud's *Lustprinzip*, his *Wiederholungszwang*, without further qualifications and supplements, is not something strongly differentiating human from nonhuman animals. If anything, quite the contrary: What are animal instincts if not, among other things, patterns of behavior compulsively repeated in obedience to evolutionary imperatives encoded in and through genes? For Freud himself, the distinction between *Trieb* and *Instinkt*, which I do not seek to abolish, manifests itself specifically in the guises of the variability of objects latched on to as well as the number and complexity of "vicissitudes" these motivators can undergo over the course of the individual psychical subject's ontogenetic life history. This distinction does not depend upon (and, as I have argued here, it is in fact not substantiated by) either the pleasure principle or repetition compulsion as isolated, freestanding concepts unto themselves (although the *Lustprinzip* and *Wiederholungszwang* indeed play roles in generating the contrast between driven humans and instinctive animals when appropriately put into connection with other concepts in analytic metapsychology). But what about my recourse, at the end of the preceding paragraph, to the endogenous and the exogenous with respect to the distinction between human and animal?

If there can be said to be cases of nonhuman animals operating "beyond the pleasure principle" (and in ways not resulting from the contrived manipulations of scientific experimenters in artificial laboratory settings), these would generally involve instances of their instincts becoming maladaptive due to changes in their environments. Particularly in light of the added emphasis on environmental factors in the Gouldian punctuated equilibrium account of evolutionary history, life forms and their instincts can go from functionality to dysfunctionality with a transformation in surrounding contexts. What is adaptive in one environment can be maladaptive in another. An organism can fail to adapt to such alterations by persistently repeating, as it tends to be condemned to do by evolution and genetics, its instinctual patterns of conduct even after contextual transformations have rendered such patterns maladaptive. Hence, such repetition *Jenseits des Lustprinzips* is exogenous in that its failure is primarily a failure to adjust in relation to external forces and factors.

Admittedly, the preceding could also be said of certain neuroses as dealt with in psychoanalysis. In some cases, what is neurotic is the adult's self-harming repetition of what originally, for the child, who is the father of this adult (to paraphrase William Wordsworth), was a self-preservative response to something encountered during childhood. With the transition from the past context of the child to the present context of the adult, the repetition of a given pattern goes from being adaptive to maladaptive.

However, if one takes seriously Freudian and Lacanian metapsychology generally and drive theory especially, one is led to shift from focusing on the exogenous (as in this characterization of particular neuroses) to focusing instead on the endogenous. Animal instincts fall into maladaptation, dysfunctionality, and failure mainly because of external environmental variables. By contrast, human drives inherently tend toward a "beyond" of the pleasure principle by virtue of their own inner configurations and workings, because of their heterogeneous constitutions, which comprise sources, pressures, aims, and objects in which neurological assemblages of drastically different natural-historical ages are thrown together tensely and uneasily side by side. In line with *Time Driven*, the split within every drive between an axis of iteration (source and pressure) and an axis of alteration (aim and object) is partly (although far from completely) rooted in differences between an evolutionarily older motivational and emotional brain stem and an evolutionarily newer cognitive neocortex.[54] This means, among other implications, that there is, at least with human beings, an *Unbehagen in der Natur* in addition to an *Unbehagen in der Kultur*, to gesture, like Žižek (as noted in chapter 4), to the title of one of Freud's best-known texts. Moreover, and resonating with many insightful Freudian observations, fixations by analysands or analysts upon exogenous contingencies and their psychical internalizations as the culprits ultimately responsible for inhibitions of and obstacles to the pleasure principle are themselves defenses against facing up to endogenous necessities rendering libidinal economies inevitably suboptimal and vulnerable to SNAFUs.

From a psychoanalytic, drive-theoretic perspective, the distinction between human and animal no only aligns with one between the endogenous and the exogenous respectively; it is also testified to by what appears to be the peculiarly human penchant for coming to weirdly enjoy certain forms of maladaptation and dysfunction, for becoming libidinally invested in various symptoms, sufferings, and the like. Setting aside instances explicable in Freudian fashions from before 1920 interpretively conforming to the assumed primacy of the pleasure principle (such as phenomena arguably involving, for example, consciously misrecognized satisfactions of repressed drives or "secondary gain from illness"), the later Freud, Lacan, and Žižek, each in his own way, pinpoint strange, stubborn attachments enigmatically perseverating in defiance of what would presumably be urged by any conceivable form of a *Lustprinzip*. A paradoxical, perverse pleasure in pain, if it can be described as such, is referred to by Freud's *Trieb als Todestrieb* and Lacan's *jouissance*.

What is to account for this? I believe a genuinely materialist demystification of this mystery should draw upon explanatory resources furnished by recent neurobiological investigations. In particular, as I spell out in detail elsewhere, the affective neuroscience of what Jaak Panksepp and some likeminded researchers label the brain's "SEEKING system" promises to shed further light on perplexing phenomena "beyond the pleasure principle."[55] That said, I want now to finally circumnavigate back to a focus on Žižek himself. Apart from his affirmations of Lear's critical recasting of Freud's death drive, Žižek's explanations for things *Jenseits des Lustprinzips* tend to rely upon the Lacanian distinction between drive and desire under discussion earlier.

Repetition and Difference: The Anorganic Libidinal Economy

With respect to Žižek's version of Lacan's contrast between *pulsion* and *désir*, my initial temptation, on the basis of *Time Driven*, is to try to out-Hegel Žižek (if that is even possible). Were I to succumb to this impulse, I would maintain that my model of *Trieb* as split between an axis of iteration and an axis of alteration is one in which, in a Hegelian manner, the distinction between drive (associated with the axis of iteration as repetitive and temporally cyclical) and desire (associated with the axis of alteration as differentiating and temporally projective-retrojective) is a distinction internal to drive itself (as distributed across and divided between its two constitutive axes). This would be to oppose a dialectical version of the distinction between desire and drive to Žižek's metadialectical one.

However, I believe such succumbing would amount to a regrettable missed opportunity insofar as its exclusive focus on *Trieb/pulsion* and *Begierde-Wunsch/désir* leaves out of consideration the topics of *Instinkt* and the differences between human and animal, as I addressed them in the preceding. The opportunity not to be missed is of a piece with my earlier-articulated thesis according to which the naturalism intertwined with Freud's drive theory ought to be viewed as self-subverting and self-sublating. That is to say, my prior problematizations of indefensibly neat-and-clean, black-and-white oppositions between the adaptational, functional natural instincts of animals and the maladaptational, dysfunctional non-/antinatural drives and desires of humans (including, on this latter side of the opposition, repetition compulsion and the pleasure principle) entail the following: the pair of drive and desire not only requires a certain amount of reconceptualization in light of critically reassessing the contrast between *Instinkt* and *Trieb*; reciprocally, the very idea of instinct itself (and related notions having to do with the natural and the animal) is compelled to open to reconsideration simultaneously in the same process. How so?

From my (quasi-)naturalist, biomaterialist (yet still nonreductive) perspective, human drives are ultimately made possible, at least in part, by multiple lines of evolutionary processes having happened to eventuate in a central nervous system in which cognitive, emotional, and motivational functions (including those of concern to psychoanalysis) are highly distributed over a diverse neuroanatomical terrain whose diversity brings together rather poorly met, mismatched neural regions and subregions (although not so ill-suited as to bring about species-ending consequences by fatally interfering at large enough aggregate population scales with survival and reproduction, at least not yet in the uncertain meanderings of human history). The drives, with their juxtaposed sources, pressures, aims, and objects, bring together, on one side, natural elements shared in

CONCLUSION

common between human and nonhuman animals alike (such as evolutionary-genetic-organic imperatives to eat, drink, excrete, and orgasm repeatedly and regularly in order to maintain physiological and affective wellbeing as homeostatic equilibrium) and, on another side, more-than-natural variables characteristically peculiar to human animals alone (such as the phenomenological and structural multifacetedness of both conscious and unconscious thinking supported by neocortical systems that, thanks to epigenetics and neuroplasticity, are mediated and molded by extrasomatic, sociosymbolic dimensions that are both inter- and transsubjective). In Freudian, Lacanian, and my terms respectively, the former side is more somatic, driving, and iterating and the latter more psychical, desiring, and altering.

One can hypothesize about the natural history behind the neural routing of evolutionarily older animal needs through the evolutionarily newer mindedness and like-mindedness unique to humans and arising from their distinctive neocortices (and, indeed, some have done so). In all likelihood, and as strongly suggested by much empirical evidence, this conferred a host of distinct evolutionary advantages upon human beings. But analytic drive theory (however knowingly or not) hints that there was, and continues to be, a price to be paid for these same advantages, that they represent a double-edged sword of sorts. Through this evolutionarily permitted, intraneural outsourcing and redistribution, what remain instincts in nonhuman animals become always already derailed, for human animals, into being drives rather than instincts. Although evolutionary theory obviously indicates that the becoming-driven of the instinctual in humanity has not been so catastrophically disadvantageous as to result in the extinction of the species (again, at least not thus far), this same theory, on a certain understanding, nonetheless allows any number of disadvantages to accompany advantages so long as the former do not jeopardize, beyond a crucial threshold, population-level survival and reproduction. Much of the human discontent (*Unbehagen, malaise*) that Freudian and Lacanian analysis powerfully illuminates is partly, although far from completely, explained by libidinal economies taking shape in relation to a kludgy evolutionary-neurobiological bodily base.

But what about Žižek and a Lacanian contrast between *pulsion* and *désir*? As seen, Žižek's rendition of this distinction nondialectically opposes drive and desire, treating this opposition as a metadialectical motor of dialectical processes. At this juncture, I would propose that Žižek's Lacanian difference between *pulsion* and *désir* is itself the fallout of, in human beings, the failure of evolved instincts, themselves symptoms of nature's weakness, its lack of strong principles, its careless sloppiness, its negligent laxness permitting proliferations of malformations that are just functional enough.

To go into more precise details, I can begin by observing that the natural history of evolution has eventuated in *homo sapiens* equipped with central nervous systems involving emotional, motivational, and cognitive functions highly distributed neurophysiologically over a diverse neuroanatomical landscape spanning the breadth from the brain stem to the neocortex. What is more, epigenetics and neuroplasticity make this same evolved brain naturally inclined to the dominance of nurture over nature, preprogrammed in somatic-biological-material terms for reprogramming in and by psychical-social-symbolic terms. These natural variables specific to human evolutionary neurobiology consequently result in, within individual human beings, what would otherwise be animal instincts always already being transubstantiated into human drives as in Freudian psychoanalytic metapsychology. By virtue of these variables, evolutionarily older instinctual-type motivational and emotional functions get connected with and mediated by evolutionarily newer cognitive functions (that is, the intertwined sentience and sapience of *homo sapiens* supported by the uniquely human neocortex).

To be even more exact about Lacan and Žižek in particular, drive and desire can be understood as the dividing and becoming-antagonistic of two sides of what remains, in nonhuman animals, internally unconflicted instinct. The instinctual would involve both the repetitive and the teleological. That is to say, instincts both demand recurrences of set patterns of intending and acting (as the repetition operative in Freudian *Triebe* does) and impel in the direction of certain ends (as the Freudian *Lustprinzip* does, with its twin aims of attaining pleasure and avoiding pain). Moreover, such animal instincts qua organic generally tend to embody harmonious syntheses of repetition and teleology—by contrast with the kludgy "anorganicity" of the peculiar human organism and its kaleidoscopic, patched-together drives. As I claimed earlier, these syntheses occasionally break apart in nonhuman animals due primarily to interferences of exogenous origins. In other words, instinctually dictated repetitions cease functioning effectively toward certain teloi if and when environmental changes cause these instincts to go from being adaptive to becoming maladaptive in relation to their changed surroundings.

CONCLUSION

But, again, maladaptation at the levels of motivational or libidinal forces and factors is the endogenous rule, rather than the exogenous exception, in human (instead of nonhuman) animals. To be more specific, Žižek's version of the Lacanian distinction between drive and desire can be recast as reflecting a coming-apart of the repetitive and the teleological (that is, of what, in the instincts of nonhuman animals, are organically coupled unless interfered with by external contingencies). Arguably, this rift is opened precisely by neurobiological evolution widely distributing animal-instinctive emotional and motivational functions across humans' heterogeneous, variegated emotional, motivational, and cognitive neuroanatomy and neurophysiology. Such distribution is perhaps a stretch too far, bringing about rips and tears in the fabric of human libidinal economies, splits and wounds that come to be organizing principles of these economies.

Put simply enough, Lacanian-Žižekian *pulsion* could be said to entail repetition-without-teleology and Lacanian-Žižekian *désir* teleology-without-repetition. According to Lacan's distinction between a drive's "aim" and its "goal" (a distinction closely related to that between drive and desire), an aim-inhibited drive can achieve satisfaction, as in Freud's main characterization of sublimation as the satisfaction of an aim-inhibited drive, precisely because it has an "aim" (that is, Lacan's "goal") other than the aim inhibited. Lacan reasons, on the basis of Freud's own claims, that if all drives aim at satisfaction and yet achieve "satisfaction" via sublimation (that is, even when these same aims of theirs are inhibited), then there must be a circuit between "aim" and "satisfaction" wired into *Trieb* separate from the one calibrated by the dialectical push and pull between the see-sawing pleasure and reality principles. The inhibitable Freudian-Lacanian (drive) aim would involve "satisfaction" à la the pleasure principle, namely, "pleasure" qua contentment, happiness, homeostasis, well-being, and so on. By contrast, the Lacanian (drive) goal consists in another "satisfaction" altogether than that of the pleasure principle's aim(s), this being nothing other than the idiotic *jouissance* of aimless repetition (that is, repetition-without-teleology). In other words, Lacan, regarding *pulsion*, clearly contrasts the aim of pleasure as satisfaction with the goal of *jouissance* as, so to speak, an Other "satisfaction."

The latter, this enjoyment of and in Žižekian stuckness as repetition sans the teleology imposed by the instinct-like *Lustprinzip*, is derived from interminably circling revolutions around, as it were, *idées fixes*. This is a *jouissance* of what sometimes even is, from the perspectives of instinct and desire alike (which, despite their significant differences, both involve teleologies), pointless, counterproductive, self-destructive, and so on. Such "enjoyment," often consciously unenjoyable, might be biomaterially made possible by (even if admittedly far from exhaustively explicable through) the neuroevolutionary opening of a rift decoupling brain stem–level emotional and motivational structures and dynamics (especially those of the so-called SEEKING system of affective neuroscience) from neocortex-level cognitive ones. The former side of this rift arguably supports affectively intense, *jouissance*-saturated repetitions without accompanying teleologies (that is, Freud's source and pressure of drive, Lacan's drive-without-aim-but-with-goal, and my axis of iteration), while the latter side of this same rift arguably supports representational, signifier-like differences and differentiations with accompanying teleologies (that is, Freud's aim and object of drive, Lacan's desire with its interrelated Thing [*das Ding, la Chose*] and object-cause [*objet petit a*], and my axis of alteration).

Within the ontogenies of singular human organisms, evolution, with its cold indifference to whether life flourishes or withers and somewhat low bar of "good enough to survive long enough to reproduce" at the scale of populations rather than individuals, permits the emergence of this far-from-optimal gap fragmenting what otherwise would be organic animal instincts into the anorganic split drives characteristic of human beings. The natural-historical genesis of such a fissuring presumably brought with it certain evolutionary advantages, namely, those accruing thanks to evolved neocortically enabled sapience. This evolutionary leap almost certainly granted sapient creatures significantly finer-grained, longer-term, and bigger-picture cooperating, planning, predicting, responding, and the like than creatures that are sentient but not sapient.

But there also seem to have been many disadvantages attributable to this very same genesis. In neuroevolutionary terms, these would be ones arising from the immanent nature- and evolution-generated deorganization and reorganization of preneocortical instincts into what thereby become drives proper via the routing of these instincts through evolved neocortically enabled sapience. In psychoanalytic terms, they are the uniquely human libidinal dysfunctions detailed in *Time Driven* as symptoms of "the splitting of the drive" referred to in that book's subtitle. However, so long as, on overall species-scale balance, such disadvantages do not result in *homo sapiens* as a whole being driven to extinction through population-magnitude aggregates biologically failing to survive and reproduce, the suboptimal, discontent-inducing mechanisms of drives are allowed to continue running their courses. What is not forbidden by natural evolution—this strict ban is harshly enforced by the punishment of the brutally simple (and historically commonplace) total failure of a species to survive and reproduce—is permitted. Exemplary of what exists with this permission (a permission that is a condition that is necessary but not sufficient for such existences) is a queer, isolated species, many of whose members are miserable wretches tirelessly but unwittingly working in myriad ways against their own happiness and flourishing. This species, as Freud famously observes in *Civilization and Its Discontents*, appears counterintuitively to be getting less, rather than more, content even as it rapidly gains in adaptive powers by virtue of the modern progress of its interlinked, coevolving scientific *savoir* and technological *savoir-faire*.

Schelling is quite relevant at this juncture. In Schelling's magisterial *Freiheitschrift*, he proposes: "Animals can never escape from unity (*Einheit*), whereas man can deliberately cut (*zerreißen*) the eternal nexus of forces. . . . It would be desirable if the rottenness in man could only go so far as animality; but unfortunately man can only stand above or beneath animals."[56] With his earlier versions of *Naturphilosophie* (those from roughly 1797 to 1804) in the background, this Schelling of 1809 suggests before these just-quoted lines that "a single organ, like the eye, is possible only in the organism as a whole (*nur im Ganzen eines Organismus möglich*); nevertheless it has a life of its own (*ein Leben für sich*), indeed a kind of freedom (*eine Art von Freiheit*)."[57] He draws parallels throughout the *Freiheitschrift* between sickness as the excessive assertion of autonomy on the part of the organ against the health of the greater organism and evil as this same excessive assertion of individual subjectivity's existence (*Existenz*) against transsubjective substantiality as this same subjectivity's ground (*Grund*).

However, the Schellingian human organism, unlike other animal organisms as organic unities themselves embedded in a larger organic unity (*Einheit*), is associated with a power (or, as Schelling might say, "potency" [*Potenz*]) of *Zerrißenheit*. This particular German word, renderable in English as "disunity," "asunderness," or "fragmentation," is central in Hegel's vocabulary, with Hegel also highlighting organic illness along similar lines.[58] For the middle- and late-period Schelling, it is associated with his notion of the *Entscheidung*, namely, the "cut" of a primordial decision, of an *Ur*-choice inaugurating a new era or order. The diseased organ's rebellion against the body of which it is a component disrupts the organic unity of this body and thereby sickens it. Likewise, the human subject, as the lone being simultaneously blessed and cursed to be the privileged locus in and through which evil as a positive reality unto itself is both possible and actual, is tied to what I would call the peculiar anorganic character of the human organism, namely, this specific living being's embodiment and manifestation of intrasubstantial, intranatural disorganizing (that is, deorganicizing) *Zerrißenheit*.

In the spirit, although not exactly the letter, of Schelling's *Naturphilosophie*, my prior interweaving of speculations pertaining to evolutionary neurobiology and psychoanalytic metapsychology indicates the potential feasibility of tracing back one of several conditions for this Schellingian cutting disunity (*Zerrißenheit*) to the species-specific kludginess of the human central nervous system (although, in place of the adjective *central*, it might be better and more accurate here to say *self-decentralizing*) and the related conflictedness of psychical subjects. And, echoing Schelling's contrasting from 1809 of humans and animals, human beings are, from my psychoanalytic drive-theoretic perspective, stranded between, at one extreme, life-enhancing success at evolutionary adaptation ("above animals," as this Schelling would say) and, at the other extreme, life-negating absolute failure to adapt evolutionarily ("beneath animals," again as this same Schelling would say). The evolution-induced sickness of the natural-historical human condition, with the accompanying discontent (*Unbehagen*, malaise) contributing its share of bread and butter for practicing analysts, leaves individual humans to limp along unhappily and dysfunctionally, stranded somewhere between maximum and minimum organic adaptation. As Olaf Breidbach suggests in his study *Das Organische in Hegels Denken*, this sort of maladaptation may in truth paradoxically be humans' peculiar form of (suboptimal) adaptation.[59]

So long as the unfeeling, savage mathematics over generations of populations does not spell doom for the contingent ongoing experiment that is *homo sapiens*, evolution alone will not put human beings out of their misery (although they themselves, through any number of means, might suicidally do so in the distant or not-so-distant future). Again, all that evolutionary nature requires is that a minimally sufficient number of

CONCLUSION

members of the species live long enough to copulate with reproductive results. Of course, psychoanalysis reveals how the more-than-natural variables of a sentient-phenomenal and sapient-structural psychical subjectivity (that is, extrabiological second natures) become more determinative of actual biological reproduction than anything strictly natural (that is, the biological "first nature" of evolution and genetics). Freud's and Lacan's indispensable insights into human sexuality suggest that, if and when this sexuality happens to eventuate in reproductive consequences as by-products or side effects of its "polymorphous perversity," this almost always is weirdly both despite and because of its inflections by nonnatural pathologies, perversions, obsessions, fixations, fetishes, conflicts, and the like. To paraphrase an earlier-mentioned German saying, *Neurotiker fickt*, if not *gut*, then, at least, *gut genug*. For this reason, if no other, natural evolution allows for these partially maladaptive, denaturalizing illnesses to persist and recur.

In addition to Schelling, two conjoined references to Marx and Lacan will also be of assistance in further clarifying some of the preceding. In the immediate aftermath of May '68, Lacan mocks some of the leftist student radicals by reminding them that "revolution" has an astronomical-celestial as well as a sociopolitical sense. Whereas these students believe themselves to be engaged in the latter (that is, a sociopolitical revolution as the overturning of the Old by the New), Lacan disparages them as self-deluded and really just engaged in the former (that is, an astronomical-celestial revolution as merely turning around in place, incessantly rotating through the same well-trodden orbital path again and again). This is the Lacan who (in)famously says to an audience of such students at Vincennes that "what you, as revolutionaries, aspire to is a Master. You will have one."[60] With this scathingly blunt statement to the effect that these malcontents' conscious intentions for change are undermined by unconscious inclinations toward repetition, Lacan approaches, so to speak, political economy via libidinal economy (as is to be expected of a psychoanalyst).

But what about complementing this approach with a reversal of its direction, instead illuminating libidinal economy via political economy? Unsurprisingly, this is where the reference to Marx enters into play. In the background of this reference, and partly motivating it, is my dialectical-materialist conviction that historical-materialist models of dialectical interrelations between social infrastructures and superstructures that are irreducible to one another contain keys not only to unlocking the secrets of human history writ large, but also to perennial philosophical problems about mind and body, freedom and determinism, nature and nurture. Despite the temporal and conceptual gulfs separating Plato from Marx, this conviction echoes the Socrates who, at the start of Plato's *Republic*, speculates that sometimes a question (in this case, that of the true form of the idea of Justice) defying resolution at the microlevel of the individual (the justness of particular acts by singular persons) can be answered via a detour through the macrolevel of the collective (the justness represented by the sociopolitical utopia of the *kallipolis*). As Socrates observes, letters writ small are harder to read than larger versions of the same.[61]

I want now to take up in this hybrid Platonic-Marxist way the macroscale, large-letter illustrative example of a socioeconomic status quo volatilized to the tipping point of political revolution. Recent history and not-so-recent history alike indicate that such revolutionary explosions are occasionally detonated precisely when a slight improvement in the living conditions of the masses occurs, raising them just above absolute misery. In other words, and somewhat counterintuitively, violent radical uprisings sometimes accompany a society's plateauing at a level far below the absolute best but somewhat above the absolute worst (in terms of poverty, oppression, and other unfairly distributed hardships). Analogously—I here move from political to libidinal economies—the volatility of human drives and desires as highlighted by psychoanalysis accompanies natural history's evolutionary plateauing in *homo sapiens* at a level between maximum and minimum functionality, optimization, and the like. Similarly, on my reconstruction of analytic drive theory, the essential, inherent libidinal-economic situation of humanity is akin to the political-economic "middle-income trap" posited by some theorists of economic development.

To quote the Marx of the *Grundrisse* again, "human anatomy contains a key to the anatomy of the ape" (as invoked in chapter 3). In this instance, historical-materialist analyses of human societies' structures and political economies furnish means to advance, in a dialectical-materialist fashion, both evolutionary-theoretic analyses of human animals and their neurobiology and metapsychological analyses of human subjects and their libidinal economies. Likewise, one also could say, with this same line from the *Grundrisse* in view, that the historical emergence of *homo sapiens*—this is evolution's revolution as the leap of natural history generating the human history of these (self-)denaturalized organic beings rebelling against both nature generally and their own natures specifically—is isomorphic to social revolutions qua, as in the mature Marx's historical-materialist critique of political economy, self-wrought outcomes of their societies' immanent dialectical-structural dynamics. Phylogeny and ontogeny, at least in certain instances, appear to mirror each other.

For a while now, I have been dwelling on the topic of drive. But what about desire according to Lacan and Žižek? As I indicated earlier, whereas Lacanian-Žižekian *pulsion* embodies repetition-without-teleology, Lacanian-Žižekian *désir* represents teleology-without-repetition. What I mean by the latter is that desire in this precise technical sense is always oriented toward select teloi in the dual guises of the always-already lost Real Thing (that is, *das Ding*) of a time-before-time ontogenetic past and the eternally-yet-to-come fantasmatic object (that is, *objet petit a*) of a forever-receding future. Furthermore, these two teloi, the irretrievably lost *jouissance* of *das Ding* and the expected-but-never-obtained *jouissance* of *objet petit a*, coconstitute each other such that object *a* is a projection forward into the future of a past Thing and, correlatively but conversely, the Thing is a retrojection backward into the past of the present and future unattainable object *a*. *Désir* à la Lacan is, among many other of its myriad features, inherently teleological, ceaselessly dissatisfied in its perpetual, restless straining beyond itself in the directions of impossible-to-reach ends. Whatever it does manage to attain, Lacanian desire's response, as Žižek rightly underscores, is invariably a disappointed "*Ce n'est pas ça*" (That's not it).

Interestingly, such desire looks as though it bears resemblances to different aspects of both instinct and drive. To be more precise, *Instinkt* and *Trieb*, as I have maintained already, share in common repetitiveness, namely, the basic imperative to think and behave in certain fixed manners again and again. Freud labels this libidinal-motivational injunction *Wiederholungszwang*. However, unlike the instincts of nonhuman animals—these are ultimately rooted in evolutionarily primitive mammalian brain-stem neuroanatomy and neurophysiology—the drives of human animals route such repetitious tendencies through the cognitive circuitries of evolutionarily advanced neocortical neuroanatomy and neurophysiology. Such intraneural mediation transforming animal *Instinkt* into human *Trieb* via (re)distribution spanning the gaping distance from brain stem to neocortex also brings with it extraneural mediations. This is because the epigenetics and neuroplasticity of the neocortex, as a certain Real, hardwire or preprogram this cortex for rewiring or reprogramming vis-à-vis more-than-corporeal, nonbiological, denaturalizing dimensions both experiential-phenomenal (that is, Imaginary) and sociostructural (that is, Symbolic). In and through these somatically intra- and psychically extrabodily distributions and redistributions and mediations and metamediations at the tangled intersections of natural and human histories, instincts are torn apart and become the split drives distinctive of humanity and distinctively theorized by psychoanalysis.

Without pretending to offer an exhaustive or even thorough delineation of Lacanian *désir* in all its multifaceted complexity, I would propose that this desire can fairly be depicted in the context of this present discussion as animal instinct transubstantiated (*als Aufhebung*) by having been always already derailed into human drive at the ontogenetic level of individual members of the species *homo sapiens*. Lacan's consistent fashion from the 1950s onward of characterizing *désir* in an interrelated triad also involving *besoin* (need) and *demande* (demand) can be construed with early-twenty-first-century (post-)Lacanian neuropsychoanalytic hindsight as anticipating what I am proposing here. According to this Lacan, need is very much akin to instinct as a natural physical imperative regularly repeating itself. For a living being thrown even well before the actual moment of biological birth into a preexistent inter- and transsubjective set of matrices of mediation, and destined thereby to become a "speaking being" (*parlêtre*), these Real needs are forced, within the surrounding strictures imposed upon the little human being by both Imaginary others and Symbolic Others, into being (mis)communicated in the form of socially recognized, language-symbolized demands. Whether as Freud's somatic drive-sources and drive-pressures (that is, my axis of iteration) or Lacan's bodily needs, aspects of the biomaterial substance of the human organism get colonized and overwritten by swarms of psychically inscribed sociosymbolic rules and renditions. Thereby, in Freudian terms, the more-than-somatic ideational representations (*Vorstellungen*) of psychical drive-aims and drive-objects (that is, my axis of alteration) denaturalize and divert drive-sources and drive-pressures. In Lacanian terms, Imaginary phenomena and Symbolic structures involving both others and Others constrain Real corporeal requirements to (mis)translate themselves into signifier-like images and words (that is, needs getting articulated as demands).

Both Freud's drive-sources and drive-pressures and Lacan's needs are features of the libidinal economy that could defensibly be described as, on their own in isolation, instinctual components of human nature. Of course, as always already channeled through and filtered by representations and signifiers in creatures naturally inclined toward the dominance of nurture over nature, these instinctual features are admittedly never encountered and dealt with directly by analytic clinicians and metapsychologists in some state of undiluted purity (both Freud and Lacan acknowledge this in various different manners). Nonetheless, in Freudian and Lacanian theoretical frameworks alike, they are posited to be unavoidable and compelling presuppositions. What is more, for any Freudian or Lacanian who is also a staunch, committed materialist (whether Žižek, myself, or whoever else), these biological constituents must be acknowledged and given their appropriate place.

In connection with Lacan's recurrent denunciations of the mistranslation of *drive* (*Trieb*) as *instinct* (*Instinkt*), he sometimes maintains that *pulsion* might best be translated as *dérive* (drift). Indeed, drive is very well depicted as drift, as natural instinct set adrift by and on more-than-natural mediators (whether as Freud's somatic sources and pressures diverted into the psychical *Vorstellungen* of aims and objects or Lacan's corporeal needs forcibly expressed in and through the extracorporeal signifiers of demands). But, again, what about *désir* à la Lacan? Within the triad of need, demand, and desire, he defines it as what remains after need has been subtracted from demand. What does this mean? As I explain in detail elsewhere:

> Through being translated into demands, needs come to be saddled with surpluses of more-than-biological significances; vital requirements take on the excess baggage of meanings over and above the level of brute, simple organic survival. Largely by virtue of what O/others add to the child's experiences of needs through superimposing interpretations of these needs as socio-symbolic demands, the meeting of the child's needs in response to his/her demands makes these needs into, first and foremost, litmus tests of where he/she stands in relation to these thus-addressed significant O/others. Being given specific items of food by a parent in response to a demand expressing hunger can indicate to the child not only that the parent understands that a need to eat has to be met, but also, and more importantly, that he/she is loved by the parent, that he/she enjoys a privileged position in relation to the parent's attention and priorities. Lacan therefore asserts that each and every demand is, at bottom, a demand for love. Returning to the equation "demand − need = desire," what is desired when a demand is

addressed to another is not so much the meeting of the thus-expressed need, but, in addition to this, the very love of another.[62]

I continue at some length:

> Parents of children are all too familiar with seemingly endless series of demands from the little ones ("I want a sandwich," "OK, here's a sandwich" ... "I want a lollipop," "OK, here's a lollipop" ... "I want a new toy," "OK, here's a new toy" ... and on and on until an exhausted parental "No" is pronounced and wearily defended against vigorous protests). Adults, whether parents or not, also are aware of a similar desiring restlessness in themselves, an inability to acquire an object or attain a success that would be "IT" (with-a-capital-I-and-T), the final be-all-and-end-all *telos* of wanting and wishing satisfying them for good forever after. Similarly, an adult in a romantic relationship never is content with being told that he/she is loved by the beloved only once; he/she insists upon repetitions *ad infinitum* of the affirmation by the significant other that, "I love you" (as if no affirmation is ever quite enough). With both children and adults, margins of dissatisfaction, perpetually resurfacing itches that never can be scratched just right, are to be explained, according to Lacan, through a clarification of the essence of the "love" demanded in all demands in excessive addition to the gratification of corresponding needs. What is being requested is an impossibility impossible on the basis of the register-theoretic version of O/otherness *à la* Lacanianism.... the non-objectifiable negativity of the kinetic, slippery heart of Real Otherness (i.e., the always-on-the-move affection, focus, etc. of the Real Other's desiring core both conscious and unconscious) being objectified as the positivity of a static, stable thing (i.e., a special object able to be gift-wrapped and handed over as part of the response to demand). Employing once again the example of hunger, while the O/other can respond to demands for food with the provision of nourishing substances answering to the need for nourishment, he/she is constitutively incapable of turning the nucleus of his/her desiring being (i.e., the non-object of his/her "love") into one tangible object among others to be bestowed along with food and the like.... Conscious and unconscious fantasies are aroused on the sides of desiring demanders—and, everyone is a desiring demander—by the necessary, inevitable dissatisfactions accompanying desires. These fantasies cover over the impossibility of bringing desires to satisfying ends. They do so by constructing scenarios in which there is a yet-to-be-(re)obtained object that really is "IT." Moreover, in these fantasmatic scenarios, answers to

CONCLUSION

questions of Real Others' inscrutable desires ("What does the Other want, and want specifically of me?") are staged.[63]

The Freudian sources and pressures of drives as well as Lacanian needs all give rise to repetition, to a well-nigh irresistible *Wiederholungszwang* buffeting desire and pushing it into its ceaseless yet vain attempts and reattempts to grasp "IT" always resulting in the disappointing sense of "That's not IT!" In addition to these relentlessly reiterated "demands for work" (to borrow Freud's phrase for the repetitious insistence of drive-sources and drive-pressures), Lacan's theory of the signifier, a theory integral to the account of demand (and therefore also the account of desire) insofar as demand essentially consists of signifiers, has it that the signifier is simultaneously a condition of possibility and impossibility for repetition. On the one hand (that is, the condition of possibility for repetition), signifier-like representations, whether as words or images, enable libidinal economies and their subjects to orient themselves toward the quest for, as Freud puts it, "refinding lost objects," toward seeking out what are marked and identified as the "same" things again and again (that is, "IT"). But, on the other hand (that is, the condition of impossibility for repetition), the structural dynamics of signifiers make it such that repetition itself engenders difference, that each refinding is a relosing, that each successive return to sameness liquidates this very same sameness (thus resulting in *"Ce n'est pas ça"*).

Lacanian desire arises from the forced (mis)translation of needs into the signifiers of demands. Hence, *désir* is, one could say, caught between two varieties of repetitiousness: first, the *Wiederholungszwang* of biological, instinct-like vital requirements as recurrently insisting upon labor at their behest; second, the iterability enabled and generated by the signifiers impressed upon a human animal who thereby becomes a *parlêtre*. I claimed earlier that desire according to Lacan can plausibly be described as involving teleology-without-repetition—by contrast with Lacanian drive as repetition-without-teleology. However, I now should nuance this by observing that desire's "without-repetition" is, more precisely, without successful, satisfying repetition (or, as the Lacan of *Seminar X* [1962–1963] would put it, desire is nevertheless "not without" [*pas sans*] repetition entirely). That is to say, Lacanian *désir*, whether thought of in relation to instinct, Freud's drive-source and drive-pressure, Lacan's need, or Lacan's *pulsion*, is constantly pushed into futile, Sisyphean efforts at reaching teloi whose unreachability tends to be misperceived by the desiring subject as contingent rather than necessary.

At least one of the tones audible in desire's cry of "That's not IT!" is contributed by lingering vestiges of the teleological leanings inherent in animal instincts. Put differently, the *Ce n'est pas ça* of desire can be heard as containing impotent (à la Hegel's *Ohnmacht der Nature* and my related "weak nature") natural instinct's feeble protest against denaturalized drive's repetition-without-teleology, namely, against the latter's "perverse" enjoyment (qua *jouissance*) of failure, of tirelessly and pointlessly skirting around never-attained aims. Whereas Lacanian drive is the enjoyment of veering off teleological course, Lacanian desire does not enjoy this, instead remaining fixated upon its ever-receding teloi past and future. Like intrinsically failed instincts always operating "beyond the pleasure principle," desires are dissatisfied and dissatisfying stucknesses in impossible, doomed teleologies.

I am tempted to suggest that the ontogeny of desire emerging through need passing into demand partly involves a recapitulation of the phylogeny of instinct becoming drive (more precisely, the evolutionary genesis of the neocortex and its assumption of mediating roles in relation to emotional and motivational brain functions). Even more, the instinct-drive phylogeny is arguably a necessary condition for the ontogeny of need, demand, and desire. In other words, the denaturalizing sociosymbolic suffusions and regulations of the libidinal economy (such as the overwriting of bodily needs by the signifiers of demands) are made possible in part by virtue of a neuroanatomy and neurophysiology in which a highly plastic neocortex genetically coded endogenously to be epigenetically recoded exogenously plays a pivotal role in relation to emotional-motivational circuits. Thanks to such a cognitive cortex receptive to influences and inscriptions impressed upon it by the living being's surrounding environments of countless sorts, instinct becomes drive. This drive itself is split between a teleology-without-repetition (that is, Freud's drive-aim and drive-object, Lacan's *désir*, and my axis of alteration, all depending upon the evolved human brain's cognitive circuitry) and a repetition-without-teleology (that is, Freud's drive-source and drive-pressure, Lacan's *pulsion*, and my axis of iteration, all depending upon the human brain's emotional and motivational circuitry as well as the entire rest of the body).

CONCLUSION

Much Ado About Nothing: Less Is More Versus More Is Less

At long last, the time has finally come to circumnavigate back to reengaging directly with Žižek himself. I will end this response to him with an attempt to demonstrate why and how my extended revisitation of psychoanalytic drive theory resolves what I contend are certain problems that his fashions of redeploying Lacan's distinction between drive and desire in *Less Than Nothing* and *Absolute Recoil* create for him. But, before closing thus, Žižek's reflections on the already-mentioned notion of stuckness are worth considering.

Along with the pair of *pulsion* and *désir*, and closely related to it, stuckness is a strikingly recurrent theme throughout both *Less Than Nothing* and *Absolute Recoil*.[64] For this theme, Žižek implicitly relies upon a feature of the Lacanian logic of the signifier I underlined earlier, namely, that, in a convergence of opposites, repetition produces difference in and through signifier-like constellations and kinetics. One of Žižek's central theses about Hegel in these books is that Hegel's dialectical-speculative philosophy fundamentally relies upon repetitions producing differences:

> We can clearly see here what is wrong with one of the basic common-sense criticisms of Hegel: "Hegel always presupposes that the movement goes on—a thesis is opposed by its anti-thesis, the 'contradiction' gets aggravated, we pass to the new position, etc., etc. But what if a moment refuses to get caught in the movement, what if it simply insists in (or resigns itself to) its inert particularity: 'OK, I am inconsistent with myself, but so what? I prefer to stay where I am . . .'" The mistake of this criticism is that it misses the point: far from being a threatening abnormality, an exception to the "normal" dialectical movement, this—the refusal of a moment to become caught in a movement, its sticking to its particular identity—is precisely what happens as a rule. A moment turns into its opposite precisely by way of sticking to what it is, by refusing to recognize its truth in its opposite.[65]

This reversal of stubborn repetition into radical difference is not only entirely in line with the Lacanian logic of the signifier; Žižek is quite correct that Hegel, contrary to various complaints and objections, indeed allows for resistances to and reactions against the dialectical-speculative trajectories he traces. However, I worry that Žižek's utilization of the repetition-difference dialectic to rebut such complaints and objections is at odds with his extremely important and admirable campaign against long-standing and widespread attributions of teleological *Weltanschauungen* to Hegel (as scrutinized in chapter 3). It seems as though Žižek is responding to those who appeal to the possibility of successful rebellions contra the purportedly necessary teleological movements of Hegelian speculative dialectics by countering that these rebellions are themselves means in and through which such movements accomplish themselves (in a kind of textbook *List der Vernunft*).[66] In other words, Žižek appears at this moment to transubstantiate antiteleological impediments into proteleological facilitations. But, insofar as he wishes to acknowledge the open contingency of Hegelian motions and establish a fundamental lack of any guarantee of the future progress of dialectical-speculative sequences, does not this doubling-down on and reinforcement of the teleological risk working against the recognition and establishment of these dimensions of Hegel's philosophy?

In *Less Than Nothing*, at the start of the seventh chapter, titled "The Limits of Hegel," Žižek indicates that the employment of a (Lacanian) dialectic between repetition and difference along the lines laid out in the preceding block quotation is a self-exonerating move not available to Hegel himself. He states:

> The fact that Hegel misses the excess of purely mechanical repetition in no way implies that he is excessively focused on the New (the progress which takes place through idealizing *Aufhebung*)—on the contrary, bearing in mind that the radically New emerges only through pure repetition, we should say that Hegel's inability to think pure repetition is the obverse of his inability to think the radically New, that is, a New, which is not potentially already in the Old and has just to be brought out into the open through the work of dialectical deployment.[67]

This "excess of purely mechanical repetition" is, for Žižek, nothing other than the Freudian-Lacanian death drive.[68] As I noted earlier, the *Todestrieb* is, in Žižek's view, an extimate core of Hegelianism, something "in Hegel more than Hegel himself."

Clearly, Žižek is convinced that post-Hegelian psychoanalytic drive theory, although of course explicitly absent from the letter of the texts of Hegel's philosophy itself, is nevertheless both compatible with and even integral to

CONCLUSION

a Hegelianism reinvented for the twenty-first century. In this vein, *Less Than Nothing* subsequently goes so far as to equate the repetition of death-drive-type stuckness with the negativity so central for Hegel himself: "We all know the Oriental principle of the cosmic Whole which reproduces itself through the incessant movement and struggle of its parts—all the parts move and thereby maintain the deeper peace of the cosmic Whole. The most elementary formula of Western negativity is the disturbance of the Whole which occurs precisely when something gets stuck, fixed, refuses to move, thereby disturbing the cosmic balance of change, throwing it out of joint."[69] He soon proceeds to add:

> Radical change (negation) overlaps with the pure repetition of the same. This means that the inertia of the Old and the rise of the New also coincide in the dialectical notion of repetition. The New emerges when, instead of a process just "naturally" evolving in its flow of generation and corruption, this flow becomes stuck, an element (a gesture) is fixed, persists, repeats itself and thus perturbs the "natural" flux of (de)composition. This persistence of the Old, its "stuckness," is the only possible site of the rise of the New: in short, *the minimal definition of the New is as an Old which gets stuck and thereby refuses to pass away.*[70]

Through Žižek's contrast with "the Orient" broadly speaking—more specifically, he likely has in mind first and foremost a favorite bête noire, namely, "Western Buddhism"—he presents his fusion of Hegelian dialectics with Freudian-Lacanian *Todestrieb* as emblematic of a "Western negativity" overall (presumably in nondialectical opposition to an Eastern, or pseudo-Eastern, positivity). Furthermore, to refer back to my earlier discussions of (death) drive and desire à la Freud, Lacan, and Žižek, it strikes me as more accurate to identify Žižek's Western negativity precisely with a death drive–like dimension of Lacanian *désir* (rather than directly with, as in Žižek, *Todestrieb* or *pulsion de mort* proper). For Lacan himself, the unattainability of pure repetition (that is, repeating as dialectically self-subverting) is associated with the logic of the signifier generally and desire specifically (with the latter, as seen earlier, emerging out of the signifiers of demand coming to encode and overdetermine need). Admittedly, *désir* perseverates in its unhappy pursuit of the impossible Real Thing wrapped in the fantasmatic disguises of *objet petit a*. Thus described, Lacan's desire indeed exhibits a *Wiederholungszwang* "beyond the pleasure principle." Hence, Žižek is not without his justifications for recurring to a death drive originating with Freud in 1920. However, given that Žižek's Western-Hegelian negativity in *Less Than Nothing* hinges entirely on a repetition sublating itself into difference or newness, the psychoanalytic inspiration for this contemporary (neo-)Hegelianism looks to be not so much the Freudian *Todestrieb* as the Lacanian *désir* of the signifier-mediated *parlêtre*.

Of course, speaking of the words *repetition* and *difference* in connection with each other in a context in which psychoanalysis and twentieth-century French philosophy are also in play cannot but conjure up the figure of Deleuze and his masterpiece *Difference and Repetition*, published in 1968. As is well known, Lacan himself has the highest praise not only for *Difference and Repetition*, but also for Deleuze's "Coldness and Cruelty" (1967) as well as *The Logic of Sense* (1969).[71] Despite the tensions and incompatibilities between Lacanian and Deleuzian orientations—as I will address shortly, the Žižek of both *Less Than Nothing* and *Absolute Recoil* pointedly mobilizes these frictions between Lacan and Deleuze about repetition, difference, drive, and desire—Lacan's enthusiasm for the non-Guattarianized Deleuze of 1967 to 1969 is not misplaced. Certain facets of Deleuze's philosophy indeed cross-resonate strikingly with Lacanian psychoanalysis. Žižek, given his equation of Hegel's negativity with the stuckness of Freud's and Lacan's drives, views the account of repetition in *Difference and Repetition* as ironically quite Hegelian on the part of its avowedly anti-Hegelian author.[72]

The first of these facets appropriate to highlight in this specific context is the Deleuzian thesis according to which repetitions are inseparably immanent to their unfurling series of difference-inducing iterations. Deleuze articulates this thesis, in *Difference and Repetition*, via a revisitation of Freud from 1920 onward (that is, when *Wiederholungszwang* and the *Todestrieb* become explicit preoccupations in Freud's writings).[73] Furthermore, at one point in *The Logic of Sense*, Deleuze states that "the death instinct" (*l'instinct de la mort*) is "*not merely one instinct among others, but the crack itself around which all of the instincts congregate*" ("qui n'est pas un instinct parmi les autres, *mais la fêlure en personne, autour de laquelle tous les instincts fourmillent*").[74] This statement, already foreshadowed in "Coldness and Cruelty,"[75] condenses and echoes a number of lines of drive-theoretic thought (Freudian, Lacanian, Žižekian, and Learian) that I touched upon earlier: the death drive is not a drive unto itself, but a trait of every drive, of *Trieb* as such (according to one

CONCLUSION

of Freud's speculations regarding the *Todestrieb*); this death(ly trait of) drive involves repetitions disrupting the pleasure principle, following a *Wiederholungszwang* beyond, behind, or beneath the *Lustprinzip*; the *Todestrieb*(-like nature of all drives) is the negativity of a "crack" (*fêlure*) forming a center of gravity within the libidinal economy. (On the basis of the drive theories of Freud and Lacan, I divide drive qua drive into axes of iteration and alteration starting in *Time Driven*, which arguably dovetails with both Deleuze's "crack" and his pairings of difference [alteration] and repetition [iteration].) When Lacan, in *Seminar XVI*, favorably gestures at Deleuze's recourse to the figure of a "blank" (*blanc*) or "lack" (*manque*) as capturing the essence of what could be called "structuralism"[76] (the Deleuze of *The Logic of Sense* as well as the related essay "How Do We Recognize Structuralism?"),[77] this hints that Deleuzian negativity (including what Deleuze, in *The Logic of Sense*, associates with a deadly fissure shaping all drives) overlaps with the Lacanian Real as what immanently perturbs Imaginary-Symbolic reality (and, especially, the big Other of the symbolic order). Žižek approvingly reads this Deleuze similarly.[78]

Deleuze's "Coldness and Cruelty," because of its focus on masochism, contains extended discussions of the *Todestrieb* à la Freudian psychoanalysis. Indeed, the tenth and penultimate chapter of it is titled "The Death Instinct" ("*Qu'est-ce que l'instinct de mort*").[79] Therein, Deleuze accurately maintains that Freud, in *Beyond the Pleasure Principle*, is not primarily concerned with this *Jenseits* in terms of an utter and complete antithesis or nullification of the *Lustprinzip*, despite various impressions and interpretations regarding this book to the contrary. Instead, Deleuze's account, amply supported by the details of Freud's text, underscores that the repetitiveness (as compulsive repetition) with which Freud closely links the death drive is "beyond" specifically as a transcendental dimension before or beneath the pleasure principle. That is to say, Deleuze associates the *Todestrieb* specifically with repetition as a condition of possibility for the consequent installation, via the "binding" (*Bindung*) that Freud identifies this repetition as bringing about (or trying to bring about), of the *Lustprinzip* as the thereafter generally dominant governing tendency of psychical life. Such compulsive repetition is the groundless ground preceding and paving the way for a libidinal economy reliably leaning toward the pursuit of pleasure and the avoidance of pain. But, as a condition for the pleasure principle, this *Wiederholungszwang* itself is not governed by the rule of law it precedes and helps establish. In other words, repetition, in enabling the *Lustprinzip*, does not necessarily obey this principle.[80] A year later, *Difference and Repetition* reiterates these points.[81]

However, a troubling question I posed earlier in this conclusion again resurfaces at this juncture to become nagging once more: When instinct-like repetitions clearly fail to serve the pleasure principle in any manner whatsoever, proving instead to be painful and self-destructive for the repeater, what explains certain instances of unyielding perseverations in these repetitions? Žižek and I each have distinct fashions of resolving this enigma that Freud forcefully confronts and bequeaths to his successors. In both *Less Than Nothing* and *Absolute Recoil*, some of Žižek's considerations of Lacan with and against Deleuze bring these issues to the fore.

In *Less Than Nothing*, Žižek, after rearticulating the Lacanian difference between drive and desire and associating the former with stuckness, favorably invokes Deleuze. Specifically, he remarks that "in trying to designate the excess of the drive, its too-muchness, one often resorts to the term 'animality': what Deleuze called the 'becoming-animal' (*le devenir-animal*) of a human being.... The paradox here is that one uses the term 'animality' for the fundamental movement of overcoming animality itself, the working over of animal instincts—the drive is not instinct but its 'denaturalization.'"[82] I would assume that such "overcoming," "working over," and "denaturalization" are, for Žižek, Hegelian qua sublational, namely, processes of surpassing also preserving some of what they surpass, as in Hegel's *Aufhebung*. If so, then *Trieb/pulsion* thus characterized is, phrased in Lacanian fashion, not without its sublated remainders of the animal, the natural, and the instinctual. This implication further justifies many of the moves I made previously in terms of comparing as well as contrasting nonhuman instincts and human drives.

However, when the topic of Lacan's and Deleuze's positions on drive and desire resurfaces in *Absolute Recoil*, Deleuze fares much worse at Žižek's hands than he did in *Less Than Nothing*. (A whole separate study, not to be undertaken here, could be written on the ambivalences operative in the Žižekian rapport with Deleuze.) Žižek leads into his critique of Deleuze by rehearsing the Lacanian distinction between *pulsion* and *désir*:

> Desire is Kantian (which is why we can think of Lacan's classic teaching from the 1950s as a kind of "critique of pure desire"), drive is Hegelian. There is no

CONCLUSION

relationship between desire and its object, desire concerns the gap that forever separates it from its object, it is about the lacking object; drive, by contrast, takes the lack itself as object, finding a satisfaction in the circular movement of missing satisfaction itself. Desire versus drive, masculine and feminine, and other similar couples (up to the duality of waves and particles in physics) form an unsurpassable parallax—the alternative is absolute and unmediated, there is no higher unity or shared ground between the two poles. What one should thus especially avoid is asserting, openly or implicitly, the primacy of one of the sides—to claim, say, that particles ultimately condense or materialize the intersection of waves, or, with regard to Lacan's opposition of the "masculine" All grounded in an exception and the "feminine" non-All, that the dispersed multiplicity of non-All gets totalized into a universal Whole through the exclusion of an exception. Does this not amount, however, to the ultimate form of transcendentalism, positing a limit beyond which we cannot reach? Is there a way to move beyond or, rather, beneath the parallactic couple? The Hegelian wager is that such a move is possible: it is possible to formulate not some shared ground between the two poles but the gap itself, the deadlock that can be formalized in two ways, "masculine" and "feminine," particle and wave, etc.[83]

The interrelated references and themes fleshing out the opposition between drive and desire are by now quite familiar components of the Žižekian theoretical repertoire: the relationship between Kant and Hegel, examples from quantum physics and sexuation à la Lacan. Moreover, the motif of parallax splits (that is, Hegelian ontologizations of Kantian antinomies) mobilized in this block quotation resonates with Žižek's thesis in his recent major philosophical works according to which the dialectical is animated by the nondialectical, by impossible-to-sublate antagonisms and incompatibilities coming to function as the metadialectical conditions of possibility for all speculative dialectics (as explained in the preface). Along these lines, *Absolute Recoil*, like *Less Than Nothing* before it, treats the Lacanian tension between *pulsion* and *désir*, an allegedly unbridgeable parallactic divide, as the metadialectical motor of the dialectics of the psychoanalytic libidinal economy.

The paragraph after the one just quoted begins addressing Deleuze about libidinal-economic matters. Žižek elaborates:

For Lacan, desire and drive are opposed with regard to their formal structure: desire drifts in an endless metonymy of lack, while drive is a closed circular movement; desire is always unsatisfied, but drive generates its own satisfaction; desire is sustained by the symbolic Law/Prohibition, while drive remains outside the dialectic of the Law. Desire and drive thus form a parallax unity of mutual exclusion: each is irreducible to the other, there is no shared space within which we can bring them together. In contrast to Lacan, Deleuze asserts the flux of desire, this endless productive movement (logically) prior to the totalizing intervention of the paternal Law, a positive assertion of life prior to all negativity.[84]

Set against the wider background of the history of Western philosophy, Žižek's remarks implicitly stage a confrontation between (neo-)Spinozism (in the guise of the anti-Oedipal Deleuze's "flux of desire, this endless productive movement, . . . a positive assertion of life prior to all negativity" as akin to Spinoza's *natura naturans*, substance-as-S) and (neo-)Hegelianism (in the guise of Lacan's "parallax unity of mutual exclusion" as akin to Hegel's *Negativ*, subject-as-$).[85] Žižek soon proceeds to stress:

> Deleuzian desire is open, drifting, expanding, productive, while the Lacanian drive is self-enclosed, repetitive. The point of the Lacanian opposition between desire and drive is that there is an alienating *vel* at work here, a choice to be made: you cannot have it both ways, have both the expanding openness *and* the positive affirmation without any lack or negativity. Paradoxically, it is the prohibitory Law itself which opens up the field, "deterritorializing" the agent, cutting off the roots which constrain it to a particular identity—what the Law prohibits is our incestuous immersion in a particular narrow territory.[86]

He continues:

> The difference between Deleuze and Lacan here is radical, concerning the basic coordinates of the ontological space. Deleuze remains within the paradigmatic modern opposition between production and (the scene of) representation: the basic ontological fact is the productive affirmative process, always in excess with regard to the scene of representation; negativity, lack, etc., enter only afterwards, through the immanent split, self-sabotage, of this process. Lacan's coordinates are wholly different, and the first indication of his difference is his surprising rehabilitation of the notion of representation ("a signifier represents the subject for another signifier"): for Lacan, representation is never a mere screen or scene that mirrors the productive process in a limited and distorted way, it is rather

CONCLUSION

the void or gap that splits the process of life from within, introducing subjectivity and death.[87]

In a nutshell, Žižek's critical maneuver is to argue that Lacanian negativity (as symbolic castration, *manque-à-être*, *objet petit a*, and the like) is the disavowed condition of possibility for Deleuzian positivity. This echoes Hegel's move of arguing that Spinoza presupposes, without being willing and able to posit, the subjective in his extreme monism of the substantial. What is more, when Žižek alleges that "Deleuze remains within the paradigmatic modern opposition between production and (the scene of) representation," this alludes to the more precise charge of a regression back behind Kant to (again) Spinoza, with the latter's arguably *Verstand*-type (or, at least, insufficiently dialectical-speculative) dichotomy between *natura naturans* (that is, Žižek's "production" as the being of Spinoza's substance) and *natura naturata* (that is, Žižek's "scene of representation" as the appearances that are Spinoza's attributes and modes).[88]

From Žižek's Hegelian-Lacanian perspective, especially in *Less Than Nothing* and *Absolute Recoil*, Deleuze's neo-Spinozism (particularly à la *Capitalism and Schizophrenia*) suffers from two of the same shortcomings that Hegel diagnoses in Spinoza's metaphysics: first, an inability or refusal to ask and answer ultimately unavoidable questions as to how and why the One of being (that is, substance) gives rise to the Many of appearances (that is, attributes and modes);[89] second, an incompleteness deabsolutizing its ostensibly absolute (qua exhaustively infinite) ontology—due to a withholding of unqualified ontological weight from appearances (as discussed in chapter 1). Žižek resolves the first Spinozist shortcoming on Deleuze's part by, as I underlined, positing the Lacanian negativity that Deleuze himself presupposes but nonetheless avoids positing (just as Hegel posits the subjectivity that Spinoza likewise presupposes without positing). Žižek's response to the second shortcoming of Deleuzian neo-Spinozism is, as I have already examined in this book (in chapter 1) and elsewhere,[90] to insist that any truly absolute ontology worthy of this adjective must admit and account for the strange being(s) of appearances as nonepiphenomenal. In this vein, Žižek's Lacan does to Deleuze what Žižek's Hegel does to Kant, namely, fully ontologizes structures and phenomena otherwise treated as ontologically secondary or sterile ("for Lacan, representation is never a mere screen or scene that mirrors the productive process in a limited and distorted way").

However, a slightly earlier moment in *Absolute Recoil* reveals that, despite appearances to the contrary seen earlier, the negativity Žižek posits as the disavowed presupposition qua condition of possibility for Deleuze's neo-Spinozist positivity of the productive, deterritorialized flux of desiring machines falls on neither side of the Lacanian opposition between drive and desire. Instead, and in line with certain of the more philosophically abstract and speculative moments of both *Less Than Nothing* and *Absolute Recoil*,[91] Žižek muses about an *Urgrund*, an ultimate origin or source, out of which is generated the very distinction between *pulsion* and *désir*. He declares: "Rather than defining the void of negativity around which the drives circulate as the 'pure' death drive, it would be more appropriate to posit a negativity/impossibility that precedes the very distinction between drive and desire, and to conceive of the drive and desire as the two modes of coping with this ontological impasse."[92]

Žižek's "ontological impasse" would be a primordial Nothingness or Void as a zero-level baseless base for, among other things, drives, desires, and their difference(s). In other contexts (including chapter 4), I have already expressed critical reservations (ones that Žižek mentions in *Absolute Recoil*)[93] about these moments in the Žižekian oeuvre when he looks to be indulging himself in what I dub (paraphrasing Sellars) "the myth of the nongiven," namely, intellectual intuitions about the "x" of an ineffable Negativity floating in an inaccessible time before time and from which all existent beings somehow emanate.[94] I now feel it to be appropriate and important to sharpen and specify these criticisms further in connection with the topic of drive and desire as explored throughout the preceding. Doing so brings this book full circle, in that the sharpening and specifying to follow involves circumnavigating back to the birth of post-Kantian German idealism as I narrated it in chapter 1.

As seen in chapter 1, Žižek rightly underscores that both Schelling (at certain points) and Hegel take leave of the Neo-Platonic and neo-Spinozist aspects of Hölderlin's nonetheless pathbreaking critique of Fichte's quasi-Kantian subjectivist transcendental idealism (that is, the critique sketched in "Über Urtheil und Seyn" in 1795). Although this Hölderlin helps inspire and launch what becomes Schelling's objective idealism and Hegel's absolute idealism—both of these idealisms leave behind Kant's and Fichte's subjective idealisms, departures initiated with "On Judgment and Being"—Hölderlin's two friends

CONCLUSION

from the *Tübinger Stift* come to consider his alternative to Kant and Fichte unsatisfactory due to its repetition of Spinoza's failures to ask and answer queries as to how and why substance manifests attributes and modes (or "becomes subject," as the Hegel of the *Phenomenology* put it). That is to say, Schelling's and Hegel's eventual dissatisfactions with this Hölderlin are ascribable to the latter's lack of explanations for how and why his "Being" (the positive of a *Sein* akin to the One of Neo-Platonism and the substance of Spinozism) breaks itself to pieces in and through "Judgment" as Being judging itself (the negative of an *Urtheil* or *Ur-Teilung* akin to the Many of Neo-Platonism and the attributes and modes of Spinozism, up to and including the reflexive, reflective metaphysical judgments of Spinoza's intellectual intuition).

Interestingly, Lacan too, on one occasion, tacitly suggests that a Neo-Platonic, Spinozistic, or Hölderlinian depiction of Freudian "primary narcissism" as the infantile basis of ontogenetic subject formation renders this same formation (that is, the emergence of subjectivity) incomprehensible and, indeed, seemingly impossible.[95] Put differently, when Freudian primary narcissism is envisioned as the libidinal-affective "paradise lost" of symbiotic fusion, the "oceanic feeling," before the negations disrupting this presumed harmony and establishing such differences as inside versus outside, me versus not-me, and self versus other, the very occurrence of these difference-instituting negations becomes unthinkable. Žižek's own problematizations of (quasi-)Deleuzian "new materialisms" (as referenced in chapter 4) knowingly echo these specific Hegelian, Schellingian, and Lacanian objections against appeals to the pure positivity of a primordial plenitude.

To take up again Žižek's musings in the previous block quotation from *Absolute Recoil*, his hypothesis about a single, sole *Ur*-source giving rise to the antinomic parallax gap between *pulsion* and *désir* strikes me as in danger of amounting to an inadvertent relapse into the Neo-Platonism and Spinozism of Hölderlin with which, as Žižek himself correctly stresses, Hegel and Schelling split. It looks as though some sort of (in a Schellingian phrasing) "un-pre-thinkable being," the "ontological impasse" of Žižek's (less than) Nothing, forms an indivisible, irreducible, and unanalyzable originary unity from which drives, desires, and everything else in existence miraculously spring. To be more precise, this risks coming across as Neo-Platonism and Spinozism merely with the signs reversed from positive (the surplus of the One or substance) to negative (the deficit of the not-One or negativity).

It might similarly be said that this is neo-Spinozism under the sign of negation in the exact Freudian sense of *Verneinung*. As such, Žižek's "less than nothing" ends up being less than (fully) Hegelian.[96] Similarly, Žižek, near the end of *Absolute Recoil*, adamantly insists that "it is . . . crucial not to . . . get stuck in a kind of theology of the symbolic which appears from nowhere."[97] I could not agree more.[98] However, I also would maintain that it likewise is crucial not to get stuck in a kind of theology of a certain version of the Real. More precisely, this would be a negative theology of a unique, original, and ineffable Nothingness or Void from which all things mysteriously emanate.

On the basis of chapters 2, 3, and 4 taken together, an uncompromisingly Hegelian alternative to this perhaps compromised Hegelianism of Žižek's recent works, with the distinction between drive and desire as a focal point, would be the replacement of the Žižekian primal Void as the groundless ground of this distinction with my grounding of this same distinction outlined earlier. My alternative account of the convergences and divergences between drive and desire as Žižek describes them mobilizes biological evidence so as to provide a science-compatible, epistemologically responsible explanation of how these convergences and divergences evolve out of the dysfunctional, unreliable, collage-like instincts of a weak nature alone in its spade-turning facticity. This requires no intellectual intuitions of intangible Nothings. Whatever these thought experiments of mine might lack in aesthetic appeal or speculative sexiness they make up for in plausibility and justifiability.

Moreover, the bulk of the main body of this book amply vouches for the Hegelian credentials of my approach, for three reasons: (1) against Žižek, Hegel's ontology in the fullest sense begins only with the start of *Realphilosophie als Naturphilosophie* coming after *Logik* (as argued in chapter 2); (2) somewhat with and somewhat against Žižek, this ontology has real being(s) begin in and through contingent actualities devoid of anything further beyond, behind, or beneath them, including a (metaphysically real) Being as Nothing (as depicted in chapter 3); (3) again against Žižek, the internal kinetics of self-sundering organic objects and processes (rather than, for instance, the nonorganic arrangements and dynamics of quantum mechanics) are the keys to nondogmatically explaining (instead of dogmatically explaining away) the various negativities associated especially with minded and like-minded human subjectivity and sociality for both Hegelian speculative-dialectical *Realphilosophie* and Marxian historical and dialectical materialisms (as maintained in chapter 4). Furthermore, my approach to drive theory is entirely in line with the sensibilities of the very inventor of this specific analytic concept of *Trieb*, namely, Freud as the founder of the psychoanalysis that is at least as dear to Žižek as Hegel's philosophy. With Freud's neurological training, hopes regarding future biology, antiromanticism (underscored by Lacan), distaste for spiritualisms (likely including anything smacking of negative theology), militant atheism, and the embrace of a scientific Weltanschauung, my alternative, quasi-naturalist reconstruction of drive theory is, I believe, also more Freudian (if not Lacanian) than that offered by Žižek in *Less Than Nothing* and *Absolute Recoil*.

To make explicit the biggest-picture ontological vision implicit in my specific version of drive theory, there are, at the outer limits of what can be discerned "in the beginning," the plural positivities of dispersed natural-material multiplicities as the ultimate factual bases of every negativity taking shape within and between these many givens (as the givenness of the Many). Combining this *Ur*-facticity with transcendental materialism's more-is-less principle, according to which negativities are generated in and through tensions and conflicts between positivities (such as, within the neuroevolution of human instincts, the negativities of drives and desires arising partly from antagonisms and incompatibilities between the kludgy brain's stem and neocortex),[99] one has available an utterly nonmystical and thoroughly postcritical (rather than precritical) foundation for a dialectical-speculative theoretical edifice integrating philosophy, psychoanalysis, and science.

Although embracing the label "transcendental materialism" in *Less Than Nothing* (as seen earlier), Žižek, two years later in *Absolute Recoil*, pointedly rejects it.[100] I am tempted to suggest that it perhaps is not entirely coincidental that, in the same book in which this rejection transpires, there also look to be lapses into a position discomfortingly resembling in modified terminological guise the basic metaphysical models of Neo-Platonism, Spinozism, and Hölderlinian Romanticism that Hegel repudiates and Žižek himself likewise seeks to surpass despite these lapses of his. So, I close with proposing the following choice: either transcendental materialism (with its weak nature alone in the forms of, among other things, contingent material facticity and the dialectics of more-is-less) or regression back behind both dialectical materialism and Hegelian dialectical speculation into the darkness of a pre-Kantian night.

Notes

Preface

1. Karl Marx, "Marx to Engels in Manchester, 16 January 1858 [London]," https://marxists.anu.edu.au/archive/marx/works/1858/letters/58_01_16.htm.
2. Ibid.
3. Karl Marx, "Marx to Ludwig Kugelmann in Hanover, 6 March 1868 [London]," http://marxists.catbull.com/archive/marx/works/1868/letters/68_03_06.htm; Karl Marx, "Marx to Ludwig Kugelmann in Hanover, 27 June 1870 [London]," http://marxists.catbull.com/archive/marx/works/1870/letters/70_06_27.htm.
4. Henri Lefebvre, *La pensée de Lénine* (Paris: Bordas, 1957), 126.
5. Johann Wolfgang von Goethe, *Faust: Parts I and II*, trans. Bayard Taylor (New York: Washington Square, 1964), pt. 1, scene 4 ("The Study [*The Compact*]"), lines 2038–2039 (65).
6. G. W. F. Hegel, *Phenomenology of Spirit*, trans. A. V. Miller (Oxford: Oxford University Press, 1977), 217–218.
7. G. W. F. Hegel, *Philosophy of Mind: Part Three of the Encyclopedia of the Philosophical Sciences with the Zusätze*, trans. William Wallace and A. V. Miller (Oxford: Oxford University Press, 1971), §467 (226).
8. H. S. Harris, *Hegel's Development*, vol. 1, *Toward the Sunlight, 1770-1801* (Oxford: Oxford University Press, 1972), 176; H. S. Harris, *Hegel's Ladder I: The Pilgrimage of Reason* (Indianapolis: Hackett, 1997), 49, 265; Klaus Düsing, *Das Problem der Subjektivität in Hegels Logik*, Hegel-Studien, Beiheft 15 (Bonn: Bouvier, 1976), 246; Crawford Elder, *Appropriating Hegel* (Aberdeen: Aberdeen University Press, 1980), 39; Bernard Bourgeois, *Hegel à Francfort ou Judaïsme-Christianisme-Hegelianisme* (Paris: Vrin, 2000), 119–120; Frederick Beiser, *Hegel* (New York: Routledge, 2005), 164.
9. G. W. F. Hegel, "Aphorismen aus Hegels Wastebook (1803–1806)," in *Werke in zwanzig Bänden*, vol. 2, *Jenaer Schriften, 1801-1807*, ed. Eva Moldenhauer and Karl

Markus Michel (Frankfurt: Suhrkamp, 1970), 551; G. W. F. Hegel, "Aphorisms from the Wastebook," trans. Susanne Klein, David L. Roochnik, and George Elliot Tucker, in *Miscellaneous Writings of G. W. F. Hegel*, ed. Jon Stewart (Evanston, IL: Northwestern University Press, 2002), 250.

10. G. W. F. Hegel, *Enzyklopädie der philosophischen Wissenschaften, Dritter Teil: Die Philosophie des Geistes mit den mündlichen Zusätzen*, in *Werke in zwanzig Bänden*, vol. 10, ed. Eva Moldenhauer and Karl Markus Michel (Frankfurt: Suhrkamp, 1970), §467 (286); Hegel, *Philosophy of Mind*, §467 (226).

11. Hegel, *Phenomenology of Spirit*, 16.

12. Ibid., 9.

13. Slavoj Žižek, *Less Than Nothing: Hegel and the Shadow of Dialectical Materialism* (London: Verso, 2012), 395.

14. G. W. F. Hegel, *Phänomenologie des Geistes*, in *Werke in zwanzig Bänden*, vol. 3, ed. Eva Moldenhauer and Karl Markus Michel (Frankfurt: Suhrkamp, 1970), 36; Hegel, *Phenomenology of Spirit*, 18.

15. Hegel, *Phänomenologie des Geistes*, 36; Hegel, *Phenomenology of Spirit*, 19.

16. Hegel, *Phänomenologie des Geistes*, 36; Hegel, *Phenomenology of Spirit*, 19.

17. Slavoj Žižek and Glyn Daly, *Conversations with Žižek* (Cambridge: Polity, 2004), 61, 64–65; Žižek, *Less Than Nothing*, 333–334, 338–339, 410, 492–493, 830; Slavoj Žižek, *Absolute Recoil: Towards a New Foundation of Dialectical Materialism* (London: Verso, 2014), 321–324; Adrian Johnston, *Žižek's Ontology: A Transcendental Materialist Theory of Subjectivity* (Evanston, IL: Northwestern University Press, 2008), 109, 125–126, 166, 178–210, 222–223, 236–238.

18. Hegel, *Phänomenologie des Geistes*, 36.

19. G. W. F. Hegel, *Science of Logic*, trans. A. V. Miller (London: George Allen and Unwin, 1969), 28.

20. G. W. F. Hegel, *Wissenschaft der Logik II: Erster Teil, Die objektive Logik, Zweites Buch; Zweiter Teil, Die subjektive Logik*, in *Werke in zwanzig Bänden*, vol. 6, ed. Eva Moldenhauer and Karl Markus Michel (Frankfurt: Suhrkamp, 1969), 285–286; Hegel, *Science of Logic*, 610.

21. Hegel, *Wissenschaft der Logik II*, 286; Hegel, *Science of Logic*, 610.

22. Hegel, *Wissenschaft der Logik II*, 287; Hegel, *Science of Logic*, 611.

23. Düsing, *Das Problem der Subjektivität in Hegels Logik*, 58.

24. Karl Marx, *Capital: A Critique of Political Economy*, vol. 3, trans. David Fernbach (New York: Penguin, 1981), 570–573.

25. Hegel, *Wissenschaft der Logik II*, 287–288; Hegel, *Science of Logic*, 612.

26. Hegel, *Phenomenology of Spirit*, 15, 51–52.

27. G. W. F. Hegel, *The Encyclopedia Logic: Part I of the Encyclopedia of the Philosophical Sciences with the Zusätze*, trans. T. F. Geraets, W. A. Suchting, and H. S. Harris (Indianapolis: Hackett, 1991), §79 (125).

28. G. W. F. Hegel, *Enzyklopädie der philosophischen Wissenschaften, Erster Teil: Die Wissenschaft der Logik mit den mündlichen Zusätzen*, in *Werke in zwanzig Bänden*, vol. 8, ed. Eva Moldenhauer and Karl Markus Michel (Frankfurt: Suhrkamp, 1970), §79 (168); Hegel, *The Encyclopedia Logic*, §79 (125).

29. G. W. F. Hegel, *Lectures on Logic: Berlin, 1831*, trans. Clark Butler (Bloomington: Indiana University Press, 2008), §79 (72).

30. Žižek, *Absolute Recoil*, 16.
31. Düsing, *Das Problem der Subjektivität in Hegels Logik*, 210.
32. Hegel, *Phänomenologie des Geistes*, 24; Hegel, *Phenomenology of Spirit*, 11.
33. Hegel, *The Encyclopedia Logic*, §80 (126-128).
34. Ibid., §80 (126).
35. Ibid., §80 (127).
36. Ibid.
37. Hegel, *Lectures on Logic*, §81 (73).
38. Harris, *Hegel's Ladder I*, 558-559.
39. Hegel, *Enzyklopädie der philosophischen Wissenschaften, Erster Teil*, §80 (172); Hegel, *The Encyclopedia Logic*, §80 (128).
40. Žižek, *Less Than Nothing*, 276-277.
41. Ibid., 277.
42. Žižek, *Absolute Recoil*, 229-230; Žižek, *Disparities* (London: Bloomsbury, 2016), 249.
43. Slavoj Žižek, *Antigone* (London: Bloomsbury, 2016), 31.
44. Hegel, *Phenomenology of Spirit*, 58-66.
45. Žižek, *Less Than Nothing*, 104-105; Žižek, *Absolute Recoil*, 237, 243-244.
46. Johnston, *Žižek's Ontology*, 125-177.
47. Jacques Lacan, *The Seminar of Jacques Lacan*, book 11, *The Four Fundamental Concepts of Psychoanalysis, 1964*, ed. Jacques-Alain Miller, trans. Alan Sheridan (New York: Norton, 1977), 207-208, 211-212, 214-215, 218-219.
48. Žižek, *Disparities*, 37.
49. *SE* 2:305.
50. Žižek, *Less Than Nothing*, 110-112, 128-129, 405, 424-425, 502; Žižek, *Absolute Recoil*, 330-331, 346-347.
51. Žižek, *Less Than Nothing*, 502; Žižek, *Absolute Recoil*, 343, 346-347, 396.
52. Žižek, *Less Than Nothing*, 279.
53. Ibid., 280.
54. Žižek, *Absolute Recoil*, 227-228.
55. Žižek, *Less Than Nothing*, 395.
56. Karl Marx, *Grundrisse: Foundations of the Critique of Political Economy (Rough Draft)*, trans. Martin Nicolaus (New York: Penguin, 1993), 142-146, 157, 164, 331, 449-450, 831-832; Karl Marx, *Capital: A Critique of Political Economy*, vol. 1, trans. Ben Fowkes (New York: Penguin, 1976), 739, 909; Karl Marx, *Capital: A Critique of Political Economy*, vol. 2, trans. David Fernbach (New York: Penguin, 1978), 185; Marx, *Capital*, 3:275, 596-597, 603; Ernest Mandel, *The Formation of the Economic Thought of Karl Marx: 1843 to Capital*, trans. Brian Pearce (New York: Monthly Review Press, 1971), 47; Žižek, *Less Than Nothing*, 244-245, 252-253, 361-364, 721-722; Johnston, *Žižek's Ontology*, 43-44, 281-283; Adrian Johnston, *Adventures in Transcendental Materialism: Dialogues with Contemporary Thinkers* (Edinburgh: Edinburgh University Press, 2014), 13-22.
57. Žižek, *Disparities*, 12-13, 32, 45-47.
58. Žižek, *Absolute Recoil*, 89.
59. Žižek, *Less Than Nothing*, 455-504.
60. Žižek, *Absolute Recoil*, 89.
61. Johnston, *Žižek's Ontology*, 109, 126, 166-167, 180-189, 192-194, 209-210, 222-223, 236-238.

62. Žižek, *Less Than Nothing*, 93.
63. Ibid., 200–206, 772.
64. Žižek, *Absolute Recoil*, 32–33.
65. Žižek, *Less Than Nothing*, 610–612.
66. Ibid., 149–153, 156–157, 159, 178–179; Johnston, *Žižek's Ontology*, 16–20, 151–152, 161.
67. Žižek, *Less Than Nothing*, 793.
68. Žižek, *Disparities*, 72.
69. Hegel, *The Encyclopedia Logic*, §24 (61–63), §82 (132–133); Žižek, *Less Than Nothing*, 138–139, 290, 294, 455–456, 482–483, 952; Žižek, *Absolute Recoil*, 118–120, 126–127, 150–151, 140.
70. Žižek, *Less Than Nothing*, 950; Johnston, *Žižek's Ontology*, 265.

1. "Freedom or System? Yes, Please!"

1. Alain Badiou, *The Adventure of French Philosophy*, ed. and trans. Bruno Bosteels (London: Verso, 2012), li–lxiii.
2. Paul Franks, *All or Nothing: Systematicity, Transcendental Arguments, and Skepticism in German Idealism* (Cambridge: Harvard University Press, 2005), 10–11.
3. F. W. J. Schelling, *Philosophical Investigations Into the Essence of Human Freedom*, trans. Jeff Love and Johannes Schmidt (Albany: State University of New York Press, 2006), 9–12.
4. Dieter Henrich, *Between Kant and Hegel: Lectures on German Idealism*, ed. David S. Pacini (Cambridge: Harvard University Press, 2003), 116–117.
5. Immanuel Kant, *Critique of Pure Reason*, trans. Paul Guyer and Allen Wood (Cambridge: Cambridge University Press, 1998), A444–451/B472–479 (484–489), A538–558/B566–586 (535–546).
6. F. H. Jacobi, *David Hume on Faith, or Idealism and Realism: A Dialogue*, in *The Main Philosophical Writings and the Novel Allwill*, trans. George di Giovanni (Montreal: McGill-Queen's University Press, 1994), 336; Henrich, *Between Kant and Hegel*, 119.
7. F. H. Jacobi, *Concerning the Doctrine of Spinoza in Letters to Herr Moses Mendelssohn*, in *The Main Philosophical Writings and the Novel Allwill*, 234; F. H. Jacobi, "Jacobi to Fichte," in *The Main Philosophical Writings and the Novel Allwill*, 519; F. H. Jacobi, "David Hume on Faith, or Idealism and Realism, a Dialogue: Preface and also Introduction to the Author's Collected Philosophical Works (1815)," in *The Main Philosophical Writings and the Novel Allwill*, 583, 586–587.
8. Jean-Marie Vaysse, *Totalité et subjectivité: Spinoza dans l'idéalisme allemande* (Paris: Vrin, 1994), 18–19, 63.
9. René Descartes, *Meditations on First Philosophy*, 3rd ed., trans. Donald A. Cress (Indianapolis: Hackett, 1993), 17; K. L. Reinhold, *Über das Fundament des philosophischen Wissens* (Hamburg: Felix Meiner, 1978), 27, 47, 68–69, 78, 89, 110–111, 114, 136–138; K. L. Reinhold, *Letters on the Kantian Philosophy*, ed. Karl Ameriks, trans. James Hebbeler (Cambridge: Cambridge University Press, 2005), 42; J. G. Fichte, "Concerning the Concept of the *Wissenschaftslehre* or, of So-Called 'Philosophy,'" in *Fichte: Early*

1. "FREEDOM OR SYSTEM? YES, PLEASE!"

Philosophical Writings, ed. and trans. Daniel Breazeale (Ithaca: Cornell University Press, 1988), 96; J. G. Fichte, "Selected Correspondence, 1790-1799," in *Fichte*, 376-377, 384, 390, 400, 406; Henrich, *Between Kant and Hegel*, 125, 127-129, 157; Frederick C. Beiser, *The Fate of Reason: German Philosophy from Kant to Fichte* (Cambridge: Harvard University Press, 1987), 226-227.

10. Friedrich Hölderlin, "Über Urtheil und Seyn," trans. H. S. Harris, in *Hegel's Development*, vol. 1, *Toward the Sunlight, 1770-1801*, by H. S. Harris (Oxford: Oxford University Press, 1972), 515-516; Vaysse, *Totalité et subjectivité*, 138; Terry Pinkard, *German Philosophy, 1760-1860: The Legacy of Idealism* (Cambridge: Cambridge University Press, 2002), 141-142; Eckart Förster, *The Twenty-Five Years of Philosophy: A Systematic Reconstruction*, trans. Brady Bowman (Cambridge: Harvard University Press, 2012), 279.

11. F. W. J. Schelling, "Presentation of My System of Philosophy," in *The Philosophical Rupture Between Fichte and Schelling*, by J. G. Fichte and F. W. J. Schelling, ed. and trans. Michael G. Vater and David W. Wood (Albany: State University of New York Press, 2012), 141-143.

12. Henrich, *Between Kant and Hegel*, 80-81, 93-98, 100-101, 240, 273, 286, 292, 295, 304-305; Frederick C. Beiser, *German Idealism: The Struggle Against Subjectivism, 1781-1801* (Cambridge: Harvard University Press, 2002), 350, 352-353, 355-363, 368-372; Brady Bowman, *Hegel and the Metaphysics of Absolute Negativity* (Cambridge: Cambridge University Press, 2013), 23-24, 227.

13. G. W. F. Hegel, *Phänomenologie des Geistes*, in *Werke in zwanzig Bänden*, vol. 3, ed. Eva Moldenhauer and Karl Markus Michel (Frankfurt: Suhrkamp, 1970), 23; G. W. F. Hegel, *Phenomenology of Spirit*, trans. A. V. Miller (Oxford: Oxford University Press, 1977), 10.

14. Nathan Rotenstreich, *From Substance to Subject: Studies in Hegel* (The Hague: Martinus Nijhoff, 1974), 20, 34, 98; Werner Marx, *Hegel's Phenomenology of Spirit: Its Point and Purpose—a Commentary on the Preface and Introduction*, trans. Peter Heath (New York: Harper and Row, 1975), xxi-xxii, 48; Klaus Düsing, *Das Problem der Subjektivität in Hegels Logik*, Hegel-Studien, Beiheft 15 (Bonn: Bouvier, 1976), 228-232; Adrian Johnston, *Adventures in Transcendental Materialism: Dialogues with Contemporary Thinkers* (Edinburgh: Edinburgh University Press, 2014), 13-22.

15. Otto Pöggeler, "Hölderlin, Hegel und das älteste Systemprogramm," in *Das älteste Systemprogramm*, Hegel-Studien, Beiheft 9, ed. Rüdiger Bubner (Bonn: Bouvier, 1982), 239-243, 245-246, 258; Otto Pöggeler, "Hegel, der Verfasser des ältesten Systemprogramms des deutschen Idealismus," in *Mythologie der Vernunft: Hegels "ältestes Systemprogramm" des deutschen Idealismus*, ed. Christoph Jamme and Helmut Schneider (Frankfurt: Suhrkamp, 1984), 126-143; Harris, *Hegel's Development*, 1:249-257; H. S. Harris, *Hegel's Development*, vol. 2, *Night Thoughts (Jena 1801-1806)* (Oxford: Oxford University Press, 1983), 15-16, 78-79, 82, 89, 557-558; H. S. Harris, *Hegel's Ladder*, vol. 1, *The Pilgrimage of Reason* (Indianapolis: Hackett, 1997), 20; Henrich, *Between Kant and Hegel*, 93-98, 100-101.

16. Dieter Henrich, "Kant und Hegel: Versuch der Vereinigung ihrer Grundgedanken," in *Selbstverhältnisse: Gedanken und Auslegungen zu den Grundlagen der klassischen deutschen Philosophie* (Stuttgart: Reclam, 1982), 188; Myriam Bienenstock, *Politique du jeune Hegel: Iéna 1801-1806* (Paris: Presses Universitaires de France, 1992),

1. "FREEDOM OR SYSTEM? YES, PLEASE!"

147; Vaysse, *Totalité et subjectivité*, 126–127; Wolfgang Bonsiepen, *Die Begründung einer Naturphilosophie bei Kant, Schelling, Fries und Hegel* (Frankfurt: Klostermann, 1997), 272–273, 281; Bowman, *Hegel and the Metaphysics of Absolute Negativity*, 38, 227, 229–230, 247–248, 257–258.

17. Johnston, *Adventures in Transcendental Materialism*, 13–49.

18. G. W. F. Hegel, "The Earliest System-Program of German Idealism," trans. H. S. Harris, in *Miscellaneous Writings of G. W. F. Hegel*, ed. Jon Stewart (Evanston, IL: Northwestern University Press, 2002), 110.

19. Ibid.

20. Heinz Kimmerle, *Das Problem der Abgeschlossenheit des Denkens: Hegels "System der Philosophie" in den Jahren 1800-1804*, Hegel-Studien, Beiheft 8 (Bonn: Bouvier, 1970), 18; Düsing, *Das Problem der Subjektivität in Hegels Logik*, 53–54, 214; Pöggeler, "Hegel, der Verfasser des ältesten Systemprogramms des deutschen Idealismus," 132–133; Johnston, *Adventures in Transcendental Materialism*, 13–49.

21. G. W. F. Hegel, "Das älteste Systemprogramm des deutschen Idealismus," in *Werke in zwanzig Bänden*, vol.1, *Frühe Schriften*, ed. Eva Moldenhauer and Karl Markus Michel (Frankfurt: Suhrkamp, 1971), 234.

22. Jean Hyppolite, *Genesis and Structure of Hegel's Phenomenology of Spirit*, trans. Samuel Cherniak and John Heckman (Evanston, IL: Northwestern University Press, 1974), 544, 557; Adrien T. B. Peperzak, *Le jeune Hegel et la vision morale du monde* (The Hague: Martinus Nijhoff, 1960), 184; Ettore Barbagallo, "Selbstbewusstsein und ursprüngliche Erscheinung des Lebens bei Hegel—im Vergleich zur Autopoiesistheorie," in *Systemtheorie, Selbstorganisation und Dialektik: Zur Methodik der Hegelschen Naturphilosophie*, ed. Wolfgang Neuser and Sönke Roterberg (Würzburg: Königshausen und Neumann, 2012), 111.

23. Robert M. Wallace, *Hegel's Philosophy of Reality, Freedom, and God* (Cambridge: Cambridge University Press, 2005), 73–75, 80–81, 83; Michael Quante, *Die Wirklichkeit des Geistes: Studien zu Hegel* (Frankfurt: Suhrkamp, 2011), 140; Sally Sedgwick, *Hegel's Critique of Kant: From Dichotomy to Identity* (Oxford: Oxford University Press, 2012), 62, 96, 126.

24. Alain Badiou, *Beckett: L'increvable désir* (Paris: Hachette, 1995), 7; Alain Badiou, "Can Change Be Thought?: A Dialogue with Alain Badiou [with Bruno Bosteels]," in *Alain Badiou: Philosophy and Its Conditions*, ed. Gabriel Riera (Albany: State University of New York Press, 2005), 242; Adrian Johnston, *Badiou, Žižek, and Political Transformations: The Cadence of Change* (Evanston, IL: Northwestern University Press, 2009), 62–63; Adrian Johnston, *Prolegomena to Any Future Materialism*, vol. 1, *The Outcome of Contemporary French Philosophy* (Evanston, IL: Northwestern University Press, 2013), 108–109.

25. Slavoj Žižek, *Absolute Recoil: Towards a New Foundation of Dialectical Materialism* (London: Verso, 2014), 240.

26. Slavoj Žižek, *On Belief* (New York: Routledge, 2001), 160; Žižek, *Absolute Recoil*, 91; Adrian Johnston, *Žižek's Ontology: A Transcendental Materialist Theory of Subjectivity* (Evanston, IL: Northwestern University Press, 2008), 12–16.

27. Slavoj Žižek, *Less Than Nothing: Hegel and the Shadow of Dialectical Materialism* (London: Verso, 2012), 7–9.

28. Ibid., 8.

1. "FREEDOM OR SYSTEM? YES, PLEASE!"

29. Ibid., 50–52.
30. Bowman, *Hegel and the Metaphysics of Absolute Negativity*, 103–104.
31. G. W. F. Hegel, *Science of Logic*, trans. A. V. Miller (London: George Allen and Unwin, 1969), 63–64; G. W. F. Hegel, *The Encyclopedia Logic: Part I of the Encyclopedia of the Philosophical Sciences with the Zusätze*, trans. T. F. Geraets, W. A. Suchting, and H. S. Harris (Indianapolis: Hackett, 1991), §9 (33), §24 (56); G. W. F. Hegel, *Lectures on Logic: Berlin, 1831*, trans. Clark Butler (Bloomington: Indiana University Press, 2008), §19 (3); G. W. F. Hegel, "Hegel to von Raumer: Nuremberg, August 2, 1816," in *Hegel: The Letters*, trans. Clark Butler and Christiane Seiler (Bloomington: Indiana University Press, 1984), 341; Žižek, *Less Than Nothing*, 49; Jean Hyppolite, *Logic and Existence*, trans. Leonard Lawlor and Amit Sen (Albany: State University of New York Press, 1997), 34–35, 51, 122, 154–158, 166; Gérard Lebrun, *La patience du Concept: Essai sur le Discours hégélien* (Paris: Gallimard, 1972), 395–412; Harris, *Hegel's Development*, 2: 178, 410–418; Düsing, *Das Problem der Subjektivität in Hegels Logik*, 22, 134, 215; H. S. Harris, *Hegel's Ladder*, vol. 2, *The Odyssey of Spirit* (Indianapolis: Hackett, 1997), 759; André Doz, *La logique de Hegel et les problèmes traditionnels de l'ontologie* (Paris: Vrin, 1987), 15–16, 18–19, 23, 298; Rolf-Peter Horstmann, *Die Grenzen der Vernunft: Eine Untersuchung zu Zielen und Motiven des Deutschen Idealismus* (Frankfurt: Klostermann, 2004), 133–134, 138–141; Frederick Beiser, *Hegel* (New York: Routledge, 2005), 53; Wallace, *Hegel's Philosophy of Reality, Freedom, and God*, 91, 93–94, 244–245; Stephen Houlgate, *An Introduction to Hegel: Freedom, Truth and History*, 2nd ed. (Oxford: Blackwell, 2005), 43–46; Stephen Houlgate, *The Opening of Hegel's Logic: From Being to Infinity* (West Lafayette, IN: Purdue University Press, 2006), 115–119, 146–147, 436–438; Bowman, *Hegel and the Metaphysics of Absolute Negativity*, 109; Förster, *The Twenty-Five Years of Philosophy*, 301–302; Stanley Rosen, *The Idea of Hegel's Science of Logic* (Chicago: University of Chicago Press, 2014), 412.
32. Žižek, *Less Than Nothing*, 11–13.
33. Ibid., 12–13, 15–16; Dieter Henrich, "Hegel und Hölderlin," in *Hegel im Kontext: Mit einem Nachwort zur Neuauflage* (Frankfurt: Suhrkamp, 2010), 37–38; Henrich, *Between Kant and Hegel*, 289, 293, 309; Dieter Henrich, "Andersheit und Absolutheit des Geistes: Sieben Schritte auf dem Wege von Schelling zu Hegel," in *Selbstverhältnisse*, 152–153; Rotenstreich, *From Substance to Subject*, 76; Düsing, *Das Problem der Subjektivität in Hegels Logik*, 66, 165–166, 250–251; Harris, *Hegel's Ladder*, 1:302, 321; Harris, *Hegel's Ladder*, 2:736–738; Vaysse, *Totalité et subjectivité*, 200, 205; Gilles Marmasse, *Penser le réel: Hegel, la nature et l'esprit* (Paris: Kimé, 2008), 23–24.
34. F. W. J. Schelling, "On the World-Soul," trans. Iain Hamilton Grant, *Collapse: Philosophical Research and Development* 6 (January 2010): 73–74, 85–86, 92–95; F. W. J. Schelling, *First Outline of a System of the Philosophy of Nature*, trans. Keith R. Peterson (Albany: State University of New York Press, 2004), 17, 39, 48, 87, 106–108, 113, 116–117, 122–123, 204–205, 213, 216, 218–220, 232.
35. Slavoj Žižek, "The Abyss of Freedom," in *The Abyss of Freedom/Ages of the World*, by Slavoj Žižek and F. W. J. Schelling (Ann Arbor: University of Michigan Press, 1997), 88–89.
36. Wolfram Hogrebe, *Prädikation und Genesis: Metaphysik als Fundamentalheuristik im Ausgang von Schellings "Die Weltalter"* (Frankfurt: Suhrkamp, 1989), 23–24, 28, 33–34, 51–55, 57, 118, 127–128.

1. "FREEDOM OR SYSTEM? YES, PLEASE!"

37. Johnston, *Žižek's Ontology*, 12–15, 69–70, 128–144, 148, 161–166, 172, 187, 200–201, 207–208, 265–267.

38. Žižek, *Less Than Nothing*, 149, 536–539, 706–707, 740, 907, 924–926; Žižek, *Absolute Recoil*, 106, 109; Žižek, *Disparities* (London: Bloomsbury, 2016), 99.

39. Žižek, *Less Than Nothing*, 268–269.

40. Ibid., 267.

41. Kant, *Critique of Pure Reason*, A297–298/B353–355 (386–387), A302/B359 (389), A305–306/B362–363 (390–391), A671–674/B699–702 (606–608); Immanuel Kant, *Prolegomena to Any Future Metaphysics That Will Be Able to Come Forward as a Science*, trans. Gary Hatfield, in *Theoretical Philosophy After 1781*, ed. Henry Allison and Peter Heath (Cambridge: Cambridge University Press, 2002), §§40–44 (119–124), §56 (138–140).

42. Beiser, *German Idealism*, 88–131.

43. Kant, *Critique of Pure Reason*, B303 (358–359), A845–847/B873–875 (698–699).

44. Žižek, *Less Than Nothing*, 269.

45. Ibid., 280–281.

46. Ibid., 195.

47. John Locke, *An Essay Concerning Human Understanding in Two Volumes*, vol. 1, ed. Alexander Campbell Fraser (New York: Dover, 1959), 25–33.

48. Adrian Johnston, "Repeating Engels: Renewing the Cause of the Materialist Wager for the Twenty-First Century," special issue, "animal.machine.sovereign," ed. Javier Burdman and Tyler Williams, *Theory @ Buffalo* 15 (2011): 155–156.

49. Adrian Johnston, *Prolegomena to Any Future Materialism*, vol. 2, *A Weak Nature Alone* (Evanston, IL: Northwestern University Press, 2018).

50. Jacobi, *David Hume on Faith, or Idealism and Realism: A Dialogue*, 336.

51. Johnston, *Žižek's Ontology*, 133–142, 152–163; Pinkard, *German Philosophy, 1760–1860*, 92; Horstmann, *Die Grenzen der Vernunft*, 55.

52. Kant, *Critique of Pure Reason*, Bxvi–xvii (110–111), Bxxii (113).

53. Bowman, *Hegel and the Metaphysics of Absolute Negativity*, 133.

54. Žižek, *Less Than Nothing*, 282–284.

55. Hegel, *Science of Logic*, 132, 134–135; Hegel, *The Encyclopedia Logic*, §60 (105–106), §92 (148); Hegel, *Lectures on Logic*, §93 (104); G. W. F. Hegel, *Philosophy of Mind: Part Three of the Encyclopedia of the Philosophical Sciences with the Zusätze*, trans. William Wallace and A. V. Miller (Oxford: Oxford University Press, 1971), §386 (23–24).

56. Žižek, *Less Than Nothing*, 226.

57. G. W. F. Hegel and F. W. J. Schelling, "Introduction for the *Critical Journal of Philosophy*: On the Essence of Philosophical Criticism Generally, and Its Relationship to the Present State of Philosophy in Particular," trans. H.S. Harris, in *Miscellaneous Writings of G. W. F. Hegel*, 211–212; G. W. F. Hegel, *The Difference Between Fichte's and Schelling's System of Philosophy*, trans. H. S. Harris and Walter Cerf (Albany: State University of New York Press, 1977), 79–83, 117, 126–127, 133, 135, 140–141, 155–158, 162–163, 172–174, 176; G. W. F. Hegel, *Faith and Knowledge*, trans. Walter Cerf and H. S. Harris (Albany: State University of New York Press, 1977), 75–77; G. W. F. Hegel, "How the Ordinary Human Understanding Takes Philosophy (as Displayed in the Works of Mr. Krug)," trans. H. S. Harris, in *Miscellaneous Writings of G. W. F. Hegel*, 229; Hegel, *Science of Logic*, 45–47, 489; Hegel, *The Encyclopedia Logic*, §24 (56–57), §41 (81), §42 (86), §45 (88–89); Hegel, *Lectures on Logic*, §43 (36); G. W. F. Hegel, *Lectures on the History of*

1. "FREEDOM OR SYSTEM? YES, PLEASE!"

Philosophy, vol. 3, trans. E. S. Haldane and Frances H. Simson (New York: Humanities, 1955), 535–536, 541–542, 551–553.

58. Hegel, *Phenomenology of Spirit*, 13–14, 55; Hegel, *Science of Logic*, 32, 106–108.

59. Hegel, *Phenomenology of Spirit*, 36; Hegel, *Science of Logic*, 28, 54–56, 832–833; Hegel, *The Encyclopedia Logic*, §82 (131–132), §91 (147).

60. Jacques Lacan, *The Seminar of Jacques Lacan*, book 7, *The Ethics of Psychoanalysis, 1959-1960*, ed. Jacques-Alain Miller, trans. Dennis Porter (New York: Norton, 1992), 139; Jacques Lacan, *The Seminar of Jacques Lacan*, book 11, *The Four Fundamental Concepts of Psychoanalysis, 1964*, ed. Jacques-Alain Miller, trans. Alan Sheridan (New York: Norton, 1977), 268; Jacques Lacan, *Le Séminaire de Jacques Lacan*, book 16, *D'un Autre à l'autre, 1968-1969*, ed. Jacques-Alain Miller (Paris: Seuil, 2006), 224–225, 249.

61. Hegel, *Lectures on Logic*, §60 (59).

62. Karl Rosenkranz, *G. W. F. Hegels Leben* (Darmstadt: Wissenschaftliche Buchgesellschaft, 1971), xiv; Hyppolite, *Logic and Existence*, 58–59; Béatrice Longuenesse, *Hegel et la critique de la métaphysique* (Paris: Vrin, 1981), 17, 19–21, 188; Robert B. Pippin, *Hegel's Idealism: The Satisfactions of Self-Consciousness* (Cambridge: Cambridge University Press, 1989), 6–7, 9, 16–17, 28–31, 79, 120–121, 132, 176, 225, 230, 248; James Kreines, "Metaphysics Without Pre-Critical Monism: Hegel on Lower-Level Natural Kinds and the Structure of Reality," *Bulletin of the Hegel Society of Great Britain* 57/58 (2008): 50; Robert Stern, "Introduction: How Is Hegelian Metaphysics Possible?," in *Hegelian Metaphysics* (Oxford: Oxford University Press, 2009), 10, 29; Robert Stern, "Hegel's Idealism," in *Hegelian Metaphysics*, 56–57; Rosen, *The Idea of Hegel's Science of Logic*, 61; Slavoj Žižek, *Tarrying with the Negative: Kant, Hegel, and the Critique of Ideology* (Durham: Duke University Press, 1993), 265–266; Slavoj Žižek, *The Metastases of Enjoyment: Six Essays on Woman and Causality* (London: Verso, 1994), 187; Slavoj Žižek, *The Ticklish Subject: The Absent Centre of Political Ontology* (London: Verso, 1999), 55, 60; Slavoj Žižek, *Organs Without Bodies: On Deleuze and Consequences* (New York: Routledge, 2004), 58.

63. Hegel, *Science of Logic*, 55–56, 190–192, 197–198, 831–833; Hegel, *The Encyclopedia Logic*, §48 (91–93), §81 (128–131); Hegel, *Lectures on Logic*, §48 (41–44), §81 (73–74); G. W. F. Hegel, "Logic [for the Middle Class]," in *The Philosophical Propaedeutic*, ed. Michael George and Andrew Vincent, trans. A. V. Miller (Oxford: Blackwell, 1986), §78 (90); G. W. F. Hegel, "Hegel to Niethammer: Nuremberg, October 23, 1812," in *Hegel: The Letters*, 281.

64. Stern, "Introduction," 4, 16–17; Robert Stern, "Individual Existence and the Philosophy of Difference," in *Hegelian Metaphysics*, 350.

65. Düsing, *Das Problem der Subjektivität in Hegels Logik*, 68.

66. Michael Theunissen, *Sein und Schein: Die kritische Funktion der Hegelschen Logik* (Frankfurt: Suhrkamp, 1980), 142.

67. Žižek, *Less Than Nothing*, 143.

68. Hegel, "Hegel to Niethammer: Nuremberg, October 23, 1812," 277.

69. Hegel, *Science of Logic*, 51; Hegel, *The Encyclopedia Logic*, §24 (56).

70. Hegel, *Science of Logic*, 61–64.

71. Schelling and Hegel, "Introduction for the *Critical Journal of Philosophy*," 214–216; Hegel, "How the Ordinary Human Understanding Takes Philosophy (as Displayed in the Works of Mr. Krug)," 231; Hegel, *The Difference Between Fichte's and*

1. "FREEDOM OR SYSTEM? YES, PLEASE!"

Schelling's System of Philosophy, 90, 95–96, 158–159; Hegel, Faith and Knowledge, 107–108, 112–113; G. W. F. Hegel, The Jena System, 1804-5: Logic and Metaphysics, ed. John W. Burbidge and George di Giovanni (Kingston: McGill-Queen's University Press, 1986), 35; Hegel, Science of Logic, 137–140, 142–143; Hegel, The Encyclopedia Logic, §§93–95 (149–152), §104 (165); Harris, Hegel's Ladder, 2:732; Johnston, Adventures in Transcendental Materialism, 23–49.

72. Hegel, Phenomenology of Spirit, 1–3.
73. Hegel, Science of Logic, 48–49, 68–69, 72–75, 78; Hegel, Lectures on Logic, §87 (93); Houlgate, The Opening of Hegel's Logic, 29–71.
74. Hegel, Phenomenology of Spirit, 9, 15–17, 28, 31–33, 35–36, 49–56.
75. Ibid., 68–70, 72–77, 87–91.
76. Hegel, Science of Logic, 71–72.
77. Žižek, The Ticklish Subject, 84–85; Johnston, Žižek's Ontology, 128–133.
78. Žižek, Less Than Nothing, 950.
79. Hegel, Phänomenologie des Geistes, 118–119; Hegel, Phenomenology of Spirit, 89.
80. Hegel, Phenomenology of Spirit, 88–89.
81. Hegel, Faith and Knowledge, 76–77.
82. Hegel, Phenomenology of Spirit, 87–88.
83. G. W. F. Hegel, Differenz des Fichteschen und Schellingschen Systems der Philosophie, in Werke in zwanzig Bänden, vol. 2, Jenaer Schriften, 1801-1807, ed. Eva Moldenhauer and Karl Markus Michel (Frankfurt: Suhrkamp, 1970), 106; Hegel, The Difference Between Fichte's and Schelling's System of Philosophy, 166.
84. Hegel, Science of Logic, 489, 499, 507; Hegel, The Encyclopedia Logic, §131 (199–200); Hegel, Lectures on Logic, §135 (149–150); G. W. F. Hegel, Encyclopedia of the Philosophical Sciences in Outline, trans. Steven A. Taubeneck, in Encyclopedia of the Philosophical Sciences in Outline and Critical Writings, ed. Ernst Behler (New York: Continuum, 1990), §81 (89), §89 (93).
85. Hegel, Phenomenology of Spirit, 87–88.
86. Ibid., 151.
87. Ibid., 100–103.
88. Slavoj Žižek, The Sublime Object of Ideology (London: Verso, 1989), 193, 195; Slavoj Žižek, Enjoy Your Symptom!: Jacques Lacan in Hollywood and Out (New York: Routledge, 1992), 53, 137; Žižek, Tarrying with the Negative, 36–37, 39, 241, 245–246; Slavoj Žižek, "Postface: Georg Lukács as the Philosopher of Leninism," in A Defense of History and Class Consciousness: Tailism and the Dialectic, by Georg Lukács, trans. Esther Leslie (London: Verso, 2000), 181; Žižek, Organs Without Bodies, 60–61, 65; Slavoj Žižek, "The Parallax View: Toward a New Reading of Kant," Epoché 8, no. 2 (Spring 2004): 259–260; Slavoj Žižek, The Parallax View (Cambridge: MIT Press, 2006), 29–30, 106; Johnston, Žižek's Ontology, 136–144, 162.
89. Žižek, Less Than Nothing, 4.
90. Ibid., 244–245, 252–253, 361–364; Johnston, Adventures in Transcendental Materialism, 13–22.
91. Alenka Zupančič, Das Reale einer Illusion: Kant und Lacan, trans. Reiner Ansén (Frankfurt: Suhrkamp, 2001), 141–142; Alenka Zupančič, The Odd One In: On Comedy (Cambridge: MIT Press, 2008), 17; Žižek, Less Than Nothing, 721–722; Johnston, Žižek's Ontology, 43–44, 281–283.

1. "FREEDOM OR SYSTEM? YES, PLEASE!"

92. Bowman, *Hegel and the Metaphysics of Absolute Negativity*, 58.
93. Schelling, *Philosophical Investigations Into the Essence of Human Freedom*, 11–14, 16–18, 21; F. W. J. Schelling, "Stuttgart Seminars," in *Idealism and the Endgame of Theory: Three Essays by F. W. J. Schelling*, trans. Thomas Pfau (Albany: State University of New York Press, 1994), 214; F. W. J. Schelling, *The Ages of the World: Third Version (c. 1815)*, trans. Jason M. Wirth (Albany: State University of New York Press, 2000), 104–105; F. W. J. Schelling, *On the History of Modern Philosophy*, trans. Andrew Bowie (Cambridge: Cambridge University Press, 1994), 64–75; F. W. J. Schelling, *The Grounding of Positive Philosophy*, trans. Bruce Matthews (Albany: State University of New York Press, 2007), 126; Hegel, *Phenomenology of Spirit*, 10–13; Hegel, *The Encyclopedia Logic*, §151 (226–227); G. W. F. Hegel, *Philosophy of Nature: Part Two of the Encyclopedia of the Philosophical Sciences*, trans. A. V. Miller (Oxford: Oxford University Press, 1970), §359 (385–386); Hegel, *Philosophy of Mind*, §415 (156); Hegel, *Lectures on the History of Philosophy*, 3:257–261, 263–264, 268–269, 280, 287–289; Düsing, *Das Problem der Subjektivität in Hegels Logik*, 50; Harris, *Hegel's Ladder*, 1:456; Pinkard, *German Philosophy, 1760–1860*, 258; Bowman, *Hegel and the Metaphysics of Absolute Negativity*, 19; Johnston, *Adventures in Transcendental Materialism*, 23–49.
94. Žižek, *Less Than Nothing*, 807–809; Žižek, *Absolute Recoil*, 77–78; Žižek, *Disparities*, 341–342.
95. Rotenstreich, *From Substance to Subject*, 69.
96. Žižek, *Less Than Nothing*, 907.
97. Herbert Marcuse, *Reason and Revolution: Hegel and the Rise of Social Theory*, 2nd ed. (New York: Routledge, 2000), 100; Hyppolite, *Genesis and Structure of Hegel's Phenomenology of Spirit*, 527; Harris, *Hegel's Ladder*, 2:567.
98. Žižek, *Absolute Recoil*, 186.
99. Herbert Marcuse, *Hegel's Ontology and the Theory of Historicity*, trans. Seyla Benhabib (Cambridge: MIT Press, 1987), 73.
100. Rosen, *The Idea of Hegel's Science of Logic*, 293.
101. Ibid., 298.
102. Düsing, *Das Problem der Subjektivität in Hegels Logik*, 69.
103. Lacan, *The Seminar of Jacques Lacan*, book 11, 103, 111–112; Johnston, *Žižek's Ontology*, 138–140.
104. Žižek, *Less Than Nothing*, 40–42; Alain Badiou, *La République de Platon* (Paris: Fayard, 2012), 9, 165, 169, 380, 383, 400–401, 526–527, 571–572, 590.
105. Žižek, *Less Than Nothing*, 31–39.
106. Ibid., 37.
107. Ibid., 96–97.
108. Hegel, *Phenomenology of Spirit*, 58–79; Hegel, *Science of Logic*, 109–156.
109. G. W. F. Hegel, "Who Thinks Abstractly?," trans. Walter Kaufmann, in *Miscellaneous Writings of G. W. F. Hegel*, 284–285; Marcuse, *Reason and Revolution*, 113; Johnston, *Adventures in Transcendental Materialism*, 60, 66, 78.
110. Hegel, *Phenomenology of Spirit*, 1, 27–28, 60; Hegel, *Science of Logic*, 600–622; Hegel, *The Encyclopedia Logic*, §6 (29–30), §20 (50–51), §24 (56–57), §70 (117–118), §142 (213–215), §164 (241–242), §212 (286); Ernst Bloch, "Über die Besonderheit bei Hegel," in *Über Methode und System bei Hegel* (Frankfurt: Suhrkamp, 1970), 90–94.
111. Žižek, *Less Than Nothing*, 235; Žižek, *Disparities*, 100.

1. "FREEDOM OR SYSTEM? YES, PLEASE!"

112. Žižek, *Less Than Nothing*, 197, 740–741.
113. Žižek, *The Parallax View*, 29; Johnston, *Žižek's Ontology*, 162–165.
114. Žižek, *Less Than Nothing*, 131.
115. Ibid., 808.
116. Ibid., 144.
117. Ibid., 141.
118. Hegel, *Encyclopedia of the Philosophical Sciences in Outline*, §75 (87); Žižek, *Tarrying with the Negative*, 38; Slavoj Žižek, *The Indivisible Remainder: An Essay on Schelling and Related Matters* (London: Verso, 1996), 139; Slavoj Žižek, "Foreword to the Second Edition: Enjoyment within the Limits of Reason Alone," in *For They Know Not What They Do: Enjoyment as a Political Factor*, 2nd ed. (London: Verso, 2002), xlix–l; Slavoj Žižek, *The Puppet and the Dwarf: The Perverse Core of Christianity* (Cambridge: MIT Press, 2003), 66; Johnston, *Žižek's Ontology*, 140–142, 160.
119. Hegel, *Phenomenology of Spirit*, 90.
120. Hegel, *Science of Logic*, 503–504.
121. Rosen, *The Idea of Hegel's Science of Logic*, 275.
122. Žižek, *Absolute Recoil*, 16–17.
123. Žižek, *Less Than Nothing*, 144–145.
124. G. W. F. Hegel, *Natural Law: The Scientific Ways of Treating Natural Law, Its Place in Moral Philosophy, and Its Relation to the Positive Sciences of Law*, trans. T. M. Knox (Philadelphia: University of Pennsylvania Press, 1975), 71, 111–112; Hegel, *The Jena System, 1804-5*, 35–36; Johnston, *Adventures in Transcendental Materialism*, 23–49.
125. G. W. F. Hegel, "Fragment of a System," trans. Richard Kroner, in *Miscellaneous Writings of G. W. F. Hegel*, 154; Hegel, *The Difference Between Fichte's and Schelling's System of Philosophy*, 156; F. W. J. Schelling, *Bruno, or On the Natural and the Divine Principle of Things*, trans. Michael G. Vater (Albany: State University of New York Press, 1984), 136, 143.
126. Žižek, *Less Than Nothing*, 906–909; Johnston, *Adventures in Transcendental Materialism*, 13–22.
127. Žižek, *Less Than Nothing*, 906.
128. Johann Gottfried Herder, "Gott," in *Schriften: Eine Auswahl aus dem Gesamtwerk*, ed. Walter Flemmer (Munich: Wilhelm Goldmann, 1960), 209–210; Johann Gottfried von Herder, "On the Cognition and Sensation of the Human Soul," in *Philosophical Writings*, ed. and trans. Michael N. Forster (Cambridge: Cambridge University Press, 2002), 216–217; Harris, *Hegel's Development*, 1:295; Beiser, *The Fate of Reason*, 159–161.
129. Salomon Maimon, *Essay on Transcendental Philosophy*, trans. Nick Midgley, Henry Somers-Hall, Alistair Welchman, and Merten Reglitz (London: Continuum, 2010), 37–38, 42–43; G. E. Schulze, "Aenesidemus," trans. George di Giovanni, in *Between Kant and Hegel: Texts in the Development of Post-Kantian Idealism*, ed. George di Giovanni and H. S. Harris (Indianapolis: Hackett, 2000), 104–135; Beiser, *German Idealism*, 240–259.
130. Johnston, *Žižek's Ontology*, 269–287; Johnston, *Adventures in Transcendental Materialism*, 13–22.
131. Žižek, *Less Than Nothing*, 905.
132. Ilya Prigogine and Isabelle Stengers, *La nouvelle alliance: Métamorphose de la science* (Paris: Gallimard, 1979), 278.

133. Terrence W. Deacon, *Incomplete Nature: How Mind Emerged from Matter* (New York: Norton, 2012), 143; Adrian Johnston, "Lacking Causes: Privative Causality from Locke and Kant to Lacan and Deacon," *Speculations: A Journal of Speculative Realism* 6 (December 2015): 19–60; Johnston, *Prolegomena to Any Future Materialism*, vol. 2.
134. Žižek, *Absolute Recoil*, 28.
135. Žižek, *Less Than Nothing*, 137–189.
136. Ibid., 104–105; Bourgeois, *Hegel à Francfort ou Judaïsme-Christianisme-Hegelianisme* (Paris: Vrin, 2000), 16.
137. David J. Chalmers, *The Conscious Mind: In Search of a Fundamental Theory* (Oxford: Oxford University Press, 1997), xii–xiii.

2. Where to Start?

1. Slavoj Žižek, *The Indivisible Remainder: An Essay on Schelling and Related Matters* (London: Verso, 1996), 13.
2. Gilles Marmasse, *Penser le réel: Hegel, la nature et l'esprit* (Paris: Kimé, 2008), 324–325.
3. Slavoj Žižek, *Less Than Nothing: Hegel and the Shadow of Dialectical Materialism* (London: Verso, 2012), 228–229.
4. Ibid., 229.
5. Robert M. Wallace, *Hegel's Philosophy of Reality, Freedom, and God* (Cambridge: Cambridge University Press, 2005), 5; Stanley Rosen, *The Idea of Hegel's Science of Logic* (Chicago: University of Chicago Press, 2014), 48, 85.
6. Rosen, *The Idea of Hegel's Science of Logic*, 98, 103.
7. Martin Heidegger, "What Is Metaphysics?," trans. David Farrell Krell, in *Basic Writings*, ed. David Farrell Krell (New York: HarperCollins, 1993), 89–110.
8. G. W. F. Hegel, *Science of Logic*, trans. A. V. Miller (London: George Allen and Unwin, 1969), 31, 83–84, 88; G. W. F. Hegel, "Preface to the Second Edition (1827)," in *The Encyclopedia Logic: Part I of the Encyclopedia of the Philosophical Sciences with the Zusätze*, trans. T. F. Geraets, W. A. Suchting, and H. S. Harris (Indianapolis: Hackett, 1991), 10; G. W. F. Hegel, *The Encyclopedia Logic*, §13–14 (37–39), §86 (138); G. W. F. Hegel, *Lectures on Logic: Berlin, 1831*, trans. Clark Butler (Bloomington: Indiana University Press, 2008), §87 (88–89); G. W. F. Hegel, *Lectures on the History of Philosophy*, vol. 1, trans. E. S. Haldane (New York: Humanities, 1955), 1–2, 4–5, 18, 29–30, 34–39, 45.
9. Hegel, *Science of Logic*, 73–75; Hegel, *The Encyclopedia Logic*, §51 (99), §85–88 (136–145); Hegel, *Lectures on Logic*, §51 (52), §87 (90–91); Karl Rosenkranz, *G. W. F. Hegels Leben* (Darmstadt: Wissenschaftliche Buchgesellschaft, 1971), xxii.
10. Stephen Houlgate, *The Opening of Hegel's Logic: From Being to Infinity* (West Lafayette, IN: Purdue University Press, 2006), 263, 266–267; Stephen Houlgate, *An Introduction to Hegel: Freedom, Truth and History*, 2nd ed. (Oxford: Blackwell, 2005), 32, 40, 43–46.
11. Dieter Henrich, "Hegels Logik der Reflexion," in *Hegel im Kontext: Mit einem Nachwort zur Neuauflage* (Frankfurt: Suhrkamp, 2010), 104–105, 114–117, 121–128, 139–141, 143–150, 152–155; Dieter Henrich, *Between Kant and Hegel: Lectures on German Idealism*, ed. David S. Pacini (Cambridge: Harvard University Press, 2003), 320–321.

2. WHERE TO START?

12. Robert B. Pippin, *Hegel's Idealism: The Satisfactions of Self-Consciousness* (Cambridge: Cambridge University Press, 1989), 6, 9, 17, 33–35, 76, 79–80, 83–85, 91, 96–98, 104, 108, 111–112, 114–115, 120–121, 124–125, 132, 139–142, 152–154, 167–170, 176, 182–183, 224–225, 241–242, 284, 304; Robert B. Pippin, "Hegel and Category Theory," *Review of Metaphysics* 43, no. 4 (June 1990): 843–844.

13. G. W. F. Hegel, "Logic [for the Lower Class]," in *The Philosophical Propaedeutic*, ed. Michael George and Andrew Vincent, trans. A. V. Miller (Oxford: Blackwell, 1986), §2 (65); G. W. F. Hegel, "Logic [for the Middle Class]," in *The Philosophical Propaedeutic*, §1 (74); Hegel, *Science of Logic*, 43–44; Hegel, *The Encyclopedia Logic*, §17 (41), §19 (45–46); Hegel, *Lectures on Logic*, §19 (1).

14. G. W. F. Hegel, "Aphorisms from the Wastebook," trans. Susanne Klein, David L. Roochnik, and George Elliot Tucker, in *Miscellaneous Writings of G. W. F. Hegel*, ed. Jon Stewart (Evanston, IL: Northwestern University Press, 2002), 249; G. W. F. Hegel, "The Science of the Concept [for the Higher Class]," in *The Philosophical Propaedeutic*, §86 (122); Hegel, *Science of Logic*, 71–72, 838–842; G. W. F. Hegel, *Philosophy of Mind: Part Three of the Encyclopedia of the Philosophical Sciences with the Zusätze*, trans. William Wallace and A. V. Miller (Oxford: Oxford University Press, 1971), §574 (313); Hegel, *Lectures on Logic*, §§235–236 (227).

15. Karl Ameriks, "Recent Work on Hegel: The Rehabilitation of an Epistemologist?," *Philosophy and Phenomenological Research* 52 (1992): 177–202; Ameriks, "Hegel and Idealism," *Monist* 74, no. 3 (July 1991): 386–402.

16. Klaus Hartmann, "Hegel: A Non-Metaphysical View," in *Hegel: A Collection of Critical Essays*, ed. Alasdair MacIntyre (New York: Anchor, 1972), 101–124; Klaus Hartmann, "Die ontologische Option," in *Die ontologische Option: Studien zu Hegels Propädeutik, Schellings Hegel-Kritik und Hegels Phänomenologie des Geistes*, ed. Klaus Hartmann (Berlin: de Gruyter, 1976), 1–30; Charles Taylor, *Hegel* (Cambridge: Cambridge University Press, 1975), 27, 39–40, 44–45, 537–571.

17. Žižek, *Less Than Nothing*, 285–286; Dieter Henrich, "Kant und Hegel: Versuch der Vereinigung ihrer Grundgedanken," in *Selbstverhältnisse: Gedanken und Auslegungen zu den Grundlagen der klassischen deutschen Philosophie* (Stuttgart: Reclam, 1982), 189.

18. Frederick C. Beiser, "Introduction: Hegel and the Problem of Metaphysics," in *The Cambridge Companion to Hegel*, ed. Frederick C. Beiser (Cambridge: Cambridge University Press, 1993), 1–24; Frederick C. Beiser, "Hegel, A Non-Metaphysician?: A Polemic," *Bulletin of the Hegel Society of Great Britain* 32 (1995): 1–13; Frederick C. Beiser, *German Idealism: The Struggle Against Subjectivism, 1781-1801* (Cambridge: Harvard University Press, 2002), 558–560; Frederick Beiser, *Hegel* (New York: Routledge, 2005), 55–57; Frederick C. Beiser, "Introduction: The Puzzling Hegel Renaissance," in *The Cambridge Companion to Hegel and Nineteenth-Century Philosophy*, ed. Frederick C. Beiser (Cambridge: Cambridge University Press, 2008), 1–14; Brady Bowman, *Hegel and the Metaphysics of Absolute Negativity* (Cambridge: Cambridge University Press, 2013), 5–7, 14–15, 18, 23–24, 36, 38, 97–98, 102–104, 109, 125, 133–135, 142–143, 145, 148–150, 153, 156, 181–182, 215–216, 219, 222–223, 227, 229–230, 238, 241, 247–248, 255–258; Markus Gabriel, *Transcendental Ontology: Essays in German Idealism* (London: Continuum, 2011), viii–ix, xii, xix–xxii, 1, 3, 54, 60; Rolf-Peter Horstmann, *Die Grenzen der Vernunft: Eine Untersuchung zu Zielen und Motiven des Deutschen Idealismus* (Frankfurt:

2. WHERE TO START?

Klostermann, 2004), 133–134, 138–141; Houlgate, *The Opening of Hegel's Logic*, 137–143; Stephen Houlgate, *Hegel's Phenomenology of Spirit* (London: Bloomsbury, 2013), 193–194; James Kreines, "Hegel's Metaphysics: Changing the Debate," *Philosophy Compass* 1, no. 5 (2006): 466–480; James Kreines, "Metaphysics Without Pre-Critical Monism: Hegel on Lower-Level Natural Kinds and the Structure of Reality," *Bulletin of the Hegel Society of Great Britain* 57/58 (2008): 48–70; Sally Sedgwick, *Hegel's Critique of Kant: From Dichotomy to Identity* (Oxford: Oxford University Press, 2012), 9–11, 62, 96, 125–126; Robert Stern, "Introduction: How Is Hegelian Metaphysics Possible?," in *Hegelian Metaphysics* (Oxford: Oxford University Press, 2009), 1–41; Robert Stern, "Hegel's Idealism," in *Hegelian Metaphysics*, 45–76; Kenneth R. Westphal, "Hegel, Idealism, and Robert Pippin," *International Philosophical Quarterly* 33 (1993): 263–272; Adrian Johnston, "The Voiding of Weak Nature: The Transcendental Materialist Kernels of Hegel's *Naturphilosophie*," *Graduate Faculty Philosophy Journal* 33, no. 1 (2012): 103–157; Adrian Johnston, *Adventures in Transcendental Materialism: Dialogues with Contemporary Thinkers* (Edinburgh: Edinburgh University Press, 2014), 13–49; Adrian Johnston, *Prolegomena to Any Future Materialism*, vol. 2, *A Weak Nature Alone* (Evanston, IL: Northwestern University Press, 2018).

19. Terry Pinkard, "The Categorial Satisfaction of Self-Reflexive Reason," *Bulletin of the Hegel Society of Great Britain* 19 (1989): 5–17; Terry Pinkard, "How Kantian Was Hegel?," *Review of Metaphysics* 43, no. 4 (June 1990): 831–838; Robert B. Pippin, "Hegel's Idealism: Prospects," *Bulletin of the Hegel Society of Great Britain* 19 (1989): 28–41; Pippin, "Hegel and Category Theory," 839–848; Robert B. Pippin, "Hegel's Original Insight," *International Philosophical Quarterly* 33 (1993): 285–295; Sally Sedgwick, "Pippin on Hegel's Critique of Kant," *International Philosophical Quarterly* 33 (1993): 273–283.

20. Beiser, *German Idealism*, 508–511.

21. Žižek, *Less Than Nothing*, 237.

22. Slavoj Žižek, *Absolute Recoil: Towards a New Foundation of Dialectical Materialism* (London: Verso, 2014), 17, 27–29.

23. Žižek, *Less Than Nothing*, 238.

24. Ibid., 239.

25. Adrian Johnston, *Žižek's Ontology: A Transcendental Materialist Theory of Subjectivity* (Evanston, IL: Northwestern University Press, 2008), 155, 162–163, 179, 209, 236, 241, 245–246, 263–265, 275; Johnston, *Adventures in Transcendental Materialism*, 25–26, 55–56, 115.

26. Rosen, *The Idea of Hegel's Science of Logic*, 8–9.

27. Žižek, *Less Than Nothing*, 393–394.

28. Žižek, *Absolute Recoil*, 29.

29. Pippin, *Hegel's Idealism*, 17–18, 35, 232; Pippin, "Hegel's Idealism," 30–31; Pippin, "Hegel and Category Theory," 843; Pippin, "Hegel's Original Insight," 288; Robert B. Pippin, "Avoiding German Idealism: Kant, Hegel, and the Reflective Judgment Problem," in *Idealism as Modernism: Hegelian Variations* (Cambridge: Cambridge University Press, 1997), 131; Robert B. Pippin, "The Kantian Aftermath: Reaction and Revolution in Modern German Philosophy," in *The Persistence of Subjectivity: On the Kantian Aftermath* (Cambridge: Cambridge University Press, 2005), 47–52; Robert B. Pippin, *Hegel on Self-Consciousness: Desire and Death in the Phenomenology of*

2. WHERE TO START?

Spirit (Princeton: Princeton University Press, 2011), 10; Ameriks, "Hegel and Idealism," 400.

30. Robert B. Brandom, *Tales of the Mighty Dead: Historical Essays in the Metaphysics of Intentionality* (Cambridge: Harvard University Press, 2002), 53–54, 216–217.

31. G. W. F. Hegel, *Wissenschaft der Logik II: Erster Teil, Die objektive Logik, Zweites Buch; Zweiter Teil, Die subjektive Logik*, in *Werke in zwanzig Bänden*, vol. 6, ed. Eva Moldenhauer and Karl Markus Michel (Frankfurt: Suhrkamp, 1969), 254–255; Hegel, *Science of Logic*, 584–585.

32. Hegel, *Science of Logic*, 585.

33. Immanuel Kant, *Critique of Pure Reason*, trans. Paul Guyer and Allen Wood (Cambridge: Cambridge University Press, 1998), B137 (249).

34. G. W. F. Hegel and F. W. J. Schelling, "Introduction for the *Critical Journal of Philosophy*: On the Essence of Philosophical Criticism Generally, and Its Relationship to the Present State of Philosophy in Particular," trans. H. S. Harris, in *Miscellaneous Writings of G. W. F. Hegel*, 212; G. W. F. Hegel, *Phenomenology of Spirit*, trans. A. V. Miller (Oxford: Oxford University Press, 1977), 142–145; Hegel, *Science of Logic*, 613–614; Hegel, *The Encyclopedia Logic*, §42 (84), §60 (107–108); G. W. F. Hegel, *Lectures on the History of Philosophy*, vol. 3, trans. E. S. Haldane and Frances H. Simson (New York: Humanities, 1955), 483; Hegel, *Lectures on Logic*, §42 (35).

35. H. S. Harris, "The Problem of Kant," *Bulletin of the Hegel Society of Great Britain* 19 (1989): 26; Sedgwick, "Pippin on Hegel's Critique of Kant," 273, 275; Stern, "Hegel's Idealism," 48.

36. Hegel, *Phenomenology of Spirit*, 88–91, 100–101; Hegel, *Science of Logic*, 121, 134–135, 490, 507; Hegel, *The Encyclopedia Logic*, §44 (87), §60 (105); Hegel, *Lectures on Logic*, §44 (37).

37. Westphal, "Hegel, Idealism, and Robert Pippin," 263–272; Thomas E. Wartenberg, "Hegel's Idealism: The Logic of Conceptuality," in *The Cambridge Companion to Hegel*, 104–107, 109–110, 117, 120, 122, 125–126, 128.

38. Hegel, *Phenomenology of Spirit*, 139–146; Hegel, *Science of Logic*, 45–47, 51, 61–64, 489; Hegel, *The Encyclopedia Logic*, §§41–42 (81–84), §§45 (88–89); Hegel, *Lectures on Logic*, §43–44 (36–37).

39. Hegel, *Science of Logic*, 45–47.

40. Herbert Marcuse, *Hegel's Ontology and the Theory of Historicity*, trans. Seyla Benhabib (Cambridge: MIT Press, 1987), 146–147.

41. Ibid., 145.

42. G. W. F. Hegel, *Wissenschaft der Logik I: Erster Teil, Die objektive Logik, Erstes Buch*, in *Werke in zwanzig Bänden*, vol. 5, ed. Eva Moldenhauer and Karl Markus Michel (Frankfurt: Suhrkamp, 1969), 39; Hegel, *Science of Logic*, 46.

43. Hegel, *Science of Logic*, 154–155; Marcuse, *Hegel's Ontology and the Theory of Historicity*, 60–61; Nathan Rotenstreich, *From Substance to Subject: Studies in Hegel* (The Hague: Martinus Nijhoff, 1974), 76; H. S. Harris, *Hegel's Development*, vol. 2, *Night Thoughts (Jena 1801–1806)* (Oxford: Oxford University Press, 1983), 566; H. S. Harris, *Hegel's Ladder*, vol. 1, *The Pilgrimage of Reason* (Indianapolis: Hackett, 1997), 81, 490; Robert Stern, *Hegel, Kant, and the Structure of the Object* (London: Routledge, 1990), 107; Stern, "Hegel's Idealism," 75; William Maker, "The Very Idea of the Idea of Nature, or Why Hegel Is Not an Idealist," in *Hegel and the Philosophy of Nature*, ed. Stephen

2. WHERE TO START?

Houlgate (Albany: State University of New York Press, 1998), 3–5, 14–15; Bernard Bourgeois, *Hegel à Francfort ou Judaïsme-Christianisme-Hegelianisme* (Paris: Vrin, 2000), 122; Beiser, *German Idealism*, 578; Paul Franks, *All or Nothing: Systematicity, Transcendental Arguments, and Skepticism in German Idealism* (Cambridge: Harvard University Press, 2005), 386; Wallace, *Hegel's Philosophy of Reality, Freedom, and God*, 53–54, 114–115; Alison Stone, *Petrified Intelligence: Nature in Hegel's Philosophy* (Albany: State University of New York Press, 2005), 22; Houlgate, *The Opening of Hegel's Logic*, 429; Michael Quante, *Die Wirklichkeit des Geistes: Studien zu Hegel* (Frankfurt: Suhrkamp, 2011), 23; Sedgwick, *Hegel's Critique of Kant*, 125; Bowman, *Hegel and the Metaphysics of Absolute Negativity*, 14–15, 18, 125, 215–216, 219; Italo Testa, "Hegel's Naturalism or Soul and Body in the Encyclopedia," in *Essays on Hegel's Philosophy of Subjective Spirit*, ed. David S. Stern (Albany: State University of New York Press, 2013), 21, 33; Rosen, *The Idea of Hegel's Science of Logic*, 144, 303; Johnston, *Adventures in Transcendental Materialism*, 13–49; Johnston, *Prolegomena to Any Future Materialism*, vol. 2.

44. G. W. F. Hegel, *The Difference Between Fichte's and Schelling's System of Philosophy*, trans. H. S. Harris and Walter Cerf (Albany: State University of New York Press, 1977), 177; Harris, *Hegel's Ladder*, 1:87.

45. G. W. F. Hegel, *Natural Law: The Scientific Ways of Treating Natural Law, Its Place in Moral Philosophy, and Its Relation to the Positive Sciences of Law*, trans. T. M. Knox (Philadelphia: University of Pennsylvania Press, 1975), 57; Marcuse, *Hegel's Ontology and the Theory of Historicity*, 23–24, 29.

46. Kant, *Critique of Pure Reason*, B136–139 (248–250); Henry Allison, *Kant's Transcendental Idealism: An Interpretation and Defense* (New Haven: Yale University Press, 1983), 144–145.

47. Kant, *Critique of Pure Reason*, A111 (234).

48. Marcuse, *Hegel's Ontology and the Theory of Historicity*, 113, 118–119, 165, 167.

49. Robert B. Pippin, "Hösle, System and Subject," *Bulletin of the Hegel Society of Great Britain* 17 (Spring/Summer 1988): 17; Pippin, *Hegel's Idealism*, 38, 91–94, 178, 256; Pippin, "Hegel's Idealism," 32; Pippin, "Hegel and Category Theory," 843–844, 847–848; Ameriks, "Recent Work on Hegel," 199–200; Harris, "The Problem of Kant," 27.

50. G. W. F. Hegel, *Phänomenologie des Geistes*, in *Werke in zwanzig Bänden*, vol. 3, ed. Eva Moldenhauer and Karl Markus Michel (Frankfurt: Suhrkamp, 1970), 178–181; Hegel, *Phenomenology of Spirit*, 139–142.

51. Hegel, *Phänomenologie des Geistes*, 181–182; Hegel, *Phenomenology of Spirit*, 142.

52. Marcuse, *Hegel's Ontology and the Theory of Historicity*, 36, 58, 165; Marmasse, *Penser le réel*, 408; Rosen, *The Idea of Hegel's Science of Logic*, 72, 242, 263.

53. Hegel, *Phenomenology of Spirit*, 144.

54. Hegel, *Science of Logic*, 155.

55. Hegel, *The Difference Between Fichte's and Schelling's System of Philosophy*, 115, 127, 165–167.

56. G. W. F. Hegel, "How the Ordinary Human Understanding Takes Philosophy (as Displayed in the Works of Mr. Krug)," trans. H. S. Harris, in *Miscellaneous Writings of G. W. F. Hegel*, 229.

57. G. W. F. Hegel, *First Philosophy of Spirit (being Part III of the "System of Speculative Philosophy" of 1803/4)*, trans. H. S. Harris, in *System of Ethical Life (1802/3) and First Philosophy of Spirit (Part III of the System of Speculative Philosophy 1803/4)*, ed. and

2. WHERE TO START?

trans. H. S. Harris and T. M. Knox (Albany: State University of New York Press, 1979), 223–226.

58. Hegel, *The Encyclopedia Logic*, §95–96 (152–153).

59. Pippin, "Hegel's Original Insight," 289.

60. Hegel, *Phenomenology of Spirit*, 142–145.

61. Hegel, *Phänomenologie des Geistes*, 184–185; Hegel, *Phenomenology of Spirit*, 144–145.

62. Kant, *Critique of Pure Reason*, B145 (253–254).

63. Galileo Galilei, "The Assayer," in *Discoveries and Opinions of Galileo*, trans. Stillman Drake (New York: Anchor, 1957), 274–278.

64. Kant, *Critique of Pure Reason*, Bii (91).

65. Ibid., Bxii (108).

66. Francis Bacon, "The Great Renewal," in *The New Organon*, ed. Lisa Jardine and Michael Silverthorne (Cambridge: Cambridge University Press, 2000), 21, 24; Francis Bacon, *The New Organon*, bk. 1, aphorisms 1–14 (33–35).

67. Kant, *Critique of Pure Reason*, Bxii–xiv (108–109).

68. Hegel, *Phenomenology of Spirit*, 208–210.

69. Jean Hyppolite, *Genesis and Structure of Hegel's Phenomenology of Spirit*, trans. Samuel Cherniak and John Heckman (Evanston, IL: Northwestern University Press, 1974), 240–241.

70. Hegel, *Phänomenologie des Geistes*, 185–186; Hegel, *Phenomenology of Spirit*, 145–146.

71. Marcuse, *Hegel's Ontology and the Theory of Historicity*, 270–271.

72. Hegel, *Phenomenology of Spirit*, 88, 170–171, 177, 178–179.

73. Hegel, *Science of Logic*, 664, 669, 826–827; Hegel, *The Encyclopedia Logic*, §24 (56–57); Ermanno Bencivenga, *Hegel's Dialectical Logic* (Oxford: Oxford University Press, 2000), 28, 35, 37–38, 56; Klaus Düsing, *Das Problem der Subjektivität in Hegels Logik*, Hegel-Studien, Beiheft 15 (Bonn: Bouvier, 1976), 251, 267; Marcuse, *Hegel's Ontology and the Theory of Historicity*, 125–126, 144–145; Sedgwick, *Hegel's Critique of Kant*, 10–11; Ludwig Siep, "Hegel's Idea of a Conceptual Scheme," *Inquiry* 34 (1991): 71, 75–76; Westphal, "Hegel, Idealism, and Robert Pippin," 268.

74. Hegel, *Phenomenology of Spirit*, 151; G. W. F. Hegel, "Phenomenology [for the Middle Class]," in *The Philosophical Propaedeutic*, §§40–42 (63–64); Hegel, *Lectures on the History of Philosophy*, 3:181–182; Hegel, *Lectures on Logic*, §§24–25 (15–18), §95 (110); Düsing, *Das Problem der Subjektivität in Hegels Logik*, 297; Willem A. DeVries, *Hegel's Theory of Mental Activity: An Introduction to Theoretical Spirit* (Ithaca: Cornell University Press, 1988), 110, 114–115, 175, 177–178, 196–197, 200; Michael Inwood, *A Hegel Dictionary* (Oxford: Blackwell, 1992), 123–128; Harris, *Hegel's Ladder*, 1:452–453, 490; Kreines, "Hegel's Metaphysics," 467; Quante, *Die Wirklichkeit des Geistes*, 31–32, 43–44, 93, 133, 147; Rosen, *The Idea of Hegel's Science of Logic*, 157–158.

75. Johnston, "The Voiding of Weak Nature," 115–118; Johnston, *Prolegomena to Any Future Materialism*, vol. 2.

76. Hegel, *Phenomenology of Spirit*, 56.

77. Ibid., 137–139.

78. Ibid., 141–142.

2. WHERE TO START?

79. Terry Pinkard, *Hegel's Phenomenology: The Sociality of Reason* (Cambridge: Cambridge University Press, 1996), 81.
80. Hegel, *Phenomenology of Spirit*, 131–132, 134–138.
81. Johnston, "The Voiding of Weak Nature," 114–115; Johnston, *Prolegomena to Any Future Materialism*, vol. 2.
82. Bacon, "The Great Renewal," 18; Bacon, *The New Organon*, bk. 1, aphorism 2 (33).
83. Hegel, *Phenomenology of Spirit*, 115–116, 117–118; Marcuse, *Hegel's Ontology and the Theory of Historicity*, 270–271.
84. Hegel, *Phenomenology of Spirit*, 139.
85. Ibid., 139, 147–149, 154; Johnston, "The Voiding of Weak Nature," 119–120.
86. Hegel, *Lectures on the History of Philosophy*, 3:175–177.
87. Bowman, *Hegel and the Metaphysics of Absolute Negativity*, 97–98.
88. Johnston, *Prolegomena to Any Future Materialism*, vol. 2.
89. Johnston, "The Voiding of Weak Nature," 118–121.
90. Houlgate, *The Opening of Hegel's Logic*, 139–143.
91. Rosen, *The Idea of Hegel's Science of Logic*, 487; Žižek, *Disparities*, 116–117, 128, 130, 132–133.
92. Myriam Bienenstock, *Politique du jeune Hegel: Iéna 1801-1806* (Paris: Presses Universitaires de France, 1992), 23.
93. Hegel, *The Encyclopedia Logic*, §42 (84–85).
94. G. W. F. Hegel, *Enzyklopädie der philosophischen Wissenschaften, Erster Teil: Die Wissenschaft der Logik mit den mündlichen Zusätzen*, in *Werke in zwanzig Bänden*, vol. 8, ed. Eva Moldenhauer and Karl Markus Michel (Frankfurt: Suhrkamp, 1970), §42 (118); Hegel, *The Encyclopedia Logic*, §42 (85).
95. Marcuse, *Hegel's Ontology and the Theory of Historicity*, 26, 113, 118–119, 165, 167; Düsing, *Das Problem der Subjektivität in Hegels Logik*, 117–118, 233; Stern, *Hegel, Kant, and the Structure of the Object*, vii, 5, 39, 42, 95–96, 107.
96. G. W. F. Hegel, "Two Fragments on Love," trans. C. Hamlin and H. S. Harris, in *Miscellaneous Writings of G. W. F. Hegel*, 116, 118–120; Georg Lukács, *The Ontology of Social Being*, vol. 1, *Hegel*, trans. David Fernbach (London: Merlin, 1978), 9.
97. Pippin, "Hegel's Original Insight," 290–291.
98. Johnston, *Adventures in Transcendental Materialism*, 13–49.
99. Hegel, *Phenomenology of Spirit*, 10–12.
100. Hegel, *Phänomenologie des Geistes*, 25; Hegel, *Phenomenology of Spirit*, 11–12.
101. Hegel, *Phänomenologie des Geistes*, 24; Hegel, *Phenomenology of Spirit*, 11.
102. Marcuse, *Hegel's Ontology and the Theory of Historicity*, 15, 42, 112, 146; Houlgate, *The Opening of Hegel's Logic*, 154.
103. Düsing, *Das Problem der Subjektivität in Hegels Logik*, 117; Quante, *Die Wirklichkeit des Geistes*, 121.
104. Hegel, *Wissenschaft der Logik*, 2:257; Hegel, *Science of Logic*, 586.
105. Hegel, *Science of Logic*, 755–760; G. W. F. Hegel, *Encyclopedia of the Philosophical Sciences in Outline*, trans. Steven A. Taubeneck, in *Encyclopedia of the Philosophical Sciences in Outline and Critical Writings*, ed. Ernst Behler (New York: Continuum, 1990), §162 (128); Horstmann, *Die Grenzen der Vernunft*, 205–206.

2. WHERE TO START?

106. Testa, "Hegel's Naturalism or Soul and Body in the Encyclopedia," 23–24, 33; Philip T. Grier, "The Relation of Mind to Nature: Two Paradigms," in Stern, *Essays on Hegel's Philosophy of Subjective Spirit*, 226–228, 239–240.

107. G. W. F. Hegel, *The Jena System, 1804-5: Logic and Metaphysics*, ed. John W. Burbidge and George di Giovanni (Kingston: McGill-Queen's University Press, 1986), 185; G. W. F. Hegel, *Philosophy of Nature: Part Two of the Encyclopedia of the Philosophical Sciences*, trans. A. V. Miller (Oxford: Oxford University Press, 1970), §376 (443–445); Hegel, *Philosophy of Mind*, §381 (8, 13–14), §388–389 (29–31), §391 (35–36), §412 (151–152).

108. Pippin, *Hegel's Idealism*, 6, 17, 35; Pippin, "Hegel's Idealism," 28–29.

109. G. W. F. Hegel, *Differenz des Fichteschen und Schellingschen Systems der Philosophie*, in *Werke in zwanzig Bänden*, vol. 2, *Jenaer Schriften, 1801-1807*, ed. Eva Moldenhauer and Karl Markus Michel (Frankfurt: Suhrkamp, 1970), pg. 9–10; Hegel, *The Difference Between Fichte's and Schelling's System of Philosophy*, 79–80.

110. Kant, *Critique of Pure Reason*, A26/B42–A49/B66 (159–171), B66–73 (188–192).

111. Ibid., A493–494/B521–522 (512), A506–507/B534–535 (519).

112. Marcuse, *Hegel's Ontology and the Theory of Historicity*, 17–18, 190, 202.

113. Hegel, *The Difference Between Fichte's and Schelling's System of Philosophy*, 81–83, 117, 133, 135, 155, 157–158, 162; Marcuse, *Hegel's Ontology and the Theory of Historicity*, 17–18.

114. Pippin, *Hegel's Idealism*, 42–44, 83, 98, 168.

115. Hegel, *The Difference Between Fichte's and Schelling's System of Philosophy*, 82–83, 157, 159–162, 165–169, 172–174.

116. Pippin, *Hegel's Idealism*, 64.

117. Marcuse, *Hegel's Ontology and the Theory of Historicity*, 18, 23, 29, 188.

118. G. W. F. Hegel, *Faith and Knowledge*, trans. Walter Cerf and H. S. Harris (Albany: State University of New York Press, 1977), 76–77.

119. Düsing, *Das Problem der Subjektivität in Hegels Logik*, 235, 237, 241–243, 299, 323; Harris, *Hegel's Development*, 2:45.

120. Rosen, *The Idea of Hegel's Science of Logic*, 5.

121. Hegel, *Science of Logic*, 843–844; Hegel, *The Encyclopedia Logic*, §244 (307); Hegel, *Lectures on Logic*, §244 (232–233); Hegel, *Philosophy of Nature*, §§253–254 (28–29), §§257–258 (34–35).

122. Hans Friedrich Fulda, *Das Problem einer Einleitung in Hegels Wissenschaft der Logik* (Frankfurt: Klostermann, 1965), 284; Sedgwick, *Hegel's Critique of Kant*, 156.

123. Slavoj Žižek, *Žižek's Jokes (Did You Hear the One About Hegel and Negation?)*, ed. Audun Mortensen (Cambridge: MIT Press, 2014), 54.

124. Ernst Bloch, "Hegel und der Humor," in *Über Methode und System bei Hegel* (Frankfurt: Suhrkamp, 1970), 136–140.

125. Žižek, *Absolute Recoil*, 154–155.

126. Hans-Georg Gadamer, "The Idea of Hegel's Logic," in *Hegel's Dialectic: Five Hermeneutical Studies*, trans. P. Christopher Smith (New Haven: Yale University Press, 1976), 88–91; Bernard Bourgeois, *La pensée politique de Hegel* (Paris: Presses Universitaires de France, 1969), 105.

127. Hegel, *The Encyclopedia Logic*, §187 (263); Hegel, *Lectures on Logic*, §§188–189 (197–198); Stern, *Hegel, Kant, and the Structure of the Object*, 115–118.

3. CONTINGENCY, PURE CONTINGENCY

128. Harris, *Hegel's Ladder*, 1:30.
129. Düsing, *Das Problem der Subjektivität in Hegels Logik*, 22, 327–328; Žižek, *Absolute Recoil*, 238–239.
130. Marmasse, *Penser le réel*, 367.
131. Harris, *Hegel's Ladder I*, 66, 81; Wallace, *Hegel's Philosophy of Reality, Freedom, and God*, 211; Hegel, *Science of Logic*, 49–50.
132. Harris, *Hegel's Development*, 2:342.
133. Louis Althusser, "The Humanist Controversy," in *The Humanist Controversy and Other Writings*, ed. François Matheron, trans. G. M. Goshgarian (London: Verso, 2003), 240–241; Louis Althusser, *Elements of Self-Criticism*, in *Essays in Self-Criticism*, trans. Grahame Locke (London: New Left Books, 1976), 135; Harris, *Hegel's Ladder*, 1:31.
134. Düsing, *Das Problem der Subjektivität in Hegels Logik*, 36–37.
135. Hegel, *Phenomenology of Spirit*, 3.
136. Ernst Bloch, *Subjekt-Objekt: Erläuterungen zu Hegel* (Frankfurt: Suhrkamp, 1977), 219.
137. Marmasse, *Penser le réel*, 314, 350, 352–354, 356–357, 368, 413; Žižek, *Absolute Recoil*, 227.
138. Hegel, *Phenomenology of Spirit*, 36; Hegel, *Science of Logic*, 54–56, 106–107; Hegel, *The Encyclopedia Logic*, §82 (131–132).
139. G. W. F. Hegel, *Elements of the Philosophy of Right*, ed. Allen W. Wood, trans. H. B. Nisbet (Cambridge: Cambridge University Press, 1991), 20–23.
140. Hegel, *Phenomenology of Spirit*, 6–7; G. W. F. Hegel, *Philosophy of History*, trans. J. Sibree (New York: Dover, 1956), 446–447; Hegel, *Lectures on the History of Philosophy*, 3:546–548, 551–552.
141. Rosen, *The Idea of Hegel's Science of Logic*, 393.

3. Contingency, Pure Contingency—Without Any Further Determination

1. Adrian Johnston, *Žižek's Ontology: A Transcendental Materialist Theory of Subjectivity* (Evanston, IL: Northwestern University Press, 2008), 123–268.
2. Friedrich Engels, *Ludwig Feuerbach and the Outcome of Classical German Philosophy*, trans. C. P. Dutt (New York: International, 1941), 11–13, 24; Georgi V. Plekhanov, "For the Sixtieth Anniversary of Hegel's Death," trans. R. Dixon, in *Selected Philosophical Works in Five Volumes*, vol. 1, ed. M. T. Ivochuk, A. N. Maslin, P. N. Fedoseyev, V. A. Fomina, B. A. Chagin, E. S. Kots, I. S. Belensky, S. M. Firsova, and B. L. Yakobson (Moscow: Foreign Languages, 1974), 468, 472, 477; V. I. Lenin, "Conspectus of Hegel's Book *The Science of Logic*," in *Collected Works*, vol. 38, *Philosophical Notebooks*, trans. Clemence Dutt (Moscow: Progress, 1976), 189–191; Nikolai Bukharin, *Philosophical Arabesques*, trans. Renfrey Clarke (New York: Monthly Review Press, 2005), 57, 114–116, 325; Georg Lukács, *The Young Hegel: Studies in the Relations Between Dialectics and Economics*, trans. Rodney Livingstone (Cambridge: MIT Press, 1976), xxvi, 275–276, 324–325, 345–348, 350, 352, 398–399, 474–476, 510–511.

3. CONTINGENCY, PURE CONTINGENCY

3. Slavoj Žižek, *Absolute Recoil: Towards a New Foundation of Dialectical Materialism* (London: Verso, 2014), 35–36.

4. Martin Heidegger, "Elucidation of the 'Introduction' to Hegel's 'Phenomenology of Spirit,'" in *Hegel*, trans. Joseph Arel and Niels Feuerhahn (Bloomington: Indiana University Press, 2015), 110.

5. G. W. Leibniz, "On Contingency," in *Philosophical Essays*, trans. Roger Ariew and Daniel Garber (Indianapolis: Hackett, 1989), 28–30; G. W. Leibniz, "Primary Truths," in *Philosophical Essays*, 30–34; G. W. Leibniz, "Discourse on Metaphysics," in *Philosophical Essays*, 35–68; G. W. Leibniz, "Principles of Nature and Grace, Based on Reason," in *Philosophical Essays*, 206–213; G. W. Leibniz, "The Principles of Philosophy, or, the Monadology," in *Philosophical Essays*, 213–225.

6. G. W. F. Hegel, "How the Ordinary Human Understanding Takes Philosophy (as Displayed in the Works of Mr. Krug)," trans. H. S. Harris, in *Miscellaneous Writings of G. W. F. Hegel*, ed. Jon Stewart (Evanston, IL: Northwestern University Press, 2002), 229, 231, 233; G. W. F. Hegel, "On the Relationship of Skepticism to Philosophy, Exposition of its Different Modifications and Comparison of the Latest Form with the Ancient One," trans. H. S. Harris, in *Between Kant and Hegel: Texts in the Development of Post-Kantian Idealism*, ed. and trans. George Di Giovanni and H. S. Harris (Indianapolis: Hackett, 2000), 330; G. W. F. Hegel, *Phenomenology of Spirit*, trans. A. V. Miller (Oxford: Oxford University Press, 1977), 27–28; G. W. F. Hegel, *Philosophy of Nature: Part Two of the Encyclopedia of the Philosophical Sciences*, trans. A. V. Miller (Oxford: Oxford University Press, 1970), §250 (23); G. W. F. Hegel, *Lectures on the History of Philosophy*, vol. 3, trans. E. S. Haldane and Frances H. Simson (New York: Humanities, 1955), 511–512; Jean-Marie Lardic, "Hegel et la contingence," in *Comment le sens commun comprend la philosophie, suivi de La contingence chez Hegel*, by G. W. F. Hegel and Jean-Marie Lardic (Paris: Actes Sud, 1989), 97; Bernard Mabille, *Hegel: L'épreuve de la contingence* (Paris: Aubier, 1999), 24, 29.

7. F. W. J. Schelling, *On the History of Modern Philosophy*, trans. Andrew Bowie (Cambridge: Cambridge University Press, 1994), 134–163; F. W. J. Schelling, *The Grounding of Positive Philosophy*, trans. Bruce Matthews (Albany: State University of New York Press, 2007), 118, 128–135, 137, 139, 145–147, 149–151, 155, 159–161, 202–205, 211; Friedrich Engels, *Anti-Schelling*, 1841, http://marxists.org/archive/marx/works/1841/anti-schelling; Jürgen Habermas, "Dialectical Idealism in Transition to Materialism: Schelling's Idea of a Contraction of God and Its Consequences for the Philosophy of History," trans. Nick Midgley and Judith Norman, in *The New Schelling*, ed. Judith Norman and Alistair Welchman (London: Continuum, 2004), 43–89; Manfred Frank, *Der unendliche Mangel an Sein: Schellings Hegelkritik und die Anfänge der Marxschen Dialektik* (Munich: Wilhelm Fink, 1992), 11–13, 33, 46, 97, 99–102, 138, 141–144, 155–156, 172, 191, 211, 219, 227–230, 234–235, 265–267, 279, 286, 290, 293, 331–332, 372–373, 389–391; Stephen Houlgate, "Schelling's Critique of Hegel's *Science of Logic*," *Review of Metaphysics* 53, no. 1 (September 1999): 99–128; Stephen Houlgate, *The Opening of Hegel's Logic: From Being to Infinity* (West Lafayette, IN: Purdue University Press, 2006), 292–296.

8. Klaus Düsing, *Das Problem der Subjektivität in Hegels Logik*, Hegel-Studien, Beiheft 15 (Bonn: Bouvier, 1976), 341–342.

9. Johnston, *Žižek's Ontology*, 126–128, 141, 221.

3. CONTINGENCY, PURE CONTINGENCY

10. Slavoj Žižek, *Less Than Nothing: Hegel and the Shadow of Dialectical Materialism* (London: Verso, 2012), 98, 467–469, 637–638.
11. Louis Althusser, "Man, That Night," in *The Spectre of Hegel: Early Writings*, trans. G. M. Goshgarian (London: Verso, 1997), 170; Ermanno Bencivenga, *Hegel's Dialectical Logic* (Oxford: Oxford University Press, 2000), 72; John W. Burbidge, *Hegel's Systematic Contingency* (Basingstoke: Palgrave Macmillan, 2007), 16–17, 41–43, 47; André Doz, *La logique de Hegel et les problèmes traditionnels de l'ontologie* (Paris: Vrin, 1987), 151; Dieter Henrich, "Hegels Theorie über den Zufall," in *Hegel im Kontext: Mit einem Nachwort zur Neuauflage* (Frankfurt: Suhrkamp, 2010), 160, 165; Jean Hyppolite, *Logic and Existence*, trans. Leonard Lawlor and Amit Sen (Albany: State University of New York Press, 1997), 174–175; Jean-Marie Lardic, "Présentation," in Hegel and Lardic, *Comment le sens commun comprend la philosophie, suivi de La contingence chez Hegel*, 28; Lardic, "Hegel et la contingence," 63; Gérard Lebrun, *L'envers de la dialectique: Hegel à la lumière de Nietzsche* (Paris: Seuil, 2004), 25–72; Lukács, *The Young Hegel*, 394; Mabille, *Hegel*, 95–96; Catherine Malabou, *The Future of Hegel: Plasticity, Temporality and Dialectic*, trans. Lisabeth During (New York: Routledge, 2005), 73–74, 160–164, 183; Herbert Marcuse, *Hegel's Ontology and the Theory of Historicity*, trans. Seyla Benhabib (Cambridge: MIT Press, 1987), 97, 102; Gilles Marmasse, *Penser le réel: Hegel, la nature et l'esprit* (Paris: Kimé, 2008), 139, 142, 146–147, 347, 410–411, 416–418; Terry Pinkard, *Hegel's Naturalism: Mind, Nature, and the Final Ends of Life* (Oxford: Oxford University Press, 2012), 119–120; Emmanuel Renault, *Hegel: La naturalisation de la dialectique* (Paris: Vrin, 2001), 60; Stanley Rosen, *The Idea of Hegel's Science of Logic* (Chicago: University of Chicago Press, 2014), 302.
12. Adrian Johnston, "The Voiding of Weak Nature: The Transcendental Materialist Kernels of Hegel's *Naturphilosophie*," *Graduate Faculty Philosophy Journal* 33, no. 1 (2012): 103–157.
13. Žižek, *Less Than Nothing*, 791.
14. Žižek, *Absolute Recoil*, 26.
15. Žižek, *Less Than Nothing*, 207, 449–450, 452–453, 525, 857–858.
16. Žižek, *Absolute Recoil*, 12.
17. Adrian Johnston, "From Scientific Socialism to Socialist Science: *Naturdialektik* Then and Now," in *The Idea of Communism*, vol. 2, *The New York Conference*, ed. Slavoj Žižek (London: Verso, 2013), 103–136; Adrian Johnston, *Prolegomena to Any Future Materialism*, vol. 2, *A Weak Nature Alone* (Evanston, IL: Northwestern University Press, 2018).
18. Joseph Dietzgen, *Excursions of a Socialist Into the Domain of Epistemology*, 1887, trans. Max Beer and Theodor Rothstein, http://marxists.org/archive/dietzgen/1887/epistemology.htm; Karl Kautsky, *Frederick Engels: His Life, His Work, and His Writings*, trans. May Wood Simmons, 1887/1888, http://marxists.org/archive/kautsky/1887/xx/engels.htm.
19. Žižek, *Less Than Nothing*, 575–576.
20. Louis Althusser, "The Underground Current of the Materialism of the Encounter," in *Philosophy of the Encounter: Later Writings, 1978–1987*, ed. François Matheron and Oliver Corpet, trans. G. M. Goshgarian (London: Verso, 2006), 188–190, 194–196; Louis Althusser, "Philosophy and Marxism: Interviews with Fernanda Navarro, 1984–87," in *Philosophy of the Encounter*, 261–262, 273.

3. CONTINGENCY, PURE CONTINGENCY

21. Althusser, "Philosophy and Marxism," 257, 275; Adrian Johnston, "Marx's Bones: Breaking with Althusser," in *The Concept in Crisis: Reading Capital Now*, ed. Nick Nesbitt (Durham: Duke University Press, 2017), 189–215; Johnston, *Prolegomena to Any Future Materialism*, vol. 2.

22. Louis Althusser, "The Humanist Controversy," in *The Humanist Controversy and Other Writings*, ed. François Matheron, trans. G. M. Goshgarian (London: Verso, 2003), 240–241; Louis Althusser, *Elements of Self-Criticism*, in *Essays in Self-Criticism*, trans. Grahame Locke (London: New Left Books, 1976), 135; Louis Althusser, *Être marxiste en philosophie*, ed. G. M. Goshgarian (Paris: Presses Universitaires de France, 2015), 71–76.

23. Althusser, "The Underground Current of the Materialism of the Encounter," 169–171, 188–190; Louis Althusser, "Correspondence About 'Philosophy and Marxism': Letter to Fernanda Navarro, 10 July 1984," in *Philosophy of the Encounter*, 217–218; Althusser, "Philosophy and Marxism," 272–273, 277–278; Louis Althusser, "Portrait of the Materialist Philosopher," in *Philosophy of the Encounter*, 290–291.

24. Louis Althusser, "On Feuerbach," in *The Humanist Controversy and Other Writings*, 88–89; Althusser, "The Humanist Controversy," 234, 241–242; Louis Althusser, *Reply to John Lewis*, in *Essays in Self-Criticism*, 54, 56; Louis Althusser, "Réponse à une critique," in *Écrits philosophiques et politiques, Tome II*, ed. François Matheron (Paris: Stock/IMEC, 1995), 378.

25. G. W. F. Hegel, "Fragments of Historical Studies," in *Miscellaneous Writings of G. W. F. Hegel*, 99; G. W. F. Hegel, *The System of Ethical Life (1802/3)*, trans. T. M. Knox and H. S. Harris, in *The System of Ethical Life (1802/3) and First Philosophy of Spirit (Part III of the System of Speculative Philosophy 1803/4)*, ed. H. S. Harris and T. M. Knox (Albany: State University of New York Press, 1979), 170–171; G. W. F. Hegel, *Elements of the Philosophy of Right*, ed. Allen W. Wood, trans. H. B. Nisbet (Cambridge: Cambridge University Press, 1991), §§244–246 (266–268), §248 (269); G. W. F. Hegel, "On the English Reform Bill," in *Political Writings*, ed. Laurence Dickey and H. B. Nisbet, trans. H. B. Nisbet (Cambridge: Cambridge University Press, 1999), 255–256; Althusser, "Philosophy and Marxism," 276.

26. Plekhanov, "For the Sixtieth Anniversary of Hegel's Death," 471–472.

27. Žižek, *Less Than Nothing*, 437–438; Žižek, *Absolute Recoil*, 23, 44.

28. Althusser, "Philosophy and Marxism," 279.

29. Hegel, *Elements of the Philosophy of Right*, 21–23; Walter Benjamin, "Theses on the Philosophy of History," in *Illuminations: Essays and Reflections*, ed. Hannah Arendt, trans. Harry Zohn (New York: Schocken, 1969), 253–264; André Tosel, "Les aléas du matérialisme aléatoire dans la dernière philosophie de Louis Althusser," in *Sartre, Lukács, Althusser: des marxistes en philosophie*, ed. Eustache Kouvélakis and Vincent Charbonnier (Paris: Presses Universitaires de France, 2005), 196; Žižek, *Less Than Nothing*, 217–223.

30. Ibid., 388–393.

31. Althusser, "Portrait of the Materialist Philosopher," 291.

32. Louis Althusser, "The Historical Task of Marxist Philosophy," in *The Humanist Controversy and Other Writings*, 188–189; Louis Althusser, "Une question posée par Louis Althusser," in *Écrits philosophiques et politiques, Tome I*, ed. François Matheron (Paris: Stock/IMEC, 1994), 346–347, 353–356; Louis Althusser, "The Transformation of Philosophy," trans. Thomas E. Lewis, in *Philosophy and the Spontaneous Philosophy*

3. CONTINGENCY, PURE CONTINGENCY

of the Scientists and Other Essays, ed. Gregory Elliott (London: Verso, 1990), 262–264; Louis Althusser, "Marxism Today," trans. James H. Kavanagh, in Philosophy and the Spontaneous Philosophy of the Scientists and Other Essays, 276–277; Louis Althusser, Initiation à la philosophie pour les non-philosophes, ed. G. M. Goshgarian (Paris: Presses Universitaires de France, 2014), 379–381; Louis Althusser, 22ᵉ congrès (Paris: François Maspero, 1977), 30–31; Louis Althusser, Ce qui ne peut plus durer dans le parti communiste (Paris: François Maspero, 1978), 91, 96; Althusser, "Correspondence About 'Philosophy and Marxism,'" 217; Althusser, "Correspondence About 'Philosophy and Marxism': Letter to Fernanda Navarro, 8 April 1986," 242; Althusser, "Philosophy and Marxism," 253–255.

33. Johnston, "Marx's Bones," 189–215; Johnston, Prolegomena to Any Future Materialism, vol. 2.

34. Althusser, "Correspondence About 'Philosophy and Marxism,'" 229.

35. Althusser, "The Underground Current of the Materialism of the Encounter," 193–194.

36. Žižek, Less Than Nothing, 11–13, 15–16, 291, 473, 528, 611, 665, 811; Žižek, Absolute Recoil, 243–244, 377.

37. Johnston, Žižek's Ontology, 126–127, 173.

38. Žižek, Less Than Nothing, 618, 629, 779; Žižek, Absolute Recoil, 187–188, 191–192.

39. Johnston, Žižek's Ontology, 126–127, 173.

40. François Matheron, "La récurrence du vide chez Louis Althusser," in Futur antérieur: Lire Althusser aujourd'hui, ed. Jean-Marie Vincent (Paris: L'Harmattan, 1997), 30–32; Tosel, "Les aléas du matérialisme aléatoire dans la dernière philosophie de Louis Althusser," 188.

41. G. W. F. Hegel, Grundlinien der Philosophie des Rechts oder Naturrecht und Staatswissenschaft im Grundrisse: Mit Hegels eigenhändigen Notizen und den mündlichen Zusätzen, in Werke in zwanzig Bänden, vol. 7, ed. Eva Moldenhauer and Karl Markus Michel (Frankfurt: Suhrkamp, 1970), 24; Hegel, Elements of the Philosophy of Right, 20.

42. Rudolf Haym, "Preußen und die Rechtsphilosophie (1857): Hegel und seine Zeit," in Materialien zu Hegels Rechtsphilosophie, ed. Manfred Riedel (Frankfurt: Suhrkamp, 1975), 365–394.

43. Plekhanov, "For the Sixtieth Anniversary of Hegel's Death," 482; Karl Löwith, From Hegel to Nietzsche: The Revolution in Nineteenth-Century Philosophy, trans. David E. Green (New York: Columbia University Press, 1991), 138; Eric Weil, Hegel et l'état: Cinq conférences, suivies de Marx et la philosophie du droit (Paris: Vrin, 2002), 24–25; Bernard Bourgeois, La pensée politique de Hegel (Paris: Presses Universitaires de France, 1969), 92–93; Allen W. Wood, Hegel's Ethical Thought (Cambridge: Cambridge University Press, 1990), 10, 218; Michael O. Hardimon, Hegel's Social Philosophy: The Project of Reconciliation (Cambridge: Cambridge University Press, 1994), 26, 53; M. W. Jackson, "Hegel: The Real and the Rational," in The Hegel Myths and Legends, ed. Jon Stewart (Evanston, IL: Northwestern University Press, 1996), 19–25; Frederick Neuhouser, Foundations of Hegel's Social Theory: Actualizing Freedom (Cambridge: Harvard University Press, 2000), 257–258; Frederick Beiser, Hegel (New York: Routledge, 2005), 221–222; Jean-François Kervégan, L'effectif et le rationnel: Hegel et l'esprit objectif (Paris: Vrin, 2007), 17–32; Rosen, The Idea of Hegel's Science of Logic, 217.

44. Hegel, Elements of the Philosophy of Right, 22.

3. CONTINGENCY, PURE CONTINGENCY

45. G. W. F. Hegel, "Hegel to Niethammer: Jena, October 13, 1806," in *Hegel: The Letters*, trans. Clark Butler and Christiane Seiler (Bloomington: Indiana University Press, 1984), 114; G. W. F. Hegel, *Enzyklopädie der philosophischen Wissenschaften, Erster Teil: Die Wissenschaft der Logik*, in *Werke in zwanzig Bänden*, vol. 8, ed. Eva Moldenhauer and Karl Markus Michel (Frankfurt: Suhrkamp, 1970), §6 (47–49); G. W. F. Hegel, *The Encyclopedia Logic: Part I of the Encyclopedia of the Philosophical Sciences with the Zusätze*, trans. T. F. Geraets, W. A. Suchting, and H. S. Harris (Indianapolis: Hackett, 1991), §6 (29–30), §9 (33); Hegel, *Grundlinien der Philosophie des Rechts*, 24–28; Hegel, *Elements of the Philosophy of Right*, 20–23; G. W. F. Hegel, *Philosophy of History*, trans. J. Sibree (New York: Dover, 1956), 17–19, 63–64, 446–447.

46. Lukács, *The Young Hegel*, 461.

47. Terry Pinkard, *Hegel: A Biography* (Cambridge: Cambridge University Press, 2000), 450–453, 532, 534.

48. Hegel, *Enzyklopädie der philosophischen Wissenschaften, Erster Teil*, §142 (279); Hegel, *The Encyclopedia Logic*, §142 (213).

49. Hegel, *The Encyclopedia Logic*, §141 (213).

50. Ibid., §143 (215); G. W. F. Hegel, *Lectures on Logic: Berlin, 1831*, trans. Clark Butler (Bloomington: Indiana University Press, 2008), §§141–143 (155–156).

51. Hegel, *The Encyclopedia Logic*, §142 (214).

52. Immanuel Kant, *Critique of Pure Reason*, trans. Paul Guyer and Allen Wood (Cambridge: Cambridge University Press, 1998), A80/B106 (212).

53. Hegel, *Lectures on Logic*, §159 (172–173).

54. Hegel, *Enzyklopädie der philosophischen Wissenschaften, Erster Teil*, §143 (283); Hegel, *The Encyclopedia Logic*, §143 (216–217).

55. G. W. F. Hegel, "Texte zur Philosophischen Propädeutik: Philosophische Enzyklopädie für die Oberklasse," in *Nürnberger Schriften*, in *Werke in zwanzig Bänden*, vol. 4, *Nürnberger und Heidelberger Schriften, 1808-1817*, ed. Eva Moldenhauer and Karl Markus Michel (Frankfurt: Suhrkamp, 1970), §48 (20); G. W. F. Hegel, "The Philosophical Encyclopedia [for the Higher Class]," in *The Philosophical Propaedeutic*, ed. Michael George and Andrew Vincent, trans. A. V. Miller (Oxford: Blackwell, 1986), §48 (133).

56. Hegel, *The Encyclopedia Logic*, §147 (220–221).

57. G. W. F. Hegel, *Science of Logic*, trans. A. V. Miller (London: George Allen and Unwin, 1969), 545.

58. Hegel, *Enzyklopädie der philosophischen Wissenschaften, Erster Teil*, §145 (286–287); Hegel, *The Encyclopedia Logic*, §145 (219).

59. Hegel, *Phenomenology of Spirit*, 145–210.

60. Adrian Johnston, "The Weakness of Nature: Hegel, Freud, Lacan, and Negativity Materialized," in *Hegel and the Infinite: Religion, Politics, and Dialectic*, ed. Slavoj Žižek, Clayton Crockett, and Creston Davis (New York: Columbia University Press, 2011), 159–179; Adrian Johnston, "Second Natures in Dappled Worlds: John McDowell, Nancy Cartwright, and Hegelian-Lacanian Materialism," in *Umbr(a): The Worst*, ed. Matthew Rigilano and Kyle Fetter (Buffalo: Center for the Study of Psychoanalysis and Culture, State University of New York at Buffalo, 2011), 71–91; Johnston, "The Voiding of Weak Nature," 103–157; Adrian Johnston, "An Interview with Adrian Johnston on Transcendental Materialism [with Peter Gratton]," *Society and Space* (October 2013): http://societyandspace.com/2013/10/07/interview-with-adrian-johnston-on

3. CONTINGENCY, PURE CONTINGENCY

-transcendental-materialism/; Adrian Johnston, "Transcendentalism in Hegel's Wake: A Reply to Timothy M. Hackett and Benjamin Berger," special issue, "Schelling: Powers of the Idea," ed. Benjamin Berger, *Pli: The Warwick Journal of Philosophy* 26 (Fall 2014): 204–237; Adrian Johnston, "Confession of a Weak Reductionist: Responses to Some Recent Criticisms of My Materialism," in *Neuroscience and Critique: Exploring the Limits of the Neurological Turn*, ed. Jan De Vos and Ed Pluth (New York: Routledge, 2015), 141–170; Johnston, *Prolegomena to Any Future Materialism*, vol. 2.

61. Hegel, *Science of Logic*, 31–33.

62. G. W. F. Hegel, *First Philosophy of Spirit (Part III of the System of Speculative Philosophy 1803/4)*, trans. H. S. Harris, in *The System of Ethical Life (1802/3) and First Philosophy of Spirit (Part III of the System of Speculative Philosophy 1803/4)*, 221–223; G. W. F. Hegel, *Philosophie des Geistes, Jenaer Systementwürfe III: Naturphilosophie und Philosophie des Geistes*, ed. Rolf-Peter Horstmann (Hamburg: Felix Meiner, 1987), 176–178; G. W. F. Hegel, *Philosophy of Mind: Part Three of the Encyclopedia of the Philosophical Sciences with the Zusätze*, trans. William Wallace and A. V. Miller (Oxford: Oxford University Press, 1971), §459 (214, 218), §461 (219), §462 (220–221); Hegel, *Philosophy of History*, 62.

63. Žižek, *Less Than Nothing*, 470.

64. Hegel, *Enzyklopädie der philosophischen Wissenschaften, Erster Teil*, §147 (289); Hegel, *The Encyclopedia Logic*, §147 (221).

65. Marcuse, *Hegel's Ontology and the Theory of Historicity*, 97, 102; Doz, *La logique de Hegel et les problèmes traditionnels de l'ontologie*, 151; Marmasse, *Penser le réel*, 142, 411.

66. V. L. Komarov, "Marx and Engels on Biology," in *Marxism and Modern Thought*, by N.I. Bukharin et al., trans. Ralph Fox (New York: Harcourt, Brace, 1935), 209–210.

67. Herbert Marcuse, *Reason and Revolution: Hegel and the Rise of Social Theory*, 2nd ed. (New York: Routledge, 2000), 138–139; Hyppolite, *Logic and Existence*, 64–65; Adrien T. B. Peperzak, *Le jeune Hegel et la vision morale du monde* (The Hague: Martinus Nijhoff, 1960), 182–185; Hans Friedrich Fulda, *Das Problem einer Einleitung in Hegels Wissenschaft der Logik* (Frankfurt: Klostermann, 1965), 196; Robert M. Wallace, *Hegel's Philosophy of Reality, Freedom, and God* (Cambridge: Cambridge University Press, 2005), 45–46; Houlgate, *The Opening of Hegel's Logic*, 425; Michael Quante, *Die Wirklichkeit des Geistes: Studien zu Hegel* (Frankfurt: Suhrkamp, 2011), 29; Pinkard, *Hegel's Naturalism*, 192, 195.

68. Slavoj Žižek, *Disparities* (London: Bloomsbury, 2016), 268.

69. Ibid., 121.

70. Rosen, *The Idea of Hegel's Science of Logic*, 375.

71. Lukács, *The Young Hegel*, 394.

72. H. S. Harris, *Hegel's Development*, vol. 2, *Night Thoughts (Jena 1801–1806)* (Oxford: Oxford University Press, 1983), 367.

73. G. W. F. Hegel, *Wissenschaft der Logik II*, in *Werke in zwanzig Bänden*, vol. 6, ed. Eva Moldenhauer and Karl Markus Michel (Frankfurt: Suhrkamp, 1969), 123; Hegel, *Science of Logic*, 478.

74. Marmasse, *Penser le réel*, 147, 347, 410.

75. Béatrice Longuenesse, *Hegel et la critique de la métaphysique* (Paris: Vrin, 1981), 191.

76. Hegel, *Science of Logic*, 603; Marcuse, *Hegel's Ontology and the Theory of Historicity*, 97; Fulda, *Das Problem einer Einleitung in Hegels Wissenschaft der Logik*, 260.

3. CONTINGENCY, PURE CONTINGENCY

77. Žižek, *Absolute Recoil*, 101.
78. Hegel, *Philosophy of History*, 79–102.
79. Georgi V. Plekhanov, *Fundamental Problems of Marxism*, ed. James S. Allen, trans. Julius Katzer (New York: International, 1969), 49.
80. Hegel, *Phenomenology of Spirit*, 217–221.
81. Hegel, *Enzyklopädie der philosophischen Wissenschaften, Erster Teil*, §143 (282–283); Hegel, *The Encyclopedia Logic*, §143 (216).
82. Hegel, *Enzyklopädie der philosophischen Wissenschaften, Erster Teil*, §143 (283); Hegel, *The Encyclopedia Logic*, §143 (216).
83. Rosen, *The Idea of Hegel's Science of Logic*, 4.
84. Leibniz, "The Principles of Philosophy, or, the Monadology," §31–32 (217).
85. David Hume, *A Treatise of Human Nature*, ed. Ernest C. Mossner (New York: Penguin, 1985), 205–223, 231–238; David Hume, *An Enquiry Concerning Human Understanding*, ed. Eric Steinberg, 2nd ed. (Indianapolis: Hackett, 1993), 21–24.
86. G. W. F. Hegel, *Faith and Knowledge*, trans. Walter Cerf and H. S. Harris (Albany: State University of New York Press, 1977), 69, 154; Hegel, "On the Relationship of Skepticism to Philosophy, Exposition of Its Different Modifications and Comparison of the Latest Form with the Ancient One," 311–362; Hegel, *The Encyclopedia Logic*, §38 (77–79), §39 (80); Hegel, *Lectures on the History of Philosophy*, 3:369–375; Hegel, *Lectures on Logic*, §§32–39 (26–30).
87. Marcuse, *Hegel's Ontology and the Theory of Historicity*, 94.
88. Wallace, *Hegel's Philosophy of Reality, Freedom, and God*, 209.
89. Plekhanov, "For the Sixtieth Anniversary of Hegel's Death," 476–477; Plekhanov, *Fundamental Problems of Marxism*, 90–92; Georgi V. Plekhanov, "The Role of the Individual in History," in *Fundamental Problems of Marxism*, 143–144, 146; Bukharin, *Philosophical Arabesques*, 116–117; Louis Althusser, "Cremonini, Painter of the Abstract," in *Lenin and Philosophy and Other Essays*, trans. Ben Brewster (New York: Monthly Review Press, 2001), 165.
90. Friedrich Engels, *Anti-Dühring: Herr Eugen Dühring's Revolution in Science* (Moscow: Foreign Languages, 1959), 157.
91. Kant, *Critique of Pure Reason*, A444/B472–A451/B479 (484–489).
92. Y. M. Uranovsky, "Marxism and Natural Science," in Bukharin et al., *Marxism and Modern Thought*, 150–151, 154.
93. Friedrich Engels, *Socialism: Utopian and Scientific*, trans. Edward Aveling (New York: International, 1975), 48–53.
94. Engels, *Anti-Dühring*, 390–393.
95. Baruch Spinoza, *Ethics*, in *Complete Works*, ed. Michael L. Morgan, trans. Samuel Shirley (Indianapolis: Hackett, 2002), pt. 1, propositions 29 (234), 32 (235), 33 (235–238), pt. 2, propositions 35 (264), 48 (272), 49 (272–277).
96. Adrian Johnston, *Adventures in Transcendental Materialism: Dialogues with Contemporary Thinkers* (Edinburgh: Edinburgh University Press, 2014), 23–64.
97. Johnston, "The Voiding of Weak Nature," 103–157; Johnston, *Adventures in Transcendental Materialism*, 23–64; Johnston, "Transcendentalism in Hegel's Wake," 204–237; Johnston, *Prolegomena to Any Future Materialism*, vol. 2.
98. Friedrich Engels, "The Part Played by Labour in the Transition From Ape to Man," in *Dialectics of Nature*, trans. C. P. Dutt (New York: International, 1940), 279–296.

3. CONTINGENCY, PURE CONTINGENCY

99. Adrian Johnston, "Repeating Engels: Renewing the Cause of the Materialist Wager for the Twenty-First Century," special issue, "animal.machine.sovereign," ed. Javier Burdman and Tyler Williams, *Theory @ Buffalo* 15 (2011): 141–182; Johnston, "From Scientific Socialism to Socialist Science," 103–136; Johnston, *Prolegomena to Any Future Materialism*, vol. 2.

100. Johnston, "The Voiding of Weak Nature," 103–157; Johnston, "Transcendentalism in Hegel's Wake," 204–237; Johnston, *Prolegomena to Any Future Materialism*, vol. 2.

101. Hegel, *Science of Logic*, 562–563.

102. Hegel, *Philosophy of Mind*, §377 (2), §381 (13); Hegel, *Elements of the Philosophy of Right*, §348 (375); Hegel, *Philosophy of History*, 29–38.

103. Hegel, *Philosophie des Geistes*, 190; Hegel, *Philosophy of Nature*, §245 (5); Hegel, *Philosophy of History*, 27.

104. Francis Bacon, "The Great Renewal," in *The New Organon*, ed. Lisa Jardine and Michael Silverthorne (Cambridge: Cambridge University Press, 2000), 24; Francis Bacon, *The New Organon*, bk. 2, aphorisms 1 (102), 3 (103), 4 (103), 17 (128), 31 (149–150).

105. Hegel, *Enzyklopädie der philosophischen Wissenschaften, Erster Teil*, §147 (290).

106. Hegel, *The Encyclopedia Logic*, §147 (222).

107. Hegel, *Enzyklopädie der philosophischen Wissenschaften, Erster Teil*, §158 (303); Hegel, *The Encyclopedia Logic*, §158 (233).

108. Hegel, *Wissenschaft der Logik II*, 427; Hegel, *Science of Logic*, 725.

109. Bernard Bourgeois, *Hegel à Francfort ou Judaïsme-Christianisme-Hegelianisme* (Paris: Vrin, 2000), 94.

110. Karl Marx, *Grundrisse: Foundations of the Critique of Political Economy (Rough Draft)*, trans. Martin Nicolaus (New York: Penguin, 1993), 105.

111. GW 8:90; SE 11:189; GW 13:400; SE 19:178; Toril Moi, "Is Anatomy Destiny?: Freud and Biological Determinism," in *Whose Freud?: The Place of Psychoanalysis in Contemporary Culture*, ed. Peter Brooks and Alex Woloch (New Haven: Yale University Press, 2000), 72–74; Adrian Johnston, *Time Driven: Metapsychology and the Splitting of the Drive* (Evanston, IL: Northwestern University Press, 2005), 177; Adrian Johnston, *Prolegomena to Any Future Materialism*, vol. 1, *The Outcome of Contemporary French Philosophy* (Evanston, IL: Northwestern University Press, 2013), 30–31.

112. Žižek, *Less Than Nothing*, 216; Žižek, *Absolute Recoil*, 242.

113. Žižek, *Less Than Nothing*, 468.

114. Hegel, *Wissenschaft der Logik II*, 206; Hegel, *Science of Logic*, 545.

115. Hegel, *Science of Logic*, 82–108; Hegel, *The Encyclopedia Logic*, §§86–88 (136–145).

116. Hegel, *Science of Logic*, 546–547.

117. Hegel, *Wissenschaft der Logik II*, 211; Hegel, *Science of Logic*, 549.

118. Hegel, *Science of Logic*, 550.

119. Hegel, *Wissenschaft der Logik II*, 213; Hegel, *Science of Logic*, 550.

120. Marcuse, *Hegel's Ontology and the Theory of Historicity*, 97.

121. Hegel, *Science of Logic*, 550.

122. Hegel, *Wissenschaft der Logik II*, 215; Hegel, *Science of Logic*, 552.

123. Hegel, *Science of Logic*, 553.

3. CONTINGENCY, PURE CONTINGENCY

124. Žižek, *Less Than Nothing*, 467.
125. Marcuse, *Hegel's Ontology and the Theory of Historicity*, 97.
126. Žižek, *Less Than Nothing*, 637.
127. Ibid., 459–460.
128. Ibid., 469.
129. Marcuse, *Hegel's Ontology and the Theory of Historicity*, 79.
130. Hegel, *Phenomenology of Spirit*, 2; Hegel, *Science of Logic*, 48; Hegel, *The Encyclopedia Logic*, 5, 7–8, §81 (130–131), §82 (132–133).
131. G. W. F. Hegel, *Wissenschaft der Logik I*, in *Werke in zwanzig Bänden*, vol. 5, ed. Eva Moldenhauer and Karl Markus Michel (Frankfurt: Suhrkamp, 1969), 82; Hegel, *Science of Logic*, 82.
132. Žižek, *Absolute Recoil*, 385.
133. Düsing, *Das Problem der Subjektivität in Hegels Logik*, 52.
134. Marcuse, *Hegel's Ontology and the Theory of Historicity*, 97.
135. Žižek, *Less Than Nothing*, 98.
136. Ibid., 220, 222–223.
137. Ibid., 217.
138. Ibid., 218.
139. Ibid., 225.
140. Johnston, *Žižek's Ontology*, 126–127.
141. Žižek, *Less Than Nothing*, 227.
142. Ibid., 218–219.
143. Ibid., 221.
144. Hegel, *Elements of the Philosophy of Right*, 21.
145. *SE* 17:85; *SE* 19:143–144, 184–185, 253; *SE* 23:203; Jean Laplanche and Jean-Bertrand Pontalis, *The Language of Psycho-Analysis*, trans. Donald Nicholson-Smith (New York: Norton, 1973), 118–121.
146. Octave Mannoni, "Je sais bien, mais quand même . . .," in *Clefs pour l'Imaginaire ou l'Autre Scène* (Paris: Seuil, 1969), 9–33; Adrian Johnston, *Badiou, Žižek, and Political Transformations: The Cadence of Change* (Evanston, IL: Northwestern University Press, 2009), 92; Žižek, *Less Than Nothing*, 983.
147. Hegel, *Philosophy of Nature*, §257–259 (33–40).
148. Hegel, *Philosophy of Mind*, §483–486 (241–243).
149. Rosen, *The Idea of Hegel's Science of Logic*, 291.
150. Lenin, "Conspectus of Hegel's Book *The Science of Logic*," 88, 227; Guy Planty-Bonjour, *The Categories of Dialectical Materialism: Contemporary Soviet Ontology*, trans. T. J. Blakeley (New York: Praeger, 1967), 50, 70.
151. Hegel, *Science of Logic*, 559, 562–563; Hegel, *The Encyclopedia Logic*, §§153–154 (227–230); Hegel, *Lectures on Logic*, §§153–157 (167–169).
152. Žižek, *Absolute Recoil*, 238–239.
153. Žižek, *Less Than Nothing*, 629, 866.
154. Žižek, *Less Than Nothing*, 440–442, 449, 455–458, 461–463, 484–485, 490, 492–493; Žižek, *Absolute Recoil*, 29–31, 34, 183–186, 199, 202.
155. Hegel, *Grundlinien der Philosophie des Rechts*, 26; Hegel, *Elements of the Philosophy of Right*, 21.

3. CONTINGENCY, PURE CONTINGENCY

156. Hegel, *Grundlinien der Philosophie des Rechts*, 12; Hegel, *Elements of the Philosophy of Right*, 10.
157. Hegel, *Phenomenology of Spirit*, 1, 3–4, 20, 22, 50–52; Hegel, *Science of Logic*, 34, 48–49, 53–54.
158. Hegel, *Science of Logic*, 31, 42, 54, 63–64; Hegel, *The Encyclopedia Logic*, §9 (33), §§12–15 (37–39), §24 (56); Hegel, *Lectures on Logic*, §19 (3).
159. Hyppolite, *Logic and Existence*, 3–4, 7.
160. Johnston, *Žižek's Ontology*, 125–268; Johnston, *Adventures in Transcendental Materialism*, 40–43; Johnston, *Prolegomena to Any Future Materialism*, vol. 2.
161. Rosen, *The Idea of Hegel's Science of Logic*, 227.
162. Ibid., 238.
163. Hegel, *Elements of the Philosophy of Right*, 21.
164. Adrian Johnston, "A Review of Frank Ruda's *Hegel's Rabble*," *Notre Dame Philosophical Reviews* (June 21, 2012), http://ndpr.nd.edu/news/31707-hegel-s-rabble-an-investigation-into-hegel-s-philosophy-of-right/.
165. Ibid.
166. Ibid.
167. Hegel, *Grundlinien der Philosophie des Rechts*, 26; Hegel, *Elements of the Philosophy of Right*, 22.
168. G. W. F. Hegel, *Phänomenologie des Geistes*, in *Werke in zwanzig Bänden*, vol. 3, ed. Eva Moldenhauer and Karl Markus Michel (Frankfurt: Suhrkamp, 1970), 46; Hegel, *Phenomenology of Spirit*, 27.
169. G. W. F. Hegel, *Vorlesungen über die Philosophie der Geschichte*, in *Werke in zwanzig Bänden*, vol. 12, ed. Eva Moldenhauer and Karl Markus Michel (Frankfurt: Suhrkamp, 1970), 529; Hegel, *Philosophy of History*, 447.
170. G. W. F. Hegel, "Hegel to Niethammer: Bamberg, October 28, 1808," in *Hegel: The Letters*, 179.
171. Hegel, *Elements of the Philosophy of Right*, 21.
172. Hegel, *Phenomenology of Spirit*, 51, 267–289; G. W. F. Hegel, *Lectures on the History of Philosophy*, vol. 1, trans. E. S. Haldane (New York: Humanities, 1955), 425–448.
173. Žižek, *Less Than Nothing*, 161–163, 388–390, 393; Žižek, *Absolute Recoil*, 351–353.
174. Hegel, *Phenomenology of Spirit*, 36, 51; Hegel, *Science of Logic*, 53–54; Hegel, *The Encyclopedia Logic*, §11 (35), §82 (131–132); Hegel, *Lectures on Logic*, §85 (79–80).
175. Engels, *Ludwig Feuerbach and the Outcome of Classical German Philosophy*, 11–13.
176. Žižek, *Less Than Nothing*, 525.
177. Ibid., 272–273.
178. Žižek, *Absolute Recoil*, 234–235.
179. Žižek, *Less Than Nothing*, 285.
180. Ibid., 468.
181. Johnston, "The Voiding of Weak Nature," 146–147.
182. Benjamin, "Theses on the Philosophy of History," 254; Johnston, *Badiou, Žižek, and Political Transformations*, xiii–xvi; Johnston, *Prolegomena to Any Future Materialism*, vol. 2.
183. H. S. Harris, *Hegel's Ladder*, vol. 2, *The Odyssey of Spirit* (Indianapolis: Hackett, 1997), 143.

184. Žižek, *Disparities*, 374.
185. Karl Marx, *A Contribution to the Critique of Political Economy*, ed. Maurice Dobb, trans. S. W. Ryazanskaya (New York: International, 1970), 21.
186. Žižek, *Less Than Nothing*, 222–223.
187. Walter Benjamin, "Theories of German Fascism," in *Selected Writings*, vol. 2, pt. 1, *1927-1930*, ed. Michael W. Jennings, Howard Eiland, and Gary Smith, trans. Rodney Livingstone et al. (Cambridge: Harvard University Press, 1999), 321.
188. Mao Tse-Tung, "On the Correct Handling of Contradictions Among the People," in *Selected Readings from the Works of Mao Tsetung* (Peking: Foreign Languages, 1971), 442–444, 446, 464; Mao Tse-Tung, "Speech at the Tenth Plenum of the Eighth Central Committee," September 24, 1962, www.marxists.org/reference/archive/mao/selected-works/volume-8/mswv8_63.htm; Mao Tse-Tung, "Speech to the Albanian Military Delegation," May 1, 1967, www.marxists.org/reference/archive/mao/selected-works/volume-9/mswv9_74.htm; Johnston, *Badiou, Žižek, and Political Transformations*, 55–57.

4. Materialism Sans Materialism

1. V. I. Lenin, *Materialism and Empirio-Criticism* (Peking: Foreign Languages, 1972), 308–318; Slavoj Žižek, *The Indivisible Remainder: An Essay on Schelling and Related Matters* (London: Verso, 1996), 165, 230–231; Slavoj Žižek, *Organs Without Bodies: On Deleuze and Consequences* (New York: Routledge, 2004), 24–25; Slavoj Žižek, *The Parallax View* (Cambridge: MIT Press, 2006), 165, 239; Slavoj Žižek, *Less Than Nothing: Hegel and the Shadow of Dialectical Materialism* (London: Verso, 2012), 807, 929; Slavoj Žižek, *Absolute Recoil: Towards a New Foundation of Dialectical Materialism* (London: Verso, 2014), 5, 73; Adrian Johnston, *Žižek's Ontology: A Transcendental Materialist Theory of Subjectivity* (Evanston, IL: Northwestern University Press, 2008), 200–203.
2. V. I. Lenin, "Conspectus of Hegel's Book *The Science of Logic*," in *Collected Works*, vol. 38, *Philosophical Notebooks*, ed. Stewart Smith, trans. Clemence Dutt (Moscow: Progress, 1976), 89, 91–93, 103–104, 110, 123, 130, 141, 147, 169, 175, 183, 189, 196–199, 201, 207, 222.
3. Karl Marx, "Theses on Feuerbach," trans. S. Ryazanskaya, in *Karl Marx: Selected Writings*, ed. David McLellan (Oxford: Oxford University Press, 1977), 156–158.
4. Žižek, *Less Than Nothing*, 657–658, 660, 905–907, 909; Žižek, *Absolute Recoil*, 31, 72–73.
5. Lenin, *Materialism and Empirio-Criticism*, 309–314, 318, 340, 342, 372, 376–378, 434.
6. Friedrich Engels, *Ludwig Feuerbach and the Outcome of Classical German Philosophy*, trans. C. P. Dutt (New York: International, 1941), 25–27, 46–47; Lenin, *Materialism and Empirio-Criticism*, 298–301; Y. M. Uranovsky, "Marxism and Natural Science," in *Marxism and Modern Thought*, by N. I. Bukharin et al., trans. Ralph Fox (New York: Harcourt, Brace, 1935), 153.
7. Žižek, *Absolute Recoil*, 1.
8. Ibid.

4. MATERIALISM SANS MATERIALISM

9. Žižek, *The Indivisible Remainder*, 189–236; Žižek, *Less Than Nothing*, 740, 744, 910, 912, 914–915, 918–926, 929, 932–933, 945–946; Žižek, *Absolute Recoil*, 222, 225, 380–381, 390–391; Adrian Johnston, *Adventures in Transcendental Materialism: Dialogues with Contemporary Thinkers* (Edinburgh: Edinburgh University Press, 2014), 165–183.

10. Adrian Johnston, *Prolegomena to Any Future Materialism*, vol. 2, *A Weak Nature Alone* (Evanston, IL: Northwestern University Press, 2018).

11. Slavoj Žižek, "Postface: Georg Lukács as the Philosopher of Leninism," in *A Defense of History and Class Consciousness: Tailism and the Dialectic*, by Georg Lukács, trans. Esther Leslie (London: Verso, 2000), 179–180; Slavoj Žižek, "Afterword: Lenin's Choice," in *Revolution at the Gates: Selected Writings of Lenin from 1917*, by V. I. Lenin, ed. Slavoj Žižek (London: Verso, 2002), 178–181; Žižek, *The Parallax View*, 168; Slavoj Žižek, "An Answer to Two Questions," in *Badiou, Žižek, and Political Transformations: The Cadence of Change*, by Adrian Johnston (Evanston, IL: Northwestern University Press, 2009), 214; Slavoj Žižek, "The Fear of Four Words: A Modest Plea for the Hegelian Reading of Christianity," in *The Monstrosity of Christ: Paradox or Dialectic?*, by Slavoj Žižek and John Milbank, ed. Creston Davis (Cambridge: MIT Press, 2009), 97, 100; Žižek, *Less Than Nothing*, 642–644, 646–647, 905–909; Slavoj Žižek and Glyn Daly, *Conversations with Žižek* (Cambridge: Polity, 2004), 96–97.

12. Nikolai Bukharin, *Philosophical Arabesques*, trans. Renfrey Clarke (New York: Monthly Review Press, 2005), 307, 328, 337, 372; Gustav A. Wetter, *Dialectical Materialism: A Historical and Systematic Survey of Philosophy in the Soviet Union*, trans. Peter Heath (New York: Praeger, 1958), 130–131; Guy Planty-Bonjour, *The Categories of Dialectical Materialism*, trans. T. J. Blakeley (New York: Praeger, 1967), 29, 79, 91, 98; Loren R. Graham, *Science and Philosophy in the Soviet Union* (New York: Knopf, 1972), 36–37.

13. Sebastiano Timpanaro, *On Materialism*, trans. Lawrence Garner (London: Verso, 1980), 33; Richard Levins and Richard Lewontin, "The Problem of Lysenkoism," in *The Dialectical Biologist* (Cambridge: Harvard University Press, 1985), 163–196; Graham, *Science and Philosophy in the Soviet Union*, 450; Helena Sheehan, *Marxism and the Philosophy of Science: A Critical History—the First Hundred Years*, 2nd ed. (Amherst: Humanity Books, 1993), 220–228; Lucien Sève, "Pour en finir avec l'anachronisme," in *Sciences et dialectiques de la nature*, ed. Lucien Sève (Paris: La Dispute, 1998), 13–14, 20–21; Lucien Sève, "Nature, science, dialectique: Un chantier à rouvrir," in *Sciences et dialectiques de la nature*, 94–107; Adrian Johnston, "Repeating Engels: Renewing the Cause of the Materialist Wager for the Twenty-First Century," special issue, "animal.machine.sovereign," ed. Javier Burdman and Tyler Williams, *Theory @ Buffalo* 15 (2011): 141–182; Adrian Johnston, "From Scientific Socialism to Socialist Science: *Naturdialektik* Then and Now," in *The Idea of Communism*, vol. 2, *The New York Conference*, ed. Slavoj Žižek (London: Verso, 2013), 103–136; Johnston, *Prolegomena to Any Future Materialism*, vol. 2.

14. Walter Benjamin, "Theses on the Philosophy of History," in *Illuminations: Essays and Reflections*, ed. Hannah Arendt, trans. Harry Zohn (New York: Schocken, 1969), 255.

15. Žižek, *Less Than Nothing*, 393–394.

16. Georg Lukács, "What Is Orthodox Marxism?," in *History and Class Consciousness: Studies in Marxist Dialectics*, trans. Rodney Livingstone (Cambridge: MIT Press,

4. MATERIALISM SANS MATERIALISM

1971), 24; Georg Lukács, "Reification and the Consciousness of the Proletariat," in *History and Class Consciousness*, 88–91, 98–99, 102–104, 109–110; Georg Lukács, "The Changing Function of Historical Materialism," in *History and Class Consciousness*, 234; Georg Lukács, "N. Bukharin: Historical Materialism," in *Tactics and Ethics: Political Writings, 1919-1929*, ed. Rodney Livingstone, trans. Michael McColgan (London: New Left Books, 1972), 136, 139–142; Georg Lukács, "Karl August Wittfogel: The Science of Bourgeois Society," in *Tactics and Ethics*, 144–145; Georg Lukács, "Tailism and the Dialectic," in *A Defense of History and Class Consciousness*, 100, 102.

17. Bukharin, *Philosophical Arabesques*, 217–218; Wetter, *Dialectical Materialism*, 449–450; Planty-Bonjour, *The Categories of Dialectical Materialism*, 1–5; Graham, *Science and Philosophy in the Soviet Union*, 60.

18. Žižek, *Less Than Nothing*, 461.

19. Žižek, *Absolute Recoil*, 93.

20. Herbert Marcuse, *Soviet Marxism: A Critical Analysis* (New York: Penguin, 1971), 115, 118–121; Timpanaro, *On Materialism*, 7, 15–16, 29, 32, 35–36, 43–45, 47–48, 56, 58, 73–74, 76, 129, 209, 216–217, 232–233; Graham, *Science and Philosophy in the Soviet Union*, 29–30, 41; Sheehan, *Marxism and the Philosophy of Science*, 255, 258–259, 263, 277–279, 282.

21. Max Horkheimer and Theodor W. Adorno, *Dialectic of Enlightenment: Philosophical Fragments*, ed. Gunzelin Schmid Noerr, trans. Edmund Jephcott (Stanford: Stanford University Press, 2002), xi–xii, xiv–xv, 3–4, 7, 65–66, 68, 201–202, 232.

22. Alfred Schmidt, *The Concept of Nature in Marx*, trans. Ben Fowkes (London: Verso, 2014), 10, 32–33, 45, 50, 69–70, 96, 98, 124–126, 134, 166–167, 213, 228; Žižek, *Less Than Nothing*, 907–908; Johnston, *Žižek's Ontology*, 150.

23. Slavoj Žižek and Renata Salecl, "Lacan in Slovenia (an Interview with Slavoj Žižek and Renata Salecl [with Peter Osborne])," in *A Critical Sense: Interviews with Intellectuals*, ed. Peter Osborne (New York: Routledge, 1996), 41.

24. Žižek, *Absolute Recoil*, 205.

25. Slavoj Žižek, *Tarrying with the Negative: Kant, Hegel, and the Critique of Ideology* (Durham: Duke University Press, 1993), 128–129.

26. Bukharin, *Philosophical Arabesques*, 337; Žižek, *Absolute Recoil*, 89.

27. Žižek, *Absolute Recoil*, 223.

28. Žižek, *Less Than Nothing*, 250–251, 857–858.

29. Ibid., 207.

30. Žižek, *Absolute Recoil*, 31.

31. Žižek, *Less Than Nothing*, 244–245, 252–253, 359–364, 395–396, 398.

32. Alain Badiou, *Logics of Worlds: Being and Event 2*, trans. Alberto Toscano (London: Continuum, 2009), 1–9.

33. Žižek, *Absolute Recoil*, 72–73.

34. Ibid., 5–6.

35. Žižek, *Less Than Nothing*, 193–194, 622–623, 663–664, 807–809, 821–826, 835–836, 842–844; Žižek, *Absolute Recoil*, 75, 77–78, 87.

36. Žižek, *Less Than Nothing*, 40–42; Žižek, *Absolute Recoil*, 80.

37. Žižek, *Less Than Nothing*, 985–986, 988.

38. Johnston, "Repeating Engels," 141–182; Adrian Johnston, "The Voiding of Weak Nature: The Transcendental Materialist Kernels of Hegel's *Naturphilosophie*," *Graduate Faculty Philosophy Journal* 33, no. 1 (2012): 103–157; Adrian Johnston,

4. MATERIALISM SANS MATERIALISM

"Reflections of a Rotten Nature: Hegel, Lacan, and Material Negativity," special issue, "Science and Thought," ed. Frank Ruda and Jan Voelker, *Filozofski Vestnik* 33, no. 2 (2012): 23–52; Johnston, "From Scientific Socialism to Socialist Science," 103–136; Adrian Johnston, "An Interview with Adrian Johnston on Transcendental Materialism [with Peter Gratton]," *Society and Space* (October 2013), http://societyandspace.com/2013/10/07/interview-with-adrian-johnston-on-transcendental-materialism/; Adrian Johnston, "Transcendentalism in Hegel's Wake: A Reply to Timothy M. Hackett and Benjamin Berger," special issue, "Schelling: Powers of the Idea," ed. Benjamin Berger, *Pli: The Warwick Journal of Philosophy* 26 (Fall 2014): 204–237; Adrian Johnston, "Marx's Bones: Breaking with Althusser," in *The Concept in Crisis: Reading Capital Now*, ed. Nick Nesbitt (Durham: Duke University Press, 2017), 189–215; Adrian Johnston, *Prolegomena to Any Future Materialism*, vol. 1, *The Outcome of Contemporary French Philosophy* (Evanston, IL: Northwestern University Press, 2013), 81–128; Johnston, *Prolegomena to Any Future Materialism*, vol. 2.

39. Slavoj Žižek, *Disparities* (London: Bloomsbury, 2016), 335.
40. Žižek, *Less Than Nothing*, 60.
41. Ibid., 399–400.
42. Žižek, *Less Than Nothing*, 374, 379–380, 707–708; Žižek, *Absolute Recoil*, 153; Žižek, *Disparities*, 38, 82–83.
43. Žižek, *Less Than Nothing*, 374.
44. Ibid., 416.
45. Žižek, *Absolute Recoil*, 140.
46. Žižek, *Disparities*, 118.
47. Žižek, *Absolute Recoil*, 140–141.
48. Žižek, *Less Than Nothing*, 826.
49. Žižek, *Absolute Recoil*, 107.
50. Žižek, *Less Than Nothing*, 333–334, 338–340, 354, 373, 410, 440–442, 449, 651–653, 744, 824–826; Žižek, *Absolute Recoil*, 66, 107–109, 140–141, 183, 202–205, 275–276, 303–304.
51. Žižek, *Disparities*, 9–10; Alenka Zupančič, "Freedom and Cause," in *Why Psychoanalysis?: Three Interventions* (Copenhagen: NSU Press, 2008), 34–35; Alenka Zupančič, "'Encountering Lacan in the Next Generation': Interview with Alenka Zupančič [with Jones Irwin and Helena Motoh]," in *Žižek and His Contemporaries: On the Emergence of the Slovenian Lacan*, ed. Jones Irwin and Helena Motoh (London: Bloomsbury, 2014), 166–167, 170.
52. Žižek, *Absolute Recoil*, 8, 12.
53. Johnston, *Adventures in Transcendental Materialism*, 139–183.
54. Johnston, "The Voiding of Weak Nature," 103–157; Johnston, *Prolegomena to Any Future Materialism*, vol. 2.
55. Žižek, *Less Than Nothing*, 400–401, 459–460; Žižek, *Absolute Recoil*, 227; Dieter Henrich, "Kant und Hegel: Versuch der Vereinigung inhrer Grundgedanken," in *Selbstverhältnisse: Gedanken und Auslegungen zu den Grundlagen der klassischen deutschen Philosophie* (Stuttgart: Reclam, 1982), 206–207.
56. Ludwig Siep, *Der Weg der Phänomenologie des Geistes: Ein einführender Kommentar zu Hegels "Differenzschrift" und "Phänomenologie des Geistes"* (Frankfurt: Suhrkamp, 2000), 66, 75–76.

4. MATERIALISM SANS MATERIALISM

57. Stanley Rosen, *The Idea of Hegel's Science of Logic* (Chicago: University of Chicago Press, 2014), 169–170.
58. Žižek, *Less Than Nothing*, 457–458, 461–463.
59. Ibid., 807.
60. Ibid., 915.
61. Lenin, "Conspectus of Hegel's Book *The Science of Logic*," 169; Uranovsky, "Marxism and Natural Science," 160–162, 164–167; Bukharin, *Philosophical Arabesques*, 141–142, 196; Wetter, *Dialectical Materialism*, 392; Žižek, *Less Than Nothing*, 909, 914–915.
62. H. S. Harris, *Hegel's Development*, vol. 2, *Night Thoughts (Jena 1801-1806)* (Oxford: Oxford University Press, 1983), 284–285; H. S. Harris, *Hegel's Ladder*, vol. 1, *The Pilgrimage of Reason* (Indianapolis: Hackett, 1997), 556; Olaf Breidbach, *Das Organische in Hegels Denken: Studie zur Naturphilosophie und Biologie um 1800* (Würzburg: Königshausen and Neumann, 1982), 132, 187–188, 190, 192–193; Michael Quante, *Die Wirklichkeit des Geistes: Studien zu Hegel* (Frankfurt: Suhrkamp, 2011), 128.
63. Johnston, *Adventures in Transcendental Materialism*, 165–183.
64. Žižek, *Less Than Nothing*, 915.
65. Johnston, "The Voiding of Weak Nature," 125–135; Johnston, *Prolegomena to Any Future Materialism*, vol. 2.
66. Žižek, *Less Than Nothing*, 400.
67. Ibid.
68. Ibid., 401.
69. Žižek, *Disparities*, 80–81.
70. Žižek, *Less Than Nothing*, 441.
71. Žižek, *Absolute Recoil*, 202.
72. Žižek, *Less Than Nothing*, 442, 449, 561–562.
73. Ibid., 298, 373.
74. Žižek, *Absolute Recoil*, 140–141, 192.
75. Ibid., 29.
76. G. W. F. Hegel, *Philosophy of Mind: Part Three of the Encyclopedia of the Philosophical Sciences with the Zusätze*, trans. William Wallace and A. V. Miller (Oxford: Oxford University Press, 1971), §§409–410 (139–147).
77. Johnston, *Žižek's Ontology*, 180–181, 191–194; Johnston, *Adventures in Transcendental Materialism*, 146–160.
78. Žižek, *Less Than Nothing*, 333–334, 338–340, 344–346, 350, 354, 356, 358, 384, 410, 886, 914–915; Žižek, *Absolute Recoil*, 44–46, 64, 66, 80, 190.
79. Johnston, "Reflections of a Rotten Nature," 23–52; Adrian Johnston, "Drive Between Brain and Subject: An Immanent Critique of Lacanian Neuropsychoanalysis," special issue, "Spindel Supplement: Freudian Futures," *Southern Journal of Philosophy* 51 (2013): 48–84; Johnston, *Prolegomena to Any Future Materialism*, vol. 2.
80. Žižek, *Absolute Recoil*, 28.
81. Ibid., 96.
82. Ibid., 107.
83. Ibid.
84. Žižek, *Disparities*, 34, 285.

85. Žižek, *Absolute Recoil*, 108–109.
86. Johnston, "The Voiding of Weak Nature," 103–157; Johnston, "Reflections of a Rotten Nature," 23–52; Johnston, "Drive Between Brain and Subject," 48–84; Johnston, *Prolegomena to Any Future Materialism*, vol. 2.
87. Žižek, *Absolute Recoil*, 202.
88. Ibid., 203.
89. Ibid., 202–203.
90. Johnston, "Transcendentalism in Hegel's Wake," 204–237.
91. Johnston, *Prolegomena to Any Future Materialism*, 1:59–77.
92. Žižek, *Absolute Recoil*, 98.

5. Bartleby by Nature

1. Slavoj Žižek, *Less Than Nothing: Hegel and the Shadow of Dialectical Materialism* (London: Verso, 2012), 457–458, 461–463.
2. Adrian Johnston, *Badiou, Žižek, and Political Transformations: The Cadence of Change* (Evanston, IL: Northwestern University Press, 2009), 144–156.
3. Žižek, *Less Than Nothing*, 121.
4. Ibid., 122.
5. Slavoj Žižek, *Absolute Recoil: Towards a New Foundation of Dialectical Materialism* (London: Verso, 2014), 321–324.
6. Žižek, *Less Than Nothing*, 123.
7. Ibid.
8. Ibid., 265–266, 310.
9. Slavoj Žižek, *The Indivisible Remainder: An Essay on Schelling and Related Matters* (London: Verso, 1996), 73; Slavoj Žižek, "Preface: Burning the Bridges," in *The Žižek Reader*, ed. Elizabeth Wright and Edmond Wright (Oxford: Blackwell, 1999), ix; Slavoj Žižek, "Liberation Hurts: An Interview with Slavoj Žižek [with Eric Dean Rasmussen]" (2003), www.electronicbookreview.com/thread/endconstruction/desublimation; Slavoj Žižek and Glyn Daly, *Conversations with Žižek* (Cambridge: Polity, 2004), 61, 64–65, 135; Žižek, *Less Than Nothing*, 492–493, 830; Adrian Johnston, *Žižek's Ontology: A Transcendental Materialist Theory of Subjectivity* (Evanston, IL: Northwestern University Press, 2008), 105, 109, 126, 166, 181–194.
10. Žižek, *Less Than Nothing*, 127–128.
11. G. W. F. Hegel, *Faith and Knowledge*, trans. Walter Cerf and H. S. Harris (Albany: State University of New York Press, 1977), 67, 73, 76–78; G. W. F. Hegel, *Philosophy of Mind: Part Three of the Encyclopedia of the Philosophical Sciences with the Zusätze*, trans. William Wallace and A. V. Miller (Oxford: Oxford University Press, 1971), §467 (226); G. W. F. Hegel, *Elements of the Philosophy of Right*, ed. Allen W. Wood, trans. H. B. Nisbet (Cambridge: Cambridge University Press, 1991), §6 (39–40), §§135–137 (162–165); G. W. F. Hegel, *Lectures on the History of Philosophy*, vol. 3, trans. E. S. Haldane and Frances H. Simson (New York: Humanities, 1955), 460–461, 471–474.
12. Žižek, *Less Than Nothing*, 209–210.

5. BARTLEBY BY NATURE

13. J. G. Fichte, "Review of *Aenesidemus*," in *Fichte: Early Philosophical Writings*, ed. and trans. Daniel Breazeale (Ithaca: Cornell University Press, 1988), 64, 75; J. G. Fichte, "Concerning the Concept of the *Wissenschaftslehre* or, of So-Called 'Philosophy,'" *Fichte*, 126; J. G. Fichte, "Outline of the Distinctive Character of the *Wissenschaftslehre* with Respect to the Theoretical Faculty," in *Fichte*, 267; J. G. Fichte, "A Comparison Between Prof. Schmid's System and the *Wissenschaftslehre*," in *Fichte*, 328; J. G. Fichte, *The Science of Knowledge*, trans. Peter Heath and John Lachs (Cambridge: Cambridge University Press, 1982), 40–42, 93, 96–98; J. G. Fichte, *The Vocation of Man*, trans. William Smith (La Salle, IL: Open Court, 1965), 70; Dieter Henrich, "Fichte's Original Insight," trans. David R. Lachterman, in *Contemporary German Philosophy*, ed. Darrel E. Christensen, Manfred Riedel, Robert Spaemann, Reiner Wiehl, and Wolfgang Wieland (University Park: Pennsylvania State University Press, 1982), 25–26, 48.

14. Žižek, *Less Than Nothing*, 214.

15. Ibid., 649.

16. Žižek, *Absolute Recoil*, 187–188, 191–192.

17. Slavoj Žižek, *Disparities* (London: Bloomsbury, 2016), 87.

18. Immanuel Kant, *Critique of Pure Reason*, trans. Paul Guyer and Allen Wood (Cambridge: Cambridge University Press, 1998), B156 (259), A346/B404 (414), A350–351 (416–417).

19. Immanuel Kant, *Groundwork of the Metaphysics of Morals*, in *Practical Philosophy*, trans. and ed. Mary J. Gregor (Cambridge: Cambridge University Press, 1996), 61–62; Immanuel Kant, *Critique of Practical Reason*, in *Practical Philosophy*, 257–258; Johnston, *Žižek's Ontology*, 63–64.

20. Žižek, *Less Than Nothing*, 147–148, 161–163, 169, 174–175.

21. Ibid., 149.

22. Quentin Meillassoux, *After Finitude: An Essay on the Necessity of Contingency*, trans. Ray Brassier (London: Continuum, 2008), 53, 91–92; Adrian Johnston, *Prolegomena to Any Future Materialism*, vol. 1, *The Outcome of Contemporary French Philosophy* (Evanston, IL: Northwestern University Press, 2013), 150.

23. Žižek, *Less Than Nothing*, 907.

24. Ibid., 185.

25. Ibid., 263.

26. Ibid., 264.

27. Žižek, *Absolute Recoil*, 18, 21.

28. Johnston, *Žižek's Ontology*, xxv, 65, 77–79, 92, 107, 111–113, 122, 148, 170–171, 179–180, 189, 208–209, 272–273, 285–287; Adrian Johnston, *Adventures in Transcendental Materialism: Dialogues with Contemporary Thinkers* (Edinburgh: Edinburgh University Press, 2014), 13–22; Adrian Johnston, *Prolegomena to Any Future Materialism*, vol. 2, *A Weak Nature Alone* (Evanston, IL: Northwestern University Press, 2018).

29. Žižek, *Less Than Nothing*, 282–284, 317.

30. Ibid., 461.

31. Ibid., 211–212.

32. Daniel C. Dennett, *Freedom Evolves* (New York: Viking, 2003), 85, 90–91, 93; Johnston, *Žižek's Ontology*, 204–208.

33. Johnston, *Adventures in Transcendental Materialism*, 13–22; Johnston, *Prolegomena to Any Future Materialism*, vol. 2.

34. G. W. F. Hegel, "The Spirit of Christianity and Its Fate," in *Early Theological Writings*, trans. T. M. Knox (Philadelphia: University of Pennsylvania Press, 1975), 234–237, 285–286; Hegel, *Faith and Knowledge*, 147; G. W. F. Hegel, *Phenomenology of Spirit*, trans. A. V. Miller (Oxford: Oxford University Press, 1977), 221–235, 392–393, 399–400, 403–404; Hegel, *Elements of the Philosophy of Right*, §13 (47); Hegel, *Lectures on the History of Philosophy*, 3:510; G. W. F. Hegel, "Review of Solger's *Posthumous Writings and Correspondence*," trans. Diana I. Behler, in *Miscellaneous Writings of G. W. F. Hegel*, ed. Jon Stewart (Evanston, IL: Northwestern University Press, 2002), 394–395; G. W. F. Hegel, "Review of Göschel's *Aphorisms*," trans. Clark Butler, in *Miscellaneous Writings of G. W. F. Hegel*, 410–411, 418.

35. Žižek, *Less Than Nothing*, 212–213.

36. Ibid., 213.

37. Ibid., 465–466.

38. *SE* 19:52.

39. Alenka Zupančič, *Ethics of the Real: Kant, Lacan* (London: Verso, 2000), 28, 39; Alenka Zupančič, *Das Reale einer Illusion: Kant und Lacan*, trans. Reiner Ansén (Frankfurt: Suhrkamp, 2001), 35, 46; Johnston, *Žižek's Ontology*, 102.

40. Johnston, *Žižek's Ontology*, 93–122.

41. Žižek, *Absolute Recoil*, 320–321.

42. Ibid., 321.

43. Žižek, *Less Than Nothing*, 553–554.

44. Žižek, *Absolute Recoil*, 318.

45. Henry Allison, *Kant's Theory of Freedom* (Cambridge: Cambridge University Press, 1990), 40; Henry Allison, "Spontaneity and Autonomy in Kant's Conception of the Self," in *The Modern Subject: Conceptions of the Self in Classical German Philosophy*, ed. Karl Ameriks and Dieter Sturma (Albany: State University of New York, 1995), 13; Johnston, *Žižek's Ontology*, 104.

46. Jacques Lacan, *The Seminar of Jacques Lacan*, book 7, *The Ethics of Psychoanalysis, 1959-1960*, ed. Jacques-Alain Miller, trans. Dennis Porter (New York: Norton, 1992), 14.

47. Harry G. Frankfurt, "Freedom of the Will and the Concept of a Person," *Journal of Philosophy* 68, no. 1 (January 14, 1971): 5–20; Adrian Johnston, "Drive Between Brain and Subject: An Immanent Critique of Lacanian Neuropsychoanalysis," special issue, "Spindel Supplement: Freudian Futures," *Southern Journal of Philosophy* 51 (2013): 81–82; Johnston, *Prolegomena to Any Future Materialism*, vol. 2.

48. Slavoj Žižek, *Le plus sublime des hystériques: Hegel passe* (Paris: Points Hors Ligne, 1988), 77; Slavoj Žižek, *The Sublime Object of Ideology* (London: Verso, 1989), 169; Johnston, *Žižek's Ontology*, 18–19, 146–148, 151–152, 160.

49. Žižek, *Disparities*, 104, 269.

50. G. W. F. Hegel, "The Philosophical Encyclopedia [for the Higher Class]," in *The Philosophical Propaedeutic*, ed. Michael George and Andrew Vincent, trans. A. V. Miller (Oxford: Blackwell, 1986), §51 (133); G. W. F. Hegel, *Science of Logic*, trans. A. V. Miller (London: George Allen and Unwin, 1969), 559; G. W. F. Hegel, *The Encyclopedia Logic: Part I of the Encyclopedia of the Philosophical Sciences with the Zusätze*, trans. T. F. Geraets, W. A. Suchting, and H. S. Harris (Indianapolis: Hackett, 1991), §§153–154 (227–230); G. W. F. Hegel, *Lectures on Logic: Berlin, 1831*, trans. Clark Butler (Bloomington: Indiana University Press, 2008), §§153–154 (167–168).

5. BARTLEBY BY NATURE

51. Slavoj Žižek, *Organs Without Bodies: On Deleuze and Consequences* (New York: Routledge, 2004), 137–138; Slavoj Žižek, *The Parallax View* (Cambridge: MIT Press, 2006), 240–241.

52. Benjamin Libet, *Mind Time: The Temporal Factor in Consciousness* (Cambridge: Harvard University Press, 2004), 42, 56, 66–67, 80–81, 101–102, 107.

53. Ibid., 139, 208.

54. Žižek, *The Sublime Object of Ideology*, 61–62; Slavoj Žižek, *The Metastases of Enjoyment: Six Essays on Woman and Causality* (London: Verso, 1994), 35–36; Slavoj Žižek, "Da capo senza fine," in *Contingency, Hegemony, Universality: Contemporary Dialogues on the Left*, by Judith Butler, Ernesto Laclau, and Slavoj Žižek (London: Verso, 2000), 227; Slavoj Žižek, *The Fright of Real Tears: Krzysztof Kieślowski Between Theory and Post-Theory* (London: British Film Institute, 2001), 101; Slavoj Žižek, *For They Know Not What They Do: Enjoyment as a Political Factor*, 2nd ed. (London: Verso, 2002), 169; Slavoj Žižek, *À travers le réel: Entretiens avec Fabien Tarby* (Paris: Lignes, 2010), 47–58; Žižek, *Less Than Nothing*, 98, 217–223, 225, 227, 459–460, 467–469, 637–638; Žižek, *Absolute Recoil*, 26; Johnston, *Žižek's Ontology*, 126–128, 221.

55. Hegel, *Science of Logic*, 545, 549–550, 553; Hegel, *The Encyclopedia Logic*, §145 (219), §147 (221–222); Hegel, *Lectures on Logic*, §147 (159–161); Johnston, *Prolegomena to Any Future Materialism*, vol. 2.

56. SE 1:233; SE 2:133; SE 10:206; SE 12:149; Jacques Lacan, "Position of the Unconscious," in *Écrits: The First Complete Edition in English*, trans. Bruce Fink (New York: Norton, 2006), 711; Žižek, *For They Know Not What They Do*, 202; Adrian Johnston, *Time Driven: Metapsychology and the Splitting of the Drive* (Evanston, IL: Northwestern University Press, 2005), xxi, xxx, 9–10, 34–35, 47, 141, 193, 218–219, 226–227, 316.

57. Jacques Lacan, *Le Séminaire de Jacques Lacan*, book 15, *L'acte psychanalytique, 1967-1968* (unpublished typescript), sessions of November 15, 1967, November 22, 1967.

58. Jacques Lacan, *The Seminar of Jacques Lacan*, book 10, *Anxiety, 1962-1963*, ed. Jacques-Alain Miller, trans. A. R. Price (Cambridge: Polity, 2014), 317; Jacques Lacan, *Le Séminaire de Jacques Lacan*, book 14, *La logique du fantasme, 1966-1967* (unpublished typescript), session of June 7, 1967; Johnston, *Badiou, Žižek, and Political Transformations*, 117.

59. Žižek, *For They Know Not What They Do*, 222; Slavoj Žižek, *In Defense of Lost Causes* (London: Verso, 2008), 314–315; Johnston, *Žižek's Ontology*, 120–121; Johnston, *Badiou, Žižek, and Political Transformations*, 117, 148.

60. Žižek, *Absolute Recoil*, 408.

61. Lacan, *Le Séminaire de Jacques Lacan*, book 14, sessions of February 15, 1967, February 22, 1967; Lacan, *Le Séminaire de Jacques Lacan*, book 15, session of November 29, 1967; Jacques Lacan, "L'acte psychanalytique: Compte rendu du Séminaire 1967-1968," in *Autres écrits*, ed. Jacques-Alain Miller (Paris: Seuil, 2001), 375.

62. Johnston, *Badiou, Žižek, and Political Transformations*, 110.

63. Alain Badiou, *Peut-on penser la politique?* (Paris: Seuil, 1985), 101, 107; Alain Badiou, "Six propriétés de la vérité II," *Ornicar?* 33 (April-June 1985): 123, 141; Alain Badiou, "On a Finally Objectless Subject," trans. Bruce Fink, in *Who Comes After the Subject?*, ed. Peter Connor and Jean-Luc Nancy (New York: Routledge, 1991), 31; Alain Badiou, "La vérité: Forçage et innommable," in *Conditions* (Paris: Seuil, 1992),

5. BARTLEBY BY NATURE

206–207; Alain Badiou, *Being and Event*, trans. Oliver Feltham (London: Continuum, 2005), 206, 209, 397–398; Johnston, *Badiou, Žižek, and Political Transformations*, 33, 58–60.

64. Johnston, *Badiou, Žižek, and Political Transformations*, 148–150.

65. Ibid., 150–156.

66. Alain Badiou, *Ethics: An Essay on the Understanding of Evil*, trans. Peter Hallward (London: Verso, 2001), 43; Johnston, *Badiou, Žižek, and Political Transformations*, 114.

67. Johnston, *Žižek's Ontology*, 108, 142–143, 165–167, 171–172, 178, 180, 189, 208; Johnston, *Adventures in Transcendental Materialism*, 13–22, 111–183; Adrian Johnston, "Slavoj Žižek," in *The Blackwell Companion to Continental Philosophy*, ed. William Schroeder, 2nd ed. (Oxford: Blackwell, 2018).

68. Žižek, *Less Than Nothing*, 744.

69. V. I. Lenin, *Materialism and Empirio-Criticism* (Peking: Foreign Languages, 1972), 338, 342.

70. Žižek, *Less Than Nothing*, 915.

71. David Hume, *An Enquiry Concerning Human Understanding*, ed. Eric Steinberg, 2nd ed. (Indianapolis: Hackett, 1993), 53–69; John Locke, *An Essay Concerning Human Understanding in Two Volumes*, vol. 1, ed. Alexander Campbell Fraser (New York: Dover, 1959), 315–328.

72. Adrian Johnston, "The Weakness of Nature: Hegel, Freud, Lacan, and Negativity Materialized," in *Hegel and the Infinite: Religion, Politics, and Dialectic*, ed. Slavoj Žižek, Clayton Crockett, and Creston Davis (New York: Columbia University Press, 2011), 159–179; Adrian Johnston, "Reflections of a Rotten Nature: Hegel, Lacan, and Material Negativity," special issue, "Science and Thought," ed. Frank Ruda and Jan Voelker, *Filozofski Vestnik* 33, no. 2 (2012): 23–52; Adrian Johnston, "Points of Forced Freedom: Eleven (More) Theses on Materialism," *Speculations: A Journal of Speculative Realism* 4 (June 2013): 95–96; Johnston, "Drive Between Brain and Subject," 48–84; Johnston, *Prolegomena to Any Future Materialism*, vol. 2.

73. Žižek, *The Indivisible Remainder*, 189–236; Žižek, *The Parallax View*, 165–173; Johnston, *Žižek's Ontology*, 195–203.

74. Žižek, *Less Than Nothing*, 918–919.

75. Ibid., 920.

76. Ibid., 921.

77. Adrian Johnston, "A Critique of Natural Economy: Quantum Physics with Žižek," in *Žižek Now*, ed. Jamil Khader and Molly Anne Rothenberg (Cambridge: Polity, 2013), 103–120; Johnston, *Adventures in Transcendental Materialism*, 165–183.

78. F. W. J. Schelling, *Ideas for a Philosophy of Nature*, trans. Errol E. Harris and Peter Heath (Cambridge: Cambridge University Press, 1988), 30–31, 33–35, 53–54; F. W. J. Schelling, *First Outline of a System of the Philosophy of Nature*, trans. Keith R. Peterson (Albany: State University of New York Press, 2004), 48, 215–217, 229–231; F. W. J. Schelling, "Presentation of My System of Philosophy," in *The Philosophical Rupture Between Fichte and Schelling*, by J. G. Fichte and F. W. J. Schelling, ed. and trans. Michael G. Vater and David W. Wood (Albany: State University of New York Press, 2012), 153, 167, 194, 199; F. W. J. Schelling, "System of Philosophy in General and of the Philosophy of Nature in Particular," in *Idealism and the Endgame of Theory: Three Essays by*

5. BARTLEBY BY NATURE

F. W. J. Schelling, trans. Thomas Pfau (Albany: State University of New York Press, 1994), 192.

79. Johnston, *Adventures in Transcendental Materialism*, 139–183; Ernst Bloch, *Subjekt-Objekt: Erläuterungen zu Hegel* (Frankfurt: Suhrkamp, 1977), 189–190, 194–196.

80. Johnston, "A Critique of Natural Economy," 103–120; Johnston, *Adventures in Transcendental Materialism*, 165–183.

81. F. W. J. Schelling, *Philosophical Investigations Into the Essence of Human Freedom*, trans. Jeff Love and Johannes Schmidt (Albany: State University of New York Press, 2006), 4, 11–13, 16–17, 21–22, 29, 31–35, 48, 68–69, 73; F. W. J. Schelling, "Stuttgart Seminars," in *Idealism and the Endgame of Theory*, 202, 207, 213, 225; F. W. J. Schelling, *Clara, or, On Nature's Connection to the Spirit World*, trans. Fiona Steinkamp (Albany: State University of New York Press, 2002), 28; F. W. J. Schelling, *The Ages of the World: Third Version (c. 1815)*, trans. Jason M. Wirth (Albany: State University of New York Press, 2000), 56–59, 61–62, 64, 77–78.

82. F. W. J. Schelling, "Of the I as the Principle of Philosophy, or On the Unconditional in Human Knowledge," in *The Unconditional in Human Knowledge: Four Early Essays (1794-1796)*, trans. Fritz Marti (Lewisburg: Bucknell University Press, 1980), 69; F. W. J. Schelling, "Treatise Explicatory of the Idealism in the *Science of Knowledge*," in *Idealism and the Endgame of Theory*, 92–93; Schelling, *Ideas for a Philosophy of Nature*, 50–51; F. W. J. Schelling, "On the World-Soul," trans. Iain Hamilton Grant, *Collapse: Philosophical Research and Development* 6 (January 2010): 70–71, 92; Schelling, *First Outline of a System of the Philosophy of Nature*, 17, 34–35, 48, 116–117, 122–123, 196, 202–203, 205, 211, 218; F. W. J. Schelling, *System of Transcendental Idealism*, trans. Peter Heath (Charlottesville: University Press of Virginia, 1978), 17; F. W. J. Schelling, "J. G. Fichte/F. W. J. Schelling: Correspondence (1800-1802): Schelling in Jena to Fichte in Berlin, November 19, 1800," in *Fichte and Schelling, The Philosophical Rupture Between Fichte and Schelling*, 44–45; Schelling, "Presentation of My System of Philosophy," 142–143, 145, 149, 203–204; F. W. J. Schelling, "Further Presentations from the System of Philosophy [Extract]," in *Fichte and Schelling, The Philosophical Rupture Between Fichte and Schelling*, 218–219; F. W. J. Schelling, *On University Studies*, trans. E. S. Morgan (Athens: Ohio University Press, 1966), 65; F. W. J. Schelling, *Bruno, or On the Natural and the Divine Principle of Things*, trans. Michael G. Vater (Albany: State University of New York Press, 1984), 125, 202–203; Schelling, "System of Philosophy in General and of the Philosophy of Nature in Particular," 186; F. W. J. Schelling, *Philosophy and Religion*, trans. Klaus Ottmann (Putnam: Spring, 2010), 8, 14.

83. Jean Hyppolite, *Genesis and Structure of Hegel's Phenomenology of Spirit*, trans. Samuel Cherniak and John Heckman (Evanston, IL: Northwestern University Press, 1974), 7, 42, 543, 582, 585.

84. Žižek, *The Indivisible Remainder*, 220–228, 231.

85. Žižek, *Organs Without Bodies*, 137–138.

86. Ibid., 138.

87. Schelling, "Stuttgart Seminars," 200, 205–207; Schelling, *Clara*, 28, 78; Schelling, *The Ages of the World*, 22–23, 38–39, 85, 100; SE 1:231, 270–271, 279; SE 3:220, 255; Žižek, *Le plus sublime des hystériques*, 221–224, 229; Žižek, *The Sublime Object of Ideology*, 168; Slavoj Žižek, *Enjoy Your Symptom!: Jacques Lacan in Hollywood and Out* (New York: Routledge, 1992), 35–36; Žižek, *The Indivisible Remainder*, 13, 33–34, 47,

5. BARTLEBY BY NATURE

53–54, 72; Slavoj Žižek, "The Abyss of Freedom," in *The Abyss of Freedom/Ages of the World*, by Slavoj Žižek and F. W. J. Schelling (Ann Arbor: University of Michigan Press, 1997), 14–15, 29–31, 33, 37, 41; Slavoj Žižek, *The Ticklish Subject: The Absent Centre of Political Ontology* (London: Verso, 1999), 318; Slavoj Žižek, *The Fragile Absolute, or Why Is the Christian Legacy Worth Fighting For?* (London: Verso, 2000), 73, 78, 93–94; Slavoj Žižek, *On Belief* (New York: Routledge, 2001), 147; Žižek, *The Fright of Real Tears*, 151; Žižek, *Organs Without Bodies*, 25–26; Žižek, *Less Than Nothing*, 273–275; Žižek and Daly, *Conversations with Žižek*, 166.

88. Žižek, *Absolute Recoil*, 194.
89. Johnston, *Žižek's Ontology*, 90–122.
90. Bruno Bosteels, "Badiou Without Žižek," special issue, "The Philosophy of Alain Badiou," ed. Matthew Wilkens, *Polygraph: An International Journal of Culture and Politics* 17 (2005): 241–242.
91. Žižek, *The Parallax View*, 240–241.
92. G. W. F. Hegel, *Philosophie des Geistes, Jenaer Systementwürfe III: Naturphilosophie und Philosophie des Geistes*, ed. Rolf-Peter Horstmann (Hamburg: Felix Meiner, 1987), 171–185; Hegel, *Phenomenology of Spirit*, 18–19, 21; G. W. F. Hegel, "The Science of Laws, Morals and Religion [for the Lower Class]," in *The Philosophical Propaedeutic*, §1 (4); G. W. F. Hegel, "Logic [for the Middle Class]," in *The Philosophical Propaedeutic*, §3 (75); Hegel, *The Encyclopedia Logic*, §§1–3 (24–27), §§8–9 (32–33), §20 (49–51), §24 (58); Hegel, *Philosophy of Mind*, §381 (11–15), §408 (128), §410 (140–141), §§413–414 (154–155), §422 (162–163).
93. Kant, *Critique of Pure Reason*, A162/B202–A218/B265 (286–321).
94. Wilfrid Sellars, *Empiricism and the Philosophy of Mind* (Cambridge: Harvard University Press, 1997), 14, 45.
95. SE 1:296–297, 306–307, 312, 317–319; SE 14:194; SE 18:26–32, 55–56, 58, 63; SE 19:19–26, 230, 238; Slavoj Žižek, "The Thing from Inner Space," in *Sexuation*, ed. Renata Salecl (Durham: Duke University Press, 2000), 216–259; Johnston, *Žižek's Ontology*, 160–161.
96. Antonio Damasio, *Descartes' Error: Emotion, Reason, and the Human Brain* (New York: Avon, 1994), 173–175, 185, 187–189, 197–198, 212–219; Antonio Damasio, *Looking for Spinoza: Joy, Sorrow, and the Feeling Brain* (New York: Harcourt, 2003), 148–150; Antonio Damasio, *Self Comes to Mind: Constructing the Conscious Brain* (New York: Pantheon, 2010), 9.
97. Libet, *Mind Time*, 6, 17, 86–87, 163, 184.
98. Ibid., 172–177.
99. Žižek, *Less Than Nothing*, 239, 374, 379–380, 399–401, 416, 459, 561–562, 595–597, 707–708, 726–727, 729–736, 905–906; Johnston, *Adventures in Transcendental Materialism*, 13–22, 111–183.
100. Libet, *Mind Time*, 28, 56, 66–67, 107.
101. Ibid., 71–72, 120–122, 208.
102. Ibid., 118–119.
103. Ibid., 115–116.
104. Ibid., 107.
105. Žižek, *Less Than Nothing*, 285–286.
106. Ibid., 185–186, 188–189.

107. Adrian Johnston, "Humanity, That Sickness: Louis Althusser and the Helplessness of Psychoanalysis," special issue, "*Reading Capital* and *For Marx*: 50 Years Later," ed. Frank Ruda and Agon Hamza, *Crisis and Critique* 2, no. 2 (2015): 248–253.

108. Žižek, *Less Than Nothing*, 333–334.

109. Ibid., 65, 414, 730, 764; Johnston, *Adventures in Transcendental Materialism*, 13–22, 111–183.

110. Johnston, *Time Driven*, xxxvi–xxxviii, 340–341; Johnston, *Žižek's Ontology*, xxv, 65, 77, 107–108, 113, 170–171, 179–180, 189, 208–209, 212–213, 269–287; Johnston, "The Weakness of Nature," 159–179; Johnston, "Reflections of a Rotten Nature," 23–52; Johnston, "Points of Forced Freedom," 93–97; Johnston, "Drive Between Brain and Subject," 48–84; Adrian Johnston, "An Interview with Adrian Johnston on Transcendental Materialism [with Peter Gratton]," *Society and Space* (October 2013), http://societyandspace.com/2013/10/07/interview-with-adrian-johnston-on-transcendental-materialism/; Johnston, *Adventures in Transcendental Materialism*, 13–22, 111–183; Johnston, *Prolegomena to Any Future Materialism*, vol. 2.

111. Johnston, *Prolegomena to Any Future Materialism*, vol. 1, 59–77; Johnston, "An Interview with Adrian Johnston on Transcendental Materialism [with Peter Gratton]."

Conclusion

1. Slavoj Žižek, *Looking Awry: An Introduction to Jacques Lacan Through Popular Culture* (Cambridge: MIT Press, 1991), 37; Slavoj Žižek, *The Indivisible Remainder: An Essay on Schelling and Related Matters* (London: Verso, 1996), 121–122; Slavoj Žižek, "Lacan Between Cultural Studies and Cognitivism," in *Umbr(a): Science and Truth*, ed. Theresa Giron (Buffalo: Center for the Study of Psychoanalysis and Culture, State University of New York at Buffalo, 2000), 29; Slavoj Žižek, "Liberation Hurts: An Interview with Slavoj Žižek [with Eric Dean Rasmussen]," 2003, www.electronicbookreview.com/thread/endconstruction/desublimation; Slavoj Žižek, *The Puppet and the Dwarf: The Perverse Core of Christianity* (Cambridge: MIT Press, 2003), 79–80; Slavoj Žižek and Glyn Daly, *Conversations with Žižek* (Cambridge: Polity, 2004), 61, 63–65; Adrian Johnston, *Žižek's Ontology: A Transcendental Materialist Theory of Subjectivity* (Evanston, IL: Northwestern University Press, 2008), 109, 126, 166–167, 178–210, 222–223, 236–238.

2. Slavoj Žižek, *Less Than Nothing: Hegel and the Shadow of Dialectical Materialism* (London: Verso, 2012), 830; Slavoj Žižek, *Absolute Recoil: Towards a New Foundation of Dialectical Materialism* (London: Verso, 2014), 89.

3. Žižek, *Less Than Nothing*, 492.

4. Ibid., 492–493.

5. Ibid., 496.

6. G. W. F. Hegel, *Science of Logic*, trans. A. V. Miller (London: George Allen and Unwin, 1969), 131–136, 139–154; G. W. F. Hegel, *The Encyclopedia Logic: Part I of the Encyclopedia of the Philosophical Sciences with the Zusätze*, trans. T. F. Geraets, W. A. Suchting,

and H. S. Harris (Indianapolis: Hackett, 1991), §§93–95 (149–151); G. W. F. Hegel, *Lectures on the History of Philosophy*, vol. 3, trans. E. S. Haldane and Frances H. Simson (New York: Humanities, 1955), 461–464.

7. Immanuel Kant, *Critique of Practical Reason*, in *Practical Philosophy*, trans. and ed. Mary J. Gregor (Cambridge: Cambridge University Press, 1996), 238–247.

8. Immanuel Kant, *Groundwork of the Metaphysics of Morals*, in *Practical Philosophy*, 49–55, 57–60, 99; Kant, *Critique of Practical Reason*, 203–204, 207, 209–210, 257–258; G. W. F. Hegel, *Phenomenology of Spirit*, trans. A. V. Miller (Oxford: Oxford University Press, 1977), 365–383.

9. Friedrich Schiller, *On the Aesthetic Education of Man*, trans. Reginald Snell (Mineola: Dover, 2004), 29, 31–32, 34, 48, 50, 68–69, 87, 97–99, 108–109, 113–115; G. W. F. Hegel, "Hegel to Schelling: Bern, April 16, 1795," in *Hegel: The Letters*, trans. Clark Butler and Christiane Seiler (Bloomington: Indiana University Press, 1984), 35–36; G. W. F. Hegel, "The Spirit of Christianity and Its Fate," in *Early Theological Writings*, trans. T. M. Knox (Philadelphia: University of Pennsylvania Press, 1975), 211–215, 244; H. S. Harris, *Hegel's Development*, vol. 1, *Toward the Sunlight, 1770-1801* (Oxford: Oxford University Press, 1972), 81, 253–254; H. S. Harris, *Hegel's Development*, vol. 2, *Night Thoughts (Jena 1801-1806)* (Oxford: Oxford University Press, 1983), 15–16, 404, 554, 561; Frederick Beiser, *Hegel* (New York: Routledge, 2005), 39–40, 47, 87, 113.

10. Kant, *Critique of Practical Reason*, 75–92.
11. Schiller, *On the Aesthetic Education of Man*, 74, 79–80, 112.
12. Žižek, *Less Than Nothing*, 638–639; Žižek, *Absolute Recoil*, 372–373.
13. Žižek, *Less Than Nothing*, 550.
14. Ibid., 496, 662; Slavoj Žižek, *Disparities* (London: Bloomsbury, 2016), 327.
15. Žižek, *Less Than Nothing*, 497.
16. Ibid., 638–639.
17. Ibid., 497–498.
18. Ibid., 498.
19. Žižek, *Less Than Nothing*, 550, 639–640; Žižek, *Absolute Recoil*, 373–374.
20. Žižek, *Absolute Recoil*, 89.
21. Ibid., 387; Žižek, *Disparities*, 38, 82–83; Adrian Johnston, *Adventures in Transcendental Materialism: Dialogues with Contemporary Thinkers* (Edinburgh: Edinburgh University Press, 2014), 13–64.
22. Žižek, *Less Than Nothing*, 499.
23. Jacques Lacan, "Some Reflections on the Ego," *International Journal of Psycho-Analysis* 34 (1953): 11–17.
24. Žižek, *Absolute Recoil*, 34.
25. Ibid.
26. Žižek, *Less Than Nothing*, 18.
27. Ibid., 440–442, 461–463, 484–485, 490, 492–493.
28. Žižek, *Disparities*, 17.
29. Žižek, *Less Than Nothing*, 499.
30. Ibid., 661.
31. Ibid., 547.
32. Ibid.

33. Žižek, *Less Than Nothing*, 499, 549, 639–640, 884; Eric L. Santner, *On the Psychotheology of Everyday Life: Reflections on Freud and Rosenzweig* (Chicago: University of Chicago Press, 2001), 8, 22, 36–37.

34. Žižek, *Disparities*, 71.

35. Žižek, *Less Than Nothing*, 131–132.

36. Žižek, *Absolute Recoil*, 122–124.

37. Adrian Johnston, "The Weakness of Nature: Hegel, Freud, Lacan, and Negativity Materialized," in *Hegel and the Infinite: Religion, Politics, and Dialectic*, ed. Slavoj Žižek, Clayton Crockett, and Creston Davis (New York: Columbia University Press, 2011), 159–179; Johnston, *Adventures in Transcendental Materialism*, 139–164.

38. Jonathan Lear, *Happiness, Death, and the Remainder of Life* (Cambridge: Harvard University Press, 2000), 85.

39. Johnston, "The Weakness of Nature," 160.

40. Ibid.

41. Ibid., 162.

42. Johnston, *Adventures in Transcendental Materialism*, 65–107.

43. Adrian Johnston, "Intimations of Freudian Mortality: The Enigma of Sexuality and the Constitutive Blind Spots of Freud's Self-Analysis," *Journal for Lacanian Studies* 3, no. 2 (2005): 222–246; Adrian Johnston, "Sextimacy: Freud, Mortality, and a Reconsideration of the Role of Sexuality in Psychoanalysis," in *Sexuality and Psychoanalysis: Philosophical Criticisms*, ed. Jens De Vleminck and Eran Dorfman (Leuven: Leuven University Press, 2010), 35–59.

44. Žižek, *Less Than Nothing*, 499, 639, 884.

45. Žižek *Disparities*, 31.

46. Adrian Johnston, *Prolegomena to Any Future Materialism*, vol. 2, *A Weak Nature Alone* (Evanston, IL: Northwestern University Press, 2018).

47. Adrian Johnston, "Transcendentalism in Hegel's Wake: A Reply to Timothy M. Hackett and Benjamin Berger," special issue, "Schelling: Powers of the Idea," ed. Benjamin Berger, *Pli: The Warwick Journal of Philosophy* 26 (Fall 2014): 226–228.

48. Friedrich Engels, *Socialism: Utopian and Scientific*, trans. Edward Aveling (New York: International, 1975), 61.

49. Adrian Johnston, "Confession of a Weak Reductionist: Responses to Some Recent Criticisms of My Materialism," in *Neuroscience and Critique: Exploring the Limits of the Neurological Turn*, ed. Jan De Vos and Ed Pluth (New York: Routledge, 2015), 141–170.

50. Adrian Johnston, "Misfelt Feelings: Unconscious Affect Between Psychoanalysis, Neuroscience, and Philosophy," in *Self and Emotional Life: Philosophy, Psychoanalysis, and Neuroscience*, by Adrian Johnston and Catherine Malabou (New York: Columbia University Press, 2013), 174–178; Adrian Johnston, *Prolegomena to Any Future Materialism*, vol. 1, *The Outcome of Contemporary French Philosophy* (Evanston, IL: Northwestern University Press, 2013), 75; Johnston, *Prolegomena to Any Future Materialism*, vol. 2; Johnston, *Adventures in Transcendental Materialism*, 142, 146, 181–182; Adrian Johnston, "Second Natures in Dappled Worlds: John McDowell, Nancy Cartwright, and Hegelian-Lacanian Materialism," in *Umbr(a): The Worst*, ed. Matthew Rigilano and Kyle Fetter (Buffalo: Center for the Study of Psychoanalysis and Culture, State University of New York at Buffalo, 2011), 76, 83; Adrian Johnston, "Points of Forced

Freedom: Eleven (More) Theses on Materialism," *Speculations: A Journal of Speculative Realism* 4 (June 2013): 96; Adrian Johnston, "An Interview with Adrian Johnston on Transcendental Materialism [with Peter Gratton]," *Society and Space* (October 2013), http://societyandspace.com/2013/10/07/interview-with-adrian-johnston-on-transcendental-materialism/; Adrian Johnston, "Reflections of a Rotten Nature: Hegel, Lacan, and Material Negativity," special issue, "Science and Thought," ed. Frank Ruda and Jan Voelker, *Filozofski Vestnik* 33, no. 2 (2012): 47–50; Johnston, "Transcendentalism in Hegel's Wake," 208–209.

51. Adrian Johnston, "Drive Between Brain and Subject: An Immanent Critique of Lacanian Neuropsychoanalysis," special issue, "Spindel Supplement: Freudian Futures," *Southern Journal of Philosophy* 51 (2013): 48–84; Johnston, "Confession of a Weak Reductionist," 141–170; Adrian Johnston, "The Late Innate: Jean Laplanche, Jaak Panksepp, and the Distinction Between Sexual Drives and Instincts," in *Inheritance in Psychoanalysis*, ed. James Godley (Albany: State University of New York Press, 2018); Johnston, *Prolegomena to Any Future Materialism*, vol. 2.

52. Johnston, "Reflections of a Rotten Nature," 23–52; Johnston, "Drive Between Brain and Subject," 48–84; Johnston, "Confession of a Weak Reductionist," 141–170; Johnston, "The Late Innate"; Johnston, *Prolegomena to Any Future Materialism*, vol. 2.

53. Gilles Deleuze, "Coldness and Cruelty," in *Masochism: Coldness and Cruelty and Venus in Furs*, by Gilles Deleuze and Leopold Sacher-Masoch, trans. Jean McNeil (New York: Zone, 1991), 54.

54. Johnston, "Drive Between Brain and Subject," 48–84.

55. Ibid., 48–84; Johnston, "Confession of a Weak Reductionist," 141–170; Johnston, "The Late Innate"; Johnston, *Prolegomena to Any Future Materialism*, vol. 2.

56. F. W. J. Schelling, *Über das Wesen der menschlichen Freiheit* (Stuttgart: Reclam, 1964), 88; F. W. J. Schelling, *Philosophical Investigations Into the Essence of Human Freedom*, trans. Jeff Love and Johannes Schmidt (Albany: State University of New York Press, 2006), 40.

57. Schelling, *Über das Wesen der menschlichen Freiheit*, 57; Schelling, *Philosophical Investigations Into the Essence of Human Freedom*, 18.

58. Johnston, *Prolegomena to Any Future Materialism*, vol. 2.

59. Olaf Breidbach, *Das Organische in Hegels Denken: Studie zur Naturphilosophie und Biologie um 1800* (Würzburg: Königshausen and Neumann, 1982), 267.

60. Jacques Lacan, "Impromptu at Vincennes," trans. Jeffrey Mehlman, in *Television/A Challenge to the Psychoanalytic Establishment*, ed. Joan Copjec (New York: Norton, 1990), 126.

61. Plato, *Republic*, trans. G. M. A. Grube, rev. C. D. C. Reeve, in *Plato: Complete Works*, ed. John M. Cooper (Indianapolis: Hackett, 1997), lines 368c–369b (1007–1008).

62. Adrian Johnston, "Jacques Lacan (1901–1981)," in *Stanford Encyclopedia of Philosophy*, 2013, http://plato.stanford.edu/entries/lacan/.

63. Ibid.

64. Žižek, *Less Than Nothing*, 499, 549, 639–640, 884; Žižek, *Absolute Recoil*, 118–119.

65. Žižek, *Less Than Nothing*, 294.

66. Ibid., 138–139.

67. Ibid., 455–456.

68. Ibid., 492–493.

69. Ibid., 482–483.
70. Ibid., 483.
71. Jacques Lacan, *Le Séminaire de Jacques Lacan*, book 14, *La logique du fantasme, 1966-1967* (unpublished typescript), sessions of April 19, 1967, June 14, 1967; Jacques Lacan, *Le Séminaire de Jacques Lacan*, book 16, *D'un Autre à l'autre, 1968-1969*, ed. Jacques-Alain Miller (Paris: Seuil, 2006), 134, 218–220, 245, 257; Jacques Lacan, *Le Séminaire de Jacques Lacan*, book 21, *Les non-dupes errent, 1973-1974* (unpublished typescript), session of February 19, 1974.
72. Slavoj Žižek, *The Metastases of Enjoyment: Six Essays on Woman and Causality* (London: Verso, 1994), 47; Slavoj Žižek, *Organs Without Bodies: On Deleuze and Consequences* (New York: Routledge, 2004), 12, 33–93; Slavoj Žižek, *In Defense of Lost Causes* (London: Verso, 2008), 324, 396.
73. Gilles Deleuze, *Difference and Repetition*, trans. Paul Patton (New York: Columbia University Press, 1994), 17–18, 115, 274, 286, 289.
74. Gilles Deleuze, *La logique du sens* (Paris: Minuit, 1969), 378; Gilles Deleuze, *The Logic of Sense*, ed. Constantin V. Boundas, trans. Mark Lester with Charles Stivale (New York: Columbia University Press, 1990), 326.
75. Deleuze, "Coldness and Cruelty," 30–31.
76. Lacan, *Le Séminaire de Jacques Lacan*, book 16, 227.
77. Deleuze, *The Logic of Sense*, 48–51, 66, 227–228; Gilles Deleuze, "How Do We Recognize Structuralism?," in *Desert Islands, and Other Texts, 1953-1974*, ed. David Lapoujade, trans. Michael Taormina (New York: Semiotext[e], 2004), 170–192.
78. Žižek, *The Metastases of Enjoyment*, 131–132; Slavoj Žižek, *The Parallax View* (Cambridge: MIT Press, 2006), 122; Slavoj Žižek, *Living in the End Times* (London: Verso, 2010), 304–305.
79. Gilles Deleuze, "Le froid et le cruel," in *Présentation de Sacher-Masoch: Le froid et le cruel*, by Gilles Deleuze and Leopold Sacher-Masoch (Paris: Minuit, 1967), 96.
80. Deleuze, "Coldness and Cruelty," 111–121.
81. Deleuze, *Difference and Repetition*, 18–19, 111, 289.
82. Žižek, *Less Than Nothing*, 884.
83. Žižek, *Absolute Recoil*, 372–373.
84. Ibid., 373–374.
85. Slavoj Žižek, *Enjoy Your Symptom!: Jacques Lacan in Hollywood and Out* (New York: Routledge, 1992), 192–193; Žižek, *Organs Without Bodies*, 52; Žižek, *Less Than Nothing*, 368–369, 374, 376, 611–612, 985; Žižek, *Absolute Recoil*, 8, 12, 387–388, 397; Johnston, *Adventures in Transcendental Materialism*, 13–107.
86. Žižek, *Absolute Recoil*, 374.
87. Ibid.
88. Johnston, *Adventures in Transcendental Materialism*, 13–107.
89. Žižek, *Absolute Recoil*, 397.
90. Johnston, *Žižek's Ontology*, 269–287; Johnston, *Adventures in Transcendental Materialism*, 13–107, 111–138.
91. Žižek, *Less Than Nothing*, 378–379, 712; Žižek, *Absolute Recoil*, 385, 391, 393–394, 410–415.
92. Žižek, *Absolute Recoil*, 207.
93. Ibid., 225–226.

94. Johnston, "Reflections of a Rotten Nature," 23–52; Johnston, "Points of Forced Freedom," 95; Johnston, *Prolegomena to Any Future Materialism*, vol. 2.

95. Jacques Lacan, *The Seminar of Jacques Lacan*, book 8, *Transference, 1960–1961*, ed. Jacques-Alain Miller, trans. Bruce Fink (Cambridge: Polity, 2015), 348; Johnston, *Žižek's Ontology*, 212–213; Johnston, "Reflections of a Rotten Nature," 34–35; Johnston, *Adventures in Transcendental Materialism*, 129.

96. Herbert Marcuse, *Hegel's Ontology and the Theory of Historicity*, trans. Seyla Benhabib (Cambridge: MIT Press, 1987), 12.

97. Žižek, *Absolute Recoil*, 396.

98. Johnston, *Prolegomena to Any Future Materialism*, 1:59–77.

99. Johnston, "Points of Forced Freedom," 95–96; Johnston, "Drive Between Brain and Subject," 48–84; Johnston, *Prolegomena to Any Future Materialism*, vol. 2.

100. Žižek, *Absolute Recoil*, 224.

Bibliography

All citations of works by Sigmund Freud are references to his *Gesammelte Werke* (German) or *Standard Edition* (English). These are abbreviated as *GW* or *SE*, followed by the volume number and the page number (*GW/SE #:#*).

Allison, Henry. *Kant's Theory of Freedom*. Cambridge: Cambridge University Press, 1990.
———. *Kant's Transcendental Idealism: An Interpretation and Defense*. New Haven: Yale University Press, 1983.
———. "Spontaneity and Autonomy in Kant's Conception of the Self." In *The Modern Subject: Conceptions of the Self in Classical German Philosophy*, edited by Karl Ameriks and Dieter Sturma, 11–45. Albany: State University of New York, 1995.
Althusser, Louis. *22ᵉ congrès*. Paris: François Maspero, 1977.
———. *Ce qui ne peut plus durer dans le parti communiste*. Paris: François Maspero, 1978.
———. "Correspondence About 'Philosophy and Marxism.'" In *Philosophy of the Encounter: Later Writings, 1978–1987*, edited by François Matheron and Oliver Corpet, translated by G. M. Goshgarian, 208–250. London: Verso, 2006.
———. "Cremonini, Painter of the Abstract." In *Lenin and Philosophy and Other Essays*, translated by Ben Brewster, 157–166. New York: Monthly Review Press, 2001.
———. *Elements of Self-Criticism*. In *Essays in Self-Criticism*, translated by Grahame Locke, 101–161. London: New Left, 1976.
———. *Être marxiste en philosophie*. Edited by G. M. Goshgarian. Paris: Presses Universitaires de France, 2015.
———. "The Historical Task of Marxist Philosophy." In *The Humanist Controversy and Other Writings*, edited by François Matheron, translated by G. M. Goshgarian, 155–220. London: Verso, 2003.

———. "The Humanist Controversy." In *The Humanist Controversy and Other Writings*, edited by François Matheron, translated by G. M. Goshgarian, 221-305. London: Verso, 2003.

———. *Initiation à la philosophie pour les non-philosophes*. Edited by G. M. Goshgarian. Paris: Presses Universitaires de France, 2014.

———. "Man, That Night." In *The Spectre of Hegel: Early Writings*, translated by G. M. Goshgarian, 170-172. London: Verso, 1997.

———. "Marxism Today." Translated by James H. Kavanagh. In *Philosophy and the Spontaneous Philosophy of the Scientists and Other Essays*, edited by Gregory Elliott, 267-280. London: Verso, 1990.

———. "On Feuerbach." In *The Humanist Controversy and Other Writings*, edited by François Matheron, translated by G. M. Goshgarian, 85-154. London: Verso, 2003.

———. "Philosophy and Marxism: Interviews with Fernanda Navarro, 1984-87." In *Philosophy of the Encounter: Later Writings, 1978-1987*, edited by François Matheron and Oliver Corpet, translated by G. M. Goshgarian, 251-289. London: Verso, 2006.

———. "Portrait of the Materialist Philosopher." In *Philosophy of the Encounter: Later Writings, 1978-1987*, edited by François Matheron and Oliver Corpet, translated by G. M. Goshgarian, 290-291. London: Verso, 2006.

———. "Une question posée par Louis Althusser." In *Écrits philosophiques et politiques, Tome I*, edited by François Matheron, 345-356. Paris: Stock/IMEC, 1994.

———. *Reply to John Lewis*. In *Essays in Self-Criticism*, translated by Grahame Locke, 33-99. London: New Left Books, 1976.

———. "Réponse à une critique." In *Écrits philosophiques et politiques, Tome II*, edited by François Matheron, 351-391. Paris: Stock/IMEC, 1995.

———. "The Transformation of Philosophy." Translated by Thomas E. Lewis. In *Philosophy and the Spontaneous Philosophy of the Scientists and Other Essays*, edited by Gregory Elliott, 241-265. London: Verso, 1990.

———. "The Underground Current of the Materialism of the Encounter." In *Philosophy of the Encounter: Later Writings, 1978-1987*, edited by François Matheron and Oliver Corpet, translated by G. M. Goshgarian, 163-207. London: Verso, 2006.

Ameriks, Karl. "Hegel and Idealism." *Monist* 74, no. 3 (July 1991): 386-402.

———. "Recent Work on Hegel: The Rehabilitation of an Epistemologist?" *Philosophy and Phenomenological Research* 52 (1992): 177-202.

Bacon, Francis. "The Great Renewal." In *The New Organon*, edited by Lisa Jardine and Michael Silverthorne, 1-24. Cambridge: Cambridge University Press, 2000.

———. *The New Organon*. Edited by Lisa Jardine and Michael Silverthorne. Cambridge: Cambridge University Press, 2000.

Badiou, Alain. *The Adventure of French Philosophy*. Edited and translated by Bruno Bosteels. London: Verso, 2012.

———. *Beckett: L'increvable désir*. Paris: Hachette, 1995.

———. *Being and Event*. Translated by Oliver Feltham. London: Continuum, 2005.

———. "Can Change Be Thought?: A Dialogue with Alain Badiou [with Bruno Bosteels]." In *Alain Badiou: Philosophy and Its Conditions*, edited by Gabriel Riera, 237-261. Albany: State University of New York Press, 2005.

———. *Ethics: An Essay on the Understanding of Evil*. Translated by Peter Hallward. London: Verso, 2001.

BIBLIOGRAPHY

———. *Logics of Worlds: Being and Event, 2*. Translated by Alberto Toscano. London: Continuum, 2009.
———. "On a Finally Objectless Subject." Translated by Bruce Fink. In *Who Comes After the Subject?*, edited by Peter Connor and Jean-Luc Nancy, 24-32. New York: Routledge, 1991.
———. *Peut-on penser la politique?* Paris: Seuil, 1985.
———. *La République de Platon*. Paris: Fayard, 2012.
———. "Six propriétés de la vérité II." *Ornicar?* 33 (April-June 1985): 120-149.
———. "La vérité: Forçage et innommable." In *Conditions*, 196-212. Paris: Seuil, 1992.
Barbagallo, Ettore. "Selbstbewusstsein und ursprüngliche Erscheinung des Lebens bei Hegel—im Vergleich zur Autopoiesistheorie." In *Systemtheorie, Selbstorganisation und Dialektik: Zur Methodik der Hegelschen Naturphilosophie*, edited by Wolfgang Neuser and Sönke Roterberg, 93-117. Würzburg: Königshausen und Neumann, 2012.
Beiser, Frederick C. *The Fate of Reason: German Philosophy from Kant to Fichte*. Cambridge: Harvard University Press, 1987.
———. *German Idealism: The Struggle Against Subjectivism, 1781-1801*. Cambridge: Harvard University Press, 2002.
———. *Hegel*. New York: Routledge, 2005.
———. "Hegel, a Non-Metaphysician?: A Polemic." *Bulletin of the Hegel Society of Great Britain* 32 (1995): 1-13.
———. "Introduction: Hegel and the Problem of Metaphysics." In *The Cambridge Companion to Hegel*, edited by Frederick C. Beiser, 1-24. Cambridge: Cambridge University Press, 1993.
———. "Introduction: The Puzzling Hegel Renaissance." In *The Cambridge Companion to Hegel and Nineteenth-Century Philosophy*, edited by Frederick C. Beiser, 1-14. Cambridge: Cambridge University Press, 2008.
Bencivenga, Ermanno. *Hegel's Dialectical Logic*. Oxford: Oxford University Press, 2000.
Benjamin, Walter. "Theories of German Fascism." In *Selected Writings*, vol. 2, pt. 1, *1927-1930*, edited by Michael W. Jennings, Howard Eiland, and Gary Smith, translated by Rodney Livingstone et al., 312-321. Cambridge: Harvard University Press, 1999.
———. "Theses on the Philosophy of History." In *Illuminations: Essays and Reflections*, edited by Hannah Arendt, translated by Harry Zohn, 253-264. New York: Schocken, 1969.
Bienenstock, Myriam. *Politique du jeune Hegel: Iéna 1801-1806*. Paris: Presses Universitaires de France, 1992.
Bloch, Ernst. "Hegel und der Humor." In *Über Methode und System bei Hegel*, 136-140. Frankfurt: Suhrkamp, 1970.
———. *Subjekt-Objekt: Erläuterungen zu Hegel*. Frankfurt am Main: Suhrkamp, 1977.
———. "Über die Besonderheit bei Hegel." In *Über Methode und System bei Hegel*, 90-94. Frankfurt: Suhrkamp, 1970.
Bonsiepen, Wolfgang. *Die Begründung einer Naturphilosophie bei Kant, Schelling, Fries und Hegel*. Frankfurt: Klostermann, 1997.
Bosteels, Bruno. "Badiou Without Žižek." Special issue, "The Philosophy of Alain Badiou," edited by Matthew Wilkens. *Polygraph: An International Journal of Culture and Politics* 17 (2005): 221-244.

Bourgeois, Bernard. *Hegel à Francfort ou Judaïsme-Christianisme-Hegelianisme*. Paris: Vrin, 2000.
——. *La pensée politique de Hegel*. Paris: Presses Universitaires de France, 1969.
Bowman, Brady. *Hegel and the Metaphysics of Absolute Negativity*. Cambridge: Cambridge University Press, 2013.
Brandom, Robert B. *Tales of the Mighty Dead: Historical Essays in the Metaphysics of Intentionality*. Cambridge: Harvard University Press, 2002.
Breidbach, Olaf. *Das Organische in Hegels Denken: Studie zur Naturphilosophie und Biologie um 1800*. Würzburg: Königshausen and Neumann, 1982.
Bukharin, Nikolai. *Philosophical Arabesques*. Translated by Renfrey Clarke. New York: Monthly Review Press, 2005.
Burbidge, John W. *Hegel's Systematic Contingency*. Basingstoke: Palgrave Macmillan, 2007.
Chalmers, David J. *The Conscious Mind: In Search of a Fundamental Theory*. Oxford: Oxford University Press, 1997.
Damasio, Antonio. *Descartes' Error: Emotion, Reason, and the Human Brain*. New York: Avon, 1994.
——. *Looking for Spinoza: Joy, Sorrow, and the Feeling Brain*. New York: Harcourt, 2003.
——. *Self Comes to Mind: Constructing the Conscious Brain*. New York: Pantheon, 2010.
Deacon, Terrence W. *Incomplete Nature: How Mind Emerged From Matter*. New York: Norton, 2012.
Deleuze, Gilles. "Coldness and Cruelty." In *Masochism: Coldness and Cruelty and Venus in Furs*, by Gilles Deleuze and Leopold Sacher-Masoch, translated by Jean McNeil, 7–138. New York: Zone, 1991.
——. *Difference and Repetition*. Translated by Paul Patton. New York: Columbia University Press, 1994.
——. "Le froid et le cruel." In *Présentation de Sacher-Masoch: Le froid et le cruel*, by Gilles Deleuze and Leopold Sacher-Masoch, 13–115. Paris: Minuit, 1967.
——. "How Do We Recognize Structuralism?" In *Desert Islands, and Other Texts, 1953-1974*, edited by David Lapoujade, translated by Michael Taormina, 170–192. New York: Semiotext(e), 2004.
——. *The Logic of Sense*. Edited by Constantin V. Boundas, translated by Mark Lester with Charles Stivale. New York: Columbia University Press, 1990.
——. *La logique du sens*. Paris: Minuit, 1969.
Dennett, Daniel C. *Freedom Evolves*. New York: Viking, 2003.
Descartes, René. *Meditations on First Philosophy*. 3rd ed. Translated by Donald A. Cress. Indianapolis: Hackett, 1993.
DeVries, Willem A. *Hegel's Theory of Mental Activity: An Introduction to Theoretical Spirit*. Ithaca: Cornell University Press, 1988.
Dietzgen, Joseph. *Excursions of a Socialist Into the Domain of Epistemology*. Translated by Max Beer and Theodor Rothstein. 1887. http://marxists.org/archive/dietzgen/1887/epistemology.htm.
Doz, André. *La logique de Hegel et les problèmes traditionnels de l'ontologie*. Paris: Vrin, 1987.
Düsing, Klaus. *Das Problem der Subjektivität in Hegels Logik, Hegel-Studien, Beiheft 15*. Bonn: Bouvier, 1976.

BIBLIOGRAPHY

Elder, Crawford. *Appropriating Hegel*. Aberdeen: Aberdeen University Press, 1980.
Engels, Friedrich. *Anti-Dühring: Herr Eugen Dühring's Revolution in Science*. Moscow: Foreign Languages, 1959.
———. *Anti-Schelling*. 1841. http://marxists.org/archive/marx/works/1841/anti-schelling.
———. *Ludwig Feuerbach and the Outcome of Classical German Philosophy*. Translated by C. P. Dutt. New York: International, 1941.
———. "The Part Played by Labour in the Transition from Ape to Man." In *Dialectics of Nature*, translated and edited by Clemens Dutt, 279–296. New York: International, 1940.
———. *Socialism: Utopian and Scientific*. Translated by Edward Aveling. New York: International, 1975.
Fichte, J. G. "A Comparison Between Prof. Schmid's System and the *Wissenschaftslehre*." In *Fichte: Early Philosophical Writings*, edited and translated by Daniel Breazeale, 307–335. Ithaca: Cornell University Press, 1988.
———. "Concerning the Concept of the *Wissenschaftslehre* or, of So-called 'Philosophy.'" In *Fichte: Early Philosophical Writings*, edited and translated by Daniel Breazeale, 87–135. Ithaca: Cornell University Press, 1988.
———. "Outline of the Distinctive Character of the *Wissenschaftslehre* with Respect to the Theoretical Faculty." In *Fichte: Early Philosophical Writings*, edited and translated by Daniel Breazeale, 233–306. Ithaca: Cornell University Press, 1988.
———. "Review of *Aenesidemus*." In *Fichte: Early Philosophical Writings*, edited and translated by Daniel Breazeale, 53–77. Ithaca: Cornell University Press, 1988.
———. *The Science of Knowledge*. Translated by Peter Heath and John Lachs. Cambridge: Cambridge University Press, 1982.
———. "Selected Correspondence, 1790–1799." In *Fichte: Early Philosophical Writings*, edited and translated by Daniel Breazeale, 355–440. Ithaca: Cornell University Press, 1988.
———. *The Vocation of Man*. Translated by William Smith. La Salle, IL: Open Court, 1965.
Förster, Eckart. *The Twenty-Five Years of Philosophy: A Systematic Reconstruction*. Translated by Brady Bowman. Cambridge: Harvard University Press, 2012.
Frank, Manfred. *Der unendliche Mangel an Sein: Schellings Hegelkritik und die Anfänge der Marxschen Dialektik*. Munich: Wilhelm Fink, 1992.
Frankfurt, Harry G. "Freedom of the Will and the Concept of a Person." *Journal of Philosophy* 68, no. 1 (January 14, 1971): 5–20.
Franks, Paul. *All or Nothing: Systematicity, Transcendental Arguments, and Skepticism in German Idealism*. Cambridge: Harvard University Press, 2005.
Freud, Sigmund. "Abstracts of the Scientific Writings of Dr. Sigm. Freud, 1877–1897." In Freud, *Standard Edition*, 3:223–257.
———. "The Aetiology of Hysteria." In Freud, *Standard Edition*, 3:187–221.
———. "Beiträge zur Psychologie des Liebeslebens II: Über die allgemeinste Erniedrigung des Liebeslebens." *GW* 8:78–91.
———. *Beyond the Pleasure Principle*. In Freud, *Standard Edition*, 18:1–64.
———. "The Dissolution of the Oedipus Complex." In Freud, *Standard Edition*, 19:171–179.
———. *The Ego and the Id*. In Freud, *Standard Edition*, 19:1–66.
———. "Extracts From the Fliess Papers." In Freud, *Standard Edition*, 1:173–280.

———. *From the History of an Infantile Neurosis.* In Freud, *Standard Edition*, 17:1–123.
———. *Gesammelte Werke.* Edited by E. Bibring, W. Hoffer, E. Kris, and O. Isakower. Frankfurt: Fischer, 1952.
———. "The Infantile Genital Organization (an Interpolation Into the Theory of Sexuality)." In Freud, *Standard Edition*, 19:139–145.
———. "The Loss of Reality in Neurosis and Psychosis." In Freud, *Standard Edition*, 19:181–187.
———. "Negation." In Freud, *Standard Edition*, 19:233–239.
———. *Notes Upon a Case of Obsessional Neurosis.* In Freud, *Standard Edition*, 10:151–320.
———. "A Note Upon the 'Mystic Writing-Pad.'" In Freud, *Standard Edition*, 19:225–232.
———. "On the Universal Tendency to Debasement in the Sphere of Love (Contributions to the Psychology of Love II)." In Freud, *Standard Edition*, 11:177–190.
———. *An Outline of Psycho-Analysis.* In Freud, *Standard Edition*, 23:139–207.
———. *Project for a Scientific Psychology.* In Freud, *Standard Edition*, 1:281–397.
———. "Remembering, Repeating and Working-Through (Further Recommendations on the Technique of Psycho-Analysis II)." In Freud, *Standard Edition*, 12:145–156.
———. "Some Psychical Consequences of the Anatomical Distinction Between the Sexes." In Freud, *Standard Edition*, 19:241–258.
———. *The Standard Edition of the Complete Psychological Works of Sigmund Freud.* Edited and translated by James Strachey, in collaboration with Anna Freud, assisted by Alix Strachey and Alan Tyson, 24 vols. London: Hogarth Press and the Institute of Psycho-Analysis, 1953–1974.
———. *Studies on Hysteria.* In Freud, *Standard Edition*, vol. 2.
———. "The Unconscious." In Freud, *Standard Edition*, 14:159–215.
———. "Der Untergang des Ödipuskomplexes." *GW* 13:393–402.
Fulda, Hans Friedrich. *Das Problem einer Einleitung in Hegels Wissenschaft der Logik.* Frankfurt: Klostermann, 1965.
Gabriel, Markus. *Transcendental Ontology: Essays in German Idealism.* London: Continuum, 2011.
Gadamer, Hans-Georg. "The Idea of Hegel's Logic." In *Hegel's Dialectic: Five Hermeneutical Studies*, translated by P. Christopher Smith, 75–99. New Haven: Yale University Press, 1976.
Galileo Galilei. "The Assayer." In *Discoveries and Opinions of Galileo*, translated by Stillman Drake, 229–280. New York: Anchor, 1957.
Goethe, Johann Wolfgang von. *Faust: Parts I and II.* Translated by Bayard Taylor. New York: Washington Square, 1964.
Graham, Loren R. *Science and Philosophy in the Soviet Union.* New York: Knopf, 1972.
Grier, Philip T. "The Relation of Mind to Nature: Two Paradigms." In *Essays on Hegel's Philosophy of Subjective Spirit*, edited by David Stern, 223–246. Albany: State University of New York Press, 2013.
Habermas, Jürgen. "Dialectical Idealism in Transition to Materialism: Schelling's Idea of a Contraction of God and its Consequences for the Philosophy of History." Translated by Nick Midgley and Judith Norman. In *The New Schelling*, edited by Judith Norman and Alistair Welchman, 43–89. London: Continuum, 2004.
Hardimon, Michael O. *Hegel's Social Philosophy: The Project of Reconciliation.* Cambridge: Cambridge University Press, 1994.

BIBLIOGRAPHY

Harris, H. S. *Hegel's Development*. Vol. 1, *Toward the Sunlight, 1770–1801*. Oxford: Oxford University Press, 1972.

———. *Hegel's Development*. Vol. 2, *Night Thoughts (Jena 1801–1806)*. Oxford: Oxford University Press, 1983.

———. *Hegel's Ladder*. Vol. 1, *The Pilgrimage of Reason*. Indianapolis: Hackett, 1997.

———. *Hegel's Ladder*. Vol. 2, *The Odyssey of Spirit*. Indianapolis: Hackett, 1997.

———. "The Problem of Kant." *Bulletin of the Hegel Society of Great Britain* 19 (1989): 18–27.

Hartmann, Klaus. "Hegel: A Non-Metaphysical View." In *Hegel: A Collection of Critical Essays*, edited by Alasdair MacIntyre, 101–124. New York: Anchor, 1972.

———. "Die ontologische Option." In *Die ontologische Option: Studien zu Hegels Propädeutik, Schellings Hegel-Kritik und Hegels Phänomenologie des Geistes*, edited by Klaus Hartmann, 1–30. Berlin: de Gruyter, 1976.

Haym, Rudolf. "Preußen und die Rechtsphilosophie (1857): Hegel und seine Zeit." In *Materialien zu Hegels Rechtsphilosophie*, edited by Manfred Riedel, 365–394. Frankfurt: Suhrkamp, 1975.

Hegel, G. W. F. "Das älteste Systemprogramm des deutschen Idealismus." In *Werke in zwanzig Bänden*, vol. 1, *Frühe Schriften*, 234–236.

———. "Aphorismen aus Hegels Wastebook (1803–1806)." In *Werke in zwanzig Bänden*, vol. 2, *Jenaer Schriften, 1801–1807*, 540–567.

———. "Aphorisms from the Wastebook." Translated by Susanne Klein, David L. Roochnik, and George Elliot Tucker. In *Miscellaneous Writings of G. W. F. Hegel*, edited by Jon Stewart, 245–255. Evanston, IL: Northwestern University Press, 2002.

———. *The Difference Between Fichte's and Schelling's System of Philosophy*. Translated by H. S. Harris and Walter Cerf. Albany: State University of New York Press, 1977.

———. *Differenz des Fichteschen und Schellingschen Systems der Philosophie*. In *Werke in zwanzig Bänden*, vol. 2, *Jenaer Schriften, 1801–1807*, 7–138.

———. "The Earliest System-Program of German Idealism." Translated by H. S. Harris. In *Miscellaneous Writings of G. W. F. Hegel*, edited by Jon Stewart, 110–112. Evanston, IL: Northwestern University Press, 2002.

———. *Elements of the Philosophy of Right*. Edited by Allen W. Wood, translated by H. B. Nisbet. Cambridge: Cambridge University Press, 1991.

———. *The Encyclopedia Logic: Part I of the Encyclopedia of the Philosophical Sciences with the Zusätze*. Translated by T. F. Geraets, W. A. Suchting, and H. S. Harris. Indianapolis: Hackett, 1991.

———. *Encyclopedia of the Philosophical Sciences in Outline*. Translated by Steven A. Taubeneck. In *Encyclopedia of the Philosophical Sciences in Outline and Critical Writings*, edited by Ernst Behler, 45–264. New York: Continuum, 1990.

———. *Enzyklopädie der philosophischen Wissenschaften, Erster Teil: Die Wissenschaft der Logik*. In *Werke in zwanzig Bänden*, vol. 8.

———. *Enzyklopädie der philosophischen Wissenschaften, Dritter Teil: Die Philosophie des Geistes mit den mündlichen Zusätzen*. In *Werke in zwanzig Bänden*, vol. 10.

———. *Faith and Knowledge*. Translated by Walter Cerf and H. S. Harris. Albany: State University of New York Press, 1977.

———. *First Philosophy of Spirit (Part III of the System of Speculative Philosophy 1803/4)*. Translated by H. S. Harris. In *The System of Ethical Life (1802/3) and First Philosophy of*

Spirit (Part III of the System of Speculative Philosophy 1803/4), edited by H. S. Harris and T. M. Knox, 187–250. Albany: State University of New York Press, 1979.

———. "Fragment of a System." Translated by Richard Kroner. In *Miscellaneous Writings of G. W. F. Hegel*, edited by Jon Stewart, 151–160. Evanston, IL: Northwestern University Press, 2002.

———. "Hegel to Niethammer: Bamberg, October 28, 1808." In *Hegel: The Letters*, translated by Clark Butler and Christiane Seiler, 178–179. Bloomington: Indiana University Press, 1984.

———. "Hegel to Niethammer: Jena, October 13, 1806." In *Hegel: The Letters*, translated by Clark Butler and Christiane Seiler, 114–115. Bloomington: Indiana University Press, 1984.

———. "Hegel to Niethammer: Nuremberg, October 23, 1812." In *Hegel: The Letters*, translated by Clark Butler and Christiane Seiler, 275–282. Bloomington: Indiana University Press, 1984.

———. "Hegel to Schelling: Bern, April 16, 1795." In *Hegel: The Letters*, translated by Clark Butler and Christiane Seiler, 35–36. Bloomington: Indiana University Press, 1984.

———. "Hegel to von Raumer: Nuremberg, August 2, 1816." In *Hegel: The Letters*, translated by Clark Butler and Christiane Seiler, 338–341. Bloomington: Indiana University Press, 1984.

———. "How the Ordinary Human Understanding Takes Philosophy (as Displayed in the Works of Mr. Krug)." Translated by H. S. Harris. In *Miscellaneous Writings of G. W. F. Hegel*, edited by Jon Stewart, 226–244. Evanston, IL: Northwestern University Press, 2002.

———. *The Jena System, 1804–5: Logic and Metaphysics*. Edited by John W. Burbidge and George di Giovanni. Kingston: McGill-Queen's University Press, 1986.

———. *Lectures on Logic: Berlin, 1831*. Translated by Clark Butler. Bloomington: Indiana University Press, 2008.

———. *Lectures on the History of Philosophy*. Vol. 1. Translated by E. S. Haldane. New York: Humanities, 1955.

———. *Lectures on the History of Philosophy*. Vol. 3. Translated by E. S. Haldane and Frances H. Simson. New York: Humanities, 1955.

———. "Logic [for the Lower Class]." In *The Philosophical Propaedeutic*, edited by Michael George and Andrew Vincent, translated by A. V. Miller, 65–73. Oxford: Blackwell, 1986.

———. "Logic [for the Middle Class]." In *The Philosophical Propaedeutic*, edited by Michael George and Andrew Vincent, translated by A. V. Miller, 74–104. Oxford: Blackwell, 1986.

———. *Natural Law: The Scientific Ways of Treating Natural Law, Its Place in Moral Philosophy, and Its Relation to the Positive Sciences of Law*. Translated by T. M. Knox. Philadelphia: University of Pennsylvania Press, 1975.

———. "On the English Reform Bill." In *Political Writings*, edited by Laurence Dickey and H. B. Nisbet, translated by H. B. Nisbet, 234–270. Cambridge: Cambridge University Press, 1999.

———. "On the Relationship of Skepticism to Philosophy, Exposition of Its Different Modifications and Comparison of the Latest Form with the Ancient One."

Translated by H. S. Harris. In *Between Kant and Hegel: Texts in the Development of Post-Kantian Idealism*, edited and translated by George Di Giovanni and H. S. Harris, 311–362. Indianapolis: Hackett, 2000.

———. *Phänomenologie des Geistes*. In *Werke in zwanzig Bänden* vol. 3.

———. "Phenomenology [for the Middle Class]." In *The Philosophical Propaedeutic*, edited by Michael George and Andrew Vincent, translated by A. V. Miller, 55–64. Oxford: Blackwell, 1986.

———. *Phenomenology of Spirit*. Translated by A. V. Miller. Oxford: Oxford University Press, 1977.

———. "The Philosophical Encyclopedia [for the Higher Class]." In *The Philosophical Propaedeutic*, edited by Michael George and Andrew Vincent, translated by A. V. Miller, 124–169. Oxford: Blackwell, 1986.

———. *Philosophie des Geistes, Jenaer Systementwüfre III: Naturphilosophie und Philosophie des Geistes*, edited by Rolf-Peter Horstmann, 171–262. Hamburg: Felix Meiner, 1987.

———. *Philosophy of History*. Translated by J. Sibree. New York: Dover, 1956.

———. *Philosophy of Mind: Part Three of the Encyclopedia of the Philosophical Sciences with the Zusätze*. Translated by William Wallace and A. V. Miller. Oxford: Oxford University Press, 1971.

———. *Philosophy of Nature: Part Two of the Encyclopedia of the Philosophical Sciences*. Translated by A. V. Miller. Oxford: Oxford University Press, 1970.

———. "Preface to the Second Edition (1827)." In *The Encyclopedia Logic: Part I of the Encyclopedia of the Philosophical Sciences with the Zusätze*, translated by T. F. Geraets, W. A. Suchting, and H. S. Harris, 4–17. Indianapolis: Hackett, 1991.

———. "Review of Göschel's *Aphorisms*." Translated by Clark Butler. In *Miscellaneous Writings of G. W. F. Hegel*, edited by Jon Stewart, 401–429. Evanston, IL: Northwestern University Press, 2002.

———. "Review of Solger's *Posthumous Writings and Correspondence*." Translated by Diana I. Behler. In *Miscellaneous Writings of G. W. F. Hegel*, edited by Jon Stewart, 354–400. Evanston, IL: Northwestern University Press, 2002.

———. "The Science of Laws, Morals and Religion [for the Lower Class]." In *The Philosophical Propaedeutic*, edited by Michael George and Andrew Vincent, translated by A. V. Miller, 1–54. Oxford: Blackwell, 1986.

———. *Science of Logic*. Translated by A. V. Miller. London: George Allen and Unwin, 1969.

———. "The Science of the Concept [for the Higher Class]." In *The Philosophical Propaedeutic*, edited by Michael George and Andrew Vincent, translated by A. V. Miller, 105–123. Oxford: Blackwell, 1986.

———. "The Spirit of Christianity and Its Fate." In *Early Theological Writings*, translated by T. M. Knox, 182–301. Philadelphia: University of Pennsylvania Press, 1975.

———. *The System of Ethical Life (1802/3)*. Translated by T. M. Knox and H. S. Harris. In *The System of Ethical Life (1802/3) and First Philosophy of Spirit (Part III of the System of Speculative Philosophy 1803/4)*, edited by H. S. Harris and T. M. Knox, 97–177. Albany: State University of New York Press, 1979.

———. "Texte zur Philosophischen Propädeutik: Philosophische Enzyklopädie für die Oberklasse." In *Werke in zwanzig Bänden*, vol. 4, *Nürnberger und Heidelberger Schriften, 1808-1817*, 9–69.

———. "Two Fragments on Love." Translated by C. Hamlin and H. S. Harris. In *Miscellaneous Writings of G. W. F. Hegel*, edited by Jon Stewart, 115–122. Evanston, IL: Northwestern University Press, 2002.
———. *Vorlesungen über die Philosophie der Geschichte*. In *Werke in zwanzig Bänden*, vol. 12.
———. *Werke in zwanzig Bänden*. Edited by Eva Moldenhauer and Karl Markus Michel. Frankfurt: Suhrkamp, 1969–1979.
———. "Who Thinks Abstractly?" Translated by Walter Kaufmann. In *Miscellaneous Writings of G. W. F. Hegel*, edited by Jon Stewart, 283–288. Evanston: Northwestern University Press, 2002.
———. *Wissenschaft der Logik I*. In *Werke in zwanzig Bänden*, vol. 5.
———. *Wissenschaft der Logik, II*. In *Werke in zwanzig Bänden*, vol. 6.
Heidegger, Martin. "Elucidation of the 'Introduction' to Hegel's 'Phenomenology of Spirit.'" In *Hegel*, translated by Joseph Arel and Niels Feuerhahn, 49–113. Bloomington: Indiana University Press, 2015.
———. "What Is Metaphysics?" Translated by David Farrell Krell. In *Basic Writings*, edited by David Farrell Krell, 89–110. New York: HarperCollins, 1993.
Henrich, Dieter. "Andersheit und Absolutheit des Geistes: Sieben Schritte auf dem Wege von Schelling zu Hegel." In *Selbstverhältnisse: Gedanken und Auslegungen zu den Grundlagen der klassischen deutschen Philosophie*, 142–172. Stuttgart: Reclam, 1982.
———. *Between Kant and Hegel: Lectures on German Idealism*. Edited by David S. Pacini. Cambridge: Harvard University Press, 2003.
———. "Fichte's Original Insight." Translated by David R. Lachterman. In *Contemporary German Philosophy*, edited by Darrel E. Christensen, Manfred Riedel, Robert Spaemann, Reiner Wiehl, and Wolfgang Wieland, 15–53. University Park: Pennsylvania State University Press, 1982.
———. "Hegels Logik der Reflexion." In *Hegel im Kontext: Mit einem Nachwort zur Neuauflage*, 95–157. Frankfurt: Suhrkamp, 2010.
———. "Hegels Theorie über den Zufall." In *Hegel im Kontext: Mit einem Nachwort zur Neuauflage*, 158–187. Frankfurt: Suhrkamp, 2010.
———. "Hegel und Hölderlin." In *Hegel im Kontext: Mit einem Nachwort zur Neuauflage*, 9–40. Frankfurt: Suhrkamp, 2010.
———. "Kant und Hegel: Versuch der Vereinigung inhrer Grundgedanken." In *Selbstverhältnisse: Gedanken und Auslegungen zu den Grundlagen der klassischen deutschen Philosophie*, 173–208. Stuttgart: Reclam, 1982.
Herder, Johann Gottfried von. "Gott." In *Schriften: Eine Auswahl aus dem Gesamtwerk*, edited by Walter Flemmer, 209–210. Munich: Wilhelm Goldmann, 1960.
———. "On the Cognition and Sensation of the Human Soul." In *Philosophical Writings*, edited and translated by Michael N. Forster, 187–243. Cambridge: Cambridge University Press, 2002.
Hogrebe, Wolfram. *Prädikation und Genesis: Metaphysik als Fundamentalheuristik im Ausgang von Schellings "Die Weltalter."* Frankfurt: Suhrkamp, 1989.
Hölderlin, Friedrich. "Über Urtheil und Seyn." Translated by H. S. Harris. In *Hegel's Development*, vol. 1, *Toward the Sunlight, 1770–1801*, by H. S. Harris, 515–516. Oxford: Oxford University Press, 1972.

BIBLIOGRAPHY

Horkheimer, Max, and Theodor W. Adorno. *Dialectic of Enlightenment: Philosophical Fragments*. Edited by Gunzelin Schmid Noerr, translated by Edmund Jephcott. Stanford: Stanford University Press, 2002.

Horstmann, Rolf-Peter. *Die Grenzen der Vernunft: Eine Untersuchung zu Zielen und Motiven des Deutschen Idealismus*. Frankfurt: Klostermann, 2004.

Houlgate, Stephen. *Hegel's Phenomenology of Spirit*. London: Bloomsbury, 2013.

———. *An Introduction to Hegel: Freedom, Truth and History*. 2nd ed. Oxford: Blackwell, 2005.

———. *The Opening of Hegel's Logic: From Being to Infinity*. West Lafayette, IN: Purdue University Press, 2006.

———. "Schelling's Critique of Hegel's *Science of Logic*." *Review of Metaphysics* 53, no. 1 (September 1999): 99–128.

Hume, David. *An Enquiry Concerning Human Understanding*. 2nd ed. Edited by Eric Steinberg. Indianapolis: Hackett, 1993.

———. *A Treatise of Human Nature*. Edited by Ernest C. Mossner. New York: Penguin, 1985.

Hyppolite, Jean. *Genesis and Structure of Hegel's Phenomenology of Spirit*. Translated by Samuel Cherniak and John Heckman. Evanston, IL: Northwestern University Press, 1974.

———. *Logic and Existence*. Translated by Leonard Lawlor and Amit Sen. Albany: State University of New York Press, 1997.

Inwood, Michael. *A Hegel Dictionary*. Oxford: Blackwell, 1992.

Jackson, M. W. "Hegel: The Real and the Rational." In *The Hegel Myths and Legends*, edited by Jon Stewart, 19–25. Evanston: Northwestern University Press, 1996.

Jacobi, F. H. *Concerning the Doctrine of Spinoza in Letters to Herr Moses Mendelssohn*. In *The Main Philosophical Writings and the Novel Allwill*, translated by George di Giovanni, 173–251. Montreal: McGill-Queen's University Press, 1994.

———. *David Hume on Faith, or Idealism and Realism: A Dialogue*. In *The Main Philosophical Writings and the Novel Allwill*, translated by George di Giovanni, 253–338. Montreal: McGill-Queen's University Press, 1994.

———. "David Hume on Faith, or Idealism and Realism, a Dialogue: Preface and Also Introduction to the Author's Collected Philosophical Works (1815)." In *The Main Philosophical Writings and the Novel Allwill*, translated by George di Giovanni, 537–590. Montreal: McGill-Queen's University Press, 1994.

———. "Jacobi to Fichte." In *The Main Philosophical Writings and the Novel Allwill*, translated by George di Giovanni, 497–536. Montreal: McGill-Queen's University Press, 1994.

Johnston, Adrian. *Adventures in Transcendental Materialism: Dialogues with Contemporary Thinkers*. Edinburgh: Edinburgh University Press, 2014.

———. *Badiou, Žižek, and Political Transformations: The Cadence of Change*. Evanston, IL: Northwestern University Press, 2009.

———. "Confession of a Weak Reductionist: Responses to Some Recent Criticisms of My Materialism." In *Neuroscience and Critique: Exploring the Limits of the Neurological Turn*, edited by Jan De Vos and Ed Pluth, 141–170. New York: Routledge, 2015.

———. "A Critique of Natural Economy: Quantum Physics with Žižek." In *Žižek Now*, edited by Jamil Khader and Molly Anne Rothenberg, 103–120. Cambridge: Polity, 2013.

——. "Drive Between Brain and Subject: An Immanent Critique of Lacanian Neuropsychoanalysis." Special issue, "Spindel Supplement: Freudian Futures." *Southern Journal of Philosophy* 51 (2013): 48–84.

——. "From Scientific Socialism to Socialist Science: *Naturdialektik* Then and Now." In *The Idea of Communism*, vol. 2, *The New York Conference*, edited by Slavoj Žižek, 103–136. London: Verso, 2013.

——. "Humanity, That Sickness: Louis Althusser and the Helplessness of Psychoanalysis." Special issue, "*Reading Capital* and *For Marx*: 50 Years Later," edited by Frank Ruda and Agon Hamza. *Crisis and Critique* 2, no. 2 (2015): 217–261.

——. "An Interview with Adrian Johnston on Transcendental Materialism [with Peter Gratton]." *Society and Space* (October 2013): http://societyandspace.com/2013/10/07/interview-with-adrian-johnston-on-transcendental-materialism/.

——. "Intimations of Freudian Mortality: The Enigma of Sexuality and the Constitutive Blind Spots of Freud's Self-Analysis." *Journal for Lacanian Studies* 3, no. 2 (2005): 222–246.

——. "Jacques Lacan (1901–1981)." In *Stanford Encyclopedia of Philosophy*. http://plato.stanford.edu/entries/lacan/. 2013.

——. "Lacking Causes: Privative Causality from Locke and Kant to Lacan and Deacon." *Speculations: A Journal of Speculative Realism* 6 (December 2015): 19–60.

——. "The Late Innate: Jean Laplanche, Jaak Panksepp, and the Distinction Between Sexual Drives and Instincts." In *Inheritance in Psychoanalysis*, edited by James Godley. Albany: State University of New York Press, 2018.

——. "Marx's Bones: Breaking with Althusser." In *The Concept in Crisis: Reading Capital Now*, edited by Nick Nesbitt, 189–215. Durham: Duke University Press, 2017.

——. "Misfelt Feelings: Unconscious Affect Between Psychoanalysis, Neuroscience, and Philosophy." In *Self and Emotional Life: Philosophy, Psychoanalysis, and Neuroscience*, by Adrian Johnston and Catherine Malabou, 73–210. New York: Columbia University Press, 2013.

——. "Points of Forced Freedom: Eleven (More) Theses on Materialism." *Speculations: A Journal of Speculative Realism* 4 (June 2013): 91–99.

——. *Prolegomena to Any Future Materialism*, vol. 1, *The Outcome of Contemporary French Philosophy*. Evanston, IL: Northwestern University Press, 2013.

——. *Prolegomena to Any Future Materialism*, vol. 2, *A Weak Nature Alone*. Evanston, IL: Northwestern University Press, 2018.

——. "Reflections of a Rotten Nature: Hegel, Lacan, and Material Negativity." Special issue, "Science and Thought," edited by Frank Ruda and Jan Voelker. *Filozofski Vestnik* 33, no. 2 (2012): 23–52.

——. "Repeating Engels: Renewing the Cause of the Materialist Wager for the Twenty-First Century." Special issue, "animal.machine.sovereign," edited by Javier Burdman and Tyler Williams. *Theory @ Buffalo* 15 (2011): 141–182.

——. Review of Frank Ruda's *Hegel's Rabble*. *Notre Dame Philosophical Reviews* (June 21, 2012). http://ndpr.nd.edu/news/31707-hegel-s-rabble-an-investigation-into-hegel-s-philosophy-of-right/.

——. "Second Natures in Dappled Worlds: John McDowell, Nancy Cartwright, and Hegelian-Lacanian Materialism." In *Umbr(a): The Worst*, edited by Matthew

Rigilano and Kyle Fetter, 71–91. Buffalo: Center for the Study of Psychoanalysis and Culture, State University of New York, Buffalo, 2011.
———. "Sextimacy: Freud, Mortality, and a Reconsideration of the Role of Sexuality in Psychoanalysis." In *Sexuality and Psychoanalysis: Philosophical Criticisms*, edited by Jens De Vleminck and Eran Dorfman, 35–59. Leuven: Leuven University Press, 2010.
———. "Slavoj Žižek." In *The Blackwell Companion to Continental Philosophy*, edited by William Schroeder. Oxford: Blackwell, 2018.
———. *Time Driven: Metapsychology and the Splitting of the Drive*. Evanston, IL: Northwestern University Press, 2005.
———. "Transcendentalism in Hegel's Wake: A Reply to Timothy M. Hackett and Benjamin Berger." Special issue, "Schelling: Powers of the Idea," edited by Benjamin Berger. *Pli: The Warwick Journal of Philosophy* 26 (Fall 2014): 204–237.
———. "The Voiding of Weak Nature: The Transcendental Materialist Kernels of Hegel's *Naturphilosophie*." *Graduate Faculty Philosophy Journal* 33, no. 1 (2012): 103–157.
———. "The Weakness of Nature: Hegel, Freud, Lacan, and Negativity Materialized." In *Hegel and the Infinite: Religion, Politics, and Dialectic*, edited by Slavoj Žižek, Clayton Crockett, and Creston Davis, 159–179. New York: Columbia University Press, 2011.
———. *Žižek's Ontology: A Transcendental Materialist Theory of Subjectivity*. Evanston, IL: Northwestern University Press, 2008.
Kant, Immanuel. *Critique of Practical Reason*. In *Practical Philosophy*, translated and edited by Mary J. Gregor, 133–271. Cambridge: Cambridge University Press, 1996.
———. *Critique of Pure Reason*. Translated by Paul Guyer and Allen Wood. Cambridge: Cambridge University Press, 1998.
———. *Groundwork of the Metaphysics of Morals*. In *Practical Philosophy*, translated and edited by Mary J. Gregor, 41–108. Cambridge: Cambridge University Press, 1996.
———. *Prolegomena to Any Future Metaphysics That Will Be Able to Come Forward as a Science*. Translated by Gary Hatfield. In *Theoretical Philosophy After 1781*, edited by Henry Allison and Peter Heath, 30–169. Cambridge: Cambridge University Press, 2002.
Kautsky, Karl. *Frederick Engels: His Life, His Work, and His Writings*. 1887/1888. Translated by May Wood Simmons. http://marxists.org/archive/kautsky/1887/xx/engels.htm.
Kervégan, Jean-François. *L'effectif et le rationnel: Hegel et l'esprit objectif*. Paris: Vrin, 2007.
Kimmerle, Heinz. *Das Problem der Abgeschlossenheit des Denkens: Hegels "System der Philosophie" in den Jahren 1800–1804, Hegel-Studien, Beiheft 8*. Bonn: Bouvier, 1970.
Komarov, V. L. "Marx and Engels on Biology." In *Marxism and Modern Thought*, by N. I. Bukharin et al., translated by Ralph Fox, 190–234. New York: Harcourt, Brace, 1935.
Kreines, James. "Hegel's Metaphysics: Changing the Debate." *Philosophy Compass* 1, no. 5 (2006): 466–480.
———. "Metaphysics Without Pre-Critical Monism: Hegel on Lower-Level Natural Kinds and the Structure of Reality." *Bulletin of the Hegel Society of Great Britain* 57–58 (2008): 48–70.

Lacan, Jacques. "L'acte psychanalytique: Compte rendu du Séminaire 1967–1968." In *Autres écrits*, edited by Jacques-Alain Miller, 375–383. Paris: Seuil, 2001.

——. "Impromptu at Vincennes." Translated by Jeffrey Mehlman. In *Television/A Challenge to the Psychoanalytic Establishment*, edited by Joan Copjec, 117–128. New York: Norton, 1990.

——. "Position of the Unconscious." In *Écrits: The First Complete Edition in English*, translated by Bruce Fink, 703–721. New York: Norton, 2006.

——. *Le Séminaire de Jacques Lacan*, book 14, *La logique du fantasme, 1966–1967* (unpublished typescript).

——. *Le Séminaire de Jacques Lacan*, book 15, *L'acte psychanalytique, 1967–1968* (unpublished typescript).

——. *Le Séminaire de Jacques Lacan*, book 16, *D'un Autre à l'autre, 1968–1969*. Edited by Jacques-Alain Miller. Paris: Seuil, 2006.

——. *Le Séminaire de Jacques Lacan*, book 21, *Les non-dupes errent, 1973–1974* (unpublished typescript).

——. *The Seminar of Jacques Lacan*, book 7, *The Ethics of Psychoanalysis, 1959–1960*. Edited by Jacques-Alain Miller, translated by Dennis Porter. New York: Norton, 1992.

——. *The Seminar of Jacques Lacan*, book 8, *Transference, 1960–1961*. Edited by Jacques-Alain Miller, translated by Bruce Fink. Cambridge: Polity, 2015.

——. *The Seminar of Jacques Lacan*, book 10, *Anxiety, 1962–1963*. Edited by Jacques-Alain Miller. Translated by A. R. Price. Cambridge: Polity, 2014.

——. *The Seminar of Jacques Lacan*, book 11, *The Four Fundamental Concepts of Psychoanalysis, 1964*. Edited by Jacques-Alain Miller. Translated by Alan Sheridan. New York: Norton, 1977.

——. "Some Reflections on the Ego." *International Journal of Psycho-Analysis* 34, (1953): 11–17.

Laplanche, Jean, and Jean-Bertrand Pontalis. *The Language of Psycho-Analysis*. Translated by Donald Nicholson-Smith. New York: Norton, 1973.

Lardic, Jean-Marie. "Hegel et la contingence." In *Comment le sens commun comprend la philosophie, suivi de La contingence chez Hegel*, by G. W. F. Hegel and Jean-Marie Lardic, 61–107. Paris: Actes Sud, 1989.

——. "Présentation." In *Comment le sens commun comprend la philosophie, suivi de La contingence chez Hegel*, by G. W. F. Hegel and Jean-Marie Lardic, 13–39. Paris: Actes Sud, 1989.

Lear, Jonathan. *Happiness, Death, and the Remainder of Life*. Cambridge: Harvard University Press, 2000.

Lebrun, Gérard. *L'envers de la dialectique: Hegel à la lumière de Nietzsche*. Paris: Seuil, 2004.

——. *La patience du Concept: Essai sur le Discours hégélien*. Paris: Gallimard, 1972.

Lefebvre, Henri. *La pensée de Lénine*. Paris: Bordas, 1957.

Leibniz, G. W. "Discourse on Metaphysics." In *Philosophical Essays*, translated by Roger Ariew and Daniel Garber, 35–68. Indianapolis: Hackett, 1989.

——. "On Contingency." In *Philosophical Essays*, translated by Roger Ariew and Daniel Garber, 28–30. Indianapolis: Hackett, 1989.

——. "Primary Truths." In *Philosophical Essays*, translated by Roger Ariew and Daniel Garber, 30–34. Indianapolis: Hackett, 1989.

———. "Principles of Nature and Grace, Based on Reason." In *Philosophical Essays*, translated by Roger Ariew and Daniel Garber, 206–213. Indianapolis: Hackett, 1989.

———. "The Principles of Philosophy, or, the Monadology." In *Philosophical Essays*, translated by Roger Ariew and Daniel Garber, 213–225. Indianapolis: Hackett, 1989.

Lenin, V. I. "Conspectus of Hegel's Book *The Science of Logic*." In *Collected Works*, vol. 38, *Philosophical Notebooks*, edited by Stewart Smith, translated by Clemence Dutt, 83–237. Moscow: Progress, 1976.

———. *Materialism and Empirio-Criticism*. Peking: Foreign Languages, 1972.

Levins, Richard, and Richard Lewontin. "The Problem of Lysenkoism." In *The Dialectical Biologist*, 163–196. Cambridge: Harvard University Press, 1985.

Libet, Benjamin. *Mind Time: The Temporal Factor in Consciousness*. Cambridge: Harvard University Press, 2004.

Locke, John. *An Essay Concerning Human Understanding in Two Volumes*. Vol. 1. Edited by Alexander Campbell Fraser. New York: Dover, 1959.

Longuenesse, Béatrice. *Hegel et la critique de la métaphysique*. Paris: Vrin, 1981.

Löwith, Karl. *From Hegel to Nietzsche: The Revolution in Nineteenth-Century Philosophy*. Translated by David E. Green. New York: Columbia University Press, 1991.

Lukács, Georg. "The Changing Function of Historical Materialism." In *History and Class Consciousness: Studies in Marxist Dialectics*, translated by Rodney Livingstone, 223–255. Cambridge: MIT Press, 1971.

———. "Karl August Wittfogel: *The Science of Bourgeois Society*." In *Tactics and Ethics: Political Writings, 1919–1929*, edited by Rodney Livingstone, translated by Michael McColgan, 143–146. London: New Left Books, 1972.

———. "N. Bukharin: *Historical Materialism*." In *Tactics and Ethics: Political Writings, 1919–1929*, edited by Rodney Livingstone, translated by Michael McColgan, 134–142. London: New Left Books, 1972.

———. *The Ontology of Social Being*. Vol. 1, *Hegel*. Translated by David Fernbach. London: Merlin, 1978.

———. "Reification and the Consciousness of the Proletariat." In *History and Class Consciousness: Studies in Marxist Dialectics*, translated by Rodney Livingstone, 83–222. Cambridge: MIT Press, 1971.

———. "Tailism and the Dialectic." In *A Defense of History and Class Consciousness: Tailism and the Dialectic*, translated by Esther Leslie, 45–149. London: Verso, 2000.

———. "What Is Orthodox Marxism?" In *History and Class Consciousness: Studies in Marxist Dialectics*, translated by Rodney Livingstone, 1–26. Cambridge: MIT Press, 1971.

———. *The Young Hegel: Studies in the Relations Between Dialectics and Economics*. Translated by Rodney Livingstone. Cambridge: MIT Press, 1976.

Mabille, Bernard. *Hegel: L'épreuve de la contingence*. Paris: Aubier, 1999.

Maimon, Salomon. *Essay on Transcendental Philosophy*. Translated by Nick Midgley, Henry Somers-Hall, Alistair Welchman, and Merten Reglitz. London: Continuum, 2010.

Maker, William. "The Very Idea of the Idea of Nature, or Why Hegel Is Not an Idealist." In *Hegel and the Philosophy of Nature*, edited by Stephen Houlgate, 1–27. Albany: State University of New York Press, 1998.

Malabou, Catherine. *The Future of Hegel: Plasticity, Temporality and Dialectic.* Translated by Lisabeth During. New York: Routledge, 2005.

Mandel, Ernest. *The Formation of the Economic Thought of Karl Marx: 1843 to Capital.* Translated by Brian Pearce. New York: Monthly Review Press, 1971.

Mannoni, Octave. "Je sais bien, mais quand même . . ." In *Clefs pour l'Imaginaire ou l'Autre Scène*, 9–33. Paris: Seuil, 1969.

Mao Tse-Tung. "On the Correct Handling of Contradictions Among the People." In *Selected Readings from the Works of Mao Tsetung*, 432–479. Peking: Foreign Languages, 1971.

——. "Speech at the Tenth Plenum of the Eighth Central Committee." September 24, 1962. www.marxists.org/reference/archive/mao/selected-works/volume-8/mswv8_63.htm.

——. "Speech to the Albanian Military Delegation." May 1, 1967. www.marxists.org/reference/archive/mao/selected-works/volume-9/mswv9_74.htm.

Marcuse, Herbert. *Hegel's Ontology and the Theory of Historicity.* Translated by Seyla Benhabib. Cambridge: MIT Press, 1987.

——. *Reason and Revolution: Hegel and the Rise of Social Theory.* 2nd ed. New York: Routledge, 2000.

——. *Soviet Marxism: A Critical Analysis.* New York: Penguin, 1971.

Marmasse, Gilles. *Penser le réel: Hegel, la nature et l'esprit.* Paris: Kimé, 2008.

Marx, Karl. *Capital: A Critique of Political Economy.* Vol. 1. Translated by Ben Fowkes. New York: Penguin, 1976.

——. *Capital: A Critique of Political Economy.* Vol. 2. Translated by David Fernbach. New York: Penguin, 1978.

——. *Capital: A Critique of Political Economy.* Vol. 3. Translated by David Fernbach. New York: Penguin, 1981.

——. *A Contribution to the Critique of Political Economy.* Edited by Maurice Dobb. Translated by S. W. Ryazanskaya. New York: International, 1970.

——. *Grundrisse: Foundations of the Critique of Political Economy (Rough Draft).* Translated by Martin Nicolaus. New York: Penguin, 1993.

——. "Marx to Engels in Manchester, 16 January 1858 [London]." https://marxists.anu.edu.au/archive/marx/works/1858/letters/58_01_16.htm.

——. "Marx to Ludwig Kugelmann in Hanover, 6 March 1868 [London]." http://marxists.catbull.com/archive/marx/works/1868/letters/68_03_06.htm.

——. "Marx to Ludwig Kugelmann in Hanover, 27 June 1870 [London]." http://marxists.catbull.com/archive/marx/works/1870/letters/70_06_27.htm.

——. "Theses on Feuerbach," Translated by S. Ryazanskaya. In *Karl Marx: Selected Writings*, edited by David McLellan, 156–158. Oxford: Oxford University Press, 1977.

Marx, Werner. *Hegel's Phenomenology of Spirit: Its Point and Purpose—a Commentary on the Preface and Introduction.* Translated by Peter Heath. New York: Harper and Row, 1975.

Matheron, François. "La récurrence du vide chez Louis Althusser." In *Futur antérieur: Lire Althusser aujourd'hui*, edited by Jean-Marie Vincent, 23–47. Paris: L'Harmattan, 1997.

Meillassoux, Quentin. *After Finitude: An Essay on the Necessity of Contingency.* Translated by Ray Brassier. London: Continuum, 2008.
Moi, Toril. "Is Anatomy Destiny?: Freud and Biological Determinism." In *Whose Freud?: The Place of Psychoanalysis in Contemporary Culture*, edited by Peter Brooks and Alex Woloch, 70–92. New Haven: Yale University Press, 2000.
Neuhouser, Frederick. *Foundations of Hegel's Social Theory: Actualizing Freedom.* Cambridge: Harvard University Press, 2000.
Peperzak, Adrien T. B. *Le jeune Hegel et la vision morale du monde.* The Hague: Martinus Nijhoff, 1960.
Pinkard, Terry. "The Categorial Satisfaction of Self-Reflexive Reason." *Bulletin of the Hegel Society of Great Britain* 19 (1989): 5–17.
——. *German Philosophy, 1760–1860: The Legacy of Idealism.* Cambridge: Cambridge University Press, 2002.
——. *Hegel: A Biography.* Cambridge: Cambridge University Press, 2000.
——. *Hegel's Naturalism: Mind, Nature, and the Final Ends of Life.* Oxford: Oxford University Press, 2012.
——. *Hegel's Phenomenology: The Sociality of Reason.* Cambridge: Cambridge University Press, 1996.
——. "How Kantian Was Hegel?" *Review of Metaphysics* 43, no. 4 (June 1990): 831–838.
Pippin, Robert B. "Avoiding German Idealism: Kant, Hegel, and the Reflective Judgment Problem." In *Idealism as Modernism: Hegelian Variations*, 129–153. Cambridge: Cambridge University Press, 1997.
——. "Hegel and Category Theory." *Review of Metaphysics* 43, no. 4 (June 1990): 839–848.
——. *Hegel on Self-Consciousness: Desire and Death in the Phenomenology of Spirit.* Princeton: Princeton University Press, 2011.
——. "Hegel's Idealism: Prospects." *Bulletin of the Hegel Society of Great Britain* 19 (1989): 28–41.
——. *Hegel's Idealism: The Satisfactions of Self-Consciousness.* Cambridge: Cambridge University Press, 1989.
——. "Hegel's Original Insight." *International Philosophical Quarterly* 33 (1993): 285–296.
——. "Hösle, System and Subject." *Bulletin of the Hegel Society of Great Britain* 17 (Spring/Summer 1988): 5–19.
——. "The Kantian Aftermath: Reaction and Revolution in Modern German Philosophy." In *The Persistence of Subjectivity: On the Kantian Aftermath*, 27–53. Cambridge: Cambridge University Press, 2005.
Planty-Bonjour, Guy. *The Categories of Dialectical Materialism: Contemporary Soviet Ontology.* Translated by T. J. Blakeley. New York: Praeger, 1967.
Plato, *Republic.* Translated by G. M. A. Grube. Revised by C. D. C. Reeve. In *Plato: Complete Works*, edited by John M. Cooper, 971–1223. Indianapolis: Hackett, 1997.
Plekhanov, Georgi, V. "For the Sixtieth Anniversary of Hegel's Death." Translated by R. Dixon. In *Selected Philosophical Works in Five Volumes*, vol. 1, edited by M. T. Ivochuk, A. N. Maslin, P. N. Fedoseyev, V. A. Fomina, B. A. Chagin, E. S. Kots, I. S. Belensky, S. M. Firsova, and B. L. Yakobson, 455–483. Moscow: Foreign Languages, 1974.

BIBLIOGRAPHY

———. *Fundamental Problems of Marxism*. Edited by James S. Allen, translated by Julius Katzer. New York: International, 1969.

———. "The Role of the Individual in History." In *Fundamental Problems of Marxism*, edited by James S. Allen, translated by Julius Katzer, 139–177. New York: International, 1969.

Pöggeler, Otto. "Hegel, der Verfasser des ältesten Systemprogramms des deutschen Idealismus." In *Mythologie der Vernunft: Hegels "ältestes Systemprogramm" des deutschen Idealismus*, edited by Christoph Jamme and Helmut Schneider, 126–143. Frankfurt: Suhrkamp, 1984.

———. "Hölderlin, Hegel und das älteste Systemprogramm." In *Das älteste Systemprogramm, Hegel-Studien, Beiheft 9*, edited by Rüdiger Bubner, 211–259. Bonn: Bouvier, 1982.

Prigogine, Ilya, and Isabelle Stengers. *La nouvelle alliance: Métamorphose de la science*. Paris: Gallimard, 1979.

Quante, Michael. *Die Wirklichkeit des Geistes: Studien zu Hegel*. Frankfurt: Suhrkamp, 2011.

Reinhold, K. L. *Letters on the Kantian Philosophy*. Edited by Karl Ameriks. Translated by James Hebbeler. Cambridge: Cambridge University Press, 2005.

———. *Über das Fundament des philosophischen Wissens*. Hamburg: Felix Meiner, 1978.

Renault, Emmanuel. *Hegel: La naturalisation de la dialectique*. Paris: Vrin, 2001.

Rosen, Stanley. *The Idea of Hegel's Science of Logic*. Chicago: University of Chicago Press, 2014.

Rosenkranz, Karl. *G. W. F. Hegels Leben*. Darmstadt: Wissenschaftliche Buchgesellschaft, 1971.

Rotenstreich, Nathan. *From Substance to Subject: Studies in Hegel*. The Hague: Martinus Nijhoff, 1974.

Santner, Eric L. *On the Psychotheology of Everyday Life: Reflections on Freud and Rosenzweig*. Chicago: University of Chicago Press, 2001.

Schelling, F. W. J. *The Ages of the World: Third Version (c. 1815)*. Translated by Jason M. Wirth. Albany: State University of New York Press, 2000.

———. *Bruno, or On the Natural and the Divine Principle of Things*. Translated by Michael G. Vater. Albany: State University of New York Press, 1984.

———. *Clara, or, On Nature's Connection to the Spirit World*. Translated by Fiona Steinkamp. Albany: State University of New York Press, 2002.

———. *First Outline of a System of the Philosophy of Nature*. Translated by Keith R. Peterson. Albany: State University of New York Press, 2004.

———. "Further Presentations from the System of Philosophy [Extract]." In *The Philosophical Rupture Between Fichte and Schelling*, by J. G. Fichte and F. W. J. Schelling, edited and translated by Michael G. Vater and David W. Wood, 206–225. Albany: State University of New York Press, 2012.

———. *The Grounding of Positive Philosophy*. Translated by Bruce Matthews. Albany: State University of New York Press, 2007.

———. *Ideas for a Philosophy of Nature*. Translated by Errol E. Harris and Peter Heath. Cambridge: Cambridge University Press, 1988.

———. "J. G. Fichte/F. W. J. Schelling: Correspondence (1800–1802)." In *The Philosophical Rupture Between Fichte and Schelling*, by J. G. Fichte and F. W. J. Schelling, edited

and translated by Michael G. Vater and David W. Wood, 21–75. Albany: State University of New York Press, 2012.
———. "Of the I as the Principle of Philosophy, or On the Unconditional in Human Knowledge." In *The Unconditional in Human Knowledge: Four Early Essays (1794-1796)*, translated by Fritz Marti, 59–149. Lewisburg: Bucknell University Press, 1980.
———. *On the History of Modern Philosophy*. Translated by Andrew Bowie. Cambridge: Cambridge University Press, 1994.
———. "On the World-Soul." Translated by Iain Hamilton Grant. *Collapse: Philosophical Research and Development* 6 (January 2010): 67–95.
———. *On University Studies*. Translated by E. S. Morgan. Athens: Ohio University Press, 1966.
———. *Philosophical Investigations Into the Essence of Human Freedom*. Translated by Jeff Love and Johannes Schmidt. Albany: State University of New York Press, 2006.
———. *Philosophy and Religion*. Translated by Klaus Ottmann. Putnam: Spring, 2010.
———. "Presentation of My System of Philosophy." In *The Philosophical Rupture Between Fichte and Schelling*, by J. G. Fichte and F. W. J. Schelling, edited and translated by Michael G. Vater and David W. Wood, 141–205. Albany: State University of New York Press, 2012.
———. "Stuttgart Seminars." In *Idealism and the Endgame of Theory: Three Essays by F. W. J. Schelling*, translated by Thomas Pfau, 195–268. Albany: State University of New York Press, 1994.
———. "System of Philosophy in General and of the Philosophy of Nature in Particular." In *Idealism and the Endgame of Theory: Three Essays by F. W. J. Schelling*, translated by Thomas Pfau, 139–194. Albany: State University of New York Press, 1994.
———. *System of Transcendental Idealism*. Translated by Peter Heath. Charlottesville: University Press of Virginia, 1978.
———. "Treatise Explicatory of the Idealism in the *Science of Knowledge*." In *Idealism and the Endgame of Theory: Three Essays by F. W. J. Schelling*, translated by Thomas Pfau, 61–138. Albany: State University of New York Press, 1994.
———. *Über das Wesen der menschlichen Freiheit*. Stuttgart: Reclam, 1964.
Schelling, F. W. J., and G. W. F. Hegel. "Introduction for the *Critical Journal of Philosophy*: On the Essence of Philosophical Criticism Generally, and Its Relationship to the Present State of Philosophy in Particular." Translated by H. S. Harris. In *Miscellaneous Writings of G.W.F. Hegel*, by G. W. F. Hegel, edited by Jon Stewart, 207–225. Evanston, IL: Northwestern University Press, 2002.
Schiller, Friedrich. *On the Aesthetic Education of Man*. Translated by Reginald Snell. Mineola: Dover, 2004.
Schmidt, Alfred. *The Concept of Nature in Marx*. Translated by Ben Fowkes. London: Verso, 2014.
Schulze, G. E. "Aenesidemus." Translated by George di Giovanni. In *Between Kant and Hegel: Texts in the Development of Post-Kantian Idealism*, edited by George di Giovanni and H. S. Harris, 104–135. Indianapolis: Hackett, 2000.
Sedgwick, Sally. *Hegel's Critique of Kant: From Dichotomy to Identity*. Oxford: Oxford University Press, 2012.
———. "Pippin on Hegel's Critique of Kant." *International Philosophical Quarterly* 33 (1993): 273–283.

Sellars, Wilfrid. *Empiricism and the Philosophy of Mind*. Cambridge: Harvard University Press, 1997.
Sève, Lucien. "Nature, science, dialectique: Un chantier à rouvrir." In *Sciences et dialectiques de la nature*, edited by Lucien Sève, 23–247. Paris: La Dispute, 1998.
———. "Pour en finir avec l'anachronisme." In *Sciences et dialectiques de la nature*, edited by Lucien Sève, 11–22. Paris: La Dispute, 1998.
Sheehan, Helena. *Marxism and the Philosophy of Science: A Critical History—the First Hundred Years*. 2nd ed. Amherst: Humanity, 1993.
Siep, Ludwig. "Hegel's Idea of a Conceptual Scheme." *Inquiry* 34 (1991): 63–76.
———. *Der Weg der Phänomenologie des Geistes: Ein einführender Kommentar zu Hegels "Differenzschrift" und "Phänomenologie des Geistes."* Frankfurt: Suhrkamp, 2000.
Spinoza, Baruch. *Ethics*. In *Complete Works*, edited by Michael L. Morgan, translated by Samuel Shirley, 213–382. Indianapolis: Hackett, 2002.
Stern, Robert. *Hegel, Kant, and the Structure of the Object*. London: Routledge, 1990.
———. "Hegel's Idealism." In *Hegelian Metaphysics*, 45–76. Oxford: Oxford University Press, 2009.
———. "Individual Existence and the Philosophy of Difference." In *Hegelian Metaphysics*, 345–370. Oxford: Oxford University Press, 2009.
———. "Introduction: How Is Hegelian Metaphysics Possible?" In *Hegelian Metaphysics*, 1–41. Oxford: Oxford University Press, 2009.
Stone, Alison. *Petrified Intelligence: Nature in Hegel's Philosophy*. Albany: State University of New York Press, 2005.
Taylor, Charles. *Hegel*. Cambridge: Cambridge University Press, 1975.
Testa, Italo. "Hegel's Naturalism or Soul and Body in the Encyclopedia." In *Essays on Hegel's Philosophy of Subjective Spirit*, edited by David Stern, 19–35. Albany: State University of New York Press, 2013.
Theunissen, Michael. *Sein und Schein: Die kritische Funktion der Hegelschen Logik*. Frankfurt: Suhrkamp, 1980.
Timpanaro, Sebastiano. *On Materialism*. Translated by Lawrence Garner. London: Verso, 1980.
Tosel, André. "Les aléas du matérialisme aléatoire dans la dernière philosophie de Louis Althusser." In *Sartre, Lukács, Althusser: des marxistes en philosophie*, edited by Eustache Kouvélakis and Vincent Charbonnier, 169–196. Paris: Presses Universitaires de France, 2005.
Uranovsky, Y. M. "Marxism and Natural Science." In *Marxism and Modern Thought*, by N. I. Bukharin et al., translated by Ralph Fox, 136–174. New York: Harcourt, Brace, 1935.
Vaysse, Jean-Marie. *Totalité et subjectivité: Spinoza dans l'idéalisme allemande*. Paris: Vrin, 1994.
Wallace, Robert M. *Hegel's Philosophy of Reality, Freedom, and God*. Cambridge: Cambridge University Press, 2005.
Wartenberg, Thomas E. "Hegel's Idealism: The Logic of Conceptuality." In *The Cambridge Companion to Hegel*, edited by Frederick C. Beiser, 102–129. Cambridge: Cambridge University Press, 1993.
Weil, Eric. *Hegel et l'état: Cinq conférences, suivies de Marx et la philosophie du droit*. Paris: Vrin, 2002.

Westphal, Kenneth R. "Hegel, Idealism, and Robert Pippin." *International Philosophical Quarterly* 33 (1993): 263–272.

Wetter, Gustav A. *Dialectical Materialism: A Historical and Systematic Survey of Philosophy in the Soviet Union*. Translated by Peter Heath. New York: Praeger, 1958.

Wood, Allen W. *Hegel's Ethical Thought*. Cambridge: Cambridge University Press, 1990.

Žižek, Slavoj. *Absolute Recoil: Towards a New Foundation of Dialectical Materialism*. London: Verso, 2014.

———. "The Abyss of Freedom." In *The Abyss of Freedom/Ages of the World*, by Slavoj Žižek and F. W. J. Schelling, 1–104. Ann Arbor: University of Michigan Press, 1997.

———. "Afterword: Lenin's Choice." In *Revolution at the Gates: Selected Writings of Lenin from 1917*, by V. I. Lenin, edited by Slavoj Žižek, 165–336. London: Verso, 2002.

———. "An Answer to Two Questions." In *Badiou, Žižek, and Political Transformations: The Cadence of Change*, by Adrian Johnston, 174–230. Evanston, IL: Northwestern University Press, 2009.

———. *Antigone*. London: Bloomsbury, 2016.

———. *À travers le réel: Entretiens avec Fabien Tarby*. Paris: Lignes, 2010.

———. "Da capo senza fine." In *Contingency, Hegemony, Universality: Contemporary Dialogues on the Left*, by Judith Butler, Ernesto Laclau, and Slavoj Žižek, 213–262. London: Verso, 2000.

———. *Disparities*. London: Bloomsbury, 2016.

———. *Enjoy Your Symptom!: Jacques Lacan in Hollywood and Out*. New York: Routledge, 1992.

———. "The Fear of Four Words: A Modest Plea for the Hegelian Reading of Christianity." In *The Monstrosity of Christ: Paradox or Dialectic?*, by Slavoj Žižek and John Milbank, edited by Creston Davis, 24–109. Cambridge: MIT Press, 2009.

———. "Foreword to the Second Edition: Enjoyment Within the Limits of Reason Alone." In *For They Know Not What They Do: Enjoyment as a Political Factor*, by Slavoj Žižek, xi–cvii. 2nd ed. London: Verso, 2002.

———. *For They Know Not What They Do: Enjoyment as a Political Factor*. 2nd ed. London: Verso, 2002.

———. *The Fragile Absolute, or Why Is the Christian Legacy Worth Fighting For?* London: Verso, 2000.

———. *The Fright of Real Tears: Krzysztof Kieślowski Between Theory and Post-Theory*. London: British Film Institute, 2001.

———. *In Defense of Lost Causes*. London: Verso, 2008.

———. *The Indivisible Remainder: An Essay on Schelling and Related Matters*. London: Verso, 1996.

———. "Lacan Between Cultural Studies and Cognitivism." In *Umbr(a): Science and Truth*, edited by Theresa Giron, 9–32. Buffalo: Center for the Study of Psychoanalysis and Culture, State University of New York at Buffalo, 2000.

———. *Less Than Nothing: Hegel and the Shadow of Dialectical Materialism*. London: Verso, 2012.

———. "Liberation Hurts: An Interview with Slavoj Žižek [with Eric Dean Rasmussen]." 2003. www.electronicbookreview.com/thread/endconstruction/desublimation.

———. *Living in the End Times*. London: Verso, 2010.
———. *Looking Awry: An Introduction to Jacques Lacan Through Popular Culture*. Cambridge: MIT Press, 1991.
———. *The Metastases of Enjoyment: Six Essays on Woman and Causality*. London: Verso, 1994.
———. *On Belief*. New York: Routledge, 2001.
———. *Organs Without Bodies: On Deleuze and Consequences*. New York: Routledge, 2004.
———. *The Parallax View*. Cambridge: MIT Press, 2006.
———. "The Parallax View: Toward a New Reading of Kant." *Epoché* 8, no. 2 (Spring 2004): 255–269.
———. *Le plus sublime des hystériques: Hegel passe*. Paris: Points Hors Ligne, 1988.
———. "Postface: Georg Lukács as the Philosopher of Leninism." In *A Defense of History and Class Consciousness: Tailism and the Dialectic*, by Georg Lukács, translated by Esther Leslie, 151–182. London: Verso, 2000.
———. "Preface: Burning the Bridges." In *The Žižek Reader*, edited by Elizabeth Wright and Edmond Wright, vii–x. Oxford: Blackwell, 1999.
———. *The Puppet and the Dwarf: The Perverse Core of Christianity*. Cambridge: MIT Press, 2003.
———. *The Sublime Object of Ideology*. London: Verso, 1989.
———. *Tarrying with the Negative: Kant, Hegel, and the Critique of Ideology*. Durham: Duke University Press, 1993.
———. "The Thing from Inner Space." In *Sexuation*, edited by Renata Salecl, 216–259. Durham: Duke University Press, 2000.
———. *The Ticklish Subject: The Absent Centre of Political Ontology*. London: Verso, 1999.
———. *Žižek's Jokes (Did You Hear the One About Hegel and Negation?)* Edited by Audun Mortensen. Cambridge: MIT Press, 2014.
Žižek, Slavoj, and Glyn Daly. *Conversations with Žižek*. Cambridge: Polity, 2004.
Žižek, Slavoj, and Renata Salecl. "Lacan in Slovenia (an Interview with Slavoj Žižek and Renata Salecl [with Peter Osborne])." In *A Critical Sense: Interviews with Intellectuals*, edited by Peter Osborne, 20–44. New York: Routledge, 1996.
Zupančič, Alenka. "'Encountering Lacan in the Next Generation': Interview with Alenka Zupančič [with Jones Irwin and Helena Motoh]." In *Žižek and His Contemporaries: On the Emergence of the Slovenian Lacan*, by Jones Irwin and Helena Motoh, 158–178. London: Bloomsbury, 2014.
———. *Ethics of the Real: Kant, Lacan*. London: Verso, 2000.
———. "Freedom and Cause." In *Why Psychoanalysis?: Three Interventions*, 31–56. Copenhagen: NSU Press, 2008.
———. *The Odd One In: On Comedy*. Cambridge: MIT Press, 2008.
———. *Das Reale einer Illusion: Kant und Lacan*. Translated by Reiner Ansén. Frankfurt: Suhrkamp, 2001.

Index

Absolute: absolute appearance coinciding with, 22, 31–32; access to, 38; actuality, 106–8; Being rejoined by, 109; caricatures of, 74; conflicts in, 16; contingency and, 76, 79–80, 107, 109, 111, 188; freedom, 163; illusion of, 29–30; Knowledge, 116; necessity, 75, 103–4, 106–11; Negativity, 16, 188–89; as result of Owl of Minerva, 79; self-reflection of, 31; as substance, 61
Absolute appearance, 22, 31–32
Absolute idealism, 20, 34, 79, 173–74, 244; deflationary approach and, 48–50, 55, 58–62, 64–66, 69–70; legacy of, 135; necessity in, 99; as realist, 143; rise of, 158; as speculation, 32–33; sublating of, 1–9
Absolute Knowing (*absolute Wissen*), xxvi, 116, 122
Absolute Recoil (Žižek): caricatures of Hegel fought in, 74; compatibilism in, 153, 163, 167, 176–77; contingency and, 90, 103, 121; deflationary approach and, 42, 45, 47; dialectical materialism reinvented by, 129–31, 133–35, 137–42, 144–45, 147–50; drive and desire in, 187, 190, 192, 196, 198, 235, 238, 240–41, 243–47; historical background of, 14–16, 36; new contributions of, 2; overview of, xiv, xxi–xxiv, xxviii, xxx–xxxii, 1–5, 7; in post-Kantian aftermath, 14–16, 32, 35–36; stuckness in, 235; on teleology, 121
Absolute Wissen (Absolute Knowing), xxvi, 116, 122
Abstract identity (*abstrakten Identität*), 91, 93
Abstract moment (*abstraktes Moment*), 91–93
Abstrakten Identität (Abstract identity), 91, 93
Abstraktes Moment (abstract moment), 91–93
Act: deferred, 111, 114, 156, 167; Lacan on, 152–55, 167–68; Žižek on, 152–56, 167–68
Actuality (*Wirklichkeit*): absolute, 106–8; Becoming enriched by, 104–5, 127; contingency and, 81–85, 88–95, 98–99, 103–8, 118–19, 123, 127; *Dasein* distinct from, 84, 88–89, 98; in "The Doctrine of Essence," 81–84, 98,

[321]

INDEX

Actuality (*Wirklichkeit*) (*cont.*) 103–8, 120; formal, 103–4, 106; modalities emerging out of, 83, 85; necessitation unnecessary for, 123; possibility and, 81, 83–85, 89–95, 98, 103–9, 113, 120–23, 127, 173, 212–13

Adorno, Theodor, 133

Aesthetics, Hegelian, 143

Aim: Kantian, 194–95, 198–99; Lacan on, 223–24

Aleatory materialism, 77–81, 109, 125

Alienation, separation distinct from, xxvii

Allison, Henry, 168, 172; incorporation thesis of, 164–66, 170; reciprocity thesis of, 49–50, 64, 66

Althusser, Louis, 5, 7, 14, 70, 76; aleatory materialism of, 77–81, 109, 125; "Portrait of the Materialist Philosopher," 79; "The Subterranean Current of the Materialism of the Encounter," 78–80

Ameriks, Karl, 42, 50

Analytic philosophical tradition, 3, 73, 161, 171, 184–85

Anatomy, 103, 213, 228

Anderen. See Other

Animality, humanity superseding, 195, 226, 240

Anthropology, Hegelian, 146, 197

Anti-Dühring (Engels), 5, 95–97, 100–102

"Antinomies of Pure Reason" (Kant), 96

Appearance: absolute, 22, 31–32; essence and, 30; Hegel on, 25–29, 46, 52; Žižek on, 22, 28–34

Après-coup: in cause and effect, 165; of Lacan, 80, 111, 114, 123, 156, 165, 167–68

Asubjective being, 18, 22, 38

Aufhebung (sublation), xix–xx, xxii, xxxii, 8, 20–21, 24, 64, 83, 85, 108, 144, 174; utopian pseudoversion of, xxxii

Authentic idealism (*echter Idealismus*), 64–65

Autonomy: loss of, 11–12; of subjectivity, 14, 33–34, 152, 154, 156–59, 161, 165–70, 173–75, 177–78, 184–85

Bacon, Francis, 53–60, 100

Badiou, Alain, 11, 29–30, 35, 132, 141; compatibilism of, 7, 167–68; *Logics of Worlds*, 134–35; ontology of, 137; Spinozism of freedom and, 14; Žižek relying on, 167–68

Badiou, Žižek, and Political Transformations (Johnston), 1

Barbagallo, Ettore, 14

Bare life, 135

Beckett, Samuel, 127

Becoming (*Werden*): actuality and possibility enriching, 104–5, 127; Hegel and, 40–41, 72; Necessity from, 89–90

Begriff (Concept), xix–xx, 41, 63, 116

Being (*Sein*): Absolute rejoining, 109; asubjective, 18, 22, 38; Hegel and, 39–41, 72, 245; names for, 6; into Nothingness, 39–41; void in, 157

Being-there. *See* Dasein

Beiser, Frederick, 42–43

Bencivenga, Ermanno, 76

Benjamin, Walter, 5, 79, 124–26, 132

Beobachtende Vernunft (Observing Reason), 53–54, 56, 87, 91

Besoin (need), 230–34

Bewußtsein. See Consciousness

Beyond the Pleasure Principle (*Jenseits des Lustprinzips*) (Freud), 154, 201–3, 205–8, 239

Big Other: barred, 159, 183; Lacan on, xxvi–xxvii, 147, 154–55, 159, 169, 202–3, 209, 211, 239; redoubling of, 203

Biology: in compatibilism, 151, 160, 162, 166, 168, 171–72, 175, 177, 180, 182; subjects arising from, 141. *See also* Neurobiology

Biopolitics, 135

Bloch, Ernst, 68

Bosteels, Bruno, 177–78

[322]

INDEX

Bourgeois, Bernard, 68
Bowman, Brady, 42
Brain: evolution of, 215, 222, 224, 229, 234; neuroplasticity of, 229–30; SEEKING system of, 215, 224. *See also* Neurobiology
Brandom, Robert, 42–43
Breidbach, Olaf, 226
Brücke, Ernst, 210
Burbidge, John, 76

Canguilhem, Georges, 79–80
Capital (Marx), xiii, xix
Capitalism: *Grundrisse* and, 101–2; monopoly, xix; rabble created by, 79–80, 117–19, 124–25
Cause and effect: *après-coup* in, 165; contingency and, 78, 96–102, 108, 114, 123; deterministic necessitation of, 213; logical status of, 165
Chalmers, David, 37
Choice of neurosis (*Neuronenwahl*), 176, 178, 183
Civilization and Its Discontents (Freud), 225
Cognitivism, 160, 176–78, 182–83
"Coldness and Cruelty" (Deleuze), 238–39
Communism: dialectical materialism and, 102, 125, 131–32; germs of, 127–28
Compatibilism: of Badiou, 7, 167–68; biology in, 151, 160, 162, 166, 168, 171–72, 175, 177, 180, 182; of Dennett, 160–62, 171–72; of dialectical materialism, 151–52, 182, 185; Fichte and, 151, 155–61, 164; of Hegel, 4–5, 96–100, 151, 154, 156–62, 164–67, 169–72, 174–75, 178–79, 182–85; of heteronomous natural substantiality and autonomous denaturalized subjectivity, 152, 166, 174, 185; incompatibilism and, 160–61, 164; Kant and, 151–61, 164–66, 168, 170–72, 177–79, 184; Lacan and, 152–56, 159–60, 163–65, 167–69, 173, 183–85;

natural science in, 151–52, 160, 162, 166, 168, 171–75, 177, 180, 182, 185; neurobiology in, 166–68, 170–72, 175–78, 180–83; psychoanalysis and, 152–55, 163–64, 166–67, 175, 177, 179–82, 184–85; quantum physics in, 151, 170–75; of Schelling, 151, 157–59, 161, 164, 173–78, 182–83, 185; of Žižek, 7, 151–86
Concept (*Begriff*), xix–xx, 41, 63, 116
Concept of Nature in Marx, The (Schmidt), 133
Concrete universality, xxviii–xxix, 20, 28
Conscience, 206
Consciousness (*Bewußtsein*): becoming Self-Consciousness, 28–29, 31, 50, 100; objectivity of, 55; in perception-consciousness system, 179–80; Reason distinguished from, 54, 58; Unhappy, 56–57
Conservatism, 118–19
Continental philosophical tradition, 3, 73, 171, 185
Contingency (*Zufälligkeit*): Absolute and, 76, 79–80, 107, 109, 111, 188; actuality and, 81–85, 88–95, 98–99, 103–8, 118–19, 123, 127; causality and, 78, 96–102, 108, 114, 123; dialectical materialism and, 74, 77–81, 96–97, 100, 102, 109, 113, 125; in "The Doctrine of Essence," 80–84, 98, 114; Engels and, 95–98; freedom and, 167–72, 174; in Hegelian System, 4, 76, 80–92, 94–96, 98, 100–107, 109–14, 116; Kant and, 83, 86, 93, 96, 110–11, 116; in *Less Than Nothing*, 75–77, 79, 103, 108, 110–11, 117, 121; nature and, 85–87, 95–103, 108, 123; necessity and, 4–5, 74–78, 80–81, 83–91, 94–111, 113–14, 120–23, 166–67, 170; possibility and, 76, 81, 83–85, 88–95, 98–99, 101–7, 113, 120–21, 123, 127; primacy of, xi, 4, 75–76, 167, 170, 188, 214; Ur-contingency, 77, 89–90, 107, 109; Žižek and, 74–81, 89–90, 103–4, 108–17, 119–23, 125, 127

[323]

Contribution to the Critique of Political Economy, A (Marx), 125
Critique of Practical Reason (Kant), 192
Critique of Pure Reason (Kant), 19, 38, 83, 178; Bacon and, 53; "The Doctrine of the Concept" on, 45–46; epistemology and ontology in, 18, 22; Jacobi dissatisfied with, 12; "Transcendental Aesthetic," 65–66; "Transcendental Analytic," 17, 23, 47, 52, 179; "Transcendental Deduction," 41, 47–50, 62–67, 179; "Transcendental Dialectic," xxvi, 15, 65–66
Critique of the Power of Judgment (Kant), 141
Culture: as Imaginary-Symbolic realities, 133–34; nature in opposition to, 173; as products of objective spirit, 102

Damasio, Antonio, 180
Darwin, Charles, 176, 212–15
Dasein (Being-there): actuality distinct from, 84, 88–89, 98; as beginning of Hegelian Logic, 40–41, 68, 72; modality introduced by, 85; possibility coemergent with, 104
Deacon, Terrence, 35–36
Death drive (*Todestrieb, pulsion de mort*): defined, 209; as extimate nucleus of Hegelian System, 187–89; Freudian-Lacanian, xv, xxx–xxxi, 7, 154, 187–88, 194–205, 208–11, 216, 219, 236–39, 244; introduction to, 7; Lear on, 201–3, 208–10, 216, 219, 228; as negativity, xv, xxx–xxxi, 194, 203, 206, 211, 216, 237–39
Deferred action, 111, 114, 156, 167
Deflationary approach, to Hegel: absolute idealism and, 48–50, 55, 58–62, 64–66, 69–70; dialectical materialism and, 45, 68, 72; dominance of, 3, 39; *Encyclopedia Logic* and, 40–41, 47, 51, 60–61, 63, 68–71; to Hegelian System, 23, 41, 50, 67–69, 71; *Phenomenology of Spirit* and, 38, 41, 48–59, 61, 69–71; of Pippin, 3, 39, 41–45, 47–52, 58–63, 65–68, 72; push-back against, 3, 42–43; Reason and, 38, 50–61, 64, 66; *Science of Logic* and, 40–42, 45, 47–49, 51–52, 58, 60, 62–64, 68, 70; subjective idealism and, 48–51, 55, 58–59, 64–66, 73; transcendental unity of apperception and, 39, 41, 46–49, 51–53, 55, 58, 60–62, 64, 66–67; Žižek and, 38–45, 47, 63, 67–68, 72–73
Deleuze, Gilles, 139; "Coldness and Cruelty," 238–39; *Difference and Repetition*, 238, 240; drive and, 217, 238–45; *The Logic of Sense*, 238–39
Demand (*demande*), 230–34
Democratic materialism, 135, 139
Democritus, 136
Dennett, Daniel, 160–62, 171–72, 177
Dérive (drift), 231
Descartes, René, 12, 23, 33, 56
Descartes' Error (Damasio), 180
Desire (*désir*): drive contrasted with, xii, 7–8, 187–88, 190–99, 219–23, 235, 238, 240–41, 245–47; Kant and, 153, 188, 190–92, 240–41; *objet petit a*, 193, 198, 224, 229, 237; Žižek on, 187, 190, 192, 196, 198, 223, 229–35, 237–38, 240–41, 243–47
Destiny (*Schicksal*), 103
Determinism: freedom and, 12, 96, 151, 160–66, 170, 177–78, 183, 185; necessity and, 212–13; self-determination distinct from, 161
Diachrony, 150
Dialectical materialism: future work of, 186; horror, 79; introduction to, xi–xii, xiv, 2–9; regression back behind, 248; Žižek reinventing, xiii–xiv, 5–9, 68, 72, 74, 77–79, 81, 109, 113, 125, 129–52, 185–86. *See also specific topics*
Dialectics: ancient art of, 15, 21; drive of, 7, 188; of Hegel, 21, 38, 121, 189, 192, 235; of libidinal economy, 241;

metadialectics, 134, 194, 220–21, 241; nondialectical ground of, 187–90; repetition-difference, 235–38
Diamat, 78–79, 99
Dietzgen, Joseph, 5
Difference, repetition and, 235–38
Difference and Repetition (Deleuze), 238, 240
Differenzschrift (Hegel), 27, 49, 51, 63–66
Ding, das (Real Thing), 229, 237
Ding an sich (thing in itself): Kant and, 12, 19–21, 52–53, 65–66, 157; transcendental subjectivity conflated with, 157
Discursive idealism, 134
Disparities (Žižek), 42, 138
Disunity (*Zerrißenheit*), 225–26
"Doctrine of Being, The" (*Die Lehre vom Sein*) (Hegel), 72, 81; Becoming in, 68, 104, 120; Houlgate and, 41, 67; Pippin and, 42, 52
"Doctrine of Essence, The" (*Die Lehre vom Wesen*) (Hegel): actuality in, 81–84, 98, 103–8, 120; cause and effect in, 114; contingent in, 80–84, 98, 114; Henrich and, 41, 67
"Doctrine of the Concept, The" (*Die Lehre vom Begriff*) (Hegel): Pippin and, 41–42, 45–47, 60, 67; Subjective Logic and, xvi, 41, 81
Doz, André, 76
Dreams, interpretation of, 206–7
Drift (*dérive*), 231
Drive (*pulsion, Trieb*): Deleuze and, 217, 238–45; desire contrasted with, xii, 7–8, 187–88, 190–99, 219–23, 235, 238, 240–41, 245–47; of dialectics, 7, 188; as drift, 231; evolution and, 200, 211–18, 220–29, 234; Freud and, xv, xxx–xxxi, 7, 154, 187–89, 194–225, 227, 229–31, 233–34, 236–40, 244–47; Hegel and, 187–92, 194–97, 236; instinct contrasted with, 194–95, 197–98, 204, 229, 231, 234; Lacan and, xv, xxx–xxxi, 7, 154, 187–205, 207–12, 214–16, 218–19, 221–24, 227, 229–45, 247; maladaptive, 210, 220, 222–23, 227; naturalism of, 210–12; ontology of, 199, 201, 215–16, 242–47; oral, 195–96; play, 192; pleasure principle and, 154, 200–11, 216–20, 222–23, 234, 237, 239–40; in psychoanalysis, xv, xxx–xxxi, 7, 154, 187–88, 194–205, 208–11, 216–19, 235–39, 244; satisfaction of, 193; subject and, 194; in *Time Driven*, 189, 209–11, 216, 218–19, 224, 239; Žižek on, 187–201, 203–4, 207–10, 212, 215–16, 218–23, 229, 235–48. *See also* Death drive
Düsing, Klaus, 30, 75

"Earliest System-Program of German Idealism, The" (Hegel), 13–14, 29, 61, 178
Early-modern rationalist substance metaphysics, 23
Eastern/Soviet Marxism, 5, 132–33
Echter Idealismus (authentic idealism), 64–65
Ecological green thinking, 139, 145
Ego psychology, 196
Elements of the Philosophy of Right (Hegel): Philosophy of the Real in, 115; preface to, 71, 79, 81–82, 111, 115–17, 119
Elsewhere, 32; absence of, 22, 159; introduction to, xx, xxv, xxvii
Emergent dual-aspect monism, 181
Emergentism, 141–42, 174, 181, 185
Encounter, materialism of, 78–80
Encyclopedia Logic (Hegel), xix–xxi, 21, 23–24; conclusion of, 143; contingent in, 4, 81–86, 88–91, 94, 96, 100–102, 104–5, 107, 110; deflationary approach and, 40–41, 47, 51, 60–61, 63, 68–71; divisions of, 41; opening of, 39–40
Encyclopedia of the Philosophical Sciences (Hegel), xvi, 75; conclusion of, 188; structure of, 112–13, 115. *See also Science of Logic*

INDEX

Engels, Friedrich: *Anti-Dühring*, 5, 95–97, 100–102; dialectical materialism of, 5–6, 96–97, 100, 102, 129, 131–33, 136, 140–41; Hegel and, xiii, 4–5, 95–102, 120; *Naturdialektik* of, 133, 136

Ent-Scheidung (unconscious decision), 176, 178, 182–83

Epigenetics, 229–30

Epistemology: of Kant, 12, 15–16, 18–19, 22–25, 157–58; ontology and, 12, 15–16, 18–19, 22–23, 25, 38, 43–45, 71, 157–59

Essay Concerning Human Understanding, An (Locke), 18–19

Ethical act, 152–53

Ethical subject, 154, 164, 166

Ethics (Spinoza), 97

Ethics, Kantian, 172, 191–92

Ethics of Psychoanalysis, The (Lacan), 152

Evental subjectivity, 168

Evolution: of brain, 215, 222, 224, 229, 234; Darwin on, 176, 212–15; drive and, 200, 211–18, 220–29, 234; in nature, 212–17, 226–27

Evolutionary materialism, 44

Existence (*Existenz*), 175; essence and, 82–83; facticity tied to, 89–90

Extended mind, models of, 183–84

Fact/act (*Tat-Handlung*), 155–56

Fascism, 126

Fatalism, 12, 100

Faust (Goethe), xiv–xv, xxii, xxix

Fechner, Gustav, 210

Feuerbach, Ludwig, 134

Fichte, J. G., 6, 49, 119; compatibilism and, 151, 155–61, 164; in post-Kantian aftermath, 12–16, 19–20, 22, 33–36, 47; Schelling breaking with, 13; on self-consciousness, 155; transcendental idealism of, 20, 53, 56, 65, 155–58, 244; *Wissenschaftslehre*, 12, 191

"First Philosophy of Spirit" (Hegel), 51

Formal actuality, 103–4, 106

For They Know Not What They Do (Žižek), 2

Frank, Manfred, 163

Freedom: absolute, 163; abyss of, 177, 183; barred big Other as condition of, 159; contingency and, 167–72, 174; determinism and, 12, 96, 151, 160–66, 170, 177–78, 183, 185; as foundational, 6; Freud on, 163; of *Geist*, 102, 143–44; as necessity, 95–97, 99–101, 162–63, 167; self-determinacy as, 142; Spinozisms of, 12–14, 16, 34–35, 178; of spontaneous subjectivity, 12–13, 33–34, 36, 96–97, 100, 152, 155–59, 161, 164–65, 169–70, 173, 175, 177–78, 183–84; system or, 11–14, 16, 19–20, 22–25, 30, 34–35, 37

Freedom Evolves (Dennett), 160–62, 171

Free will, 160–61, 166, 171, 175

Freiheitschrift (Schelling), 15, 225

French Revolution, 6, 11, 82, 119

Freud, Sigmund: on anatomy and destiny, 103; *Beyond the Pleasure Principle*, 154, 201–3, 205–8, 239; *Civilization and Its Discontents*, 225; Darwin and, 214–15; drive and, xv, xxx–xxxi, 7, 154, 187–89, 194–225, 227, 229–31, 233–34, 236–40, 244–47; on freedom, 163; *The Interpretation of Dreams*, 206–7; Lacan and, 74, 164; Libet and, 182–83; on libidinal economy, 189, 195, 204, 220–25, 227, 229–31, 233–34, 245; *Nachträglichkeit* of, 80, 111, 114, 123, 156, 167; naturalism of, 210–12, 220; *Neuronenwahl* of, 176, 178, 183; perception-consciousness system of, 179–80; pleasure principle of, 153–54, 200–11, 216–20, 222–23, 234, 237, 239–40; *Three Essays on the Theory of Sexuality*, 204; *Wiederholungszwang* of, 200, 204, 208, 217, 220, 229, 233, 237–40

Fulda, Hans Friedrich, 67

Future metaphysics, 24

[326]

INDEX

Gabriel, Markus, 42
Gadamer, Hans-Georg, 68
Geist (Spirit), 4, 24, 62–64, 69–70; emergence of, 96–97, 143, 147, 150; freedom of, 102, 143–44; future of, 116–17, 120; independent existence of, 143; *Natur und*, 29, 70, 97, 130, 138, 140, 143–47, 149–50; quantum physics and, 173
Geistesphilosophie (Philosophy of Mind): evolutionary theory in, 212; of Hegel, xv, 69–70, 72, 75, 113–15, 130, 140, 146, 212; *Naturphilosophie* linked to, 146
German idealism: crucial problem of, 39; defined, 11; first-person perspective of, 44; history of, 2–7, 14–15. *See also specific topics*
Gewohnheit (Habit), 146–47
Glauben und Wissen (Hegel), 26
Goal: Hegelian, 190, 193–95, 198–99; Lacan on, 223–24
Goethe, Johann Wolfgang von, xiv–xv, xxii, xxix
Graham, Loren R., 132
Greece, fetishization of, 40
Grenze (simple external limit), 119–20
Grundrisse (Marx), xiii, 101–2, 213, 228

Habit (*Gewohnheit*), 146–47
Haeckel, Ernst, 91
Harris, H. S., 13, 47, 50
Hartmann, Klaus, 42
Haym, Rudolf, 81
Hegel, G. W. F.: contemporary relevance of, 125–28; introduction to, xi–xxxiii, 2–9; regression back behind, 248; resurrected, 114–15; return to, xi, xxvi, xxxiii, 7, 38–39, 74, 142. *See also specific topics*
"Hegel and Humor" (Bloch), 68
Hegelian System: architectonic of, xxii, 3–4, 112–13, 212; caricatures of, 74–75, 112; contingency in, 4, 76, 80–92, 94–96, 98, 100–7, 109–14, 116; death drive as extimate nucleus of, 187–89; deflationary approach to, 23, 41, 50, 67–69, 71; dialectical materialism and, xii, 2–8, 72, 74, 77–78, 81, 96–97, 109, 129–30, 133–38, 140–47, 149–50; flaws of, 2; introduction to, xi–xxxiii, 2–9, 23; irrational core of, 120; sexuality accommodated by, 197; start of, 23, 41, 67
Hegel on Self-Consciousness (Pippin), 43
Hegel's Idealism (Pippin), 43
Hegel's Practical Philosophy (Pippin), 43
Hegel's Rabble (Ruda), 79, 117–18
Heidegger, Martin, 40, 188
Henrich, Dieter, 41, 67, 76
Heteronomous natural substantiality, autonomous denaturalized subjectivity compatible with, 152, 166, 174, 185
Historical materialism, 45, 247; dialectical materialism and, 5, 133; Hegel and, 72, 91, 96; predictive power of, xii, 4, 79, 111, 116, 124–25
History and Class Consciousness (Lukács), 133
Hogrebe, Wolfram, 16
Hölderlin, Friedrich, 247; "On Judgment and Being," 12–13, 16, 29, 61, 244–45; Schelling and, 12–13, 178, 244
Holy Spirit, 57
Horkheimer, Max, 133
Horstmann, Rolf-Peter, 42
Houlgate, Stephen, 41–42, 59, 67
"How the Ordinary Human Understanding Takes Philosophy (as Displayed in the Works of Mr. Krug)" (Hegel), 51
Humanity: animality superseded by, 195, 226, 240; history of, 90–91, 102, 185, 228; Nature and, 146–50; organisms and, 172
Hume, David, 93, 158
Hyppolite, Jean, 14, 76

Id, unconscious conflated with, 163–64
Idealism. *See* German idealism
Ideational logic, xviii, 22, 62, 136
Identity (*Identität*), 104–6, 149; abstract, 91, 93; subjectivity and, 152–53
Illness, 219, 225, 227
Imaginary-Symbolic realities, 153, 169; culture as, 133–34; disruption of, 167, 239; Other and, 230
Immortality, 99, 190–91
Impossibility: possibility paired with, xxxi–xxxii, 4, 22, 44, 83, 88, 232–33, 244; void as, 148
Incompatibilism, 160–61, 164
Incorporation thesis, 164–66, 170
In Defense of Lost Causes (Žižek), 1
Indeterminacy: quantum, 142, 170–71, 175; self-determinacy conflated with, 170, 172–73
Indivisible Remainder, The (Žižek), 5, 39, 173, 175
Innere als übersinnliche Jenseits (inner world), 26–28, 31
Inner-party disputes, xi, 9
Inner world (*Innere als übersinnliche Jenseits*), 27–28
Instinct (*Instinkt*): drive contrasted with, 194–95, 197–98, 204, 229, 231, 234; in libidinal economy, 220–24, 229–31, 233–34; maladaptive, 217–18, 222; *Wiederholungszwang* as, 217
Interpretation of Dreams, The (Freud), 206–7

Jacobi, F. H.: Kantianism and, 11–12, 19, 34–35, 157; on Spinoza, 12; on systems, 11–12
Jenseits des Lustprinzips (*Beyond the Pleasure Principle*) (Freud), 154, 201–3, 205–8, 239
Johnston, Adrian: *Badiou, Žižek, and Political Transformations*, 1; "The Voiding of Weak Nature," 122–23; *Žižek's Ontology*, 1–2, 16, 76, 189, 199. *See also* Time Driven
Jokes, 67–68
Jouissance, 153, 219, 223–24, 229, 234

Kant, Immanuel: aim of, 194–95, 198–99; "Antinomies of Pure Reason," 96; compatibilism and, 151–61, 164–66, 168, 170–72, 177–79, 184; contingency and, 83, 86, 93, 96, 110–11, 116; *Critique of Practical Reason*, 192; *Critique of the Power of Judgment*, 141; desire and, 153, 188, 190–92, 240–41; dialectics revived by, 15, 21; *Ding an sich* and, 12, 19–21, 52–53, 65–66, 157; epistemology of, 12, 15–16, 18–19, 22–25, 157–58; ethics of, 172, 191–92; German idealism emerging from, 2; Hegel subtracting from, xiv, xxiv, 17–18, 21–22, 116, 191; incorporation thesis and, 164–66, 170; introduction to, xiv, xxvi–xxvii, 2–3, 6–7, 11; Jacobi and, 11–12, 19, 34–35, 157; Lacan paired with, 152–56, 159–60, 168, 188, 191–92, 240–41; metaphysics of morals of, 154, 165, 192; ontology and, 12, 15–25, 38; Other of, xxvi; Pippin and, 39, 41, 43–45, 47–49, 59–63, 65–67, 72, 179; reciprocity thesis and, 49–50, 64, 66; regression back behind, 248; transcendental idealism of, 11–15, 17–25, 27, 33, 38, 43, 48, 51–53, 56, 58–59, 62–66, 70, 155–58, 244; Žižek and, 14–18, 20–22, 24–25, 28–37. *See also Critique of Pure Reason*; post-Kantian aftermath
Kautsky, Karl, 5
Kervégan, Jean-François, 42
Knowledge: absence of, 157–58; Absolute, as distinct from Absolute Knowing, 116
Kojève, Alexandre, 4, 114
Kreines, James, 42
Krug, W. T., 75

INDEX

Lacan, Jacques, 21, 150; on acts, 152–55, 167–68; on aim, 223–24; *après-coup* of, 80, 111, 114, 123, 156, 165, 167–68; on big Other, xxvi–xxvii, 147, 154–55, 159, 169, 202–3, 209, 211, 239; compatibilism and, 152–56, 159–60, 163–65, 167–69, 173, 183–85; on death drive, xv, xxx–xxxi, 7, 154, 187–88, 194–205, 208–11, 216, 219, 236–39, 244; Deleuze praised by, 238–39; desire and, 223, 229–35, 237; drive and, xv, xxx–xxxi, 7, 154, 187–205, 207–12, 214–16, 218–19, 221–24, 227, 229–45, 247; *The Ethics of Psychoanalysis*, 152; Freud and, 74, 164; on goals, 223–24; *jouissance* of, 153, 219, 223–24, 229, 234; Kant paired with, 152–56, 159–60, 168, 188, 191–92, 240–41; on libidinal economy, 189, 195, 219, 221–24, 227, 229–34; negativity of, 242–43; *objet petit a* of, 193, 198, 224, 229, 237; Owl of Minerva of, 189; *Seminar XVI*, 239; on sexuality, 227; signifier theory of, 233–35, 237–38, 242; "Some Reflections on the Ego," 196; Žižek relying on, xiii, xxvi–xxvii, 2, 14–15, 148, 167, 189, 198

Language: for nature, 147–49; quantum physics and, 173; thinking bound by, 87–88

Laplace's demon, 170, 178, 185

Lardic, Jean-Marie, 76

Lear, Jonathan: on death drive, 201–3, 208–10, 216, 219, 228; on pleasure principle, 201–2

Lebrun, Gérard, 76

Lehre vom Begriff, Die. See "Doctrine of the Concept, The"

Lehre vom Sein, Die. See "Doctrine of Being, The"

Lehre vom Wesen, Die. See "Doctrine of Essence, The"

Leibniz, Gottfried Wilhelm, 74, 84–87, 93

Lenin, V. I.: dialectical materialism of, 5–6, 129–34, 137; *Materialism and Empirio-Criticism*, 5, 129–32, 171; *Philosophical Notebooks*, 129, 132; on *Science of Logic*, 129; Žižek and, 5, 129–34, 137, 171

Less Than Nothing (Žižek): appearance in, 28–34; caricatures of Hegel fought in, 74; compatibilism in, 151–52, 154–59, 162–64, 166–67, 169–72, 175, 181; contingency in, 75–77, 79, 103, 108, 110–11, 117, 121; deflationary approach and, 39, 41–43, 45, 47, 63, 68, 72; dialectical materialism reinvented by, 129–31, 133–40, 143–46, 151; drive and desire in, 187–88, 190–98, 235–38, 240–41, 243–47; historical background of, 14–16, 36; new contributions of, 2; overview of, xiii–xv, xxii–xxv, xxvii–xxviii, xxx–xxxii, 1–5, 7; in post-Kantian aftermath, 14–16, 18, 20–22, 25, 28–31, 33–36; stuckness in, 235; on teleology, 121–22

Letters on the Aesthetic Education of Man (Schiller), 191–92

Lévi-Strauss, Claude, 15

Libet, Benjamin: compatibilist naturalization of Kant via, 172; Freud and, 182–83; neurobiological research of, 166–68, 170–72, 175–78, 180–83; ontology of, 181; in *Organs Without Bodies*, 175–76; in *The Parallax View*, 178–79

Libidinal economy: anorganic, 219–34; crack in, 239; dialectics of, 241; Freud theorizing, 189, 195, 204, 220–25, 227, 229–31, 233–34, 245; instinct in, 220–24, 229–31, 233–34; Lacan theorizing, 189, 195, 219, 221–24, 227, 229–34; Marx and, 227–28; political economy illuminating, 227–28; Žižek reconstructing, xii, 189, 219–23, 229, 231, 239–41

Life sciences: Marxism and, 141; as proving grounds, 132, 174–75, 216. *See also* Biology

INDEX

Limitation proper (*Schranke*), 119–20
Locke, John, 18–20
Logic (*Logik*): beginning of, 40–42, 45, 67–72; caricatures of, 75, 112; categories, unfolding of, 140; conclusion of, 143; ideational, xviii, 22, 62, 136; importance of, 4; independence of, 115; introduction to, xii–xiii, 4; metaphysics and, 69–70; Objective, 23–24, 41, 81; *Phenomenology of Spirit* related to, 41; Real and, 115–16, 120; *Realphilosophie* and, xii, 69, 71–72, 75, 88, 112–16, 143; revision and, 115; strict logical abstractness of, 105; Subjective, xvi, 41, 50, 62, 81; *Ur*-contingency prioritized by, 89. *See also Encyclopedia Logic; Science of Logic*
Logic of Sense, The (Deleuze), 238–39
Logics of Worlds (Badiou), 134–35
Logik. See Logic
Lukács, Georg, 5, 76, 89, 133–34
Lustprinzip. See Pleasure principle
Lysenko, Trofim Denisovich, 132

Mabille, Bernard, 76
Maimon, Salomon, 35
Malabou, Catherine, 76
Mannoni, Octave, 112
Marcuse, Herbert, 30, 76
Marmasse, Gilles, 39, 76
Marx, Karl, 4, 28, 43, 96, 196; *Capital*, xiii, xix; contemporary relevance of, 125–27; *A Contribution to the Critique of Political Economy*, 125; *Grundrisse*, xiii, 101–2, 213, 228; Hegel and, xiii, 134, 142; libidinal economy and, 227–28; rabble and, 79
Marxism: Darwinism criticized in, 213; dialectical materialism, 77, 130, 185, 247; Eastern/Soviet, 5, 132–33; Hegelianism contrasted with, 74, 95, 117–19, 134; life sciences and, 141; nonaleatory materialisms in, 78; Western-European, 5, 133. *See also* Historical materialism

Materialism: third-person perspective of, 44; for twenty-first century, 189–90. *See also specific topics*
Materialism and Empirio-Criticism (Lenin), 5, 129–32, 171
Matter: disappearance of, 129; materialism without, 129, 135–37, 139–40; spiritualized, 135
McDowell, John, 43, 179
Meditations on First Philosophy (Descartes), 56
Meillassoux, Quentin, 34, 141, 157–58
Melancholia, 206
Metadialectics, 134, 194, 220–21, 241
Metaphysics: beginnings of, xi–xii; deflationary approach to, 38–43, 48, 53, 57, 59, 65–66, 69–73; early-modern rationalist substance, 23; future, 24; Hegel and, 3, 38–43, 48, 53, 57, 59, 65–66, 69–74, 82–83, 89, 110, 115–16, 120, 140; Logic and, 69–70; of morals, 154, 165, 192; philosophical approach of, 32; Platonic, 136, 139–40; in post-Kantian aftermath, 12–13, 15–24, 26–27, 30–33; Spinozan monistic substance, 12; as transcendental realism, 32–33; Žižek and, 38–40, 139. *See also* Deflationary approach, to Hegel
Miller, Jacques-Alain, 155
Mind-body problem, 151
Modal categories: of Hegel, 4, 85, 95, 98, 103, 108, 110, 114; introduction to, 4. *See also specific categories*
Möglichkeit. See Possibility
Monism, 12, 34, 97, 181–82, 243
Monopoly capitalism, xix
Moore, G. E., 3
Morals, metaphysics of, 154, 165, 192
More-is-less principle, 247–48
Myth of the nongiven, 244

Nachträglichkeit, 80, 111, 114, 123, 156, 167
Natur. See Nature
Natural history, xii, 185, 212–15, 221–22, 228

INDEX

Natural science, 35–36, 99, 102, 140; as artificial configuration, 133; Bacon and, 53; in compatibilism, 151–52, 160, 162, 166, 168, 171–75, 177, 180, 182, 185; German idealism combined with, 151–52, 154–55, 157–58, 161, 163–68, 170, 172–73, 175, 179–80, 184–85; life sciences, 132, 141, 174–75, 216; *Naturdialektik* combined with, 96; necessitarian worldview of, 87; Newtonian physics, 31, 130, 178; Soviet, 132; subjectivity proven in, 173–75. *See also* Biology; Quantum physics

Naturdialektik, 5, 133, 136, 141

Nature (*Natur*): as artificial configuration, 133; contingencies and, 85–87, 95–103, 108, 123; culture in opposition to, 173; de-naturalization of, 138–39, 144, 148; evolutionary, 212–17, 226–27; *Geist* and, 29, 70, 97, 130, 138, 140, 143–47, 149–50; humanity and, 146–50; independent existence of, 143, 146; language for, 147–49; as macro-/mega-Subject, 150; maladaptation in, 217–18; naturalism of, 172; as not-all barred Other, 211; as Real, 70, 133–34, 136, 147; as self-shattering, 145–46; spiritualized, 138–39, 144; weakness of, 87, 137, 139, 149, 212, 234

Naturphilosophie (Philosophy of Nature): evolutionary theory in, 212, 214; *Geistesphilosophie* linked to, 146; of Hegel, xi, 3, 6, 13, 69–72, 75–76, 96–97, 113, 130, 133, 136, 141–45, 159, 246; of Schelling, 16, 141, 159, 173, 178, 225–26

Navarro, Fernanda, 79

Necessity (*Notwendigkeit*): absolute, 75, 103–4, 106–11; in absolute idealism, 99; from becoming, 89–90; broadness of, 101; contingency and, 4–5, 74–78, 80–81, 83–91, 94–111, 113–14, 120–23, 166–67, 170; of destiny, 103; deterministic, 212–13; formal, 106; freedom as, 95–97, 99–101, 162–63, 167; looseness of, 213–14; in natural sciences, 87; of past, 121, 123; "Pleasure and Necessity" figure and, 91; process of, 88–89; *Ur*-necessity, 89, 107; world-historical individuals and, 99

Need (*besoin*), 230–34

Negativity: Absolute, 16, 188–89; death drive as, xv, xxx–xxxi, 194, 203, 206, 211, 216, 237–39; of Hegel, 31, 75, 111, 114, 117, 124, 179, 188–89, 191–92, 194, 238, 242, 247; introduction to, xv–xvii, xxi, xxiv–xxvii, xxx–xxxii, 7–8; Lacanian, 242–43; power of, xv, xvii, 117, 138; of pre-human real, 149; Western, 237–38

Neo-Platonism, 8, 16, 244–45, 247

Neo-Spinozism, 8, 242–47

Neurobiology: in compatibilism, 166–68, 170–72, 175–78, 180–83; Damasio investigating, 180; German idealism synthesized with, 168; Libet researching, 166–68, 170–72, 175–78, 180–83

Neuronenwahl (choice of neurosis), 176, 178, 183

Neuroplasticity, 229–30

Neuroses, 176, 178, 183, 218

New, rise of, 121

New Organon (Bacon), 53

Newtonian physics, 31, 130, 178

Niethammer, Friedrich Immanuel, 22

Nihilism, 12

Nirvana principle, 200

Nominalism, 30

Nonaleatory materialisms, 78

Nongiven, myth of, 244

Not-all barred Other, nature as, 211

Nothingness/Void, xii; Being passing into, 39–41; Hegel and, 40, 72; as impossibility, 148; materialism without matter and, 136; negative theology of, 246; Real as, 35, 147–49, 244, 246; rise of New and, 121

Notwendigkeit. *See* Necessity

Object-cause of desire (*objet petit a*), 193, 198, 224, 229, 237
Objective idealism, 6, 20, 32–33, 158, 244
Objective Logic, 23–24, 41, 81
Objective spirit (*objektive Geist*): culture as products of, 102; Hegel on, 63, 102, 113, 147, 159, 183–84, 197
Objet petit a (object-cause of desire), 193, 198, 224, 229, 237
Observing Reason (*Beobachtende Vernunft*), 53–54, 56, 87, 91
Ohnmacht der Natur (weakness of nature), 87, 137, 139, 149, 212, 234
"On Judgment and Being" ("*Über Urtheil und Seyn*") (Hölderlin), 12–13, 16, 29, 61, 244–45
Ontology: of Badiou, 137; beginnings of, xi–xii, 246–47; of drive theory, 199, 201, 215–16, 242–47; epistemology and, 12, 15–16, 18–19, 22–23, 25, 38, 43–45, 71, 157–59; Hegel-inspired, 3, 39–40, 43–45, 49–50, 53, 61–62, 66, 69–72, 201, 246; incomplete, 35–36, 169, 243; Kant and, 12, 15–25, 38; of Libet, 181; realist post-Kantian, 38; as unavoidable, 22; of Žižek, xxix–xxx, 7, 138–39, 177, 215, 244
Oral drive, 195–96
Organische in Hegels Denken, Das (Breidbach), 226
Organs Without Bodies (Žižek), 175–76, 182–83
Other (*Anderen, Autre*), 50, 52, 54, 109; Imaginary and Symbolic, 230; Kantian, xxvi; lack in, 159; nature as, 211; nonalienated, xxvii; of the Other, 203, 209; Real, 232–33; satisfaction, 223. *See also* Big Other
Owl of Minerva: Absolute as result of, 79; Darwinism similar to, 214; hindsight of, xv, xxviii, 70–71, 79, 110, 112, 116–17, 120, 122, 189, 197, 214; Lacanian, 189

Panksepp, Jaak, 219
Panpsychism, 139–40, 142, 144, 149

Pantheism controversy (*Pantheismusstreit*), 12
Parallax View, The (Žižek), 1, 175, 178–79
Parmenides (Plato), 15
Peperzak, Adrien, 14
Perception (*Wahrnehmung*), 26–27, 54, 58
Perception-consciousness system, 179–80
Phenomenology of Spirit (Hegel), xiv–xvi, xx, 245; absurd rationalizations in, 87; appearance in, 25–29; deflationary approach and, 38, 41, 48–59, 61, 69–71; innovations of, 38; introductory role of, 115; Logic related to, 41; Observing Reason in, 53–54, 56, 87, 91; "Pleasure and Necessity" figure in, 91; preface to, xxi, 13, 61, 83, 118; starting point in, 23–24
Philosophical Notebooks (Lenin), 129, 132
Philosophy of History (Hegel), 107, 119; fatalism in, 100; prediction in, 124–25; Žižek on, 90–91, 110, 112
Philosophy of Mind. *See Geistesphilosophie*
Philosophy of Nature. *See Naturphilosophie*
Philosophy of Subjective Spirit, 197
Philosophy of the Real. *See Realphilosophie*
Phrenology, 54, 87
Phylogenetics, 69, 91, 184–85, 229
Physics. *See* Newtonian physics; Quantum physics
Pinkard, Terry, 42, 76
Pippin, Robert: deflationary approach of, 3, 39, 41–45, 47–52, 58–63, 65–68, 72; "The Doctrine of Being" and, 42, 52; "The Doctrine of the Concept" and, 41–42, 45–47, 60, 67; as foil for Žižek, 3, 42–45, 47, 63, 163; *Hegel on Self-Consciousness*, 43; *Hegel's Idealism*, 43; *Hegel's Practical Philosophy*, 43; Kant and, 39, 41, 43–45, 47–49, 59–63, 65–67, 72, 179

Plato, 30, 119; metaphysics of, 136, 139–40; Neo-Platonism and, 8, 16, 244–45, 247; *Parmenides*, 15; *Republic*, 228
Play drive (*Spieltrieb*), 192
"Pleasure and Necessity" figure, 91
Pleasure principle (*Lustprinzip*): drive and, 154, 200–211, 216–20, 222–23, 234, 237, 239–40; failures of, 205–7, 210, 216; of Freud, 153–54, 200–11, 216–20, 222–23, 234, 237, 239–40; Lear on, 201–2; *Beyond the Pleasure Principle* on, 154, 201–3, 205–8, 239
Plekhanov, Georgi, 79
Pöbel (rabble), 79–80, 117–19, 124–25
Pöggeler, Otto, 13
Political economy, libidinal economy illuminated by, 227–28
"Portrait of the Materialist Philosopher" (Althusser), 79
Possibility (*Möglichkeit*): actuality and, 81, 83–85, 89–95, 98, 103–9, 113, 120–23, 127, 173, 212–13; Becoming enriched by, 104–5, 127; contingency and, 76, 81, 83–85, 88–95, 98–99, 101–7, 113, 120–21, 123, 127; *Dasein* coemergent with, 104; empty, 93; formal, 106; impossibility paired with, xxxi–xxxii, 4, 22, 44, 83, 88, 232–33, 244
Post-Fichtean idealism, 20, 29
Post-Kantian aftermath: *Absolute Recoil* in, 14–16, 32, 35–36; Fichte in, 12–16, 19–20, 22, 33–36, 47; Hegel in, 2, 12–36; idealism in, 2, 11–15, 17, 19–23, 25, 27–35, 244–45; *Less Than Nothing* in, 14–16, 18, 20–22, 25, 28–31, 33–36; metaphysics in, 12–13, 15–24, 26–27, 30–33; realist ontology in, 38; Schelling in, 12–16, 19–20, 29, 31, 33, 157
Post-traumatic stress disorder (PTSD), 206–7
Potencies (*Potenzen*), 173–75

Practical, primacy of, 12, 35, 191
Prädikation und Genesis (Hogrebe), 16
Pre-human real, 35, 147–49
Prigogine, Ilya, 35–36
Primary narcissism, 245
Principle of sufficient reason, 87, 93, 162, 169
Process of necessity (*Prozeß der Notwendigkeit*), 88–89
Psychoanalysis: compatibilism and, 152–55, 163–64, 166–67, 175, 177, 179–82, 184–85; dream interpretation in, 206–7; drive in, xv, xxx–xxxi, 7, 154, 187–88, 194–205, 208–11, 216, 219, 236–39, 244; evolutionary nature and, 212; freedom and determinism in, 163; German idealism tied to, 155; neuroses in, 176, 178, 183, 218; role of, 217. *See also* Freud, Sigmund; Lacan, Jacques
PTSD. *See* Post-traumatic stress disorder
Pulsion. See Drive
Pulsion de mort. See Death drive
Pythagorianism, 136, 139

Quantum physics: compatibilism of, 151, 170–75; *Geist* and, 173; indeterminacy in, 142, 170–71, 175; language and, 173; materialism and, 129, 131; Schelling and, 149–50, 173–75; Žižek and, xii, 5, 129, 131, 141–42, 149, 151, 170

Rabble (*Pöbel*), 79–80, 117–19, 124–25
Radical left, 118, 127, 132, 227
Rationality (*Vernünftigkeit*), 82
Real: barred, 136, 139, 142, 159, 169; Logic and, 115–16, 120; nature as, 70, 133–34, 136, 147; as Nothingness, 35, 147–49, 244, 246; Other, 232–33; pre-human, 35, 147–49; of *Realphilosophie*, 67, 69–70; shielding of, 44; Thing, 229, 237; transformations of, 120

[333]

INDEX

Realism: absolute idealism as, 143; Platonic metaphysical, 136, 139–40; of post-Kantian ontology, 38; transcendental, 32–33
Really Existing Socialism, 79, 132
Realphilosophie (Philosophy of the Real), 43, 97, 127, 247; defined, 115; *Elements of the Philosophy of Right* and, 115; knowing in, 116; *Logik* and, xii, 69, 71–72, 75, 88, 112–16, 143; natural and spiritual realities of, 140; ontology beginning with, 246; Real of, 67, 69–70; revision of, 114–15
Real Thing (*das Ding*), 229, 237
Reason (*Vernunft*): Bacon and, 53–60; consciousness distinguished from, 54, 58; deflationary approach and, 38, 50–61, 64, 66; Observing, 53–54, 56, 87, 91; principle of sufficient, 87, 93, 162, 169; Understanding and, xiv–xxxiii, 17, 20, 25–28, 51, 62, 64–65, 109, 194, 212
Rechtsphilosophie, 82, 115, 117, 119, 127
Reciprocity thesis, 49–50, 64, 66
Redding, Paul, 42
Reinhold, K. L., 12, 35, 47, 49
Relativity theory, 131–32
Renault, Emmanuel, 76
Repetition compulsion. *See Wiederholungszwang*
Repetition-difference dialectic, 235–38
Republic (Plato), 228
Retroaction, 116, 162; *après-coup* and, 80, 111, 114, 123, 156, 165, 167–68; crucial role of, 80, 113–14, 167; *Nachträglichkeit* and, 80, 111, 114, 123, 156, 167; teleology and, 121–22
Revolutionary rationality, 82
Romanticism, xvi, 40, 247
Rosen, Stanley, 30, 40, 73, 76, 89, 116
Ruda, Frank, 79, 117–18
Russell, Bertrand, 3

Santner, Eric, 200
Sartre, Jean-Paul, 5, 7, 14, 125

Schelling, F. W. J.: compatibilism of, 151, 157–59, 161, 164, 173–78, 182–83, 185; *Ent-Scheidung* of, 176, 178, 182–83; Fichte and, 13; *Freiheitschrift*, 15, 225; against Hegelianism, 75, 105, 245; Hölderlin and, 12–13, 178, 244; importance of, 65–66; middle-period, 7–8, 15–16; *Naturphilosophie* of, 16, 141, 159, 173, 178, 225–26; in post-Kantian aftermath, 12–16, 19–20, 29, 31, 33, 157; quantum physics and, 149–50, 173–75; *System of Transcendental Idealism*, 66
Schicksal (destiny), 103
Schiller, Friedrich, 191–92
Schmidt, Alfred, 133
Schranke (limitation proper), 119–20
Schulze, G. E., 35
Science (*Wissenschaft*), 5, 30; Bacon and, 53–60, 100; Hegelian, 47, 69, 71, 115; predictive power of, 213–14. *See also* Natural science
Science of Logic (Hegel): beginning of, 22–24, 40; conclusion of, 143; contingent in, 4, 81, 85, 87–89, 91, 101–3, 105–6, 110, 116; deflationary approach and, 40–42, 45, 47–49, 51–52, 58, 60, 62–64, 68, 70; Lenin on, 129; overview of, xvi–xviii, xix–xx, xxii, 4; three major divisions of, 41. *See also* "Doctrine of Being, The"; "Doctrine of Essence, The"; "Doctrine of the Concept, The"
Scientific socialism, 5, 96, 99, 119
Sedgwick, Sally, 42, 47, 67
SEEKING system, 215, 224
Seele (soul), 146, 190–91
Sein. See Being
Sein an sich, 29, 44
Self-Consciousness (*Selbstbewußtsein*), 61–63; consciousness becoming, 28–29, 31, 50, 100; Fichte on, 155; slavery and, 57; Unhappy Consciousness and, 56–57; unity of, 47

INDEX

Self-determinacy: determinism distinct from, 161; as freedom, 142; indeterminacy conflated with, 170, 172–73; spontaneous, 12, 161, 164–65, 169–70
Self-grounding, 109
Self-relating spontaneity, 36
Sellars, Wilfrid, 179, 244
Seminar XVI (Lacan), 239
Sense-Certainty (*sinnliche Gewißheit*), 26–27, 30, 54–55, 58
Separation, alienation distinct from, xxvii
Sexuality, 197, 227
Signifier, theory of, 233–35, 237–38, 242
Simple external limit (*Grenze*), 119–20
Sinnliche Gewißheit (Sense-Certainty), 26–27, 30, 54–55, 58
Slavery, 57
Socialism, xix; Really Existing, 79, 132; scientific, 5, 96, 99, 119
Socrates, 228
Somatic marker hypothesis, 180
"Some Reflections on the Ego" (Lacan), 196
Soul (*Seele*), 146, 190–91
Soviet Union: Marxism in, 5, 132–33; natural science in, 132; Really Existing Socialism in, 79, 132; Stalin in, 78–79, 99, 125, 132
Speculative idealism, 44
Speculative materialism, 34
Spieltrieb (play drive), 192
Spinoza, Baruch, 33, 86, 149, 175; *Ethics*, 97; monistic substance metaphysics of, 12
Spinozisms: of freedom, 12–14, 16, 34–35, 178; neo-Spinozism, 8, 242–47
Spirit. *See* Geist
Spontaneity: of self-determination, 12, 161, 164–65, 169–70; of subjectivity, 12–13, 33–34, 36, 96–97, 100, 152, 155–59, 161, 164–65, 169–70, 173, 175, 177–78, 183–84
Stalin, J. V., 78–79, 99, 125, 132
Stengers, Isabelle, 35–36

Stern, Robert, 42, 47
Structuralism, 14, 136, 139–40, 148, 239
Stuckness: Santner on, 200; Žižek on, xxxii, 200, 207–8, 223, 234–35, 237–38, 240
Subject: biology and, 141; drive and, 194; ethical, 154, 164, 166; introduction to, 7–8; Nature as, 150; substance and, 8, 13–14, 33–34, 61, 137–39, 141, 152, 166, 174, 185, 194, 201
Subjective idealism, 17, 20, 32, 244; deflationary approach and, 48–51, 55, 58–59, 64–66, 73; precise sense of, 83
Subjective Logic, xvi, 41, 50, 62, 81
Subjectivity: appearances and, 33; autonomous, 14, 33–34, 152, 154, 156–59, 161, 165–70, 173–75, 177–78, 184–85; denaturalized, 152, 154, 156–59, 161, 165–70, 173–75, 177–78, 184–85; emergence of, 36–37, 141–42, 150, 152; ethical, 154, 164, 166; evental, 168; identity and, 152–53; introduction to, 2–3, 6–8; natural sciences as proving grounds for, 173–75; spontaneous, free activity of, 12–13, 33–34, 36, 96–97, 100, 152, 155–59, 161, 164–65, 169–70, 173, 175, 177–78, 183–84; transcendental, 12–13, 36, 155–59, 169
Substance: Absolute as, 61; in early-modern rationalist substance metaphysics, 23; in Spinozan monistic substance metaphysics, 12; subject and, 8, 13–14, 33–34, 61, 137–39, 141, 152, 166, 174, 185, 194, 201
"Subterranean Current of the Materialism of the Encounter, The" (Althusser), 78–80
Symbolic: barred, 159; Other, 230; virtual, 176, 182–84. *See also* Imaginary-Symbolic realities
Synchrony, 150

INDEX

System: freedom or, 11–14, 16, 19–20, 22–25, 30, 34–35, 37; Jacobi on, 11–12. *See also* Hegelian System
System of Transcendental Idealism (Schelling), 66

Tat-Handlung (fact/act), 155–56
Taylor, Charles, 3, 42
Teleology: repetition and, 223, 229, 233–34; Žižek on, 5, 110, 121–24
Theodicy, Hegel and, 74, 82, 84, 86, 93, 105
Theoretical physics, 141, 170
Theory of everything, 112
"Theses on the Philosophy of History" (Benjamin), 79, 124–25, 132
Thing in itself. *See* Ding an sich
Thinking, as language bound, 87–88
Three Essays on the Theory of Sexuality (Freud), 204
Time, concept of, 113–14
Time Driven (Johnston): drive in, 189, 209–11, 216, 218–19, 224, 239; reliance on, 189
Todestrieb. *See* Death drive
"Transcendental Aesthetic" (Kant), 65–66
"Transcendental Analytic" (Kant), 17, 23, 47, 52, 179
"Transcendental Deduction" (Kant), 41, 47–50, 62–67, 179
"Transcendental Dialectic" (Kant), xxvi, 15, 65–66
Transcendental idealism: of Fichte, 20, 53, 56, 65, 155–58, 244; of Kant, 11–15, 17–25, 27, 33, 38, 43, 48, 51–53, 56, 58–59, 62–66, 70, 155–58, 244; philosophical approach of, 32–33
Transcendental materialism, 9, 174, 181, 190; cogency of, 36–37; defined, 34; future of, 37, 247–48; more-is-less principle of, 247–48; rejection of, 247–48
Transcendental realism, 32–33
Transcendental subjectivity, 12–13, 36, 155–59, 169

Transcendental unity of apperception: deflationary approach and, 39, 41, 46–49, 51–53, 55, 58, 60–62, 64, 66–67; introduction to, 3
Trieb. *See* Drive
Truth (*Wahrheit*), xxi, 50, 52, 54
Twenty-first century materialism, 189–90

"Über Urtheil und Seyn" ("On Judgment and Being") (Hölderlin), 12–13, 16, 29, 61, 244–45
Unconscious, id conflated with, 163–64
Unconscious decision (*Ent-Scheidung*), 176, 178, 182–83
Understanding (*Verstand*): introduction to, xiv–xxix, xxxii; Reason and, xiv–xxxiii, 17, 20, 25–28, 51, 62, 64–65, 109, 194, 212
Unhappy Consciousness, 56–57
Ur-contingency, 77, 89–90, 107, 109
Ur-necessity, 89, 107
Ur/Un-Grund, 175

Vernunft. *See* Reason
Vernünftigkeit (Rationality), 82
Verstand. *See* Understanding
Veto power, 166, 168, 170, 172, 175–78
Virtual symbolic order, 176, 182–84
Void. *See* Nothingness/Void
"Voiding of Weak Nature, The" (Johnston), 122–23
von Helmholtz, Hermann, 210
Von Herder, Johann Gottfried, 34

Wahrheit (truth), xxi, 50, 52, 54
Wahrnehmung (Perception), 26–27, 54, 58
Wallace, Robert, 40
Weakness of nature (*Ohnmacht der Natur*), 87, 137, 139, 149, 212, 234
Werden. *See* Becoming
Western-European Marxism, 5, 133
Western Negativity, 237–38
Westphal, Kenneth, 42–43
"What Is Metaphysics?" (Heidegger), 40

INDEX

Wiederholungszwang (repetition compulsion): as animal instinct, 217; of Freud, 200, 204, 208, 217, 220, 229, 233, 237–40; of Lacanian desire, 237
Wirklichkeit. *See* Actuality
Wish fulfillment, 207
Wissenschaft. *See* Science
Wissenschaftslehre (Fichte), 12, 191
Wittgenstein, Ludwig, 68
Wolff, Christian, 23

Wood, Allen, 42
Wordsworth, William, 218

Zerrißenheit (disunity), 225–26
Žižek, Slavoj. *See specific topics*
Žižek's Jokes (Žižek), 67–68
Žižek's Ontology (Johnston), 1–2, 16, 76, 189, 199
Zufälligkeit. *See* Contingency
Zupančič, Alenka, 28, 139, 152, 163

GPSR Authorized Representative: Easy Access System Europe, Mustamäe tee 50, 10621 Tallinn, Estonia, gpsr.requests@easproject.com

www.ingramcontent.com/pod-product-compliance
Lightning Source LLC
Chambersburg PA
CBHW021931290426
44108CB00012B/797